Prejudice
Its Social Psychology

Second Edition

Rupert Brown

WILEY-BLACKWELL

A John Wiley & Sons, Ltd., Publication

This second edition first published 2010
© 2010 Rupert Brown

Blackwell Publishing was acquired by John Wiley & Sons in February 2007. Blackwell's publishing program has been merged with Wiley's global Scientific, Technical, and Medical business to form Wiley-Blackwell.

Registered Office
John Wiley & Sons Ltd, The Atrium, Southern Gate, Chichester, West Sussex, PO19 8SQ, United Kingdom

Editorial Offices
350 Main Street, Malden, MA 02148-5020, USA
9600 Garsington Road, Oxford, OX4 2DQ, UK
The Atrium, Southern Gate, Chichester, West Sussex, PO19 8SQ, UK

For details of our global editorial offices, for customer services, and for information about how to apply for permission to reuse the copyright material in this book please see our website at www.wiley.com/wiley-blackwell.

The right of Rupert Brown to be identified as the author of this work has been asserted in accordance with the UK Copyright, Designs and Patents Act 1988.

Library of Congress Cataloging-in-Publication Data

Brown, Rupert, 1950–
 Prejudice : its social psychology / Rupert Brown. – 2nd ed.
  p. cm.
 Includes bibliographical references and index.
 ISBN 978-1-4051-1306-9 (hardcover : alk. paper) – ISBN 978-1-4051-1307-6 (pbk. : alk. paper)
1. Prejudices. 2. Prejudices in children. 3. Stereotypes (Social psychology) 4. Social psychology.
I. Title.
 BF575.P9B74 2010
 303.3'85–dc22

                              2010001885

A catalogue record for this book is available from the British Library.

Set in 10/12.5pt Galliard by SPi Publisher Services, Pondicherry, India
Printed and bound in Malaysia by Vivar Printing Sdn Bhd

1 2010

Praise for *Prejudice*, Second Edition

'In the 15 years si... e been
many exciting adv... econd
edition of *Prejudi*... ion of
these advances. Th... ooks is
now the definitive ... s item
bibliography and ... or the
specialist.'

... Cruz

'Like an adept foo... urces,
and yet retained th... k. It is
an approachable an... lars.'

... versity

'Brown's *Prejudic*... mpor-
tance, not only to ... policy
makers. This revise... ed by
its integrative app... h and
cutting-edge devel... l new
ideas. This new ed... of different perspectives ... terna-
tional research in t... ppeal
to a broad audienc... f psychological work o... luable
resource for resear...

... versity

'This top-notch, re... target
people as interchan... ed by
conflict and power... ,

... versity

'Brown's original b... field.
Fifteen years on an... ains a
superbly written, comprehensive, excellently organised and thoroughly absorbing
survey of the social psychology of prejudice. It has been worth waiting for.'

Dominic Abrams, University of Kent

To Hannah and Rosa

The two newest and dearly loved members of my favourite ingroup

Contents

Preface

This is a book about prejudice: that state of mind, feeling or behaviour that involves some disparagement of others on account of the group they belong to. This is my second attempt to write about prejudice. The other was made fifteen years ago, when the first edition of this book came out. In the meantime there have been many significant advances in the social psychology of prejudice: new theories have been proposed; clever techniques for its measurement have been devised; we have begun to realize the important role that unconscious processes can play in its determination; we now focus not just on the perpetrators of prejudice but also on those who are its victims; and we know much more than we did about effective measures to reduce it.

I have tried to do justice to these developments in this second edition. In Chapter 1 I engage with current debates as to how exactly we should define prejudice. Chapter 2 contains now an enlarged discussion of personality theories of prejudice, reflecting the revival of interest in this approach in recent years. In Chapters 3 and 4 there is an expanded coverage of the still dominant socio-cognitive perspective on prejudice. I discuss there the critical role played by categorization (Chapter 3) – the cognitive foundation of all forms of prejudice. Categorization processes give rise to stereotyping (Chapter 4), one of the ways in which people make sense of, and justify, their social world. The study of how prejudice develops in childhood has also enjoyed a renaissance over the past decade, and I have expanded and revised Chapter 5 accordingly. Chapter 6, the theoretical heart of the book, analyses prejudice as an intergroup phenomenon stemming from groups' material interests and perceptions of entitlement, deprivation and threat. Centrally implicated in all these intergroup relations are people's identities as members of ethnic or religious groups, gender groups, and many others. Chapter 7 focuses on contemporary techniques for the assessment and measurement of prejudice. It has been extended to include the burgeoning topic of the relationship between conventional pencil-and-paper measures of prejudice and other, more implicit, indicators. Chapter 8, dealing with the effects of prejudice on its targets, is entirely new. It reflects a growing appreciation amongst social psychologists that we need to view prejudice in a wider, more dynamic perspective, in which both the perpetrators and their victims are kept clearly in the field of view. Finally, in Chapter 9 I offer the latest thinking on how we can combat prejudice. Here, too, there is much new material to consider, most of it published only in the past ten years or so. Reflecting my own current concerns, I have dwelt at length here on some of the more promising practical applications of social psychology for the reduction of prejudice.

If much of the content of this edition has changed from the earlier version of the book, I hope that the style in which it is written has not. Throughout the exposition of theory and the presentation of research findings, I have liberally sprinkled the text with illustrations from newspapers, novels, films – and sometimes with anecdotes from my own life. I have also adopted a more personal style than is common in academic writing. My students tell me that they find this approach more accessible than conventionally written textbooks, and so I have continued with it. In other respects, though, the format of the book is orthodox enough. In each chapter I have chosen to highlight a few key studies, sometimes with a table or figure to show the actual findings. At the end of each chapter there is a Summary of the main issues covered and some Further Reading where more in-depth treatments of certain topics can be found. A References chapter, which contains approximately 1,000 entries, is to be found at the end: I want this volume to be a source of reference as well as a readable book.

Acknowledgements

This book has many creditors. Two – and intellectually the most important – are, sadly, no longer alive: Gordon Allport and Henri Tajfel. I first read Allport as an undergraduate and then, as now, I was profoundly impressed by the depth of his thinking and the lucidity of his writing. I still recommend his *The Nature of Prejudice* as one of the best books on the subject ever written. I studied with Tajfel as a post-graduate; and he, more than anyone else, was responsible for my abiding interest in problems of intergroup relations. His life-long (and personally experienced) concerns with identity issues, coupled with passionate intellectual ambitions for social psychology, provided me with an irresistible academic role model.

Others, too, have made significant contributions to this book. Over the course of my career I have been extremely fortunate to have benefited from the wise counsel, emotional support and superb collaboration of many colleagues, several of whom I now count amongst my closest friends. They have variously commented on draft chapters, worked with me on joint projects and, more generally, sustained in me a belief in the importance of what we do. Especially deserving of mention here are: Jens Binder, Raff Calitri, Lindsey Cameron, Sabina Čehajić, Laura Ferraresi, Roberto González, Ginette Herman, Miles Hewstone, Lorella Lepore, Joke Meeus, Amelie Mummendey, Sam Pehrson, Jenny Roth, Adam Rutland, Pablo De Tezanos Pinto and Hanna Zagefka. I am also grateful to four anonymous reviewers who made several very helpful comments on the original manuscript, and to Megan Hurst for compiling the indices so meticulously.

Finally, a word on how the book was written. I recently saw a film called *Duplicity*. Although this was an entirely forgettable cinematic experience, one line from it has stayed with me. One of the characters, on learning that his boss still uses a fountain pen to write memos to his staff, shouts, 'How frickin' pretentious is that?!'. I dare say some of my colleagues and students might share this same thought. Well, pretentious or not, it still works for me. Every word of this book was written first in long-hand, mostly using a beautiful Waterman fountain pen given to me many years ago as a gift. I find the enduring craftsmanship of the Waterman Pen Company and the reassuring immutability of Parker Permanent Black ink to be wonderfully refreshing antidotes to today's disposable society. Still, I must admit that my persistence with such unfashionable writing technology has only been possible thanks to the excellent secretarial skills of Tiffany Bancel and Charlotte Rea, who so quickly and uncomplainingly turned my appalling hand-writing into something that the rest of the world could read.

List of Figures

1

The Nature of Prejudice

In 1954 a Harvard social psychologist called Gordon Allport published a book from which this chapter takes its title (Allport, 1954). Brilliantly written and encyclopaedic in its scope, the book has rightly come to be regarded as point of departure for modern investigators into the nature of prejudice and into methods for its reduction. Allport provided not only an incisive analysis of the origins of intergroup discrimination, anticipating some discoveries in social cognition and group behaviour that have only recently been made (see Chapters 3–6), but also a series of influential policy recommendations for its elimination (see Chapter 9). Indeed, it is no exaggeration to say that most practical attempts to improve intergroup relations in over the past fifty years have had their basis in Allport's theorizing.

It is thus entirely appropriate that in this first chapter we should take another look at some of the definitions and assumptions that guided Allport's scholarship. After presenting a few contemporary illustrations of prejudice in action, I examine how the term 'prejudice' has traditionally been defined. Though finding much to agree with in these conventional accounts, I propose a simpler and more inclusive definition, which eschews any reference to the putative 'falsity' of a prejudiced thought, word or deed. After this terminological discussion, I outline in broad terms the perspective to be adopted in the remainder of the book – a perspective that simultaneously seeks to treat prejudice as a *group process* and as a phenomenon that nevertheless can be analysed at the level of *individual* perception, emotion and action. Finally, I relate this social psychological approach to the analyses offered by other disciplines – history, politics, economics, sociology and so on. I conclude that each of these various perspectives can independently offer valuable insights into the nature of prejudice without being subservient or reducible to some more fundamental level of analysis. At the same time, I recognize that ultimately – in some future social scientific utopia – each level of analysis will need to be consistent with the others and may well impose conceptual and empirical constraints on theorizing in those other domains.

What Is Prejudice?

It is 5 o'clock in the afternoon somewhere in Bristol, in the West of England, in the mid-1980s. Geoff Small, a black man in his twenties, has just been shown round a flat that is being offered to let by a white landlord.

> SMALL: Am I the first one to see it?
> LANDLORD: ...Yes, you are actually but there are several other people coming round, you know. Well, another one in a moment – ten past – and some more at six.
> SMALL: Ah, right. Then what's your criterion for allotting the place?
> LANDLORD: Well, I'm going to see the people who come along. Then, you know, give them a call and let them know ...

Ten minutes later a second man, also in his twenties, calls round to the same flat. His name is Tim Marshall. He happens to be white. After being shown round, he asks how the landlord will decide on who will be the tenant.

> MARSHALL: Is it on a first come, first served ... that is, if I wanted it ...?
> LANDLORD: (hesitating) ... er ... yeah ... well ... yes ... someone sort of suitable I would say yes, I would. But ... otherwise I might say 'I'll let you know' (embarrassed laugh).
> MARSHALL: Ok, I do actually like it. But I have got ...
> LANDLORD: ... got others to see, have you?
> MARSHALL: Yes, two places. But I mean ... have I got any competition? I mean, does anyone else want it?
> LANDLORD: Well, the situation is that I came back at four o'clock. There's a chap coming round at six o'clock – between six and seven – and ... um ... being a bit of a racist ... but he was black – nice enough chap – but I thought he might create problems so I said look, I'd let him know.
> MARSHALL: Would you not have a black ...?
> LANDLORD: No. He was a nice chap, you know. But on the other hand, he was a big bloke and he'd be a bit of a handful. But I thought he might create problems, you know.
> MARSHALL: Damn. I don't know what to say. I don't want to lose it but I don't want to say yes for sure.
> LANDLORD: Well, I've got another room ... which I let as well.
> MARSHALL: Well, I'll take my chances because you're saying the black guy is not going to get it?
> LANDLORD: That's right.

On the way downstairs to show Marshall out, the landlord continues his justification for not wanting to let to the previous applicant, at one point describing him as 'a bit arrogant'.

These two encounters were covertly filmed by the two prospective tenants, who were in reality making a television documentary (*Black and White*, BBC Television, 1987). Armed with hidden microphones and cameras, they went looking for accommodation, jobs and leisure entertainment. The documentary was, in fact, a televised replication of a well-known piece of research initiated by a committee appointed by the British Government in 1965 (Daniels, 1968). As in the television programme, one of the research techniques was to dispatch three interviewers, who purported to be genuine applicants, in search of housing, jobs and a variety of other services. In most respects the interviewers were similar – similar age, appearance, qualifications – but there were some crucial differences: the first applicant to any vacancy happened to have somewhat darker skin than the other two because he was West Indian or Asian; the second applicant's skin was white, but he was from Hungary; and the third applicant was always white and English.

The results were dramatic: out of 60 landlords approached, the West Indian received identical treatment to the others on just 15 occasions (Daniels, 1968). On 38 of the 45 other occasions he was told that the flat had gone when both other applicants were told later that it was still vacant. When applying for jobs, an equally stark discrimination occurred: 40 firms were approached. On no less than 37 occasions, the West Indian or Asian applicants were told that there was no vacancy. The white English received only 10 such outright refusals, and the Hungarian 23. Direct offers of jobs or encouragement to apply showed a similar bias.

It is tempting to dismiss such findings on grounds of their antiquity. Surely, one might ask, it would be difficult to witness such overt discrimination today, after four decades of successive race relations and equal opportunities legislation? I would not be so sanguine about it. There was, after all, that television documentary, which revealed repeated instances of a differential treatment of black and white reporters. That such discrimination lingers is confirmed in some more recent reports. One was a study by Bertrand and Mullainathan (2004) in which 5,000 applications were sent out in response to various job advertisements in American newspapers. Half of the applicants purported to have typically white-sounding names like Allison or Greg, the remainder had typical African American names like Ebony or Leroy. Independently of the names at the top of the résumé, some applicants seemed to have more skills and experience relevant to the job, others less. Of course, the vast majority of these applications did not elicit a response from the employers. However, those with white-sounding names were about 50 per cent more likely to yield a reaction than those with the African American names: the response rates were 9.6 per cent and 6.4 per cent respectively. Even worse, for the applications from the 'white' candidates, the quality of the résumé made a noticeable difference to the likelihood of a response, whilst it had virtually no effect for the 'black' candidates. Similar evidence of job discrimination, simply on the basis of applicants' names, has been found in Britain, where applicants with Asian names are less likely to be short-listed than those with white names (BBC, 2004; Department for Work and Pensions, 2009; Esmail and Everington, 1993). And in Chile, too, workers with high-status Castillean Spanish names are likely to earn around 10 per cent more than their colleagues with lower-class or indigenous names, even when holding constant (or, in technical terms, controlling for) their academic achievement level on graduating from university (Nunez and Gutierez, 2004). In the field of housing, it seems that people from ethnic minorities in Britain still face discrimination when they look for property to rent. According to the British Commission for Racial Equality, as many as 20 per cent of private accommodation agencies were still discriminating in the allocation of rented property in the late 1980s – a situation which still persists in some places, according to a recent report in a Belfast newspaper (CRE, 1990; Irish News, 30 October 2004).

Behind these statistics lies a grim reality of daily verbal abuse, harassment and threat of physical attack for many members of minority groups. Perhaps the following will serve as one last illustration that prejudice can sometimes – perhaps often – contain elements of overt hostility and violence. In 2009, the BBC sent two British Asian reporters, Tamann Rahman and Amil Khan, to live for two months on a working-class housing estate in Bristol ('Panorama', BBC 1 TV, 19 October 2009; see http://news. bbc.co.uk/panorama/hi/front_page/newsid_8303000/8303229.stm). Posing as a married couple, the two covertly filmed how they were received by their neighbours and other people in the community. Their treatment was truly shocking. They were frequently called names in the street – 'Paki', 'Oi, you Taliban', 'Who's got a bomb?', 'Iraq's that way' are some of the more printable insults that they received. They were physically assaulted, sometimes by quite young children. An 11-year-old boy tried to mug Ms Rahman, pretending to have a gun, then a knife, and finally actually producing a rock with which he threatened her until a passer-by intervened. She had rocks, bottles and cans of drink thrown at her. Mr Khan was similarly abused, and on one occasion he was punched on the side of his head, in a completely unprovoked attack. Such is life for some ethnic minorities living in parts of twenty-first-century Britain.

These are all instances of a particular kind of prejudice: prejudice towards members of ethnic minorities. There are, of course, many other common varieties of prejudice – against women, against gay people, against people with disabilities – as will become clear in the pages of this book. But what exactly do we mean by the word 'prejudice'? It is conventional at this point to refer to a dictionary in which we can find prejudice typically defined as 'a judgement or opinion formed beforehand or without due examination' (Chambers English Dictionary, 1988).

Definitions like this one have led many social psychologists to emphasize features such as 'incorrectness' or 'inaccuracy' in their attempts to define prejudice. For example Allport wrote: '[e]thnic prejudice is an antipathy *based upon a faulty and inflexible generalization*. It may be felt or expressed. It may be directed toward a group as a whole or toward and individual because he is a member of that group' (Allport, 1954, p. 10; my emphasis); or, more recently, Samson: 'prejudice involves an *unjustified*, usually negative attitude towards others because of their social category or group membership' (Samson, 1999, p. 4; my emphasis).

Such social psychological definitions have much to recommend them over more formal lexical accounts. In particular, they accurately convey one essential aspect of the phenomenon of prejudice – that it is a social orientation either towards whole groups of people or towards individuals *because* of their membership of a particular group. The other common factor between these definitions is that they stress the negative flavour of group prejudice. Of course, logically, prejudice can take both positive and negative forms. I, for example, am particularly favourably disposed towards all things Italian: I love Italian food, Italian cinema, and I lose no opportunity to try out my execrable Italian on anyone who will listen (much to the embarrassment of friends and family). However, such harmless infatuations hardly constitute a major social problem, worthy of much of our attention as social scientists. Rather, the kind of prejudice that besets so many societies in the world today and which so urgently requires our understanding is usually the negative variety: the wary, fearful, suspicious, derogatory, hostile or ultimately murderous treatment of one group of people by another. Thus, practically speaking, I think it is usually most useful to concern ourselves with what governs variations in these different forms of antipathy. Still, it will be necessary to revisit this question of 'positive' prejudice when I present my definition below.

However, I do not believe it is necessary to imply – as these definitions do – that prejudice must be regarded as a 'false' or 'irrational' set of beliefs, a 'faulty' generalization, or as an 'unwarranted' disposition to behave negatively towards another group. There are three reasons for taking issue with this point of view. First, to say that an attitude or belief is 'faulty' implies that we could have some way of establishing its 'correctness'. In some rather special circumstances it might be possible to do this, but only if the belief in question refers to some objectively measurable criterion (Judd and Park, 1993; Lee et al., 1995; Oakes and Reynolds, 1997). But how often would this be possible? Prejudiced statements are typically couched in much more vague and ambiguous terms. Take the landlord quoted earlier in the chapter: how could we hope to establish the truth or falsity of his beliefs that blacks are likely 'to create problems'? By devising some procedure to measure people's scores on this index against some normative standard of 'peaceableness'? Even to pose the question seems to me to high-light the insurmountable difficulties that would be encountered in trying to answer it. And, even if such a comparative test were possible and, let us suppose hypothetically, it did show a greater incidence of 'problem creation' among the black population, would this justify regarding that landlord's statement as unprejudiced? There is a myriad of possible explanations for the hypothetical statistic – for example reactions to provocation by whites, response to unjust social deprivation, and so on – any one of which could suffice to refute the imputation of blacks' supposed propensity 'to create problems'. The fact remains that the sentiments expressed by that landlord – and their social consequences – would be no less negative (and prejudicial) for having some (alleged) basis in reality.

A second problem with including any 'truth value' element in a definition of prejudice stems from the peculiarly relativistic nature of intergroup perception. It has long been observed – and we shall see ample confirmations in later chapters – that, for groups even more than for individuals, 'beauty is in the eye of the beholder'. In other words, one group may view very differently what another group finds to be 'pleasant', or 'virtuous', or even self-evidently 'true'. So, if one group regards itself as 'thrifty', is that view more, or is it less, at variance with reality than the view of another group, who regards the former as 'stingy'? Of course, it is impossible to say. The important distinction between the two views lies not in their relative 'correctness' but in their implied connotations of value.

A third point to make about some of these traditional definitions of prejudice is that they often seem to pre-empt the analysis of the origins and functions of prejudiced thinking. Thus, when Allport (1954) refers to an 'inflexible generalization', or when Ackerman and Jahoda (1950) talk of prejudice serving an 'irrational function', they are presupposing more in their definitions than it may be wise to allow. It may well be, as we shall see in subsequent chapters, that much prejudice does have an apparently immutable and dysfunctional quality to it. But equally, as these chapters will also reveal, to think of prejudice as being impervious to change, or as having no rational function for its adherents, is to fail to do justice to the variety and complexity of the forms it can take and to its surprisingly labile quality in many situations.

Let us now return to the restriction, encountered in traditional definitions, that prejudice should refer to a negative orientation. For many years this restriction was uncontroversial (Aboud, 1988; Jones, 1972; Sherif, 1966). Indeed in the first edition of this book I adopted it myself (Brown, 1995). However, some recent analyses have argued that social psychological definitions of prejudice should, after all, include some apparently positive beliefs, sentiments and actions. Thus Jones, in a revision of his earlier book, now defines prejudice as 'a *positive or negative* attitude, judgement or feeling about a person that is generalized from attitudes or beliefs held about the group to which the person belongs' (Jones, 1997, p. 10; my emphasis). And Glick and colleagues (2000) argue that 'subjectively favourable attitudes towards women can themselves be a form of prejudice in that they serve to justify and maintain women's subordination' (Glick et al., 2000, p. 764).

What is the thinking behind these more inclusive definitions? In a nutshell, the argument runs like this: many intergroup attitudes, whilst superficially positive in character, serve to perpetuate an outgroup's subordinate status position, since they accord value to the outgroup only on specific and, typically, less 'important' attributes. Moreover, these attributes may help to define members of that outgroup as being particularly suitable for more servile roles in society. Thus, however positive and genuine the feeling underlying such attitudes may be, their net effect is to reinforce rather than to undermine any pre-existing intergroup inequalities. An important stimulus in the development of this argument came from some findings reported by Eagly and Mladinic (1994) which showed that, in North America at least, men (and women) tended to hold more favourable stereotypes of women than of men. These stereotypes were most evident in various communal and expressive attributes (such as 'helpful', 'warm', 'understanding'), and they were somewhat – but not completely – counterbalanced by less favourable evaluations on such agentic and instrumental attributes as 'independent', 'decisive' and 'self-confident'. Subsequently Glick and Fiske (1996) found that, on average, men are happy to endorse such positive sounding opinions as these: 'men are incomplete without women'; 'women, compared to men, tend to have a superior moral sensibility'; or 'a good woman should be set on a pedestal by her man'. However 'benevolent' such sentiments seem to be, Glick and Fiske (1996, 2001) argue that their ultimate effect is to define women as dependent on, and hence subordinate to, men (see Chapter 7 for a fuller treatment of benevolent and hostile sexism). Part of their reasoning stems from the fact that people who agree with such statements will also tend to endorse more 'obviously' sexist attitudes: 'benevolent' sexist attitudes are generally positively correlated with 'hostile' ones, weakly at an individual level (around +.3) but strongly at a national sample level (around +.9) (Glick et al., 2000).

Jackman (1994) has extended this argument to ethnic and class relationships. In her book, tellingly entitled *The Velvet Glove* (which disguises the iron fist within), she sets out 'to examine the ways that dominant groups subvert conflict by befriending or at least emotionally disarming those whom they subordinate' (p. 2). She goes on to advocate that 'the concept of prejudice be abandoned in favour if a conception of interracial attitudes that views them as politically motivated communications to defend group interests rather than as expressions of parochial negativism' (p. 41).

These arguments have more than a ring of plausibility about them. Members of minority or subordinate groups have since times immemorial complained of paternalistic treatment by dominant groups, a treatment that often comes disguised as a benevolent yet demeaning concern for their welfare, or as attitudes which are as patronizing as they are 'favourable'. As a consequence, I believe it may be wise to amend the traditional definition of prejudice so as to capture not just the direct expressions of a negative orientation, but also these more indirectly negative intergroup attitudes. As a working definition for this book, therefore, **prejudice** will be regarded as *any attitude, emotion or behaviour towards members of a group, which directly or indirectly implies some negativity or antipathy towards that group.*

To this definition I would add the following three additional comments. First, while directly negative manifestations of prejudice are relatively simple to identify, the indirect forms may be more problematic, and even impossible to specify in advance. I have already mentioned that I happen to hold generally positive stereotypes about things Italian, including the people – for example, that Italians seem to me rather stylish, hospitable and open, especially when compared to my fellow Britons. Now, does this reveal a progressive shift from the overtly negative way my parents' generation might have viewed them seventy years ago (when Italy and Britain were at war), or does it betray a not-so-subtle northern European snobbery against southerners, represented as an emotional but feckless people – an attitude which comfortably relegates them to subordinate status in the European order? A priori it is difficult to say. Probably the best way to find out would be to assess the co-variation of such seemingly positive attitudes with more obvious indicators of a negative intergroup relationship, and also to observe the reaction of the target to the expression of the positive attitudes. If there is some positive correlation and the recipients respond adversely, then an inference of prejudice would be warranted.

The second comment is that, in this rather wide sense in which I shall be using the term, prejudice can be regarded as roughly synonymous with several others such as **sexism**, **racism**, **homophobia**, **ageism** and the like. There are some who would restrict the application of certain terms, for instance 'racism', to ideologies or practices that are justified by reference to presumed biological group differences (for example van den Berghe, 1967; Miles, 1989). However, from the social psychological perspective adopted here, I believe it is more useful to regard all the phenomena encompassed by these terms as special cases of the more general phenomenon of prejudice. In this way we do not exclude from our discussion important intergroup antipathies such as class prejudice and some forms of religious bigotry, which do not have any obvious biological component.

The third point is that prejudice is not to be regarded as just a cognitive or attitudinal phenomenon; it can also engage our emotions, as well as finding expression in behaviour. Thus I shall not be drawing any firm distinctions between biased attitudes, hostile feelings and discriminatory behaviour. Which is not to say that these different forms of prejudice are all identical, or are necessarily highly intercorrelated; we shall review evidence which suggests that, in fact, the relationship between them is often quite complex. But it is still possible to say that attitudes, feelings and actions *are* all facets of a general prejudiced orientation. This multiple-level emphasis is deliberate and stands in contrast to some trends in modern social psychology, which have tended to stress the cognitive aspects of prejudice and rather to overlook its affective and behavioural components (for example Hamilton, 1981 – but compare Mackie and Hamilton, 1993; Mackie and Smith, 2002; Smith, 1993). This cognitive analysis is undoubtedly important; indeed I shall be devoting two whole chapters to it (Chapters 3 and 4). However, to ignore the emotionally laden – one might even say saturated – nature of prejudice as it is actually perpetrated and experienced in everyday life is, it seems to me, to overlook something rather fundamental about it. Thus a recurring theme in the pages that follow will be the interplay between the cognitive, the affective and the behavioural processes implicated in prejudice.

A Social Psychological Approach

Having defined what I mean by prejudice, I should say a few words about the general approach I shall be adopting throughout the book. At this stage, I shall outline the perspective only in rather broad terms, without very much supportive evidence and argumentation. Its more detailed documentation will be left to subsequent chapters.

The first point to make is that I see prejudice as primarily a phenomenon originating in group processes. There are three closely related reasons why this is so. *First*, it is, as I have chosen to define it, an orientation towards whole categories of people rather than towards isolated individuals. Even if its target in any concrete instance is only a single individual (as in the example with which I began the previous section), nevertheless that person's individual characteristics matter much less than the markers that allocate him or her to one group rather than another – by name, by accent, by skin colour, and so on. The *second* reason why prejudice should be regarded as a group process is that it is most frequently a socially shared orientation. That is to say, large numbers of people in a segment of society will broadly agree in their negative stereotypes about any given outgroup and will behave in a similar way towards its members. Although, as we shall see in the next chapter, there are some grounds for believing that in its most chronic and extreme forms prejudice may be associated with particular types of personality, we cannot escape the conclusion that it is too widespread and too prevalent a phenomenon to be consigned to the province of individual pathology. The *third* reason follows directly from the first two. Insofar as prejudice is usually directed *at* particular groups *by* some other groups, we should not be too surprised to discover that the relationships between these groups play an important role in determining it. Thus intergroup relations such as conflict over scarce resources, or power domination of one group by another, or gross disparities in numerical size or status can all, as I will show in later chapters, have crucial implications for the direction, level and intensity that the prejudice will display. Indeed, it is this *intergroup* nature of prejudice that really forms the leitmotif of the whole book.

The second general point about the perspective to be taken is that the focus of my analysis will predominantly be the individual. I shall be concerned, in other words, with the impact that various causal factors have on *individuals'* perceptions of, evaluations of, and behavioural reactions towards, members of other groups. These causal factors may take a variety of forms. Some may themselves be individually located (as in the case of certain personality and cognitive processes – see Chapters 2–4). On the other hand, many of the most powerful causal agents, as we shall see, stem from characteristics of the social situation in which people find themselves (for example social influence from peers, or the nature of intergroup goal relationships: see Chapters 6 and 9). Still others may have their origin in the wider society, as our discussion of socialization influences (Chapter 5) and our analysis of new forms of prejudice (Chapter 7) will reveal. But still, in all these instances, my concern as a social psychologist is with the effects of such causal factors on individual social behaviour.

Now, since this approach seems rather to contradict my earlier claim that prejudice was essentially a group process, a little further elaboration is necessary. Actually, as I have argued elsewhere, this contradiction is apparent rather than real (Brown, 2000a). To assert the causal importance and distinctiveness of group-based processes within social psychology is merely to recognize that individuals and individual behaviour can be transformed in group settings, much as the behaviour of a metallic object can be affected by the presence of a magnetic field. The presence of the magnetic field – something external to the object itself – does not prevent us from describing and predicting what will happen to the object. In the same way it is possible to analyse individuals' behaviour as part of a coherent pattern of group processes.[1] Consider the actions of protestors during a gay rights demonstration or in an episode of ethnic conflict. To be sure, the actions of these people – their form, direction and intensity – are likely to be shaped by the norms and goals of those around them and by the relationships between the groups concerned. However, those actions are no less incidences of social behaviour by individual persons for that, and as such they fall squarely in the province of social psychology.

We can now see the resolution to the apparent contradiction between wanting to study prejudice, simultaneously, as a *group*-based phenomenon and as a phenomenon located at the level of *individual* cognition, emotion and behaviour. The key is to recognize that I am not proposing the simultaneous study of individual behaviour and group behaviour in themselves; these are indeed rather different levels of analysis. Rather, I wish to distinguish between *individuals acting as group members* – that is, in terms of their group memberships – and *individuals acting as individuals* (Sherif, 1966; Tajfel, 1978a). It is with the former class of behaviours – with people acting as 'women' or 'men', as 'gays' or 'straights', as 'blacks or 'whites' – that I shall be mainly concerned throughout this book.

In arguing for this kind of social psychological approach, I should immediately make it clear that I do not for one minute believe that social psychology has any privileged disciplinary position in providing explanations and remedies for prejudice. A complete understanding of the phenomenon is, surely, only possible if we also take account of the complex mix of historical, political, economic and social structural forces at work in any given context. History is important because it is this that bequeaths to us our language, our cultural traditions and norms, and our social institutions. All these play a significant part in the way we come to construe our world in terms of different social categories, which is the first and indispensable precursor to all forms of prejudice (see Chapter 3). Likewise, political processes cannot be ignored; for these help to determine a country's legislation on basic civil rights, or its immigration policies (to name but two issues). Apart from directly affecting the lives of minority groups (usually to their detriment), such policies contribute to the ideological frameworks in which various ethnic (and other) groups are differently valued in society. Miles (1989), for example, has described how the European settlement of Australia and the subsequent development of a 'white Australia' policy in the early years of this century were historically accompanied by the emergence of various racial terms, both in official and in everyday language. It is something of a tragic irony that the 'success' of that 'white Australia' policy in perpetrating a systematic assault on, and oppression of, the aboriginal people has resulted in its virtual obliteration from all the official 'histories' of the continent (Pilger, 1989). Economic factors can play an important – some would say overriding – role in governing relations between groups in society. When one group has the means and the will to appropriate whole territories from another for the purposes of economic exploitation, as in the case of Britain's colonization of large parts of Africa, Asia and Australia, then racist beliefs are often developed in justification (Banton, 1983). In Simpson and Yinger's (1972) pithy summary: 'prejudice exists because someone gains by it' (p. 127).

Though not easily separable from the factors just discussed, the very structure of society, its organization into sub-groups and the social arrangements of those groups can play their part in the manufacture and maintenance of prejudice. As an example, consider the difference between societies composed of groups of ever-increasing size and inclusiveness (family, religion, region and so on), and those in which groups cut across one another (for example societies where norms prescribe that people should marry outside their immediate community, thus creating an overlap between family and village groupings). Drawing on extensive anthropological sources, LeVine and Campbell (1972) suggest that the latter type of society is less given to internal conflict because of the competing loyalty structures created by the criss-crossing of different groups (see Chapter 3). Other kinds of societal analyses reveal how institutions and social practices can exist to regulate the access to goods and services by different groups in society. Such differential access can then perpetuate, and perhaps even accentuate, existing disparities that, in turn, can generate their own self-fulfilling justification for prejudice against particular groups. Take access to education. In Britain someone's chances of going to university are strongly related to the social class of that person's parents. According to recent figures, nearly 50 per cent of entrants to university in Britain in 2000 were from social classes I and II, who comprise only 43 per cent of the population. In contrast, less than 20 per cent of the entrants were of classes IIIM to V, who make up over 40 per cent of the population (Department for Education and Skills, 2003). Such a skew in the class composition of university students results in similar imbalances in recruitment to different occupations and in the likelihood of unemployment. From there it is an easy step to the perpetuation of prejudiced images of working-class people as 'uneducated', 'stupid' and 'lazy'.

It is clear, then, that there are several different levels at which prejudice can be analysed, and the social psychological perspective is but one of these. But if, as Allport (1954) elegantly put it, 'plural causation is the primary lesson we wish to teach' (p. xii), what is the relationship between these different causal factors? Can the different levels of analysis be reduced to some more fundamental perspective? Consider two social scientists' views. They are talking about war, but it could just as well have been prejudice:

> To attempt to explain war by appeal to innate pugnacity would be like explaining Egyptian, Gothic, and Mayan architecture by citing the physical properties of stone. (White, 1949, p. 131)

> Dealings between groups ultimately become problems for the psychology of the individual. Individuals decide to go to war; battles are fought by individuals; and peace is established by individuals. (Berkowitz, 1962, p. 167)

Each of these scholars is claiming the theoretical priority of one discipline over another. For White, an anthropologist, it is the societal analysis that is fundamental; Berkowitz, a psychologist, believes that a microscopic approach is ultimately more valuable. In fact neither form of reductionism is necessary. It is possible, as LeVine and Campbell (1972) have persuasively argued, to pursue these various lines of enquiry treating them more or less as independent of one another, in the spirit of what these authors call 'optional autonomy' (p. 26). In their view, no one level of analysis can make any claim of superiority or priority over another. Disciplinary preference should simply be dictated by the nature of the problem with which one is confronted. Thus, in order to analyse the effect of discriminatory hiring practices on unemployment levels in different ethnic groups, a macroscopic level of analysis is obviously appropriate. But if one's concern were with the actual social dynamics of employment selection procedures, then a social psychological approach would probably be more fruitful. Each analysis can be conducted relatively unencumbered by the other. However, this is not to propose a form of intellectual anarchy. In the last analysis the different approaches will have to be 'congruent' with one another – to use LeVine and Campbell's term again. That is, a valid theory of employment discrimination pitched at the economic or sociological level will have to be consistent with social psychological conclusions drawn from studies of individual social behaviour in job interviews, *and vice versa*.

This is the position I have taken in this book. By accident of training I am a social psychologist, and it is this perspective that I attempt to develop in the following chapters. But I hope that, by the time the final page is reached, it will be clear that social psychology, whilst it contains the potential to contribute significantly both to the dissection and to the dissolution of prejudice, can never do more than explain a part – and perhaps only a small part – of the phenomenon as a whole.

Summary

1   Prejudice is often defined as a faulty or unjustified negative judgement held about members of a group. However, such definitions run into conceptual difficulties because of problems in ascertaining whether social judgements are at variance with reality. Instead, prejudice is here defined simply as an attitude, emotion or behaviour towards members of a group which directly or indirectly implies some negativity towards that group.

2   Because prejudice involves judgements of some groups made by others, and because it can be shown to be affected by the objective relationships between these groups, prejudice is appropriately regarded as a phenomenon originating in group processes. However, such a perspective is not incompatible with a social psychological analysis that is primarily concerned with individual perceptions, evaluations and actions. Such an analysis sees individuals acting as group members, as part of a coherent pattern of group dynamics.

3   A social psychological analysis is but one in a number of valid scientific perspectives on prejudice. Each discipline can usefully pursue its own research problems more or less independently of the others, although ultimately these diverse analyses will have to be compatible with each other.

Note

1 Actually the analogy with magnetic fields is not quite precise because, unlike inanimate objects, human beings have the ability to alter and recreate the 'magnetic' fields of the group they find themselves in. But the point is that their attempts to do so can still be analysed as individual constituents of an organized system (Asch, 1952; Steiner, 1986).

Further Reading

Allport, G. W. (1954) *The Nature of Prejudice*, chs 1, 14, 15. Reading, MA: Addison-Wesley.
Brown, R. J. (2000) *Group Processes*, ch. 1. Oxford: Basil Blackwell.
Jones, J. M. (1997) *Prejudice and Racism*, 2nd edn, ch. 17. NY: McGraw Hill.
Sherif, M. and Sherif, C. W. (1969) *Interdisciplinary Relationships in the Social Sciences*, ch. 1. Chicago: Aldine.

2

Prejudiced Individuals

Some years ago one of my colleagues had a leaflet pushed through his letter box. It contained a few hundred vitriolic words complaining that the British Home Secretary had not prevented the visit to Britain of a Mr Sharpton, a black activist from the United States. The gist of the leaflet was that Mr Sharpton was here to incite black rioting and that the media were conspiring to give him free publicity. Here are a few selected but quite representative extracts from that leaflet:

> Already black violence is on a massive scale here with thousands of our *women having been viciously raped and our elderly brutally attacked*.

> We know the Press is Jew-owned (Maxwell and Murdoch are Jews from Russia) and that a former Director of the BBC stated 'We are all Marxists at the BBC'. We know too that the Home Secretary is a stooge of the Board of Jewish Deputies.

> We hope through this series of leaflets to alert you that millions of hostile racist aliens are not here by accident but that they are here through conspiracy; a conspiracy against YOU.

When one is presented with such blatant and obviously offensive racism, a common reaction is to label its author as a 'crackpot' or as having some kind of personality problem. Indeed, for many – lay people and psychologists alike – the phenomenon of prejudice is exactly this: a manifestation of a particular and probably pathological personality type. In this chapter I consider this hypothesis in some detail. I begin with the best known version of it, which proposes that the origins of prejudice can be sought in the psychological make-up and functioning of the individual, and these factors are thought to be the product of a certain familial history. A particular upbringing, so this theory claims, produces someone with a strongly deferential attitude towards authority, a rather simplistic and rigid cognitive style, and a strong tendency to be susceptible to right-wing and racist ideas. This theory can be extended to include a general syndrome of intolerance, whether on the left or right; and in a second section I examine approaches which have developed this thesis. I then examine a more recent theory, which claims that prejudice can be traced to a general orientation of social dominance. In this account, hierarchical (or dominance) relationships are a universal feature of human existence, they have evolutionary origins and they manifest themselves at societal, intergroup and individual levels. I conclude by identifying a number of difficulties all of these individualistic approaches run into, difficulties which, I believe, render them rather inadequate as accounts of the causes of prejudice.

The Authoritarian Personality

The best known attempt to link prejudice to a particular personality type was provided by Adorno and colleagues (1950). This theory – a unique blend of Marxist social philosophy, Freudian analysis of family dynamics, and quantitative psychometrics – quickly established itself as a reference point for a whole generation of researchers into the nature of prejudice.

Its basic hypothesis was simple: an individual's political and social attitudes cohere together and are 'an expression of deep lying trends in personality' (Adorno et al., 1950, p. 1). Prejudiced people are those whose personalities render them susceptible to those racist or fascist ideas prevalent in a society at a given time. The theory did not try to explain the origins of those ideas at a societal level; this, asserted its authors, was a problem for sociological or political analysis. Rather, they were concerned to account for individual differences in *receptivity* to those ideas.

According to Adorno and his team, these personality differences can be traced to the family in which the child is socialized. Much influenced by Freudian thinking, these researchers believed that the child's development involves the constraints of social existence. The earliest and most powerful agents of this socialization process are, of course, the parents, and in the 'normal' case they strike a balance between allowing the child some self-expression – for example tolerating occasional outbursts of temper or exuberance – and imposing some flexible limits of acceptable and unacceptable behaviour. The problem with prejudiced people, argued Adorno and his colleagues, was that they had been exposed to a family regime which was overly concerned with 'good behaviour' and conformity to conventional moral codes. The parents in such families – especially the fathers – used excessively harsh disciplinary measures to punish the child's transgressions. As a result – or so Adorno and his colleagues believed – the child's aggression towards the parents (which is an inevitable effect of its 'natural' urges being frustrated) is displaced away from them, because of anxiety about the consequences of displaying it so directly, and *onto* substitute targets. The most likely choice of scapegoats would be those seen as weaker or inferior to oneself – for example anyone who deviated from the societal norm. Ready candidates for this cathartic release of aggression were thought to include members of minority ethnic groups or of other socially devalued categories such as homosexuals or convicted criminals.

Adorno and his colleagues proposed that this syndrome was not just reflected in the content of the person's social attitudes; it also manifested itself in the cognitive style in which those attitudes were constructed and expressed. They believed that, on account of the parents' disciplinary zeal and strictly conventional morality, the child develops a simplistic way of thinking about the world in which people and their actions are rigidly categorized into 'right' and 'wrong'. This tendency was thought to generalize into a cognitive style which is marked by the consistent use of very clearly demarcated categories and by intolerance to any 'fuzziness' between them. Of course, such a way of thinking also readily lends itself to the endorsement of distinctive and immutable stereotypes about social groups.

The end result, then, is a person who is over-deferential and anxious towards authority figures (since these symbolize the parents), who sees the world – often literally – in black and white, being unable or unwilling to tolerate cognitive ambiguity, and who is overtly hostile to anyone who is not obviously an ingroup member. Adorno and his colleagues called this type of person the **authoritarian personality**, and the author or authors of the leaflet with which we began this chapter would constitute an excellent example of just such a type. The combination of crudely anti-black, anti-Semitic and anti-communist invective, laced with undercurrents of sexual violence and fear of powerful conspiracies, is precisely the kind of constellation of attitudes which the prototypical authoritarian is thought to endorse.

To substantiate their theory, Adorno and his colleagues initiated a huge research project, which combined large-scale psychometric testing and individual clinical interviews. The psychometric work was initially concerned with designing some objective measures of various forms of overt prejudice (for example **anti-Semitism**, or general **ethnocentrism**). This then evolved into the construction of a personality inventory which, it was hoped, would tap into the central aspects of the underlying authoritarian personality syndrome. This measure, the most famous to emerge from the project, they called the 'F-scale', so labelled because it was intended to measure 'pre-fascist tendencies'. It consisted of thirty items which, after a careful process of screening and pre-testing, were all designed to reflect various aspects of the authoritarian person's hypothesized make-up. For example there were questions concerned with authoritarian submission ('obedience and respect for authority are the most important virtues children should learn'), with aggression towards deviant groups ('homosexuals are hardly better than criminals and ought to be severely punished'), and with the projection of unconscious, especially sexual, impulses ('the wild sex life of the Greeks and Romans was tame compared to some of the goings-on in this country, even in places where people might least expect it'). The scale had good internal reliability and, just as its authors had predicted, it correlated well with their previous measures of intergroup prejudice, despite the fact that it contained no items specifically referring to ethnic groups.

In an attempt to validate the F-scale, small sub-samples of very high and very low scorers on it were selected for intensive clinical interviews. These consisted of detailed questioning of the respondents' recollection of their early childhood experiences, of their perceptions of their parents, and of their views on various social and moral issues of the day. These interviews did seem to confirm many of Adorno and his team's theoretical suppositions about the origins and consequences of **authoritarianism**. For instance high scorers on the F-scale tended to idealize their parents as complete paragons of virtue. At the same time they recalled their childhood as a time of strict obedience to parental authority, with harsh sanctions for any minor misdemeanours. Their current attitudes corresponded well to their answers on the F-scale items: very moralistic, openly condemnatory of 'deviants' or social 'inferiors', and exhibiting sharply defined categorical stereotypes, often openly prejudiced. The low scorers, by contrast, painted a more equivocal and balanced picture of their early family life and typically presented a more complex and flexible set of social attitudes.

Whether due to the ambitiousness of its theoretical and applied goals or to the range of methodologies it employed, *The Authoritarian Personality* excited much interest amongst social psychologists in the 1950s. A review article which appeared just eight years after its appearance cited over 200 published studies investigating correlates of authoritarianism with such psychological phenomena as leadership, impression formation, problem solving, social acquiescence, psychopathology, cognitive style and, of course, prejudice (Christie and Cook, 1958).

It is the latter two topics that are of interest to us here. What independent empirical support is there for Adorno and colleagues' hypothesis that the authoritarian is characterized by an over-rigid cognitive style, which does not easily accommodate ambiguities and equivocation and which, when translated into social attitudes, shows as hostility towards minority groups?

One of the earliest experiments designed to examine the association between authoritarianism and mental rigidity was carried out by Rokeach (1948). His technique was to present participants with a series of simple arithmetic problems. In the practice trials these problems required at least three separate operations for their solution. However, in the test trials, the problems, although superficially similar to those presented in the practice sessions, could be solved by a simpler, one-step procedure – in addition to the previously rehearsed longer solution. The key question was whether participants would solve these subsequent problems by the faster method or whether they would persevere rigidly with the less direct technique they had learned in practice. Rokeach also measured their ethnocentrism, which normally correlates well with authoritarianism. Just as he (and Adorno and colleagues) had hypothesized, those who scored highly (that is, above the median) on ethnocentrism showed consistently a higher mental rigidity than those who scored below the median. However, after several unsuccessful attempts to replicate these findings, Brown (1953) concluded that the link between authoritarianism and rigidity only emerged when the testing situation was important for participants. By experimentally manipulating the presumed social, scientific and personal significance of the arithmetic problems, Brown found a clear-cut association between authoritarianism and rigidity only in the 'ego-involving' conditions, and not in the 'non-involved' group.

These studies were early forerunners to many others, which were to investigate the correlations between authoritarian or right-wing attitudes and cognitive styles. Jost and colleagues (2003a) identified over eighty such studies and concluded that, indeed, people with authoritarian attitudes did seem to display particular ways of thinking. In addition to the **intolerance of ambiguity** hypothesized by Adorno and his team, Jost and colleagues (2003a) also found evidence of less **integrative complexity**, increased uncertainty avoidance, greater need for more **cognitive closure** and heightened feelings of fear and threat amongst more conservatively oriented individuals. To be sure, not all of these associations were large – over all the nine indicators examined, the mean correlation was .29; but, given that these were typically averaged over several independent samples, they were all statistically highly reliable. In sum, therefore, there is evidence that more authoritarian (in other words, more prejudiced) people do have a tendency to think in certain ways.

What about the link between authoritarianism and prejudice? As already noted, Adorno and colleagues (1950) found substantial correlations (usually greater than 0.6) between their earlier measure of outright ethnocentrism and the F-scale, correlations which thus confirmed the proposed link between prejudice and personality. Subsequent investigations have borne out this relationship. For instance, in a sample of US students, Campbell and McCandless (1951) found a similar-sized correlation between authoritarianism and their own measure of **xenophobia**, which tapped hostility towards blacks, Jews, Mexicans, Japanese, and English people. Studies outside the USA have also found associations between authoritarianism and prejudice. Pettigrew (1958) found reliable correlations (of between 0.4 and 0.6) between the F-scale and anti-black prejudice, a finding to which I shall return later. In the Netherlands, Meleon and colleagues (1988) reported consistent and substantial correlations between authoritarianism and ethnocentrism, and similar relationships between authoritarianism, sexism and support for extreme right-wing political groups. In India, Sinha and Hassan (1975) found that religious prejudice against Muslims, caste prejudice against Harijans and sexist prejudice were all predictable from the authoritarianism of some high-caste Hindu men. Moreover, the three indices of prejudice also correlated highly amongst each other, further supporting the idea of an underlying prejudiced personality. Also consistent with *The Authoritarian Personality* are the correlations which have been observed between authoritarianism and attitudes towards stigmatized or deviant sub-groups. For example, Cohen and Streuning (1962), then Hanson and Blohm (1974) found that authoritarians were less sympathetic than non-authoritarians towards mentally ill people, even when, as was the case in the former study, the respondents were actually staff in psychiatric institutions. In a similar vein, attitudes towards people with AIDS may be less positive amongst authoritarians (Witt, 1989). Finally, as we will see shortly, a modern variant of the F-scale also correlates reliably with prejudice towards a variety of other outgroup targets (Altemeyer, 1988, 1996).

Despite this range of supportive evidence, research findings on the link between authoritarianism and prejudice have not been entirely unequivocal. Some of the observed correlations are not very strong, usually explaining less than half, and sometimes less than a fifth, of the variance in prejudice scores. Thus, whatever the contribution of personality disposition to expressed prejudice may be, there are clearly other processes at work too. A second problem is that, occasionally, zero correlations have been reported between authoritarianism and outgroup rejection. One interesting example is Forbes' (1985) study of the link between authoritarianism and intergroup attitudes in Canada. Amongst English-speaking respondents there was (as predicted) a significant correlation between authoritarianism and anti-French feeling, although it was very weak (< 0.2). However, the same group showed a *negative* correlation between authoritarianism and a measure of nationalism, and no correlation at all with *inter*nationalism. Even more problematic were the consistent null relationships observed amongst the francophones.[1]

Ironically enough, the explosion of research interest stimulated by *The Authoritarian Personality* quickly identified a number of rather damaging methodological and theoretical flaws in the whole project (Brown, 1965; Christie and Jahoda, 1954; Rokeach, 1956). Since many of these criticisms are both well known and better articulated elsewhere, I shall do no more than rehearse what I see as the most damning of those early arguments, leaving for a later section a more general critique of the attempt to explain prejudice in personality terms.

At a methodological level, most of the critical attention focused on the design and validation of the F-scale (Hyman and Sheatsley, 1954; Brown, 1965). Three problems in particular came to light. The first was that Adorno and his colleagues had used rather unrepresentative samples of respondents on whom to develop and subsequently refine their questionnaires. Despite the impressive size of some of these samples – over 2,000 respondents in the development of the F-scale alone – they were drawn mainly from formal (and predominantly middle-class) organizations. These, Hyman and Sheatsley (1954) suggested, might well attract a particular kind of personality type and, in any case, hardly constituted a sound empirical base from which to construct a general theory of prejudice. A second and perhaps more serious problem concerned the construction of the F-scale itself. In common with other scales devised by Adorno and colleagues, all its items were worded in such a way that agreement with them indicated an authoritarian response. The obvious drawback of this procedure, as Brown (1965) pointed out, was that authoritarianism so measured can easily be distinguished from a general tendency to agree with seemingly authoritative sounding statements (see also Bass, 1955). Finally, the steps taken to validate the F-scale through those in-depth clinical interviews with high and low scorers left much to be desired. Particularly worrisome was the fact that the interviewers knew in advance the score of each respondent, a fact which raised the possibility that, unconsciously or not, they could have influenced the answers they elicited. As psychology was later to discover, even the behaviour of laboratory rats can be affected when one's research assistants are aware of the experimental hypotheses under test (Rosenthal, 1966).

There was other, more substantive criticism to be made of *The Authoritarian Personality* project. This centred on the correlations which Adorno and colleagues reported between authoritarianism and such variables as intelligence, level of education and social class, correlations which were observed still more strongly in later research (Christie, 1954). The theoretical significance of these correlations is that they suggest an alternative explanation for the genesis of authoritarianism. Perhaps the latter simply reflects the socialized attitudes of particular sub-groups in society and does not, as Adorno and colleagues contended, have its origins in personality dynamics deriving from a certain kind of family upbringing (Brown, 1965). This could explain why Mosher and Scodel (1960), when they measured the ethnocentrism of children and their mothers, and also the mothers' attitudes towards authoritarian child-rearing practices, found a reasonable correlation between the two measures of ethnocentrism, but absolutely no association at all between the mothers' child-rearing attitudes and their children's prejudice levels. This strongly suggests some direct socialization of attitudes rather than an indirect shaping of a prejudiced personality by parenting style. However, as we shall see in Chapter 5, even the direct socialization model is not without its problems.

Right-wing authoritarianism: An old wine in a new bottle?

In the face of these criticisms, perhaps it was not surprising that the quest for the prejudiced personality lapsed into relative obscurity in the second and third decades after the publication of *The Authoritarian Personality*. It might have remained there, had it not been for the efforts of Altemeyer (1988, 1996, 1998). Like others before him (for instance Lee and Warr, 1969), Altemeyer set his sights on rectifying the psychometric imperfections of the F-scale. In particular, he sought to correct its most glaring deficiency: the presence of an **acquiescence response set** (all the items worded in the same 'authoritarian direction'). Over the years, Altemeyer has developed a number of versions of what he calls a **right-wing authoritarianism** (RWA) scale, the most recent and now widely accepted of which contains thirty items balanced for the direction of their wording (Altemeyer, 1996). These items, selected from a much larger number, are intended to capture what Altemeyer sees as the three essential ingredients of the authoritarian character: submission (to authorities), aggression (towards deviants or 'outsiders'), and conventionalism (adherence to orthodox moral codes). The following examples will give a flavour of the items in the scale:

Our country will be great if we honour the ways of our forefathers, do what authorities tell us to do, and get rid of the 'rotten apples' who are ruining everything.

A lot of our rules regarding modesty and sexual behaviour are just customs which are not necessarily any better or holier than those which other people follow. [Reverse item: in other words, this item actually measures the *opposite* of authoritarianism and needs to be reversed before being aggregated with the other items.]

Our country will be destroyed someday if we do not smash the perversions eating away at our moral fibre and traditional beliefs. (Altemeyer, 1996, p. 13)

Notice how these statements typically seek to tap two or more of the core constructs at the same time. In the first one quoted, the initial phrase links to conventionalism; in the second one, to authoritarian submission; and in the final one, to authoritarian aggression. As a result, most of the statements are quite long and express several ideas simultaneously. Not surprisingly, since they are purporting to be measuring similar constructs, some of the RWA items bear some resemblance in tone, if not in exact content, to those of the original F-scale. Gone, though, are those items with a strong psychoanalytic flavour, since, for Altemeyer (1996), one of the distinctive features – and virtues – of the RWA scale is that it is freed from the Freudian trappings of its F-scale predecessor.

The RWA scale has good psychometric properties. It has high **internal reliability**, reflected in the fact that all the items correlate respectably with the total score. Its **test/re-test reliability** also appears to be good, typically in the 0.7–0.9 range (Altemeyer, 1996, p. 319). This is prima facie evidence that the scale is measuring a relatively stable personality trait, although, as we shall see, it is not definitive evidence of this. Finally, as evidence for its validity, the scale correlates predictably and positively with a wide range of outgroup prejudice measures, including prejudice towards ethnic minorities, homophobia and (negative) attitudes towards the homeless and law breakers (Altemeyer, 1996). As we have come to expect, these correlations are of 'moderate' magnitude (that is, 0.4–0.6), which leaves more than half of the variance in prejudice unaccounted for by the RWA scores.

Some of Altemeyer's (1996) other claims about his version of authoritarianism are also noteworthy. Eschewing the psycho-dynamic approach of Adorno and colleagues (1950), Altemeyer argues that the origins of authoritarianism lie not in the parent–child dynamics in early childhood but in the wider social learning experiences of the individual, particularly those leading into adolescence. Although he does not have any direct developmental evidence for this hypothesis, Altemeyer does find that high RWA scorers tend to recollect their life experiences as more narrowly conventional and more marked by strict discipline than low RWA scorers do. In other words, people learn to be authoritarian as an adaptation to social environments of particular kinds, and not just as a result of being subjected to the attentions of overbearing parents. One piece of evidence in support of this thesis is that people's RWA scores correlate more strongly (around .70) with a scale tapping experiences with authority situations than with their parents' RWA scores (around .40). Other evidence consistent with this social learning account is the fact that people's RWA scores can be observed to change over their life-span. For example the experience of higher education tends to lower RWA scores, whilst parenthood seems to increase them.

Finally, Altemeyer (1996) also records that he has observed some striking cohort differences in RWA over a twenty-three-year period. Although Altemeyer interprets these fluctuations as evidence for the sensitivity of the RWA scale to detect changes in his students' typical individual life experiences, ironically they can also be viewed as evidence *against* the kind of traditional personality theory that he espouses. I will return to this point in the concluding section of the chapter.

What, then, should be concluded about Altemeyer's attempt to update and improve on the original project of locating the personality type prone to be prejudiced? At a technical level, there is no doubt that the RWA scale is superior to the F-scale. It is balanced for affirmative and negative items and it shows reasonable internal and test/re-test reliabilities. Still, it is not without its flaws. As we saw, many of its items are double-barrelled or even treble-barrelled in form, and normally such complex formulations should be avoided because it is unclear which part of the statement the respondent is (dis)agreeing with (Robinson et al., 1991). Moreover, despite Altemeyer's claim that the RWA measures a single construct, authoritarianism, albeit one with three sub-components (aggression, submission, conventionalism), more careful analysis suggests that these sub-scales should indeed be distinguished (Funke, 2005). Not only does a tripartite structure seem to fit the observed pattern of correlations amongst the items, but the three dimensions can be differentially related to social attitudes. Funke showed how the level of punishment proposed by participants for a hypothetical offender was positively related to the aggression dimension of authoritarianism, but *negatively* to the conventionalism and submission dimensions. Moreover, the aggression and submission dimensions were strongly and negatively related to an 'integration' acculturation orientation (Berry, 1984), whilst the conventionalism dimension was unrelated to that same orientation (Funke, 2005). In short, authoritarianism may be a more complex constellation of personality factors than Altemeyer (1996) surmises.

There is a final potential criticism of the concept of right-wing authoritarianism, one which it shares with the original *Authoritarian Personality* idea: both deal only with one variant of authoritarianism – that siding with the political right. Could it not be that people with other political views are also authoritarian, and hence also prejudiced? This argument was first advanced by Shils (1954), and it was properly developed into a more systematic theory by Rokeach (1956, 1960).

Prejudice on the Left and Right: The Psychology of Dogmatism

Rokeach's (1956) analysis began by distinguishing between the *content* of what a prejudiced person believes in – that is, the specific constellation of intolerant attitudes and the outgroups to which these are directed – and the underlying organization or *structure* of those beliefs. According to Rokeach, the theory and associated measuring instruments of Adorno and colleagues really dealt only with prejudice amongst right-wingers towards conventional conservative targets such as Communists, Jews, and other 'deviant' minority groups. Perhaps, argued Rokeach, it would be possible to find manifestations of outgroup rejection amongst left-wingers as well, albeit towards different targets.[2] The virulent rejection of Trotskyists and other so-called revisionists by supporters of Stalin would be a case in point (Deutscher, 1959). On Rokeach's hypothesis, these apparently very different kinds of prejudice had in common a similar underlying cognitive structure, in which different beliefs or belief systems were well isolated from one another, so that mutually contradictory opinions could be tolerated. Furthermore, such belief systems would be rather resistant to change in the light of new information and would be characterized by their holders' use of appeals to authority to justify their correctness. Rokeach labelled this syndrome of intolerance the 'closed mind' or dogmatic personality, in contradistinction to the 'open minded' or non-prejudiced person (Rokeach, 1960).

To substantiate his theory, Rokeach (1956) devised two new scales. One was the 'opinionation scale'; it consisted of a series of rather extreme social attitude statements, worded both in a right-wing and in a left-wing direction. This was designed to give a measure of intolerance. The other was the '**dogmatism** scale': this one, while intended to be closely related to the opinionation scale, aimed to tap general authoritarianism. Although some of the items of this second scale bore a marked resemblance to the earlier F-scale items and shared the latter's positive response set, it was Rokeach's hope that the dogmatism measure would be a more content-free index of authoritarianism than Adorno and his colleagues had been able to devise. As we shall see, there are grounds for doubting whether he was successful in this.[3]

Using standard psychometric procedures, Rokeach established that these scales were internally reliable. He then attempted to demonstrate their **validity**. This he did in a variety of ways, with – it has to be said – mixed success. In two small studies he compared the dogmatism scores of groups of students judged by their professors or their peers to be especially dogmatic or very open-minded. When the professorial judgements were taken as the criterion, there were no reliable differences between the groups on measured dogmatism, although the scale did prove more discriminatory when peer ratings were used as the bench-mark (Rokeach, 1960). In further studies of the same book, Rokeach compared the dogmatism scores of groups which, on a priori grounds, he considered to be more dogmatic than average (for example non-believers, political liberals). At the same time he also measured their authoritarianism and ethnocentrism using the instruments devised by Adorno and colleagues (1950). Some of these comparisons did indeed support his contention that dogmatism was a more general measure than authoritarianism. For instance, his (admittedly rather small) group of Communists scored the same as the Conservatives on dogmatism, but considerably lower on authoritarianism. On the other hand, these same Communists scored marginally higher than liberals on dogmatism, but lower than them on author- itarianism; this suggested that it might be possible to distinguish general intolerance from a right-wing political position in a way that the F-scale seemed not to do. This hypothesis was further corroborated by evidence from several earlier studies in which dogmatism consistently correlated with both left *and* right-wing opinionation and, of course, with authoritarianism and ethnocentrism (Rokeach, 1956). The latter two measures, however, only correlated with right-wing opinionation. Against this gener- ally supportive pattern of evidence, though, stood the comparisons amongst religious groups, some of which failed to show the expected differences in dogmatism (ibid.).

What are the origins of the dogmatic personality? Here Rokeach followed Adorno and colleagues (1950) in believing that they lay in early family socialization experi- ences, and particularly in the relationships between child and parents. He thus expected 'close-minded' (or dogmatic) people to show the same exaggerated glorifi- cation of their parents and the same other symptoms of repressed anxiety (for exam- ple, nail-biting, nightmares, and so on) that Adorno and his colleagues had described in their portraits of authoritarians. Consistent with this, Rokeach (1960) did find that 'open-minded' students were more likely to describe their parents in equivocal or ambivalent terms and to recollect fewer symptoms of childhood anxiety. However, somewhat surprisingly, it was the 'intermediate' rather than the extremely 'close- minded' group that showed the biggest contrast with the 'open-minded' group.

How useful is the concept of dogmatism for predicting prejudice? Unfortunately, the amount of research addressing this question is rather sparse. Rokeach himself, as we have seen, demonstrated that dogmatism was correlated with the generalized rejection of outgroups measured by the scale of ethnocentrism. Maykovich (1975) also found that a measure of dogmatism was correlated with whites' anti-black attitudes in the USA, even after the effects of major social variables such as geographi- cal region, education, and socio-economic status had been accounted for. Amongst fundamentalist religious groups in Israel, dogmatism was found to be correlated, although not strongly, with anti-Arab prejudice (Kedem et al., 1987; see also Hoge and Carroll, 1973). Finally, in a rare experimental study, Dion (1973) found that dyads composed of high-dogmatic subjects showed no greater discrimination towards a rival dyad in reward allocations; nor were their intergroup evaluations any more biased than those of dyads composed of less dogmatic subjects. In this experiment the mere division into groups seemed more important than the personalities of the groups' members – a phenomenon to which we shall return in Chapter 3.

What of Rokeach's general claim that extremists of the left and right share some personality attributes and have similar cognitive styles? The data from Rokeach's own research are not very convincing. The key study comparing respondents at opposite ends of the political spectrum is based on some very small samples indeed (for exam- ple just thirteen Communists) and, perhaps because of this, none of the crucial 'extremist' versus 'centrist' comparisons on dogmatism are in fact statistically signifi- cant (Rokeach, 1960). McFarland and colleagues (1992) studied the levels and correlates of authoritarianism in the former Soviet Union and in the USA. Although the sampled Russian respondents tended to score lower on authoritarianism than their American counterparts, the pattern of correlations suggested that authoritarianism was *positively* correlated with an endorsement of communist ideals in the former group, and negatively correlated in the latter. In other words, there was no simple link between left and right extremes and authoritarianism; the relation between them depended on the cultural context. Other evidence for the idea that ideologies of left and right share similar psychological characteristics has been provided by Tetlock (1983, 1984). Analysing the rhetoric of both conservative and socialist politicians in the USA and Britain, Tetlock has shown how their arguments tend to be less complex than those of their more centrist counterparts, which supports the idea that the former two groups may see the world in more stark and rigidly defined terms. Whether this difference in cognitive style can be attributed to personality functioning is arguable, however, since it is possible that at least some of it may be determined by whether such a group's party is in government or opposition. When in opposition, politicians tend to make speeches which are less qualified and circumspect than the ones they make when they are in power (Tetlock, 1984). Moreover, a subsequent systematic analysis of the cognitive style of individuals on the left and right of the political spectrum concluded that the balance of evidence supported the view that extreme right-wingers are cognitively more rigid than extreme left-wingers, with little sign of the U-shaped function that Rokeach predicted (Jost et al., 2003a).

Perhaps the most trenchant criticism of attempts to equate extremists of different political persuasions has been made by Billig (1976). He points out that measuring instruments adopted in this kind of research, far from being politically neutral (and thus able to detect purely psychological distinctions), actually contain items which are ideologically heavily laden. He concludes that any differences – or similarities – observed between groups are thus attributable to the aggregation of political attitudes elicited by the particular mix of items on any given scale. To demonstrate this point, Billig and Cochrane (1979) showed that members of the Communist Party and of the National Front Party in Britain *could* be clearly distinguished through a careful analysis of the individual items they endorsed on Rokeach's (1973) value survey instrument – which thus contradicted the idea that they could be regarded as belonging to a common psychological category.

Prejudice as Social Dominance

The final approach that I want to consider in this chapter is a little different in form and scope from the ones we have examined so far. More than just a personality theory, this approach is held by its proponents to be a synthesis of the psychological, sociological and evolutionary processes which conspire to create and maintain hierarchical social systems the world over. According to this view, all forms of prejudice and discrimination are simply manifestations of a universal human tendency to form group-based structures of social dominance, in which members of some groups have the means and the desire to subjugate members of others. What is more, this theory also proposes that members of socially subordinate groups very often acquiesce to, or even actively collaborate in, their own oppression; such is the all-embracing nature of dominance relationships. These are bold claims indeed. Who has made them and why?

Social dominance theory, as this approach is called, has been promulgated by Sidanius and Pratto (1999). They start with the observation that all known human societies seem to be hierarchically organised, some groups having power over others. Of course, the composition of these hierarchies varies widely. In some places they are organized by clan, elsewhere by religion, ethnicity or any of the myriad social categories that human beings find it expedient to employ in order to make sense of their social worlds (see Chapter 3). Which groups are significant in any particular cultural context is a rather arbitrary matter, and for that reason Sidanius and Pratto label them as 'arbitrary set' distinctions. However, in contrast to the huge diversity of arbitrary set systems in existence, there are two categorical dimensions that Sidanius and Pratto believe to be functionally significant everywhere: age and gender – especially gender. The authors argue that, for reasons which they attribute to 'evolutionary survival value', the near universal tendency for older and male members of societies to have more power and privilege than their younger and female counterparts gives these two category systems a privileged status in their theory. Thus they predict that, in general, we should expect to find men displaying greater proclivity for dominance than women and, maybe less generally, we should expect older people to show more dominance than younger people.

But why are group-based hierarchies, whether based on arbitrary sets or on age and gender, inevitable? Sidanius and Pratto (1999) adduce a mixture of evolutionary and social functionalist arguments to sustain their claim. They argue that sexual competition and the biological vulnerability of human infants can help to explain the emergence of gender and age as prevalent dominance relations. Furthermore, as societies produced economic surpluses, other arbitrary divisions would emerge, presumably as a result of competition for the control of those surpluses. Finally, hierarchically organized societies are presumed to be more stable than egalitarian ones, which gives them a 'functional' advantage in the long run. A further implication of such reasoning is that group-based hierarchies will tend to be self-perpetuating, developing various mechanisms to ensure their continuation. Moreover, because it is held to be more socially functional to live in stratified rather than horizontal systems, even members of lower status groups will usually collaborate in their own subordination: 'group oppression is very much a cooperative game', as Sidanius and Pratto (1999, p. 43) put it.[4]

Although the main tenor of social dominance theory is to stress the inevitability and stability of hierarchical systems, its authors do allow that there can sometimes be tensions within those systems, such that some groups, or some individuals within groups, will seek to attenuate rather than enhance the existing inequalities. The measure of **social dominance orientation** (SDO), the most intensively investigated component of Sidanius and Pratto's theory, seeks to capture precisely such differences, both among groups and among individuals, in the degree of their preference for inequalities.

The SDO scale consists of a number of statements (sixteen in its most recent version) affirming or denying the desirability of group inequality. Here are some examples:

To get ahead in life, it is sometimes necessary to step on other groups.
Sometimes other groups must be kept in their place.
We would have fewer problems if we treated people more equally. [Reverse item.]

People's degree of agreement with items like these tends to be quite consistent, producing a scale which satisfies the usual criteria for internal reliability. Sidanius and

Pratto propose that this scale measures the general extent to which individuals value unequal intergroup relationships, and that this preference will in turn translate itself into the endorsement of whatever the contextually relevant form of prejudice may be (for instance into racism or nationalism). In social dominance theory, such prejudices are regarded as myths which help to legitimize the unequal status quo; ultimately they will be reflected in discriminatory behaviour that will reinforce the existing social hierarchy. The SDO scale can also be used at an aggregate level, to test the theory's hypotheses about the relative propensity for dominance between different groups (for example the hypothesis that men score higher than women).

What are the determinants of someone's level of SDO? In contrast to the detailed aetiological theory provided by the originators of *The Authoritarian Personality*, Sidanius and Pratto (1999) do not have a very well specified account of the origins of SDO. They suggest that it stems in part from the person's socialization experiences in a particular stratum of society – for example one may be socialized as white, middle-class and male, to choose a configuration that should produce high levels of SDO according to the theory. In addition, SDO may partly derive from more ideographic life experiences (a certain method of child-rearing); and it may also depend, to a certain extent, on situational factors (the particular intergroup status differences that are psychologically salient in a given context). As we shall see, this last point is rather controversial, because it seems to undermine Sidanius and Pratto's claim that people's levels of SDO reflect *stable* predispositions to agree with (or reject) prevailing ideologies of racism, sexism or whatever. If SDO is so contextually labile, how can it be cross-situationally consistent? There is one final point to make about SDO. Unlike other measures of individual difference I have considered in this chapter, Sidanius and Pratto are at pains to point out that a person's (high) level of SDO is not a marker of pathology or an indication that they are aberrant in some way. Instead, SDO 'reflects normal human variation, in combination with normal socialization experiences, and partly from inherited personality dispositions' (Sidanius and Pratto, 1999, p. 74).

We are now in a position to assess how well social dominance theory can explain prejudice. Not surprisingly perhaps, most research attention has concentrated on the predicted relationship between SDO and various measures of prejudice, and rather less on the larger – and harder to test – claims about the universality and inevitability of group-based hierarchies. Thus Pratto and colleagues (1994) found consistent correlations between SDO and racism, sexism and nationalism (averaging around .50) in several samples of American college students. Importantly, SDO was only very weakly correlated with right-wing authoritarianism and, even controlling for the latter variable, the relationships with various indicators of prejudice were still robust. As expected also, men scored slightly higher in SDO than women. Similar relationships between SDO and different forms of prejudice have been observed by several other investigators (Duckitt, 2001; Duriez et al., 2005; Whitley, 1999). In all these studies SDO was reliably associated with prejudice, even after any effects of RWA have been removed, a result which implies that SDO and RWA are relatively independent correlates of prejudice. Indeed, SDO and RWA are usually only correlated at around the .20 level, although in some contexts the correlations can be noticeably higher or lower (Duckitt, 2001; Duriez et al., 2005).

So a co-variation between SDO and prejudice is well established. But this still leaves open the nature of SDO itself and its causal connection with prejudice. Is it, as Pratto and colleagues (1994) imply in the title of their article, just another 'personality variable predicting social and political attitudes'?[5] Altemeyer (1998) certainly thinks so: he suggests that SDO measures a form of authoritarianism complementary to that of RWA: the dominating rather than the submissive aspect of autoritarianism. Such a conceptualization of personality, at least in its strict form, would mean that people's level of SDO was a rather stable part of their make-up and was a root cause of prejudice, being more or less invariant from situation to situation. It would also imply that different levels of SDO (and prejudice) typically observed among occupational groups (for instance police officers versus social workers) would be a result of self-selection (more dominant people seeking out 'dominating' roles), of institutional selection (organizations employing people whose personalities matched their roles), or of both (Pratto et al., 1997; Sidanius et al.,1994).

However, there are reasons to doubt whether SDO is such a fixed predisposition. Duckitt (2001) has pointed out that the SDO scale, like its RWA cousin, is really a measure of social attitude rather than of personality. The SDO items reflect a general ideological outlook in which the world is seen as a place full of competing groups, with inevitable winners or losers. The RWA items, in contrast, seem to portray the world as a dangerous and threatening place, in which we need the protection of strong ingroup moral values and revered authorities. Although Duckitt (2001) himself links these different world views to underlying personality traits – toughmindedness (Eysenck, 1954) and social conformity (Saucier, 1994) respectively – it is also plausible to suppose that such belief systems could equally well *arise from* certain situations or events, or from being socialized into an institution with a particularly competitive or egalitarian ethos. If this is true, then SDO should no longer be viewed as a primary cause of various prejudices but, instead, as an ideological response to the circumstances people find themselves in. This reaction may well go on to generate a particular intergroup attitude, but it cannot really be regarded as its originator.

Evidence for this alternative conception of SDO has been provided by Schmitt and colleagues (2003) and by Guimond and colleagues (2003). In one of their studies, Schmitt and colleagues (2003, Study 2) first pre-tested their participants for their levels of racism and sexism some time before the experiment proper. Then, in the actual study, they made either ethnicity or gender salient for the participants by asking them to answer five questions on why it felt natural to be a member of their ethnic (or gender) group. They then filled out an SDO scale. Now, if SDO reflects some general predisposition to prefer dominance relations and hence to show prejudice, one would expect it to correlate equally well with both racism and sexism, irrespective of experimental condition. In fact, it correlated only with racism in the ethnicity salient condition, and only with sexism in the gender salient condition. This strongly suggests that SDO was a reaction to situational contingencies (which dictated which identity was salient at the time) rather than an underlying cause of general prejudice. Guimond and colleagues (2003) investigated the possibility that SDO results from differential group socialization. They measured SDO and prejudice in an elite group of students (Law) and in a lower-status group (Psychology), obtaining samples both from first-year and from third- or fourth-year students of these respective disciplines. According to social dominance theory, those bound for a superior status career (the lawyers) should manifest both higher social dominance and (hence) more prejudice. Well, so

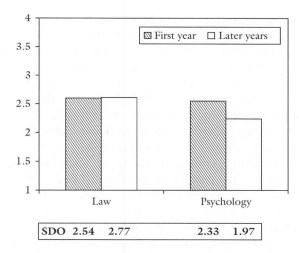

Figure 2.1   Social dominance orientation and prejudice in elite (Law) and non-elite (Psychology) groups of students. Numbers in bold below each bar give the corresponding levels of social dominance orientation for each group. Adapted from Figure 2 in Guimond et al., 2003

they did, but not in quite such a straightforward way. The Law students did generally score higher in SDO than the Psychology students, but this difference was especially pronounced amongst the more senior students. Crucially, though, amongst the first-year students, although there was still a disciplinary difference in SDO, there was *no difference at all* in their levels of prejudice; such a difference only emerged in the older samples (see Figure 2.1). Guimond and colleagues interpret these results as showing that it took some time for the law (or psychology) students to become acculturated to the harshly competitive (or more communal) worlds of their chosen careers, their SDO levels increasing (or decreasing) as a result. Lest it should be thought that there could have been 'cohort effects' – that is, something specific to the particular groups of students studied – Guimond and colleagues (2003) found analogous results using experimentally created groups of differential status.

One last feature of social dominance theory deserves discussion, and this concerns the hypothesis which links social dominance relations to evolutionary processes. As we saw earlier, this link leads Sidanius and Pratto (1999) to the conclusion that group-based hierarchies and the legitimizing ideologies (or prejudices) which accompany them are culturally universal and hence somewhat inevitable. In particular, the theory holds that the sex differences expressed in SDO should be universal. Sidanius and colleagues (2000) did indeed find that men were always more socially dominant in each of the six countries they sampled (China, Israel, Palestine, New Zealand, USA, former USSR), despite substantial differences between these countries on other indicators of inequality. However, other research has been less supportive of this so-called 'invariance hypothesis'. Wilson and Liu (2003) found that the sex difference in SDO only obtained for men and women who identified strongly with their gender categories; for less strongly identified people, they found that women scored higher than men on SDO. Thus it seems that men's and women's social dominance orientation is more contextually dependent than Sidanius and Pratto had surmised.

As for the broader claim that group-based hierarchies are inevitable, this has attracted trenchant criticism, as much for its pessimistic political implications as for its evidential basis (Reicher, 2004; Turner and Reynolds, 2003). As Reicher (2004) put it, 'my concern with theories that posit the inevitability of unequal status relations is not that they are true, but that they might become so' (p. 42). It is true that evolutionary hypotheses are notoriously difficult to falsify, and this alone might give us pause for thought before we incorporate them too eagerly into our theories. Still, we can also have some sympathy for the social dominance theorists' defence that, in attempting to describe and explain hierarchical systems, they are by no means seeking to justify them: 'evolutionarily informed analysis of human behaviour is no more a moral endorsement of that behaviour than geology is a moral endorsement of earthquakes, epidemiology a moral endorsement of Ebola outbreaks, or psychiatry an endorsement of madness' (Sidanius et al., 2004, p. 862). In this they are surely right. Sometimes social science does throw up uncomfortable truths, and our response should be to find ways to combat or circumvent their effects rather than simply to deny their existence.

The Limitations of a Personality Approach to Prejudice

Let me now turn from the discussion of particular theories and consider the wider argument that it is possible to explain the variation and occurrence of prejudice by reference to individual differences in personality. There are, it seems to me, four major limitations to this thesis (see also Billig, 1976 for a similar critique).

The *first* is that it underestimates the power and importance of the immediate social situation in shaping people's attitudes. It is by now almost a truism in social psychology that our opinions and behaviour are strongly influenced by such factors as the attitudes of others around or near to us, the norms of our group, and the relationships between our group and others (Brown, 2000a). So it is with the expression of prejudice. Take, for example, a study by Siegel and Siegel (1957). In one of social psychology's rare true field experiments, Siegel and Siegel were able to observe the change in authoritarianism over a one-year period amongst two groups of American women students. One group had resided in very conservative and traditional sorority housing, whilst the other had lived in dormitories where more liberal norms prevailed. The beautiful feature of this study from a methodological point of view was that the housing assignments had been made on a properly random basis, which thus ensured that at the beginning of the year the two groups would be equivalent in terms of personality and other characteristics. True to form, the students who had been exposed to the more progressive group norms showed a marked decline in their authoritarianism, whilst the sorority group changed hardly at all (see Table 2.1).

The ironic feature of this study is that its measure of prejudice, which proved sensitive enough to detect changes in the respondents' attitudes as a result of their group experiences, was, in fact, the F-scale, supposedly an index of people's temporally and situationally *stable* personality!

Recall, too, the work of Guimond and colleagues (2003) discussed in the previous section. As I noted there, they found that students' levels of SDO and prejudice changed substantially according to the degree subject they ended up studying.

Table 2.1 Changes in authoritarianism after exposure to liberal or conservative group norms

	Time 1	Time 2 (one year later)
Conservative sorority	103.0	99.1
Liberal dormitories	102.1	87.3

Source: Adapted from Table 2 in Siegel and Siegel, 1957

Guimond and colleagues were also able to change SDO and prejudice by means of a short-term experimental manipulation. Further evidence for the situational specificity of prejudice and for its underpinnings has been provided by Verkuyten and Hagendoorn (1998). They had the insight that a personality variable like authoritarianism might only be influential in determining prejudice in situations where people's group affiliations were not particularly salient. In contrast, they argued, when group identities were psychologically foremost, such personality determinants would give way to factors such as ingroup norms or stereotypes about an outgroup. In their studies they managed to activate people's personal or social identities by asking them a series of questions *either* about their individual characteristics (appearance, hobbies, and so on) *or* about their nationality. This simple procedure was enough to change radically the correlation between authoritarianism and prejudice: the correlation was positive and significant in the personal identity condition (the first group tested) but negligible in the social identity condition (the second group tested). In the latter group it was ingroup stereotypes that reliably predicted prejudice, a relationship completely absent in the personal identity condition (see also Reynolds et al., 2001).

The *second* limitation of the thesis that prejudice can be explained by reference to individual differences in personality is an extension of the above argument to a broader cultural or societal level. The seminal study here is the cross-cultural research undertaken by Pettigrew (1958), who examined prejudice in South Africa and the USA. Unsurprisingly, he found that white South Africans showed very high levels of anti-black prejudice, as did whites from the southern USA. However, whilst there was a correlation at an individual level between authoritarianism and prejudice in both places, the overall means for authoritarianism given by the sample were no higher than in other, less prejudiced groups. In other words, in terms of overall distribution of personality types, the sampled populations were rather similar to 'normal' ones, despite their overtly racist attitudes. Pettigrew's conclusion was that the origin of this racism lay much more in the prevailing societal norms to which these respondents were exposed than in any personality dysfunction. This conclusion was reinforced by the consistently high correlations he observed between prejudice and measures of social conformity.

Over the years, South Africa has been a particularly interesting context in which to study the determinants of prejudice because of its institutionally racist structure during the apartheid era. The apartheid system, founded as it was on the twin premises of ethnic segregation and white supremacy, provided a fertile breeding ground for the generation and transmission of racist ideas. Following Pettigrew's (1958) research, several other studies have examined the origins of prejudice there. In general, the

Table 2.2 Ethnic discrimination in English children: Percentage of allocation
strategies adopted

| | Ethnic origin of children | | | |
Patterns of sweets allocation[a]	White	West Indian	Asian	All
Ethnocentric	59.8	41.4	39.8	50.2
Fair	24.7	36.0	25.8	27.8
Outgroup favouring	0.4	0.8	1.6	0.8

Notes: [a] According to the definition adopted in this experiment, 'ethnocentric' were those children
who gave at least three out of the four sweets to their own group; 'fair' were those who distributed
two sweets to each of the ethnic groups; 'outgroup favouring' was the behaviour of those who
predominantly favoured another group at the expense of their own.
Source: Adapted from Table 9.2 in Davey, 1983

existence of an intra-individual correlation between authoritarianism and prejudice
has been confirmed, although not always strongly (Colman and Lambley, 1970;
Duckitt, 1988; Heaven, 1983). Perhaps more important, however, is the finding that
socio-demographic variables have been consistently good predictors of levels of prejudice, independently of the levels of authoritarianism. For example Afrikaans-speakers
and groups of lower socio-economic status have tended to be more prejudiced than
English-speaking or middle-class groups (Duckitt, 1988; Pettigrew, 1958). The existence of these large sub-cultural differences further strengthens the argument that
social norms rather than individual personality dynamics determine overall levels of
prejudice in particular groups.

The *third* difficulty with any personality account is its inability to explain the
uniformity of prejudiced attitudes across whole groups of people. The very nature
of such theories – explaining prejudice via individual *differences* among people –
makes them particularly unsuited to explain how prejudice can become virtually
consensual in certain societies. In pre-war Nazi Germany – or, until the early 1990s,
in modern-day South Africa – consistently racist attitudes and behaviour were
observable amongst hundreds of thousands of people, who must surely have differed
on most other psychological attributes. For a contemporary and more systematic
illustration of the pervasiveness of prejudice, albeit in a milder form, Davey's (1983)
study of interethnic attitudes amongst English children will serve well. Part of this
research involved having children share out some sweets between unknown members of different ethnic groups shown in photographs. As can be seen in Table 2.2,
of the 500 or so children participating, fully 50 per cent were ethnocentric in their
distribution of sweets – that is, they gave more to the ingroup photographs than to
other group members. Of the white children, nearly 60 per cent showed this
discrimination. It is difficult to imagine that so many of these children, coming as
they did from a variety of perfectly ordinary backgrounds, had all been exposed to
a particular kind of family dynamics, or childhood socialization, alleged to give rise
to the prejudiced person (see also Chapter 5).

A *fourth* problem concerns the historical specificity of prejudice. If uniformities of
prejudice are hard to explain with a personality model, the sudden rises and falls of

prejudice over time are equally problematic. For instance the growth of anti-Semitism under Hitler occurred over the space of only a decade or so, much too quickly for a whole generation of German families to have adopted the child-rearing practices necessary to engender authoritarian and prejudiced children. The attitudes of the Americans towards the Japanese before and after the bombing of Pearl Harbour in 1942 would be another, even more telling case (Seago, 1947). The changes here, both at a personal and at an institutional level – including the establishment of large prison camps for Asiatic Americans – took place over a matter of months (Nakanishi, 1988). In more recent times, the rise of islamophobia in many countries after the events of 11 September 2001 would serve as another example (see for instance Kaplan, 2006).

Another two recent and systematic studies underline this point. Recall the changes in authoritarianism observed over a twenty-three-year period, between 1973 and 1996, with successive cohorts of Canadian undergraduates (Altemeyer, 1996). As we saw earlier in the chapter, Altemeyer observed considerable variations in authoritarianism over this period. Significantly from an **aetiological** point of view, over the same period the parents of those students changed hardly at all in their levels of authoritarianism. Even more impressive were the results of a longitudinal study of over 900 Dutch adolescents (Vollebergh, 1991). Tracing the changes in authoritarianism over a two-year period, Vollebergh observed a small but highly reliable decrease in authoritarianism. Moreover, this phenomenon could be observed at each of the five age levels she studied. Temporal changes such as these are, as I have already noted, rather awkward for explanations which trace the origins of prejudice to family dynamics. These historical changes pose a still more critical problem for the personality approach, because they suggest that authoritarianism and social dominance may actually be an effect of changing social conditions rather than deriving from particular histories of socialization. If this is so, then, as every student of introductory statistics is constantly reminded, the commonly observed correlations between personality variables and prejudice, rather than indicating a causal relationship between them, may actually stem from their joint dependence on these wider societal factors.

This interpretation is rendered more plausible by a series of archival studies which have examined historical co-variations between different economic indices and several societal indicators of authoritarianism. The first of these studies was conducted by Sales (1973), who proposed that an important source of authoritarianism, in adults as much as in children, is the existence of threatening factors in society. Chief amongst these are the prevailing economic conditions: when times are hard, people feel under greater threat than they do in periods of prosperity. Sales reasoned that such feelings of threat would manifest themselves in people's attraction towards more authoritarian forms of religion. Conversion rates to various American churches between 1920 and 1939, a period spanning the boom years of the 1920s and during the great depression of the 1930s provided some support for this hypothesis. There were reliable negative correlations between income levels and conversion rates to 'authoritarian' religions like Catholicism and Seventh-Day Adventism, but positive associations for the 'non-authoritarian' churches like the Presbyterian. Thus, to paraphrase Marx's famous dictum, it is especially authoritarian religions that are the 'opiates of the people' in times of economic recession. Sales (1973) then extended his analysis by ingeniously devising some other indicators of authoritarianism. For example he suggested that, in a

threatening climate, popular culture icons like comic strip characters should emphasize power and toughness; there should be a growth in the popularity of astrology and
other superstitious beliefs; and people's choice of pet dogs should veer towards aggressive hunting breeds such as Dobermann Pinschers and German Shepherds. All these
indices showed reliable associations with economic variables. Similar archival studies
of Germany in the pre-war period and of the US in the 1970s and 1980s have largely
supported Sales' conclusions (Doty et al., 1991; Padgett and Jorgenson, 1982). More
recently still, Perrin (2005) observed a noticeably more authoritarian tone in letters
to American newspapers after the 11 September terrorist attacks. Interestingly, and
probably as a counter-reaction, there was also a (smaller) increase in non-authoritarian
letters in the same period.

   This idea that authoritarianism might be a collective response to group-related
threats has been advanced by Duckitt and Fisher (2003) and by Stellmacher and
Petzel (2005; see also Duckitt, 1989). Duckitt and Fisher (2003) asked their New
Zealand participants to read one of three 'future scenarios' for New Zealand as it
might be in ten years time. One of them depicted a socially and economically threatening future (high levels of unemployment and crime, political instability); another,
a secure and prosperous future (economic growth and social harmony); and the
third one, a 'neutral' status-quo-prevails outcome. As expected, reading these different scenarios reliably altered participants' world views and levels of authoritarianism
and, though less evidently, their levels of social dominance. Stellmacher and Petzel
(2005) took the argument further by developing a *group* authoritarianism scale, an
instrument which, they believe, measures collective reactions to identity threatening
situations. In their model, they still retain individual predispositions to authoritarianism as a starting point, predispositions which then interact with the strength of
group identification and with the social threat, to produce an increase in authoritarian group reactions (conformity to group norms, obedience to leaders and xenophobia). In an experiment in which psychology students' career prospects were
threatened (or not), Stellmacher and Petzel did indeed observe such an interaction
between individual levels of authoritarianism, identification and threat: group
authoritarianism was highest amongst students who were initially high in individual
authoritarianism, who also identified strongly as psychologists and were in the high
threat condition.

   It seems to me that these are promising developments and offer the prospect of
rescuing a purely personality-based approach to prejudice from the cul-de-sac that it
ran into. Adorno, Rokeach and others after them believed that the answer to the
problem of prejudice lies in the structure of the individual's personality: children
experiencing particular upbringing would grow up to be deferential towards authority, to be rigid in their thinking and, above all, to be hostile towards minority groups
and foreigners. However, as we have seen, such a personalistic approach runs into
problems when it comes to accounting both for the pervasiveness of prejudice in
some times and places and for its almost complete absence in others. If personality
factors are important at all, then it is probable that they are so for those at the two
extremes of the distribution of prejudice: the perpetually tolerant and the unremit-
ting bigot. For the remaining large majority, personality may be a much less important determining factor of prejudice than the many and varied *situational* influences
on behaviour. Furthermore, for these people it may even be more appropriate to

regard variables like authoritarianism and social dominance as effects of those same social and cultural variables rather than as causal agents in their own right.

Summary

1   A common explanation of prejudice attributes it to some special type of personality. The most famous example of such an explanation within psychology is the theory proposed in *The Authoritarian Personality*. This model proposed that certain family conditions, particularly the experience of excessively harsh and moralistic parenting, produce an outlook on life which is over-deferential towards authority, socially conservative, hostile towards minority or 'deviant' groups, and dominated by a simplistic cognitive style. This approach was widely criticized on methodological grounds and has been supplanted by Altemeyer's (1996) right-wing authoritarianism theory.

2   An extension of work on authoritarianism is Rokeach's hypothesis that intolerance and mental rigidity are not the exclusive prerogative of the political right but can be observed in extreme left-wingers also. This theory, too, is not without its empirical difficulties.

3   Social dominance theory seeks to explain prejudice as an expression of social dominance – an orientation which is inherent in all hierarchically organized societies. The existence of group-based hierarchies is also a universal feature of human existence according to this theory. However, the causal status of social dominance orientation has been questioned in recent research.

4   Personality accounts of prejudice are limited because of their tendency to downplay situational factors and to neglect the influence of societal or sub-cultural norms. Furthermore, they cannot readily explain the widespread uniformity of prejudice in some societies or groups. Nor can they easily account for historical changes in the expression of prejudice. Recent analyses view authoritarianism and social dominance as responses to changing intergroup conditions rather than as prime causes of prejudice.

Notes

1   Given the size of the samples (both larger than 600), it seems unlikely that the absence of any strong relationships in this study is attributable to a lack of statistical power.

2   Another attempt to link personality to prejudice but to separate it from political conservatism was made by Eysenck (1954).

3   Somewhat surprisingly, the work on prejudice for which Rokeach is most well known did not employ dogmatism as an independent variable. This is his 'belief congruence theory', which is dealt with more fully in Chapter 3.

4   This kind of argument has much in common with system justification theory (e.g. Jost et al., 2004: see Chapter 8).

5   In subsequent versions of social dominance theory, Sidanius and Pratto modified their position somewhat (Sidanius and Pratto, 1999; Sidanius et al., 2004). Although they still wish to claim that SDO reflects some underlying personality trait, they do allow for its variation as a function of situationally relevant variables. Still, they argue that, even if absolute levels of SDO can change in different contexts, *relative* levels – that is, the rank order of individuals along the SDO dimension – should not change.

Further Reading

Billig, M. (1978) *Fascists: A Social Psychological View of the National Front*, ch. 3. London: Harcourt Brace Jovanovich.

Duckitt, J. (2001) A dual-process cognitive–motivational theory of ideology and prejudice. *Advances in Experimental Social Psychology* 33: 41–113.

Sidanius, J., and Pratto, F. (1999) *Social Dominance: An Intergroup Theory of Social Hierarchy and Oppression*, chs 2–3. Cambridge: Cambridge University Press.

3

Social Categorization and Prejudice

Already in the first two chapters we have encountered several examples of prejudice which, though they have all differed widely in their intensity and mode of expression, have all had one thing in common: they all involved some negative sentiment directed *towards a particular group of people, or at least towards representatives of that group*. It will be recalled from Chapter 1 that this is one of the defining characteristics of prejudice: it has this categorial basis, as opposed to other forms of antipathy, which are more interpersonal or idiosyncratic in character. Viewing prejudice in this way is important, because it emphasizes its social consequences for those who are its target. Prejudice is not something hat happens to isolated individuals; potentially it can affect *any* member of the outgroup in question.

Such a categorial definition is also important for another reason. It underlines the fact that the perpetrators of prejudice are very likely to have engaged in a certain kind of cognitive activity before, or perhaps as, they formed their prejudiced judgement or performed their discriminatory deed. When someone makes a racist or sexist remark, or when an employer chooses to employ someone because s/he is a member of his/her own group, in preference to someone equally well qualified from another group, they have mentally invoked one or more social categories. They have used that categorization as the starting point of inferring some attributes about the people in question and then, often, in order to justify their actions towards them. Indeed, so central is the categorization process to the operation of prejudice that some have argued that it is the *sine qua non* without which prejudice could not exist (Allport, 1954; Tajfel, 1969a).

In this chapter, which is the first of two devoted to the cognitive processes underlying prejudice, I begin by considering the most direct consequences of **categorization**: **intercategory differentiation** and **intracategory assimilation**. In subsequent sections I consider what happens when more than one categorial dimension is psychologically salient. First I show how and when the differentiation and assimilation processes combine in situations where the categories cut across each other. Next I focus particularly on the intracategory assimilation process, a process which leads to members of the same group being seen as more similar to each other than they really are. In intergroup contexts, this process seldom operates symmetrically; usually one group is seen as more homogeneous than the other. Next I consider what factors govern the choice of different available categorizations for making sense of any given situation. Finally, and by way of a direct contrast, I consider a theory which proposes that category differences are less important for intergroup attitudes than is commonly supposed.

Sorting Out the World: Social Categorization, a Fundamental Cognitive Process

The idea that social categorization is a necessary precursor of prejudice is crucial because it emphasizes prejudice's ordinary or common-place nature (Allport, 1954). Categorization is a cognitive process which does not just occur in bizarre circumstances or in certain pathological cases. It is, as Bruner (1957) suggested some years ago, an inescapable feature of human existence. Why is this? It is so because the world is simply too complex a place for us to be able to survive without some means of simplifying and ordering it first. Just as biologists and chemists use classification systems to reduce nature's complexity to a more manageable number of categories, linked together in scientifically useful ways, so we, too, rely on systems of categories in our everyday lives. We simply do not have the capability to respond differently to every single person or event that we encounter. Moreover, even if we did have that capacity, it would be highly dysfunctional to do so, because such stimuli possess many characteristics in common with each other, as well as attributes which distinguish them from other stimuli. By assigning them to categories on the basis of these similarities and differences, we can deal with them much more efficiently. This is one reason why human languages are all replete with complex systems of categories and sub-categories; they permit ready reference to whole classes of people and objects, without constant need for particularistic description. In Allport's memorable phrase, categories are 'nouns that cut slices' through our environment (Allport, 1954, p. 174).

To give an example: suppose I visit some foreign city and I need to find my way to some famous landmark. It is much more useful for me, in order to ask for directions, to be able to recognize particular categories of people (for example police, taxi drivers, local residents) than simply to ask the first person I meet (usually an equally lost fellow tourist). What is a matter of mere convenience in this mundane example can become literally a question of life or death in more threatening environments. To be able to recognize and behave appropriately towards members of 'our' and 'their' side in the streets of Baghdad or Jerusalem can make the need for fast and accurate categorial judgements more than a little important for one's personal survival.

Exaggerating and overlooking differences: Differentiation and assimilation

If categories are to be useful simplifying and ordering devices, then it is important that they help us to discriminate clearly between those who belong and those who do not. One of the first people to recognize this was Campbell (1956), who, in a rarely cited paper, observed that an important facet of stereotyping was an enhancement of the contrast between groups. Then, by eliciting such a contrast effect in a simple physical judgement task, he demonstrated that this was a rather basic consequence of categorization. He asked his participants to learn the physical location of some nonsense syllables (on every trial, a given syllable was always presented in the same position along a horizontal line). Within the stimuli there were two implicit categories of nonsense syllable, one in which the central letter was always 'E', the other which always ended in an 'X'. The 'E' group were always presented towards the left, the 'X' group to the right, although they overlapped in the middle. Campbell found that participants made consistent errors in estimating the position of these overlapping syllables: the 'E' stimuli were moved to the left, the 'X' stimuli to the right, so that the physical locations of the two categories of stimuli were even more clearly separated.

This principle was later formalized by Tajfel (1959) into two hypotheses concerning the cognitive consequences of categorization. The first hypothesis claimed that, if a category distinction is imposed on a set of stimuli – whether these be physical objects, sensory events, or people – such that some of the stimuli fall into class A and the remainder into class B, then this will have the effect of enhancing any pre-existing differences between the members of the two resulting categories A and B. The second hypothesis, really a corollary of the first, was that differences *within* the categories will be attenuated. Or, put less formally, members of different groups will be seen as more different from each other than they really are, whilst members of the same group will be seen as more similar than they really are.

The first direct test of these hypotheses was carried out by Tajfel and Wilkes (1963). Like Campbell (1956), they studied judgements of physical stimuli. They asked their participants simply to estimate the length of a series of lines, presented one at a time. There were in fact eight different lines, each differing from its neighbour by a constant amount (a bit less than 1 cm). This is an easy enough task and, sure enough, people in the control conditions made quite accurate estimates. However, in the experimental conditions one small new piece of information was made available to participants as they made their judgements. On each card containing the stimulus line, the letter 'A' or 'B' appeared. It so happened that the four shorter lines were labeled 'A', the four longer lines 'B'. The addition of this simple A/B categorization had a curious effect on the participants' judgements: most of their estimates remained accurate, with the exception of the perceived difference between the longest 'A' line and the shortest 'B' line (that is, the two lines marking the boundary of the A/B dichotomy). Consistently, this difference was seen by participants to be twice its actual size (around 2 cm). In other words, just as Tajfel had hypothesized, the perceived difference between the two categories had been exaggerated. However, contrary to his second hypothesis, there was much less evidence that differences *within* the categories were reduced.

Stimulated by these experiments, others have confirmed the category differentiation effect in a variety of different tasks, including sound patterns comprising speech phoneme categories, judgements of area, estimates of temperature in different months of the year, impressions of faces, and the evaluation of attitude statements (Doise, 1976; Eiser and Stroebe, 1972; Krueger and Clement, 1994). The last two judgemental tasks are interesting because they are more social in content and hence imply that, as Campbell (1956) had surmised, the effects of the categorization process may apply in a rather wide range of situations. Moreover, other experiments have confirmed the existence of the intracategory assimilation effect also. McGarty and Penny (1988), using a judgement paradigm devised by Eiser (1971), found evidence of both category differentiation *and* assimilation. Participants had to judge a series of statements expressing various political views, rating each one for how left-wing or right-wing it was. In one of the categorization conditions, all the right-leaning statements were attributed to 'Author A' and all the left-leaning statements to 'Author B'. In a second condition, these uninformative categorial attributions were elaborated upon by 'A' being described as an 'American right-wing political candidate' and 'B' as a 'Canadian Marxist Sociologist'. The presence of these informative labels should act so as to enhance any accentuation or assimilation processes because of the extra political connotations they convey. And, of course, there was a condition in which the statements were unlabelled. Participants' judgements were reliably affected by the labeling of the statements: the perceived differences between the left-leaning and the right-leaning statements were magnified when labels were attached to the statements as compared to control, and this effect was even stronger with the informative labels; on the other hand the differences *among* the two types of statement were correspondingly diminished, again especially in the informative labels condition (see also Doise et al., 1978).

Us and Them: Social categorization and intergroup discrimination

So far we have seen that introducing a principle of categorization into an otherwise undifferentiated situation has some predictable distorting effects on people's perceptual and cognitive functioning. But, it might reasonably be objected, surely most of these phenomena are rather far removed from the kinds of social judgements and behaviour involved in intergroup prejudice? Is there any evidence that social categorization has any more meaningful consequences for people's attitudes and behaviour towards members of their own and other groups? Indeed there is. In later sections we shall encounter several other instances where categorization processes are seen to have some quite complex and profound effects on intergroup relations; but before dealing with these there is one further consequence of the mere fact of categorization itself which needs describing. This is that categorization seems to provide the sufficient condition for people to begin to favour their own group over others, whether in the form of biased evaluative judgements or through some kind of concrete behavioural **intergroup discrimination**.

One of the first studies to demonstrate this idea was Rabbie and Horwitz (1969). Dutch school children who were strangers to one another were randomly divided into groups of four, labelled 'green' and 'blue', allegedly for administrative reasons. They then worked on their own on some irrelevant tasks for a few minutes. Then, depending on experimental conditions, one of two things happened. Some of the children learned that one of the groups was to receive a reward (some new transistor radios) for helping with the research, whilst the other would not, apparently due to a shortage of resources. This 'common fate' would be decided through the toss of a coin. However, for other children – in the control condition – this piece of information was omitted; hence they had nothing in common with each other than their colour label. The participants were then asked to rate each other on a number of socio-metric scales. The question was: would these impressionistic ratings of what were more or less complete strangers be influenced by those flimsy labels, 'green' and 'blue'? The results showed that in the conditions where the children experienced some interdependence – the unexpected and arbitrary reward or deprivation – there was clear evidence that those from the ingroup were rated more favourably than those coming from the other group. In the control condition, on the other hand, the ratings appeared to show no such bias. Rabbie and Horwitz initially concluded that mere classification was not itself sufficient to influence people's intergroup judgements; what seemed to be necessary was some additional feeling of interdependence. Actually, as they later conceded, that conclusion was premature (Horwitz and Rabbie, 1982). In a follow-up study, where they increased the size of that control group, they did find some (statistically significant) evidence of ingroup–outgroup differentiation. Here, then, was the first evidence that simply placing people into one of two, albeit pretty meaningless, categories could have predictable effects on their judgements of real peers (and not just of physical stimuli or of hypothetical others).

This conclusion was confirmed, in an even more dramatic fashion, in a series of experiments initiated by Tajfel and colleagues (1971). These researchers set out to discover if simply belonging to a group, and nothing else, might be enough to instigate a rudimentary form of behavioural prejudice – that is, the differential treatment of ingroup and outgroup members. To this end, they devised what has come to be known as the **minimal group paradigm**, so called because it sought to create groups which had been stripped bare of all the usual concomitants of group life – face-to-face interaction, an internal group structure, a set of norms, relationships with other groups, and so on (see Brown, 2000a). All that remained, in fact, was the knowledge of having been placed in one category rather than another. To achieve this rather bizarre situation, experimental participants are usually invited to take part in a 'decision-making' experiment, the first part of which consists of showing them some pairs of abstract paintings and making them indicate which of each pair they prefer.[1] Supposedly on the basis of these preferences, each person is then allocated to one of two groups; in the original experiments these were called Klee and Kandinsky, named after the painters of the pictures. An important feature of this group allocation procedure is that it is done privately; nobody knows who else is in their (or in the other) group. In this way the anonymity of the groups is preserved, and possible contaminating factors like having particular friends in one of the groups are avoided. The next part of the 'decision-making' experiment is then introduced. This consists of the participants allocating money to various other people, identified only by code numbers and group membership, by using especially prepared booklets of reward matrices[2] (see Table 3.1). To eliminate self-interest as a motive, the participants are never able to award money to themselves.

What strategies might they use? An examination of Table 3.1 reveals that there is a number of possibilities. One perfectly reasonable objective might be always to try to give the two anonymous recipients as near as possible the same amount, on the grounds that there was really nothing to choose between them – who *were* numbers 72 and 47 after all? Another rational strategy would be to choose the box that totaled the highest sum, with the aim of maximizing the amount that would eventually be dispensed to everyone. Still another possibility would be to choose at random, since the whole situation was so devoid of cues for action that this was as sensible as anything. Or, finally, one could choose to discriminate systematically between recipients on the

Table 3.1 Two sample matrices from the minimal group paradigm

	Reward points[a]												
Matrix 1[b]													
Member 72 of Klee group	18	17	16	15	14	13	12	11	10	9	8	7	6 5
Member 47 of Kandinsky group	5	6	7	8	9	10	11	12	13	14	15	16	17 18
Matrix 2[b]													
Member 74 of Klee group	25	23	21	19	17	15	13	11	9	7	5	3	1
Member 44 of Kandinsky group	19	18	17	16	15	14	13	12	11	10	9	8	7

Notes. [a] On each page participants must choose one pair of numbers which stand for real monetary rewards.
[b] These are two of several types of matrix used. Matrix 1 was designed to measure general ingroup favouritism, while Matrix 2 was designed to measure the tendency to maximize the difference between ingroup and outgroup recipients. In the experiment, these matrices would be presented to each participant at least twice: once as above, and once with the group affiliations of the two recipients reversed.
Source: Adapted from Tables 2 and 7 in Tajfel et al., 1971

basis of their group membership. In fact the evidence shows that only the first and the last of these strategies are used with any regularity (Branthwaite et al., 1979; Turner, 1980). The usual pattern is for people to make some effort to be fair in their allocations but, at the same time, to show a reliable tendency to award more money to ingroup members than to outgroup members. Thus in the original experiments, in Matrix 1 in Table 3.1, over 70 per cent of participants made choices favouring their own group, with a mean response from people in the Klee group (say) of between the 14/9 and 13/10 boxes (Tajfel et al., 1971).

This was true even when, in absolute terms, that ingrouper would be worse off. For example, in Matrix 2 the mean response from those in the Kandinsky group was somewhere between the 13/13 and 12/11 options (Tajfel et al., 1971). Note that this choice results in the Kandinsky recipient receiving 6–7 points less than s/he might otherwise have done; but, crucially, s/he thereby receives *more* than the Klee recipient. This **maximizing difference** strategy, as it is known, has been a consistent feature of findings from minimal group studies (Turner, 1981).

Such intergroup discrimination in minimal group settings has proved to be a remarkably robust phenomenon, having been replicated more than twenty times in several different countries by a wide range of participants (Brewer, 1979; Diehl, 1990; Tajfel, 1982). Nevertheless, despite this empirical consensus, there are two intriguing exceptions to this apparent 'generic' (minimal) social discrimination. The first concerns social situations in which there is more than one outgroup. Although in the real world outside the laboratory intergroup relationships are often reducible to a dichotomous 'us' and 'them' division, other arrangements can be found. For example, in the Balkans War in the 1990s there were at least three participating groups: Bosniaks (that is, Bosnian Muslims), Serbs and Croats (or four, if one includes the United Nations). As I write, Iraq is embroiled in a war involving the occupying armies of USA, Britain, and Shia and Sunni Muslim groups. What happens in the minimal group paradigm if the usual two-group scenario is extended to include a third group? The short answer seems to be: not very much! Hartstone and Augoustinos (1995) tried to replicate the standard findings of intergroup discrimination in point allocations in a situation in which participants were faced with two outgroups instead of one. Few signs of the usual ingroup favouring biases were observed (see also Spielman 2000, Study 2).

The second anomalous finding has emerged from minimal group experiments that have substituted sanctions for rewards in the allocation phase of the procedure. For example, Mummendey and colleagues (1992) adapted the classic paradigm, so that participants were asked to distribute, to ingroup and outgroup members, what they thought would be durations of an unpleasantly high pitched tone or time to be spent on a boring task. The use of this measure seemed to eliminate ingroup favouritism completely, and strategies of equalizing outcomes (fairness) or minimizing the total aversive experience were much more in evidence. Only in special circumstances – for example when participants are placed in a low-status minority group – does the 'usual' ingroup favouritism appear. This difference between positive and negative forms of discrimination seems to be rather pervasive and can also be observed in people's inter-group judgements on positively and negatively worded value dimensions (Buhl, 1999; Mummendey and Otten, 1998). What gives added significance to this **positive–negative asymmetry effect** (as it is called) is that most forms of prejudice actually involve some kind of negative treatment or judgement of outgroups.

I will return shortly to these exceptional findings; but, for now, it is worth noting that the apparently spontaneous discrimination observed in the standard minimal group paradigm is quite consistent with the more general differentiation phenomena associated with the categorization process (Doise, 1976). Consider the situation confronting the experimental participants. For the few minutes of the experiment there is little for them to distinguish their fellow participants. The code numbers are apparently random and hence uninformative. Faced with this ambiguity, they latch on to the only other available piece of information – the Klee and Kandinsky category memberships – and then they use it to make sense of the situation. Once that particu-lar (and only) classification has been adopted, the inevitable category differentiation occurs, and it occurs in the only way possible here: by allocating different amounts to ingroup and outgroup recipients. This is why it is so significant that participants often seem to be as concerned with maximizing the differences between the categories as they are with favouring the ingroup in an absolute fashion. Here is, at a socially mean-ingful behavioural level, apparently the same phenomenon that can be observed in physical and social judgements.

What should we make of the fact that discrimination is so much harder to observe in multigroup contexts, or when sanctions rather than rewards are at stake? It is possible, but by no means certain, that such findings are still explicable through the operation of categorization processes. In the two (or more) outgroup situation – especially in the socially stripped-down minimal paradigm – it is conceivable that the categories lose some of their psychological utility as cognitive organizing devices. In an extreme case, would one expect people to attach much significance to a division of twenty or thirty of their class-mates into five, or even ten groups? Probably not. In the case of the asymmetry between allocations of rewards and punishments, it seems likely that what happens when participants in minimal group experiments are asked to administer negative outcomes is that they recategorize the situation into 'us' (*all* the participants, whatever their group membership) versus 'them' (the experimenter(s)). This could be caused by the unusualness – not to say, inappropriateness – of being

Table 3.2 Rewards and punishments in the minimal group paradigm: Levels of discrimination and relative category importance

	Experimental condition			
	Rewards		*Punishments*	
	Allocate	*Remove*	*Allocate*	*Remove*
Discrimination[a]	2.14	−0.77	0.60	1.13
Relative category importance[b]	0.21	2.54	2.33	0.43

Notes: [a]Positive scores indicate discrimination that favours the ingroup; scores close to zero indicate little or no discrimination.
[b]Identification with school minus identification with Klee.
Source: Adapted from Tables 2 and 5 in Gardham and Brown, 2001

asked to inflict unpleasant experiences upon one's peers. If such a recategorization did occur, then it would follow from categorization principles that differences amongst participants (for instance between members of Klee and Kandinsky groups) would be reduced, while differences between participants and the experimenter would be accentuated. We have found some evidence for this explanation (Gardham and Brown, 2001). We elaborated Mummendey and colleagues' (1992) design, so that participants in different experimental conditions were asked either to allocate or to withhold rewards or punishments. We found that the positive–negative asymmetry effect also extends to the withdrawal of rewards, as well as to the infliction of punishments (see Table 3.2). What is more, the participants' sense of the relative significance of the artificial Klee/Kandinsky groups and of the real-life superordinate school group perfectly mirrored the pattern of discrimination levels (see Table 3.2, lower half). Indeed we could show that the relative importance of the two groups statistically accounted for the discrimination findings.

Unconscious ingroup favouritism

The experiments I have just discussed all involved people making conscious decisions about the treatment of ingroup and outgroup members. As we have seen, there is a good deal of evidence to show that these decisions reveal ingroup favouritism, even when the groups concerned are essentially meaningless. But such ingroup preference is not limited to the conscious domain; it can also be observed in our automatic or unconscious responses. One study which showed this was by Perdue and colleagues (1990). In their experiment they first presented some pronouns with ingroup or outgroup connotations ('we', 'us', 'they' and so on). But the exposure of these pronouns was so brief (55 milleseconds (ms)), and they were so rapidly overwritten on the screen by another word, that few would have been able to detect what had actually been presented. The participants' task was simply to indicate as quickly as they could whether the second word was a positive or a negative description. Only that.

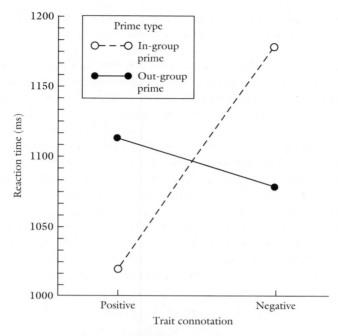

Figure 3.1 Unconscious ingroup favouritism: Reaction times for positive and negative words preceded by subliminal ingroup/outgroup primes. Source: Perdue et al., 1990, Figure 2

The rather dramatic finding was that people's reaction times to make that decision were systematically affected by the first **subliminally** presented pronoun. As can be seen in Figure 3.1, reaction times for positive words were noticeably shorter when the word in question had been primed by 'we' or 'us' than they were for negative words with the same primes. The subliminal priming of the implied outgroup labels had less effect – a finding confirmed in a subsequent experiment.

The same kind of ingroup positivity bias was observed by Otten and Moskowitz (2000) using a rather different technique. In this experiment participants were first assigned to one of two minimal groups. In a subsequent task they had to read some sentences that described some everyday behaviours of either ingroup or outgroup members. Each sentence could be taken to imply a particular positive or negative trait, although the word for that trait never actually appeared in the sentence. After each sentence had been removed form the screen, a trait word appeared and participants had to decide whether or not that word had actually appeared in the previous sentence.

Sometimes the trait word was relevant to the sentence, at other times it was irrelevant. Regardless of this, the participants' correct response should always have been to indicate that the word had *not* appeared. However, Otten and Moskowitz believed that, in the case of sentences about ingroup members displaying positive behaviours, participants would suffer some interference with their decisions, especially by comparison with sentences about ingroup negative behaviours. And the researchers were proved to be right. Response times in the former trials were over 100 ms longer than in the latter trials.

For the outgroup behaviours there was no corresponding difference. The point is that the participants' judgements were made entirely spontaneously, with little time spent in deliberation.

These studies, like the earlier ones involving reward allocations to minimal ingroup and outgroup members, are important because they suggest that at least some of the origins of prejudice are to be found in the operation of normal cognitive processes. This idea of prejudice as essentially normal or ordinary is, of course, in marked contrast to the approaches considered in Chapter 2, where the emphasis was much more on prejudice as a deviant or pathological syndrome. As I argued there, the personality perspective, while potentially useful to explain prejudice in some of its more extreme forms, was limited precisely because of its inability to account for its more common-garden, every-day manifestation. However, let me hasten to add, this recognition of the 'ordinariness' of prejudice should not lead us too quickly to assume its inevitability. Whilst it is true that the world is replete with categories of different kinds – men and women, employed and unemployed, old and young, black and white – as we shall see later, there are still complex issues to unravel in ascertaining which of these categories will come into play when, and what happens when different category systems operate simultaneously.

When people belong to more than one group: The effects of crossed categorizations

I have a friend who works in a Canadian university. Naturally she has both male and female colleagues, though the latter are rather fewer. As in many Canadian public institutions, both English and French may be used in the teaching and administration of the university and, in fact, both anglophones and francophones[3] work there. Let us imagine a hypothetical committee of academics at this university evaluating some job applications for a research position. The composition of this committee, let us assume not too implausibly, is almost entirely male anglophones. How, we may ask ourselves, might they react, were they to be confronted with a succession of candidates some of whom were anglophones, some francophones, some male and some female? In due course, I shall present some empirical data which we collected to answer just such a question as this; but let us first analyse the situation theoretically, from what we know of the operation of categorization processes. As we saw in the previous section, we should expect an enhancement of the between-category differences and a diminution of the within-category differences. Doise (1976) has argued that, in the case where two categories cut across one another (in our example, gender and language preference), any differentiation in terms of the original categories will be reduced, because of the simultaneous operation of the between-category and within-category effects on both dimensions. As Figure 3.2 illustrates, the differentiation and assimilation processes should effectively cancel each other out, and the end result should be lessened bias – or perhaps even completely abolished – in terms of gender or language.

There is a good deal of evidence which supports this hypothesis. Social anthropologists have often noted how societies which are characterized by cross-cutting kinship and tribal systems seem to be less prone to internal feuding than those with a more pyramidal structure. Gluckman's (1956) analysis of the Nuer people from the Sudan showed how their kinship system reduces the likelihood of severe intergroup

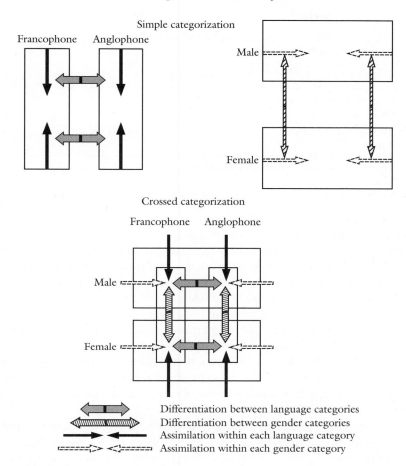

Figure 3.2 Effect of crossed categorizations

conflict. For example, marriage rules prohibit intermarriage with any relative less than seven generations distant, thus effectively requiring people to marry outside their immediate community. Such exogenous marriage conventions create a complex web of loyalties between neighbouring groups, since any village is likely to contain relatives by marriage. Of course, not everything is perfectly harmonious. Gluckman noted that, while cross-cutting structures may alleviate *internal* tensions, they can heighten aggression towards 'real' outsiders (those with no kinship ties at all). Thus Nuer rules of warfare carefully constrain the kinds of weapons permitted and impose limits on the violence between tribes; but they contain no such prescriptions where 'foreigners' are concerned. Quantitative analyses comparing 'matrilocal' societies (such as the Nuer) with other types of arrangement confirm this correlation between crossed categorization, internal cohesion and external aggression (LeVine and Campbell, 1972).

The first attempts to examine this same idea experimentally told a similar story. Deschamps and Doise (1978) asked some teenage girls to rate 'young people' and 'adults', and 'males' and 'females', on a number of stereotypical traits. Half of the

Table 3.3 Effect of cross-cutting gender and ethnicity on intergroup liking in Hong Kong[a]

Ethnicity	Same-sex targets[b]	Opposite sex targets[b]
Cantonese (own group)	3.2	2.5
Shanghai	3.0	2.4
American	2.8	2.2
Indian	2.5	1.9

Notes: [a]Participants were Cantonese children.
[b]Scale 1–4.
Source: Adapted from Table 1 (collapsing across boys and girls) in Brewer et al., 1987

girls rated these groups as dichotomous pairs. This was the simple categorization condition. The remainder rated the categories in conjunction: 'young females', 'male adults', and so on. This was the crossed categorization condition. In the latter, the perceived differences, both between the age and between the gender categories, were consistently smaller than in the simple categorization condition. In a second study, in which groups of young girls and boys were subdivided into 'red' and 'blue' groups, an even more dramatic reduction in bias occurred. With just a simple categorization, both boys and girls showed ingroup favouritism in their judgements of task performance; in the crossed condition, that gender bias completely disappeared. In fact even those who were of the opposite gender *and* belonged in the other colour group were rated as favourably as those who were in the same category – and on both criteria.

These experiments stimulated a number of others. Using two artificial and hence equally (un)important categories, Brown and Turner (1979) found that some bias persisted in the partially overlapping case (that is, when one membership was shared but not the other) and was magnified in the completely non-overlapping case (that is, when neither category was shared). With an occasional exception, that pattern has been replicated in other studies, which used ad hoc groups (Crisp and Hewstone, 2000, 2001; Migdal et al., 1998; Urban and Miller, 1998). That particular configuration of bias has been labeled the 'additive' pattern, because it is as if the two dimensions of categorization combine together to create the most favourable evaluations of double ingroupers, the least favourable of double outgroupers, and intermediate evaluations of those in the overlapping cases (Hewstone et al., 1993). Indeed, that finding is so common that it has been labeled the baseline or default pattern in crossed categorization situations (Crisp et al., 2002). However, as we shall see, once we venture outside the laboratory, other patterns of bias are also likely to occur as a result of crossing categorizations.

In a study undertaken in Hong Kong, for instance, Brewer and colleagues (1987) asked some Cantonese boys and girls to express their liking for each of eight hypothetical peers. The 'stimulus' children were either male or female and were from one of four different ethnic groups: Cantonese (like the participants under study), Shanghai, American, and Indian. The participants' liking ratings showed two things clearly (see Table 3.3). First and foremost, they preferred those of their own gender. This was the strongest single element. They also showed a clear preference for the two Chinese groups over the other two, but this preference was slightly stronger when evaluating same-gender targets than opposite gender targets. Brewer and colleagues interpreted their findings as showing that, for these children, gender assumed greater importance than ethnicity and that, unlike in Deschamps and Doise's (1978) laboratory experiment, the addition of the second (ethnic) dimension was not enough to eliminate that potent gender bias. Notice that even Cantonese (ingroup) children of the opposite gender were viewed no more favourably than Indian children of the same gender.

This tendency for one categorial dimension to dominate in real-life contexts was confirmed in a study conducted amongst Bangladeshi Muslims and Hindus (Hewstone et al., 1993). Here the cross-cutting categories were religion (Muslim versus Hindu), nationality (Banglasdeshi versus Indian) and, in a second study, language use (Bengali versus other languages). In the Hong Kong study above, gender had dominated; here it was religion. If people were seen as sharing the same religion, they were always evaluated positively. If not, the ratings dropped sharply, no matter if they were of similar nationality or spoke the same language. Across the border in India, religious distinctions also tend to dominate (Hagendoorn and Henke, 1991). In the early 1990s there was significant civil unrest in several cities in India, sometimes sparked off by disputes over the ownership of particular religious sites. The nature of the religious prejudice underlying this unrest is well caught in the following extract from an interview with a middle-class Hindu Indian:

> To be honest, Muslims who stayed behind in India at the time of partition were riff-raff. There are exceptions, of course, but in general Indian Muslims are not very intelligent. The elite went to Pakistan. And in Bombay, Muslims are the underworld, the mafia if you like. They are the gold smugglers, the drug dealers, the illegal currency, that sort of criminal thing. And they think of themselves as Muslims first and Indians second – never the other way round. (*Independent*, 13 December 1992)

The field studies serve as important reminders that the question of which category dimension will assume pre-eminence in any situation is dependent on particular local circumstances. In Northern Ireland, Iraq and the Indian sub-continent, religion is often crucial. Elsewhere, however, other social divisions come into the fore – as in Rwanda, in the 1994 genocide. Indeed so various are the complexities of intergroup situations in the real world that social psychologists continue to be preoccupied with disentangling the processes at work in multiple categorization contexts. Hewstone and colleagues (1993) identified several different possible intergroup outcomes from such situations, of which, as we have seen, the 'additivity' and 'category dominance' are two common patterns. Another pattern is where the double ingroup serves as a baseline and *any* categorial deviation from it (that is, partial or whole) causes a decrease in evaluation or liking. This is sometimes called a 'category conjunction' effect. Surveying the literature, Urban and Miller (1998) and Migdal and colleagues (1998) have identified some factors which seem to be associated with these different patterns. As I have already indicated, both papers agree that the 'additive' pattern is the most commonly occurring outcome. If situational factors are such as to create cognitive overload or negative mood in people, then this tends to shift the outcome away from the 'additive' pattern towards a 'category conjunction' effect (Urban and Miller, 1998). On the other hand, and rather self-evidently, the more the category dimensions differ in psychological importance, the greater the likelihood is of a 'category dominance' outcome. And if factors are present that will lead to a greater emphasis on individuals and to a lessening of the salience of intergroup boundaries – a constellation known as 'personalization' – then this tends to shift the outcome towards the original pattern observed by Deschamps and Doise (1978): an 'equivalence' of evaluations of all category combinations, or a general reduction in bias (Ensari and Miller, 2001).

There is one final factor worth mentioning, and it concerns the effect of having present *several* cross-cutting category dimensions simultaneously. After all, a moment's reflection reminds us that we belong to many different groups, and these member-ships may overlap (or not) with those of potential outgroup members. So how would a young Afro-Caribbean man, who happens to be gay, who is studying science at university X and who also supports the West Indies cricket team, judge an elderly (or young) Bengali man (or woman) who is straight (or gay), who studies law (or science) at university Y (or X) and who supports the Indian cricket team? The effects of such multiple, potentially overlapping (or excluding) categories have been studied by Crisp and colleagues (2001) and by Hall and Crisp (2005). Initially they found that the simultaneous presence of several category dimensions tended to reduce (though not to eliminate) the amount of bias shown towards someone who was an outgroup member on at least one dimension (for instance different university). Intriguingly, there was no greater bias if that person was an outgrouper on all dimensions than if he or she was an outgrouper on one dimension but an ingrouper on the remainder (Crisp et al., 2001, Study 2). It may well have been that the presence of so many bases of categorization led the participants to cease seeing the situation in categorial terms. Still, such a result seems slightly at variance with our earlier conclusion that those who are double (or treble) outgroupers will typically be viewed rather unfavourably (Brown and Turner, 1979; Hewstone et al., 1993). The resolution of this apparent disparity may well have been provided by Hall and Crisp (2005), who spotted that the benefi-cial effect of having many categories present is only manifest if those categories are unrelated to each other. If, as so often happens in the real world, the different dimen-sions are correlated (for example, ethnicity, nationality and religion often co-vary together), then being a multiple outgroup member no longer confers any benefits – quite the reverse (Hewstone et al., 1993, Study 2).

Thus the complexities of intergroup situations in the real world, particularly where the groups are of different size or status and may be co-operatively or competitively interdependent, should lead us to be cautious about the efficacy of criss-cross arrange-ments for reducing prejudice. As one final illustration, let me return to the Canadian personnel selection situation with which I began this discussion. In the course of a survey of university academics, we included a hypothetical scenario in which six candidates (described in brief curricula vitae) were applying for a research assistantship (Joly et al., 1993). The CVs had been carefully prepared: there were four equally good ones, differing only in gender and language preference, and two obviously infe-rior ones, both from men, one anglophone, one francophone. Our respondents, who also included both male and female anglophones and francophones, were asked to indicate their recommendation for a payment rate for these six candidates. Not surprisingly, the two weaker candidates were generally allocated lower salaries (see Table 3.4). However, amongst the 'good' candidates there was some evidence of bias against francophones – even, it has to be said, from the francophones themselves!

Table 3.4 Effect of cross-cutting categories in a Canadian university: Recommended payment rates for research assistant candidates[a]

'Strong' candidates[b]				'Weak' candidates	
Female anglo.	Male anglo.	Female franco.	Male franco.	Male anglo.	Male franco.
5.7	5.4	4.9	3.8	3.6	2.8

Notes: [a]Summed across M, F, anglophone and francophone respondents. Scale 1–7, where 1 = $19 per interview, 7= $25 per interview.
[b]Amongst the 'strong' candidates both the anglo vs. franco and the male vs. female differences are significant.
Source: Joly et al., 1993

(Breaking Table 3.4 down into different types of respondent did not produce a markedly different picture.) Once again, then, the presence of two cross-cutting categories did little to diminish the historically rooted perception of francophones as a lower-status group. In addition, and perhaps somewhat surprisingly, the female candidates fared slightly better than the male candidates, though this gender bias was less strong than the language bias. Once again, we have an example of one category dimension dominating, rather than being cancelled out by, the other.

Why do they all look the same? Perceived intragroup homogeneity

The two fundamental effects of categorization are the exaggeration of intergroup differences and the enhancement of intragroup similarities. As the study of these effects was extended to a wider range of settings, particularly settings involving the categorization of people, it became clear that the effects were not symmetrical; there were consistent differences in how the ingroup and the outgroup were perceived. In this section I want to focus on asymmetries in the second effect: the assimilation of within-category differences, or **perceived intragroup homogeneity**.

Everyday observation suggests that, if there is a bias in the perception of intragroup homogeneity, it is in the direction of seeing the outgroup as more homogeneous, its members more alike one another, than the ingroup: 'they are all alike, *we* are all different'. Here is John Motson, a well-known (white) football commentator making a revealing remark during a radio interview:

> There are teams where you have got players who, from a distance, look almost identical. And, of course, with more black players coming into the game, they would not mind me saying that it can be very confusing [...] if there were five or six black players in the team and several of them are going for the ball it can be difficult. (*Independent*, 5 January 1998)

Hamilton and Bishop (1976) observed something similar among the white residents they interviewed in neighbourhoods in Connecticut, into each one of which a new family, either black or white, had recently moved. The respondents were more likely to mention the arrival of the new family if it were black than if it were white. However, despite this greater awareness, they seemed to know less about the new black families. After one month, only 11 per cent knew the last name of the new black family, by comparison with 60 per cent who knew the name of the new white family. Apparently the black families continued to be seen in categorial terms, as blacks, with little to distinguish them, whilst the white families were seen more as individuals.

One of the first attempts to study this phenomenon systematically was by Jones and colleagues (1981), who asked members of university clubs to rate the members of their own club as to how similar they were on a number of trait dimensions. The exercise was repeated for members of other clubs. Jones and colleagues found a consistent tendency for members of outgroups to be seen as more similar to one another than members of the ingroup. Similar results have been obtained in several other studies (Linville et al., 1989; Ostrom and Sedikides, 1992; Quattrone, 1986).

What is the explanation for this **outgroup homogeneity effect** (as the phenomenon is known)? On one view, it stems from the different amount of information we have about ingroup and outgroup members (Linville et al., 1989). We usually know more individuals in our own group, we may interact with them more and, as a result, be more aware of the differences between them. Members of the outgroup, on the other hand, because they are known less well, are likely to be seen in a more undifferentiated fashion. A second model adopts a slightly different perspective, suggesting that it is not information about a number of specific exemplars that is important, but the nature of the category as a whole (Park et al., 1991). According to this view, people hold in their heads, not a tally of specific ingroup or outgroup people known, but more abstract conceptions of the categories as a whole, modeled on the prototypical member of each and on some estimate of the variability around this typical person. The reason why the ingroup may be seen as more variable is that the conception of that category is more important (because it contains the self), more concrete (again, because there is there at least one case very well known to us), and more provisional (because of a presumed greater motivation to form an accurate impression about those who are close to us psychologically).

Although intuitively plausible, the first view – call it the familiarity hypothesis – does not have much empirical support. Linville and colleagues (1989) did find that over the period of a semester members of a university course rated their fellow class-mates as increasingly more variable, and then they demonstrated in a computer simulation that greater perceived variability can be associated with changes in familiarity. However, these findings stand against a number of other studies, which have either found either no effects for familiarity, or even an inverse correlation. For example, in Jones and colleagues' (1981) study referred to above, there was no association between the number of members known in each group and the estimates of that group's variability. Another problem for the familiarity hypothesis is that the outgroup homogeneity effect can still be observed in minimal group situations, where there is equal and near-zero information about both ingroup and outgroup, because the groups concerned are anonymous (Wilder, 1984b). Even more problematic is the evidence from some research of ours, which examined variability judgements during the process of group formation (Brown and Wootton-Millward, 1993). We studied groups of student nurses over a year of their training. These groups were small (typically less than twenty) and their members had extensive daily face-to-face contact with one another. If Linville and colleagues are right, the greater mutual acquaintanceship afforded by this experience should have led to enhanced perceived variability within the ingroup over time, and thus to a more pronounced outgroup homogeneity effect. In fact there was *no* consistent tendency towards greater perceived ingroup variability over time and, still worse for the familiarity hypothesis, on at least two judgemental dimensions it was the ingroup, and not the outgroup, that was seen as more homogenous.

With respect to the last finding, this was only one in a series of studies which have shown that the outgroup homogeneity effect is far from being the universal feature of intergroup perception that it is sometimes claimed to be (Simon, 1992a). Curiously enough, one of the first – and often overlooked – studies of perceived homogeneity also found evidence of *ingroup* homogeneity (Stephan, 1977). Stephan studied the mutual perceptions of black, white and Chicano school children in the South-West of the USA. Contrary to the many studies which came after, Stephan found that all three groups saw their own group in *less* differentiated terms than they saw the other two groups. Noting that at least two of the groups in Stephan's study were minorities, we speculated that an ingroup's size relative to other groups might be an important factor in determining whether ingroup or outgroup homogeneity would be observed (Simon and Brown, 1987). Perhaps, we thought, where an ingroup is in the minority, it may feel its identity to be under threat from the larger majority group. One response to such a threat might be a greater need to protect the cohesion and integrity of the ingroup by seeing it in more homogeneous terms – a kind of psychological closing of ranks. Using a minimal group paradigm, we independently varied the size both of the ingroup and of the outgroup and discovered, as we had expected, that those who found themselves in a relatively smaller group showed a clear ingroup homogeneity; those in the non-minority groups showed the usual outgroup homogeneity effect (see Figure 3.3). Two further details from the experiment confirmed our suspicion that people's identities might be involved in this reversal. One was the data from the control conditions: there exactly the same judgements were made, but with one crucial difference – the participants were not themselves allocated to a group, and hence they were acting as neutral 'observers'. These participants showed no tendency to see smaller groups as more homogeneous, thus ruling out the possibility that our results could be explained as simply an effect of group size (see also Bartsch and Judd, 1993). A second and clinching point was the finding that those in the minority groups identified more strongly with their ingroup than members of larger groups.

The discovery that minority groups typically display **ingroup homogeneity** has been confirmed in several other studies, both inside and outside the laboratory (Mullen and Hu, 1989; Simon, 1992a). Two examples will suffice here. One comes from an educational setting and exploits the fact that in most universities women form a distinctive minority (in this case they are outnumbered by about 8:1; Brown and Smith, 1989). Judgements from male and female staff in the British university studied replicated the earlier Simon and Brown (1987) finding: men (the majority) showed outgroup homogeneity, women showed ingroup homogeneity. In a follow-up study conducted both in British and in Italian universities, Hewstone and colleagues (2006) confirmed these results, and also showed that the extent of the homogeneity bias, whether ingroup or outgroup, depended on the proportions of men and women in each academic department: the more skewed that proportion, the larger the bias.

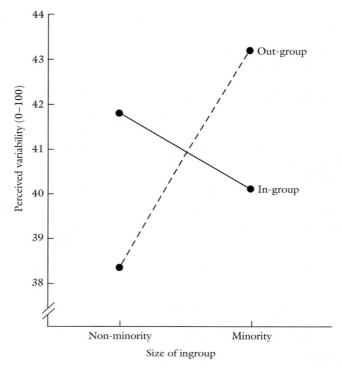

Figure 3.3 Perceived intragroup homogeneity in minority–majority contexts. Derived from Table 1 in Simon and Brown, 1987

Similarly, in a study of heterosexual and homosexual men, it was found that the latter saw their fellow gays as more similar to each other than members of the majority out-group; heterosexuals, on the other hand, generally showed outgroup homogeneity (Simon et al., 1991). In neither the Brown and Smith (1989) nor the Simon and col-leagues (1991) studies was there any consistent relationship between perceived homo-geneity and the number of group members known to a respondent – which, once again, contradicted the familiarity hypothesis.

We have seen, then, that people's direct knowledge of ingroup and outgroup members cannot satisfactorily explain these differences in the perception of intra-group homogeneity. Moreover, the existence of *ingroup* homogeneity in certain intergroup contexts also raises problems for the second explanation, which posits more abstract conceptions of ingroup and outgroup (Park et al., 1991). What other explanations might there be? One clue comes from the finding in the Simon and Brown (1987) experiment already referred to: the idea that group identity is more important for minority group members. Turner and colleagues (1987) have suggested that the process of identifying with a group involves the simultaneous operation of two other processes: that of matching oneself to what is seen to be the key defining, or 'criterial', attributes of the ingroup prototype; and that of maximizing the distance between this prototype and the outgroup prototype. It is the first process that is of interest here. To the extent that people strive to make themselves more similar to some idealized conception of what a 'good member' should be, this will tend to induce an enhanced perception of ingroup similarity, at least along certain dimensions.

The dimensional specificity of homogeneity perceptions is by now well established. Kelly (1989), in her study of British political parties, found that party members saw their own party as being more homogeneous on those issues which were central to their party's ideology, but less homogeneous on more general criteria. Similarly, in our study of student nurses, we found ingroup homogeneity on dimensions relevant to nursing ('care and understanding', 'communication'), but the opposite on criteria more relevant to the doctors' outgroup (for example 'professional independence'; see Brown and Wootton-Millward, 1993). Both of these studies replicate the same basic pattern found in more controlled laboratory conditions (Simon, 1992b). All in all, therefore, it seems reasonable to suppose that an important factor contributing to asymmetries in group homogeneity perceptions consists in processes stemming from people's identities as members of certain groups and not of others (see Chapter 6).

When, Where and How Do We Categorize? Factors Governing Category Use

As we have seen, in most social situations there is more than just one categorial dimension available to participants. When I bring to mind a typical lecture class, for instance, I recall that it consists of rather more women than men; there is a majority of white British students and a sprinkling of people from various other ethnic and national minorities; most are between the ages of 18 and 21, but there is usually a handful of older students, often noticeable because they sit together; I remember, too, that not all are studying for psychology degrees, since our courses are routinely taken by students from other disciplines too; there may also be a couple of my colleagues sitting in on the lecture, as part of the new university appraisal system; finally, there will be a diversity of sartorial styles – a very occasional jacket and tie, maybe a 'goth' or two, both making a striking contrast to the jeans and t-shirts worn by the more conventionally attired students. Which of these categories are most likely to be uppermost in my mind as I give my lecture and what factors govern that choice?

The first point to note is that there are different *levels* of categorization, some more inclusive than others. In the example above, the most inclusive category would be 'student' or, perhaps, if I wished to include my colleagues and me, 'members of the university'. Several other categories would have been much less global and might consist of combinations or partitions of categories – for instance, 'mature psychology students'. According to Rosch (1978), when people categorize the physical world of objects they are most likely to use what she calls 'basic' level categories – for example 'chairs' and 'tables' – rather than 'superordinate' or 'subordinate' levels (for example 'furniture' or 'bar stool' respectively). Extending this argument to the social domain, Turner and colleagues (1987) suggest that, in general, the basic level for categorizing people is that of the social group, whatever it happens to be in any situation. The corresponding superordinate and subordinate levels are those of 'human beings' and of 'individual differences' respectively.

Shortly I shall examine some of the factors that determine which of the available groupings are selected on any particular occasion; for now, it is worth emphasizing that there is growing evidence to the effect that what constitutes commonly used basic social categories is in fact, quite often, not broad undifferentiated groups but rather sub-types within them. Brewer and colleagues (1981) asked (young) college students to sort some photographs into piles in any way they wished. The set of photographs contained various pictures of elderly people and some of people the students' own age. Analysis of the sorting strategies used by the students indicated that these typically did not comprise a simple 'old' versus 'young' dichotomy but were responsive to apparent sub-divisions within the elderly category (for example 'senior', 'elder statesman'). As we shall see in Chapter 5, this use of sub-sets of a larger category is also prevalent in younger children.

This tendency to use sub-types was confirmed by Stangor and colleagues (1992) using a less direct method. In their experiments they showed participants a series of photographs of black and white men and women. Associated with each photograph was a statement which that person had purportedly made. The participants' job was subsequently to recall which statement had been made by whom. If they used either of the ethnic or gender categories to assist them in this memory task, one would expect systematic confusion errors amongst members of the same category – for example thinking that 'Mark' had said something which had in fact been attributed to 'David' – but fewer errors between different categories – for example confusing a statement of 'Mark' with that of 'Joan'. The pattern of errors showed clearly that both principal categorizations were used (though gender more strongly than ethnicity); but they seemed to be used in conjunction with each other, so as to form sub-categories (for example 'white women', 'black men', and so on). This was revealed by the fact that the highest number of errors was made in the within-sex within-ethnicity combination – roughly twice as many as in the other combinations. There was one further interesting result from this research: more prejudiced participants (as determined by a pre-test on a prejudice scale) were slightly more inclined to make within-ethnicity confusion errors than less prejudiced participants – a phenomenon suggesting that, for the prejudiced participants, ethnicity was a particularly important category. I shall return to this finding in a moment, since it bears on the question of which categories are chosen when.

Knowing that people prefer to use more refined groupings than simply 'old' and 'young', 'black' and 'white', does not in itself help us to predict which of the many possible ways of carving up the world will actually be chosen on a given occasion. To do this we need to know more about the people who perceive the situation (What are their habitual ways of seeing things? What are their needs and goals?), and more about the situation they are confronted with (What are the actual similarities and differences amongst the people in it? What happened immediately before which might have 'triggered' one set of categories rather than another?). These insights were provided by Bruner (1957), who suggested that the categories most likely to be used are those which are most 'accessible' to a person – this is shorthand for the first set of questions – and those which best **fit** the stimuli he or she is faced with – the second set of questions (see also Higgins, 1989).

To illustrate these ideas of '**accessibility**' and 'fit', let me return to my (not so) hypothetical classroom context. In that situation, as we saw, there is a multiplicity of categories and of cues associated with them. As a teacher, perhaps the most obvious thing I will do is to classify the room into 'students' and 'staff'. This division might be particularly likely on this occasion because I am uncomfortably aware of the presence of my two colleagues at the back of the room. Because I am being evaluated on that day, my self-awareness as a teacher and my need to perform well are especially salient to me. On other occasions, however, the student/staff division may be less useful to me. In the usual run of things I may be more attentive to national differences in the class, simultaneously monitoring the level of understanding amongst those for whom English is not their first language and the level of boredom amongst the native English speakers (should I go too slowly or repeat myself too often). I might make further divisions. In an earlier chapter I confessed my affinity for things and people Italian. This could lead me to identify the two or three students from Italy amongst the larger group of foreign students and perhaps to address an example or joke (in my bad Italian) in their direction. My habitual or 'chronic' interest in this domain makes that particular category especially accessible to me. Moreover, a joke from me, or a remark in that spirit, will probably draw my audience's attention to the same group division, even if only temporarily.

But, whatever categories I bring with me to the classroom because of my idiosyncratic predispositions or temporary task goals, they will only be useful to me if they match the actual people in front of me in some way. It is thus rather likely that the categories Catholic and Protestant will be used. As far as I am aware, few of my students are religious and this particular categorization simply would not discriminate amongst them.[4] On the other hand, a categorization by gender or nationality does actually correspond to some real differences amongst the class members. Of course, some of these differences are more clear-cut than others. Campbell (1958) and Rosch (1978) pointed out that most stimuli in our environment do not form themselves into perfectly defined groupings, but nearly always have an element of approximation or 'fuzziness' about them. Campbell (1958), in particular, identified some of the factors which seem to lead to discrete entities (that is, people) being seen as groups – a property he called '**entitativity**'. These are common fate, similarity, and proximity. People who move around together or to whom similar things happen (who have a common fate) can be said to form a category, much as – to use Campbell's example – the close spatial and temporal interdependence of the molecules of a stone leads to its being seen as a single object. Likewise, people who are similar to one another in some respects (for example they speak the same language) are likely to be classified together. Those who are often physically near one another or in proximity – the mature students in my example – may also be regarded as a group for some purposes. In sum, there are some real physical, psychological and cultural differences between people to which categories must correspond, even if only approximately, if these categories are to be functional for us.

'Accessibility' and 'fit' are not independent of each other. Since, as we shall see, which categories are most accessible can change from situation to situation, this shift has implications for their 'fit' with the real differences between the things being perceived. Also, not all the categories are psychologically equivalent for us: we are members of some and *not* members of others. Turner and colleagues (1987) have noted that this introduces an element of asymmetry into the accessibility–fit combination. According to Turner and colleagues, the categorization which is more likely to be adopted in any situation is that which simultaneously minimizes the difference between self and the most prototypical member of the ingroup and maximizes the difference between that prototypical ingrouper and the prototypical outgroup member. This they have formalized into what they call the optimal '**meta-contrast ratio**'; and the important point they stress is that this ratio does not have a fixed formula for the perceiver in any situation. If, for whatever reason, a different ingroup identity becomes salient, a different metacontrast ratio becomes operative. As we saw above in discussing accessibility, my identity in that classroom might switch from 'teacher' (versus student) to 'English' (versus 'foreign'), depending on immediate contextual needs and cues.

Let me now examine some of the empirical research which has investigated this question of the choice of categorization. First I deal with three features of the immediate situation which have been found to be important: the entitativity of potential category members; their perceptual distinctiveness; and the recent external evocation of a category. These are all directly relevant to the 'fit' component of Bruner's (1957) theory. Then I turn to the 'accessibility' component by considering some aspects of the perceiver which have also been found to determine category usage.

Category fit: Situational factors and the choice of categories

As we have seen, Campbell (1958) suggested that the way people (as stimuli) actually stand in relation to each other influences whether they are perceived as members of the same group. One of the clearest demonstrations of the truth of this statement was provided by Gaertner and colleagues (1989), in a study investigating how ingroup bias can be reduced. Gaertner and his colleagues reasoned that, if members of two categories could be perceived as belonging to a single superordinate group or, alternatively, as separate individuals, then any ingroup bias associated with these categories would be reduced. Accordingly, in three different experimental conditions they sought to maintain a two-group division, to subsume it in a larger category, or to eliminate group cues altogether. Through the use of artificial group labels (different colour tags), six participants were initially assigned to one of two groups and had to work together in those groups. The two groups were then brought together to work on a further task, and the nature of this encounter was systematically varied. In the 'two-group' condition, the members of the group sat opposite each other at a table, keeping their original group labels, and interacted mainly amongst each other, with a view to winning a prize for the best single solution to the task. In contrast, in the 'one-group' condition the members of the two groups sat in alternate places around the table, devised a new group label for the larger entity formed through the joining of the groups, and worked with each other to win a prize for the best joint group solution to the task. And in the 'individual' condition each person sat at a separate table, was asked to think up an idiosyncratic name, and worked towards the best individual solution. Notice how this experimental manipulation incorporated all three of Campbell's (1958) criteria for entitativity: physical proximity (where they sat), similarity (the labels) and interdependence of fate (the reward outcomes). Table 3.5 shows how the manipulation affected the participants' perception of the situation. It is clear (from the percentages along the upper left to lower right diagonal) that it had a

Table 3.5 Situational effects on perceived entitativity (% of participants in each condition choosing each cognitive representation of the situation)

Cognitive representation	Experimental condition		
	Two groups	*One group*	*Separate individuals*
Two groups	80.0	21.7	16.7
One group	18.9	71.7	15.8
Separate individuals	1.7	6.7	67.5

Source: Gaertner et al., 1989, Table 1

marked effect on the way participants categorized each other. And, as expected, these altered perceptions were also associated with differences in ingroup bias, being least observed in the 'one-group' case, most in the 'two-group' condition. (I shall return to this experiment in Chapter 9.)

Of course, there were many cues that can elicit perceptions of entitativity. Magee and Tiedens (2006) found that seeing a number of individuals showing similar emotional expressions (whether happy or sad) was more likely to lead to a judgement of entitativity than a situation where they displayed different emotions. Lickel and colleagues (2000) asked people to rate the entitativity of a large number of naturally occurring groups (forty; for instance sports teams, families, ethnic groups) as well as the occurrence of various other attributes of those same groups (for instance group member similarity, common outcomes, amount of intragroup interaction). The attribute that correlated most strongly with perceived entitativity was the amount of interaction: the more group members did stuff with each other, the more of a group they were seen to be. Having common outcomes and goals and being seen to be similar also led to perceptions of groupness, if less strongly.

Another situational factor which some have argued may determine which categories get cognitively 'triggered' is the perceptual distinctiveness of certain people. Kanter (1977), for instance, suggested that people who constitute a numerical minority in an organization can become the focus of attention for the majority. Kanter herself was particularly interested in how women were perceived and treated in predominantly male work situations. She describes how, in one company where women were outnumbered by 15:1, such 'token' representatives of the category 'woman' seemed to be easily noticed and were sometimes the object of exaggerated sex-role stereotyping from their male colleagues. Kanter's data were somewhat impressionistic, but they were followed up by some experimental studies undertaken by Taylor and her colleagues (Taylor et al., 1978; Taylor, 1981). In these experiments participants listened to a tape-recorded discussion among six people, whose pictures were shown during the recording at the time of their oral contributions. The composition of the group was systematically varied. In one experiment it consisted of one black and five whites, five blacks and one white, or three of each (Taylor, 1981). In another, gender was the categorization variable and the group consisted of single-sex participants and all other possible sex ratios (Taylor et al., 1978). Both studies provided some, but not unequivocal, evidence of the cognitive drawing power of numerical distinctiveness.

Taylor (1981) reports that memory for the black person's contributions was better in the 'solo' black condition than in the case of the black people in the group where blacks and whites were equally balanced (3:3), although he was not seen in a particularly (black) stereotypical fashion. Similarly, Taylor and colleagues (1978) found that 'solo' men and women were seen as more assertive than men and women in a balanced group. However, they were not seen in more sex-stereotyped ways, which would have been a clearer indication that the gender category was at work.

A further investigation of the alleged distinctiveness of 'solos' was reported by Biernat and Vescio (1993). In two studies using the same paradigm as Taylor and colleagues (1978) with black and white participants, they found that the pattern of memory errors indicated that the black–white category was actually more likely to be evoked in the 'balanced' conditions, since the difference between 'within-race' and 'between-race' errors – a key indicator of category usage – appeared to be greater there than in the 'solo' conditions (see Oakes, 1994; Biernat and Vescio, 1994). Indeed, in one of the experiments, one of the 'solo' conditions failed to show any reliable 'within' versus 'between' differences in recall errors.

Thus it seems that just being in a minority is not a very reliable or potent source of distinctiveness. There are other sources, however. People with a physical disability or some visible bodily disfigurement often complain about how frequently they are stared at. One reason for this may be that, for most people, the sight of a disabled person may be a fairly novel event and this novelty may itself catch people's attention. So argued Langer and colleagues (1976) when they arranged for various photographs of people with and without disabilities to be displayed in a public foyer. They unobtrusively measured how long passers-by stopped and looked at the pictures and found that those of people with a physical disability (a woman in a leg brace, or a hunchbacked man) were consistently looked at longer than those of people with no such visible stigma.[5] In a follow-up study reported in the same paper, Langer and colleagues also found that participants chose to sit further away from a physically disabled person than from a non-disabled person. This difference disappeared if they had had a prior opportunity to view the disabled person, which thus presumably reduced her novelty for them.

It is not just the stimulus properties of the situation that can activate one category rather than another. If some event has occurred very recently which is evocative of a particular categorization, then it is likely that subsequent events or situations will also be interpreted in terms of that same category system. Thus, if we see a news item alleging some racial harassment by the police, this heightens our sensitivity to ethnic issues in subsequent reports of police malpractice. We may be more ready to look for evidence of racial discrimination than we would be, had the prior report not come to our notice. In technical terms, this preparation is known as **priming**. The powerful effects of priming were shown in two experiments by Skowronski and colleagues (1993). They studied the effects of two types of prime on people's recall and impressions of a person described in a short story. The primes used were adjectives or labels designed to evoke the category 'mentally handicapped'. One type of prime was administered covertly by having words like 'stupid' and 'dumb' embedded amongst a large number of neutral words shown to the participants before they read the story. The other kind of prime was a much more overt label, 'mentally retarded', which was used to describe the character in the story. Because it was so much more obvious, this second type of prime might have been expected to elicit more socially desirable responses in the participants than the covert one. Indeed, this is what happened. With the addition of explicit labels, participants tended to remember more items from the story that were stereotypically *incongruent* with mentally handicapped people and to evaluate the principal character more positively. With the more subtle primes, however, the effects generally went in the opposite direction: so long as there was no overt label, participants recalled more stereotypical attributes about the person and generally evaluated him more negatively.

There is even some evidence that the activation of a category by a prime can occur below the level of conscious awareness and, moreover, that activating one category seems to have the effect of *inhibiting* the use of another. This was shown in an ingenious experiment by Macrae and colleagues (1995). The study comprised three apparently unrelated experiments. In the first phase, women participants undertook what they thought to be a vigilance task. On each trial a nonsense string of consonants was flashed up somewhere on the periphery of the computer screen and the participants' job was simply to press one of two keys to indicate whether it had appeared on the left or the right of the central fixation point. Unbeknownst to them, however, on each trial another real word was flashed up for 75 ms, being immediately masked by the nonsense word. For a third of the participants that real word was 'woman', for another third 'Chinese', and for the remainder (the control group) no word was presented. Presenting stimuli this way, briefly and parafoveally,[6] is one method of ensuring that they are not consciously perceived. In the second phase, participants watched a short video clip of a Chinese woman reading a book. The crucial question for the researchers was, 'how would that person be categorized, as a woman or as Chinese?' To answer it they subjected their ever patient participants to a third task, in which various words were shown on the screen, this time clearly visible, and their job was simply to judge as quickly as possible whether each word was a real word or not, again by pressing one of two keys. Of the real words, some were stereotypical attributes of women ('emotional', 'romantic'), others, stereotypical of Chinese ('trustworthy', 'calm'), and some neutral. Macrae and colleagues reasoned that, if a particular category has been 'activated' by the subliminal primes, then words stereotypically associated with that category should be recognized faster; conversely, if a category has been 'inhibited', then words associated with it should be more slowly recognized. As can be seen from Figure 3.4, this is exactly what happened. Those primed initially with 'Chinese' recognized the stereotypically Chinese attributes faster than the stereotypically feminine attributes; for those in the 'woman' prime condition the reverse occurred. Note, too, that, compared to the control participants, who had not been primed with either category, the two other conditions showed both facilitation (faster response times) and inhibition (slower) on their respective stereotypical and non-stereotypical words.

The fact that a category can be made to 'fit' a situation even without our knowledge underlines the ever-readiness of our cognitive system to cope with the world it is confronted with. Moreover, the simultaneous inhibition of one category when another is activated points to the functionality of attentional processes. Given that cognitive resources are limited, it makes sense that mental energy is concentrated on a single dominant category and not dissipated on two (or more). At this point it may be worth revisiting the work on crossed categorizations that I discussed earlier in this chapter.

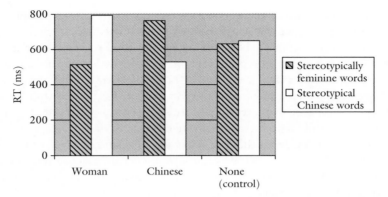

Figure 3.4 Category activation and inhibition following subliminal priming. The figure shows response times (RTs) in recognizing different kinds of words. Adapted from Table 1 in Macrae et al., 1995

There, it will be recalled, it was not uncommon for one category dimension to domi-nate to the exclusion of others. Although there are usually deep-rooted cultural and historical reasons for such category dominance in each particular situation, it is interesting that a similar pattern can be observed in the operation of automatic cognitive processes.

Category accessibility: Personal factors and category choice

If transitory situational factors can influence the categories which best 'fit' a given set of stimuli, it is no less true that some attributes of the perceiver can also contribute to the ease or difficulty with which categories are accessed. Three in particular have been found to be important: the current task or goal of the person doing the categorizing, his/her ingroup–outgroup relationship to the target people, and the extent to which certain categories are chronically accessible for the person, either due to some personal or social needs or because of a specially high frequency of prior usage (Higgins, 1989).

The importance of task demands for category selection was demonstrated by Oakes and Turner (1986). Using the same paradigm as Taylor and colleagues (1978) that I described earlier, they showed how giving participants certain instructions can over-ride any distinctiveness properties associated with 'solo' stimuli. Like Taylor and colleagues, Oakes and Turner varied the sex composition of a tape-recorded discus-sion group. Half the listeners were warned that they would be asked to describe just a single person; the remainder were told to concentrate on the group as a whole. In the latter conditions, reasoned Oakes and Turner, the sex category would be the most likely to be used – not in the 'solo' case, but in the 'balanced' groups (three males: three females), where it would be a better fit for the task at hand. This, indeed, seemed to be the case. The evaluation of the same male target was more stereotyped in the 'balanced' than in the 'solo' conditions, which implies that the sex category was more readily accessed there (see also Biernat and Vescio, 1993).

A further and more direct demonstration of the importance of the perceiver's task was provided by Stangor and colleagues (1992). Presented with a series of men and women, some dressed casually and some more formally, participants made recall errors which showed, as usual, that the sex category had been used (since many more 'within-sex' than 'between-sex' errors were made). Style of dress (formal versus casual) was used as a secondary classification. However, when this same procedure was imposed in a personnel selection task for the choice of a 'media representative', the participants used the dress style category significantly more. Nevertheless, there are limits to the extent to which experimental instructions like this can influence people's use of categories. In the two other experiments by Stangor and colleagues (1992), in which the most functional categorizations were ethnicity and sex – presumably two well rehearsed categories, accessed regularly, as a matter of habit – attempts to change participants' category usage through direct instructions or by indirect means (a prime) proved ineffectual. I shall return to this issue again shortly.

The influence of the perceiver's current goal was also examined by Pendry and Macrae (1996) by using reaction times to measure category activation in a lexical decision task. Here all the participants (except those in the control group) were shown a short videotape of a woman working in an office. Some participants were asked to pay particular attention to the video, since later on they would be asked to justify to a third party the impression they formed of the person in the tape. This instruction was designed to maximize the information processing goal of participants and hopefully to activate the more differentiated category of 'businesswoman' instead of merely 'woman'. Other participants were instructed to focus on the target person's height, since they would be required to provide an estimate of it later; others were told to focus only on the technical quality of the videotape. In these latter two conditions it was assumed that the lack of an explicit goal to form an impression of the target person would lead to the default activation of the 'woman' category. Response times to words stereotypically associated with 'businesswoman' and 'woman' bore out these expectations. Only in the first condition was there noticeable facilitation in the recognition of 'businesswoman' traits; in the other two conditions 'woman'-related traits words were identified faster.

A second factor influencing category usage is the potential intergroup relationship of the target person to the perceiver. Here the issue is not which category system is likely to be used, but into which category the target person will be placed: the perceiver's own, or another? Introducing this factor reminds us that *social* categorization is crucially different from the categorization of the physical world. For when we categorize in the social domain we ourselves are often implicated in the outcome, in a way which does not hold when we classify different kinds of fruit or pieces of furniture. Leyens and Yzerbyt (1992) have suggested that one consequence of group membership is that we can become especially vigilant about who else is classified with us; psychologically we find it easier to misclassify a real ingrouper as a member of an outgroup than to run the risk of 'letting in' a member of the outgroup. They call this the '**ingroup over-exclusion effect**', and they demonstrated it in an experiment conducted amongst French-speaking Walloon participants in Belgium. In Belgium there has been a long history of tension between the Walloons and their Flemish-speaking compatriots. Setting their study in this Walloon–Flemish context, Leyens and Yzerbyt presented their participants with profiles of a number of people. The way they did it was to present one piece of information at a time (to a maximum of ten items) for each target person. The participants were asked to stop the presentation whenever they felt they had enough information to classify the person as a Walloon. The information had been carefully presented so as to be either positive or negative, and confirmatory or disconfirmatory of the Walloon stereotype. The results showed that participants needed consistently more information before classifying the target as a fellow Walloon – that is, more information of the confirmatory and positive kind – than they did when the information was clearly disconfirming and negative, which quickly led them to categorize the target as Flemish. This phenomenon was corroborated by another study, which used language as the categorial clue (Yzerbyt et al., 1995).

Thus far we have considered some general factors which seem to affect the accessibility of categories. However, it is also the case that there are people for whom a given categorization is perpetually or 'chronically' accessible. These are likely to be people with especially high prejudice levels; almost any situation will be interpreted by such people via their favoured categories (Lepore and Brown, 2000). Evidence for this claim comes from a number of sources. Allport and Kramer (1946) presented equal numbers of photographs of Jewish and non-Jewish people to participants who had been pre-tested on a measure of anti-Semitism. The more anti-Semitic participants identified a greater number of photographs as Jewish than the less prejudiced participants, and were also more accurate. In our terms, ethnicity was a chronically accessible categorization for the prejudiced participants and, as a consequence, they applied it more readily – and, it seems, with greater precision – than the less prejudiced participants. This experiment has been replicated several times since, though not always with the same results (Tajfel, 1969b). Nevertheless, one consistent finding has been the tendency for more prejudiced people to be more willing to classify people as belonging to the outgroup, even if sometimes erroneously. This is still further evidence of the ingroup over-exclusion effect.

This thesis was most elegantly demonstrated by Quanty and colleagues (1975), who applied a signal detection analysis to the facial recognition paradigm. Like Allport and Kramer (1946), they asked highly and moderately prejudiced people to classify photographs as Jewish or non-Jewish. Then, in an interesting variation, they promised some of the participants a financial reward for identifying correctly either Jewish or non-Jewish faces. The remainder received no incentives for accuracy. Once again, highly prejudiced participants classified more photographs as Jewish than the less prejudiced participants, as is accounted for by the generally lower threshold criteria levels of the former. Interestingly, only the latter group was affected by the different task incentives. In this group the accessibility of the Jewish/non–Jewish category could be affected by different perceptual goals, whereas for the more prejudiced people ethnicity was chronically accessible, and this was apparently enough to leave it unaffected by such a temporary task set.

Another demonstration that more prejudiced people may be especially vigilant about ethnic categorizing was provided by Blascovich and colleagues (1997). To a selection of people with high and low levels of prejudice, they presented a set of faces and oval shapes that were either clearly back or white, or rather more ambiguously coloured. The task was simply to report the colour of each stimulus. Not surprisingly, all ambiguous stimuli took longer to classify than unambiguous ones. More interesting were the different times that high-prejudice and low-prejudice people took to classify ambiguous and unambiguous *faces*: that difference was much sharper for the more highly prejudiced participants, suggesting that they were taking special care to categorize the ambiguous faces (there was no comparable effect of prejudice level in the oval stimuli). This extended time seems to reflect general caution on their part, since Blascovich and colleagues report that the delay held equally for decisions to classify the stimuli as 'black' or 'white'. Castano and colleagues (2002) used a similar paradigm to study northern Italians' decisions to classify faces as 'northern' or 'southern' Italian. The facial stimuli were produced by computer morphing: prototypically 'northern' and 'southern' faces were morphed in different proportions. Overall, the northerners showed a slight reluctance to classify the faces as 'northern', but this ingroup over-exclusion was especially evident amongst the more highly identified *settentrionali* ('northeners'). In this case, strong attachment to the ingroup apparently made the north–south division particularly salient for one category of participants.

Not only ethnicity can become chronically accessible. Stangor (1988) showed that gender, too, can make a more readily available category for some people than for others. Stangor made a preliminary assessment of people's general tendency to use gender concepts in the descriptions of others. On this basis, pre-tested participants were classified as 'chronically accessible' for gender (or not). In a subsequent memory task in which male and female target were seen to perform various behaviours, there was clear evidence that the 'chronically accessible' participants made more 'within-sex' than 'between-sex' recall errors than the less gender-prone participants. (This anticipated a similar result in Stangor et al., 1992 described earlier, where, it will be recalled, ethnically prejudiced participants made more 'within-race' errors than the less prejudiced participants.) Similar effects on memory tasks involving gendered stimuli have been observed by using the degree of sex-typing (that is, the degree to which respondents resorted to typologies based on sex) as an index of chronic accessibility (Frable and Bem, 1985; Taylor and Falcone, 1982; although compare Beauvois and Spence, 1987).

In summary, then, the accessibility of different social category systems is not a fixed or immutable property of our cognitive system, since it depends on the nature of our immediate purposes, on the intergroup relationships between perceiver and perceived and on personal factors contributing to our chronic use (or neglect) of various categories.

Is It the Group or What They Believe In? Categorization versus Belief Similarity as a Basis for Prejudice

The final issue to be considered in this chapter is whether we have exaggerated the importance of categorization as the basis for different kinds of prejudice. Perhaps, after all, despite the theory and evidence which I have discussed above, the perception of someone as belonging to a different group from our own matters less than some other factor in paving the way for negative intergroup attitudes and discrimination. Such was the claim made by Rokeach (1960), who argued that the crucial 'other factor' was the degree of similarity or 'congruence' between our belief system and that of the other person. Following Festinger (1954), Rokeach believed that similarity of opinion between two people leads to mutual attraction, because of the validation that such agreement provides. On the other hand, disagreement leads to dislike, because of the threat to our belief system that is posed by that discord (see Brown, 2000a). Rokeach then extrapolated from this well-founded hypothesis and proposed that various group prejudices do not have much to do with people's memberships of those groups and their associated norms, stereotypes and intergroup relations, but are principally the result of **belief incongruence**, a perception that the people concerned hold belief systems incompatible with our own. To quote him directly, 'belief is more important than ethnic or racial membership as a determinant of social discrimination' (Rokeach, 1960, p. 135).

To test this idea, Rokeach and colleagues (1960) devised an experimental paradigm in which group membership and belief congruence were independently varied. Thus participants typically had to express their liking for various people who allegedly belonged either to the same or to a different group from their own and who were also seen to hold similar or different beliefs. In a number of studies using this basic technique, the 'belief' factor usually emerges as a more powerful determinant of attitude than the categorial variable. Thus white people will often claim that they prefer a black person with similar beliefs to a white person with dissimilar beliefs (Byrne and Wong, 1962; Hendrick et al., 1971; Rokeach and Mezei, 1966; Rokeach et al., 1960). The exceptions to this tendency appear to be accounted for by rather stronger measures of attraction (for example by the desire to have a close friendship) – a situation where several studies have found that the category difference assumes greater importance than belief dissimilarity (Insko et al., 1983; Stein et al., 1965; Triandis and Davis, 1965).

Despite the empirical support for Rokeach's theory, there are several grounds for doubting whether it offers an adequate account of prejudice, at least in the strong form in which he originally formulated it. To begin with, we should note that the theory involves some sleight of hand in explaining the occurrence of any kind of intergroup prejudice. If it is the case, as Rokeach argued, that we dislike people (that is, we are prejudiced against them) because we perceive them to hold different beliefs from ours, why should we assume that members of outgroups hold those different beliefs? Surely, if social categories are unimportant, then our liking for a person should be on a case-by-case basis, decided by that person's similarity to us. There should be no a priori reason why a whole group of people (for example blacks, if we happen to be white) should share the same beliefs. And yet, prejudice *is* manifestly patterned along categorial lines, as the dozens of examples we have already encountered in this book testify so clearly. Thus, for Rokeach's theory to hold water, we need to add the extra and *category-based* assumption that members of another group are likely to believe in different things from the ones we believe in. In fact, there is some evidence that this is exactly what people do perceive; but, note, such a perception is first predicated on the psychological reality of the ingroup–outgroup category difference (Allen and Wilder, 1979; Wilder, 1984a).

A second difficulty with Rokeach's theory is that it is limited by an important qualification. From the beginning he wished to exempt from the belief-congruence explanation those situations in which the prejudice has become institutionalized by law or social custom, or where there exists significant social support for its expression. There, he conceded, people's respective group memberships would override belief congruence as the basis for prejudice (Rokeach, 1960, p. 164). Thus, for many of the most widespread and virulent manifestations of prejudice – against Muslims in many parts of Europe and of the USA; between different religious sects in parts if the Middle East; between members of different castes in India, and so on – it seems that Rokeach's theory is simply inapplicable.

Table 3.6 Categorization vs similarity as causes of intergroup discrimination[a]

	No categorization	*Categorization*
No similarity	−0.2	+2.0*
Similarity	+1.0	+3.9*

Notes: [a]Discrimination could range from −12 to +12, positive score indicating ingroup favouritism. Asterisk indicates that score was significantly greater than zero.
Source: Adapted from Figure 1 in Billig and Tajfel, 1973

A third criticism of the belief-congruence approach hinges on the typical experimental methodology used to substantiate it. I have presented this critique in more detail elsewhere (Brown and Turner, 1981), so here I will do no more than briefly reiterate the main argument. The central point of this critique is that the race-belief paradigm (as it has come to be known) does not usually present a proper intergroup situation to the experimental participants. Typically, participants are confronted with a series of individuals (real or hypothetical) who just happen to endorse this or that set of beliefs and who, almost incidentally, share (or not) a category membership with the participant. In such circumstances, I have argued, it is little wonder that one of the major determinants of *interpersonal* attraction (that is, attitudinal or belief similarity) comes to the fore as the principal casual factor. On the other hand, where the group-like nature of the situation is given equal weight to considerations of interpersonal similarity, the evidence for Rokeach's theory is much less strong.

Perhaps the direct example of this comes from an experiment by Billig and Tajfel (1973), which employed variants of the minimal group paradigm I described earlier in the chapter. Their objective was to examine the effects of different methods of group formation on intergroup discrimination. In one condition, participants were informed only that some recipients were more similar to them than others because they had preferred the same kind of painting in the pre-test. There was no mention made of groups. This, therefore, constituted a 'pure' similarity condition. In a second condition, by contrast, there was no mention of any similarity; participants were simply told that they had been assigned to two groups by the toss of a coin. This was a 'pure' categorization condition. In a third variant, the first and second conditions were combined so that similarity of picture preferences formed the basis for categorization. Finally, in the control condition there was neither similarity nor categorization. The first two conditions are the critical ones. If Rokeach is correct, one would expect discrimination in the first, but not the second. If, however, categorization does have an independent influence, then one would expect more discrimination in the second than in the first. Table 3.6 summarizes the main results, and it is clear that the latter interpretation received more support: in the two conditions where a categorization was present, ingroup favouritism in the reward allocations was visible. The main effect of the similarity variable, although statistically significant, was much weaker than the categorization effect. Other experiments using the minimal-group paradigm have also generated findings which are difficult to reconcile with belief-congruence theory (Allen and Wilder, 1975; Diehl, 1988).

It seems clear, therefore, that the original form of Rokeach's (1960) hypothesis is not tenable as an explanation for prejudice. In situations in which group memberships are psychologically salient – which, as I argued in Chapter 1, are exactly the ones that are of most interest to students of prejudice – the idea that dissimilarity of beliefs is a more potent force than categorial differences simply cannot be sustained. Nevertheless, there is a weaker version of Rokeach's theory which may be more consistent with the evidence. In this form, some division into ingroup and outgroup is taken as read, and what is then at issue is the effect of different degrees of intergroup similarity (Brown, 1984b). Do people typically display less prejudice against outgroups which are seen as endorsing similar attitudes to those which prevail in the ingroup than against outgroups which seem to believe in quite different things? The answer to this question is a qualified 'yes'. However, to understand how I arrive at this conclusion requires some consideration of the consequences of group membership for a person's social identity. Since this is not treated until Chapter 6, I shall postpone further discussion of the alternative form of Rokeach's theory until then.

Summary

1   A fundamental aspect of human cognition is people's need and ability to categorize the world. This need arises because of the enormous amount and complexity of information we have deal with. This is as true of the social world as it is of the physical world. Associated with the simplificatory function of categorization are a number of biases which have important implications for understanding prejudice and how it can be reduced.

2   One direct outcome of categorization is a cognitive accentuation of differences between categories and a diminution of the difference within categories. These processes of differentiation and assimilation have been shown to affect intergroup perceptions, attitudes, and behavioural discrimination. Some of these processes may operate outside of our awareness.

3   When two or more systems of categorization operate simultaneously, the effect can be to reduce the biases associated with any single one of them, taken in isolation. This is most evident in laboratory settings. In naturalistic contexts one categorization will often dominate over the other(s).

4   Once a given categorization comes into play, differences within groups are attenuated. This is usually not a symmetrical process – outgroups may be seen as being more homogenous – although in certain intergroup contexts, particularly in those involving minorities or values central to a group's identity, the reverse is observed.

5   The adoption of a particular categorization in a given situation depends upon the ease of its cognitive *accessibility* to the person concerned and upon the degree of *fit* between that category system and the actual differences and similarities between people in that situation. Factors affecting accessibility and fit include the person's needs, goals and habitual dispositions, or features of the stimuli such as visibility, proximity and interdependence.

6   Some have claimed that categorial differences are a less important basis for prejudice than perceived differences in beliefs. This claim is only tenable in those

situations where group memberships are not psychologically salient. Otherwise the evidence shows that categorization factors are more important than interpersonal difference in belief.

Notes

1 This is but one in a variety of different procedures which have been used for allocating people to groups. Others include: musical preferences (Brown and Deschamps, 1981), dot estimation tasks (Tajfel et al., 1971), and even, most minimally of all, the simple toss of a coin (Billig and Tajfel, 1973).
2 The techniques for scoring these matrices and the various measures which can be derived from them are described by Bourhis and colleagues (1994).
3 The terms 'anglophone' and 'francophone' refer to people whose preferred language is English and French respectively.
4 Of course, if I am giving the lecture in Northern Ireland, the same dichotomy might be much more functional!
5 The difference was eliminated in one experiment by making the passers-by aware that they were being observed. Apparently, then, the 'attention grabbing' properties of novelty can be easily counteracted by social desirability factors.
6 'Parafoveally' means outside of the central part of a person's visual field. Subliminality is achieved because it takes some milleseconds for the eye to move from the central fixation point to the stimulus, by which time the stimulus has disappeared behind the mask. When people are shown primes like this one, they are usually unable to report what they have seen, apart from the nonsensical string itself.

Further Reading

Crisp, R. J, Ensari, N., Hewstone, M., and Miller, N. (2002) A dual-route model of crossed categorization effects. *European Review of Social Psychology* 13: 35–74.

Diehl, M. (1990) The minimal group paradigm: Theoretical explanations and empirical findings. *European Review of Social Psychology* 1: 263–92.

Oakes, P. (2001) The root of all evil in intergroup relations? Unearthing the categorisation process. In R. Brown and S. Gaertner (eds), *The Blackwell Handbook of Social Psychology: Intergroup Processes*, 3–21. Oxford: Blackwell.

Tajfel, H. (1981a) *Human Groups and Social Categories*, chs 4–6. Cambridge: Cambridge University Press.

Voci, A. (2000) Perceived group variability and the salience of personal and social identity. *European Review of Social Psychology* 11: 177–221.

Wilder, D. (1986) Social categorization: Implications for creation and reduction of intergroup bias. *Advances in Experimental Social Psychology* 19: 291–355. New York: Academic Press.

4

Stereotyping and Prejudice

The observation in the last chapter that perceived differences amongst members of the same category often become blurred leads naturally to a phenomenon at the heart of the study of prejudice: that of **stereotyping**. To stereotype someone is to attribute to that person some characteristics which are seen to be shared by all or most of his or her fellow group members. A stereotype is, in other words, an inference drawn from the assignment of a person to a particular category. Despite its popularity in everyday and in scientific usage, the word 'stereotype' has a curious origin. It actually derives from an aspect of the printing process in which a mould is made so as to duplicate patterns or pictures on to the page. It was Lippman, a political journalist, who first saw the aptness of the term to describe the way people use cognitive moulds to reproduce in their own minds images of other people or of events – the 'pictures in our heads', as he called them (Lippman, 1922, p. 4).

In any discussion of stereotypes, three questions invariably arise: Where do they come from? How do they operate and with what effects? How can they be changed? Accordingly, I have organized this chapter around these same three themes. Because we are interested in the implications of stereotyping processes for prejudice, I shall naturally concentrate on unfavourable group stereotypes. But being unfavourable is by no means a universal feature of group stereotypes. Just as the categories on which they are based are not, in themselves, positive or negative, so it is perfectly possible for stereotypes, too, to have positive, negative, or even neutral overtones.

Origins of Stereotypes

During the height of the debate over the Maastricht Treaty and the future of the European Community in 1992, a student of mine gave me a cartoon cut from a German newspaper. Surrounding the circle of twelve stars (the logo of the Community) there is a caption, '*Der perfekt Europäer ist …*', and then come twelve images, each capturing or humorously contradicting some well-known national stereotype: '*kocht … wie ein Engländer*' ('cooks…. like an Englishman'), '*übt Selbstbeherrschung … wie ein Italiener*' ('is self-controlled … like an Italian'), '*humorvoll … wie ein Deutscher*' ('full of humour, like a German') – and so on (*Lippische Landeszeitung*, 28 October 1992). A few days later, another newspaper reported the results of a cross-national survey conducted in six European countries. It recorded how the respondents viewed Germans as above average in the traits of 'hardworking', 'aggressive', 'ambitious', 'successful' and 'arrogant', but below average in being 'humorous' and 'untrustworthy'. The British, on the other hand, were depicted as 'boring', 'arrogant', but 'humorous', whilst not faring so well in 'ambition' and 'hard work'. The latter defects, together with 'untrustworthiness', were also perceived in Italians, where they were somewhat compensated for by 'stylishness' and 'humour' (*The European*, 12–15 November 1992). Such are some of the 'pictures in the heads' of late twentieth-century Europeans. Where do such images come from?

Socio-cultural origins

The simplest answer is that they are embedded in the culture in which we are raised and live, and that they are conveyed and reproduced in all the usual socio-cultural ways – through socialization in the family and at school, then through repeated exposure to images in books, television and newspapers – images just like the ones I have just reproduced. Allport (1954) was in no doubt that these were potent sources of prejudicial stereotypes, and he devoted no less than four chapters in his classic book to the societal socialization and perpetuation of prejudice. I shall examine some of these influences in the next chapter; but for now we can note that one of the strongest pieces of evidence for this socio-cultural view of the origins of stereotypes is their persistence over long periods of time. This was demonstrated by some research inspired by one of the earliest studies of ethnic and national stereotypes (Katz and Braly, 1933). Katz and Braly's technique was simple in the extreme. They asked their participants – who were Princeton University students – to indicate, for each of ten groups, how many attributes from a long list seemed 'typical' of the group in question. They found that, for each group, there were three or four adjectives which were ticked by a quarter or more of their respondents. In some cases there was remarkable consensus. For example, 78 per cent and 65 per cent respectively believed that Germans were 'scientifically minded' and 'industrious'; 84 per cent and 75 per cent rated negroes as 'superstitious' and 'lazy'. Some twenty years later, then forty, the same procedure was used again, with subsequent cohorts of Princeton students (Karlins et al., 1969; Gilbert, 1951; see also Madon et al., 2001a). The results from these follow-up studies revealed, simultaneously, evidence of change and evidence of stability in the endorsement of group stereotypes. The clearest sign of change was the greatly reduced rate of consensus on the most obviously negative stereotypes. For example, those percentages seeing negroes as 'superstitious' and 'lazy' declined to 13 per cent and to 26 per cent by 1967. There were also changes in the content and complexity of some stereotypes. Some previously dominant images were replaced by others, and typically more traits were included in each group's stereotype. However, despite these changes, it was noteworthy how many of the same old attributes recurred in the later studies. For example the 'scientific/industrious' German stereotype was still very much in evidence in 1967, with 47 per cent and 59 per cent respectively endorsing these two traits. Recall, too, that in the survey data with which I began this discussion 'hard-working' was still regarded as a typical German trait amongst

Europeans in 1992. The persistence of these stereotypes over several generations seems most plausibly attributable to some process of socio-cultural transmission.

But what of the changes that Gilbert (1951) and Karlins and colleagues (1969) reported? As I shall show later in this chapter and elsewhere (see Chapter 6), there are good reasons why we should expect stereotypes to change in response to different inter-group situations or disconfirming information. However, one other obvious explanation for the changes observed in those Princeton studies is simply that the normative climate in American society has changed over the years. Thus what might have been socially acceptable to express publicly in the pre-war years – for example a belief like 'Negroes are lazy' – became progressively less acceptable in the decades after the war, which were marked by anti-discrimination legislation and by social policies of desegregation. Indeed, both Gilbert and Karlins and colleagues note anecdotally that some of their respondents resisted having to attribute traits wholesale to a group. Hence we must leave open the possibility that at least some of the changes in group stereotypes recorded by these rela-tively simple techniques are attributable to factors of social desirability rather than to internalized changes in attitude. I shall return to this issue in Chapter 7.

A 'grain of truth'?

One explanation for the origin of stereotypes is that they derive, however tenuously, from some aspect of social reality. This does not mean that any particular stereotype of an outgroup is in some way objectively 'true' in the sense of describing accurately that group's actual characteristics. There are circumstances in which accuracy can be assessed, which I shall discuss shortly. Rather, the suggestion is that a group's culturally distinctive patterns of behaviour, or the particular socio-economic circumstances in which it finds itself, could provide the seed-bed in which certain stereotypical percep-tions about it would readily flourish. This is sometimes known as the 'grain of truth' theory of the origin of stereotypes (Allport, 1954; Brewer and Campbell, 1976).

How might this theory work? Let us suppose that a given ethnic group occupies an economically disadvantaged position in society. It has poor wage levels, high unem-ployment rates, crowded and impoverished housing conditions, low levels of educa-tional achievement; and it shows similar deviations on other indices. It is not too difficult to see how these visible and objective indicators of a group's social position could rather easily get translated into perceptions of that group as 'poor', 'lazy', and 'stupid'. Given what we know about the cognitive differentiation effects associated with categorization (see Chapter 3), it is but a short step to such attributes becoming exaggerated still further, into full-blown stereotypes that constitute prejudice. Some evidence for this socio-economic basis for stereotypes was obtained by Brewer and Campbell (1976) in their ethnographic study of thirty ethnic groups in East Africa. One of the more economically developed of these groups, the Kikuyu tribe in Kenya, was consistently described by other groups in the area as 'intelligent' and 'progressive' or, less flatteringly, as 'pushy' and 'proud'.

Social psychologists have traditionally been more interested in the valence, operation and mutability of stereotypes than in whether they are veridical or not. This is because the consequences of stereotypical thinking – whether for the perceiver, for the target or for the relationship between them – probably stem from how positive or negative any particular mental representation of a group is and how it affects social judgements and behaviour more than from how accurate it might be. Still, some researchers have concerned themselves with the question of stereotype accuracy (Judd and Park, 1993; Jussim, 2005; Ryan, 2002). A prerequisite for investigating accuracy is to have some objective criterion against which the stereotype can be compared. As I noted in Chapter 1, for very many prevailing stereotypes, this poses an insuperable problem: psychology simply does not have the tools reliably to assess 'humourousness', 'trustworthiness' or 'stylishness' (to cite three of the European national stereotypes mentioned above). In some cases such criteria may exist, particularly with regard to socio-economic data (for example wealth, educational achievement) or in especially contrived laboratory settings. In such instances, stereotypical accuracy can mean that judgements about the central tendency of the group (for example its median income level), or about variability within the group (for example the gap between the wealthiest and poorest members), or about both, approximately correspond to the *actual* median and range of wealth of the group (Judd and Park, 1993). Interestingly enough, one of the stereotypical phenomena discussed in Chapter 3 – variations in the perceived relative group homogeneity in groups of different size or status – may have some basis in reality.

Guinote and colleagues (2002) created high and low-power groups artificially, in the laboratory, and compared intergroup perceptions of homogeneity with the actual behaviour of the two groups. It turned out that members of high-power groups were not only seen to be more variable, but actually did behave less uniformly. This can happen in the 'real' world too, since members of more powerful groups often have greater autonomy (in other words they may be less constrained by social norms), and also have the means to impose uniformity on others (since they usually control the rewards and sanctions contingent on conformity and deviance).

Still, when all is said and done, the question of whether stereotypes are 'objectively' (in)accurate is only of marginal interest to most students of prejudice. For, even if any given group stereotype – say, that 'Xs' do less well at school than 'Ys' – turned out to be accurate, the socially and psychologically more important issue concerns the attributed reason or cause of that group difference: Is it because Xs are fundamentally stupid, or are there situational factors which caused the disparity? For reasons like this (as well as for other reasons), many social psychologists continue to be critical of the value of focusing unduly on stereotype accuracy (Fiske, 1998; Oakes and Reynolds, 1997; Stangor, 1995).

Another variant of the 'grain of truth' theory explains the origins of stereotypes by reference to the over-representation of different groups in certain socially prescribed roles. Eagly and Steffen (1984) have argued rather convincingly that some gender stereotypes seem to derive more from the requirements of fulfilling the traditional feminine roles of 'homemaker' and 'caregiver' than from any inherent properties of women themselves. They showed this by demonstrating that the consensual stereotypes of women as being more 'kind', 'warm' and 'understanding' than men (but less 'active', 'self-confident' and 'competitive') could be eliminated, and even reversed, if a woman was described as being also an employed person. Similarly, men were seen to be just as interpersonally 'sensitive' as women if they were described as 'homemakers'. In a similar demonstration, Eagly and Wood (1982) showed how the common view of women as being more compliant than men stemmed from a perception of them as typically occupying subordinate status positions in employment settings. A woman described as a 'manager', on the other hand, was perceived to be just as independent as her male counterpart. It seems, therefore, that people draw inferences about men's and women's attributes by observing them in their typical roles. Note, too, that this role typicality is not itself spurious; in most industrialized countries more women than men do actually have responsibility for child care and other domestic work, and if they work outside the home they are more likely to do so in jobs where they will be taking orders from men – as secretaries, nurses and the like.

Stereotypes as ideologies

The fact that groups occupy very different positions in society, some having manifestly more wealth, power and privilege than others, suggests a third origin of stereotypes. This origin is related to the fact that stereotypes can serve an ideological function, justifying the status quo. For to depict a deprived minority group as 'lazy' or 'stupid' helps to rationalize the social system, which may have created that deprivation in the first place, and simultaneously endorses the dominant group's right to its privileged position (Devine and Sherman, 1992).

This justificatory function of stereotypes was well demonstrated by Hoffman and Hurst (1990). Inspired by Eagly and Steffen's (1984) social roles hypothesis, Hoffman and Hurst invented a fictitious world for their participants: a world populated by two groups, Orinthians and Ackmians. The two researchers presented their participants with individual descriptions of fifteen members of each of these groups. The descriptions indicated each person's group membership, included three personality traits and, crucially, mentioned that each person was either a city worker or a child raiser. Only the latter social role ascription differed systematically between the groups: the Orinthians were mostly described as city workers and the Ackmians as child raisers (or vice versa, in a counterbalanced condition). The personality characteristics, in contrast, were randomly distributed amongst the thirty individuals so that, as a group, the Orinthians should have been characterized equivalently to the Ackmians. Having read these thirty vignettes, participants were asked to rate the two groups in 'general' on six agentic (and typically 'masculine') traits – for instance assertive, competitive – and six communal (and typically 'feminine') traits – emotional, gentle. Prior to this stereotyping task, half the participants were asked to think of an explanation why the Orinthians and the Ackmians occupied their respective roles; the other half did not have to do this. Hoffman and Hurst (1990) reasoned first of all that, despite the actual equivalence between the fifteen Ackmians and the fifteen Orinthians, participants would be inclined to attribute to the two groups traits stereotypically consistent with their predominant social role (agentic traits to the city worker group and communal traits to the child rearing group). Moreover, the degree of this (false) stereotyping was expected to be greater for those participants who were first asked to think of an explanation for the social role differentiation. So it proved. The group composed mainly of city workers was seen in much more 'masculine' terms than the group composed primarily of child raisers. In addition, and consistently with the idea that stereotypes serve to justify the perceived status quo, those participants who first had to try and think of why the two groups occupied different roles in the fictitious society showed a greater tendency to stereotyping than those who had not had to do so.

This idea – of stereotypes originating from, and then being used to, justify existing intergroup relationships – also lay behind some research of Alexander and colleagues

(1999). Drawing on an idea from political science that the stereotypical images which nations hold of each other reflect their political inter-relations, Alexander and colleagues speculated that there could be four basic outgroup images: 'enemy', 'ally', 'dependent', 'barbarian'. The precise content of these images is thought to vary from context to context, but, broadly speaking, it should reflect the relationship implied by the name. That is, 'enemies' will usually be seen as hostile and untrustworthy; 'allies' as peaceful and trustworthy; 'dependents' as childlike and incompetent; and 'barbarians' as ruthless and irrational. According to this perspective, the four stereotypical images are functional for maintaining (or improving) the ingroup's standing in relation to the other group. So, if the ingroup has colonized another group – as for example Britain did so successfully in the eighteenth and nineteenth centuries – it will serve that ingroup's interests well to regard its colonial peoples as weak dependents, the better to justify taking control of them and all their resources. Alexander and colleagues tried to show the generality of this approach by presenting different intergroup scenarios to their college participants. All of these involved the participants' own college or a neighbouring one. In the scenario presented to them, the relationship between these colleges was described as *competitive* (they were of equal status and vying for resources and for students), *co-operative* (having equal status but collaborating over resources), *dependent* (the outgroup was weaker and reliant on the ingroup), or overtly *hostile* (the outgroup was stronger and threatening towards the ingroup). Having read the scenario, participants then formed an impression of the outgroup college by means of a questionnaire that contained the different ingredients of the four outgroup images. As expected, participants' views of the other group broadly corresponded to the intergroup relationship that they had been presented with, although the 'barbarian' image was not much in evidence and was not always the most prevalent one chosen by participants in the hostility condition. These kinds of findings imply that stereotypes are rooted in the web of social relations between groups and do not derive solely, or even mostly, form the workings of our cognitive systems (Tajfel, 1981b). This viewpoint has been argued forcibly by Oakes and colleagues (1994) and it is one to which we return in Chapter 6.

The fact that at least some of our stereotypes may have some distant basis in real – albeit illegitimate – differences between groups should not come as too much of a shock. A recurring theme of the previous chapter was that the human brain is rather adept at simplifying and making sense of the vast and complex array of social information confronting it. It would be rather surprising – and not a little discomforting – if the inferences it allowed us to draw were completely at variance with reality. Nevertheless, it is not a perfect system and in those inferential processes biases and distortions do occur. I shall catalogue them in some detail in the next section; but one such cognitive bias is of interest here because it points to a fourth origin of stereotypes.

What you remember is not what you saw: Stereotypes as illusory correlations

The bias in question is a peculiar sensitivity we seem to have towards statistically infrequent events or attributes. Things which are less common than average or which happen only rarely seem to attract a disproportionate share of our attention and may be remembered more readily than more commonplace occurrences. The discovery that

Table 4.1 Statistical infrequency as a source of illusory correlation

	Group	
	A	B
Distribution of behaviours between two groups in the stimuli		
Desirable	18.0 (67%)	9.0 (33%)
Undesirable	8.0 (67%)	4.0 (33%)
Distribution of behaviours between two groups as perceived by participants		
Desirable	17.5 (65%)	9.5 (35%)
Undesirable	5.8 (48%)	6.2 (52%)

Source: Adapted from Table 1 in Hamilton and Gifford, 1976

the psychological distinctiveness of infrequency could give rise to stereotyping was first made by Hamilton and Gifford (1976). Drawing on some earlier work by Chapman (1967) which reported that people overestimated the degree of association between words which were paired together infrequently, Hamilton and Gifford presented to their participants a number of sentences in which individuals belonging to one of two groups ('A' and 'B') were described as performing desirable or undesirable behaviours. In the stimuli there were always twice as many people in group A as in group B, so the latter was a minority group. Similarly, desirable behaviours outnumbered undesirable behaviours by just over 2:1. The upper portion of table 4.1 shows that in the stimuli there was no correlation between group membership and the behaviours; the likelihood of a group B person performing an undesirable act was the same as that of a group A person. When asked to recall the frequency with which different behaviours had been performed by members of the two groups, participants were fairly accurate in assigning the positive behaviours but showed a consistent tendency to attribute too many of the less frequent undesirable behaviours to the numerically smaller – and hence more distinctive – group B, and too few to group A (see lower half of Table 4.1). In other words, they formed an 'illusory correlation' between group membership and undesirable behaviour. If we extrapolate this phenomenon outside the laboratory, it suggests that, in a predominantly white country, people will more readily remember relatively rare anti-social behaviours (for example physical assaults) committed by blacks (the minority group) than they will remember instances of the same acts perpetrated by whites. In this way an incorrect stereotypical perception of a correlation between aggressiveness and skin colour could arise. In this first demonstration of illusory correlation, the stereotype formed of group B was a negative one because the undesirable attributes happened to be the infrequent ones. Of course, statistically speaking, this need not be so, and in a subsequent experiment Hamilton and Gifford (1976) confirmed that the same effect could be found with positive attributes.

Other studies, too, have replicated the effect in a variety of contexts, suggesting that it is a fairly general phenomenon (see Hamilton and Sherman, 1989). In a study we conducted in a university setting where 'women' and 'senior academic staff' were the two rare occurrences, we too found that people consistently over-estimated the number of senior women staff (Brown and Smith, 1989).

Nevertheless, despite these demonstrations that the illusory correlation effect can be observed for positive as well as for negative traits – which thus suggest the operation of some affectively neutral information-processing bias – the phenomenon may not be quite so simple. Schaller and Maass (1989) pointed out that, in most real-life settings, people are not detached observers, recording and recalling information about groups; typically they belong to one of the groups in question. Schaller and Maass argued that such group affiliations would motivate people to be more likely to perceive illusory correlations if these would result in a favourable stereotype of their group, but to be less susceptible to the phenomenon if the ingroup stereotype would be unfavourable (for example if one was a member of group B in Table 4.1). They showed this to be the case in a series of experiments: the size of the perceived correlations could be predictably exaggerated or attenuated through the simple device of assigning participants to one of the two groups in the usual experimental paradigm and of varying the relative frequency of the desirable and undesirable traits (Schaller and Maass, 1989; Schaller, 1991).

So far I have presented the illusory correlation phenomenon as being caused by some psychological bias in favour of 'distinctive' stimuli and by some identity-serving process of optimizing the favourability of the image of the participant's ingroup. However, it is possible that neither of these two processes is involved; moreover, perceptual 'distinctiveness' may not underline the bias at all. McGarty and colleagues (1993), for example, discovered that it is possible to obtain the illusory correlation effect *without first presenting the stimulus materials to participants*. All that is required, apparently, is to inform the participants *either* that there will be twice as many statements about group A as about group B *or* that half the statements will describe positive behaviours performed by group A. Then, when asked to attribute some behavioural sentences to group A or to group B, the participants display an illusory correlation effect at least as large as, if not larger than, those obtained in the conventional recall paradigm (McGarty et al., 1993, experiment 1). This is puzzling indeed for the accepted explanation that the illusory correlation is based on differential ease of attention or recall. McGarty and colleagues argue that what causes the illusory correlation effect is not in fact the 'distinctiveness' of one cell of the 2×2 contingency table; the illusory correlation is rather a result of the participants' categorization activity. What happens, they suggest, is that participants use the group labels 'A' and 'B' to try to make sense of the stimuli. Since there is, in fact, a greater absolute number of positive statements associated with group A, participants form an initial hypothesis of the general form 'group A is good'. Then, through the usual process of trying to optimize the meta-contrast ratio between group A and group B (see Chapter 3), they bias their attribution of statements to A and to B so as to sharpen the differences between the two groups. According to this view, the formation of stereotypical associations between groups and attributes is a result of people's attempts to impose some order on the stimuli through categorization rather than being an automatic property of the stimuli themselves.

Yet another explanation of illusory correlation phenomena has been offered by Fiedler and colleagues (2007). They propose that illusory correlations can be more persuasively traced to a cognitive confusion between correlations at group level and correlations at individual level. Thus, to borrow from Eagly and Wood's (1982) social role study discussed earlier, it may be that the majority of managers are men, and it may be that the majority of managers are also assertive. But these two (skewed) base rates should not logically lead to a conclusion that there is also a correlation between

Table 4.2 How correlations at a group level can give rise to illusory perceived correlations at an individual level

Student	'Ability' score	'Motivation' score
	Blue Group[a]	
1	8	2
2	8	2
3	8	8
4	8	8
5	5	8
6	5	8
7	5	8
8	5	8
	Red Group	
9	5	2
10	5	2
11	5	2
12	5	2
13	2	2
14	2	2
15	2	8
16	2	8

Notes: [a] The Blue group scores on average higher than the Red group on both 'ability' and 'motivation'. However, there is no actual correlation between 'ability' and 'motivation' scores at an individual level, even if observers often conclude – wrongly – that there is.
Source: Adapted from Table 1 in Fiedler et al., 2007

maleness and assertiveness; except that *psychologically* it seems to. Fiedler and colleagues (2007) showed this through the ingenious creation of a computer-simulated classroom setting peopled by sixteen (virtual) students. These students were divided equally into two groups of Blue and Red, and the 'teacher' participants were given a series of questions to put to the class. The computer programme then controlled which of the virtual students raised their hands to answer, and it also controlled the (in)correctness of their answers. By varying the frequency of these two factors across the class members, the programme could convey the students' apparent motivation (hand-raising) and ability (correctness). In one experiment, Fiedler and colleagues (2007) arranged that most of the students in the Blue group were highly motivated and were also of high ability, even though at the individual level there was no actual correlation between motivation and ability. (Table 4.2 indicates how this was achieved. Note that, for each value on the ability dimension, there was an equal number of high and low values on the motivation dimension.) After the mock lesson, the 'teacher' participants were asked to remember (estimate) the proportion of each individual student's answers that were correct and the proportion of the questions to which they raised their hands. Strictly speaking, there should have been no correlation between the two estimates (Table 4.2); but in fact participants falsely perceived such a correlation (of between .4 and .6). They erroneously concluded that, just because the Blue group contained both a majority of high ability and high motivation students, the two attributes must have been correlated. In a later study, Fiedler and colleagues (2007) also demonstrated that such illusory correlations could be obtained in the same way by using real groups – for example, gender. They conclude, with Eagly (1987), that many social stereotypes derive from real-world social structures in which skewed base rates on a categorial attribute (ethnicity, gender) co-occur with skewed base rates on some other attribute(s) (criminality, leadership ability).

Seeing individuals as a group: Group entitativity as a source of stereotypes

One last potential source of stereotyping derives from a perceptual feature of groups themselves. It will be recalled from Chapter 3 that the likelihood of any given collection of people coming to be categorized as a group depends in part on their perceived entitativity: the extent to which they are seen to be a unit (Campbell, 1958). Some groups are perceived to have rather high entitativity – for example families and small work groups – while others have very little – for example a collection of people waiting in a doctor's surgery (Lickel et al., 2000). Social categories like ethnicity or gender are usually seen to have intermediate entitativity, although this does vary from situation to situation according to the 'fit' between the category and the context (Oakes et al., 1994; see Chapter 3).

It turns out that perceived entitativity does not just affect the probability of being categorized as a group; it also means that the members of the group will be more readily stereotyped and, as a consequence, confused with each other. This was shown by Crawford and colleagues (2002). In their study they presented participants with brief behavioural vignettes, each apparently describing some episode in thirty-two people's life (and photos were attached, to add realism). These thirty-two people were said to be members of two groups, and the members of each group were alleged to be very similar to (*or* very different from) each other; thus the groups were made to have high and low entitativity respectively. There was also a control condition, where no mention of groups was made. The behavioural descriptions were so arranged that each group did seem to be typified by two general traits, one positive and one negative (for instance honest and aggressive). After getting these descriptions and performing an intervening filler task, the participants were given a paired associates memory task. In this task, each of the stimulus photos was paired with a trait word, which either matched its original behavioural vignette or was actually related to one of the other vignettes. Regardless of the nature of this combination, the participants had still to remember which photo was paired with which trait word. A few minutes later, after another filler task, the participants' recall of these pairings was tested. The researchers reasoned that the original presentations of the vignettes, together with the added information about entitativity (or the lack of it), would create two stereotypes for each group (a positive one and a negative one). The two indications that this had happened would be a *reduction* in participants' ability to recall correctly which word had been paired with which photo (since stereotyping implies a lessened attention to individual pieces of information) and an *increase* in their tendency to associate (incorrectly) the stereotypic trait of the 'other' group with one of the members of the same group (since stereotyping also gives rise to a generalization of attributes from one group member to the next). This is exactly what happened. Participants in the high entitativity condition made fewer correct inferences and more generalizations than those in the other two conditions, who did not differ from each other.

The fact that perceived entitativity can facilitate stereotyping is interesting because it suggests that even members of small face-to-face groups, which are high in entitativity, will often be seen by each other (and by others) in stereotypical terms, despite the fact that such members will also have a good deal of individualized information about each other. This is worth remembering, because we usually associate stereotypes only with larger social categories like class, ethnicity or gender. Spencer-Rodgers and colleagues (2007) showed that both large social categories and small task groups are liable to be seen in stereotypic terms and, moreover, that the entitativity of these different kinds of groups was a crucial determinant of the degree of stereotyping.

One reason why entitativity gives rise to stereotyping may be that, when we see a collection of people as an entity – a group – we will often attribute to that entity some underlying essential property, something 'possessed' by most of its members (Yzerbyt et al., 2001). Sometimes that 'essence' is some learned skill or attribute (for instance, plumbers may all be seen to possess manual dexterity and a knowledge of the mysterious properties of water and gas); on other occasions the 'essence' may be something more fixed, or biological (as in the case of the racist, who believes that there is something 'in the blood' that makes a particular ethnic group inferior or repugnant). The latter form of essentialist belief is particularly pernicious and may be associated with overtly prejudiced views held about ethnic minorities and foreigners (Keller, 2005; Pehrson et al., 2009a; but see Haslam et al., 2002 for contrary evidence).

Stereotypes in Use

Once a stereotype has been acquired, what are its effects on people's judgements about the social world and, more importantly still, on their behaviour towards others? What factors seem to inhibit or encourage its use? To answer these questions, I want first to examine the large literature which has been concerned with the **expectancies** and biases observed to associate with stereotypes. These expectancies and biases include both overt judgements and perceptions, presumably made under conscious control, and more subtle effects, which may occur even without our awareness. I shall also examine how the stereotypes we have of various groups – our own and others – are described in rather different linguistic forms. Then I shall discuss some of the psychological and contextual factors which have been shown to lead to increased or reduced use of stereotyping. Many of these effects occur in people's minds – as biases in perception, cognition, memory or causal attribution – but it is important to recognize that they have behavioural consequences too. As we shall see in the final part of this section, in everyday social situations the operation of stereotypes can have very real implications for those who are its targets.

Stereotypes and judgements of others

A stereotype, whether prejudiced or not, is a cognitive association of a social category with certain characteristics. Most straightforwardly, then, we might expect that someone who possesses a stereotype about a group will, when encountering a particular individual from that group, attribute to that person the relevant stereotypical characteristics. On the basis of that attribution we might anticipate further consequences: the person concerned might be evaluated differently (in accordance with the stereotype) and hence judged to be a more or less suitable employee, tenant or whatever.

The matter is a little more complicated than this, however. When we meet a real person we have at our disposal not just our preconceptions about their group membership, but also information about the way that person actually appears, dresses and behaves which may not be consistent with the group stereotype. How do we integrate these different pieces of information? This was one of the questions which Locksley and colleagues (1980) set out to investigate. They presented their participants with the transcript of a telephone conversation between two people, one of whom came across from his/her remarks either as decidedly assertive or as someone lacking in confidence. The sex of this target person was also varied. Subsequently participants were asked for their impression of the target's personality and had to predict how the target would behave in some other hypothetical situations. If the participants' sex stereotypes were operative, their judgements of the target should have been affected simply by switching the target's sex (it is a widely held stereotype that men are more assertive than women). Surprisingly, altering the alleged sex of the target had almost no effect whatsoever on the judgements of him/her. The overriding factor was the behaviour of the person implied by the telephone conversation: in the 'assertive' condition the person was subsequently rated as more assertive and more masculine *irrespective of their sex*, and, in the 'passive' condition, as more passive and feminine. Locksley and colleagues optimistically concluded that in real situations, where we have 'individuating' information about the person, 'social stereotypes may not exert as powerful an effect on social judgements of people as has been traditionally assumed' (Locksley et al., 1980, p. 830).

However, there are several grounds for doubting the general validity of this conclusion. First, the absence of stereotyping in Locksley and colleagues' study may have been specific to the judgemental context they employed. Nelson and colleagues (1990), for instance, found that people's estimates of the heights of men and women portrayed in photographs were reliably influenced by the sex of the person depicted, even when there was no actual sex difference in height in the stimulus photographs themselves. In another experiment using a similar paradigm, these authors also suggested that the apparent absence of a stereotype effect reported by Locksley and colleagues (1980) might have been due to different judgemental standards being employed for rating men and women (Biernat et al., 1991). They showed how the sex stereotype effect on height judgements could be eliminated by replacing an objective height judgement (in feet and inches) with the instruction to estimate the people in the photographs *in comparison with others of the same sex*. It is possible that a similar within-sex subjective standard was used by participants in Locksley and colleagues' experiment to estimate assertiveness.

Moreover, as Kunda and colleagues (1997) have shown, the same trait (say, 'aggressive') can have very different behavioural implications depending on the group with which it is associated. Thus, on the basis of some 'individuating' information about how two people reacted to a provocative social situation, we might conclude that each was equally 'aggressive', irrespective of their social class (perhaps one person might have been a construction worker, the other a lawyer). However, if we are then asked to predict how likely certain subsequent behavioural reactions might be, we may well infer that the construction worker would be more likely to get into a physical fight, whilst the lawyer would probably engage in a verbal argument. The same trait may well have different stereotypic connotations in the two occupational groups, and these would result in radically different behavioural manifestations (Kunda et al., 1997).

Secondly, Krueger and Rothbart (1988) point out that the absence of stereotypical effects in the Locksley and colleagues study might have been due to their pitting rather strong individuating information about the assertiveness of each person, against the weaker information about assertiveness conveyed by the gender stereotype. It would be strange indeed if we did ignore very clear-cut information about people in forming impressions of them. However, if the relative potency, or what Krueger and Rothbart call the 'diagnosticity', of individuating and group stereotypical information is changed, then we should find that its effects on judgements vary accordingly. The authors found that estimates of the aggressiveness of a target person, as derived from a brief behavioural description, of course correlated strongly with the content of that description (that is, with whether the actions depicted were aggressive to a greater or smaller extent), but also varied according to the category label applied (for example male versus female), particularly when the individuating information implied aggressiveness only weakly.

Finally, there are several studies which have clearly demonstrated how stereotypes do affect judgements, even when information is available about the individual characteristics of the person being judged. Grant and Holmes (1981) presented Canadian participants with mini-character sketches of a person whose nationality (as Chinese, Irish or Somalian) was also evident. The portraits implied someone who was either somewhat similar to the Chinese stereotype ('scientific', 'ambitious') or similar to the Irish stereotype ('happy go lucky', 'talkative'). Grant and Holmes found that merely altering the presumed nationality of the person had a significant influence on the judgements made about him, even if the character sketches themselves had an even more powerful independent effect (see also Locksley et al., 1982). Glick and colleagues (1988) also found a reliable sex stereotyping effect in a more realistic personnel selection context.

Perhaps most vividly of all, Darley and Gross (1983) found that social class stereotypes can influence people's judgements of children's academic performance. In their experiment, participants were first shown a videotape of a 9-year-old girl (called Hannah). The tape depicted her either as coming from a deprived working-class background or as enjoying a more privileged middle-class environment. This was designed to generate, respectively, negative and positive expectancies of her academic performance on account of the well-known correlation between class and educational achievement. The impact of these stereotypical expectancies was assessed in two separate conditions: in one, no further information was available; in the other, a second tape was shown in which Hannah undertook some tests, but these presented a rather ambiguous and inconsistent picture of her abilities. In all these cases participants were asked to predict Hannah's future performance in different academic domains. In the second condition participants had some further and potentially individuating information; hence, if Locksley and colleagues (1980) were right, we should expect to find less impact of the social class stereotype amongst them. In fact, exactly the opposite happened. Those who had access to the additional information contained in the second tape projected their class stereotypes onto Hannah's future performance more strongly than those who only ever saw the first tape. For that second group of participants, 'middle-class' Hannah was estimated to achieve a whole grade point higher than 'working-class' Hannah.

Darley and Gross (1983) concluded from their experiment that we do not use stereotypes in an undiscriminating or unthinking way; rather, stereotypes serve as tentative hypotheses for which we then seek out further information. Without that further information, as in the 'no information' conditions of their experiment, we hesitate to apply them too firmly (see also Leyens et al., 1992, 1994).

The idea of stereotypes as 'hypotheses' about the world is an appealing one and in itself would not be a cause for concern. After all, some philosophers of science have long advocated that an optimal strategy for scientists is to derive hypotheses from their theories and then to set about trying to falsify them by reference to empirical data (Popper, 1963). What more could we ask of lay people going about their daily lives? Unfortunately, neither scientists nor ordinary people follow such Popperian ideals very often. Instead of attempting to falsify their hypotheses, people usually seek out information that will confirm them. This was observed some time ago, in research on logical reasoning (Wason and Johnson-Laird, 1972). It turns out that in our social reasoning such confirmatory biases are also the norm (Snyder, 1981; Stangor and Ford, 1992).

One of the most compelling demonstrations of this phenomenon was given by Snyder and Swann (1978). They led their participants to believe that the person they were about to interview was in one instance an extrovert, or an introvert in another. Then, during the interview itself, the participants could select from a range of questions in order to discover whether the target person really did fit the designated personality type. Those holding the 'extrovert' hypothesis systematically chose more questions likely to reveal extrovert tendencies (for example 'What would you do if you wanted to liven things up at a party?'); those holding the alternative hypothesis chose more questions indicative of introversion (for example 'What factors make it hard for you to really open up to people?'). Such confirmation-seeking tendencies persisted even when, in another experiment, participants were offered a substantial reward for the most accurate diagnosis. And, perhaps most disturbing of all, in a further study the interviewees themselves started to display the very tendencies, be they extrovert or introvert, which their interviewers had been primed to expect – even though, of course, everyone (both interviewers and interviewees) had been randomly assigned to the different expectancy conditions. I shall return to this self-fulfilling characteristic of stereotypes shortly.

However, whilst stereotypical expectancies can often mislead us by biasing our search for and receptiveness to information, they may also be very functional, by allowing us to perceive some things more readily or, equally usefully, by freeing up cognitive resources in order to make us concentrate on more immediately pressing concerns. This renewed emphasis on the cognitive benefits of stereotyping has been given prominence in an ingenious series of studies by Macrae and his colleagues (Macrae et al. 1994a; Macrae et al. 1994b). In one experiment, the task facing participants was to recognize words as they became progressively less degraded by reducing the density of a covering mask. The set of words contained references to stereotypical traits (and, for counterbalance, to non-stereotypical traits) associated with two categories of social deviants: child abusers and soccer hooligans. Prior to the word-recognition task, participants were primed for one of these two categories by being asked to generate a list of characteristics of the typical abuser or hooligan. This prior procedure facilitated their subsequent recognition of the stimulus words that were stereotypical for the primed category (Macrae et al., 1994b). In other experiments it has been shown that the presence of an activated stereotype in one task permits an improved performance in a simultaneous task (Macrae et al., 1994a). A typical experimental procedure asks the participants to undertake an impression formation task (that is, to recall as many attributes as possible about a variety of stimulus people) whilst *at the same time* monitoring some factual geographical information presented to them aurally. Half the participants are given a category label alongside each stimulus person (and, of course, several of the attributes are stereotypical for that category); the remainder do not have this label. Macrae and colleagues argued that the presence of the category label would activate a stereotype, which would mean that the relevant traits would be more readily assimilated. This phenomenon would subsequently allow them to concentrate better on the contemporaneous task. And indeed, this seemed to happen. Participants in the 'category label' condition recalled significantly more of the geographical information than those in the 'no label' condition. The same happened in a second study, even when the labels were presented subliminally.

Stereotyping processes are not only cognitively functional; they can also serve motivational ends, protecting our fragile egos from criticism or feeding them with praise. One circumstance where this can happen is when there is more than one categorial stereotype available for activation and use. Sinclair and Kunda (1999) demonstrated this thesis by exposing white Canadian participants to either negative or positive feedback on their performance on an interpersonal skills task. This feedback was delivered by someone purporting to be a doctor – a high-status occupation with mainly positive stereotypic associations. In half the conditions this 'doctor' was white, in the remainder he was black. Sinclair and Kunda speculated that, when the criticism was received from the black doctor, it would be particularly hard for the participants to take it because of the prevailing negative stereotypes of black people in Canada. In such cases, Sinclair and Kunda argued, participants might seek to discount the feedback by activating the black stereotype and disparaging the evaluator ('Who cares what he says, he's only a black'). In contrast, when *praised* by a black doctor, participants would be more motivated to activate their doctor stereotype ('If he says I'm good, I really must be because he should know, he's a doctor') and simultaneously to inhibit the black stereotype. Something of this kind did, indeed, seem to happen, because the participants had rather different response times in a subsequent lexical decision task where they were required to decide if a given stimulus was (or was not) a real word. Response times to words redolent of the black stereotype ('black', 'rap', 'aggressive') were recognized faster in the negative feedback black doctor condition than in the positive feedback black doctor condition (there was little difference between the two white doctor conditions). On the other hand, words more associated with doctors ('doctor', 'patient', 'hospital') were recognized faster in the positive black doctor condition than in the negative black doctor condition.[1]

Stereotypes not only influence our expectations for the future, but they can bias our recall of the past as well. This was shown by Hamilton and Rose (1980), who presented participants with a series of slides depicting some occupational groups (for example stewardess, salesman) associated with some traits ('attractive', 'talkative'). In the slides, each trait accompanied each occupation exactly the same number of times. However, when asked to recall what they had seen, participants erroneously remembered a greater number of stereotypical associations (for example 'attractive stewardess') than of non-stereotypical pairings (for example 'attractive salesman'). Information consistent with occupational stereotypes was more readily remembered – even over-remembered – than inconsistent information. Although this finding fits well with the idea of stereotypes as hypotheses waiting to be confirmed, in one sense it is slightly counter-intuitive. One could argue that it is information *inconsistent* with the stereotype that should be recalled better, because it is more distinctive and hence more likely to attract our attention (Wyer and Gordon, 1982). Recent reviews of the by now large literature on personal memory have, in fact, found that in general there is a consistent memorial advantage for information which is incongruent with prior expectation (Rojahn and Pettigrew, 1992; Stangor and McMillan, 1992). However, a more careful examination of this body of work reveals that the better memory for inconsistent information is usually associated with memory for individuals and their associated attributes; when groups are the target, people recall stereotype-consistent information better (Stangor and McMillan, 1992; but compare Rojahn and Pettigrew, 1992, who reached a slightly different conclusion). One reason for this individual–group difference could be that people may expect at least some individual variation within a group, and hence the 'inconsistent' pieces of information can more easily be overlooked; within a single person, on the other hand, we may expect greater coherence and so any 'inconsistencies' are more remarkable (Fiske and Taylor, 1991).

The selective effects of group stereotypes on memory occur even in the most primitive conditions. Howard and Rothbart (1980) asked participants to recall various statements about behaviours which had previously been associated with members of two experimentally created groups. The participants themselves had also been assigned to one of these two groups. The behaviours to be recalled were both favourable and unfavourable and, of course, both types were exactly balanced between the two groups. However, the participants' memories were not so well balanced. While they were equally good at recalling the group provenance of the favourable behaviours, when it came to the unfavourable behaviours they were much better at recalling those associated with the outgroup than with the ingroup (see Figure 4.1). Just like in the line from that old Simon and Garfunkel song, 'a man hears what he wants to hear and disregards the rest', it seems that having a few minutes' minimal psychological investment in a group is enough to bias what we remember about it. How much stronger would such an effect be in the case of a lifetime identification with a religious or ethnic group?

Being prejudiced without realizing it: Stereotyping at an automatic level

This experiment of Howard and Rothbart reminds us that the stereotypes we hold of different groups are often not evaluatively neutral but are biased in particular directions. Indeed, the central interest of stereotypes for students of prejudice lies precisely in this feature. There is now mounting evidence that many such biases may be automatic in their operation; quite literally, we may not even need time to think if we are to display some kind of differential reaction to group-associated stimuli.

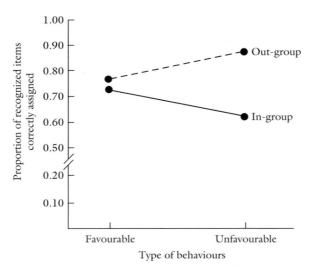

Figure 4.1   Selective recall for ingroup and outgroup information. Source: Howard and Rothbart 1980, Figure 1

The first hint that this might be so came from two experiments performed by Gaertner and McGlaughlin (1983), which measured how long (white) participants took to decide whether two strings of letters presented on a screen were real words. Some of them were actually nonsense syllables (such as KUPOD, ZUMAP), but others were real words (including BLACK, WHITE), three positive adjectives (for instance CLEAN), and three negative adjectives (for instance STUPID). The key question was how long participants would take to acknowledge the pairing of BLACK and WHITE with these negative and positive words. In the event there was no difference in reaction time to the negative pairings with the ethnic labels, but real *positive* words were responded to consistently faster when they were associated with WHITE than when they were associated with BLACK. Notice that the task was very easy: the participants were not required to say that they endorsed any of the word pairings, they were only asked to identify them as real words or not. And this was even easier in the presence of the familiar, psychologically comfortable association between the ingroup and things positive (see also Lalonde and Gardner, 1989).

An even more startling discovery was made by Devine (1989). Using a parafoveal priming procedure (see Chapter 3), Devine first subliminally presented the participants with various words, both directly descriptive of African Americans (for example 'blacks') and stereotypically associated with them, sometimes in quite negative ways (such as 'lazy', 'nigger'). Those in the experimental condition were exposed to many such words, those in the control condition only to a few, although, given the subliminal nature of the presentation, they would not have been aware of this difference. Shortly afterwards, all participants took part in an apparently unrelated study, in which they had to read a short vignette about a man engaging in some ambiguous behaviours and then to form an impression of him by rating the extent to which he possessed various traits ('hostile', 'dislikeable', 'unfriendly'). Rather remarkably, the participants in the experimental condition rated this target person as significantly more hostile than those in the control condition; on other traits there was little difference between the two conditions. Devine (1989) also found that this subliminal priming effect seemed to work equally well for all participants, no matter whether they scored high or low on an explicit prejudice measure administered well before the study.

Devine's explanation for this automatic stereotyping effect of the subliminal priming was that the experience of being brought up and of living in a culture – in this case, the USA – where ethnicity is a highly salient category ensures that everyone will have some knowledge of the (mostly negative) stereotypes associated with African Americans. Devine believed that this knowledge is represented cognitively by associative links between the category in question ('African Americans') and various stereotypic traits ('aggressive', 'lazy', and so on). Thus, whenever the category is activated – for example by meeting a black person, or through a laboratory priming procedure – then *potentially* those stereotypical associations will also be activated. However, Devine argued that in everyday life we are usually aware of that activation and will have the time and motivation to inhibit the negative associations and to replace them with other, socially more acceptable ones. This is especially true of less prejudiced people, whose conscious beliefs about African Americans may be neutral or even positive in valence. But in her experiment, where the activation happened without the participants' knowledge, such inhibition could not occur, and everyone – highly and less prejudiced alike – showed the same automatic stereotyping effects due to those deeply embedded knowledge structures. Thus, Devine concluded, at this primitive or automatic level prejudice is more or less inevitable.

Devine's (1989) experiment and her conclusions from it have won wide acceptance in the field. Indeed, many textbooks routinely and uncritically cite them as demonstrating that prejudice is always with us at an unconscious level, whether we like it or not. Shortly I will discuss several studies which challenge that conclusion; but, before doing so, let us consider some other research, which shows that automatic stereotyping effects can be found in people's actual behaviour and also in decision-making contexts with potentially lethal consequences.

Bargh and colleagues (1996) took Devine's (1989) argument one step further. If it is possible to activate an ethnic stereotype subliminally and thereby to influence people's subsequent judgements about an ambiguous person, perhaps, they argued, the automatic activation might spread to certain behavioural constructs that are also associated with the stereotype. Once activated in their turn, these behavioural constructs might then trigger in the person actual behaviour of a similar kind. With this reasoning in mind, Bargh and colleagues (1996) asked their participants to take part in a rather tedious visual judgement experiment in which, on each trial, their job would be to estimate whether an odd or even number of circles had been presented on the computer screen. Unbeknownst to the participants, before each set of circles was displayed, a black or a white face (depending on the experimental condition) was flashed up for around $20\,ms^2$ and then immediately masked by a cross-hatched pattern followed by the circles. Presenting the faces as briefly as this meant that they would be invisible to the participants. After 130 trials of this procedure, the computer displayed an error message and indicated that the participant would have to start over again from the beginning. We can well imagine how annoyed the participants would have felt at this point, and Bargh and his colleagues recorded their annoyance by means of a hidden video camera. Subsequent ratings of those video tapes by judges revealed that those participants who had been primed with the black faces displayed significantly more hostility than those in the white prime condition. Apparently this hostility was unaffected by the participants' prejudice level as measured by a racism scale administered after the experiment. Thus, just as in Devine's (1989) experiment, automatically activating the category of African American also activated the associated stereotype of hostility, which this time was expressed directly in behaviour.

Similar automatic behaviour effects have been observed after subliminally or unobtrusively priming various other categories. Thus people have been observed to walk more slowly or to respond more slowly in a reaction time task after being primed with the category 'elderly' (Bargh at al., 1996, Study 2; Dijksterhuis et al., 2001); students performed better (or worse) in a general knowledge task after being primed with the category 'professor' (or 'football hooligan') (Dijksterhuis and van Knippenberg, 1998); and people became more long-winded after priming with the category 'politician' (Dijksterhuis and van Knippenberg, 2000).

Lest it be thought that these automatic phenomena are confined to rather trivial laboratory tasks, let me now turn to some research with some potentially rather serious social implications. To set the scene for this work, consider the following newspaper report:

> A black do-it-yourself enthusiast was arrested by armed police and held in custody for 10 days after neighbours mistook his cordless drill for a gun [...] Mr Sealy, 50, a former Barbados police officer, [...] heard his name being called over a loud-hailer by armed officers who had surrounded his house. He was ordered out of the building and told to lie on the ground while he was searched and handcuffed. He was charged with possessing a firearm with intent to endanger life even though no weapon was discovered [...] North Wales Police said it had received information from more than one source that a man was walking down the street with a firearm. (*Independent*, 30 January 2001)

Charges against Mr Sealy were eventually dropped and he received financial compensation for wrongful arrest. Mr Diallo, an African man living in New York City, was less fortunate. When stopped by the police, he reached into his pocket and was then shot dead by a fusillade of bullets from the officers. No gun was found on him (*New York Times*, 6 February 1999).

We may hazard a guess that incidents like this are not uncommon in countries like Britain and the USA, where there is a prevailing stereotype linking black people to violent crime, even if we can hope that the usual outcome is not as tragic as it was for Mr Diallo. In fact, social psychological research gives us some clues as to how such mistakes come to be made. Payne (2001) set his participants a simple task: to identify on each trial whether a picture, presented for 200 ms, was a hand tool (pair of pliers, electric drill) or a hand gun. However, before each trial, another picture was also briefly presented: the face of a black or a white man, which participants were told to ignore. When Payne (2001) measured how long participants took in the identification task he found that they were consistently faster at identifying guns when these were preceded by a black face than when they were preceded by a white face, and an exactly opposite difference occurred for the speed of identifying the tool. In a following study, when he put more time pressure on the participants to respond, he found a systematic pattern of errors being made: participants were more likely to misidentify

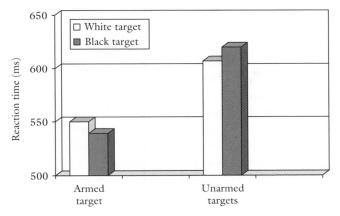

Figure 4.2 Reaction times for 'correct' response to shoot an armed target or not shoot an unarmed target. Adapted from Table 1 in Correll et al., 2002

a tool as a gun when this object was paired with a black face than with a white face, as Mr Sealy discovered to his cost in the incident described above.

Even more worrying were the results of a subsequent experiment undertaken by Correll and colleagues (2002). They created a video game in which at some point a black or a white man appeared carrying either a gun or some other, less threatening object (a camera, a mobile phone, or the like). In each trial of the game, participants had to make a quick decision about the object in the target's hand and press one button (marked 'shoot') if they thought it was a gun, or a different button ('don't shoot') if they believed it was something else. When they analysed the response times for the 'correct' decisions, Correll and colleagues found a consistent bias against the black targets. As can be seen in Figure 4.2, when the target was armed, participants were quicker to shoot at black targets than at white targets; on the other hand, when he was unarmed, they took longer to decide *not* shoot at a black target than at a white target. Moreover, they were twice as likely to shoot an unarmed black target than an unarmed white target. These ethnic biases in the decision to 'shoot' or not were not correlated with how prejudiced participants were, but were (weakly) associated with their beliefs about the cultural pervasiveness of the 'aggressive' black stereotype and with how much contact they had had with African Americans.

In another study, Correll and colleagues (2002, Study 4) found that reaction time bias to black and white targets was also shown by African American participants. The fact that neither the participants' prejudice level nor their ethnicity moderated the magnitude of the decision bias led Correll and colleagues rather to the same conclusion as Devine (1989): that most members of US society, black or white, prejudiced or not, will manifest similar automatic stereotypical associations between the category 'black' and the trait 'hostile' and, in time-pressured or ambiguous circumstances, will act accordingly.

The precise mechanisms underlying these decision-making biases are still not clear. Do the well learned stereotypical associations cause a misperception, so that a drill is actually 'seen' as a gun in the hands of a black person, or do they instead interfere in some way with the capability to control (and to correct) an erroneous response to a veridical perception? So far we do not have a definitive answer to these questions, although there is some evidence in favour of the latter view (Payne et al., 2005).

Let me now return to that provocative conclusion of Devine (1989) that automatic **stereotype activation** and its effects are rather generic amongst members of a given society and do not show much symptomatic variation unless people have sufficient time, motivation and cognitive resources to control them. Although, as we have seen from Devine's work and that of others, there seems to be evidence for this position since people's own level of prejudice sometimes does not appear to qualify automatic priming effects, there is a growing literature demonstrating the exact opposite: that, even at an automatic level, highly and less prejudiced people respond differently.

One of the first such demonstrations was an experiment I did with Lepore (Lepore and Brown, 1997). The inspiration for this study was Lepore's careful analysis of Devine's (1989) priming procedure. She noted that the primes used by Devine were neutral category words (for instance 'blacks'), and also some rather negative nouns and adjectives ('nigger', 'lazy'). Thus, in reality, Devine primed both the category *and* a set of negative stereotypes. Perhaps, then, it was not so surprising that such a priming procedure induced a generally negative impression of the target person who was to be judged in the second part of the experiment. Lepore argued that, if *only* the neutral category labels were primed, then it should be possible to observe differential stereotypical associations with those categories, as a function of people's habitual level of everyday prejudice. After all, a highly prejudiced person who routinely disparages ethnic minorities is likely to build up a very different cognitive representation of those groups from a more tolerant person, who may regularly view them and interact with them in positive ways. So it proved. We adapted Devine's (1989) priming procedure so that the negative words were removed and only neutral category labels remained ('blacks, 'West Indians'). We also modified the subsequent impression formation task so that both the stereotypically positive ratings (outgoing, athletic) and the stereotypically negative ones (aggressive, lazy) could be made. When we analysed these ratings as a function both of the experimental condition (prime versus no prime) and of the participants' prejudice level (high versus low), we found that the subliminal primes had different effects on highly prejudiced and on less prejudiced people (see Figure 4.3): more prejudiced participants reacted to the primes by rating the target both more negatively and less positively; crucially, less prejudiced people in the prime condition rated the target higher on the positive stereotypic traits, and showed little difference on the negative traits. Thus, contrary to Devine (1989), we showed that automatic activation of an ethnic minority category does not lead inevitably or generally to a negative or prejudiced response; the result depends on people's prior or habitual personal beliefs.

Several other studies have found similar moderating effects of people's level of explicit prejudice on various automatic stereotyping phenomena. Thus, people differing in their levels of expressed prejudice have also been found to differ in the speed with which they recognize positive and negative words preceded subliminally by the single word 'black' or 'white' (Wittenbrink et al., 1997); they also display differences in the speed with which they can *pronounce* positive and negative words when the latter are paired with the same ethnic labels – and this happens even under conditions which would have made it impossible to control their responses (Kawakami et al., 1998); they show different patterns of interference in identifying the colour of words stereotypical or not of Australian Aborigines in a Stroop task,[3] – a paradigm which is generally considered to reflect **automatic processes** (Locke et al., 1994); finally, people's competitive behaviour

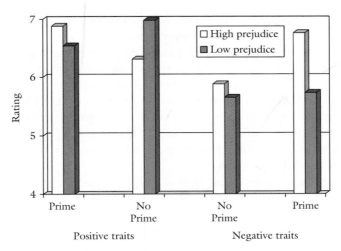

Figure 4.3 Differential effects of automatic category activation in high and low prejudiced people. Source: Lepore and Brown, 1997, Figure 1

in a 'prisoners' dilemma' game can be reliably affected both by their level of prejudice and by their having been subliminally primed with black or white faces – the highly prejudiced being more competitive after black primes, the less prejudiced being more competitive after white primes (Brown et al., 2003). All these findings were consistent with a view which suggests that highly and less prejudiced people have rather different mental representations of the ethnic (or other) groups they care about. Over many months or years, people who are generally tolerant or generally prejudiced build up different patterns of cognitive associations between the relevant category and various positive and negative attributes. As several studies now show, these differential associations can reveal themselves even at an automatic level.

Why did they do that? Stereotypes and social attributions

Earlier on I introduced the idea of stereotypes as hypotheses about the characteristics of groups – albeit biased and confirmation-seeking hypotheses. This suggests another important function that stereotypes serve: that of influencing people's explanations of social events (Tajfel, 1981b). Let me suppose that I witness a black person in the street giving someone a push. How should I interpret this action? Was it a friendly shove or was it more aggressively intended, a prelude to some more violent interchange? Further, should I infer that the perpetrator of the act consistently behaves like that, or maybe was provoked by some temporary situational factor? These, of course, are the classic questions with which **attribution theory** has been concerned, although not often from the standpoint of intergroup prejudice (for an exception, see Hewstone, 1989). What role might group stereotypes play in the attribution process? In the example above, there is an obvious possibility: if, as is the case in Britain and in the USA, one of the prevailing stereotypes of black people is that they are aggressive, this might lead more readily to an interpretation of the action as a hostile one, which perhaps derives from a dispositional (that is, internal) tendency to get involved in fights.

This, anyway, was Duncan's (1976) hypothesis when he prepared two similar videotapes showing a heated argument between two men which culminated in one of them shoving the other. In half of the tapes the perpetrator was black, in the remainder he was white. The ethnicity of the victim was also varied. White observers of this scene, believing it to be a real exchange, were asked to interpret what had happened. In the versions with a black perpetrator, over 90 per cent of participants judged the action to be 'violent' or 'aggressive' and tended to attribute it to some internal cause; in the white perpetrator versions, less than 40 per cent coded it as violent or aggressive, and they were more inclined to believe in some situational cause for the action (see also Sagar and Schofield, 1980).

The influence of stereotypes on attributional judgements has been observed in other intergroup contexts. Macrae and Shepherd (1989) found that people's explanations for two criminal actions (assault and embezzlement) varied according to whether these actions were allegedly performed by a labourer or an accountant. In each case the action was attributed to some internal cause if the criminal stereotypically fitted the crime (for example if the embezzling was perpetrated by an accountant), less so if the two were inconsistent. And Furnham (1982) found that employed people were most likely to believe that those out of work do not try hard enough to get jobs or are unwilling to move to do so – an internal attribution consistent with the stereotype of the unemployed as lazy, propagated by some popular newspapers and right-wing politicians. Not surprisingly, unemployed workers themselves were more likely to attribute their plight externally (for example to 'an influx of immigrants').

The fact that people on different sides of an intergroup divide often offer very different explanations for the same phenomenon was noted by Pettigrew (1979). Drawing on Ross's (1977) idea of the 'fundamental attribution error', according to which people tend to assume internal causes for others' behaviour but external causes for their own, Pettigrew suggested that group members were susceptible to an **ultimate attribution error**: negative behaviours by outgroup members will be seen as internally caused ('they are like that'), while the same behaviours, when coming from the ingroup, will be justified with reference to some external cause ('we were provoked'). Positive behaviours will tend to be explained in just the opposite fashion.

Several studies have supported this hypothesis. Taylor and Jaggi (1974) presented Indian (Hindu) office workers with some scenarios in which a Hindu or a Muslim behaved in a desirable or undesirable manner. When Hindus were depicted in a positive light, the desirable behaviour was attributed mainly internally; the same behaviour, when adopted by Muslims, was attributed externally. For negative behaviours the reverse occurred. A similar phenomenon was observed in Northern Ireland by Hunter and colleagues (1991), in Catholics' and Protestants' explanations for various violent events in the region. Nevertheless, despite the commonness of this 'ultimate attribution error', its effect is far from universal. Some research done by Hewstone and his colleagues has revealed that such intergroup attribution biases may be most typical of dominant or majority groups (Hewstone and Ward, 1985; Islam and Hewstone, 1993b). For example, whilst Muslims in Bangladesh (a majority group) consistently attributed positive ingroup and negative outgroup outcomes mainly to internal factors, the same was not true of the Hindu minority (Islam and Hewstone, 1993b).

It is not just the content of causal attributions that may alter according to whether we are explaining positive or negative ingroup or outgroup behaviours; the very language we use may also change. Maass and colleagues (1989) asked members of rival quarters (*contrade*) of an Italian city to describe what was happening in some cartoons depicting members of their own and of the other *contrada*. The studies were conducted in the weeks prior to an annual horse race (*palio*) involving intense competition between the *contrade*. When the descriptions were analysed linguistically, it became apparent that positive ingroup behaviours were described using words more indicative of enduring dispositional states than the words used to describe the same behaviours as performed by outgroup members. The latter tended to be more concrete and situationally specific terms. For negative behaviours, exactly the opposite occurred. This **linguistic intergroup bias** phenomenon, as Maass calls it, has been observed in a wide range of intergroup contexts, including newspaper reports of sporting events or political situations, several inter-nation or interethnic settings and relations between the sexes (Maass, 1999). As Maass points out, these linguistic biases in people's intergroup accounts may have important implications for stereotype maintenance and change. For, by their nature, more abstract and general conceptions are typically quite resistant to modification in the light of new information – unlike very concrete representations, which may be disconfirmed by a single or a few contrary instances. To the extent that positive ingroup and negative outgroup stereotypes veer in the direction of abstraction whilst negative ingroup and positive outgroup images are usually more concrete, the outlook for attempts to change mutually derogatory intergroup stereotypes does not seem very optimistic. I return to this issue of stereotype change later in the chapter.

Factors affecting stereotype activation and use

So far we have considered the various ways in which stereotypes influence our judgements or recollections of social situations. From the ease and frequency with which such influences have been observed, it would be easy to conclude that, in any context in which social categories are psychologically available, stereotypes will come into play more or less automatically. Though plausible, such a conclusion may not quite do justice to the complexity of people's social cognition. I want now to consider some of the factors which inhibit – or encourage – reliance on stereotypical expectancies.

One such factor is the extent of our mental preoccupation with concerns other than the situation at hand, what Gilbert and Hixon (1991) have called '**cognitive busyness**'. Since one primary function of stereotypes is to act as mental short-cuts designed to save us the trouble of having to investigate and apprehend in depth each person we encounter, one simple hypothesis is that, the more we are distracted with some other cognitive task, the more we will need to rely on those stereotypical short-cuts in our judgements. This was Macrae and colleagues' (1993) prediction when they showed their participants a short videotape depicting a woman talking about her lifestyle and interests. Half the participants believed that the woman was a doctor, the remainder were told she was a hairdresser. In addition, some were given a distracting task to perform (rehearsing and then recalling an eight-digit number), others were not. When asked to remember as much as they could about what the woman had said, the participants who had the additional mental task recalled more items which were consistent with her occupational stereotype than those who did not. They also rated her in more stereotypical terms. Those without the distracting task displayed exactly the reverse pattern.

While these data perfectly support the notion of the stereotype as 'the (mental) slug-gard's best friend' (Gilbert and Hixon, 1991, p. 509), there is one further wrinkle to the story. Gilbert and Hixon point out that cognitive busyness will lead to more stereotyp-ing only if some appropriate category has actually been engaged; prior to this – let us say, in the first few moments of an interaction – such cognitive distraction might actually prevent the activation of a stereotype. In an elegant experiment they provided some evidence that this might be the case. The experiment began with an Asian or a white woman (depending on the experimental condition) holding up cards on which some word fragments were printed (for example POLI-E, N-P), and the participants had a few seconds to think of as many words as possible that the fragments could belong to. Half of them were distracted by having an eight-digit number to remember. The word completions revealed an intriguing pattern: when the stimuli were presented by the Asian confederate, the *non-distracted* participants were more likely to dream up words associated with the Asian stereotype (for example, 'polite', 'nip') than when the white confederate presented them. The distracted participants, on the other hand, were unaf-fected by the ethnicity of the confederate. Then, in a second task, both groups listened to apparently the same confederate talking about her daily life and, again, a half of each group were distracted by some other task during this monologue. In the subsequent ratings of the confederate, only one sub-group of participants rated the Asian confeder-ate as more stereotypically Asian than the white confederate. This was the group who had initially not been distracted (thus allowing the stereotype to be *activated*), but who were distracted in the second phase (thus encouraging the stereotype to be *used*).

A similar result was obtained by Stroessner and colleagues (1992). They observed that emotional arousal can disrupt stereotype formation, in this case by interfering with the perception of an illusory correlation. It turns out that emotions also play a rather important role in stereotype use, in an exactly analogous way to the effects of cognitive busyness. In short, when we are upset or anxious about something we are more likely to fall back on familiar, and hence readily available, stereotypes in our social perceptions. Stephan and Stephan (1985) were among the first to draw this fact to our attention. They pointed out that interactions between members of different groups can sometimes be anxiety-provoking affairs, whether because of pre-existing conflict between the protagonists or merely through tension born out of ignorance, embarrassment or misperception. Drawing on the well established research findings concerning the disruptive effects of emotion on information processing ability (Easterbrook, 1959), they suggested that encounters between members of different groups can become breeding grounds for the growth of stereotypical judgements.[4]

Other studies of interethnic relations have underlined this important role that affect plays in intergroup situations. Dijker (1987) found that the anticipation of meetings with ethnic minority people was associated with feelings of anxiety and irritation in a sample of Dutch respondents. Similarly, contact between Hindus and Muslims in Bangladesh was found to be correlated with feelings of anxiety which, in turn, were associated with perceived greater outgroup homogeneity and negative outgroup atti-tudes (Islam and Hewstone, 1993a). This apprehension, which can be associated with intergroup contact, has important implications for attempts to reduce prejudice – a point to which I return in Chapter 9. Laboratory studies, too, have confirmed how heightened emotionality can increase the likelihood of stereotypical judgement (Mackie et al., 1989; Wilder and Shapiro 1989a and b).

Whilst we are discussing the interplay of stereotypes and emotions, it is worth reflecting on the link between stereotypes and behaviour. Implicit in much of what I have presented thus far has been the assumption that negative stereotypes give rise to prejudiced behaviour. But, according to Cuddy and colleagues (2007), that link between stereotype and behaviour may not be so direct. Their analysis starts from the idea that the manifold varieties of group stereotypes around the world can be organized into a simple two-dimensional taxonomy: groups seem to vary in the extent to which they are depicted as competent (or not), and also in how warm (or cold) they are thought to be (Fiske et al., 2002). The position of groups in this taxonomy is thought to derive from their status in society – for instance high-status groups are usually perceived to be more competent – and also from their functional relationship with the perceiver's own group – for example those with whom we are co-operating or who depend on us are typically seen to be warmer than our competitors. These different types of stereotypical beliefs are thought to generate various intergroup emotions (such as admiration for 'competent' and 'warm' groups; contempt for 'incompetent' and 'cold' groups); and it is these, rather than the stereotypes themselves, that are presumed to be the primary determinants of how we behave towards other groups. Although the evidence provided by Cuddy and colleagues (2007) is as yet preliminary and indirect – it was all derived from people's *estimates* of how others would perceive and react to outgroups – it is consistent with other research, which suggests that affect may be a more powerful predictor of discrimination than stereotypes (see Dovidio et al., 1996; Schütz and Six, 1996; Stangor et al., 1991; see also Chapters 8 and 9).

The degree to which people are cognitively or emotionally preoccupied is an incidental feature of social situations. To that extent, such factors offer little promise for consciously altering people's reliance on prejudiced stereotypes in their judgements. However, there is a third factor which may affect the likelihood of stereotype use, and that is the degree to which they, and the target of their judgement, are positively interdependent. Put less formally, if one person depends on another for the achievement of something, they may be more inclined to look for information specific to that person and less reliant on a group stereotype. Some preliminary evidence for this statement – although it is far from conclusive as yet – has been provided by Neuberg and Fiske (1987). They led people to believe that they would shortly be interacting with a former schizophrenia sufferer. It had previously been established that this category of mental illness was on the whole disliked, and also liable to arouse some anxiety among students. The interaction anticipated was described as one in which students would be outcome-dependent (or not) on this stigmatized person to win some monetary prize. The effect of varying the interdependence between them in this way seemed to make participants pay greater attention to information about the person and, sometimes, to anticipate liking him more, though is has to be said that the observed effects were not always very strong or consistent. Moreover, subsequent research by Pendry and Macrae (1994) suggests that the possibly individuating effects of interdependence are easily disrupted by cognitive distraction. Nevertheless, as we shall see in a later chapter, there are other benefits that accrue from co-operative intergroup encounters like this, which are broadly consistent with these findings on the positive outcomes of interdependence (see Chapter 9).

Creating the world in one's own image: Stereotypes as self-fulfilling prophecies

Thus far I have been solely concerned with the effects of stereotypes on us, the perceivers; how and when they influence our perceptions, recollections, and evaluations of others. To conclude this section, I want to consider their effects on those being stereotyped. I shall show that stereotypes are not merely hypotheses for which we selectively seek out confirmatory evidence; they may themselves create the very conditions in which that confirmatory evidence is more readily forthcoming (Darley and Fazio, 1980; Snyder, 1981). This altogether more dynamic view of stereotypes as **self-fulfilling prophecies** has support from a number of studies.

Take for example an early experiment of Word and colleagues (1974). There white participants had to role-play the position of a job interviewer. Half the interviewees were white and half black, but in either case they were confederates of the experimenters, who had carefully trained them to react in a standardized way throughout the interview. Careful observation of the interviewers' behaviour revealed that they acted in a subtly different way with the black as compared to the white interviewee: they sat further from them and tended to lean further back in their seats; the interviews were also fully 25 per cent (or three minutes) shorter and contained more speech disfluencies (for example stuttering, hesitations). One can easily imagine what effect these differences in non-verbal behaviour might have on a real job interviewee; but Word and colleagues did not leave this to our imagination. In a second experiment they reversed the roles. This time the *interviewers* (always white confederates) were trained to act in one of two ways: *either* to sit closer to the interviewee, make fewer speech errors, and make the interview last longer, *or* do the opposite. These were, of course, the very differences in behaviour elicited by the black and white confederates in the first experiment. This time it was the behaviour of the interviewees, again all white, that was carefully monitored and evaluated by independent judges. The striking finding was that their behaviour seemed to reciprocate that of the interviewers: when they were sat closer to and talked to more fluently they responded in the same way, and noticeably differently from the other experimental condition. As a result, they were judged to be reliably calmer and also to be more suitable for 'job' they were being interviewed for. A similar self-perpetuating effect was observed by Snyder and colleagues (1977). They led men to believe that the person they were speaking to on the telephone was either an attractive or an unattractive woman. The men's image of their partner seemed to elicit different behaviours from her: her interaction style was subsequently judged by independent observers to be more friendly, likeable and sociable in the 'attractive' than in the 'unattractive' condition (see also Snyder, 1981).

The rather subtle nature of these expectancy induced effects on the targets of stereotyping leads us to suspect that the parties to them, perceiver and perceived alike, may not be very aware of them. This suspicion is reinforced by the results of an experiment carried by Chen and Bargh (1997), in which the perceivers' stereotypes were activated subliminally. Using the same kind of subliminal priming procedure as the one followed by Bargh and colleagues (1996), Chen and Bargh exposed their white participants to repeated images of black or white faces under the guise of another task. Following this priming phase, the same participants took part in a word guessing game with a second participant, who was located in another room. The interaction took place over a voice intercom. The audiotapes of these interactions were then coded by independent observers for how much hostility each participant displayed. As expected, and consistently with the findings of Bargh and colleagues (1996), the 'perceivers' (that is, those who had been exposed to the subliminal primes) displayed reliably more hostility in their verbal behaviour when they had been exposed to the black faces than when they had received images of the white faces. However, it was not just their behaviour that altered. Their partners in the game showed identical effects: when they were paired with a 'perceiver' from the black faces condition, they, too, were verbally more aggressive than their counterparts in the white faces condition. What is remarkable – and methodologically ingenious – about this experiment is that everyone – experimenter, 'perceivers', 'targets' and judges – was 'blind' as to the condition to which each 'perceiver' had been allocated. Truly, the self-fulfilling prophecy effects that were observed took place outside everyone's awareness. I suspect that many such expectancy confirming phenomena that can be found in people's everyday interaction also occur without our knowledge. Whether we like them or not or are aware of them or not, our stereotypes do seem to help to create a world in their own image.

Such findings are not restricted to the artificial confines of the laboratory. The self-fulfilling nature of stereotypes has also been observed in naturalistic contexts, with very real important consequences for those concerned. Some of the most compelling evidence has come from school settings – a line of research inspired by Rosenthal and Jacobson's (1968) famous experiment in an American elementary school. In this school, like in others around the country, children were regularly assessed through various intelligence and achievement tests. During the year of their study, Rosenthal and Jacobson obtained permission to add a new measure to the battery of tests: the 'Harvard test of inflected acquisition'. Despite its rather grandiose name, this was actually a perfectly ordinary and well standardized non-verbal intelligence test. However, the true nature and results of this test were only known to Rosenthal and Jacobson. After its first administration, the researchers randomly selected around one fifth of the children from each year and designated them as children who would be likely 'to show a significant inflection or spurt in their learning within the next year or less than will the remaining 80 per cent of the children' (Rosenthal and Jacobson, 1968, p. 66). The names of these likely 'bloomers' were then passed on to the teachers (and only to the teachers), with a brief explanation sheet outlining the researchers' (bogus) expectations. One year later, Rosenthal and Jacobson re-tested all the children with that same 'test of inflected acquisition'. The results, which captured the imagination of social psychologists and educators then and ever since, are shown in Figure 4.4. In the first two grades, the 'experimental' children – those arbitrarily labelled as showing special promise – did actually significantly increase their scores on the intelligence test.[5] For the remaining grades, the comparisons between the 'experimental' and 'control' children showed negligible differences. What was so remarkable about these increases was that they could only be attributed to the teachers' expectations, for they were the only ones in the schools who knew the identities of those allegedly 'bright' children; the children themselves had not been informed of their 'superior' ability.

The small numbers of children involved, the lack of consistent IQ gains in the older grades and a variety of methodological difficulties with the study have produced the result that Rosenthal and Jacobson's findings have not always been universally accepted

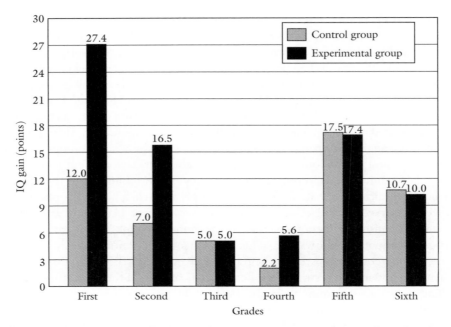

Figure 4.4 Effects of teacher expectations on student achievement levels. Source: Rosenthal and Jacobson, 1968, Figure 7.1

(see Elashoff and Snow, 1971; Jussim and Harber, 2005; Thorndike, 1968). Nevertheless, since that pioneering effort, other research has confirmed that teachers' expectations do have a consistent and measurable effect on student performance. One of the most convincing demonstrations of this was Crano and Mellon's (1978) cross-lagged panel analysis of some longitudinal data collected from seventy-two British junior schools and involving over 5,000 children.

The logic behind cross-lagged analysis is simple. Suppose we have two variables – in the present case, teachers' expectations (E) and pupil performance (P) – and we find that they are positively correlated. As we have all had it drummed into us a hundred times, correlation does not imply causality, and hence we cannot infer that E is giving rise to P; it would be equally plausible to conclude that the students' performance was actually responsible for the teachers' future expectations of them. However, suppose that we obtain our measures of E and P at two points in time ($t1$, $t2$). If E is genuinely causing P rather than the other way around, then we should expect the correlation between $E1$ and $P2$ to be stronger than the equivalent correlation between $P1$ and $E2$. This, then, was the basis of Crano and Mellon's analysis. They had access to teachers' evaluations of their charges on some behavioural, motivational, and academic criteria; they also obtained the scores of those same students on a variety of standardized achievement tests. And both kinds of data were available at two points in time, which were separated by a year. The pattern of correlations Crano and Mellon obtained was very clear. Out of 84 possible comparisons between the correlations $E1P2$ and $E2P1$, nearly three quarters of them revealed the former to be higher than the latter, which was clear evidence of a *causal* effect of expectations on subsequent performance (see also Jussim, 1989 and Smith et al., 1999).

Even if sometimes modest in size, these self-fulfilling expectancy effects are, never-theless, potentially important for the preservation of prejudiced stereotypes. Eccles-Parsons and her colleagues have pointed out that parental expectations related to their children's competencies are influenced by the child's sex even when the child's actual capabilities are taken into account, and these expectations are related in turn to the children's own self-perceptions of their abilities in different domains (for example girls see themselves as better at English but worse at mathematics: Eccles-Parsons et al., 1982; Eccles et al., 1990). From there it is but a short step to the children's selection of academic and career options consistent with these self-concepts, a process which thus perpetuates gender stereotypes about the relative linguistic and technical (dis)abilities of men and women.

Another interesting feature of self-fulfilling prophecy effects is that the direction of influence may not be one way only. There is some evidence that the self-concepts of the 'targets' of expectancy effects can influence the perceivers' subsequent expecta-tions. This was shown by Madon and colleagues (2001b) in a cross-lagged panel study of students and teachers over a one-year period. The researchers elicited both the teachers' perceptions of their students' mathematical ability and the students' estimates of their own ability. As usual, the teachers' perceptions at *t1* predicted the students' self-conceptions at *t2* (controlling for prior actual performance). Intriguingly, however, the students' self-concepts at *t1* also predicted teacher perceptions at *t2*. Neither correlation was very strong, and the latter was a little (though non signifi-cantly) weaker than the former; but both were reliable. In other words, the teachers and the students were mutually influencing each other.

Institutional practices within schools may compound expectancy effects, and may even create some of their own. For instance in many schools there is streaming by ability. In such situations students from socio-economically disadvantaged back-grounds, which will often include disproportionate numbers of ethnic minorities, are usually over-represented in the lower ability groups. There is thus some correspond-ence between academic categorization ('slow' band) and other category labels (for example 'working class' or 'black'), a phenomenon thus helping to preserve the nega-tive stereotypes of intellectual inferiority associated with the latter. This problem is well illustrated by evidence from Epstein's (1985) study of a large number of American schools, which found that teachers with more negative ethnic attitudes were also more likely to use some kind of 'tracking' system in their classrooms. Such practices would inevitably place more blacks (and other minority groups) in the 'slower' tracks, thus conveniently bolstering the teachers' prejudiced beliefs.

As a final example of stereotypes as self-fulfilling prophecies, let us consider a cross-cultural study by Levy and Langer (1994). Levy and Langer were interested in the cognitive capacities of elderly people. A 'common-sense' view, at least in many west-ern cultures, is that, as we get older, our various physical and intellectual capabilities irreversibly decline: we become less active, more forgetful, and so on. Accepting, of course, that there are biological changes associated with ageing,[6] Levy and Langer speculated that at least some of these deficits are attributable to culturally prevalent stereotypes associated with elderly people. Perhaps, they argued, society *expects* a deterioration in old age and helps to contribute towards that deterioration by not permitting elderly people to remain as physically and mentally active as they are able to be. Furthermore, the elderly themselves may internalize that same stereotype and sometimes model their own behaviour on what they see as the group prototype (Turner et al., 1987). To assess the extent of this social contribution to cognitive decrements associated with ageing, Levy and Langer (1994) compared the memory performance of six different groups: a sample of hearing American adults, a sample of Americans with a profound hearing disability, and a sample of Chinese adults. A half of each sample consisted in 'young' people (15–30 years), the other half were 'old' (59–91 years). In addition, participants were also tested for their stereotypical attitudes towards elderly people. The selection of the hearing-disabled and Chinese samples was important because in each of these two groups there is a markedly different stereotype of old people. In China, for instance, old people are revered and expected to contribute much more fully to social and political life than is common in the West. Deaf people, too, have an independent value system, relatively insulated from mainstream cultural beliefs, and they tend to hold old people in high esteem. Levy and Langer's results certainly bore this out. Both these groups had significantly more positive attitudes towards ageing then the American hearing sample. Furthermore, the elderly participants (but not the young) in the same two groups outperformed the elderly American hearing group on four memory tasks. Finally, to show the link between stereotypical attitudes and memory, the correlations were positive in the elderly participants (the more favourable the attitude, the better the memory performance) but negative amongst the young. I will return to this influence of prevailing cultural stereotypes on the task performance of stigmatized groups in a later chapter, when I discuss the burgeoning literature on what has come to be called 'stereotype threat' (Steele et al., 2002; see Chapter 8).

Stereotype Change

In this chapter I have emphasized the view of stereotypes as guides to judgement and action. I have argued that they, and the categories with which they are associated, are indispensable cognitive devices for understanding, negotiating and constructing our social world. If this is the case, they would be poor guides indeed if they were completely immutable, unable to change in response to new and maybe contradictory information. In this final section, then, I want to discuss some of the factors which give rise to stereotype change. This will not be an exhaustive treatment, however, since I want to return to this issue in greater detail in Chapter 9, when I consider how prejudice can most successfully be reduced. The focus there will be on the situational variables and social practices which are most likely to lead to a diminution of negative stereotypes and intergroup discrimination. Here I want to concentrate on how people deal with information which is inconsistent with their stereotypes. When does this lead to a revision of those beliefs and when, on the other hand, is it simply ignored or assimilated so as to leave the prejudiced ideas intact?

In the mid-1990s the British Open Golf tournament was held at Sandwich, a few miles from my then office. The particular course on which it was played, the Royal St George, was at that time one of the several golf clubs around the country to which women were still not permitted to belong. The proximity of this bastion of male chauvinism and the temporal coincidence of an all-male sporting event – belying the supposedly 'open' nature emphasized in its title – suggested to me that an example from the world of golf would be an appropriate way to begin this discussion. Here is Bill Raymond, a male golfer with some very clear ideas about men's and women's abilities at the game:

> Women don't play golf, they play at it [...] the average woman doesn't need 14 clubs. They could hit any of the bloody clubs from 100 yards. The average lady is much worse than the average man. They play a different game. They can't play as quickly or as accurately. Everything's got to be right from the head gear to the furry golf covers. (*Independent*, 19 December 1990)

The question I want to consider is this: what kind of information about women's golfing capabilities would it take to modify Mr Raymond's belief in their inferiority?

Gurwitz and Dodge (1977) formulated two possibilities. On the one hand, they suggested, he might encounter many women golfers, each one of whom failed to confirm his stereotype in some respect. Perhaps one might be a prodigious hitter; another might be able to hit her three-irons to land on a sixpence; another might care little for her appearance and break par on every round. The accumulation of such inconsistencies against his derogatory stereotype of women golfers might eventually lead him to change his view. On the other hand, another force for change might be for him to meet just a few very striking counter-examples to his stereotype; two or three champion golfers who can hit the ball long and straight, always break par, play quickly, and dress conventionally. Perhaps such obvious contradictions would compel him to revise his stereotype. Gurwitz and Dodge found some evidence for the latter process. In the context of stereotypes about college sorority members, they presented participants with information about three sorority members and asked them to predict what a fourth one, their friend, would be like. In the experimental conditions of interest to us here, several pieces of information about the friends were presented which disconfirmed the traditional sorority stereotype. This information was either 'dispersed' amongst all three friends or 'concentrated' in just one of them. The participants' ratings of the missing fourth woman were significantly less stereotypical in the latter case, which suggests that the 'glaring exception' can indeed induce a change in a group stereotype.

This will not always be the case, however, as was demonstrated by some subsequent experiments undertaken by Weber and Crocker (1983). Following Rothbart (1981), they called the change induced by a few strong exceptions 'conversion', and the change induced by many discrete disconfirmations 'book-keeping' (since it implied that stereotypes were modified by simply adding up the amount of inconsistent information). To these two models they added a third one, 'sub-typing', which they suggested could act to promote *or* to inhibit change in an overall group stereotype. To illustrate this effect, let us return to our beleaguered Mr Raymond. Suppose he does indeed witness some outstanding golfing feats by two women players. One convenient strategy for him is to place those two players in a special sub-group – perhaps 'professional women golfers'– which then allows him to leave his more general stereotype of 'ordinary women golfers' intact. In a typically apt phrase, Allport (1954) called this process '**refencing**' and suggested that it was a common cognitive device which permits people to sustain their prejudiced beliefs even when they are confronted with contradictory evidence. However, **sub-typing** can also have positive

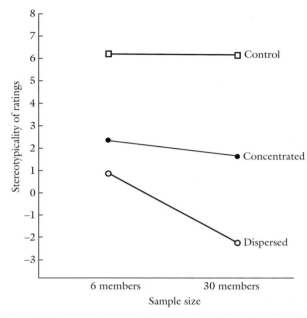

Figure 4.5 Effects of different amounts and patterns of disconfirming information on subsequent stereotypical ratings. Lower scores indicate less stereotypical judgement and hence more evidence of stereotype change. Source: Weber and Crocker, 1983, Figure 1

effects on stereotype change. Suppose Mr Raymond is continually faced with dozens of women golfers who do not fit his stereotype. Perhaps he sub-types some of them as 'professionals', others as 'low handicap golfers', others as 'good around the greens' – and perhaps some even as 'sensibly dressed'. The proliferation of sub-types, necessitated by his exposure to a wide range of counter-examples, begins to render his original superordinate category of the 'woman golfer' (who dresses inappropriately and cannot play well) rather less useful to him. As a result, the global and negative stereotype becomes fragmented and hence less potent.

Weber and Crocker (1983) modified Gurwitz and Dodge's (1977) procedure for providing disconfirming information, which was either 'concentrated' in a few members or 'dispersed' across several; this time the object was two occupational groups. They also varied the size of the sample of evidence from each group: there were six members in one condition, thirty in another (notice that both groups are larger than the group of three which Gurwitz and Dodge had used). In their subsequent judgements of the occupational groups, the participants were clearly influenced by the size of the sample, and hence by the absolute amount of disconfirming information. However, this cannot have been a simple 'book-keeping' type of change, since an even more significant factor was *how* the information was distributed across the sample. When it was dispersed across many members, it produced a less stereotypical view of the occupational group than when it was concentrated, even though the gross amount of inconsistent information was the same in each case (see Figure 4.5; see also Johnston and Hewstone, 1992). Weber and Crocker also showed that sub-typing could help to explain the changes they observed. In a subsequent task participants were asked to sort the 'stimulus persons' into groups. In the conditions where the disconfirmations were all concentrated into a few cases, participants typically formed only one sub-group (which consisted of those counter-examples); in the 'dispersed' conditions, by contrast, between two and four sub-groups were formed.

In another experiment, Weber and Crocker (1983) further clarified the role that this sub-typing process plays in stereotype change. They varied the representativeness of the disconfirming group members. Some were seen as highly typical of the group in spite of their manifesting counter-stereotypical characteristics; the others were seen as unrepresentative. The former class produced more evidence of stereotype change than the latter – a finding which was replicated in other research (see Hewstone, 1994). I shall return to this issue in Chapter 9, where it will be seen that the typicality of outgroup members with whom we have contact plays an important role in modifying our intergroup attitudes.

Gurwitz and Dodge (1977) found that concentrating all the contradictory information into one highly salient counter-example was more effective than dispersing it; Weber and Crocker (1983) and Johnston and Hewstone (1992) showed the opposite. What could account for this discrepancy? One obvious factor is the size of the sample from which the consistent and inconsistent information is drawn. In Gurwitz and Dodge the experiment contained only three samples; in the other studies these varied between six and thirty. It seems, then, that the 'conversion' mode of stereotype change is only likely to occur when we have relatively few examples on which to make up our mind (notice that in Figure 4.4 the 'benefits' of dispersed information are most noticeable in the large sample). If the target group in question is also highly homogenous (as well as small), this composition is another factor which could favour the 'conversion' process. In this case, one or two striking counter-examples seem to be particularly effective in inducing stereotype change (Hewstone et al., 1992).

Until now we have only considered how the amount and patterning of disconfirming information can affect the revision of stereotypes. To conclude, we ought also to note that some stereotypes are easier to change than others. Rothbart and Park (1986) asked people to estimate how many instances of observable behaviour it would take to confirm or disconfirm that somebody (or some group) possessed each of a large list of traits. They also had to rate the favourability of each trait. One of the clearest findings which emerged from their study was that, the more favourable a trait was, the greater the number of occasions needed to confirm it would have to be – and correspondingly the smaller the number of occasions needed to *disconfirm* it. The opposite held true for unfavourable traits. In other words, as Rothbart and Park (1986) put it, 'unfavourable traits are easier to acquire and harder to lose than are favourable traits' (p. 135). If we add this assessment to Maass' (1999) linguistic analysis of ingroup and outgroup descriptions, which we discussed earlier – recall how she discovered that descriptions of negative outgroup behaviour tend to be couched in rather general and hence not easily falsifiable terms – then we are forced to a rather sobering conclusion about the difficulty of changing prejudiced outgroup stereotypes.

So far I have discussed how one might try to change the derogatory stereotypes of someone like Mr Raymond by exposing him to people or information that might contradict them. As we have seen, we should not be overly optimistic about the ease with which this can be done. But maybe another strategy would be more effective. Just as enlightened educators and managers might seek to curb racist or homophobic opinions in the classroom or workplace, could we not try to convince Mr Raymond to suppress his rather chauvinistic views on women golfers? Unfortunately such an approach might prove to be counter-productive, if we are to believe the findings of some research conducted by Macrae and his colleagues.

In a first series of studies, Macrae and his team (1994c) asked their participants to describe a typical day in the life of a skinhead who was shown in a photograph. Half of them (the experimental groups) were asked to do this whilst actively avoiding thinking or writing about their stereotypical preconceptions about skinheads. The remainder (the control groups) were given no such **stereotype suppression** instructions. Sure enough, the experimental participants seemed able to comply with the suppression instructions they had been given, *at least temporarily*. The brief passages they wrote about the skinhead contained reliably fewer stereotypic references. However, that was not the end of the story (or of the experiment). Macrae and colleagues (1994c) were really interested in what would happen later, once the participants stopped monitoring themselves for unwanted stereotypic thoughts about skinheads. Drawing on some earlier work by Wegner and colleagues (1987), who had found that, when people were specifically asked not to think of a certain idea, they subsequently showed an even greater preoccupation with that idea,[7] Macrae and colleagues predicted a similar **rebound effect** with the stereotypes of skinheads. They reasoned that the mental process of suppression requires some constant internal monitoring ('am I thinking about skinhead stereotypes as I write this?'), and this internal monitoring is likely to render those same stereotypical constructs more accessible. Whilst the (experimental) participants continue to exercise control over what they think and write, they will, indeed, be able to restrain themselves. However, once that control is relaxed – let's say, when they think the experiment is over – those now hyper-accessible stereotypes are likely to rebound into action with renewed vigour. And so it proved. In one study, participants were led to an adjoining room where they expected to meet the skinhead whom they had been writing about. A jacket and a bag were left on a chair; the experimenter remarked that the skinhead must have popped out of the room for a minute and invited the participant to take a seat (seven other chairs were available in a line, away from the 'occupied' chair). Remarkably enough, those participants who had previously suppressed their skinhead stereotypes on average chose to sit nearly a whole chair further away from the 'occupied' chair than did the control participants. In another experiment, the subsequent activity was a lexical decision task in which participants had to identify stereotypical and non-stereotypical words from non-words. Those in the suppression condition were reliably faster at recognizing words related to the stereotype of skinheads than those in the control condition. Apparently the suppression experience had made those stereotypical words much more readily available to their consciousness (see also Macrae et al., 1998).

Fortunately, the news is not all bad for those who would attempt deliberately to suppress their own (or others') less palatable stereotypes. Monteith and colleagues (1998a) have pointed out that ironical rebound effects of suppression are by no means inevitable. For one thing, the outgroups used as targets for stereotyping in the studies of Macrae and his colleagues were mostly those for which there were no strong norms about the undesirability of expressing prejudice against them (for example skinheads, hairdressers). Perhaps with politically more sensitive groups (like black people or gays) the socially prescribed everyday suppression would have become sufficiently habitual to prevent the occurrence of any rebound effects (Monteith et al., 1998b; but compare Liberman and Förster, 2000). With such outgroups, it is possible that only dispositionally more prejudiced people, for whom the outgroup in question is likely to be more readily accessible anyway, will show any rebound effects towards them (Monteith et al., 1998b). There is also evidence that rebound effects will only occur if people are sufficiently distracted cognitively to permit the unintended stereotypes to 'leak out' (Wyer et al., 2000).

An optimistic note on rebound effects has also been sounded by Förster and Liberman (2004). Contrary to the explanation of the phenomenon favoured by Macrae and colleagues (1994c) – heightened accessibility due to continuous internal monitoring – Förster and Liberman suggest that the ironical effects of stereotype suppression are better understood as a consequence of inferences that the participants in these experiments make about their own thought processes. According to Förster and Liberman (2004), participants in the classic 'suppression' conditions of the experiments may indeed find it hard to suppress their unwanted stereotypical thoughts. But the heightened accessibility that results then stems not from some internal and automatic monitoring process, but from a more deliberative inference about themselves. The two authors explain the participants' reasoning thus:

> It is hard to write this story, and everything I can think of is, somehow, however remotely, related to the stereotype. It must be so difficult for me to write the story because I cannot use stereotypes. Without this restriction, it would have been much easier for me. It must be the case, then, that I really need to use stereotypes. (Förster and Liberman, 2004, p. 9)

This attribution of difficulty then enhances the motivation to think about the suppressed stereotype and, by so doing, increases its accessibility in the rebound phase.[8] In a rather convincing confirmation of their theory, Förster and Liberman (2001) showed that the usual rebound effect of suppression could be eliminated through the simple expedient of telling participants that avoiding stereotypes was 'difficult', that some degree of stereotyping was 'only natural' and did not indicate that a person was prejudiced. Armed with this alternative explanation for their experiences in the suppression phase of the experiment, these participants showed very similar behavioural and attitudinal reactions to those of the participants in the no suppression control conditions, and markedly different responses from those of the participants who had only received the conventional suppression instructions.

For a final observation on the feasibility of persuading people to change their prejudiced ways, let me turn to the work of Kawakami and her colleagues (Kawakami et al., 2000; Kawakami et al., 2005). They had the idea that it would be possible to train people to change their automatic cognitive associations between certain outgroup categories and various negative stereotypic traits. Their training method was simple: participants had repeatedly to respond affirmatively to the paired presentations of a picture of an outgroup member (say, skinhead) and a counter-stereotypical trait (for example 'frail', 'afraid'), but negatively to pairings of the same photograph with stereotypical traits (such as 'nasty', 'dangerous'). By having their participants just say 'yes' or 'no' respectively in literally hundreds of trials (480 to be precise), Kawakami and colleagues (2000) hoped that the old (bad) stereotypic habits would be weakened and replaced by new counter-stereotypical associations. To measure if this had happened, they used a version of the Stroop task. Remarkably enough, those in the stereotype negation training condition did show a significant reduction in their Stroop interference responses, whilst those in the control condition did not. Furthermore, this training effect could still be observed up to twenty-four hours later, which thus proved that it was not merely a transitory phenomenon. In other studies, Kawakami and colleagues observed similar outcomes using blacks as the target group. They also reduced gender discrimination in a mock personnel selection task (Kawakami et al., 2000; Kawakami et al., 2005).

Two points are especially noteworthy about these pioneering studies. One is that the training programme seems to be having an effect on people's *automatic* stereotypic activation. Remember that responses in the Stroop task are thought not to be readily amenable to conscious control. This, then, provides a nice addendum to our discussion, earlier in this chapter, of the supposed inevitability of automatic prejudice effects. It seems that such automatic cognitive responses, far from being immutable, can be modified by an intensive bout of reprogramming. Presumably even more dramatic and long-lasting changes could be effected by a sustained re-education intervention. The second point worthy of noting concerns the similarity between the procedure used by Kawakami and colleagues (2000) and the stereotype suppression paradigm developed by Macrae and colleagues (1994c). A close reading of the procedure developed by Kawakami and colleagues (2000) makes it clear that this was, in fact, a form of stereotype suppression instruction:

> Participants in the Skinhead Negation Condition were instructed to *try not to* think of cultural associations when seeing the photograph of the skinhead. Accordingly, they were asked to press 'No' on a button box when they saw the photograph of the skinhead and under it a word associated with skinheads. (Kawakami et al., 2000, p. 873, emphasis in original)

Thus, while a single episode of actively attempting to suppress stereotypes may prove counter-productive, many repetitions of the same suppressive act seem to break the stereotype mould. Here as in other walks of life, practice does seem to make (almost) perfect.

In this chapter I have confined myself mainly to a cognitive level of analysis – how information about groups is attended to, acquired, processed, forgotten and recalled. In later chapters I shall also consider how more social and motivational processes can be brought to bear on intergroup relations so as to change the way in which members of different groups feel and act towards each other (see Chapters 6 and 9).

Summary

1   A stereotype is the perception that most members of a category share some attribute. Stereotyping arises directly from the categorization process, particularly the assimilation of within-group differences.

2   Stereotypes can originate from the culture in which people are socialized, and also from real cultural and socio-economic differences between groups. For historical, political and socio-structured reasons, members of different groups often occupy different social roles in society. Stereotypes can arise from the inferences that people make about the psychological attributes necessary for the performance of these roles. Such stereotypes will often serve as ideologies designed to justify the status quo.

3   Stereotypes may also stem from a cognitive bias which causes the perception of an illusory correlation between minority groups and infrequently occurring attributes. This bias was originally thought to lie in the 'distinctiveness' of infrequent conjunctions, but recent research suggests that it may derive just as much from a categorial differentiation process or from a falsely perceived correspondence between actual correlations at a group level and correlations at an individual level.

4   The perceived entitativity, or 'groupness', of a social category can facilitate stereotyping, perhaps because it gives rise to a perception that the members of that group all possess some fundamental 'essence'.

5   Stereotypes can influence people's judgements of individuals, but this depends on the relative salience of individuating and group-based information.

6   A useful way of viewing stereotypes is as hypotheses in search of confirmatory information. Much evidence exists for this confirmation-seeking nature of stereotypic expectancies.

7   The activation and operation of stereotyping processes can occur below the level of conscious awareness; this is the so-called 'automatic' stereotyping. People can be subliminally or unobtrusively primed with category-related stimuli, and this can affect their stereotypic judgements of others and their behaviour towards them. Some have concluded that this means that some (unconscious) forms of prejudice are inevitable. However, subsequent research has shown that automatic stereotyping phenomena depend on people's prior and habitual level of prejudice.

8   Stereotypes also generate attributional judgements about the causes of ingroup and outgroup actions. A typical finding is that positive and negative behaviours adopted by the ingroup are attributed internally and externally respectively; for outgroup behaviours the reverse applies.

9   Stereotypes may be used more if people are cognitively or emotionally preoccupied with other concerns. Such distractions are thought to consume their cognitive resources, thus paving the way for the labour-saving afforded by stereotypes.

10   Stereotypes can have self-fulfilling properties, creating in their targets the very attributes which are hypothesized to exist in them. Such self-fulfilling prophecies have been intensively investigated in educational settings.

11   Stereotypes may change in response to disconfirming information, but the patterning of that information (which can be concentrated in a few exemplars or dispersed across many) and the valence of the stereotype undergoing revision are important factors in determining the extent of change.

12   Conscious attempts to suppress stereotypes can ironically result in their stronger reappearance later on – the so-called 'rebound effect'. This may happen because the internal self-monitoring involved in suppression causes a covert priming of the very stereotypical constructs one is trying to inhibit. However, prolonged training in the dissociation between category and stereotype can result in lessened subsequent stereotyping.

Notes

1   Although these results are intriguing, some caution is in order because over 20 percent of the original participants in this experiment had to be dropped from the analysis for various reasons (Sinclair and Kunda, 1999, p. 896).

2   Note that this exposure time is much briefer than in parafoveal priming procedures. This is because the stimuli in this case were presented in the central part of the visual field, where our perceptual system is better able to detect objects.

3   In a typical Stroop task the participants' task is to name the colour in which a stimulus word is presented. When the semantic content of that word is consistent with the ink colour in which the word is written (e.g. 'green' is written in green ink), or when the word has no special connotation for the participant (e.g. 'table'), then colour naming proceeds relatively fast. On the contrary, if the meaning of the word conflicts with the ink colour (e.g. 'red' is written in green ink) or is especially significant for the participant (e.g. it is stereotypical of a previously indicated group – 'Aborigines', in the case of Locke and colleagues (1994)), then one typically observes a slowing down in the response. The difference between the first and the second kind of trials is a typical measure of the Stroop interference effect (Stroop, 1935).

4   The causal links here may also be reciprocal. That is, those who saw the outgroup most stereotypically may well be more anxious over the contact. I am grateful to Tom Pettigrew for pointing this out.

5   These findings have always seemed particularly compelling to me. Many years ago I taught in a secondary school. My subject then was mathematics, which, at that school, was streamed by 'ability' after the first year. An abiding, and still saddening, memory from that experience was that of witnessing the systematic decline in numeracy over the different year groups. The contrast between the least able members of the first year mixed-ability class – always trying, always believing they would eventually master the subject – and their elder peers in the fourth and fifth-year 'bottom' sets – sullen, bored, convinced of their ineptitude – was striking indeed. The label 'no good at maths' had stuck with them, and also with us, their teachers, and we all – students and teachers alike – behaved accordingly.

6   Of which, regrettably, I myself am becoming only too aware!

7   I seem to recall a hilarious episode of *Friends*, the long running television show, which drew on this idea. As I remember it, much to his dismay, Chandler began to have erotic dreams about his prospective mother-in-law. And the more he tried to stop himself dreaming of her, the more vivid and disturbing the dreams became.

8   This account is rather reminiscent of Bem's (1972) self-perception explanation of forced compliance cognitive dissonance effects.

Further Reading

Fiedler, K., and Walther, G. (2004) *Stereotyping as Inductive Hypothesis Testing*, chs 3, 4, 7. Hove: Psychology Press.

Förster, J., and Liberman, N. (2004) A motivational model of post-suppressional rebound. *European Review of Social Psychology* 15: 1–32.

Hewstone, M. (1994) Revision and change of stereotypic beliefs: In search of the elusive sub-typing model. *European Review of Social Psychology* 5: 69–109.

Maass, A. (1999) Linguistic intergroup bias: Stereotype-perpetuation through language. In M. Zanna (ed.), *Advances in Experimental Social Psychology*, Vol. 31, 79–121. New York: Academic Press.

Macrae, C. N., Stangor, C., and Hewstone, M. (eds) (1996) *Stereotypes and Stereotyping*, chs. 2, 4, 5, 6, 7, 9. New York: Guilford.

Spears, R., Oakes, P. J., Ellemers, N., and Haslam, S. A. (eds) (1997) *The Social Psychology of Stereotyping and Group Life*, chs 3, 7, 8. Oxford: Blackwell.

5

The Development of Prejudice in Children

In an earlier chapter I examined a theory which traces the roots of adult prejudice back to childhood socialization experiences (see Chapter 2). The thrust of that approach, as we saw, was to identify certain patterns of family dynamics which would give rise to an authoritarian or dogmatic personality. Notwithstanding the historical importance of that approach, from the angle of a developmental social psychology of prejudice it suffered from two crucial weaknesses. One was that it was essentially a theory of the deviant personality. Only some children, those unfortunate enough to have been brought up in a particularly strict family, with domineering and moralistic parents, were thought likely to be predisposed to develop into prejudiced adults in later life. The remainder – presumably the majority? – because they were not so afflicted, were eased out of the theoretical field of view. The second drawback was that, despite the interest of that theory in the childhood origins of prejudice, remarkably little of the research it inspired actually studied children themselves. With the exception of Frenkel-Brunswik (1949, 1953) and one or two others, most work in this tradition studied adults and relied heavily on their retrospective reports of their childhood. However interesting these may be, they are no substitute for the direct observation of children's own attitudes and behaviour.

In this chapter I want therefore to turn the spotlight fully on children, particularly in the first ten years of their lives. What is known about prejudice in children and what can this tell us about prejudice in us, adults? Are children bound simply to reproduce the racist, sexist and ageist norms of the society into which they are born – little chips off their prejudiced elders' blocks? Or might they contribute something themselves, developing some attitudes and stereotypes of their own, from categorial attempts to systematize and control their social environment? These are some of the questions I shall be pursuing in this chapter.

Following Goodman's (1952) lead, I have divided the chapter into three main sections, which deal respectively with children's awareness of social categories; their identification with and preference for some of those categories rather than others; and then their full-blown intergroup attitudes and behaviour. In a final section I discuss the origins of these phenomena, debating the extent to which the aetiology suggested by these origins should be regarded as unidirectional (that is, running from society to the child) or, alternatively, as a reciprocal process, in which children play their part too.

Awareness of Social Categories

A little girl of about 9 or 10 years of age looks at the dozen photographs of children spread out in front of her and sorts them into three piles, according to the similarities that she sees among them. When asked why she sorted them as she did, she replies: 'They're girls, they're boys, and they're handicaps' (Maras, 1993, p. 140). For her, the way to impose some order onto that array of strange faces was to classify them by sex and disability. In order to do that she clearly must have been *aware* of the existence of those particular categories.

This issue of **category awareness** has always been a central preoccupation of researchers interested in children and prejudice. In part this is because, as we saw in Chapter 3, any kind of prejudiced perception, attitude or action necessarily implies the prior application of some categorial distinction. One cannot be sexist (say) without first having categorized people as male and female. This in itself makes the phenomenon of awareness interesting to prejudice researchers. What has given it added importance was the discovery of the age at which social categorizations emerge reliably for the first time and the capacity to ascertain how their usage develops over the course of childhood. To the extent that such categories can be observed very early on in life, the idea of a *tabula rasa* onto which adult ideas are written becomes difficult to sustain.

One of the earliest attempts to study category awareness was made by Clark and Clark (1947). They developed a paradigm which was taken up by generations of subsequent researchers in the field. It involves presenting the child with two (or more) dolls, one of which is 'white' in colour and has yellow hair, the other being 'brown' with black hair. The child is asked a series of questions about these dolls, and the two most relevant to his or her ethnic awareness are those which simply ask the child to give the researcher the doll 'which looks like a white[/coloured] child'. Clark and Clark posed this question to black children from 3 to 7 years of age and found that, even at the youngest age, over 75 per cent of the children correctly identified the ethnicity of the doll.[1] By the age of 5, well over 90 per cent were doing so.

One might quickly object that presenting a child with such a forced choice between just these two predetermined categories does not very sensitively assess their spontaneous awareness and use of different categories. Fortunately, however, such an objection can be quickly countered by other studies, which have used different techniques and have produced broadly similar findings. Horowitz and Horowitz (1938), for instance, presented white American children with a whole series of five pictures, of which three were similar on two criteria and the remaining two differed on one criterion. Take for example three white males, one black male and one white female: which is the odd one out? The children's choices give us a clue as to which category is most salient for them. By combining ethnicity, gender, age and socio-economic status in different ways, Horowitz and Horowitz were able to discover which category predominated. Ethnicity seemed to be dominant in most of the combinations in which it occurred. Gender was the second most potent category, and socio-economic status was generally the least important. Williams and Morland (1976), who reviewed several studies using photographic stimuli in which more than just one black and one white person were portrayed, also confirmed the presence of considerable ethnic awareness in children as young as 4 years of age, although the figure was somewhat higher for whites than for blacks.

Research with the other major social category, gender, has produced similar results. Thompson (1975) found that over 75 per cent of the 2-year-olds he studied could correctly classify photographs into male and female, and the proportion was rising to 90 per cent by the age of 3. Similar findings have been obtained by other researchers through slightly different techniques (see Duveen and Lloyd, 1986; Slaby and Frey, 1975; Yee and Brown, 1994). Moreover, in memory tasks – for example in the task of recalling which child had said what in some prior stimulus presentation – children of 5 years and upwards often show patterns of errors which are consistent with having encoded the information along gender lines (Bennett and Sani, 2003; Bennett et al., 2000).

Other studies have examined category awareness in more open-ended tasks and in these, too, clear evidence of the early availability of ethnic and gender concepts has been found. A popular technique has been to present children with a series of photographs and to ask them to sort them into groups according to how they 'belong together' or 'look alike'. Sometimes the task is constrained by researchers forcing the child to classify sequentially into dichotomous clusters; others allow the child to use as many categories as he or she wishes, simultaneously. Within the stimulus photographs there are usually several cues which the child could use as sorting criteria – for example there may be adults and children, males and females, different ethnic groups, and so on. Davey (1983) used gender, age, ethnicity and style of dress (to convey socio-economic status) in his study of 7–10-year-old British children. By far and away the most frequent sorting criterion was ethnicity, used as a first resort by nearly half the children. Gender was the next most popular; style of dress was used very rarely.

We used a similar technique with white children aged from 3 to 9 years (Yee and Brown, 1988). Within the photographs we systematically varied gender, ethnicity (Asian Indian and white) and age, and there were also some other possible sorting criteria (for example hair colour). The youngest children tended simply to place all the photographs in a single large category; but, by the age of 5, ethnicity was clearly emerging as a criterion (it was used by over a third of that age group), and in the two oldest groups it completely predominated (it was used by two thirds of them). More detailed analysis of the sorting strategies used by these older children revealed that ethnicity was indeed the primary dimension – children usually placed all the Indian photographs together – and then there were some subdivisions within the white stimuli (for example by dark and light hair). This is strongly reminiscent of the outgroup homogeneity phenomenon that I discussed in Chapter 3: the Indian outgroup is perceived as a single category; the white ingroup is seen in more differentiated terms.

In these two studies, although gender was clearly available to the children as a categorization, it was seldom used. This might suggest that gender is generally less potent a social cue than ethnicity. However, such a conclusion may be premature. Changing the context – for example the micro-context of the categorization task, or the broader cultural milieu in which the research is conducted – can dramatically affect the likelihood of different categories being used. Davey (1983), for instance, followed up his open-ended task with a more structured series of questions, in which the children had to 'match' two pairs of photographs 'to play together'. Faced with this task, the children used gender rather than ethnicity as the predominant category: they were much more likely to match up two pairs of girls (or boys) than to put together children from the same ethnic group (see also Verkuyten et al., 1995). As we shall see later in this chapter, such gender segregation is a remarkably pervasive and precocious feature of children's play behaviour.

In different contexts different categories may assume importance. This was revealed by Ferraresi (1988), in a study of 4/5-year-old Italian children which used the same photographs as Yee and Brown (1988). Here ethnicity was used much less frequently than it had with British children. If anything, the children tended to sort the photographs by hair colour, and secondarily by gender. Intriguingly, when we revisited the same nursery twenty years later, using the same set of photographs, a very similar pattern of responses emerged (Ferraresi and Brown, 2008). This is interesting because over those twenty years the ethnic composition of the city where we conducted the research had changed dramatically. In the late 1980s it was virtually all white; now it has some 20 per cent immigrants, mostly from North Africa. These demographic changes were reflected in similar changes in the ethnic composition of the nursery where we conducted the research. Despite these changes, the children still did not make much use of ethnicity as a sorting criterion.

Maras and Brown (1996) employed a similar technique in order to explore children's awareness of disability. This time only photographs of the same (white) ethnicity were used, and several of the people in them had various kinds of obvious physical and learning disabilities. Asked to sort these photographs, the children (aged 8–10) invariably categorized them by gender and disability and tended to make few distinctions amongst the children with disabilities, despite the fact that these were clearly visible (for example two were in a wheelchair, two had hearing aids, and so on). Some of the children then participated in a contact intervention programme which involved a weekly visit to a school for children with disabilities. After three months of such contact, these children revealed a more differentiated category structure, with subgroups of different kinds of disabilities being formed (see Chapter 9 for other effects due to this intervention programme).

Because all of these studies were concerned with children's awareness of social categories and with their ability to use and articulate that awareness verbally, the age groups studied were seldom younger than 2½–3 years. However, there is some evidence to suggest that even infants of a few months are capable of categorial distinctions among human stimuli. Kelly and colleagues (2005) employed a simple preferential looking paradigm to examine whether infants, from a few days old up to three months of age, would spend more time looking at faces of the same ethnicity than at faces from a different ethnic group. The researchers paired up faces of Caucasian adults with faces of Middle Eastern, Asian and African adults. The faces were equated for attractiveness and any distinctive features. New-born white babies looked at each picture of the pair equally often and for approximately the same length of time, thus indicating that they could not differentiate between – or did not show a preference for any of – the various ethnicities. However, by three months of age a clear own-ethnicity preference was observed. Now the white babies preferred to look at Caucasian faces 59 per cent of the time, a reliable deviation from the chance 50 per cent level. The preference was most marked for the Caucasian–African pairing but was evident in the other two pairings too. In a follow-up study with Chinese infants of the same age, again a clear own-group preference was observed, with an overall preference for Chinese faces of 62 per cent (Kelly et al., 2007).

The fact that this ingroup preference was not visible in new-borns and emerged around three months would seem to indicate that it is a learned preference, perhaps acquired through repeated exposure to caretakers from the same ethnic group. Further

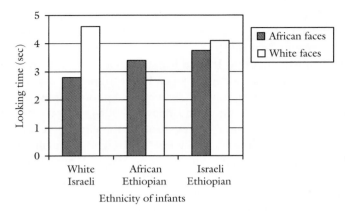

Figure 5.1   Infants' preference for own ethnicity faces as a function of intergroup contact.
Source: Bar-Haim et al., 2006, Figure 1

evidence in favour of this explanation was provided by a cross-cultural study by Bar-Haim and colleagues (2006). They compared the looking preferences for African and white faces in three groups of three-month-old infants. One group was comprised of (white) Israeli babies; a second group consisted of Ethiopian babies living in Ethiopia; the third group was made up of Ethiopian babies born to Ethiopian immigrants to Israel, who were living in 'absorption centres' where there was a great deal of exposure to whites, primarily through contact with absorption centre staff and other white immigrants. As can be seen from Figure 5.1, the patterns of looking were very different in these three groups. Both the Israeli and the Ethiopian-based Ethiopian babies showed a significant own-ethnicity preference. However, the Ethiopian immigrant babies showed no clear preference for either ethnicity. Apparently their greater exposure to *both* ethnic groups was sufficient to eliminate the usual own-group looking preference.

That selective exposure to different adults lies behind these looking preferences in young babies was confirmed in further work on gender preference. Quinn and colleagues (2002) presented pairs of faces of men and women to three-month-old children. Generally the babies seemed to prefer looking at pictures of women. Quinn and his colleagues reasoned that this may be because most babies are still looked after mainly by women. When they tested a small group of babies whose primary caretakers were men, they found that the preference for female faces had disappeared.

It seems that these familiarization effects occur quite quickly. Sangrigoli and de Schonen (2004) employed a **habituation paradigm** with young white infants, again of three months of age. In a habituation paradigm one stimulus face is shown repeatedly, until the baby appears to be a little bored (or habituated). Then the same face is shown together with a new 'test' face. If the baby fixates the test face for longer than the original stimulus, it is assumed that it sees something novel in it. In Sangrigoli and de Schonen's studies, the test face was always of the same ethnicity as the original stimulus (either white or Asian). In the first experiment, the infants showed a preference for the novel test face only in the 'own ethnicity' trials; when the face they were habituated to and the test face were both Asian, the infants looked at the two equally often. This, then, is an early example of outgroup homogeneity, since these white babies did not seem to (want to) differentiate between different outgroup faces (see Chapter 3).

However, this outgroup homogeneity effect could be quickly eliminated by the simple method of familiarizing the babies with several examples of Asian faces prior to the habituation and test trials. Just six familiarization exposures of twenty seconds each were sufficient to change the results in the habituation and test trials; now the infants looked longer at the novel test face, both in the white and in the Asian conditions.

In sum, then, the evidence from this wide variety of studies shows quite clearly that children are alert from an extremely early age to the categorial divisions current in their social environment and can be quite adept at using them. Although results are not conclusive, the existence of this capability so early in the child's life does not seem to suggest that such distinctions are simply or directly imposed on children by adults, but are picked up by the children themselves. Furthermore, the sensitivity of children's preferred categorizations both to task variations and to cultural variations suggests that categorizations are used by them in an active and strategic manner. This is consistent with our earlier discussion of the important social psychological functions of categorization (see Chapter 3). Adults use categories to simplify and make sense of their environment; apparently children do the same.

Who Am I and Whom Do I like? Category Identification and Preference

So far we have only considered the onset and development of children's *awareness* of different social categories. However, awareness does not necessarily imply an identification with, or a preference for, one category over others. In this section, therefore, I examine what is known about the development of children's **category preferences**, concentrating mainly on ethnicity and gender, since these have been the focus of most research attention. As we shall see, there is a wealth of evidence to indicate that children, from ages as young as 3 years (and possibly even younger), identify with these categories and express clear evaluative preferences for one over another. However, the nature and direction of those preferences seem also to depend on the social standing of their group in the wider society: children from dominant or majority groups often respond quite differently from children belonging to subordinate or minority groups.

Ethnic, national and other categories

A 4-year-old white British girl looks at the photographs of four girls in front of her: an Afro-Caribbean, a South Asian, an East Asian and a white.

INTERVIEWER: 'Do you think any of them would be kind?'
  The girl points to the photograph of the white girl.
INTERVIEWER: 'Do you think any of them are mean?'
  The girl points to the ethnic minority photographs.

In another sequence, a 4-year-old Afro-Caribbean boy looks at four photographs, this time of other boys: again, three have an ethnic minority background and one is white.

INTERVIEWER: 'Which one do you like the best?'
The boy points to the photo of the white boy.
INTERVIEWER: 'Do you think that any of these children snatch things?'
The boy points to the Afro-Caribbean photograph. (Taken from *A Child of Our Time*, BBC TV, 4 May 2005)

This sequence, recorded for a major television documentary, was based on a classic research paradigm, which has been used to investigate ethnic identification for more than sixty years. Typically, children are shown pictures or dolls which are chosen to represent different ethnic groups, and they are asked which one most closely resembles them, which one they would like to play with, which one looks 'nice/bad', and so on. The early research by Clark and Clark (1947) and Goodman (1952) provided the inspiration for literally dozens of subsequent studies. Questions about self-identifications revealed that a majority of children at the ages studied (between 3 and 7 years) identified themselves with the doll appropriate to their ethnic group – that is, black children identified with the darker coloured stimuli, white children with the lighter ones. However, beneath this general trend lay some important differences. Perhaps the most important one was what seemed to be an asymmetry between the identifications of the minority (black) children and those of the white majority. Clark and Clark (1947) found that only about two thirds of the black children identified with the darker doll. Goodman (1952) found a similar percentage, but a much higher figure (over 95 per cent) of the white children identifying with the white stimuli. In addition to these ethnic group differences there were some developmental effects, particularly amongst the black children. Clark and Clark (1947) observed that over 60 per cent of the 3-year-old black children actually identified with the *lighter doll*, a figure in striking contrast to the 87 per cent of 7-year-olds identifying with the darker doll.[2]

These findings on identification were underlined by some even more marked ethnic differences when it came to questions about play preferences and to evaluative judgements. In one of the earliest studies, Horowitz (1936) found that in four different samples of white children there was a consistent preference for white photographs in response to the question 'show me the one you like the best' (the children had to rank in order a series of twelve photographs of black and white children). This preference, already evident in kindergarten children, seemed to increase with age, levelling off around the age of 9/10. However, the few black children in Horowitz's study also preferred the white photographs. The percentage of pro-white preference was lower amongst them than amongst the white children, but it was still reliably above chance level (or no preference level). This finding was confirmed by Clark and Clark (1947). At every age in the groups of the black children they studied, there was a majority showing a preference to play with the *white* doll and also indicating that this was the one which 'looked nice'. These differences were not always significantly different from the chance level, but they were highly consistent and, because they favoured the 'outgroup', they were radically different from the pro-ingroup preferences shown by the white children in the Horowitz (1936) study.

In the following three decades similar results were reported from a number of studies in the USA. Using a variety of different techniques – for example actual photographs rather than line drawings, or tasks more complex than binary choices – a consistent pat-

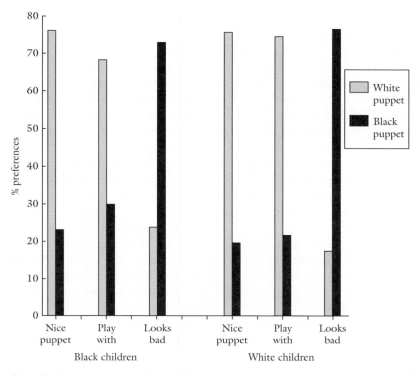

Figure 5.2 Black and white preferences for black and white puppets. Adapted from Table 1 in Asher and Allen, 1969

tern emerged: white children showed a very strong and definite preference for stimuli which represented their own ethnic group, whilst black children seemed to be much more ambivalent, often showing a preference for, and in some cases an identification with, the outgroup – that is, with whites (Brand et al., 1974; Milner, 1983; Porter, 1971; Williams and Morland, 1976).

The prevalence and strength of this outgroup preference amongst black children has been a matter of some debate, and it is true that in some of the studies the black children's choices did not deviate significantly from the 50 per cent chance level (Banks, 1976). But what is beyond doubt in these early studies is the clear discrepancy between the black and the white children's responses: the strong ingroup preference in the latter, as opposed to no preference, or outgroup preference, in the former. A study by Asher and Allen (1969) conducted in the mid-1960s captures this well. They tested a large number of black and white children aged between 3 and 8 years using both black and white researchers to control for any possible experimental demand effects. Adopting a similar 'doll methodology' to that devised by Clark and Clark (1947), they found a clear preference for the lighter coloured puppet in *both white and black children* (see Figure 5.2). In addition to these overall strong pro-white preferences, Asher and Allen observed some age effects. In both groups the pro-white bias seemed to increase from 3–4 years to reach a peak at 5–6 years, and then to decline again in the 7–8-year-olds. As we shall see, this curvilinear pattern, with its maximum around the age of 6, may be developmentally quite significant.

Up until now I have concentrated on research carried out with black and white American children between the 1930s and the 1960s. However, the patterns of children's ingroup and outgroup favouring preferences observed in those studies are by no means restricted to those ethnic groups, that country or that era. In several other societies, too, researchers noted a consistent tendency for children from (dominant) majority groups to show strong ingroup identification and preference, whilst the identification of children from (subordinate) minority group with their ingroup was much weaker and often paralleled by evaluative preferences for stimuli symbolic of the majority group. Vaughan (1964a and b) found that white New Zealand children (aged 4–12) showed strong ingroup identification and made clear ingroup favouring trait attributions, while Maori children tended to favour the outgroup. As in other studies, the peak for pro-white preference seemed to be in the 6–8 age range, declining somewhat as the children grew older.

A similar pattern has been found in Britain amongst West Indian and Asian children, although more strongly for the former than the latter (Jahoda et al., 1972; Milner, 1983; Richardson and Green, 1971). And that same trend seems to be persisting even to the present day, as we saw from the TV excerpt at the start of this section. The examples I gave there were actually reasonably representative of the 200 or so ethnic majority and minority children who were tested. Aboud (1977) found that a clear majority of white Canadian pre-school children applied an appropriate ethnic label to themselves, while only a half and a third respectively of Chinese and native Indian children did so. Griffiths and Nesdale (2006) found that Anglo-Australian children showed stronger ingroup preference over Pacific Islanders than vice versa, though both groups were strongly biased against aboriginal people. Finally, Enesco and colleagues (2005) found that Spanish children (aged 7–11 years) were strongly biased against Latin American immigrants to their country, and even more biased against gypsies. In contrast, Latin American children favoured the *Spanish* as a group vis-à-vis their own (in other words, they showed outgroup preference) and were also biased against gypsies. In respect of the latter target group, both sets of children displayed clear negativity.

Thus far, a fairly consistent finding has been that of a strong pro-white (or majority) ingroup preference amongst white children and of a more ambivalent attitude on the part of minority group children. However, the latter phenomenon has not always been observed. In particular historical contexts, especially in periods when relations between the relevant ethnic groups are in flux, it has sometimes been found that even subordinate or minority group children show ingroup preference. Thus Hraba and Grant (1970), conducting their research at the end of a turbulent decade of black–white relations in the USA, found that both black and white children made pro-ingroup choices in the standard doll-choice paradigm. Other studies conducted shortly afterwards, both in the USA and elsewhere, also found pro-ingroup preferences in minority children (Aboud, 1980; Braha and Rutter, 1980; Epstein et al., 1976; Stephan and Rosenfield, 1978; Vaughan, 1978). These findings serve as a timely reminder that social psychological phenomena are rarely immutable, unaffected by developments in the wider society.

I have reviewed work on ethnic categories and, as we have seen, there is ample evidence that children value these categories differently, suggesting that ethnic preference emerges at quite an early age. What of nationalism: do children show a similar preference for their own nationality? Does it emerge at an equally early age? The answer to the first question is an unequivocal 'yes', although, again, the strength of the preference varies somewhat across countries. Regarding the second question, the matter is harder to judge because most of the relevant studies have used slightly older children (6 years and upwards). Moreover, although the degree of own-nationality preference does show developmental change, the pattern of that change is itself quite variable and context-dependent.

One of the landmark studies in this area was a cross-national project by Lambert and Klineberg (1967). These researchers surveyed over 3,000 children of ages varying from 6 to 14 years in eleven countries. One of the early questions in the interview was: 'What are you?' The most common response to this open-ended question mentioned gender; ethnicity or nationality were mentioned only rarely. The use of social categories in these self-definitions seemed to increase somewhat between the ages of 6 and 10 years, then to level off. Despite the low frequency with which ethnicity and nationality were mentioned spontaneously – a finding confirmed by others (Jahoda, 1963; McGuire et al., 1978) – when the children were specifically asked about their own and other national groups, they were able to answer quite easily, even when they were as young as 6. In the vast majority of cases, children used positive adjectives to describe their own country (two exceptions being the Japanese and the black South Africans). Furthermore, when asked which nationality other than their own they would most and least like to have, there was a remarkable consensus across the eleven countries: the preferred nationalities were American, British and French (in that order). The only noticeable variation came from the black South Africans, who most often mentioned 'white' as their preferred alternative nationality. The *least* preferred nationalities were Russian, African, Chinese and German, although there was less consensus over these. Once again, the black South African children stood out as being the most prominent rejectors of their own ethnic group; 35–55 per cent of this sample mentioned African tribal nationality as their least preferred choice. The parallels between these reactions and those of children from subordinate groups in the doll and picture preference studies discussed earlier are striking (see also Tajfel et al., 1972).

A similarly ambitious cross-national comparative study was conducted by Barrett and his many colleagues (Barrett, 2007). Notable for its size (over 4,000 children, aged 6–15 years), for the range of countries sampled (seven nation–states with several sub-groups within them, including countries from western Europe and the former Soviet Union), and for the sophistication of the measures employed (for example positive and negative group evaluations were separately measured), this study provides many important, albeit also complex, insights into the nature of children's internation attitudes: *first*, children of all ages (including 6-year-olds) in all countries showed an obvious preference for their own country. *Secondly*, children's evaluations of other countries, though less favourable than those of their own country, were generally not especially negative. There were some notable exceptions – for example children in Azerbaijan clearly did not care much for Russians, nor Georgians for Azeris or Ukrainians for Georgians; but on the whole the children did not express much outgroup denigration.

Beyond these two conclusions, the picture becomes fuzzier. There were, it is true, many reliable changes in these intergroup attitudes with age, but they were frustratingly inconsistent, sometimes showing linear increases, sometimes decreases, and, more than once, a curvilinear pattern (especially on the topic of liking for the ingroup). However, even this latter finding – an increase from 6 to 9 years of age and then a decline – was far from universal, and several other configurations were also visible. Furthermore, there was considerable variation in the kind and direction of intergroup bias expressed. With children from some of the countries, it often seemed to be the case that one particular outgroup was out of favour; for example in several of the western European samples Germany was not much liked. But in the eastern European samples there was greater heterogeneity or variety in the outgroup(s) singled out for disapproval – here Russians, there Azeris. Barrett (2007) suggests that this situation reflects vestiges of historical or current intergroup relations between the various countries. For instance Germany's involvement in the Second World War may still be affecting children's attitudes towards it. If this is the case, then it suggests that the many socio-cultural processes involved in the transmission of images of different groups (for example through books, television or computer games) are as important an influence on the development of children's national attitudes as any generic social psychological dynamics.

There is one final feature of Barrett's (2007) findings that deserves comment. Children were generally more inclined to differentiate among countries on positive attributes than on negative ones. My own re-analysis of two of the tables presented by Barrett suggests that the range of the maximum and minimum number of positive adjectives attributed to the most favoured country (nearly always the children's own) and the least favoured country was, on average, over 50 per cent higher than the range of the maximum and minimum number of negative attributes. This turns out to be a massively significant difference, and it is not much affected by age or country. This greater willingness to use positive rather than negative means of discriminating amongst groups seems to be a rather general phenomenon and is in fact graced with its own label: the 'positive–negative asymmetry effect' (Mummendey and Otten, 1998; see Chapter 3). There are various plausible explanations for this effect (Gardham and Brown, 2001; Mummendey and Otten, 1998); but one, in particular, seems to be relevant to its occurrence in children. The asymmetry may reflect a normative difference in the acceptability of expressing positive and negative sentiments. As we are all aware, it is (just about) acceptable to say that one likes this or that person (or group) more than another. However, it is very much *not* the done thing to say that one *dis*likes a particular person (or group).

Although there did not appear to be any age differences in the positive–negative asymmetry that I found in Barrett's (2007) data, this may have been so because of the relatively large intervals separating the age groups (three years). It is possible that there is some significant developmental change in the positive–negative asymmetry effect, and that this change occurs around 7 years of age. Or so we have found in a study of British children's attitudes towards Germany (Rutland et al., 2007). As usual, ingroup bias was observed at all ages, especially on the number of positive traits attributed to Britain and Germany. However, on negative traits, children from 8 years on showed no intergroup differentiation. But *7-year-olds* clearly attributed more negative traits to Germany than to Britain. It looks as if the younger children had not yet learned the social inappropriateness of making negative evaluations of another country. This conclusion was confirmed in a follow-up study where we found that the age difference in the asymmetry effect was partially mediated by how

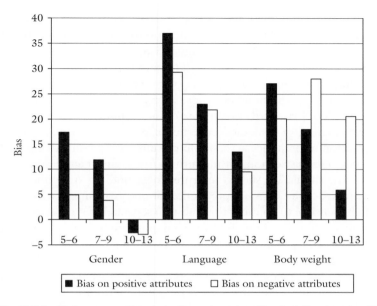

Figure 5.3   Children's intergroup biases in three domains. Bias is defined as the difference in the percentage of traits attributed to the ingroup and to the outgroup (ingroup–outgroup for positive traits, outgroup–ingroup for negative traits). Age groups are shown on the x-axis. Adapted from Table 1 in Powlishta et al., 1994

appropriate the children thought it was to exclude German children from various ingroup activities (ibid.). As we shall see, children's increasing sensitivity to social norms may well underlie several of the developmental trends that have been observed to be present in prejudice.

We have now considered biases along *ethnic* and *national* lines. In the next section I will be discussing *gender* biases in some detail. However, these three categories by no means exhaust the range of socially meaningful dimensions along which children use to make discriminations. An attribute that seems to be increasing in social importance is body weight – a phenomenon perhaps not unconnected to the twin influences of societal obsessions with ideal, thin-body images (Dittmar, 2007) and of growing concerns amongst health professionals about a global obesity pandemic (World Health Organization, 2000). There seems to be little doubt that children, starting from as young an age as 3 or 5 years, show a preference for 'normal' weight peers in comparison to 'overweight' peers (Cramer and Steinwert, 1998; Penny and Haddock, 2007; Powlishta et al., 1994). The study by Powlishta and colleagues (1994) is especially interesting because it compares children's attitudes in the domain of body size with those in language, ethnicity (the study was conducted in Quebec, Canada and examined the attitudes of anglophone children towards francophones) and gender (see Figure 5.3).

Bias was evident in all three domains and was on the whole more obvious on the positive than on the negative attributes (here is another manifestation of positive–negative asymmetry). This bias declined with age, especially on the positive attributes. But notice how the pattern of bias is rather different in the body-weight domain: although positive bias declined, bias on negative attributes here remained high in all three age groups, which perhaps indicates that fewer social proscriptions are attached to expressing derogatory feelings and attitudes towards overweight people. Two other findings from this study, not shown in Figure 5.3, were of interest. First, girls were markedly more gender biased than boys – a finding which, as we shall see in the next section, is rather prevalent. Secondly, there was very little correspondence between a child's levels of bias in different domains; nearly all the inter-domain correlations amongst measures of bias were close to zero. This reminds us yet again of the weakness of an explanation of prejudice in terms of personality, which would predict a general disposition to prejudice across different intergroup contexts (see Chapter 2).

Before I conclude this section, let me turn to one issue which deserves further discussion. Just how should we should interpret these findings on ethnic, national and other preferences: does a consistent preference for one group imply a derogation of the other? It will be sensible to consider this question separately for children from majority (or higher-status) groups and for children from minority (or lower-status) groups.

Taking the majority group first, we must immediately recognize that, in a binary choice task ('which of these pictures do you prefer?'), we cannot infer that a preference for one stimulus implies an active rejection of the other. Thus one reading of the substantial pro-ingroup preference shown by these children in nearly every study is simply that they feel more positive about their own group and either only slightly less positive or at worst neutral about the other. This, then, would not indicate the existence of any overt prejudice on their part. And indeed, the general conclusion emerging from the many more recent studies that have employed separate ingroup and outgroup evaluations on both positive and negative attributes, or on interval measures of like–dislike, is that children are consistently positive about the ingroup and only rarely negative about the outgroup (see for instance Aboud, 2003; Barrett, 2007; Black-Gutman and Hickson, 1996; Chiesi and Primi, 2006; Enesco et al., 2005; Griffiths and Nesdale, 2006; Powlishta et al., 1994; Rutland et al., 2007).

Although I believe this to be a fair representation of the available evidence, it is important that we do not rush to an overly benign conclusion about the nature of most majority children's intergroup attitudes. For one thing, even a pro-ingroup orientation (rather than an anti-outgroup one) can be socially divisive if it manifests itself in exclusive play and friendship preferences (Aboud and Sankar, 2007; Aboud et al., 2003). Secondly, there is actually some evidence of explicit negativity towards outgroups even in very young children, as we have seen – for example, towards some national outgroups and towards overweight peers (Barrett, 2007; Cramer and Steinwert, 1998; Powlishta et al., 1994). Finally, some anecdotal observations suggest that not everything in the playground is rosy. Goodman (1952) reported that around a quarter of the 4-year-old children she interviewed made clearly prejudiced comments. More recently, Katz (2003) reported the following conversation with a 3-year-old white child:

> *Q*   Which child is going to be reprimanded by the teacher?
> *A*   The black child.
> *Q*   Which child threw the garbage on the floor?
> *A*   The black child.
> *Q*   Why?
> *A*   Because he (or she) is black.

(Katz, 2003, p. 897)

Interestingly in relation to what I will discuss in a later section, this child's mother apparently held rather progressive interethnic attitudes and was rather shocked by her daughter's replies.

I recently read an article describing some of the consequences of sectarian divisions in Gaza. Here is one mother's experience:

> I once took my primary school age daughter out to a park, and there was this other little girl there. My daughter came to me and said the other girl kept saying how Hamas was better than Fatah. I told her to go back and talk about school things and play. But the other girl just carried on […] It is damaging everything, this hatred. What will happen when these five year olds become 18? All these children will remember is how Fatah and Hamas fought. That is why I am worried for the future. (*Observer*, 10 February 2008)

When we consider minority or lower-status group children, we must first remember the greater variability of their responses, which range from strong ingroup preference to almost as strong a preference for the outgroup. It is the latter response that excited the greatest amount of controversy amongst psychologists and educationalists, because it seemed to imply a misidentification with their ethnic group, perhaps even some kind of 'self-hatred'. Once again, the preference data derived from binary choice do not support this idea by themselves, though it is noteworthy that the proportion of minority group children showing ingroup preference is nearly always considerably smaller than that displayed in the majority group. The difficulty with the 'self-hatred' thesis was underlined by Stephan and Rosenfield (1978) in their study of interethnic attitudes and self-esteem amongst white, black and Mexican–American elementary school children. All three groups were ethnocentric, the white somewhat (though non-significantly) more so than the other two groups. The white and black children had roughly equivalent levels of self-esteem, while the Mexican–Americans had lower ones, perhaps as a result of social class. In other words, there was little sign of a general 'self-rejection' on the part of minority group children (see Chapter 8). Nevertheless, there was a correlation between self-esteem and ethnocentrism among the black children: the less ethnocentric they were (that is, the less they favoured blacks relative to whites), the lower was their self-esteem.

Still, some anecdotal evidence suggests that outgroup preferences may indeed imply ingroup rejection, at least for some children. Here are some of the reasons black children gave for not choosing the black doll in Clark and Clark's (1947) study: 'Because he's ugly'; 'Because it don't look pretty'; ''Cause him black' (p. 316). And even, in stronger language coming from a 4-year-old black girl in Goodman's (1952) research, 'black people – I hate 'em' (p. 46). Remember, too, the comment made by the Afro-Caribbean child in the television extract with which I began this section.

Maya Angelou, the celebrated Afro-American writer, recalls that one of her earliest childhood fantasies was 'to look like one of the sweet little white girls who were everybody's dream of what was right with the world' (Angelou, 1969, p. 4). And saddest of all are reports that black children have occasionally been observed attempting to 'wash themselves clean' of their skin colour. This has been related to me on more than one occasion, by people who had first-hand experience of looking after black children; and the same sort of thing was recounted in a popular magazine article on racism in Britain where an Asian woman is quoted as saying: 'my nine year old daughter goes into the bathroom and scrubs her skin until it bleeds because the neighbours say she's dirty' (*Living*, June 1992, p. 25).

It would be a mistake to generalize from these fragmentary observations and to conclude that minority group children have always had, and will always have, a negative view of themselves and of their group; it is clear that there are many important cultural and historical variations in these self-perceptions. Nevertheless, the consistency with which differences in minority and majority children's intergroup preferences have been observed does suggest that the experience and consequences of growing up as the member of a subordinate or of a dominant group are not the same, and that our theories of prejudice development would do well to pay heed to this.

Gender identification and preference

With very occasional exceptions, the typical study of ethnic identification has presented children with just two target stimuli and asked them to make a choice between them. Most often the stimuli were implicitly of the same gender. Arguably, therefore, the children were more or less obliged to differentiate between them on ethnic grounds if they were to discriminate at all. Such a procedure also precludes the investigation of one other major social category – perhaps the most important category of all: that of gender. Preference studies which include gender information in their stimuli are of particular interest because they permit an assessment of the relative importance of gender and ethnicity (or other categories) for the particular sample of children under study. One such study was by Katz and Zalk (1974), and it asked the usual questions asked of 4/5-year-old children about *four* dolls: two black and two white, two of each gender. Contrary to the studies reviewed earlier, Katz and Zalk found little ethnocentric preference from either black and white children. On the other hand there were some signs of own-gender preference, but only from the girls.

That gender identity and corresponding gender preferences are important for children from an early age on has long been suspected (Kohlberg, 1966; Mischel, 1970). Indeed, as Maccoby (1988) has pointed out, it would be strange if gender were not frequently used as a social psychological construct, in view of its ubiquity as a social category in just about every known language and culture. Certainly the empirical evidence, albeit mainly from western societies, bears this out. Thompson (1975) found that, while 2-year-olds were still uncertain about their gender identity (only about half of them answered correctly that they were a boy or a girl), by 2½ to 3 years of age gender identity was much more firmly established (well over 80 per cent in these age groups were correct). However, knowing one's gender at this age does not imply a full understanding of the gender concept. Kohlberg (1966) suggested that children's thinking about gender would parallel their thinking in other domains. Just as children below the age of 5 or 6 can be easily misled by the physical appearance of things – they can believe for example that a tall thin glass contains more liquid than a short wide glass – so their perceptions of gender might be rather unstable. Slaby and Frey (1975) demonstrated this by asking 2–5-year-olds a number of questions about the ramifications of being a boy or a girl. After establishing, like Thompson (1975), that the vast majority (over 90 per cent) knew their own gender, they went on to ask such questions as what would happen if they wore clothes normally worn by the opposite sex, or if they played games typical of the opposite sex. Slaby and Frey found that there was a clear progression in the acquisition of what they called 'gender constancy': the younger children could not easily understand that changing one's clothes did not mean that

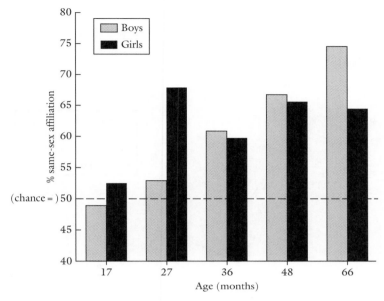

Figure 5.4 Gender segregation in children at play. Adapted from Figure 1 in La Freniere et al., 1984

one underwent a sex change! It was not until the age of 5 that significant numbers of children demonstrated complete constancy (see also Yee and Brown, 1994).

In fact children show a preference for their own sex well before they have a clear sense of gender identity. Anyone who has worked in a pre-school nursery or in a primary school will tell you that boys prefer to play with boys and, even more notice-ably, girls with girls. This early gender segregation has been observed in several stud-ies. One of the most intensive was conducted in a Montreal day-care centre and involved the careful observation of the affiliative behaviour of children from 18 months to 5½ years (La Freniere et al., 1984). Figure 5.4 shows how the percentage of same-sex affiliative acts increased with age. With the youngest children there is little gender segregation, but by just over two years the girls are already showing a clear same-sex preference, directing twice as many affiliative acts towards their fellow girls than towards boys. By the age of 3, boys have 'caught up' and thereafter both boys and girls continue to display marked own-gender preference (see also Jacklin and Maccoby, 1978).

There is nothing sacred about the age of 3 to 4 for the onset of gender segregation, however. In other cultures, which have different patterns of family life and different social norms, this phenomenon may occur at a different age. Harkness and Super (1985), for example, found that gender segregation in a rural Kenya community did not occur until 6 or 9 years. They attributed this later appearance to the greater family and economic responsibilities which typically fall on these children's shoulders: they routinely assist with child care, cattle supervision and other domestic chores, and these activities usually take place in mixed-sex groups. Once they approach or reach adulthood, which is often marked by some formal ceremony, the division of labour and social interaction along gender lines becomes much sharper.

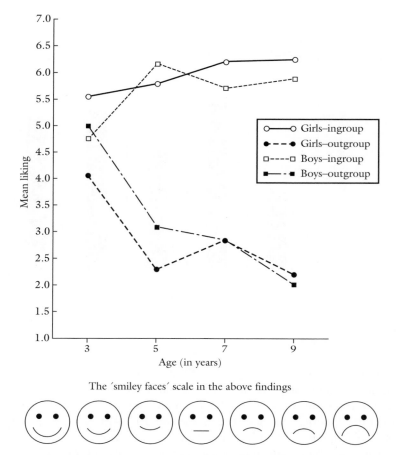

Figure 5.5 The development of own-gender bias. Adapted from Table 1 in Yee and Brown, 1994

Nor is gender segregation immutable. Serbin and colleagues (1978) showed how positive reinforcement by nursery school teachers could alter the frequency with which 4–5-year-old children engaged in cross-sex co-operative play. During the two-week 'intervention' phase of the study, teachers systematically praised those children who were found playing co-operatively with a member of the opposite sex. This had the effect of increasing the amount of time for which children played like this. However, they reverted to their preferred same-sex activities immediately after the intervention period was over.

Hayden-Thomson and colleagues (1987) used a different methodology. They asked children to 'post' photographs of known class-mates into one of three boxes, according to how much he or she liked each peer. On each box was a picture: a happy face (for children they liked a lot), a neutral face, or a sad face (for those they did not like). The children regularly posted more of their same-sex peers into the 'happy' box and, in one of the studies at least, the girls showed this gender bias earlier (at kindergarten age) than the boys (see also Powlishta et al., 1994). Extending the number of faces to seven (see Figure 5.5), we asked 3–9-year-old children what they thought of boys and girls (Yee and Brown, 1994). We also asked them to think of some 'nice' and 'not so nice' things about each gender.

As can be seen in Figure 5.5, by the age of 5, both boys and girls are showing massive favouritism for their own gender. Note that the ratings for the outgroup are well below the notional mid-point of the scale (= 4). Note, too, that the girls (though not the boys) showed this bias even when they were as young as 3 years.

In sum, then, there is ample evidence testifying to the psychological importance of gender categories for young children. The latter very quickly learn which gender they are and, although that identity is not secure until the age of 5 or 6 (at least in western children), they show very consistent preferences for peers of the same gender as themselves from an even earlier age. This gender prejudice – if that is what we want to call it – seems to reach its peak at around 5 or 6 and maintains that level until adolescence.

Intergroup Discrimination in Children

In the last section I reviewed the evidence on the ontogeny of children's identification with and preference for various ingroup categories. Inevitably, many of those data were comparative in nature, children expressing more positive orientations towards one group that towards another. In this section I want to develop that theme further and to examine children's attitudes in a wider variety of intergroup situations; in particular, I wish to investigate the development of behavioural discrimination between groups. Just as in the previous section, two themes will recur in this discussion: one is the comparatively early age at which biased attitudes and behaviour can be observed in children; the other is the period between the ages of 5 and 8 years, during which children seem to be especially group-centric and prejudiced, becoming less so as they grow older.

It may be recalled from Chapter 2 that a particularly convincing demonstration of the pervasiveness of discrimination in children was provided by Davey (1983). There I reported how, in a study of over 500 British primary school children, over half showed signs of ethnocentrism in the distribution of sweets to (unknown) children from their own and from other ethnic groups.

Similar evidence of children's propensity to favour their own ethnic group was provided by van Avermaet and McLintock (1988), this time in the context of speakers of a different language, in Belgium. The study was conducted with Flemish children aged between 6 and 10. It began with a short video (without sound) of another class of children, alleged to be either Flemish or French speakers. This gave the children a pretext to distribute rewards (some jars of attractive colour-pens) to their own classmates and to members of the other class. In the first intergroup evaluation the children were fairly positive about the other class, but they were invariably more positive about it when they were told that its children spoke Flemish, like themselves. This ingroup bias was most evident in the intermediate age group (children 8 years old). In the subsequent reward distributions, the children under study showed themselves to be biased against the other class: they kept six jars of pens for themselves and gave the other group only just over two. This unequal distribution was affected by how well the children thought the two classes had done in the task: they gave more to the other group if it had done better. However, such equitable behaviour was much less likely to be displayed if they thought that the other class was French-speaking.

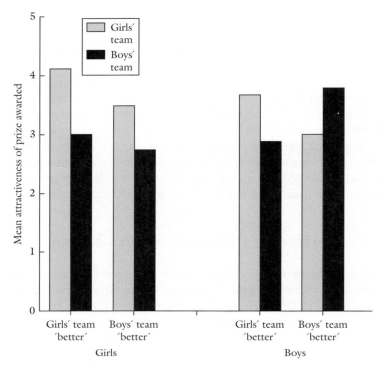

Figure 5.6 Gender discrimination in young children. Adapted from Table 3 in Yee and Brown, 1994

This balance between equity and ingroup favouritism was a feature in an experiment we conducted with young girls and boys (Yee and Brown, 1994). In the context of a competition over making collages out of scrap materials, we showed the children two collages and elicited their preference for one or the other. Depending on experimental condition, the preferred collage was alleged to have been made by a team of girls (or boys); the other – the less preferred one – by a team of boys (or girls) – in other words, the opposite to the first. The children then allocated prizes to the two teams (some attractive toys). As can be seen from Figure 5.6, the boys seemed to use some kind of equity principle in their allocations, giving more attractive prizes to the 'better' team. The girls, on the other hand, always gave the girls' team the better prizes, no matter how it had done. One other finding from this study was of interest. The extent of the gender bias in these prize allocations was positively correlated with one component (stability) of gender constancy – as indeed was the bias in their gender attitudes reported in the previous section (see Figure 5.5).

Children's biased outlook can also be observed in the kinds of interpretations they make of ambiguous social situations involving peers of differing ethnicity. McGlothlin and Killen (2006) presented white primary school children (aged 7–10 years) with various pictures which could be interpreted as one child having done something bad to another. For example one picture showed a child sitting on the ground by a swing, with pain on her face, while another child is standing behind the swing. The ethnicity of the two children was systematically varied. McGlothlin and Killen found that situations in which the 'perpetrator' was black and the 'victim' white were more likely to be interpreted as cases where something bad had happened, and the black 'perpetrators' were viewed more negatively and were judged to be more likely to behave badly in the future than white 'perpetrators'. These observations are resonant of the 'ultimate attribution error' and of the 'linguistic intergroup bias' phenomena, which we encountered in Chapter 4 (see also Maass, 1999; Pettigrew, 1979). When one of 'them' does something potentially negative, we are more likely to attribute the cause of that behaviour to some internal disposition.

The children in McGlothlin and Killen's (2006) study attended ethnically homogeneous schools and, perhaps because of this, had very few African American friends. This lack of outgroup contact may well have played a part in the development of their discriminatory attitudes, because McGlothlin and colleagues (2005) found no such prejudice using the same materials in a similar, if slightly younger, sample of children who were attending ethnically *mixed* schools. As we shall discover in Chapter 9, the greater opportunities for intergroup contact afforded by diverse social institutions encourage the development of cross-group friendships and thereby a lessening of prejudice.

In most of these studies the attitudes were elicited in response to photographic or pictorial stimuli. A still more compelling demonstration of how children's attitudes and behaviour can be altered by the perception that a peer belongs to a stigmatized category was provided by Harris and colleagues (1992). Testing the self-fulfilling prophecy hypothesis (see Chapter 4), they paired elementary school boys with other boys whom they did not know, and asked them work on two tasks. Half the boys were led to believe that their partner suffered from some hyperactive behaviour disorder and were warned to expect that he might be difficult to play with; the remainder were given no such expectancy information. In fact, unbeknown to these subjects, only half of their partners – but equally in *both* conditions – had been diagnosed as having the disorder; the other partners were 'normal'. These expectancies had a powerful influence on the boys' attitudes and behaviour. Those who had been told that they were interacting with a hyperactive partner (whether or not they actually were) found the task harder than those who had been given no expectancy information. They were also less willing to give their partner credit for doing well and, from observations of their actual behaviour, they acted in a less friendly way towards him. The 'target' children's attitudes were the mirror image of this treatment. Those designated as hyperactive (especially when in fact they were not) enjoyed the experience less than those not so stigmatized, presumably in response to the perceivers' unfriendly behaviour. Once again, we see how social stereotypes have the unfortunate tendency to manufacture the world in their own image.

All the intergroup phenomena we have discussed thus far have been associated with real life categories such as ethnicity, gender and disability, all of which are imbued with deeply ingrained cultural values and meanings. How general are these biases and, in particular, is it possible to disentangle them from the particular social relationships in which they occur? To answer these questions it can sometimes be helpful to create *ad hoc* groups and observe affiliations and behaviour. One such attempt was made by Vaughan and colleagues (1981). They adapted the minimal group paradigm (see Chapter 3) for use with 7- and 11-year-old children. After the normal picture preference task – only, this time, with children's paintings rather than those of Klee and Kandinsky – the children were divided into two groups. They were then asked to allocate money to these groups (but never to themselves personally). These reward allocations showed the usual intergroup discrimination: children gave more to their own group than to the other, particularly when this would establish a *relative* difference between the groups. There were no consistent age effects. A similar minimal group paradigm was adopted by Wetherell (1982), who compared the responses of 8-year-old European, Maori, and Polynesian children in New Zealand. Like Vaughan and colleagues (1981), she observed intergroup discrimination in all three groups. However, there were some interesting cultural differences. The Polynesian and Maori children were more generous to members of the outgroup than the Europeans were, and the Polynesians in particular seemed to favour allocation strategies whereby *both* groups benefited rather than the ingroup gained by comparison to the outgroup.

It is just possible that the age of 7 is something of a watershed for displaying discrimination in these very spartan minimal group situations. Spielman (2000) created a similar minimal group paradigm for use with 5–6-year-olds. In the standard situation, where there is literally no other information available to the children apart from the recipients' group memberships, Spielman (2000) found little evidence of intergroup discrimination with this younger age group. However, the provision of the merest hint of competition, when the experimenter told the children a little story about two children running a race, was enough to re-elicit discrimination.

As its name implies, the minimal group paradigm is a pretty minimalist social situation. Nothing much happens, except that people are told they are in one group and not another. But, of course, in real life our group memberships are much more consequential than this: the colour of our skin or the nature of our religious beliefs will usually mean that others see and treat us in particular ways. In technical terms, we experience a **common fate** with others in our group (Rabbie and Horwitz, 1969). Sometimes that fate is to enjoy some privileges or to suffer certain privations not experienced by other groups, and shortly I will discuss what happens when children find themselves in higher or lower-status groups. Before I do so, though, let me consider the effect of common fate itself. This can be examined by creating minimal groups and then imbuing them with some social significance, having teachers (or others in authority) use them to organize the children's activities.

Such was the procedure adopted by Bigler and her colleagues in a series of studies based this time not within the confines of the psychological laboratory but in the natural environment of a children's summer school programme (Bigler et al., 1997; Brown and Bigler, 2002; Patterson and Bigler, 2006). Thus Bigler and colleagues (1997) arranged for these children (aged 6–9 years) to be given one of two different coloured T-shirts for the duration of the summer school (usually six weeks). In the control classrooms no further use or mention was made of the T-shirts. In one group of experimental classrooms, however, the teachers consistently used the colour groups to organize the children's activities, seating arrangements and so on. Because the T-shirts in this condition were distributed to the children on a random basis, they labelled this condition random. In a second group of experimental classrooms, the T-shirts were allocated according to a biological criterion: dark-haired children received one colour, fair-haired children another. In other respects, the teachers' behaviour was the same as in random. In the event, there were few noticeable differences between the random condition and the biological condition. However, these children did differ from the control children, most noticeably in their intergroup evaluations. They were significantly more biased in favour of their own colour group than the control children, who were even-handed in their intergroup evaluations. Still, when asked whether they would like to change groups, even the control children indicated that they would *not*, which suggested the presence of some elementary ingroup preference. Patterson and Bigler (2006) found some similar effects of consequential classification even in children as young as 3 years: children in the experimental conditions (this time just a random classification procedure) showed a greater preference than children in the control conditions for having peers from their own colour group rather than from the other colour group as play partners. Interestingly, in neither of these studies was the amount of ingroup favouritism noticeably correlated with the children's cognitive ability to classify. As we shall see in the next section, this is theoretically significant.

Two things are remarkable about the findings from these studies. The first is that mere categorization alone (the control conditions) was not generally sufficient to elicit much ingroup bias. Unlike in the very controlled situations of a 'true' minimal group paradigm, where people neither know nor interact with others (Tajfel et al., 1971), in the normal hurly-burly of the school classroom and playground the different T-shirts simply lost their social significance. Not until the teachers started using and referring to the colour groups (in the experimental conditions) did the children begin to discriminate. The second interesting feature of the results is that it seemed to be the experience of common fate itself – being recognizably in one group and not in another – rather than any linkage to fixed biological characteristics that caused the discrimination. This is yet another reminder, if reminders were needed, that prejudice can be patterned along *any* line of social division, not just along those correlated with immutable physiognomic differences.

In these studies, as in the minimal group experiments before them, the two groups were of equal status; but such parity seldom exists in the real world. What of children's reactions to being in a 'better' or 'worse' group? This was the issue we addressed in an experiment which exploited that game much loved by organizers of children's fêtes and parties: the egg-and-spoon race (Yee and Brown, 1992). Each child was given first a practice session at egg-and-spoon running and some performance feedback (the same for all children). They were then allocated to one of two teams of same-sex but unknown children. According to the experimental condition, each child was put in a team full of children who were obviously egg-and-spoon experts, since apparently they had all done as well as, or better than, the child him/herself, and clearly better than the rival team. Alternatively, they were put in the other, less good, team. When asked to evaluate the teams' likely performance in a forthcoming egg-and-spoon race, the children's ratings were strongly affected by their team assignment: those in the so-called 'fast' team all had a more favourable opinion of their own team than of the other. The interesting findings came from the 'slow' team. Now most of the children reversed their ratings, evaluating the outgroup more favourably than the ingroup. But there was one important exception. The 5-year-olds (actually nearer to 5½) maintained and even increased slightly their ingroup favouritism, despite being told that they were in a less good team! The group morale measure ('Do you want to stay in your team or move to the other?') told a similar story: over 80 per cent of those in the 'fast' team were happy to stay where they were; on the other hand, 70 per cent of the 'slow' teams (excluding the 5-year-olds) wanted to change teams. Not the 5-year-olds, however: over two thirds of them wanted to remain in the lower-status team.

Notwithstanding this question about moving teams, the group boundaries in the Yee and Brown (1992) study were fixed and the children did not believe that they could change teams. What might happen if such 'social mobility' was a real possibility? Nesdale and Flesser (2001) explored this question in a study with young Australian children aged 5–8 years. As in our study, the children were put in a group of high or not high status ('excellent' drawers or merely 'good' drawers). Some of them were told that they might be able to move to the other team if they wanted; others were told that this couldn't happen. The main measure of interest in this study was how much the children *liked* members of their own team and of the other; and, not surprisingly, they showed the usual strong ingroup bias in these ratings. However, the amount of bias shown depended on the children's age, on the status group they were in, and also on the possibility of mobility. The 5-year-olds were especially sensitive to status and mobility, showing the most bias of all when they were in a high-status group and mobility was not possible, but the opposite pattern when mobility *was* possible (now the lower-status groups were somewhat more biased). The 8-year-olds, in contrast, seemed only responsive to status: they simply showed more bias when they were in higher-status teams, irrespective of the possibility of mobility.[3]

Experiments like these and others, which I shall consider shortly, are significant because they show that even very young children (as young as 3) are apparently able to make the kinds of social comparisons necessary to enable them to utilize information about the relative standing of their group. This is important at a theoretical level, because some have argued that children of this age are not able or disposed to make such comparisons (Ruble et al., 1980; Suls and Mullen, 1982). As we saw earlier with ethnic groups and here with artificial groups, the evidence seems to be that such children are sensitive to intergroup status differences.

Of course, status differences are not the only important factors governing real world intergroup relationships. Nesdale (2004) has argued that the degree of conflict or threat posed by an outgroup will be an important stimulus for prejudice in children. As we shall see in the next chapter, ample theory and evidence consistent with this idea has been gained from adolescents and adults (see for example Sherif, 1966; Stephan and Stephan, 2000). Children, like their elders, are also sensitive to the material well-being of their ingroups. Nesdale (2004) suggested that the emergence of true prejudice – that is, actual dislike or denigration of the outgroup – may also depend on how strongly children identify with their ingroup and on what they regard as appropriate behaviour (in other words, on what they perceive the ingroup norms to be). Those children for whom a particular ingroup is especially important are likely to react more sharply to competitive outgroups, especially if they sense that their peers are similarly ill-disposed.

In some ingenious studies, Nesdale and his colleagues have put these ideas to the test. In one of them, a large number of 5–11-year-old white Australian children were allocated into a high-status group of 'excellent' drawers: two other children of the same age and ethnicity, unknown to them (Nesdale et al., 2005a). Half the children were led to believe that they would work well together in this team. This was designed to promote greater identification. The children were then shown another group, less good drawers than their own group, with whom they would shortly be competing.

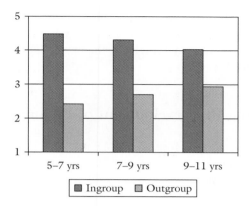

Figure 5.7 Age effects in intergroup liking. All means differed from the neutral point of scale (3.0), except for outgroup liking in the 9–11-year-old group. Adapted from Table 1 in Nesdale et al., 2005a

In some conditions the children were told that this other group didn't like them and thought that the drawing judges had been unfair in their initial judgements. This was designed to create a threatening intergroup situation, especially by comparison to the control conditions, where no information was revealed about the outgroup. There were several striking findings from this experiment. First, as expected, the more highly identified children showed more bias in their liking ratings than the less identified children, although in fact both *disliked* the outgroup. Furthermore, and even more starkly, the perception of threat also increased the bias, and now only those in the high threat conditions showed active dislike of the outgroup; in the low threat condition the liking for the outgroup hovered close to the mid-point of the scale. Finally – and importantly from a developmental perspective – there was a clear diminution of prejudice with age (see Figure 5.7). The most prejudiced were the youngest, the 5–7-year-old group, who were not only greatly enamoured with their own group but clearly disliked the outgroup. The 7–9-year-olds were only slightly more tolerant, and it wasn't until the eldest group that dislike for the outgroup disappeared. This is not the first time that we have noted such an inverse relationship between age and prejudice (recall Clark and Clark, 1947; Powlishta at al., 1994; Rutland et al., 2007); nor will it be the last.

Nesdale and colleagues (2005b) used a similar paradigm. However, instead of manipulating group identification, they varied ingroup norms about the appropriateness of liking outgroup members and working with them. Again, a threatening outgroup elicited much greater dislike than a non-threatening one. Norms to exclude the outgroup also led to greater prejudice, but especially with the younger children in this study (aged 7 years); for the 9-year-olds, the exclusionary norms needed to be combined with outgroup threat before a clear -dislike for the outgroup was observed (see also Abrams et al., 2007 for further evidence on children's sensitivity to ingroup norms).

In summary, then, it should by now be apparent that children are capable of displaying intergroup discrimination by as early as 5 or 6 years of age, and occasionally even earlier. Moreover, that discrimination sometimes manifests itself as some clearly negative attitude or behaviour towards the outgroup rather than as a mere preference for the ingroup. Finally, the good news is that this prejudice seems to dissipate, though not to disappear altogether, by the time children reach 9 or 10 years of age. In the next section I want to consider what might be the most plausible explanations for this developmental trajectory.

Understanding the Development of Prejudice in Children

'Don't you simply hate being a girl?' asked George.
'No, of course not,' said Anne. 'You see, I do like pretty frocks and I have my dolls and you can't do that if you're a boy.'
Enid Blyton, *Five on a Treasure Island*, 1942, 1989;
recording by EMI Records Ltd

The most obvious explanation for the appearance of prejudice in children is that it is acquired through direct socialization, from their parents and from other sources, for instance by peer group influence and through the usual means of cultural transmission. This would be the hypothesis made by learning theories of child development and, very probably, by many lay people, too, in their accounts (see for example Bandura, 1977; Mischel, 1966; Sears et al., 1957). Superficially, such an explanation would have much to commend it. Few would deny that the home environment has some influence on the development of the child, even if arguments still rage as to the exact nature and extent of this influence (see Harris, 1995; Plomin, 1990). The frequent depiction of men, women and certain minority groups in stereotypical roles in the media and in children's literature is by now a well documented phenomenon (Durkin, 1985; Graves, 1999; Milner, 1983). I am sure I cannot be the only parent who, while reading his children their favourite bed-time stories, has winced at the crude reproduction of conventional stereotypes which seem to pervade their pages (see the Enid Blyton extract above). What more natural conclusion to draw than that all these socio-cultural influences should directly determine our children's social attitudes?

Unfortunately the truth is not so simple. True, such a conclusion is reinforced by studies which have provided evidence of the direct effect of parentally influenced socialization on children's attitudes, or have observed correlations between exposure to mass media sources and children's prejudicial and stereotypical thinking. One of the earliest such studies was the pioneering research of Horowitz and Horowitz (1938). In addition to their findings on ethnic awareness, they carried out interviews with both parents and children. Some of the published extracts from these interviews give a revealing, if anecdotal, picture of direct parental influence on the socialization of racist attitudes in a southern state in pre-war America. Here is, for example, a 7-year-old white girl discussing her playmates: 'Mother doesn't want me to play with colored children, 'cause they colored men. Might have pneumonia if you play with them. I play with colored children but mamma whips me' (Horowitz and Horowitz, 1938, p. 333). Such direct control was openly admitted by some parents: 'I always played with other children. Yes, I used to tell her not to play with some. Just told her, never gave her any reasons. She never played with negro children, I didn't have to tell her that' (ibid., p. 335).

However, more systematic research has not always confirmed these early observations. It is true that Bird and colleagues (1952) and Mosher and Scodel (1960) found correlations between the ethnocentrism of white parents and their children's negative attitudes towards ethnic groups, a finding which is consistent with the idea of direct transmission across the generations. The correlations were, however, not very strong. On the other hand, Branch and Newcombe (1980), adopting a similar approach of correlating parental and child attitudes in black families, found some rather surprising inverse relationships: for the 4–5-year-olds there was a negative correlation between parental ethnocentrism (that is, pro-black attitude) and the child's pro-black choices on doll-choice type tasks. Only for the 6–7-year-olds did this relationship become positive, and then only weakly (and non-significantly) so. Likewise, in the study discussed earlier, Davey (1983) found little evidence of a strong link between the intergroup attitudes of parents (which were superficially tolerant) and those of the children, which, as we saw, were quite prejudiced (see also Aboud and Doyle, 1996; Spencer, 1983).

In the domain of gender attitudes a similar ambiguity exists. It is, of course, well known that from birth onwards, boys and girls receive very different treatment from their parents and caretakers (Maccoby, 1980). What is less clear is whether these different experiences involve, or result in, the direct transmission or gender attitudes from parents to child. One study which *did* find a relationship between parental (sex role) attitudes and children's tendency to show gender stereotyping in toy preferences and occupational choices was conducted by Repetti (1984). Another finding of interest was that, whilst the *total* amount of television the children watched was completely unrelated to their stereotypical judgements, the amount of *educational* television was negatively related to their stereotyping. I return to the possible effect of the media shortly.

In contrast to Repetti's findings, other research has found little or no evidence of direct parental influence on socialization. Perhaps the most systematic work has been done by Maccoby and Jacklin (1974, 1987). In their earlier review of sex differences in behaviour, they found very little relationship between the parents' own-sex typing and that of children, which suggested that the acquisition of sex differences by child–parent imitation was not a straightforward affair (Maccoby and Jacklin, 1974). Their later studies of gender segregation in pre-school children cast further doubt on the influence of parents. Two findings, in particular, were significant (Maccoby and Jacklin, 1987). Although same-sex play preferences were widespread, they were not very stable across time for each individual child. This would be unlikely if certain children had been strongly influenced by their parents to adopt particular gender attitudes. The second finding was the lack of any strong evidence showing a link between parental behaviour and the children's preference for gender-segregated play. The only correlation was between the roughness of fatherly play with their daughters and the latter's preference for female playmates. Admittedly, these findings of Maccoby and Jacklin (1987) were 'null results' and hence are inherently uninterpretable; moreover, they were based on rather small samples. Nevertheless, they do cast some doubt on the idea that parents transmit gender attitudes to their children in any direct fashion.

If the evidence for direct parent–child transmission of prejudice is weak and inconsistent, some recent research has discovered that there may, after all, be a link between parental and child attitudes; but the link is subtle and relies on non-verbal information, as well as being affected by the nature of the parent–child relationship. Castelli and his colleagues (2009) measured the explicit interethnic attitudes of 3–6-year-old children and of their mothers and fathers. In addition, they measured the implicit attitudes of the parents by using the **implicit association test** (IAT: Greenwald et al., 1998; see Chapter 7). With a measure like the IAT, the claim is that people's attitudes are less under conscious control, and hence less prone to be influenced by social desirability and self-presentational concerns (Greenwald et al., 1998). The interesting issue for Castelli and his colleagues was the relationship between the parents' prejudiced attitudes, both the explicit ones and the implicit ones measured by IAT, and their children's explicit interethnic attitudes. As usual, the parents' explicit attitudes were unrelated to those of their children. But the intriguing discovery was that the mothers' IAT scores – and only the mothers'; the fathers' scores were unpredictive – were significantly correlated with their children's intergroup attitudes. With a concurrent correlation we cannot be sure about the causal direction, but a plausible interpretation is that the children were picking up various unconscious signals from their mothers about what they felt – in this case – concerning a black outgroup. The lack of a similar correlation between fathers and children may have had to do with the fact that the mothers were reported to have been the primary caretakers, and hence a more constant source of information for the children.

This suspicion, that children are sensitive to subtle cues from adults, was borne out of some other research by Castelli and his colleagues (Castelli et al., 2008). Here Castelli and colleagues showed videos of an interethnic interaction between two adults to young children (3–7 years). The nature of these videos was experimentally controlled. In half of them, the white protagonist (Gaspare) spoke favourably to his partner (Abdul) about blacks; in the remainder, Gaspare spoke only about a neutral topic (work). In this way the researchers manipulated the verbal content of the interaction. Orthogonally to this, they also arranged for Gaspare to display very different non-verbal behaviour. In half of the videos, he greeted Abdul warmly, shook his hand vigorously, sat close to him and often established eye contact with him; in the remaining videos Gaspare behaved much less positively, shaking his hand reluctantly, sitting further away from him and avoiding eye contact. After watching these videos, the children were asked various questions about Gaspare's attitude towards Abdul, how many sweets he would give him, and so on. On all four measures there was a discernible effect of the non-verbal factor (significant in three quarters of the analyses): irrespective of what Gaspare actually said to Abdul, if his non-verbal behaviour indicated friendliness, then the children detected this and reflected it in their replies. In contrast, the verbal factor was generally ineffective (significant in only a quarter of the analyses) in changing the children's views. In a follow-up study, Castelli and colleagues (2008) found that the effects of those positive non-verbal behaviours also carried over to a new situation, where Gaspare met a different black person.

Another factor that will affect whether children become little chips off their parental blocks is the extent of their identification with their parents. If children want to be like their parents and enjoy spending time with them, one might expect a closer correspondence in the intergenerational attitudes than if they don't. This was, at any rate, the hypothesis of Sinclair and colleagues (2005) when they tried to match the parents' explicit interethnic attitudes with their children's explicit and implicit attitudes (again, using the IAT). In neither case was there any noticeable correlation until the researchers took into account the children's identification with their parents. This latter factor clearly modulated the parent–child associations: in the case of the children's implicit attitudes there was a positive correlation with their parents' explicit attitudes *only* when they identified with them; low identifiers showed no relationship at all. With the children's explicit attitudes the parent–child correlations actually reversed: again, they were positive for high identifiers, but clearly negative for low identifiers: the less prejudiced the parents were, the more racist were their children.

Of course, parents are not the only influences in a child's life. In many parts of the world children grow up immersed in ideas and images from books, comics and especially television. The evidence for the effects of these media on children's prejudice is also equivocal (Graves, 1999). One of the first studies was by Himmelweit and colleagues (1958) and it focused on the 10–14 age group. Because it was conducted in an era when television was nowhere near as widespread as it is now, it was possible to achieve a good matching of 'viewing' and 'non-viewing' children and to compare these two groups on a number of measures. One set is of interest to us here because in that experiment the researchers were concerned with children's ideas about foreigners and ethnic groups. Three slightly contradictory findings emerged. One was that the viewers' judgements about outgroups were more objective and factual and less value-laden than those of the controls. On the other hand, in another part of the study, there was evidence that viewers saw some foreigners (though not all) in more stereotypical terms (for example they saw the French as 'gay and witty'). Finally, more viewers than controls disagreed with the xenophobic statement 'my country is always right'. Perhaps one reason for the conflicting nature of these results is that the researchers restricted their sample to homes which could only receive one channel, the BBC, and at that time this channel carried a number of documentaries depicting life in other countries. Such a situation could have had the effect of providing factual information about those cultures and, simultaneously, of reinforcing certain popular and stereotypical images.

Subsequent research on the effects of television on children's social attitudes tended to confirm this ambiguous conclusion. Zuckerman and colleagues (1980) correlated parental reports of their children's television watching with measures of ethnic and gender prejudice. For the sample as a whole there were few reliable correlations, although there were indications that girls were more susceptible than boys to the influence of television (see also Morgan 1982).

However, Williams (1986) studied the impact of introducing television into a community for the first time and observed significant increases in *both* boys' and girls' sex-role differentiation after a two-year period. In an intervention study, Johnston and Ettema (1982) examined the effects of a thirteen-week educational television series whose explicit aim was to promote counter-stereotypical images of males and females. The series significantly altered elementary school children's sex-role attitudes in the direction of making them less stereotypical, and some of these changes persisted for as long as nine months.

However, more recent research has yielded more equivocal results concerning television exposure. Cole and colleagues (2003) looked at young (4–5 years) Palestinian and Israeli children's attitudes before and after the showing of an adaptation of *Sesame Street* (*Rechov Sumsum/Shar'a Simsim*), a children's television programme which presented messages of tolerance and understanding between Israelis and Palestinians. The Palestinian children's attitudes towards Jews were much more negative than the Israeli children's attitudes towards Arabs, and they deteriorated still further, four months after the series had begun broadcasting. In contrast, the Israeli children's intergroup attitudes became more favourable. In a naturalistic study like this, without the possibility of a control group, it is impossible to attribute these changes unambiguously to the television programme; it is just as probable that they reflected the impact of some recent events in that perpetually troubled area.

In sum, therefore, as Durkin (1985) concluded some years ago, the effects of the mass media on children's stereotypes are seldom consistent and unidirectional relationships where the one element directly gives rise to the other. In fact I believe this is also the conclusion to which we are forced when we consider the whole class of explanations which assume some kind of simple determination of children's prejudice by social agencies, whether these be parents or wider cultural influences like the media. There are at least four facts which point to this conclusion.

The first fact is the very early appearance of social category awareness and use by children. Recall that earlier on we noted how children as young as 2½–3 years, and occasionally even younger, show evidence of being aware of gender (especially) and of ethnic differences, and also of discriminating between them behaviourally. Whilst not conclusive in themselves, such precocious signs of social differentiation suggest that the children themselves are contributing something to the process.

The second fact is the apparently non-linear trajectory of the growth of prejudice in children. As we saw earlier, there are several studies which point to a period between 5 and 7 years of age during which ingroup favouritism of various kinds seems to reach a peak, only to decline afterwards, in the pre-adolescent period. A recent meta-analysis of over a hundred studies confirms that this is indeed a general trend (Raabe and Beelman, 2009). If the socialization of prejudice simply involved the incremental acquisition of ideas and values from the child's social environment, one would not anticipate such an inverted U-shape for its developmental time course.

Thirdly, as Aboud (1988) noted, there have been some marked changes in measured prejudice levels in adults over the past forty years (see Chapter 7), and yet recent studies of children's interethnic attitudes have shown that children below the age of 10 still continue to manifest various forms of prejudice. The same argument can be made for gender, where, again, it seems that levels of overt sexism have fallen in adults (Kahn and Crosby, 1985; Sutton and Moore, 1985), but apparently not in children, as we saw earlier. As I shall discuss later (Chapter 7), there may be more to these changes in adult attitudes than meets the eye; but, still, the discrepancy between generations remains a problem for any kind of linear socialization model.

Finally, and related to the third point, are the generally low correlations which have been observed between parental and child intergroup attitudes. If transmission was as direct as assumed by a simple socialization model, one would have hoped to explain more than 10 per cent or so of the variance which is implied by the typical correlations of 0.3 or less.

Confronted with these kinds of problems, social psychologists have developed theoretical models that link the development of prejudice to more general cognitive social and affective changes, which occur in children in the first ten years of their life (Aboud, 1988; Cameron et al., 2001; Katz, 1983; Maccoby and Jacklin, 1987; Nesdale, 2004). Although there are undoubted differences in emphasis between these various theories, the latter have in common the assumption that the child plays a more active role in the developmental process than the traditional socialization explanation allows. In particular, all attribute primary importance to the cognitive capacity for categorization: it both assists children to make sense of their environment and provides them with various social identities.

Aboud's (1988) theory is a good example of this approach. She posits a three-stage model, in which the early years (up to about 5) are dominated by perceptual and affective processes. Children classify the world crudely, into broad categories – male and female, familiar and strange – and associate these categories with different emotional responses, presumably derived from a mixture of their own personal experiences and the vicarious observation of the experiences of others. They also quickly learn to classify themselves as belonging to some categories and not to others. Thinking at this stage is egocentric and dominated by perceptual cues – the appearance of things and people (Piaget, 1954). The combination of these affective and cognitive processes could create the basis for the early emergence of own-ethnic (and presumably other) group preferences. From 5 to 7 years, however, children's thinking becomes more sophisticated as it progresses through the **concrete operational period** (ibid.). The immature concepts of groups, which have been hitherto dominated by physical attributes such as clothing and skin colour and which manifest themselves in uncertainty about the possibility of changing sex and ethnicity, give way at this second stage to cognitions in terms of more abstract and internal attributes. At this point, paralleling the achievement of conservation in the physical domain, children recognize that many major social category memberships are relatively stable and do not change with superficial changes of appearance or with age. At about this same time (5–7 years) children's social orientations also undergo a shift, from the earlier, egocentric preoccupation with the self to a strong focus on the group, a strong affection for the familiar and the similar (ingroups) and a suspicion and dislike of the unfamiliar and different (outgroups). Thus early ingroup preferences evolve into fully-fledged stereotypes in which less obviously observable attributes and traits are associated with particular categories, sometimes being coupled with explicit outgroup derogation. According to Aboud, the co-occurrence of these social and cognitive changes is likely to facilitate a particularly high degree of ethnocentrism among 5–7-year-olds. Finally, as the child acquires properly operational thinking, there is a recognition of the possibility of individual variation within groups, and the initially rather rigid stereotypes become more flexible and amenable to change in response to counter-stereotypic or individuating information. This is what is thought to underlie the frequently observed decline in prejudice as the child move into adolescence.

Although Aboud (1988) was specifically concerned with ethnic prejudice, there seems no reason to suppose that similar socio-cognitive processes might not underlie the development of gender (and other kinds of) prejudice too, especially in view of the many similarities between them (Katz, 1983).

If Aboud is right in linking change in children's intergroup attitudes to their developing cognitive skills, one should expect to find reliable correlations between measures of **conservation** – that is, the veridical perception of certain invariant properties of objects and people despite changes in appearance – and children's prejudiced attitudes. However, the evidence for such correlations is rather mixed. Clark and colleagues (1980) found a negative association between a measure of conservation and ethnocentrism in 5–7-year-olds, but only when a black tester was used. Doyle and colleagues (1988) found that flexibility of intergroup attitudes was positively related to conservation, but not to ethnic constancy, in children of similar age. In a rare longitudinal study, Doyle and Aboud (1995) found *no* correlation between conservation and ethnic bias in 6–9-year-olds, even though their bias did show the usual decline over this age span. Moreover, classification ability, another important cognitive skill, seems not to be related to ingroup favouritism (Bigler et al., 1997; Patterson and Bigler, 2006). Meanwhile, Corenblum and Annis (1993), Yee and Brown (1994) and Rutland and colleagues (2005a) all observed *positive* correlations between measures of cognitive development and intergroup biases.

Thus the link between the acquisition of certain cognitive capacities and prejudice seems not to be a straightforward one. One explanation for these inconsistencies may lie in the very different age groups studied. With younger children, particularly in the years leading up to the attainment of concrete operations, one might indeed expect a positive correlation between **ethnic constancy**, conservation and prejudice, since it would be difficult to imagine children holding clear-cut intergroup attitudes if they believed that a person's gender or ethnicity could change with a change of clothing or hair style. With older children, who are in the process of acquiring more sophisticated abstract thinking, including the ability to comprehend that members of other groups may see the world differently from them, negative associations between cognitive skills and prejudice would be more likely.

A further troublesome fact for Aboud's theory is the extreme variability of children's prejudices throughout the duration of the developmental period. As we have seen, there are many studies – perhaps a majority – which do show a 'peaking' of prejudice around the concrete operational period (5 to 7 years of age; see Asher and Allen, 1969; Doyle et al., 1988; Doyle and Aboud, 1995; Nesdale et al., 2005a; Powlishta et al., 1994; Rutland et al., 2007; Yee and Brown, 1992). However, there are several others which show no such curvilinear trend. In the realm of gender, for instance, biases appear much earlier and seem to continue unabated into adolescence (Katz, 1983; Maccoby and Jacklin, 1987; Yee and Brown, 1994). Minority group children also seem often to show a very different pattern of preferences, ranging from outgroup favouritism, through 'fairness', to ingroup favouritism, and for them the apex of ethnocentrism seems either to be delayed by a year or two or not to happen at all (see Asher and Allen, 1969; Brand et al., 1974; Clark and Clark, 1947). And, as Barrett (2007) has found, children's national attitudes show a bewildering variety of age trends, depending on the cultural contexts in which they are elicited.

Partly in reaction to these different developmental trajectories of prejudice, other theories have been proposed which place less emphasis on a fixed sequence of socio-cognitive development and more on children's identification with their various ingroups and on the intergroup relationships in which those ingroups are embedded. One such theory is Nesdale's (2004) social identity development theory.[4] In this account, there are two crucial stages in children's social development: their awareness of social categories (such as ethnicity or gender) and then their incorporation of some of these categories into their social identity. The first stage occurs earlier, typically around 3 years of age according to Nesdale, whilst the second has usually been reached by 7/8 years. Importantly, Nesdale does not believe that at either of these stages children are likely to show much prejudice in the sense of displaying overtly negative attitudes or behaviour towards outgroups. Instead, he argues, what happens is that they will develop a strong affinity with their ingroups, a reflection of their emerging need for a positive social identity (Tajfel and Turner, 1986; see Chapter 6). Thus ingroups will often be liked and evaluated more favourably than outgroups in these early childhood years; but those outgroups will not actually be disliked or viewed derogatorily but merely neutrally (see Cameron et al., 2001 for a similar position).

What, then, in Nesdale's view, gives rise to prejudice in older children? He argues that there are two main factors which will determine whether or not outgroups will be seen or treated in a negative fashion. One is the strength of the child's identification with the particular ingroup that is contextually relevant or salient. The stronger that identification is, the more likely it will be that the child will incorporate the norms and stereotypes prevailing within the ingroup into his/her own way of thinking and behaving. If, as is sometimes unfortunately the case, these norms and stereotypes are negative, then prejudice will result. A second factor is the nature of the intergroup relationship between the ingroup(s) and outgroup(s). If this is conflictual or otherwise threatening to the ingroup, then one would expect children to react negatively, both in defence of their ingroup's interests (Sherif, 1966; see Chapter 6) and as a consequence of the heightened ingroup identification that usually results from external threats. In other words, Nesdale rejects the idea of a fixed time-course for the emergence of prejudice in children and places much more emphasis on individual factors (identification) and on contextual variables (intergroup conflict). As he puts it: 'At any time, children's attitudes towards members of ethnic out-groups might increase, decrease, or remain the same, depending on their prevailing social group identification' (Nesdale, 2004, p. 233).

This theory has much to recommend it. As we saw earlier, Nesdale and his colleagues have shown how group identification, peer group norms and explicit threats from an outgroup can all instigate clear prejudice in children, both independently and in combination. Moreover, the theory can help to explain why Barrett (2007) was able to observe such different patterns of intergroup attitudes in the various countries he sampled. Perhaps these variations can be traced to the kinds of positive and negative intergroup relationships existing between the countries concerned. A similar analysis could be applied to intergroup attitudes of ethnic minority children, which, as we have seen, are often rather less biased in favour of the ingroup than majority children's attitudes are. The prevailing intergroup relations, of domination or subordination, of more or less status, become reflected in the children's social comparisons from different sides of the intergroup divide. Vaughan (1987) has made a similar analysis of the effect of the advent of such political movements as the rise of Black Power in the United States and of Brown Power in New Zealand on minority children's attitudes between the 1960s and 1970s. Finally, Nesdale's (2004) theory is coherent with Maccoby and Jacklin's (1987) account of the development of gender prejudice in children. As I noted earlier in the chapter, not only does such prejudice seem to emerge earlier than other group biases; it also seems to follow a different time-course and to show some marked gender differences (girls generally being more prejudiced than boys, at least early on in childhood). Maccoby and Jacklin (1987) suggest that this gender segregation can be traced to the different styles of play of boys and girls and to the distinctive cultures and identities of boys' and girls' peer groups which these styles give rise to. If each gender finds it own way of playing to be more more congenial than that of the other, then this behavioural differentiation could also form the basis of subsequent attitudinal biases. And the fact that girls show gender segregation earlier than boys might be attributable to a 'defensive' reaction on the girls' part against the typically more boisterous rough-and-tumble play of their male peers.

As I say, I find Nesdale's (2004) theory rather convincing. However, not even this one is without its difficulties. One problem for it is the by now well documented incidence of explicit prejudice in children as young as 5 years, or even younger. Nesdale himself has provided some of that evidence in a study I reviewed earlier (Nesdale et al., 2005a); and so have others (Cramer and Steinwert, 1998; Powlishta et al., 1994; Yee and Brown, 1994). The fact that one can observe such negativity so early in life is difficult to reconcile with Nesdale's claim that at that stage one should only observe ingroup preference rather than outgroup derogation. A second weakness, in my opinion, is that Nesdale's theory – and still less Aboud's (1988) – does not give sufficient emphasis to children's developing awareness of societal norms which proscribe any explicit expression of prejudice, in word or deed. As I have noted several times elsewhere in this chapter, there is now considerable evidence that intergroup differentiation, whether merely ingroup favouritism or the rare but still observable outgroup derogation, undergoes a steady decline between 7 and 12 years of age. Is this because, as Aboud would have it, children are becoming sufficiently sophisticated cognitively to be able to individuate outgroup members and to view the ingroup more dispassionately? Perhaps. Or is it, as Nesdale might argue, that in the normal run of things most children do not either manifest very strong ingroup identification or experience regular threats from outgroups? Possibly. But I find it equally plausible to suppose that the decline in prejudice in this pre-pubescent phase is also connected to children's growing understanding that it is not usually appropriate to express such prejudice openly.

Evidence that this may be the case has come from recent studies comparing age changes on explicit measures of intergroup bias with changes on a more subtle measure of prejudice, like the IAT. Rutland and colleagues (2005b) asked children and adolescents (6–16 years) to provide some explicit judgements either about ethnic groups or about nationalities. They did this either whilst they were being filmed, with their image relayed back to them over a monitor, *or* with no such self-consciousness-inducing manipulation (the video camera and monitor were turned off). Rutland and colleagues reasoned that being filmed in this way would increase their awareness of what was the 'right thing to do', and hence should reduce their levels of prejudice. Finally, participants undertook a specially adapted IAT procedure (see Chapter 7). As usual, the explicit intergroup attitude measures showed a clear-cut decline in bias with age. This was especially evident in the control conditions, where the camera was switched off; in the high self-focus conditions, the differences between the youngest and the oldest participants were attenuated. This pattern of results is consistent with a normative explanation of prejudice: older participants were more aware of the social undesirability of expressing prejudice than younger children; this age difference could be counteracted by the situationally induced sensitivity to norms in the self-focus conditions, so that even younger children realized that they should not show bias. Crucially for this normative account, the IAT results showed *absolutely no* age effect: all participants demonstrated clear and roughly equivalent levels of implicit bias. Baron and Banaji (2006) found identical results.

Thus on explicit measures, where people can monitor and control their responses, one finds a decline in prejudice with age; on implicit measures, where it is thought that one's responses are less amenable to self-control, prejudice levels remain unchanged with age.

In summary, then, what can we say of prejudice in children? Obviously much remains to be understood, but at least this much is clear: children cannot be regarded as empty vessels into which the prevailing prejudices of adult society are steadily poured. Such a view simply is not compatible with the very early emergence of category awareness and use, the curvilinear nature of the growth of prejudice in childhood, and the weak evidence for a unidirectional parent–child or society–child transmission of intergroup attitudes. Instead, the work I have reviewed in this chapter points to a much more dynamic developmental process in which children, just like their parents, are actively seeking to understand, evaluate and control their social world with the (sometimes limited) cognitive means at their disposal. Since that world is itself partitioned in socially meaningful ways – for example by gender, ethnicity or age – it should not surprise us too much if the children's beliefs and behaviour become patterned along these same lines. Thus, the biases and preferences which we can so easily observe are not the result of some passive indoctrination by the adult world, but the natural outgrowth of an interaction between that world and the psychological processes of categorization, identification and comparison in the minds of our children.

Summary

1   Prejudice presupposes the awareness and use of social categories in perception, judgement and behaviour. There is evidence that children, from as young as 3 years of age, are aware of two of society's major social categories: gender and ethnicity. Primitive behavioural discriminations in terms of ethnicity and gender may even be made as early as three months of age.

2   From 3 years upward, children also readily identify with some categories rather than others and demonstrate clear attitudinal and behavioural preferences amongst these categories. Generally speaking, they prefer membership of their own group to belonging to other groups. This has been demonstrated most clearly with gender, but also with ethnicity, nationality and stigmatized groups such as overweight people.

3   There are some important variations in this own-group preference. One is the tendency for members of ethnic minorities to show it much less strongly than members of dominant and majority groups. In a number of studies, members of minority groups demonstrate a clear *outgroup* preference.

4   Children can also sometimes show clearly negative attitudes and discriminatory behaviour towards outgroups. Again, gender and ethnicity have been the most frequently studied categorial bases for this prejudice, although the latter has also been found with *ad hoc* groupings. Results indicate that girls may show own-gender favouring biases earlier on and more strongly than boys. Also, a common finding has been a 'peaking' of prejudice around the period between 5 and 7 years of age, and a decline after this.

5   Explanations for the growth of prejudice in children which assume a passive absorption by them of the prejudices they find in adult society are not easy to reconcile with the early appearance of category differentiation in children, the non-linear

nature of prejudice development and the weak or inconsistent correlations between parental and child attitudes or between exposure to mass media and prejudice.

6   More promising explanations may lie in linking the development of prejudice to other aspects of the child's social and cognitive development. Such approaches, with their emphasis on the child's changing abilities to categorize and understand the world and then to identify with some groups and not with others, regard the acquisition of prejudice as a more dynamic process: an interaction between children's developing socio-cognitive capacities and the socially structured environment which they have to deal with.

Notes

1   Note that in this task, as in many others reported in this chapter, when one is presented with a binary choice like this one there is a 'chance' level of responding of 50%. Nevertheless, with the sample size used by Clark and Clark (1947), the 77% rate of 'correct' responding by even the youngest children was significantly above this chance level.
2   It is worth noting that these findings of Clark and Clark (1947) were cited directly in a footnote to the famous 1954 US Supreme Court decision outlawing segregated schools (Clark et al., 2004). This must be one of the few occasions where social psychology can fairly claim to have had an influence on public policy.
3   These results were rather different from those obtained by Yee and Brown (1992), who found that ingroup bias in liking was little affected by age and team status. It is likely that several differences in procedure (methods of team allocation, mobility manipulation) account for these differences.
4   Nesdale (2004) focuses on explaining the development of ethnic prejudice. I am taking the liberty here of exploring the utility of this study for other kinds of prejudice too.

Further Reading

Aboud, F., and Amato, M. (2001) Developmental and socialization influences on intergroup bias. In R. Brown and S. Gaertner (eds), *Blackwell Handbook of Social Psychology: Intergroup Processes*, 65–85. Oxford: Blackwell.
Bennett, M., and Sani, F. (2004) *The Development of the Social Self*, esp. chs 4, 8 and 9. Hove: Psychology Press.
Maccoby, E. (1998) *The Two Sexes: Growing Up Apart, Coming Together*, esp. chs 1–7. Cambridge, MA: Harvard University Press.

6

Prejudice and Intergroup Relations

It is 2009, some fifteen years since I wrote the first edition of this book. In the introduction to the chapter corresponding to this one, I was then pointing to a world seemingly riven with intergroup conflicts such as genocides in Rwanda and Bosnia or continuing bloodshed in Palestine and Northern Ireland, not to mention the dozens of other incidents insufficiently bloody or not involving enough of western interests to catch the eye of newspaper and television editors. The world we live in is scarcely more harmonious now. It is true that Rwanda is rebuilding itself and, through its system of Gacaca courts, has made much progress towards intergroup reconciliation; in Bosnia–Herzegovina there is a civil society which functions again, even if tensions between Bosnian Serbs and Muslims continue to simmer not far from the surface; and Northern Ireland is finally returning to normality, after thirty years of the 'Troubles'. But the West Bank and the Gaza Strip remain war zones in all but name; Iraq and Afghanistan are now countries occupied by foreign armies; hundreds of thousands of people in Darfur live in terror for their lives as they flee murderous attacks from the Janjaweed and other militia groups; in Zimbabwe, a despotic regime clings to power through vote-rigging and ruthless political oppression; and here, in Europe, asylum-seekers and other migrant groups suffer daily discrimination at the hands of state authorities – and no little prejudice from ordinary citizens as well. The histories and dynamics of all these intergroup situations are various and complex, but they have at least one thing in common: they can all be viewed as the playing out of the material interests of the groups involved. Whether the outcome is peace or war, tolerance or bigotry, it is usually possible to trace that result, at least in part, to the groups' respective economic and political concerns.

This idea forms the starting point for the present chapter, in which we consider prejudice as originating in the social relationships between groups. The first section will therefore concentrate on objective goal relationships: What are the interests of the groups concerned? Are they in conflict or do they coincide? Viewed from this perspective, the rise and fall of prejudice at different times and in different places become more comprehensible. However, as we shall see, such variations may not be completely explicable from a consideration of groups' objective interests; we may need to pay heed to their social psychological interests also. One important factor in this respect turns out to be a groups' social standing in relation to other groups. Such intergroup comparisons can take place on many different dimensions, both concrete (for example wealth) and less tangible ones (such as social esteem). These intergroup relations are important because they have implications for the social identities of the group members concerned. Where these identities are secure and positive, often because the group has sufficient status and distinctiveness, the consequential intergroup attitudes and behaviour are likely to be very different from what they might be if the identities were ill-defined or unsatisfactory in some way. These processes of maintaining or achieving social identities provide the topic of the second section. In the third section the theme of intergroup comparisons continues, as we consider their implications for people's sense of deprivation. Here the discussion returns to material issues such as income levels and living standards, but these are viewed firmly from a *relative* rather than an absolute perspective. The conclusion from this section on relative deprivation is that prejudice springs from how badly off we *think* we are as much as it springs from conditions of objective oppression and disadvantage. In a final section I draw these three threads together, to show how prejudice can often be regarded as a response to intergroup threats: threats to the ingroup's material interests; threats to its identity; or threats to its social position.

Conflicting Group Interests: When We Lose, You Win

The idea that it is possible to analyse intergroup behaviour – and in prejudice we surely have an example par excellence of intergroup behaviour – by identifying the nature and compatibility of group goals has a long and distinguished history. In an influential article, Campbell (1965) surveyed a number of theories in sociology, anthropology and social psychology dating at least from the turn of the last century (Sumner, 1906), which are based on this premise. Noting that a common theme of these approaches is the idea that some group conflicts are 'rational' or 'realistic' in the sense of being based on a real competition for scarce resources, Campbell labelled the perspective the '**realistic group conflict theory**'. The principal hypothesis of this theory is that intergroup attitudes and behaviour will tend to reflect group interests. Where these are mutually incompatible, where what one group gains is at the expense of another, the social psychological response is likely to be negative: prejudiced attitudes, biased judgements, hostile behaviour. Where they are mutually compatible – or, even better, complementary, so that one group can only gain with the assistance of another – the reaction should be more positive: tolerance, fairness, amicability. Campbell's anthropological colleague LeVine summed it up thus: 'Describe to me the economic intergroup situation, and I shall predict the content of the (intergroup) stereotypes' (as recalled by Tajfel, 1981a, p. 224).

Within social psychology, the most influential proponent of this realistic group conflict theory is Sherif (1966). Like Campbell, Sherif was concerned to rebut the idea that prejudice could be understood primarily as a problem of individual psychology (see Chapter 2). Instead, he placed the causal emphasis squarely on to the nature of intergroup goal relationships. Prejudice, in his view, had its roots in the real or perceived conflicts of interests between one group and others. To demonstrate this thesis, Sherif, together with his colleagues, conducted a series of justly famous field experiments, which have come to be known collectively as the 'summer camp studies', so called because they were run under the guise of a summer holiday camp for boys (Sherif and Sherif, 1953; Sherif et al., 1955, 1961). The students who participated were some 12-year-old boys who had initially been screened to ensure that they all came from stable and non-deprived family backgrounds and that none of them knew any of the others prior to coming to the camp. These rather elaborate procedures were designed to ensure that no subsequent behaviour could be attributed to any pre-existing deprivation or personal relationships amongst the boys.

In the first stage of the experiments the children were split up into two groups, care being taken to match these as closely as possible. In two of the experiments it was also arranged that the majority of each boy's friends, those that had been made in the first day or two on the camp, should be in the *outgroup*. In the third experiment the boys never actually met initially, but were simply in their groups from the very start, camping at some distance from each other and unaware of the other group's existence. For a few days the children participated in some activities in these groups, but the groups themselves had little to do with each other. Despite this independence, the observers did record some instances of comparisons between the group in which, according to Sherif (1966, p. 80), 'the edge was given to one's own group'. Moreover, in the third study, on learning of the existence of the other group, several boys spontaneously suggested challenging it to some contest. As we shall see, it is significant that these instances of intergroup rivalry occurred *before* any explicit competition between the groups had been introduced.

The researchers then implemented the second stage of the study. They organized a series of competitions between the groups (for example softball, tug-of-war), and announced that the overall winner in these competitions would receive a cup and that each member of the successful group would also get an attractive new penknife. The losers would receive nothing. Thus an objective **conflict of interests** was introduced, since what one group gained, the other lost; the groups had moved from a state of independence to being negatively interdependent. This innovation produced a dramatic change in the boys' behaviour. From their initial, relatively peaceful coexistence, they quickly turned into two hostile factions, constantly berating and sometimes even physically attacking each other. Their perceptions and judgements of the two groups showed marked evidence of ingroup bias, and friendships became almost exclusively confined to members of their own group. Such favouritism is all the more noteworthy when it is recalled that in two of the studies the boys friends had been placed in the *other* group. This was a vivid illustration of the power of a single *intergroup* relationship to transform a number of interpersonal relationships almost at the drop of a hat.

Having so easily generated animosity between the groups, Sherif and his colleagues then attempted to reduce the conflict. Starting from the same theoretical premises which had led to the design of the second stage of the experiments, they reasoned that, to reduce the hostility between them, the groups must move from being negatively interdependent on each other to a state of *positive* **interdependence**. Accordingly the experimenters created a series of situations in which the two groups had a *superordinate goal*, a goal which both desired but neither could attain on its own (see Sherif, 1966). For example, on one occasion the camp truck was made to break down some miles away from the camp. It was too heavy to be 'bump started' by a single group of boys on its own; but the two groups together could (and did) get it started. After a series of such scenarios – apparently occurring naturally, but in fact carefully engineered by the researchers – the two groups became much less aggressive towards each other and their attitudes much less prejudiced.

On the face of it, the summer camp studies seem to provide some powerful evidence for an explanation of prejudice through realistic group conflict. Here were some ordinary children whose behaviour could be shown to vary predictably simply by changing the intergroup goal relationship. Such changes were too generic and too rapid to be attributable to some personality variable (see Chapter 2); nor could the prejudice be explained through dissimilarity of beliefs among the participants (see Chapter 3). The groups were carefully composed so as to be as similar as possible; if anything, for any ingroup boy, there were outgroup members who were more similar to that boy than his fellow ingroupers were – because, remember, in two of the studies each boy's friends (made in the first days of the camp) had been put into the *other* group.

In the decades following Sherif's pioneering research, laboratory studies of intergroup relations largely confirmed his basic findings. When the interdependence between groups is experimentally controlled so as to be negative, neutral, or positive, then the results are quite consistent: one observes more ingroup bias, less intergroup liking and stronger intergroup discrimination when the groups are objectively in competition than when they must co-operate over some joint goal (Brown, 2000a; Doise, 1976; Turner, 1981).

Indeed, it may even be enough to recall or imagine a brief competitive episode, not necessarily involving someone from an outgroup, for an increase in prejudice to occur. Sassenberg and colleagues (2007) asked some white American students to remember or imagine a situation in which they had either co-operated or competed with somebody. When subsequently tested, those in the competition condition showed more prejudice towards African Americans than those in the co-operation condition. Similar results were obtained in East Germany with prejudice towards West Germans and Muslims, after the participants took part in a brief game which was respectively competitive, co-operative or individual.

Findings from outside the laboratory in several quite different contexts have also been generally supportive of the realistic group conflict approach. Prevailing national stereotypes often undergo sharp changes for better or worse according to developments in international relations, as new alliances are forged or wars are declared. Seago (1947) found that stereotypes of Japanese people among American college students became very much less favourable after the Japanese attack on Pearl Harbour in 1941.

In their ethnographic study of thirty tribal groups in East Africa, Brewer and Campbell (1976) found that twenty-seven of these groups rated themselves more favourably than any other group being rated, whereas nearby groups were rated somewhat lower than more distant groups. Such a correlation is consistent with realistic group conflict theory, since neighbouring groups are more likely to become embroiled in disputes over grazing land, access to water and other scarce resources (see Brewer, 1986).

Perhaps the context par excellence which reveals the operation of realistic conflict motives underlying prejudice is that of immigration. Britain, like many other industrialized countries in recent decades, has experienced considerable migration activity at its borders, both inwards and outwards. Of course, it is the process of immigrating rather than that of emigrating that seems mostly to excite concern. In answer to a question posed in the 2003 British Social Attitudes Survey, which uses a representative national sample, 74 per cent of respondents indicated that they thought that the number of immigrants to Britain should be reduced (McLaren and Johnson, 2007). What underlies such anti-immigrant sentiment? A more recent poll, conducted for the BBC, gives us some clues. In response to some statements about new immigrants, 19 per cent asserted that the newcomers had 'put my jobs at risk'; 29 per cent, that they 'made it harder to get a fair wage for the work I do'; and 82 per cent, that 'they have put pressure on public services like schools, hospitals and public housing' (Populus, 2008). Those percentages were somewhat higher amongst working-class respondents, who are perhaps typified by Gary Unwin in the Shirland Miners Welfare Club, author of the following comments:

> We've got far too many immigrants coming over into this country now. If they want a house and they've got five or six kids, they get one before the English do. They're paying them a lot less money than they've got to pay the Englishman so they take them on and the English men can't find jobs. They hold the Englishman back from getting a job. (www.bbc.co.uk/newsnight, 6 March 2008)

In other words, from the point of view of many British people, there is a direct competition between themselves and immigrants for such scarce resources as jobs, housing and public services, and this seems to be fuelling their anti-immigrant prejudice.

Some survey research is consistent with this presumed link between conflicting group interests and prejudice towards immigrants. Quillian (1995) analysed some data from the 1988 Eurobarometer Survey, which was collected from over 11,000 people in twelve European countries. He reasoned that economic competition between host society members and immigrants would be intensified as the proportion of immigrants in a country increased, and also as the economic climate in a country worsened. According to realistic conflict theory, both these factors should lead to an increase in prejudice. There was some evidence for the first factor (proportion of immigrants), which was indeed positively correlated with anti-immigrant prejudice: for example Germany, France and Belgium had the highest proportions of immigrants and also the highest levels of prejudice; Spain, Ireland and Portugal had the fewest immigrants and the lowest levels of prejudice. The economic climate factor proved to be much less influential, although there were indications that it interacted with the proportion of immigrants: the effects of a high proportion of immigrants were relatively more pronounced in countries with a lower GDP. A similar positive association between an economic indicator (unemployment) and anti-immigrant attitudes has been observed in the USA (Espenshade and Hempstead, 1996; see Deaux, 2006).

Of course, findings from country level surveys like this one are only indirect evidence for the realistic conflict perspective, since we don't know how people in those countries actually perceive the intergroup relationships. Indeed, as I shall discuss later in this chapter, other researchers using similar data sets have reached a rather different conclusion about the robustness of these correlations at country level between immigrant proportions and prejudice, once they took into account some individual level variables (McLaren, 2003). Moreover, the data are correlational, which always renders causal inferences problematic. Esses and her colleagues avoided both of these problems in a series of studies conducted in Canada (Esses et al., 1998; Esses et al., 2001). In two of these, participants were presented with (false) magazine articles about a fictitious immigrant group, the Sandirians. In one condition the article highlighted the scarcity of jobs in Canada and the success of immigrants in the labour market; in the control condition only neutral information was given. As expected, attitudes towards Sandirians and immigration in general were less favourable in the 'competition' condition.

The realistic group conflict theory, as we have seen, provides a powerful explanation for many examples of prejudice. Moreover, it has the advantage, which is conspicuously lacking in some theories (see Chapter 2), of being able to account for the ebb and flow of prejudice over time or across different social contexts: these can often be attributed to changing economic and political relations between the groups concerned. Nevertheless, despite the theory's undoubted merits, its perspective presents a number of empirical and theoretical difficulties which, as Turner (1981) has noted, mean that this theory is unlikely by itself to provide a complete explanation for all forms of prejudice.

One problem is that, while it is clear that when groups are competing over some scarce resource they are likely to harbour more negative and biased intergroup attitudes than when they are co-operating with each other, such biases do not disappear altogether in the latter kind of situation. A number of studies have demonstrated that ingroup favouritism is remarkably hard to eradicate, even when groups have a material interest in its elimination (see Brown, 1978, 1984a; Ryen and Kahn, 1975; Worchel et al., 1977).

A second difficulty is that an explicit conflict of interests may not be necessary for the arousal of ingroup favouritism. Ironically enough, one of the first hints of this was provided by Sherif himself. Recall the observation he made in one of the summer camp studies that, even before they had explicitly introduced the competition phase of the experiment, the boys had shown an interest in trying to 'best' the other groups in various activities. Such apparently gratuitous intergroup rivalry was demonstrated still more conclusively in the minimal categorization experiments described in Chapter 3 (Rabbie and Horwitz, 1969; Tajfel et al., 1971). The main finding from those studies – that people will readily favour members of their own group as a consequence of mere categorization – poses a serious problem for realistic group conflict theory. For here is evidence that neither an immediate objective conflict of interests nor a prior history of intergroup competition are, in fact, necessary for the arousal of a rudimentary form of prejudice.

A third problem with realistic group conflict theory is that it takes little account of how intergroup power and status differences might influence people's responses to conflictual or co-operative intergroup relations. This issue has been taken up in in political science, in a branch of theorizing known as **image theory** (Alexander et al., 1999; Hermann et al., 1997). In this account, the functionalist perspective of realistic group conflict theory is elaborated upon, in order to specify the kinds of stereotypic images, intergroup affect and behavioural responses that are likely to be associated with different intergroup power relationships. Borrowing from international relations (Boulding, 1959), image theory identifies four types of relationship: 'enemy' – equal status and power groups in competition; 'ally' – equal status and power groups in co-operation;

'dependent' – greater status and power of the ingroup than of the outgroup, as in a colonial situation; and 'barbarian' – ingroup's perception of its own moral superiority, in spite of the considerably greater power of the outgroup. These relationships are thought to give rise to corresponding images of, and action tendencies towards, the outgroup. For example, people are likely to see an 'enemy' in hostile and aggressive terms and then to use those stereotypical images to justify attacking it. On the other hand, a 'barbarian', though also likely to be viewed negatively, may elicit more appeasing kinds of behaviour, because of its greater power and hence because of the potential damage it can inflict upon the ingroup. In a series of studies using carefully constructed hypothetical scenarios, some support for this theory has been garnered, although it seems that some of the predicted outcomes need the additional factor of emotional arousal to manifest themselves (Alexander et al., 1999; Hermann et al., 1997).

A final ambiguity in the theory concerns whether the **negative interdependence** which it assumes to underlie prejudice need always be based on real conflicts over such concrete things as land, money or political power. Perhaps it could derive instead from *perceived* conflicts of interests of some kind, or even merely from a competition over some rather less tangible assets – such as prestige, or 'being the winner'. Sherif himself was deliberately vague on this point, defining group interests as '[a] real or imagined threat to the safety of the group, an economic interest, a political advantage, a military consideration, prestige, or a number of others' (Sherif, 1966, p. 15).

Allowing perceived conflicts to have a similar causal status to that of actual conflicts helps to explain why some manifestations of racism (for example) take the form of 'they (immigrants) are taking all our jobs/houses and so on', even though unemployment and homelessness rates amongst immigrant groups are frequently higher than those found in the host community. The cognitive beliefs may sometimes be more important than the demographic facts.

However, sensible though such a broad interpretation of conflicting interests may be, it does pose a theoretical problem to us, students of prejudice. If perceptions of competing goals can underlie prejudice, and if such perceptions are not always correlated with the groups' actual relations, where do they come from? One obvious explanation is that such beliefs stem from ideological attempts by powerful interest groups to manufacture social divisions, presumably as part of some long-term 'divide and rule' political strategy (Billig, 1976; Reicher, 1986). Although such an argument has a ring of plausibility about it, particularly in relation to some real world intergroup tensions which do not seem to be founded in objective conflicts, it is not one for which it is easy to find conclusive empirical support. Moreover, the occurrence of such 'non-realistic' perceived conflicts, even in the rather more ideologically aseptic environment of the laboratory, suggests that there may be other origins to such subjective competitive orientations. It is to these that we now turn.

Social Identity

What social psychological processes might give rise to prejudice independently of, or in conjunction with, the objective factors just considered? Some obvious candidates are the cognitive processes considered in Chapters 3 and 4. As we saw, there are good reasons for supposing that social categorization and its byproducts of differentiation and stereotyping underlie much prejudiced thinking and judgement. However, despite the undoubted importance of these cognitive processes, there is one feature of most intergroup phenomena that they cannot readily account for: there is usually an asymmetry in people's attitudes and behaviour, such that the ingroup (and not the outgroup) comes off best. Theoretical models based solely on the cognitive activity of the person can explain why groups are perceived as being more different from each other than they really are and why they may be seen in crude and oversimplified terms. But they cannot so easily account for why those perceptions typically have a positive flavour when they refer to the ingroup and a negative, or at least a less positive hue when they focus on the outgroup. To understand this pervasive **ingroup bias**, we must turn to a further concept, that of social identity.

What do we mean by '**social identity**'? According to the architects of the theory which first gave it prominence in the field of intergroup relations, social identity 'consists [...] of those aspects of an individual's self image that derive from the social categories to which he perceives himself belonging' (Tajfel and Turner, 1986, p. 16). In other words, we invoke a part of our social identity whenever we think of ourselves as being of one gender/ethnicity/class rather than another.

Tajfel and Turner (1986) further assume that people generally have a preference for seeing themselves positively rather than negatively. Since part of our self-image is defined in terms of our group memberships, this implies that there will also be a preference to see our ingroups in a more positive light than those groups to which we do not belong. It is this general tendency to make biased intergroup comparisons which serves as the motivational core of Tajfel and Turner's theory. From it they derive their key hypothesis that the achievement or maintenance of a satisfactory identity requires that group members will search out various forms of **positive distinctiveness** for their ingroup. Where this is not possible, they may seek alternative group memberships, which offer greater scope for positive self-evaluation.

These, then, are the bare bones of **social identity theory** (SIT). Before we examine it in greater detail and explore its implications for understanding prejudice, let us look at some research which has substantiated these basic tenets. First, take the idea that group membership has implications for people's self-concept, particularly if the group is perceived to have done well (or badly) in relation to other groups. An early study by Zander and colleagues (1960) showed this quite well. They created cohesive and non-cohesive laboratory groups and set them to work on a fashion design task. Subsequently, half the groups were told that they had done well relative to other groups, while the remainder were alleged to have performed badly. For the cohesive groups – those which mattered to their members – the group's apparent success or failure resulted in raised or lowered levels of self-esteem in its members. This phenomenon of 'basking in the reflected glory' of one's group was also demonstrated in a clever field study by Cialdini and colleagues (1976). They observed college football supporters on the days immediately following intercollegiate games. If their college had won, college scarves and insignia were much more in evidence around campus than if it had lost. The students' willingness to be identified as belonging to the group seemed to be associated with the group's fortunes in intergroup encounters (see also Snyder et al., 1986).

What of the proposition that people evaluate their group mainly by means of intergroup comparisons? As we shall soon see, there is no shortage of research demonstrating people's readiness to engage in comparisons of this sort when asked to do so, and they are usually as manifestly biased as the theory predicts. However, there is a surprising dearth of studies which have attempted to examine the prevalence of *spontaneous* (that is, unbidden) comparisons. An exception was a survey of international attitudes we conducted in six European countries (Brown and Haeger, 1999). In the very first question of this survey we invited respondents to write down whatever came into their mind when they thought of their own country. Analysis of these spontaneously generated images revealed that some 20 per cent of them contained comparative references to other countries (for example 'people are free and have a comfortable standard of living compared to other countries'; 'because we have the best kitchen of the world, the nicest beaches of the world and the most corrupt government of the world'). Interestingly, a further 11 per cent of respondents made another kind of comparison – a comparison in time (either with the past or the future): 'right-wing radicalism has increased a great deal in the last few years'; 'future: looking grim'. However, the frequency with which different kinds of group comparisons spontaneously occur seems to depend greatly on context. In two diary studies conducted in the USA, Smith and Leach (2004) found that intergroup comparisons occurred relatively rarely (less than 8 per cent of all comparisons made), and temporal comparisons by group members were almost never made (less than 2 per cent). Interestingly from the point of view of SIT, intergroup comparisons were made more frequently by those with a higher level of ethnic identification. I shall return later to this issue of people's readiness to make different kinds of comparisons; but, for now, these findings provide some preliminary evidence that intergroup comparisons do figure in people's conceptions of their own group, even if not as often as SIT originally seemed to imply (see also Brown and Zagefka, 2006).

Of course, once other groups are clearly in people's psychological field of view, then biased intergroup comparisons are remarkably easy to observe: in perceptions of group attributes, in evaluations of group performances, in degrees of liking and in behavioural treatments, the ingroup almost invariably emerges more favourably than the outgroup (see reviews by Brewer, 1979; Hewstone et al., 2002; Mullen et al., 1992; Turner, 1981). Rather than retread the ground covered by those reviews, let me take two exemplary studies at the opposite ends of the spectrum of artificiality.

One is the – by now familiar – minimal group paradigm of Tajfel and colleagues (1971; see Chapter 3). How does the concept of social identity help to explain the persistent tendency for people to display intergroup discrimination, even in as barren a social context as this? Consider again the situation: subjects have been placed in one of two trivial groups. They know next to nothing about those groups, except that they are in one and that others (identified only by code numbers) are similarly categorized. Given this anonymity, the only possible source of identity, primitive though it might be, is the group they have been placed in ('Klee' or 'Kandinsky'). However, that group is not easily distinguishable from the other, and hence is contributing little positive to it members' self-concepts. It is for this reason that pressures for group distinctiveness are presumed to come into play, and group members try to differentiate their ingroup positively from the outgroup by allocating more money or points to fellow ingroupers than to outgroupers.

In this explanation there is a presumed link between discrimination and the identity of the group members showing it. In the second study I want to consider, the connection between ingroup bias and group identification was examined more directly.

Table 6.1 Biased intergroup ratings in a British political context. Adapted from table 1 in Kelly, 1988

Political party	Ratings of own party		Mean ratings of other parties[a]	
	Evaluation	Liking	Evaluation	Liking
Conservative	5.6	4.9	2.2	3.0
Labour	6.0	5.8	2.1	2.9
Liberal	5.8	5.4	2.8	3.5
Social Democrat	6.1	5.3	2.7	3.0
Communist	6.7	5.8	3.2	2.9

Note: [a]All ratings are on a 1 (negative) to 7 (positive) scale.
Source: Adapted from Table 1 in Kelly, 1988

This was a study of intergroup attitudes amongst members of different political parties in Britain (Kelly, 1988). Two of Kelly's measures are of interest: how much sympathy they had with each other's political views (a general evaluative measure), and how happy they would be at the prospect of spending an evening with a supporter from each party (a measure of liking). Table 6.1 shows how strongly these members differentiated between their own party and all the others, on these two indices. Ratings of the ingroup were nearly all at 5 or above, while rating of the outgroups were all well below 4 (the notional 'neutral' point of the scale). Kelly then correlated these indices of ingroup bias (ingroup–outgroup differences) with measures of group identification and perceived goal incompatibility between the parties. Consistent with both the social identity and the realistic group conflict approaches, levels of identification and of goal conflict were independently and positively correlated with the amount of bias the respondents displayed. Here, then, is some definitive evidence connecting biased intergroup judgements with social identity. I shall have occasion to return to this relationship later on, because it turns out that it may not hold true for all kinds of groups; but this is a complexity that can wait for the moment.

Social identity processes and prejudice

Social identity theory (SIT), then, holds that an important motive behind intergroup attitudes and behaviour is the creation or maintenance of a satisfactorily distinctive – and positive – identity. From this it follows that threats to that distinctiveness should be responded to by increasing the attempts to differentiate the ingroup from outgroups. If the distinctiveness threats are severe enough, such differentiation may evolve, from the mild expressions of bias typically observed in laboratory settings, where both ingroup and outgroup are evaluated positively (only the former more so than the latter), to more openly derogatory attitudes, which can properly be called prejudice.

There have been three main issues that have preoccupied researchers in considering the main implications of SIT for our understanding of prejudice. The first issue concerns how people will react to intergroup similarity; the second focuses on status relationships between groups; and the third concentrates on the process of identification itself, either as a causal agent in its own right or as a moderator of the effects of other variables. I will now consider each of these issues in turn. Later on in the chapter I will discuss the concept of 'threat' more generally. As we shall see, threats, whether to identity, cultural values or group interests, prove to be powerful determinants of prejudice.

Intergroup similarity

A straightforward prediction that can be made from SIT is that, if an outgroup becomes too similar to the ingroup, it threatens the latter's distinctiveness, and hence it should instigate greater ingroup bias and perhaps more dislike for that outgroup (Brown, 1984b). As long ago as 1921, Freud labelled this phenomenon 'the narcissism of small differences' (Freud, 1921). He was commenting on the tendency of some religious or cultural groups to devote enormous amount of intellectual and emotional energy to their mutual denigration. Despite the fact that, to an outside observer, the groups seem to be almost indistinguishable in their creeds or ideologies, to the members of those groups themselves the differences are often desperately important.

Although it is not difficult to think of examples illustrating this 'small difference narcissism' hypothesis – the bitter factionalism of left-wing political groups springs to mind – the research evidence in its favour is rather more equivocal. For example, Brewer and Campbell (1976) found that ethnic groups in East Africa that were independently judged to be similar to one another tended to express friendlier intergroup attitudes than culturally more disparate groups. Similarly, Berry and colleagues (1977), in a large survey of Canadian interethnic attitudes, found a moderately strong and positive correlation between respondents' evaluations of nine ethnic groups and these groups' perceived similarity to their own. Other field studies have also recorded positive associations between intergroup difference and ingroup bias or hostility (Henderson-King et al., 1997; Struch and Schwartz, 1989). All these findings are rather inconsistent with the idea that, the closer or more similar groups become, the more they will seek to differentiate themselves.

Laboratory research, on the other hand, has produced a more mixed set of results (Jetten et al., 2004). Many years ago I conducted a series of experiments on the effects of intergroup similarity (Brown, 1984a; Brown and Abrams, 1986). In these we led school children to believe that they were undertaking a task with members of another school. Depending on experimental condition, that school was alleged to be similar to them in status in the sense that they seemed to perform about as well as them academically; or it was alleged to be better or worse than them. In addition, the prevailing attitudes towards different academic subjects in the two schools were depicted as being either similar or different. Both variables had effects on the children's intergroup attitudes. The outgroup thought to hold similar attitudes was generally liked better than the outgroup that was believed to be different (Brown, 1984a; Brown and Abrams, 1986; see also Grant, 1993). A second finding was that, when the children believed they were about to co-operate with the other school, their levels of ingroup bias against the similar-status group were lower than the average of their biases against the higher-status and the lower-status group (Brown, 1984a). Both of these findings, again, contradicted the SIT prediction that similarity would provoke a greater search for positive distinctiveness. However, a third finding was more in line with that hypothesis. This finding was, namely, that, where the outgroup was very similar indeed to the ingroup, both in attitudes *and* in status, the amount of bias increased (Brown and

Abrams, 1986). It was as if a certain threshold of similarity had been crossed, beyond which the ingroup felt threatened by the psychological proximity of the outgroup (see also Diehl, 1988; Roccas and Schwartz, 1993).

In seeking to reconcile the conflicting findings on the effects of intergroup similarity, Jetten and Spears (2003) suggest that there are two countervailing processes at work. One is the SIT-inspired notion of **reactive distinctiveness**, in which group members react to a perception that the ingroup is insufficiently well defined from other groups. The other is **reflective distinctiveness**, which is a more veridically based judgement whereby objectively different groups are seen as indeed distinct. Jetten and Spears argue that the joint operation of these two processes gives rise to a curvilinear relationship between intergroup similarity and ingroup bias: at extremes of similarity and difference the two processes might cancel each other out; at intermediate levels one might expect some moderate levels of bias (see Brewer, 1991 for a similar argument from her optimal distinctiveness theory).

Some support for this inverted U-shaped relationship was obtained in two studies by Jetten and colleagues (1998). In a clever manipulation of similarity, they varied both the distance between two groups in their alleged perceptual styles or beliefs (as indexed by the group mean scores), and the distributions of each group's score around those means (they were said to be either very heterogeneous or rather homogenous). By the simultaneous manipulation of these two factors, the experimenters were able to create two groups that were extremely *similar* (similar means and heterogeneous distributions, so that the two groups overlapped), very *different* (different means and homogeneous groups), or in between (the other two combinations). As they had predicted, Jetten and colleagues found most bias in the latter two conditions and the least bias at the two extremes.

Jetten and colleagues (2004) note one other complicating factor: the strength of group members' identification with the ingroup. In their meta-analysis of thirty-nine experimental tests of the similarity hypothesis, they concluded that the *overall* relationship between group similarity and various indicators of intergroup differentiation was effectively zero (it revealed neither 'reflective' nor 'reactive' distinctiveness). However, for those people who highly identified with their group and hence presumably cared more about its distinctiveness from others, clear signs of 'reactive distinctiveness' (that is, of similarity leading to more bias) could be observed (see also Jetten et al., 2001). As we shall see shortly, this is but one instance in many, where the strength of group identification proves to play an important moderating role.

This discussion of intergroup similarity recalls a similar debate in Chapter 3, where I examined the relative effect of categorization and belief similarity – the so-called 'race-belief controversy' (Rokeach, 1960). However, note the important difference in the studies we have been considering here: in these experiments the question is not whether the similarity of interpersonal belief or the sharing of a common category membership is the more potent antidote to prejudice. Instead different category memberships are taken as given, and the question is whether two similar groups enjoy friendlier relations than groups which are different. As we have seen, at this intergroup level, the effects of similarity are far from being consistent: sometimes similarity seems to instigate more friendliness and to lessen bias, sometimes the opposite. A key moderator affecting this relationship may well be the strength of group identification, as Jetten and colleagues (2004) have suggested. Perhaps in the majority of studies showing a similarity–attraction relation the participants' group memberships were not so strongly engaged as to make them feel too close for comfort to another group and hence experience the need to react adversely to it.

Group status relations and prejudice

In some of the experiments described above, I noted that we manipulated not just the similarity of attitudes prevailing in the groups, but also how close together the groups were on some dimension of status (Brown and Abrams, 1986). From the perspective of SIT, the relevance of status relations is obvious. Since group distinctiveness – feeling superior in some respect – derives principally from intergroup comparisons, it follows that the standing of the ingroup in its immediate social hierarchy should have important implications for its members' identities and, hence for their intergroup attitudes. Whether it be white ethnic groups in many western societies (as compared to groups with darker skins), or people in work (as compared to unemployed people), or people who have no obvious physical or learning disabilities (as compared to those who have), one can all too easily find examples of groups who enjoy very different access to resources, power and, above all, public esteem. From the logic of social identity theory, members of these groups should feel very differently about themselves, and hence about other groups. Park (1924), the famous sociologist, anticipated this idea many years ago: 'Prejudice [...] seems to arise when, not our economic interests, but our social status is menaced' (p. 344). What are the consequences for social identity of belonging to a dominant or subordinate group and, most importantly for our present purposes, what implications do these consequences have for people's intergroup attitudes?

Let us take the case of privileged groups first. On a whole host of comparative criteria, such groups emerge as superior to other groups in society. Thus, if we follow the simple logic of SIT, members of such groups have few identity problems. They can satisfactorily view their ingroups as enjoying the desired state of positive distinctiveness, a perception with comfortable ramifications for their own view of themselves. At first glance, then, one might expect members of high-status or powerful groups not to need to manifest much evidence of intergroup differentiation or prejudice. However, while this does follow from a strict interpretation of social identity considerations, there are other reasons why we should not expect such an outcome.

In an important contribution, Scheepers and colleagues (2006) have pointed out that ingroup bias can serve several different functions. One of these is instrumental in nature: such bias aims to assist or motivate the ingroup to achieve some particular goal. This idea, as we saw earlier in the present chapter, underlies much of the thinking behind the realistic group conflict approach to prejudice, and we will return to it again shortly. However, another important function that ingroup bias serves is that of identification; and this function can itself be subdivided into **expressive** and **creative** modes (ibid.). In its expressive form, ingroup bias is all about reflecting – and hence confirming or validating – social reality. Clearly such 'expressive' bias is most likely to be displayed by members of higher-status groups as a form of 'gloating' over their superiority (Leach et al., 2002): 'we are better than you, and don't you forget it'. In contrast, 'creative' bias, as its name implies, is more about creating a *different* social reality, one in which the ingroup might be seen in a less unfavourable light. Such forms of bias might be more readily found in similar or subordinate-status groups, although, as we shall see, there may be circumstances when even higher-status group members resort to them.

From such an analysis, one quickly comes to the conclusion that members of dominant groups should manifest ingroup bias as a demonstration of their elevated social position; and indeed the research evidence clearly supports this. In two meta-analyses conducted a decade apart, the second comprising over 90 studies, the unambiguous conclusion was that high-status groups showed markedly more ingroup bias than low-status groups (Bettencourt et al., 2001; Mullen et al., 1992). There are some very particular intergroup contexts where this does not hold – and I will discuss them shortly – but, for now, let me illustrate this general trend with two studies, one set in the artificial world of the minimal group paradigm, the other, in the very real world of relations between occupational groups.

Sachdev and Bourhis (1987) modified the minimal group paradigm so that the two groups were of equal or unequal ability on a creativity measure. Participants then had to evaluate the creativity of the groups on another task. Both the high-status and the equal-status groups showed very clear ingroup bias in their evaluations, while the lower-status groups tended to favour the outgroup. The group members' satisfaction with their ingroup (roughly equivalent to their strength of identification) was similarly correlated with status (see also Sachdev and Bourhis, 1991). Why did the equal and the high-status groups show roughly similar levels of ingroup favouritism? This could well have been an illustration of the two different kinds of bias suggested by Scheepers and colleagues (2006). For the higher-status group, this may have been an expression, a restatement, of their socially defined superiority. The equal-status groups, in contrast, may have been attempting to achieve, or to create, some positive distinctiveness. This bifurcation also recalls the distinction made by Jetten and Spears (2003) between 'reflective' and 'reactive' modes of distinctiveness, which we encountered in the previous section.

The second example is an early study of mine in which I examined the relationships among three groups of engineering workers (Brown, 1978). By virtue of their longer training and of the labour market scarcity, one of these groups (the toolroom) had historically been seen as having higher status than the other two groups (development and production). And, consistently with our earlier analysis, this higher-status toolroom group showed the most ingroup bias towards outgroups.

So far I have considered high-status and equal-status groups. What about groups of subordinate status? At first glance, members of such groups would seem to have an unenviably negative social identity. If, as SIT suggests, they attempt to evaluate their groups in comparison to others in society, they will frequently discover that they earn less (if they have a job at all), they live in poorer accommodation, they enjoy fewer educational opportunities, and may be consensually derogated on a number of other criteria. Thus, materially and psychologically, they will experience disadvantage, and such unfavourable comparative outcomes should result in them having an unsatisfactory identity.

Tajfel and Turner (1986) suggest that one response to this situation is for members of such groups to abandon their current social identity. In the spirit of 'if you can't beat 'em, join 'em', they may seek to leave their ingroup and to join another, apparently more prestigious group. Recall how the lower-status group members in Sachdev and Bourhis' (1987) experiment expressed lower levels of satisfaction with their ingroup.

This phenomenon of members of 'inferior' groups distancing themselves psychologically from their group is strongly reminiscent of some of the research findings on ethnic preferences among minority group children that I reviewed in Chapter 5. In many studies from Clark and Clark (1947) onward, minority (often black) children showed a preference for the dominant (usually white) group stimuli.

Nevertheless, as we also saw in Chapter 5, such a response is not inevitable. Members of subordinate groups may not always be so willing (or able) to reject their identity. For instance, if the boundaries between the categories are fixed and impermeable, as is the case with many ascribed group memberships like gender and ethnicity, then the option to leave the subordinate group may not be open.[1]

In such cases, Tajfel and Turner (1986) suggest that other tactics may be adopted. One is to restrict oneself to making comparisons with other, similarly subordinate-status groups, so that the outcome of those comparisons may be more favourable to the ingroup. Rosenberg and Simmons (1972), for example, found that self-esteem amongst blacks who made comparisons with other blacks was higher than amongst those who compared themselves with whites. On the other side of that ethnic divide, it is often reported that white respondents from poorer socio-economic backgrounds show more overt prejudice than more middle-class samples (Brown, 1965; Vollebergh, 1991). Such a 'poor white racism', as it is sometimes called, may also be motivated in part by the desire to avoid identity damaging comparisons with wealthier social classes and to seek positive distinctiveness in a relation to a similarly deprived group.

Another strategy is to side-step those dimensions of comparison on which the subordinate groups is regarded as inferior and to find new dimensions, or new values of the old dimensions, so that the group can achieve some prestige. Lemaine (1966), in a study conducted – like Sherif's – in a children's camp, found that the potential losers in a hut-building contest discovered additional attributes to emphasize (for example, the hut's surrounding garden). Jackson and colleagues (1996), in a series of experimental studies, observed the same phenomenon. For example smokers, who had been led to believe that they were orally fixated and likely to posses a number of negative personality characteristics, saw themselves as more competent and likable than control participants who had not been given such identity threatening information. This is another example of the 'creative' bias I discussed above (Scheepers et al., 2006): the smokers could have been attempting to compensate for the devaluation of their group implied in the 'orally fixated' label. Importantly, Jackson and colleagues (1996) found that such compensatory strategies were even more in evidence in groups with impermeable boundaries, where individual escape routes were not open to group members. The values and lifestyles of such varied cultural sub-groups as the 'hippies' of the 1970s, the 'punks' of the 1980s, and the 'goths' and 'chavs' of more recent decades, all of which could be characterized by a rejection of the dominant society's cultural and moral norms, may be other examples of the same phenomenon.

None of these responses, with the possible exception of this last one, are completely satisfactory for members of a lower-status group, because they leave the unequal relationship between themselves and the dominant group essentially unchanged. Hence the possibility of unfavourable comparisons with that group remains, with all the likely consequences for social identity that they entail. Why, then, do such groups not confront the dominant group's superiority directly, by agitating for social and economic change and by refusing to accede to the consensually accepted definitions of their group's worth? Such a directly competitive intergroup orientation would be the most obviously predictable reaction from the premise of social identity theory, which is that people generally strive for a positive identity and avoid a negative one. It turns out that subordinate groups *do* sometimes opt for this strategy; examples are the various movements for civil rights in the 1960s, instigated by black people in the USA and followed by Maoris in New Zealand and aboriginal people in Australia, Canada and South America and, most dramatically of all, the abolition of apartheid in South Africa, brought about by the African National Congress in the 1990s. However, for this phenomenon to happen, it may be necessary for members of those lower-status groups to be able conceive of the existence of some alternatives to the current state of affairs (Tajfel and Turner, 1986). Until they can imagine that the old order is neither fair nor inevitable, such groups may be unlikely to engage in the psychologically risky comparisons with the 'superior' group.

What are the circumstances which encourage the generation of these 'cognitive alternatives'? There are probably several such factors; but, to date, the three most powerful circumstances have been found to be the following: first, the one in which the boundaries between the groups are relatively **impermeable**; secondly, the one in which the status differences between them are somewhat **unstable** and likely to change; and, thirdly, the one in which these differences are perceived as **illegitimate**, founded on unfair and arbitrary principles. In such circumstances, the 'normal' finding that high-status groups show more bias than low-status groups disappears and one observes increased levels of bias from *both* groups (Bettencourt et al., 2001; Brown and Ross, 1982; Caddick, 1982; Turner and Brown, 1978). That these effects are often observed to be as strong in the 'superior' group as they are in the 'inferior' group suggests that destabilizing and delegitimating status relations also present a threat to the higher-status group's identity, and its members react with enhanced attempts to defend their now fragile superiority.

These findings may help us to understand the historical changes in minority group children's ethnic preferences reported in Chapter 5. Most minority groups occupy a subordinate position in their respective societies. In North America (as in other countries), the 30–40 year period prior to the 1960s can fairly be represented as one of stasis as far as the position of such groups was concerned. It is true that there was tremendous social and economic upheaval wrought by the Second World War, but it must be remembered that, in many southern states of the USA, the black–white segregation was widespread and officially sanctioned in all spheres of life. In theoretical terms, we might depict this situation as one where the status relations between blacks and whites were legitimate and stable and where there was little chance of mobility between the groups (boundaries were impermeable). In accordance with this analysis, most studies of ethnic preference during this period showed that minority group children usually made *outgroup* favouring choices and judgements. Contrast this picture to the turbulent period of the late 1960s and early 1970s. The Civil Rights Movement had been outstandingly successful in challenging the worst excesses of institutionalized discrimination; there were several incidents of social unrest in cities as far apart as Los Angeles, Detroit and Newark. And all of this was underpinned by an articulate ideology of black consciousness which consistently rejected the values and legitimacy of the white majority. Such a situation could be described as *un*stable and *il*legitimate, though still one characterized by relatively impermeable social boundaries. Perhaps this is why it was in this period that several of the studies reporting *in*group favouring choices and preferences amongst black children were published (see also Vaughan, 1978).

It seems, then, that we can understand some of the attitudes of higher and lower-status groups towards each other by considering the identity processes involved in those different group memberships. However, useful though such a social identity analysis may be, the research it has inspired has generally suffered from a rather crucial defect from the perspective of arriving at a better understanding of prejudice. In this research the main focus has usually been on various measures of ingroup bias, whether in evaluative judgements or in reward allocations. There is a good reason for this: since the theory posits the need for a positive and a distinctive identity, the obvious indices to choose from, from a research standpoint, are those which reflect some positive intergroup differentiation on the part of one's respondents. The question is, however: Do these commonly used measures of ingroup bias really represent prejudice, as we are using the term (however loosely!) in this book? In Chapter 1 I defined prejudice as any attitude, emotion or behaviour towards members of a group, which directly or indirectly implies some negativity or antipathy towards that group. How well does ingroup bias of the kind we have discussed repeatedly in this chapter correspond to this definition?

To begin with, we should note that 'ingroup bias' literally means a more favourable evaluation or treatment of the ingroup *than* of the outgroup; in other words, it is an index of relative favouritism rather than one of absolute derogation of the outgroup. Indeed in many studies *both* ingroup and outgroup are evaluated (or treated) positively, only the former more so than the latter (Brewer, 1979). Moreover, ingroup and outgroup ratings may actually be positively rather than negatively correlated with each other (Turner, 1978). A further complexity was added by the discovery that ingroup biases in evaluative judgements are usually not correlated at all to affective measures, that is, to feelings of liking or dislike for the outgroup (Brewer, 1979; Brown, 1984b; Turner, 1981). All in all, as Brewer (1999) has wisely noted, we cannot assume that ingroup love (ingroup favouritism) is equivalent to – or even leads to – outgroup hate (prejudice). Thus in the next section, and indeed in the remainder of this chapter, I will focus more on intergroup attitudes and emotions which have a more obviously negative quality.

The role of group identification
The third and perhaps most durable contribution of SIT to our understanding of prejudice has been to push the construct of group identification to the forefront of researchers' investigations. One way in which it has done this, as we shall see the in the concluding part of this chapter, has been to underline the importance of the process of identification itself. Central to social identity theory and to its descendant, **self-categorization theory**, is the idea that, once someone identifies with a group, its fortunes, its attributes and its actions become incorporated as that person's fortunes, attributes and actions (Tajfel and Turner, 1986; Turner et al., 1987). But, of course, that identification process is seldom an all-or-nothing affair: people identify with their ingroups to different degrees. Thus the group and its outcomes matter to its members according to the strength of their attachment or identification with it. From this plausible assumption, two kinds of question can be asked: Do more highly identified people generally show more ingroup favouritism and/or prejudice? And do factors

which impact psychologically on members of a group do so more for those that are more highly identified? Translated into the more precise – or perhaps just more technical – language of the researcher, such questions imply either a direct causal role between the strength of group identification and prejudice (question 1), or a moderating role, such that some other causal agents of prejudice operate differently – more strongly or in an opposite direction – for high and low identifiers (question 2). In this section I want to consider what answers we can find to each of these questions.

By way of preamble, we had better survey first the various ways in which social psychologists have attempted to measure the strength of **group identification**. An early instrument was devised by Driedger (1976), which aimed to measure people's identification with their ethnic group. We adapted and shortened this scale so that it could be conveniently used for any kind of group (Brown et al., 1986). In selecting the items for our ten-item scale, we had in mind the different aspects of social identity mentioned in Tajfel's (1978b) definition of the construct: the awareness, evaluation and emotional significance of a person's group membership. Thus we included such items as 'I see myself as belonging to the X group', 'I consider the X group important' and 'I am glad to belong to the X group'. This admittedly rather rough-and-ready scale was used in various modified forms over the next decade and seemed to correlate reasonably well to other constructs (Jackson and Smith, 1999; Smith et al., 1999). Subsequently, more sophisticated multi-component instruments have been developed (Ellemers et al., 1999a; Leach et al., 2009). In these, typically, it is the emotional investment or commitment sub-scale that is most reliably correlated to intergroup attitude measures.

How well do measures like these correlate to, or even predict (in a causal sense), levels of ingroup bias and prejudice? The short answer is: rather variably. Sometimes, as I noted earlier in the chapter, there is a respectable positive association between strength of identification and ingroup bias, as there should be according to SIT (Kelly, 1988).[2] In other contexts, that correlation is much weaker, sometimes indistinguishable from zero, and occasionally even negative (Hinkle and Brown, 1990). There is also a dearth of longitudinal studies that could help determine the direction of causality; in other words, does an enhanced ingroup identification actually *lead to* a more negative attitude towards an outgroup? A rare exception is a study by Duckitt and Mphuthing (1998) conducted in South Africa, before and after the 1994 parliamentary election, with black school and university students. They administered a measure of ingroup identification and various intergroup attitude measures (for instance attitudes towards the white Afrikaans group) at both time points. If a heightened identification causes negative intergroup attitudes, one would expect that identification levels before the election would predict attitudes afterwards. In fact, all such correlations were non-significant.[3] Instead, pre-election attitudes predicted post-election identification – exactly the opposite causal direction to that suggested by SIT! In summary, then, the evidence for a straightforward connection between how much an ingroup matters to its members and their prejudice towards outgroups is neither very strong nor very consistent.

Faced with this inconsistency, researchers have sought to identify additional factors that might determine when identification does indeed lead to prejudice and when it does not. One suggestion of ours was to speculate that the psychological processes proposed by SIT may not be operative in all groups. Instead, they may depend on

Table 6.2 The relationship between national identification and xenophobia depends on the comparative context. This table shows the correlation between national identification and derogation of foreigners, averaged across four studies.

Condition		
Social comparison	Temporal comparison	Control
.44***[a]	.05	.11

Note: [a] *** means: p <.001.
Source: Adapted from Table 3 in Mummendey et al., 2001a

dynamics of
IG + conformity

prevailing levels of individualism or collectivism in the group or among its members, and on the latter's inclination (or lack of it) to engage in intergroup comparisons (Hinkle and Brown, 1990). We hypothesized, and subsequently confirmed in three empirical studies, that one would only expect a strong link between group identification and ingroup favouritism in groups which can be simultaneously characterized as 'collectivist' – that is, where there is an emphasis on intragroup co-operation and group achievements – and 'relational' – that is, where there is a concern for the ingroup's standing relative to other groups (Brown et al., 1992).

It is fair to say that this combination of collectivism and relationalism has not always yielded positive correlations between identification and bias (see for example Brown et al., 1996; Capozza et al., 2000). Nevertheless, the idea that identification will only be strongly linked to prejudice when the context encourages intergroup comparisons does seem to hold more water. In four separate studies we asked people to do one of three things before filling out a questionnaire which contained measures of national identification and xenophobia (Mummendey et al., 2001a). In one condition we asked them to write down several ways in which their country was a better country to live in than others (*social* comparison condition). In another, we asked them to write down several ways in which their country was a better country to live in now than it used to be (*temporal* comparison condition). In a third condition we simply asked them to write down why their country was a good one to live in (*control* condition). We reasoned that framing the way participants thought about their countries in these different fashions would temporarily construct a different kind of national identity, with correspondingly different implications for xenophobia. So it proved. In the social comparison condition, the correlation between national identity and xenophobia was generally positive and significantly higher than in the other two conditions, where it was close to zero (see Table 6.2). There is even some evidence that this same kind of experimental manipulation can affect identification's relationship with implicit measures of intergroup attitude (Calitri, 2005).

These experimental findings bear out a distinction made by some political psychologists between **patriotism** and **nationalism** (Kosterman and Feshbach, 1989; Schatz et al., 1999). Both are forms of national identification. The first consists of a strong but not uncritical attachment to one's country, its culture or its physical geography. The second form of national identification is equally positive about one's own country – perhaps even more so, because it manifests itself almost in a 'my country right or wrong' attitude – but now it is allied to a belief in the superiority of that country over all others. In other words, nationalism involves a strong element of social comparison, somewhat akin to what we had manipulated in the study above.

Because they share a common affinity with the ingroup, patriotism and nationalism are usually moderately well correlated to each other. However, where they differ is in their relationship to prejudice towards foreigners: nationalism tends to be clearly and positively correlated to xenophobia, whilst patriotism is only weakly so related, if at all (Blank and Schmidt, 2003; Calitri, 2005; see also Roccas et al., 2006).

This idea – that people's attachment to their country can take different ideological forms, with correspondingly different implications for attitudes towards outgroups – has, of course, been well understood and exploited by political elites for millennia (see for example Reicher and Hopkins, 2001). In this same vein, one can find disputes about how nationality itself should be defined. Should the ownership of a particular nationality be restricted to those who can claim a 'biological' or some other relatively fixed cultural connection with the country in question, possessing, if you like, some fundamental 'essence' of what it is to belong to that group? Or, instead, should a national identity be open to anyone who endorses, and confirms to, some consensually agreed social practices (such as respect for civic procedures and adherence to laws)? In political science, these two conceptions of nationality are sometimes called 'ethnic' and 'civic' nationalism, and it seems that countries have adopted formal designations of nationality that contain differing admixtures of ethnic and civic components (Smith, 2001).

This socio-legal distinction between different ways of defining nationality finds a psychological counterpart in the ways groups are typically perceived. Sometimes we are prone to see the members of certain groups as sharing some inner 'essence', various relatively fixed attributes that define them as belonging to that group; other groups may be perceived no less as groups, but they are seen in a less 'essentialist' fashion – perhaps because they happen temporarily to possess some common attribute, or merely because they are acting in concert at the same place and time (for further discussion of categorial perception and entitativity, see Haslam et al., 2000; see also Chapter 3). Thus ethnic, gender and disability groups are typically perceived in an essentialist fashion, whilst occupational and political groups may be seen rather less so (Haslam et al., 2000).

We wondered whether these different constructions of what a group is might affect the relationship between strength of identification and prejudice (Pehrson et al., 2009a). Perhaps, we thought, for people who thought of their (national) ingroup in a more 'ethnic' or 'essentialist' way, there would be a clear positive correlation between national identification and having negative exclusionary attitudes towards asylum seekers, potential new members of the ingroup. For those who saw their country in a more 'civic', less 'essentialist' way, a similar level of national identification would not translate into prejudice. Our results bore out our suspicions: the correlation between identification and prejudice was clearly positive in the first group and negligible in the second (Pehrson et al., 2009a). We found a similar pattern at a more macroscopic country level of analysis (Pehrson et al., 2009b). In this study we used data from a survey of thirty-one countries, in which measures of national identification, perceived 'ethnic' or 'civic' definitions of nationality and anti-immigrant prejudice had been administered. At an individual level the overall correlation between identification and prejudice was weakly positive, even if it was statistically significant on account of the

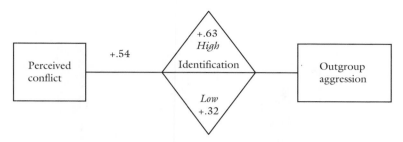

Figure 6.1 Identification moderates the relationship between perceived intergroup conflict and outgroup aggression. The figure represents the standardized coefficients obtained from: regressing aggression on perceived conflict; identification; and their interaction. Source: Struch and Schwartz, 1989

large sample (over 37,000 participants). However, the really interesting finding was that this correlation became even weaker when we took into account the average endorsement of a 'civic' conception of nationality in a country. And, in contrast, it became stronger when we took into account the average country-level endorsement of a more linguistic (akin to 'ethnic') form of nationality definition. In other words, the prevailing country-wide ideological view of how to define nationality significantly affected the individual level correlation between national identification and prejudice.

In summary, then, it is clear that there is no simple relationship between the strength of a person's attachment to their ingroup and their inclination to disparage outgroups. Instead, we need also to consider the nature or content of that group identification and the context in which it is being expressed. If intergroup comparisons are highly salient either in the person's view of their identity or in a given situation, or if the identity is constructed in a strongly essentialist way, then indeed we can expect a strong association between identification and prejudice. But there will be other occasions, other ways of seeing the ingroup, in which identification may be no less strong, but where there is little or no tendency to denigrate those who 'do not belong'.

The strength of group identification does not just determine prejudice in a direct fashion, however. Perhaps more frequently, it operates in a more indirect way, so as to amplify the effects of other causal agents. The reason for this is simple. If a particular factor is found to influence outgroup attitudes – for example by providing instrumental reasons to denigrate the outgroup or to promote the 'ingroup' – then that factor should have even greater impact on more highly identified group members, for whom the interests of the ingroup are closest to their hearts. Examples of this moderating role of identification are not hard to find. Struch and Schwartz (1989) surveyed two neighbourhoods in Jerusalem which had experienced an influx of ultra-orthodox Jews – a threatening outgroup for members of these neighbourhoods. Amongst the measures administered were an index of perceived conflict between their group and the ultra-orthodox Jews, a measure of aggressive intentions towards the latter and an ingroup identification scale. Consistent with realistic conflict theory, perceived conflict was strongly correlated with aggression, but that correlation was even stronger for those who identified highly with their ingroup (see Figure 6.1).

Struch and Schwartz (1989) measured variations in *perceived* intergroup conflict. In a field study conducted some years later, we were able to observe identification

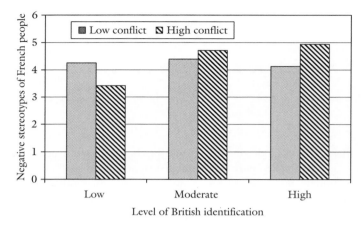

Figure 6.2 Identification moderates the effect of an actual intergroup conflict on negative outgroup stereotypes. Negative stereotypes were 'opinionated', 'unreliable', 'arrogant' and 'rude' (1–7 scale). Adapted from Table 2 in Brown et al., 2001

similarly moderating the effects of an *actual* intergroup conflict (Brown et al., 2001). This study was conducted among British passengers of a ferry going to France. On the first day of data collection, there happened to be a strike of French fishermen, who were blockading the French Channel ports; this meant that the British passengers could not travel that day. This we labelled the 'high conflict' group, and we were able to compare it to a 'low conflict' group, which we surveyed some days later, when the strike had been called off. The effects of this naturally occurring conflict on our British participants' negative stereotypes of French people were again moderated by the strength of national identification. As can be seen in Figure 6.2, the consequences of the strike were most evident in the high and moderate identifiers, and they were actually benign in the low identification group (see also Jackson, 2002; Livingstone and Haslam, 2008; and Morrison and Ybarra, 2008).

The moderating effects of group identification are not restricted to conflict; they have also been found to change group members' responsiveness to ingroup norms regarding how outgroups should be treated (Jetten et al., 1997). Jetten and colleagues varied identification experimentally, by leading psychology students to have a more or less favourable view of their group. They also led those same students to believe that their fellow ingroup members were typically fair in their dealing with members of other university departments *or* usually favoured psychology students. By varying the perceived ingroup norms in this way, the researchers hoped to discourage participants from showing ingroup favouritism in a resource allocation task, or to encourage them to show it. In the event, only those in the high identification condition followed the ingroup norms, displaying nearly twice as much bias against business students in the favouritism norm condition as in the fairness norm condition. More authoritarian people may have internalized a general norm to show prejudice towards outgroups (see Chapter 2); they will do this even more when they identify especially strongly with their ingroup (Duckitt, 1989; Stellmacher and Petzel, 2005).

Lastly, group identification is likely to affect the way people react to the knowledge that other members of their ingroup have treated an outgroup unfairly in the past.

A possible, but by no means inevitable, response to such awareness of intergroup past misdeeds is to feel some collective guilt, and hence to seek to make reparations to the outgroup or at least to show less prejudice towards it (Branscombe and Doosje, 2004). Indeed there is evidence that this often happens (Brown et al., 2008; Brown and Cehajic, 2008; McGarty et al., 2005; Pederson et al., 2004; Swim and Miller, 1999). However, to feel guilt on behalf of one's group is not without its psychological costs, since it implies an admission of moral failure and hence of damage to the ingroup's positive public image. This may be a particularly bitter pill to swallow for those who strongly identify with the ingroup. This, at any rate, was Doosje and colleagues' (1998) reasoning when they conducted a study with Dutch participants who were reminded of some historical atrocities committed towards Indonesia in the Dutch colonial period. So long as those reminders were somewhat ambiguous, so that information about the atrocities was tempered by some alleged benefits of colonization, the more strongly nationalistic Dutch participants showed less guilt and offered less by way of material reparations than their less strongly identified peers. It seems that those high identifiers sought to defend themselves from the uncomfortable psychological ramifications of feeling guilt by concentrating on the more favourable rather than on the darker side of their country's history (see also Doosje et al., 2006).

In sum, therefore, there are several strands of research that show how people's degree of attachment to their group greatly affects their reaction to different intergroup factors. If a particular variable is likely to cause people to be prejudiced, then it is a reasonably safe bet that more highly identified group members will be even more prejudiced. Thus the role of social identity processes in determining prejudice is somewhat different from what had been envisaged in the original version of SIT (Tajfel and Turner, 1986). There the emphasis was much more on the implications of different socio-structural arrangements for the group members' search for some positive distinctiveness for their group. Typically, researchers focused on how this search manifested itself in variations in different forms of ingroup bias, and they paid little attention to explicitly negative or affectively tinged intergroup attitudes – which are, after all, crucial components of prejudice. There was, however, one other idea in SIT which has proved enduringly influential: the concept of 'threats' to identity. In fact the whole notion of 'intergroup threat' is sufficiently important to the understanding of prejudice to deserve a section of its own. Before we reach that, I need to examine another powerful intergroup determinant of prejudice: relative deprivation.

Relative Deprivation

Between 1882 and 1930 there were 4,761 reported cases of lynchings in the United States. Of these, over 70 per cent were lynchings of black people and the majority occurred in southern states, for so long the heart of American slavery. Such a statistic is a sombre reminder of the awful extremes which prejudice can sometimes reach. Hovland and Sears (1940), who brought these grisly facts to the attention of social science, noticed that there was a considerable annual variation in the killings, which ranged from a high of 155 (in 1892/3) to a low of seven (in 1929). They also observed that there was a remarkable correspondence between this variation and different economic indicators of farming (farming being the principal industry in southern states): as the economy receded and times got hard, the number of lynchings increased (but compare Hepworth and West, 1988 and Green et al., 1998).

What might account for this apparent co-variation of economic recession with anti-black violence? Hovland and Sears (1940) themselves believed that it was caused by frustration. Drawing upon Dollard and colleagues' (1939) **frustration–aggression theory**, they hypothesized that the hardships generated by a depressed economy raised people's levels of frustration, which in turn generated increased aggression. Using the psychoanalytic concept of **displacement** in the same way as Adorno and colleagues (1950) were to do ten years later (see Chapter 2), Hovland and Sears suggested that the aggression would not be directed at the true source of the economic frustration (that is, the capitalist system which produced it), but would be diverted towards more vulnerable and easily accessible targets such as members of 'deviant' and minority groups (see Billig, 1976 and Brown, 2000a for more extended treatments of this argument).

Other attempts to confirm this so-called 'scapegoat' theory of prejudice[4] have had mixed success. Miller and Bugelski (1948) conducted an experiment with a group of young American men at a camp. One evening, when the men were eagerly anticipating a night on the town, the experimenters suddenly announced that the evening out was cancelled and the men would be required to undertake some uninteresting tasks instead. As it happened, they had also measured the men's ethnic attitudes towards Mexicans and Japanese before this frustrating event, and they did it again afterwards. Analysis of these attitudes revealed that the participants became significantly less favourable after the frustration; a control group experiencing no frustration showed no such change. This was a nice confirmation of the 'displacement' hypothesis, since these two minority groups could have had no conceivable responsibility for the men's plight.

However, other experiments have yielded more equivocal results. For instance Stagner and Congdon (1955) failed to find increases in prejudice in students after the frustration of failing some academic tests. Cowen and colleagues (1958), using a similar methodology, *did* find an increase in negative affect towards blacks, but this did not generalize to increases in more general ethnocentrism against other minorities. Even more problematically for the frustration–aggression theory, Burnstein and McRae (1962) found *more* favourable evaluations of a black team member following task failure, and this was particularly evident in highly prejudiced subjects, who should have been the most eager to denigrate him.

It was inconsistencies like these, as well as some other conceptual and empirical difficulties (Berkowitz, 1962; Billig, 1976), that led to the decline in popularity and utility of the frustration–aggression theory as an explanation of prejudice. In its place, and very much influenced by some of its central ideas (Gurr, 1970), there emerged a theory which placed much less emphasis on *absolute* levels of hardship and frustration but stressed instead the importance of *relative* **deprivation**. The inspiration for this new approach – relative deprivation theory (RDT), as it is known – came from some serendipitous observations made in the course of a large-scale social psychological study of morale and social attitudes in the American army (Stouffer et al., 1949). These researchers discovered that dissatisfaction was higher in certain sections of the military (for example in the air force), where prospects for career advancement were good, than in others (for example in the military police), where the chances of promotion were poor. How so? Certainly not due to absolute levels of frustration, because on that basis the military police (MP) should have been less happy than the air force. The answer, suggested Stouffer and colleagues, may lie in the different levels of *relative* frustration (or deprivation): the air force personnel, although objectively better off, had a ready and superior standard of comparison to hand – their promoted colleagues – and thus felt more aggrieved about their position; the MPs, with fewer such comparisons available, did not feel their deprivation so acutely. A contemporary example of this same phenomenon can be observed amongst some footballers in the top flight of the English Premier League. Frank Lampard, it is rumoured, was most disgruntled in 2008 to discover that one of his Chelsea team-mates was earning £30,000 *per week* more than him. The fact that he was already earning over £100,000 per week himself, four times more than most British people earn *in a year*, was apparently of little consolation to him. As we shall see, this idea, that advantaged people or groups can be as vulnerable to feelings of relative deprivation as their less privileged counterparts, is a crucial insight of RDT.

The idea that deprivation is always relative to some standard forms the centrepiece of all theories of relative deprivation (Crosby, 1976; Davies, 1969; Davis, 1959; Gurr, 1970; Runciman, 1966; Walker and Smith, 2002). Gurr (1970), who has done much to formalize the theory and to test its implications empirically, proposed that relative deprivation arises when people perceive a discrepancy between the standard of living they currently have and the standard of living they believe they *should* be enjoying. It is this gap between 'attainments' and 'expectations' that is thought to lie behind social discontent and prejudice.

Before we examine how this concept has been used to explain prejudice, an important distinction must be clarified. In some versions of relative deprivation theory – particularly those, like Gurr's (1970), which derive directly from the earlier frustration–aggression theory – the stress is on the individual's direct experience of relative deprivation: what I enjoy/suffer relative to what I expect. However, there is another kind of deprivation, one which derives from people's perception of their *group*'s fortunes relative to what they expect for their group. Runciman (1966) labelled this '**group** (or **fraternalistic**) **deprivation**', to distinguish it from the other form, '**individual**' (or 'egoistic'). A nice illustration of this distinction was provided by Caplan (1970), who noted how many black supporters of Black Power in the USA in the 1960s came from middle and upper income brackets rather than from the poorer (and most individually deprived) groups. Their own personal advantage relative to other blacks did not prevent them from perceiving the relative *disadvantage* of blacks, as a group, compared to whites. As Walker and Pettigrew (1984) have pointed out, the fact that group-relative deprivation is based so firmly on group outcomes rather than on individual ones makes it much more suitable a construct than individual deprivation for the analysis of an intergroup phenomenon like prejudice. Recalling the previous section, it is also important to note that a sense of group deprivation cannot arise without some prior identification with the ingroup. In order to feel that our group is not doing well (enough), we must first identify with that group sufficiently for its fortunes to matter to us.

What gives rise to relative deprivation? At the most general level, as just noted, relative deprivation is caused by a gap between expectations and achievements. Crawford

Table 6.3 Black militancy and relative deprivation

		Relative deprivation[a] (%)	
Attitude item		Low	High
Do you think that riots help	Help	28	54
or hurt the Negro cause?	Hurt	60	38
Do you approve or disapprove	Approve	38	64
of Black Power?	Disapprove	36	22
Will force or persuasion be	Force	40	51
necessary to change White	Persuasion	52	35
attitudes?			

Note: [a] Perceived discrepancy between 'actual' and 'ideal' life.
Source: Crawford and Naditch, 1970, Table 1 ('don't knows' omitted).

and Naditch (1970) used a direct measure of this gap in their survey of black residents in Detroit, shortly after some rioting there. Respondents were asked to indicate on a vertical eleven-step ladder where their present life-style was in relation to their 'ideal life' (at the top of the ladder). The discrepancy between these two points was taken as a measure of deprivation. As can be seen from Table 6.3, there was a clear relationship between the level of deprivation and their attitudes towards the riots and black militancy. Those high in deprivation (putting themselves on step 4 or below) showed more sympathy with the objectives of black militants than those scoring low (at step 5 or above).

The next question is: what determines people's aspirations for their ideal life? In RDT, these aspirations are thought to derive from either or both of two kinds of comparisons. One is temporal in nature and concerns one's recent past. Davies (1969) proposed that people extrapolate from their own (group's) experience of affluence or poverty and expect the future to be similar. If living standards rise steadily over a period, this will generate an expectation of future increases. From this, Davies derived his famous **J-curve hypothesis**, which suggests that dissatisfaction will be most likely to come not after a period of prolonged deprivation, but after a period in which people's living standards rise over a number of years, followed by a sudden downturn. It is this sharp drop that produces the gap between actual and expected living standards which is necessary for the arousal of deprivation.[5] A second source of expectations are comparisons with other groups. When we perceive another group to be doing better or worse than our own, especially when that group is similar or in some way relevant to the ingroup, its fate is likely to generate expectations for how well we think our group should be doing. In turn, we will feel respectively deprived or gratified (Runciman, 1966). Again, the ingroup's absolute standing is not important; it is the relative element that counts.

A recent study of income distribution in Britain graphically illustrates both of these types of deprivation (Jones et al., 2008). This study charted the weekly levels of different income groups in the UK over a period of thirty years. Figure 6.3 shows the results. All groups, including the poorest, enjoyed a rise in income. However, notice how the gap between the richest and the poorest has steadily widened over

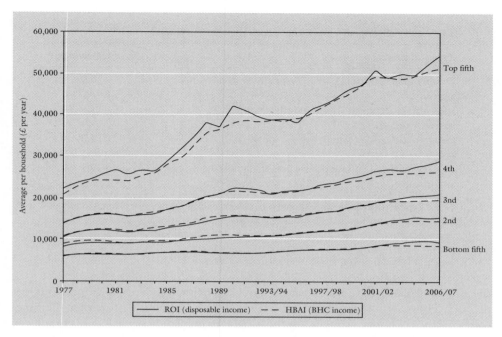

Figure 6.3 Changes in UK income distribution 1977–2007 (by quintiles). Figures show average weekly household disposable income in quintiles of the UK income distribution (adjusted to 2006/7 prices). Source: Jones et al., 2008, Figure 2

the years. Such a situation is a classic breeding ground for increased feelings of group relative deprivation on the part of the poorer group. The changes in income also reveal the potential for temporal deprivation in the wealthier group. Notice how its incomes rose sharply between 1984 and 1990, and then experienced an actual downturn until 1995/6. This is a demonstration of Davies' (1969) J-curve, and the fact that it did not result in any widespread discontent among Britain's middle classes is probably due to the revival of their fortunes in the late 1990s (Brewer et al., 2008).

What are the effects of **temporal relative deprivation** and group relative deprivation on prejudice? There has been little research on the former. Hepworth and West (1988) re-analysed the same data used by Hovland and Sears (1940) and found a correlation between one year's lynchings of black people and the decline in economic prosperity from the previous year. However, Green and colleagues (1998) found that adding just eight more years' data (1930–8), which included the Great Depression, considerably reduced the correlation between the economic index and anti-black violence. Moreover, when they attempted to correlate the unemployment rate in four New York boroughs with the incidence of hate crimes over a nine-year period (1987–95), they could find very few reliable associations, however long or short the time lags were.

Other attempts to link intergroup events to temporal changes in groups' living standards have proved similarly controversial. Davies (1969), the originator of the J-curve hypothesis, tried to explain the incidence of black urban rioting in the USA in

Table 6.4 Group and individual deprivation and prejudice

Type of deprivation	Prejudice measure[a]
Doubly gratified (doing well personally *and* as a group)	–20.9
Individually deprived (doing poorly personally but well as a group)	–13.9
Group deprivation (doing well personally but poorly as a group)	+14.3
Doubly deprived (doing poorly personally *and* as a group)	+29.1

Note: [a] Typical prejudice items included: 'would object if family member wanted to bring a negro friend home for dinner'; 'would mind if negro family with about the same income and education moved next door'; 'thinks white and black students should go to separate schools'. The higher the score, the greater the prejudice.
Source: Adapted from Table 9 in Vanneman and Pettigrew, 1972

the 1960s by reference to the rise and fall of black living standards in the previous two decades. However, others have disputed his analysis, arguing that neither the time-course of the economic changes nor the variability in black living standards fitted well with it (Crosby, 1979; Davies, 1978, 1979; Miller et al., 1977; Miller and Bolce, 1979). In short, the link between temporal relative deprivation and intergroup prejudice has proved rather elusive.

Much more attention has been paid to the effects of relative deprivation (RD) stemming from unfavourable *social* comparisons. A classic study demonstrating the link between relative deprivation and prejudice was undertaken by Vanneman and Pettigrew (1972). They surveyed over 1,000 white voters in four US cities and asked whether these respondents felt they were doing better or worse economically than other white workers like them (individual RD), and also how well whites were doing compared to blacks (group RD). On the basis of these two questions, Vanneman and Pettigrew divided their sample into four groups, according to whether their participants could be described as being 'gratified' (doing better than others) or 'deprived' in either or both of the individual and group senses (see Table 6.4). On the main measure of prejudice they administered, those who were group or doubly deprived were the ones who showed most anti-black sentiment.

These findings have since been confirmed by several other studies. Tripathi and Srivastava (1981) studied Muslim attitudes towards Hindus in India. Muslims are now a disadvantaged minority in India, although prior to partition (in 1947) they were in fact the ruling group. This change in their status might be expected to lead to strong feelings of deprivation, and indeed another study found that they did show more deprivation than the Hindus (Ghosh et al., 1992). Tripathi and Srivastava (1981) found a clear correlation between group deprivation and ingroup bias against Hindus. Similar correlations between group deprivation and prejudice have been observed in South Africa (Appelgryn and Nieuwoudt, 1988) and in several countries in Europe (Pettigrew and Meertens, 1995). In truth, the correlations that have been found are not always very large, and this may be because the measures of RD employed have often focused solely on the *perception* of discrepancy rather than on people's (negative) *feelings* associated with the discrepancy. If more affectively oriented measures of RD are used, the correlations with prejudice tend to be higher (Smith and Ortiz, 2002; Taylor, 2002; Walker and Pettigrew, 1984).

All these studies used cross-sectional correlational designs, and so the evidence they have produced is subject to all the usual difficulties of causal interpretation in such studies: did the deprivation lead to an increase in prejudice, or did heightened prejudice lead to feelings of deprivation? Fortunately there is also longitudinal survey and experimental evidence, which points firmly in the direction of deprivation causing prejudice. Duckitt and Mphuthing (2002) measured black South Africans' perceptions and feelings of deprivation and their prejudiced attitudes towards Afrikaans people before and after the 1994 transitional election in South Africa. They found that pre-election levels of affective (or emotional) RD were significantly related to post-election levels of prejudice, but *not vice versa*, which implied that it was the blacks' feelings of deprivation that were determining their subsequent levels of prejudice.

Experimental research also supports a causal link between group RD and prejudice (Grant and Brown, 1995). We asked groups of women to work on a brainstorming task for which they expected to receive around $10 each, although they were warned that this payment would depend on their evaluation by another group. That evaluation, of course, constituted our experimental manipulation of deprivation: half the groups learned that the other group had given them a poor evaluation and recommended that they should only receive $4; the remainder were evaluated positively and were told they would receive their expected $10. The participants reacted strongly to this manipulation. Compared to those who received what they expected, the deprived group showed markedly higher levels of ingroup bias against the other group, expressed consistently higher levels of dislike for them and, from careful observation of their videotaped post-feedback interactions, expressed more derogatory remarks about them.

I want now to return to an issue raised by Vanneman and Pettigrew (1972): that of the respective roles played by personal and group deprivation in the genesis of prejudice. We saw from their data that personal deprivation seemed not to be related to increases in prejudice. Other research, too, has found that only group deprivation seems to be systematically related to intergroup attitudes and behaviour, while personal deprivation seems more linked to individual outcomes like personal unhappiness, stress and depression (Guimond and Dube-Simard, 1983; Koomen and Fränkel, 1992; Walker and Mann, 1987). It would be tempting to conclude that feeling more or less personally deprived has few implications for how prejudiced a person is. Tempting, but mistaken. For one thing, personal deprivation has sometimes been found to be associated with prejudice. Ellemers and Bos (1998), in their study of Dutch shopkeepers, found that both personal and group deprivation predicted negative attitudes towards immigrant shopkeepers, independently of each other. While such a finding may not be typical, it is possible that feeling personally deprived is a first step towards a more collective sense of grievance (Tougas and Beaton, 2002). Presumably in order for this to happen, there needs to be a sufficiently strong sense of group identification to connect the 'me' to the 'us'. If that precondition is satisfied, this argument suggests that, if personal deprivation has any effects on prejudice, it does so *through* group deprivation. Pettigrew and colleagues (2008) uncovered

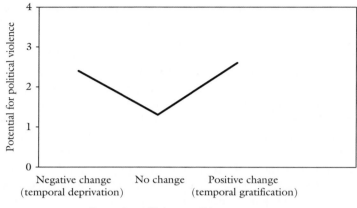

Figure 6.4   The V-curve hypothesis: relative gratification and political violence. Adapted from Table 7 in Grofman and Muller, 1973

evidence for such a mediation process in several large European surveys of anti-immigrant prejudice. Individual RD was weakly correlated to prejudice, but that correlation disappeared altogether once group RD was controlled for. On the other hand, group RD was more strongly correlated to prejudice, and that association remained even when individual RD was controlled. Such a pattern of correlations is consistent with the idea that the individual RD prejudice link is mediated by group RD, but not vice versa.

Before I conclude this discussion of relative deprivation and prejudice, there is one last issue to consider. In 1973, just one year after Vanneman and Pettigrew published their classic paper on personal and group deprivation and gratification, there appeared another paper, by Grofman and Muller, with the intriguing title 'The strange case of **relative gratification** and potential for political violence: The **V-curve hypothesis**'. This article reported the results of a survey conducted in a small mid-western US town which had experienced some serious civic disorder just three years before. In addition to being asked some standard questions about their present, past and expected future life conditions (as compared to an ideal situation),[6] respondents were also asked about their support for various forms of civil disobedience and violence. Overall, Grofman and Muller found no straightforward relationship between how deprived people felt and their propensity for political violence. However, when they divided their sample into three groups – respondents who perceived a deterioration over time, no change, or an improvement over time – a consistent pattern emerged: those who experienced a negative change were, as expected from considerations of temporal deprivation (for example the J-curve hypothesis), more likely to favour political violence than those who perceived no change. However, those who perceived a positive change – temporal relative *gratification* – showed a similar endorsement of political violence (see Figure 6.4). Given the shape of the graph depicted in Figure 6.4, Grofman and Muller labelled it 'the V-curve'.

This rather surprising finding went virtually unnoticed for thirty years, until Guimond and Dambrun (2002) decided to see if it could be replicated experimentally and applied to prejudice. They led psychology students to believe that the future job prospects for psychologists would either be better (or worse) than those for students in economics and law. Then they measured those students' level of prejudice against various immigrant groups. Consistently with the V-curve hypothesis, they found more prejudice both in the deprived and in the gratified conditions, as compared to a control group which had been given no information about psychologists' future conditions. In fact, those in the gratification condition seemed to show slightly more prejudice than even the participants in the deprivation condition. Dambrun and colleagues (2006) followed this up with a survey conducted in South Africa, and again they found that, both for those who felt things were getting worse *and* for those who felt things were getting better, prejudice tended to increase (see also Guimond et al., 2002).

What might explain this seemingly paradoxical phenomenon? Leach and colleagues (2002) have reflected on the phenomenology of belonging to an advantaged group, and they speculate that people's emotional reactions and subsequent behavioural responses could depend on several factors. Of most relevance to the relative gratification effect is Leach and colleagues' suggestion that a perception that the ingroup's advantaged position is temporary or unstable could prompt members of that group to display enhanced pride in the ingroup and/or disdain for the outgroup. These reactions are thought to be psychological defences against an eventual decline in the ingroup's status position (see my earlier discussion about the social identity implications of belonging to a superior-status group). In this respect, it is noteworthy that most studies documenting the V-curve effect have employed manipulations or measures of gratification that imply some temporal instability, albeit initially in the ingroup's favour (Dambrun et al., 2006; Grofman and Muller, 1973; Guimond and Dambrun, 2002). The argument of Leach and colleagues (2002) is that these emotions of pride and disdain have the potential to lead to negative attitudinal and behavioural responses towards outgroups (see Harth et al., 2008 for a partial test of these hypotheses).

Intriguing though these ideas are, the V-curve effect still lacks a completely convincing explanation. For one thing, it is not clear whether the effects of relative gratification generalize to all outgroups or pertain mostly to those outgroups likely to pose a future threat to the ingroup's status position. Dambrun and colleagues' (2006) findings suggest the latter, because the effect of gratification in higher socio-economic status South Africans seemed mainly targeted at European (rather than African) immigrants, since this group might be regarded as a greater potential economic threat to them. On the other hand, Guimond and Dambrun (2002) found that the relative gratification of psychologists vis-à-vis lawyers and economists produced an increase in prejudice towards North African immigrants, a group hardly likely to be competitors with professional psychologists.

Finally, it is clear that the negative effects of relative gratification on prejudice do not always occur. As we saw earlier, Vanneman and Pettigrew (1972) observed that the least prejudice of all was coming from their relatively gratified sub-group of respondents (see Table 6.4). Note that their gratification was defined in social rather than temporal terms, and so perhaps the crucial element of perceived instability of the intergroup status relations was not present (although compare Guimond et al., 2002).

Threat as a Cause of Prejudice

Reviewing the determinants of prejudice discussed in the previous three sections, it is possible to discern a common thread running through the theories and research I have presented. The linking idea is that prejudice seems to be the result of threat: threats to the material interests of the group (realistic conflict theory), threats to the distinctiveness or integrity of the group (social identity theory) and threats to the group's social position (relative deprivation theory). In this section, then, I want to focus directly on the concept of threat and to show further how extensively it is implicated as a cause of prejudice. I begin by reviewing several studies that have tackled the problem directly, by experimentally manipulating different kinds of threat, and then by examining their effect on people's attitudes or behaviour. I then consider how perceptions of different kinds of threat can have an impact on our emotions, and hence to our likely behavioural reactions towards outgroups. Finally, I discuss an influential model of threat and prejudice that seeks to integrate some of the different approaches that we have encountered in this chapter and earlier on in the book.

First, by way of introduction, here are two newspaper articles reporting on some intergroup tensions in two very different contexts. The first, under the headline 'The rise of mosques becomes catalyst for conflict across Europe', reports on local opposition, in the Swiss town of Wangen, to the planned building of a mosque by the town's Turkish community. One Wangen citizen, Roland Kissling, was particularly vocal in his opposition to the mosque: 'It's the noise, and all the cars. You should see it on a Friday night. I've got nothing against minarets. But in the city. Not in this village. It's just not right. There's going to be trouble' (*Guardian*, 11 October 2007).

Elsewhere in the article one reads that this anti-Islamic sentiment has been greatly stimulated by a right-wing political party, which was even seeking a referendum on a constitutional amendment that would outlaw the building of minarets in Switzerland. The second article reports a more extreme outbreak of intergroup violence. The headline reads 'Hunted by gangs, migrants flee the flames', and the article records how Zimbabwean immigrants to South Africa have been the target of vicious attacks by South Africans in Johannesburg, Cape Town and other cities (*Guardian*, 24 May 2008). It seems that much of this anti-immigrant feeling has been stoked by fears that the Zimbabwean migrant workers would be unfairly competing in the labour market. As one South African put it: 'They give the jobs to Zimbabweans because they will work for cheap wages. We are South Africans. We know our rights and demand to be paid properly' (*Guardian*, 24 May 2008).

Social psychological research confirms that the kinds of threat described in these two examples – the one focusing on the perceived threat to Swiss culture posed by symbols of Islam, the other highlighting the results of a sense of economic threat – have powerful effects on intergroup attitudes. Duckitt and Fisher (2003) led some of their New Zealand participants to believe that the future of their country was rather gloomy (high levels of unemployment, rising crime rates, civil disorder). Others, in contrast, were told that the future was rosy (economic prosperity, low crime and civic harmony). The former group responded to the threatening information by showing significantly higher levels of authoritarianism, a measure usually highly correlated with prejudice (see Chapter 2). Incidentally, it is worth noting that those in the low threat condition showed relatively low levels of authoritarianism and were indistinguishable from a control group. Parenthetically, we can also note that this finding is inconsistent with the V-curve hypothesis.

But threats do not have to be to tangible things, like standards of living or physical security; threats to identity can be just as potent sources of prejudice, as a series of studies has shown. A crucial aspect of many cultural groups' identity is bound up with the language they speak. When this linguistic identity is threatened – for example by an outgroup member deriding it – people may react sharply, emphasizing their own language still further and trading insults with the outgroup (Bourhis and Giles, 1977; Bourhis et al., 1978). Breakwell (1978) studied threats to identity among football fans. She arranged for some participants (teenage boys) to learn that they were not 'genuine' supporters because they had attended only a few games. This was made to seem plausible by some official-sounding statements from some well-known football managers. This group was then compared to another group of boys, who believed themselves to be genuine fans. Breakwell reasoned that the former group would react negatively, because their identity as real football lovers had been called into question. Their responses to subsequent questions about the relative merits of their own and another team's supporters seemed to bear this out: they showed more ingroup bias compared to the latter group (see also Breakwell, 1988).

Even artificial groups in the laboratory can be induced to show derogatory attitudes towards an outgroup as a result of threat to the ingroup. We arranged for group members to receive feedback from another group, which was openly derogatory, casting aspersions on the ingroup's intellectual abilities; only slightly negative; or mildly positive (Brown and Ross, 1982). The reactions to those different levels of threat were quite consistent: in the high and moderate threat conditions, annoyance with the outgroup significantly increased; in the low threat participants it decreased. Grant (1992) has found similar reactions to identity threatening communications in the context of male–female relations, as has Voci (2006) in the context of relations between northern and southern Italians.

Sometimes the identity threat needs only to be implied rather than overtly expressed. Branscombe and Wann (1994) asked their American participants to watch a short film clip of a boxing match in which one fighter defeated the other (the clip was actually taken from the film *Rocky IV*). Half of them believed that the loser was Russian, the other half thought he was American. The blow to national pride experienced by the latter group resulted in members being more disparaging towards Russians, but this happened only to those participants for whom national identity was important.

Identification also moderates the effects of threats to gender identity. This was shown by Maass and colleagues (2003) in their innovative research on sexual harassment by men. Maass and her colleagues believe that men's offensive sexual behaviour towards women is often motivated by the offenders feeling that their gender identity is threatened. To demonstrate this thesis, Maass and colleagues (2003) devised a laboratory paradigm in which male participants interacted with what they believed to be a female participant (she was actually an experimental confederate) in an experiment on 'visual memory'. This experiment required each participant to select images from a number of computer files and to send these to the other participant, supposedly to be memorized for a future recall task. The file icons were labelled 'nature', 'animals', 'models' and 'porno'. The latter file was of particular interest, because it

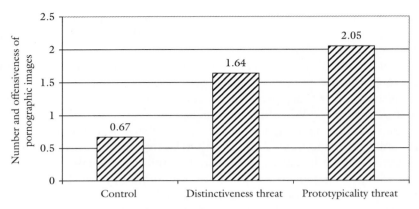

Figure 6.5   Sexual harassment as a response to identity threat. Source: Maass et al., 2003

contained sexually explicit images that independent judges had previously rated for offensiveness. The measure of sexual harassment was the number and offensiveness of images selected from the 'porno' file to be sent to the female confederate, who, by the way, clearly expressed her displeasure (via a chat line) at being sent any pornographic images at all. How did Maass and colleagues make their male participants feel threatened? In one study this was effected through the simple expedient of having the female confederate reveal herself to be a feminist (*or* a woman with more traditional gender role attitudes). The 'feminist' confederate was thought to pose a greater threat to the male participants because she was seen to challenge conventional gender inequalities. In the event, this 'feminist' confederate got sent significantly more – and significantly more offensive – pornographic images than the 'traditional' confederate. This effect of the threat was even more apparent for those men who identified more strongly with their gender.[7] In another study, the threat was manipulated either by implying that the male participant's score on a previously administered sex-role inventory placed him inside the distribution of *female* scores (and outside the male distribution), or – in a more group-based way – by suggesting that the male and female distributions were becoming increasingly similar. These two forms of threat were labelled, respectively, 'prototypicality threat' (because the first suggested that the participant was not prototypically masculine) and 'distinctiveness threat' (because the second suggested that the men of the group were no longer distinctively different from women). These two conditions were compared to a control group where it was stated that the participant's score was normal. The manipulations had predictable effects on the number and offensiveness of pornographic images sent to the woman: participants in the threat conditions, and especially in the prototypicality threat condition, sent more offensive pictures that those in control (see Figure 6.5). Again, these differences were exacerbated among the men who identified more highly with their gender.

Thus far we have considered prejudice as an undifferentiated negative intergroup reaction to threat. In fact, this may oversimplify things somewhat. A similar level of prejudice in two groups may mask very different underlying emotions. This is, anyway, the conclusion which resulted from some theoretical analyses of **intergroup emotions** (Cottrell and Neuberg, 2005; Iyer and Leach, 2008; Mackie and Smith, 2002; Smith,

1993). Although they differ somewhat in their emphases, these intergroup emotions theories share some common assumptions. The first one is that a person can experience emotions vicariously, through the group(s) that he or she belongs to. In other words, people do not have to experience some event directly – a threat, let's say – to feel some emotion; if they perceive their group to be in a particular situation, then they may well feel emotions *on behalf of that group*. For this to happen, there is one minimum precondition: that they identify sufficiently with that group for its fortunes to matter to them. This is, of course, by now a familiar idea to us from the discussion of social identity theory earlier in this chapter (Tajfel and Turner, 1986). A second common assumption of intergroup emotions theories is that the emotions which group members feel in any situation depend on how they perceive the ingroup in relation to some outgroup(s): Is an outgroup seen to be more powerful or weaker than the ingroup? Does the outgroup threaten the economic resources of the ingroup, or is it seen to be instead a source of 'contamination' because of the prevalence of harmful diseases or 'alien' values within it? For example, if the ingroup is seen as stronger than the outgroup, then anger might be a more probable emotion than fear (Smith, 1993). If the outgroup is perceived as a source of contamination rather than an economic threat, then disgust is more likely to result (Cottrell and Neuberg, 2005). A third shared assumption – and a critical one for us, students of prejudice – is that different emotions lead to different intergroup behaviours. Thus anger and contempt are thought to generate hostility, whilst fear and disgust are more likely to lead to avoidance (Cottrell and Neuberg, 2005; Smith, 1993).

This intergroup emotions perspective has started to generate an impressive literature (see Branscombe and Doosje, 2004; Iyer and Leach, 2008; Mackie and Smith, 2002). Let me present two examples of the research it has inspired which are relevant to our current concern with threat and prejudice. Mackie and colleagues (2000) arranged for their participants to read a series of newspaper headlines related to the issue of greater civil rights for gay people. Depending on experimental condition, the majority of these headlines supported gay rights *or* opposed them, thus conveying the impression to these student participants, all of whom were in favour, that their group's position in the country at large was either strong or weak. Participants then expressed various emotions towards the outgroup (opponents of gay rights) and indicated whether they would want actively to confront them or to avoid them instead. Recall that, according to intergroup emotions theory, being in a strong ingroup (vis-à-vis an outgroup) should lead to anger and confrontation, whilst being in a weak ingroup should lead to fear and avoidance. The results only partially bore out these predictions. Those in the 'strong' ingroup condition did show more anger than those in the 'weak' condition. However, the fear and avoidance reactions were less consistent with Mackie and colleagues' (2000) hypothesis. These emotions did not differ between the conditions, and indeed participants in the 'strong' condition showed even marginally more avoidance than those in the 'weak' condition (see also Dumont et al., 2003).

Cottrell and Neuberg (2005) took a different approach. They asked their white American participants to report how much they disliked and how negatively they evaluated each of nine outgroups (African Americans, Asian Americans, gay men, fundamentalist Christians, and so on). They also elicited their emotional reactions to each of these groups (anger, disgust, fear), as well as the extent to which they believed that it posed a threat to the ingroup in various ways (to its health, physical safety, social values). On the general measure of prejudice (or dislike) there were, unsurprisingly, some substantial differences between outgroups: fundamentalist Christians, feminist activists and gay men attracted most prejudice; native Americans, Asian Americans and African Americans elicited least. The interesting part, however, was that outgroups with similar prejudice scores were associated with very different emotional reactions and perceptions of threat. For example the levels of prejudice towards Asian and African Americans were indistinguishable. However, African Americans aroused markedly more fear and anxiety than Asian Americans, and this fact was linked to perceptions of threat in connection with physical safety and property. Likewise, gay men and fundamentalist Christians were disliked in equal measure, but the former group elicited more disgust, perhaps because they were perceived to be a greater threat to health. Since similar levels of prejudice were masking such different emotions and perceptions of threat, it is plausible to conclude that people's behaviour towards the different groups might also have differed, although Cottrell and Neuberg (2005) did not investigate this aspect of the situation.

To conclude the section on threat, let me return to those two newspaper cuttings with which I began: islamaphobia in Switzerland and xenophobia in South Africa. The threats underlying these two antipathies are somewhat different. In the first case, what seems to be worrying many Swiss people is the potential impact of Islamic ideas and values on the Swiss way of life, on their cultural identity as a western Judeo-Christian nation. In the second case, the concerns are more concrete and economic: Zimbabwean immigrants are seen to be taking South African jobs or to be undercutting South African wages. Stephan and Stephan (2000) have incorporated both types of threat into their **integrated threat theory** (see also Stephan and Renfro, 2003). They labelled threats of the first type **'symbolic threats'**, which include any perceived threats to the way the ingroup chooses to define itself and to symbolize its identity. Such threats would include different religions, worldviews, cultural values or languages. The second type they called **'realistic threats'**, a phrase borrowed from the name of the realistic group conflict theory, which we encountered previously. These include economic competition, conflicts over land or other scarce resources and threats to the physical safety or survival of the ingroup. To these two classes of threat, Stephan and Stephan (2000) add **intergroup anxiety** – an apprehension about anticipated encounters with outgroup members, which is due to uncertainty as to how to behave, fears about how one will be treated (Stephan and Stephan, 1985) and negative stereotypes of the outgroup.[8] All four variables are thought to lead in the same direction: to more prejudicial attitudes and increased intergroup discrimination.

This integrated threat theory has been tested in a wide variety of intergroup contexts, generally with supportive results (Curseu et al., 2007; Meeus et al., 2008; Stephan et al., 1998, 1999, 2000, 2002, 2005). Sometimes symbolic threats prove to be the more powerful predictor of prejudice; sometimes it is realistic threats that take centre stage. Occasionally both kinds need to be simultaneously present in order for prejudice to be found (Stephan et al., 2005). Intergroup anxiety, where it has been included, is nearly always a reliable correlate of prejudice, as are negative stereotypes. Even work conducted outside the integrated threat framework finds reliable support for the role both of symbolic and of realistic threats (McLaren, 2003; McLaren and

Johnson, 2007). McLaren's (2003) study is particularly interesting because it involved a very large sample (over 6,000 respondents), representative of seventeen European countries. In this instance the measure of prejudice was anti-immigrant sentiment, as indexed by the desire to deport immigrants back to their country of origin. Both realistic and symbolic threats posed by minority groups were assessed, as well as a number of other potentially important variables (such as the number of minority group friends) and the percentage of immigrants in the country (another potential source of threat). In the event, the three most robust correlates of prejudice were realistic and symbolic threat (both positive) and contact (negative). Once these three variables are controlled, the percentage of immigrants in each country bears no relationship to prejudice (see Quillian, 1995). Moreover, potential sources of threat at an individual level (risk of becoming unemployed, income level risk) were mostly unrelated to prejudice, once those three powerful factors had had their effects. Finally, in an attempt to discover what led to feelings of threat (symbolic and realistic, combined), McLaren (2003) conducted further analyses. This time the percentage of foreigners in each country was reliably correlated with perceptions of threat (higher percentage being associated with more threat) but, crucially, this relationship was qualified by the contact variable: the percentage of foreigners was only clearly related to perceived threat for those who had no minority group friends; for those with many minority group friends, the foreigner variable was completely unrelated to threat. Here, then, intergroup contact can be seen to provide an important 'buffer' against a potentially threatening demographic variable like the proportion of foreigners. In Chapter 9 I shall have occasion to provide many other examples of the positive effects of intergroup contact.

Before concluding this chapter, there is one aspect of the integrated threat theory which deserves closer attention. It will be recalled that one of the threats proposed by Stephan and Stephan (2000) is that of negative stereotypes about the outgroup. I must say I have always been rather puzzled by this. To my mind, it is a little odd to have as a hypothesized predictor of prejudice a variable which many regard as a component of prejudice itself! It is interesting that the status of negative stereotypes in the model has not escaped the attention of researchers. Stephan and colleagues (2002) themselves, in perhaps the most comprehensive test of the model, found that, empirically, this variable sat more comfortably as an *antecedent* of threat rather than as a form of threat itself. An even more plausible suggestion has been made by Curseu and colleagues (2007). In their study of Dutch employees' attitudes towards immigrant workers, they found little support for the Stephan and Stephan's (2000) hypothesis that negative stereotypes act as a threat alongside other threats (symbolic, realistic, anxiety). Instead, their data indicated that negative stereotypes should be considered as an *intervening* variable, partially mediating the effects of the other threats on prejudice.

In this chapter I have been concerned with the origins of prejudice, which lie in the relationships between groups. As we have seen, intergroup relations have implications for the groups' material well-being and physical safety, for the social identities of their members, for their sense of satisfaction or dissatisfaction with their group's social position, and for how secure or threatened they feel. If I am asked, as I sometimes am, to identify the most important factors in the genesis of prejudice, it is to the material in this chapter that I point. Prejudice is above all an intergroup phenom-enon, and so it should not surprise us if intergroup variables are pre-eminent in its causation.

Summary

1   Prejudice can usefully be regarded as the outcome of conflicting group goals. Research shows that groups competing for scarce resources typically display more biased attitudes and greater mutual animosity than groups which are co-operating to achieve jointly desired objectives.

2   Conflicting interests are not, however, necessary for the arousal of mild forms of prejudice. Groups show a tendency towards intergroup discrimination in the most minimal group situations. One explanation of such spontaneous ingroup favouritism is based on the need for a positive social identity. Social identities are thought to be maintained by making positively biased intergroup comparisons, so as to achieve some distinctiveness for the ingroup.

3   Social identity processes are relevant in two main ways for understanding preju-dice. Groups which are very similar to each other may be more biased in order to enhance their mutual distinctiveness, but only if group members identify with them sufficiently strongly. Groups of unequal status do not show the same levels of ingroup favouritism; typically, higher-status groups are more biased than low-status groups – unless destabilizing or delegitimating factors are at work, tending to undermine the status hierarchy.

4   Strength of group identification plays an important role in explaining preju-dice, but not in the obvious way – through the claim that greater identification leads to more prejudice. This claim is true only if intergroup comparisons are salient, or if the ingroup is defined in an essentialist way (in other words, if its definition implies that the ingroup has some fixed essence). More importantly, group identification *moderates* the effects of other variables: people who are more strongly attached to their ingroups usually react more sharply to other factors known to instigate prejudice.

5   Prejudice towards an outgroup can also be caused by a sense of relative dep-rivation – the perception that one's own group is not doing as well as one believes it should be doing. Such expectations can derive from one's memory of recent gains/losses made by the ingroup or, more often, from comparing the ingroup's position with that of an outgroup. Much research confirms the importance of rela-tive deprivation in determining prejudice, although occasionally a paradoxical effect of relative gratification has also been observed: groups expecting to do well in the future are sometimes more prejudiced than those anticipating little change.

6   An overarching cause of prejudice is threat. Threats may take material forms (as threats to economic well-being or to physical safety), or they may be more symbolic in nature (like threats to cultural values or identity). Particular threats often instigate specific emotional responses in group members, and these, in turn, lead to different behaviours towards outgroups.

Notes

1 Except in relatively rare circumstances, such as choosing to have a sex change operation or artificially changing the colour of one's skin. In any case, such extreme 'passing' strategies can be fraught with difficulties (see Breakwell, 1988).

2 This is a matter of some dispute. According to one of the architects of SIT, the theory never stated or implied this hypothesis (Turner, 1999). However, without wishing to enter into a protracted textual dispute with my one time collaborator and still greatly respected colleague, I think it is fair to say that not everyone shares his view (see Brown, 2000b and Mummendey et al., 2001b for further discussion of the matter).

3 In fact the analysis was a little more complex than this. When analysing longitudinal data to test a causal hypothesis, it is necessary to control for the dependent measure – in this case, attitude – at the earlier time point. Thus the crucial non-significant relationships were actually partial correlations between pre-election identification and post-election attitude, controlling for pre-election attitudes (see Finkel, 1995).

4 According to my dictionary, this term stems from a Jewish religious custom whereby a high priest symbolically laid the sins of a people on to a goat, which was then allowed to escape into the wilderness (*Chambers 20th Century Dictionary*, 1979). How ironic, therefore, that Jews themselves have so often become the scapegoats for the 'sins' of racist societies throughout human history.

5 The 'J' in the J-curve hypothesis comes from considering a graph of this rise and fall in standards. It resembles the curve of a letter 'J' laid upside down and at an angle.

6 The measures were focused on the respondents' *personal* life conditions rather than on the conditions of their group. Thus the measures of deprivation and gratification are at an individual level, which makes the results obtained from these measures all the more surprising.

7 The participants' social dominance orientation also magnified the effects of experimental condition.

8 Although intergroup anxiety and negative stereotypes featured prominently in the original model (Stephan and Stephan, 2000) and in many empirical tests of it, they are given slightly less emphasis in the revised model (Stephan and Renfro, 2002).

Further Reading

Ellemers, N., Spears, R., and Doosje, B. (eds) (1999) *Social Identity: Context Commitment, Content.* Oxford: Blackwell.

Mackie, D. M., and Smith, E. R. (eds) (2002) *From Prejudice to Intergroup Emotions: Differentiated Reactions to Social Groups.* Hove: Psychology Press.

Scheepers, D., Spears, R., Doosje, B., and Manstead, A. S. R. (2006) The social functions of ingroup bias: Creating, confirming or changing social reality. *European Review of Social Psychology* 17: 359–96.

Sherif, M. (1966) *Group Conflict and Cooperation: Their Social Psychology*, chs 1, 2, 5, 6. London: Routledge.

Tajfel, H. (1981a) *Human Groups and Social Categories*, chs 11–15. Cambridge: Cambridge University Press.

Walker, I., and Smith, H. (eds) (2002) *Relative Deprivation: Specification, Development and Integration.* Cambridge: Cambridge University Press.

7

Prejudice Old and New

In this chapter I want to pick up three themes which have recurred in various places earlier in the book. The first is that prejudice is not a static phenomenon. As I noted in Chapters 4 and 5, there is a good deal of research to show that the plainly pejorative stereotypes of some minority groups that were commonplace fifty years ago are much less in evidence today. This is as noticeable from casual observation of people's everyday conversations as it is from the results of more systematic opinion surveys. The second theme is that prejudice is not a monolithic concept. This should already be clear from the different chapter headings which have identified its characterological, cognitive and social dimensions, but it emerged especially strongly in the last chapter, where I noted that different measures of prejudice – ingroup bias, outgroup dislike, and so on – are often poorly correlated. The third theme is that there may be more to prejudice than meets the eye: there are some aspects of it that are outside our awareness or our control. We encountered these issues in Chapter 3 and 4, where I discussed several phenomena with automatic or unconscious characteristics.

These three themes come together in this chapter. I consider first whether prejudice is really on the wane. As I shall demonstrate, there is much evidence that it is, at least in western Europe and North America, where it has been most intensively studied, and at least at the level of publicly expressed attitudes. However, other evidence indicates that it is far from being extinct. Less obtrusive measures still reveal that people's behaviour towards members of an outgroup is often not the same as it is towards members of their ingroup. In the second part of the chapter I discuss various theories and associated prejudice measures which have been proposed to explain these changes in the way prejudice manifests itself. Although some of these are substantively different, what they all have in common is an assumption that new societal norms and changing political, economic and social relations between groups have combined to create a climate in which novel forms of prejudice can flourish. Underlying all these new kinds of prejudice is some residual negative affect associated with the outgroup. In the final section I address what has come to be something of a *cause célèbre* amongst many social psychologists: the relationship between explicit (pencil and paper) measures of prejudice and more implicit measures, which usually rely on different response

Table 7.1 Historical changes in white American ethnic stereotypes and attitudes

	1933[a]	1969[b]	2001[c]	
(A) Percentage of participants selecting negative traits to describe black Americans (student samples):				
Superstitious	84	13	2	
Lazy	75	26	12	
Ignorant	38	11	10	
Stupid	22	4	2	
Physically dirty	17	3	0	
Unreliable	12	6	5	
	1963	1977/8	1990	1996/7
(B) Percentage of participants endorsing prejudiced attitude statements (national surveys):[d]				
If black people came to live next door would you move?	45	14	5	2
There should be laws against mixed marriages between blacks and whites	62	29	21	13
Blacks and whites should go to separate schools	35	14	-	4[(1995)]

Note: [a] Katz and Braly (1933).
[b] Karlins et al. (1969).
[c] Madon et al. (2001a).
[d] Schuman et al. (1997).

times to undertake various speeded decision tasks. Should one type of measure be regarded as a 'truer' and more valid index of prejudice than the other?

Is Prejudice Declining?

It is relatively rare nowadays to hear prejudiced views in public, at least in the circles in which I live. By and large, people's conversations and interactions give every appearance of being models of tolerance and understanding. Surveys over past decades suggest that this is not a completely subjective impression. They indicate that intergroup attitudes and stereotypes have indeed become more positive. Table 7.1 presents some of these findings from the USA, and it would seem that there has been a progressive increase in tolerance over time. In the domain of gender, similar changes in attitudes towards women have occurred; research reveals less obviously sexist attitudes and greater support for gender equity in the workplace (Eagly and Mladinic, 1994; Kahn and Crosby, 1985; Sutton and Moore, 1985; Twenge, 1997).

It seems to me that these are real advances. Whatever the reasons for the changes and however many doubts we may harbour about their genuineness (as we shall see), it is no small achievement of sixty years of anti-racist and anti-sexist campaigning and social reform that people are actually less openly bigoted and discriminatory than they used to be. If we couple these attitudinal changes with an increase in the representation of women and of minority groups in non-stereotypical roles in the media (Gaertner and Dovidio, 1986), and with encouraging trends in their participation in professional occupations and managerial positions (Bureau of Labor, 2005; EOC, 2006; Morgan, 1988; Pettigrew, 1985; Ministry of Industry, 2005), then there is some reason not to feel completely pessimistic about the prospects for intergroup relations, at least in the domains of ethnicity and gender.

However, it would be foolish to feel too complacent about these changes. Other research reveals that everything in the garden is far from being rosy. To begin with, while it is true that some under-privileged groups have made advances in real terms in such areas as housing, education and employment, closer analysis reveals that in *relative* terms (that is, in relation to some other groups – see Chapter 6) inequalities are continuing, and may even be increasing in some respects (Pettigrew, 1985; US Department of Labor, 1992). Secondly, it is possible that the decreases in prejudiced attitudes observed towards minority groups and women may not be mirrored in similar increases in tolerance towards other groups. A series of surveys carried out in twelve European countries over a twelve-year period revealed a clear rise in anti-foreigner sentiment in the 1990s (Semyonov et al., 2006). In other words, the gains registered in the public acceptance of some groups seem to be matched by increases in prejudice towards others. Moreover, even if the so-called 'glass ceiling' for women aspiring to join the ranks of senior management has become more porous in recent years, it may be the case that it is being replaced by a 'glass cliff' – a metaphor used to describe the apparent tendency to appoint women to top executive positions when the business or organization faces a particularly challenging time (Ryan and Haslam, 2007). This may result in a disproportionate number of women being blamed for their organization's subsequent poor performance – a situation which sets them up to fail, as it were (ibid.).

There are other reasons for concern. Some commentators, faced with the evidence of decreasing prejudice in surveys, have suggested that much of this decrease is apparent rather than real (Crosby et al., 1980; Dovidio and Fazio, 1992). They point out that changes in societal norms and the existence of anti-discrimination legislation in many countries have made it increasingly unacceptable to express prejudice openly. Thus, the argument runs, people may only be paying lip-service to greater tolerance whilst really holding on to their prejudiced beliefs as fast as they ever did. There are several lines of evidence which point in this direction.

The first comes from research employing an experimental paradigm devised to reduce the social desirability effects which might be involved in responding to social sensitive attitude or stereotype measures (Sigall and Page, 1971). The paradigm is known as the **bogus pipeline**, because it involves connecting the participant, via skin electrodes, to an elaborate apparatus which supposedly can detect 'true' feelings. The experimenter goes to considerable lengths to convince the participant of the genuineness of the equipment which, in fact, is a complete façade. Then, under the guise of wishing to validate the machine, the experimenter presents the participant

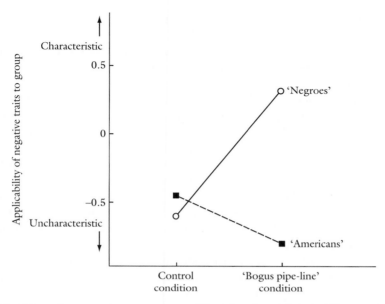

Figure 7.1 Measuring negative stereotypes with reduced social desirability contamination. This figure shows the mean for the six negative traits given in Table 2.1 (−3 to +3 scale). Adapted from Table 1 in Sigall and Page, 1971

with the critical measures and asks him/her to predict what reading the machine will give on each one. People's responses under this 'pipeline' condition are then compared to other peoples' responses, given without the benefit of all the technological trickery (control condition). The assumption is that participants in the 'pipeline' condition will be likely to 'predict' responses for the machine which are more in line with what they really believe than the responses of those in the control condition are. To illustrate this effect, consider the six negative adjectives used to describe blacks in Table 7.1. Sigall and Page used them (and several others) in order to obtain stereotypical judgements about 'negroes' and 'Americans' under 'pipeline' and control conditions. Figure 7.1 presents the mean scores for just those six traits, showing how characteristic of the two groups concerned white American participants thought they were. Notice that, in the normal control condition, these participants rated 'Americans' slightly more negatively than 'negroes'. On the other hand, in the 'bogus pipeline' condition the means were dramatically reversed: now 'negroes' are reported as being more 'ignorant', 'stupid', 'lazy' and so on than 'Americans'. Other studies have reached similar results (Roese and Jamieson, 1993).

A second body of research which suggests that intergroup attitudes, as measured by conventional techniques, may not be all that they seem to be is one which has used unobtrusive methods to observe people's actual behaviour towards outgroup members. Crosby and colleagues (1980) collated a number of studies which had observed helping behaviour in interethnic settings. Many of these studies were naturalistic studies in which participants were unaware that they were taking part in an experiment. In just under a half of the studies, more help was given to a recipient of the same ethnicity as the donor than to an outgroup recipient. (This was equally true for black and for white donors). Thus, whatever these participants might have *said* about blacks and whites as groups, when it came to the crunch significant numbers of them were *behaviourally* discriminating between 'needy' ingroup and 'needy' outgroup members.

Crosby and colleagues (1980) discovered one other interesting fact. When they examined only the studies which used white participants, they noticed that there was a noticeable tendency for higher intergroup discrimination in settings which did not involve direct, face-to-face contact with a potential black recipient. In such settings, three quarters of the studies found that significantly more help was given to fellow whites. In contrast, when the situation involved more immediate contact between donor and recipient – and hence when a refusal to help would be more publicly visible – only about one third of the studies registered pro-white bias in helping. As we shall see, this difference between people's behaviour in immediate and in more remote settings may be theoretically significant.

A third area of work relevant to this issue has focused on the disparity between people's public, and presumably rather controlled, responses on attitude scales and the like, and their more covert, and perhaps more spontaneous, non-verbal behaviours. One of the first attempts to study this disparity in an interethnic setting was made by Weitz (1972). Weitz asked her white college students to record a brief message for a later participant, of whom they had been given a short description. This description contained information about the target person's ethnicity (black or white), and also about his occupation (law student or petrol station attendant). Ratings of anticipated liking for this person were obtained, together with a series of less direct socio-metric measures (for example the choice of a task on which to interact with the person, the tasks varying in intimacy). Weitz analysed the voice tone of the recorded message for such features as warmth and admiration and then correlated the presence of these paralinguistic cues with the other measures of friendliness. Some of these correlations were intriguing. For those participants who anticipated interacting with a black person, there were *negative* correlations between the verbal rating of friendliness and the other indices (for example voice warmth and admiration, choice of task). The more friendliness they said they felt, the less actually came across in their non-verbal behaviours.

A similar disparity between obtrusive and unobtrusive measures of interethnic proximity was observed by Hendricks and Bootzin (1976). In their experiment, white women participants arrived at the laboratory and were casually invited to take a seat in a room. One of the seats was already occupied by a black or by a white confederate. The first and least obtrusive measure was simply which of the eight vacant seats was chosen by the participant. Then followed the more direct measure of proximity. The participant and the confederate had to stand at increasingly close distances from each other and to rate the degree of discomfort they felt. On the latter measure, where social desirability norms were probably very salient, no effect was found for the ethnicity of the confederate. However, the more covert seating measure revealed that participants chose to sit approximately one seat further away from the black confederate than from the white confederate – a significant difference. Recall also the experiment by Word and colleagues (1974) which I described in Chapter 4. There, too, whites chose to sit closer to a fellow white interviewee, talked longer to him/her and

Table 7.2 Correlations between measures within and outside participants' control

	Verbal	Self	Implicit	Non-verbal	Confederate	Observers
Explicit prejudice	.40*	.33*	−.09	.02	−.14	−.12
Verbal behaviour		.36*	.04	.08	−.17	−.15
Self-perception			.05	−.07	.11	.12
Implicit prejudice				.41*	.40*	.43*
Non-verbal behaviour					.34*	.32*
Confederate perception						.52*

Note: * indicates significant correlation (p<.05); all others n.s.
Source: Adapted from Table 1 in Dovidio et al., 2002 (modified)

made fewer speech errors than they did when the interviewee was black (see also Heinmann et al., 1981; Kleck et al., 1966).

More recently, Dovidio and his colleagues have provided further insights into this mismatch between what we say, what we do and how we come across to others in intergroup encounters (Dovidio et al., 2002). White participants, who had earlier filled out a standard questionnaire measure of prejudice, first undertook a computer-based task in which they had to make rapid decisions to positive and negative words; but these had been preceded by subliminally presented black or white schematic faces (see the techniques used to assess automatic stereotype activation discussed in Chapter 4). From the response times to make these decisions, Dovidio and colleagues constructed a measure of implicit prejudice – it was called this way because participants were quite unaware of the potential influence of the black and white faces. After this task, participants met with a black and then with a white confederate (or vice versa) and engaged them in a brief conversation, which was videotaped. After each conversation, participants had to record their impression of their own and their partners' behaviour; the confederates did likewise. Finally, at a later stage some independent observers coded both the verbal and the non-verbal behaviour displayed in each session (there were separate observers for the two types of behaviour). From this set of measures collected from the interactions, a series of bias scores was computed, each score representing a difference between the conversation with the black confederate and the conversation with the white confederate: differences in the participants' verbal behaviour, in their non-verbal behaviour, in their self-perceptions, in the perceptions of the confederates – and, lastly, the observers' global impressions. These bias scores were then correlated to the participants' scores on the explicit and implicit prejudice measures, which had been collected beforehand.

The pattern of these intercorrelations could not have been clearer. All the measures under the participants' conscious control correlated significantly with each other (see top left portion of Table 7.2); all the measures *outside* their control correlated with each other (see bottom right portion of Table 7.2); but members of these two classes of measure were quite unrelated. These findings raise two intriguing questions: which class of measure provides the 'truer', or the more valid, indicator of prejudice? How are we to understand the apparent dissociation between the two classes of measures? Answers to these questions have stimulated so much interest amongst social psychologists in recent years that they deserve a separate section to themselves. So I will return to them later in the chapter, after I will have considered other theories and methods that sought to understand how contemporary forms of prejudice have changed, and to provide new ways of measuring them.

New Forms of Prejudice

The observation that levels of overt prejudice were falling whilst other forms of discrimination continued has stimulated a number of new conceptualizations of prejudice over the past thirty years. The new forms of prejudice come in a multitude of guises: **symbolic**, **modern**, **aversive** and **ambivalent racism**, **subtle prejudice**, **modern** and **ambivalent sexism**, **neo-sexism**. Although there are important differences between these various constructs, they all have enough in common to justify my treating at least some of them together, under the same headings. For simplicity's sake I have kept these headings to three.

The first focuses on those approaches which claim that 'old-fashioned' or 'red-neck' prejudice is gradually being supplanted by a 'modern' form, in which the antipathy towards outgroups is expressed symbolically or indirectly. Although there is little consensus amongst the proponents of these new forms of prejudice as to their content or their origins, the proponents themselves do share a perspective focused on individual differences, in the sense that the goal has been to find reliable ways of distinguishing people who score high or low on some psychometric scale and then to examine correlates of that distinction. The second cluster of approaches places greater emphasis on situational factors. One of the main themes here has been that prejudice nowadays often takes the form of an 'aversive' response, sometimes as a reaction to anxiety-provoking situations. Thus, so long as there are no very explicit norms governing what should be said or done, people may display their prejudice by interacting in ways which subtly distance them from the outgroup person. The third set of approaches regards prejudice as having being transformed from a simple negative attitude or antipathy into something more ambivalent, an attitude with both negative and positive components, even if the positive aspects may be more apparent than real.

Modern prejudice

The first suspicion that some new kind of prejudice might be afoot came from a study of voting behaviour in the 1969 Los Angeles election for city mayor (Sears and Kinder, 1971). That election was essentially between a conservative white incumbent mayor and a liberal black city councillor. Sears and Kinder found, to their surprise, that people's preference for the former candidate was not reliably correlated to their prejudice level as measured on conventional attitude items – which tap into beliefs about black intellectual inferiority, opposition to school integration, and the like (see Table 7.3 for typical items). On the other hand some other questions, which were concerned more with the alleged economic and social advances made by minority groups and with social policies aimed at the redressing of past inequalities, were predictive of an electoral preference for the more conservative politician.

Findings like these led Sears and his colleagues to propose that a new form of racism had supplanted the older and more blatant kinds of bigotry, familiar from the 1930s

Table 7.3 Some items used to measure modern and old-fashioned racism

Modern racism

1 Over the past few years, blacks have received more economically then they deserve.
2 Over the past few years, the government and news media have shown more respect for blacks than they deserve.
3 Blacks are getting too demanding in their push for equal rights.
4 Discrimination against blacks is no longer a problem in the United States.

Old-fashioned racism

1 If a black family with about the same income and education as you moved next door, would you mind it a lot, a little, or not at all?
2 How strongly would you object if a member of your family had friendship with a black – strongly, somewhat, slightly or not at all?
3 Generally, do you feel blacks are smarter, not as smart, or about as smart as whites?
4 Generally speaking, I favour full racial integration (reversed item).

Source: Adapted from Tables 2 and 4 in McConahay, 1986

and the 1940s (Henry and Sears, 2002; McConahay, 1986; Sears, 1988). According to these authors, there were several reasons for this phenomenon. As we have already noted, changing societal norms meant that open expressions of prejudice were now socially frowned upon. Thus the predictive utility of traditional prejudice measures was reduced as a result of the influence of these factors of social desirability. Nevertheless, given the long history of racism in the United States and elsewhere, it was to be assumed that some residual anti-black affect would still comprise the socialization experience of most whites. In addition, the political demands of minority groups and the introduction of such policies as compulsory school bussing and positive discrimination threatened traditional western values based on meritocratic principles – like individual freedom of choice and equality of opportunity. The perceived violation of these abstract values, then, was thought to be an important component of the new form of prejudice, especially when coupled with the culturally socialized negative affect towards blacks. McConahay (1986) has summarized the modern racist's outlook on the world thus: discrimination no longer exists, because all groups enjoy the same civil and economic rights; blacks are making too many demands too quickly; these demands are unfair; therefore any gains they have made are undeserved.

Before we examine how this construct has been measured, three further features of the approach should be mentioned. The first is that modern racists are to be distinguished from 'old-fashioned' racists mainly through their beliefs about the attributes of blacks as a group. It is true that they share with **old-fashioned racists** some negative feeling towards blacks, but it is presumed that they do not endorse the traditional negative stereotypes of blacks as 'stupid' and 'lazy'; nor do they necessarily agree with Deep South segregationist views about separate schools, mixed marriages and the like. The second feature consists in the importance attached to the violation of deeply held western values among the factors which drive the modern racist's attitude. Indeed the conflict of values, rather than any immediately perceived threat to personal interests, is the core component of the ideology. Thus it is thought that what upsets modern racists is not so much that blacks may be going to the same school as their children, but that the educational policy of enforced bussing, designed as it is to achieve better ethnic balances within city schools, contradicts or denies the parents' 'right' to choose a school for their children. Finally, it is claimed that the techniques used to measure modern racism are less reactive than conventional instruments because they tap into subtle and indirect aspects of prejudice rather than into its more blatant features. This, it is felt, makes them less prone to the kinds of bias related to social desirability response which I considered in the last section.

Some of the items used to measure modern racism are presented in Table 7.3, where they are contrasted with more traditional racism items. When such items are factor analysed, it turns out that these two clusters of items tend to load on separate factors – which supports the distinction between the two types of prejudice that modern racism theorists have made (McConahay, 1986). However, the separation is not complete and modern and old-fashioned racism are usually substantially correlated to each other (ibid.; Henry and Sears, 2002). This correlation can be read two ways. It could mean that the two constructs are not as different as it is claimed, or it could support the idea, circulated in modern racism theory, that both types of prejudice share a common origin in negative feelings towards black people. One way to decide which of these two interpretations is the more tenable one is by seeing how well, the different scales can predict other attitudes and behaviour towards black people that could reasonably be interpreted as prejudiced, or at least as illiberal.

One study designed to examine this question was undertaken by McConahay (1982). He used both kinds of measures in order to try to predict people's attitudes against compulsory bussing in Kentucky, USA. In addition, he attempted to assess the extent to which respondents had a direct personal interest in the bussing issue – for example by having children of school age. The results were clear-cut. The largest single correlate of negative attitudes to bussing was modern racism. Old-fashioned racism was also a reliable predictor, as was a simple feeling about blacks 'thermometer' measure, but both of these correlations were much weaker than that obtained for the modern racism scale. Self-interest did not correlate at all (see also Jacobson, 1985, Kinder and Sears, 1981, Kluegel and Smith, 1983 and McConahay, 1986). The ability of these new scales of prejudice to predict people's attitudes towards governmental policies on ethnic integration was subsequently confirmed in three large surveys conducted in California which used a short version of the symbolic racism scale – a close cousin of the modern racism scale (Henry and Sears, 2002). Symbolic racism was correlated to an opposition to ethnic policies independently of old-fashioned racism and conservative political beliefs (see also Sears and Henry, 2005 and Tarman and Sears, 2005).

The idea that prejudice may have developed new disguises is not confined either to the United States or to the black–white context in which it originated. Researchers in other geographical and social domains have also found that scales of modern prejudice have usefully predicted people's intergroup judgements. In Australia, Augoustinos and colleagues (1994) adapted McConahay's (1986) scale to focus on whites' attitudes towards aboriginal Australians. They found that this measure correlated with the degree of endorsement of positive and negative attributes associated with aborigines. We, too, have developed a modern racism measure, this time for use in a British context, and we have also found that it correlates with various

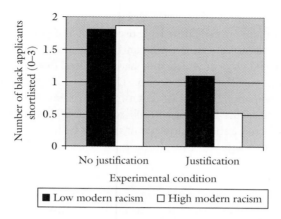

Figure 7.2 Modern racism and 'legitimate' justification to discriminate. Adapted from Table 1 in Brief et al., 2000

non-reactive measures of intergroup bias (Lepore and Brown, 1997). An adaptation of the modern racism scale to measure prejudice against Arab peoples was correlated with people's willingness to join an anti-Islamic organization (Echebarria-Echabe and Guede, 2007).

Modern (or symbolic) racism measures have proved to be remarkably durable and useful tools for social psychologists in a wide variety of contexts. A common use of these measures considers them *independent* variables, in an attempt to see if they predict people's responses in intergroup settings. We have already encountered this usage in Chapter 4, where such a measure was used to see if it could differentiate people's automatic stereotypic reactions (Devine, 1989; Lepore and Brown, 1997; Wittenbrink et al., 1997). A more applied example of such usage has been provided by Brief and colleagues (2000). These researchers reasoned that, characteristically, modern racists will not discriminate in an obvious way; they will only do so if they can find some 'legitimate' justification, which is in line with their traditional values. Accordingly, Brief and colleagues presented their participants (who had previously been tested for modern racism) with the hypothetical employment decision of choosing three candidates from a pool of ten: the three were to be shortlisted for a marketing position. Half of the ten applicants (three black, two white) appeared to be well qualified, the remainder (all white) were clearly unqualified. In one condition participants read a memo from the chief executive of the company which indicated that, because very few of their customers were from ethnic minorities, it would be preferable to select white personnel for the marketing position; in the other condition there was no such memo. Brief and colleagues (2000) believed that the presence of such a direct instruction from a legitimate authority would provide modern racists with the 'excuse' they were looking for to reveal their prejudice; without it, showing discrimination would be untenable. The results confirmed this hypothesis. In theory the participants could have chosen up to three black candidates, and indeed they should have chosen at least one, because five of the white candidates were manifestly unsuitable. In the event, they chose an average of just over one (1.4), but this varied both according to condition and according to their modern racism scores. As can be seen from Figure 7.2, the high and the low racists only differed in the 'justification' condition: the modern racists on average selected well under one black candidate.

But, since the various modern racism scales were intended as indicators of prejudice, it is no surprise that many investigators have used them as *dependent* measures, to assess the impact of other variables. Branscombe and colleagues (2007) asked white participants to think of all the ways in which they had benefited from (*or* had been *dis*advantaged by) belonging to their ethnic group. The intention of this instruction was to highlight these participants' feelings of illegitimate privilege – which, as we learned in Chapter 6, might constitute a threat to their social identity. As a defence against that threat, they might increase their endorsement of such beliefs as 'discrimination against blacks is no longer a problem' or 'over the past few years, blacks have received economically more than they deserve' – core components of the modern racism scale (see Table 7.3). So it proved: those in the 'advantaged' condition showed more modern racism than those in the 'disadvantaged' condition, and this was particularly so for participants who identified strongly with their ethnic group (Branscombe et al., 2007).

Because modern racism scales were designed to capture a kind of prejudice that is symbolic rather than direct in nature, one might expect them to react to events that are emblematic of race relations in a country. One such notable event was the 1995 murder trial of O. J. Simpson. Simpson was an extremely prominent African American sportsman who had been accused of murdering his wife. The trial dominated the news media in the USA (and around the world) for weeks, and the announcement of the verdict ('Not guilty') provoked still further discussion throughout the country. Three social psychologists had the foresight to realize that people's reactions to the verdict might reflect, *or be reflected by*, their attitudes to modern racism (Nier et al., 2000). Accordingly, they measured white students' modern racism one week before, one week after, and then again nine weeks after the jury's decision. At the second testing point they divided their sample into three groups, according to whether the students agreed with the verdict (about 17 per cent), believed that O. J. Simpson should have been found guilty (55 per cent), or were undecided (28 per cent). Would it have been possible to predict who was in each group just by knowing their modern racism scores two weeks earlier (that is, one week before the verdict)? Not at all! The three groups had virtually identical pre-verdict modern racism scores. But did their modern racism scores change after the verdict? Indeed they did! Those in the 'guilty' or 'undecided' groups showed strong increases in modern racism scores immediately after the trial, increases which persisted for the next two months. Those in the 'not guilty' group showed little reliable change (Nier et al., 2000).

A distinction similar to the one between modern and old-fashioned has been proposed by Pettigrew and Meertens (1995) (see also Meertens and Pettigrew, 1997). Their labels are **subtle** and **blatant racism**. The latter corresponds to old-fashioned prejudice. Subtle racism has much in common with modern racism, since it, too, consists in part of a defence of traditional individualistic values together with beliefs that minority groups are in receipt of undeserved favours. However, Pettigrew and Meertens also propose that subtle racism also includes a perceived exaggeration of the cultural differences between the majority ingroup and the minority outgroup ('How different or similar do you think West Indians living here in Britain are to other British people like yourself?' – different, that is, in values, sexual values and practices, religious beliefs and practices, and language), and a denial of any positive emotional response towards outgroup members ('Have you ever felt sympathy/admiration for West Indians living here?'). In contrast to blatant racists, subtle racists do not express overtly negative feelings towards minority groups; they merely withhold any positive feelings. On the basis of a large survey conducted in four European countries, Pettigrew and Meertens found some support for their hypothesized distinction (see Meertens and Pettigrew, 1997; Pettigrew and Meertens, 1995). Their scales of blatant and subtle racism were, as usual, quite well correlated, but they did seem to load on two separate factors[1] in a **factor analysis**. Both scales were positively correlated to general ethnocentrism, support for racist political organizations and fraternalistic relative deprivation (although the correlations with the latter two measures were generally weaker for subtle racism) and negatively correlated to intergroup contact (Pettigrew, 1998; Voci and Hewstone, 2003). There was also some evidence that subtle and blatant racists had different views on various immigration and deportation policies: blatant racists happily endorsed forced wholesale emigration for all minority groups; subtle racists supported deportation only for those who had no immigration papers or had committed crimes.

So far I have only considered modern prejudice towards ethnic groups. However, some have proposed that a similar symbolic form of prejudice is emerging in other intergroup contexts. Benokraitis and Feagin (1986), for example, suggested that women, too, are often the victims of covert forms of discrimination – what the authors called 'modern sexism'. Bearing in mind the idea of trying to measure this new kind of gender prejudice, we developed a scale of neo-sexism (Tougas et al., 1995). The items for this scale were drawn from some existing modern racism scales (see Table 7.3), adapted to the gender domain; and we added some items of our own. We used this scale, together with a scale of old-fashioned sexism (Rombough and Ventimiglia, 1981) and a measure of men's collective interests in the employment domain, to predict the attitudes of male students towards affirmative action programmes for women. We found that, whilst old-fashioned sexism and neo-sexism were positively correlated, out of the two only the latter one reliably predicted attitudes towards affirmative action: the higher the sexism score, the less positive the attitudes. In contrast to what was found in some of the research on modern racism reviewed earlier, here the collective interest measure[2] was also an important factor, correlating positively with both kinds of sexism but negatively with affirmative action policies. A follow-up study of male employees in a firm which had recently implemented an affirmative action programme produced essentially the same results (Tougas et al., 1995). Contemporaneously, Swim and colleagues (1995) devised a modern sexism scale. The rationale for this measure is very similar to that for the neo-sexism scale, and indeed the two measures tend to co-vary quite closely and to correlate similarly to other indicators (Campbell et al., 1997).

Some current attitudes towards stigmatized groups may also be construed as modern prejudice. One such group is that of fat people in the United States, who are the subject of enough social, educational and employment discrimination to have formed their own National Association to Advance Fat Acceptance (Crandall, 1994; *Independent*, 13 June 1994). Crandall (1994) has devised a measure of anti-fat prejudice – a measure which he believes to be conceptually similar to scales of modern racism. Like the latter, his scale has two correlated components: a measure of anti-fat affect and a measure tapping into the tendency to attribute excess weight to the lack of willpower in the fat person. Crandall also found that the two main sub-scales of his anti-fat measure were correlated to individualistic and conservative value orientations but not at all with the respondent's own obesity, thus apparently mirroring the correlations noted earlier between low personal self-interest and modern racism. Cowan and colleagues (2005) have come up with measures of old-fashioned and modern heterosexism, a development much in line with the other measures of contemporary prejudice discussed above. It is likely that, as social psychologists widen the scope of their enquiries, similar patterns will emerge in prejudice towards groups such as the elderly, people with Aids and people with disabilities.

The many variants of the modern prejudice thesis have not escaped criticism. Most of these critiques have focused on modern *racism*, but I shall try to generalize their arguments so as to make them apply to other new forms of prejudice too. Three issues dominate these debates.

The first issue is: How distinct are these new forms of prejudice from their old-fashioned counterparts? As I noted earlier, the two kinds of prejudice – modern (or symbolic) and old-fashioned, subtle and blatant – consistently co-vary, usually at around the 0.6 level. Now, although this is in line with what theories of modern prejudice predict, because both scales have in common an anti-outgroup component, some have argued that the two measures should be regarded as tapping into a single construct[3] (Sniderman and Tetlock, 1986). Much of this argument is highly technical and centres on how one should conduct and then interpret factor analyses of items which purport to measure the two kinds of prejudice (Coenders et al., 2001; Meertens and Pettigrew, 1997; Pettigrew and Meertens, 2001; Sniderman et al., 1991; Tarman and Sears, 2005). The rancorous debate between Coenders and colleagues (2001) and Pettigrew and Meertens (2001) encapsulates the nub of the matter. Coenders and colleagues (2001) re-analysed the same data set as Pettigrew and Meertens (1995) using some slightly different assumptions and analytic techniques. They concluded that the so-called subtle and blatant items did not fall neatly into two clear factors, as Pettigrew and Meertens (1995) had claimed. Instead, most of the subtle items seemed to factor together with the blatant items, with the exception of the four items tapping into perceived cultural differences (I shall have more to say on those items presently). Moreover, the correlates of the prejudice items (for instance educational level, relative deprivation, conservatism) were also generally rather different from the correlates of the cultural difference items. In response, Pettigrew and Meertens (2001) queried what they called Coenders and colleagues' atheoretical approach to data analysis and offered a variety of further statistical arguments in defence of their original formulation. However, for me, more important than these statistical disputes is the fact the two types of prejudice do have reliably distinct predictive uses. Scales of modern prejudice correlate with attitudes towards such issues as school bussing, affirmative action programmes, immigration and the harmfulness of homophobic hate speech in ways that old-fashioned measures simply do not; or the latter correlate to such attitudes, but do so less strongly or in a different direction (Cowan et al., 2005; Henry and Sears, 2002; Meertens and Pettigrew, 1997; Tougas et al., 1995). Ultimately, it is this **discriminant validity** of modern prejudice measures that is the strongest argument in their favour.

A second issue is: How subtle or indirect are these new measures of prejudice? Are they really less liable to socially desirable ways of responding than the older varieties? Considering just the surface content of the items comprising the scales, it seems doubtful. It is usually fairly obvious what the 'socially correct' direction to answer is.

Moreover, sample mean scores typically tend to be skewed towards the non-prejudiced end of the scale (Augoustinos et al., 1994; Cowan et al., 2005; Devine et al., 1991; Lepore and Brown, 1997; Tougas et al., 1995; Locke et al., 1994). However, more encouragingly for the scales' proponents, Ratazzi and Volpato (2003) found that neither blatant nor subtle prejudice was reliably correlated with an individual tendency to present oneself in a desirable light, and judges' ratings of the individual items indicated that blatant items were regarded as slightly – but significantly – less socially acceptable than subtle items. Nevertheless, if these modern measures of prejudice are truly indirect or subtle, then scores on them should not be affected by the ethnicity of the researcher administering the test or by having participants answer privately (anonymously) or in public. McConahay and colleagues (1981) conducted two experiments in which they varied the ethnicity of the experimenter and found that only old-fashioned racism was affected by the presence of a black (rather than a white) experimenter; modern racism scores did not differ between the experimenters.

Unfortunately, with the passage of time others have found modern racism scales to be more reactive than this. Fazio and colleagues (1995) repeated McConahay and colleagues' (1981) experiment of varying the ethnicity of experimenter. Participants first completed the modern racism scale in an anonymous and collective testing session. Then two to three months later they completed it again, this time individually, in the presence of a white or black experimenter. Everyone's scores declined somewhat the second time round, but those in the black experimenter condition showed a more dramatic decrease (by fully four points, as compared to only one point in the white condition). Moreover, the test/re-test correlation was also much lower in the black experimenter condition, indicating not only that the overall mean had dropped, but also that the rank ordering of participants within that condition had changed. In a subsequent experiment, Fazio and colleagues (1995) also found that there was a correspondence between modern racism scores and an implicit measure of prejudice only for participants who had earlier indicated that they were not much motivated to control their expression of prejudice in public. Lambert and colleagues (1996) found further evidence of the modern racism scale's sensitivity to social desirability. They asked participants to form some judgements about a hypothetical black person described in a brief paragraph. Half the participants believed that they would be required to discuss their judgements with some of their peers (public condition); the remainder were told that their judgements would remain confidential (private condition). In the latter condition there was little correspondence between their modern racism scores and their judgements of this one black individual; in fact, the correlation was, if anything negative. However, in the public condition the modern racism scores and individual judgements were positively correlated. The strong suspicion is that, when answering the modern racism scale, participants were trying to present themselves as non-prejudiced, presumably as they would have done in the 'public' judgemental task.

A third issue concerns the interpretability of responses to some items in modern prejudice scales. Focusing particularly on the symbolic racism construct, Sniderman and Tetlock (1986) point out that an item like 'It is wrong to set up quotas to admit black students to college who don't meet the usual standards' (Kinder and Sears, 1981), to which agreement is taken to indicate symbolic racism, could arguably be used as an indicator of a *non-racist* response. For example, it is possible to imagine liberal objections to ethnic quotas and affirmative action on the grounds that such measures are patronizing towards minority groups and undermine their subsequent academic or professional achievements. Similarly, in Pettigrew and Meertens' (1995) subtle racism scale there are four items measuring perceived cultural differences (high difference is scored in the racist direction). Yet the position of many ethnic minorities and progressive policy-makers concerned with developing multicultural awareness is precisely to stress the importance of recognizing and respecting intergroup differences as an antidote to the cultural annihilation implied by assimilationist philosophies. And it is significant, I think, that the cultural differences sub-scale is often more weakly correlated (if at all) to other theoretically relevant predictors of prejudice (relative deprivation, contact, educational level; see Coenders et al., 2001; Pettigrew, 1997).

A related criticism has been made by Sniderman and colleagues (1991). These authors have extended their argument about the interpretability of modern racism scales so as to contend that such scales may, in fact, be measuring instead a kind of principled conservatism. This is an ideological position closely tied to the defence of traditional values (a component of modern racism scales) but not necessarily racist in outlook. I don't find this argument very convincing, for the simple reason that most recent studies examining correlates of modern prejudice routinely control for political attitude and yet still find highly reliable associations of prejudice with other variables of interest (Meertens and Pettigrew, 1997; Sears and Henry, 2005; Tarman and Sears, 2005).

Ambivalent prejudice

As we have seen, theories of modern prejudice propose that contemporary expressions of prejudice are determined by a mixture between a strong adherence to an ideology of individualism, a desire not be seen as being obviously prejudiced and an underlying anti-outgroup feeling. These sometimes conflicting motives are thought to drive people's intergroup attitudes and behaviour, most usually in a negative or discriminatory fashion. A second group of theories also posits that current intergroup attitudes derive from conflicting processes, but this time associated with simultaneously held positive and negative attitudes towards outgroups. Because of their focus on contemporaneous positivity and negativity, these theories can be called theories of *ambivalent* prejudice. I will deal with two such theories: racial ambivalence (Katz et al., 1986) and ambivalent sexism (Glick and Fiske, 1996). As we shall discover, although they share a nomenclature, these two theories differ sharply in their analysis of the psychological underpinnings of prejudice and the likely outcomes of it.

It was Myrdal (1944) who first suggested that white American intergroup attitudes might reflect a conflict between two values central to North American culture: *egalitarianism* (all should be equal under the law, everyone should have an equal chance in life) and *individualism* (one should only get what one works for or deserves). The first value might be expected to lead to concern for under-privileged groups (say, ethnic minorities) and to a desire to see greater social equality; the second might lead to 'victim' blaming or derogatory attitudes towards disadvantaged groups: if these are poor, uneducated and so on, this can only be due to a lack of effort on their part. Katz and colleagues (1986) picked up on this idea and suggested that many majority group members simultaneously hold both positive and negative attitudes towards ethnic minorities and that resolving the contradiction posed by these two sets of attitudes would often lead them to behave in an unstable and extreme fashion towards members of those groups: very favourably or very derogatorily.[4] Which direction this response will take, inspired as it is by ambivalence, is thought to depend on several factors, some specific to the situation (for instance cues that plausibly lead to particular attributions about the outgroup members' behaviour), some more related to the perceiver's own behaviour and self-image (for instance defences against ego-threatening inferences about whether s/he was responsible for the outgroup members' plight). Two ideas are central to this theory of racial ambivalence: the first is that the positive attitudes towards the outgroup are genuinely held, rather than being mere 'lip service', as in the 'modern prejudice' accounts; the second is that, when the ambivalence becomes highlighted, the experience is emotionally discomforting and people will work to reduce this discomfort. Again, this contrasts with 'modern prejudice' theories, which hypothesize that holders of modern prejudiced attitudes are either unaware of any underlying conflicting values or have already resolved them in a discriminatory fashion.

Several early experimental studies provided some nice illustrations of this ambivalence. Gergen and Jones (1963) arranged for participants to interact with someone who was alleged to be 'mentally ill' (or not). This is a classic example of a social category towards which many people may hold ambivalent attitudes – sympathy, but also fear or revulsion. This confederate's behaviour was made to seem predictable or unpredictable. When his behaviour had consequences for the participants, their subsequent evaluations of the confederate revealed just the kind of **response amplification** predicted by ambivalence theory: they became more favourable to the 'mentally ill' person in the predictable (positive outcome) condition (as compared to the 'normal' person), and less favourable in the unpredictable (negative outcome) condition (again, relative to the 'normal' confederate). Gibbons and colleagues (1980) observed exactly the same phenomenon, this time using a confederate with an apparent physical disability. *Behavioural* amplification has also been observed. Katz and colleagues (1979) led the participants to believe that they had unintentionally upset or inconvenienced a member of a stigmatized group (blacks, people with physical disability). When subsequently given the opportunity to help the 'victim', they did so to a greater degree than when the 'victim' had been white or without a disability.

In these studies the attitudinal ambivalence was assumed to be responsible for the extreme reactions, but this was never actually demonstrated to be so. The next step was to measure people's ambivalence directly. Accordingly, Katz and Hass (1988) administered separate scales of pro and anti-black attitudes to several samples of white participants, along with scales measuring humanitarian–egalitarian and protestant ethnic (individualist) values. They found that the pro-black and anti-black scales were only very weakly correlated (negatively), which thus indicated that the scales were picking up on *separate* positive and negative orientations towards blacks. Moreover, the pro-black scale was positively correlated to humanitarian–egalitarian values, whilst the anti-black scale was associated with individualism. Subsequently, Hass and colleagues (1991) constructed a measure of ambivalence by multiplying the pro and anti-black scale scores with each other (after some statistical transformation). This measure provides a good index of the extent to which people's scores on the two scales are simultaneously similar and extreme – an operational definition of ambivalence. Hass and colleagues (1991) showed that this ambivalence measure was positively correlated to the evaluation of a black collaborator in a 'success' condition, but negatively correlated in a 'failure' condition (see also Hass et al., 1992). Moreover, and consistently with the theorizing underlying the concept, the racial ambivalence scale (as measured by Hass and team, 1991) seems to be associated with emotional discomfort in a way in which modern racism does not (Monteith, 1996). To support the distinctiveness of ambivalent and modern prejudice, these two measures were quite uncorrelated (ibid.).

Although the racial ambivalence measure has not proved as popular a research tool as scales of modern, symbolic or subtle racism, it seems to me that it does capture something valuable about people's intergroup attitudes – namely the fact that they are not always homogeneously negative, but are sometimes an amalgam of favourable and unfavourable elements. A weakness of ambivalence theory is that it does not specify very clearly the direction the polarized response will take. As we have seen, ambivalence can lead both to greater denigration *and* to greater pro-sociability towards the stigmatized group member, and it is not easy to predict which one is most likely to occur.

In Katz and colleagues' (1986) formulation, the ambivalence that we may feel in relation to outgroups is a real one, because any positive intergroup attitudes are thought to be genuinely held and any outgroup sympathy is assumed to be honestly felt. Jackman (1994) offers a very different and altogether more sinister account of ambivalence. Like Katz and colleagues, her point of departure is that contemporary attitudes of dominant groups towards subordinate groups often contain clearly positive elements: whites may express admiration for what they see as the blacks' superior athletic or musical prowess; men will often profess affection, or even love, for women, extolling their supposed virtues of warmth and sensitivity. But in Jackman's analysis these seemingly favourable attitudes are something of an ideological charade; their real purpose is to maintain and reinforce existing power inequalities between the groups. Although at first glance this may seem rather paradoxical, Jackman argues that in most modern societies exerting one's dominance by brute force and coercion is either simply not feasible (for constitutional reasons) or too costly (not least because subordinate groups would be highly resistant). A strategy by far cleverer is to use persuasion, to offer lower status groups whatever blandishments are needed in order for them to accept their subordination. Sweet talk them into submission, in other words.[5]

Glick and Fiske (1996) reasoned in a similar way when developing their ambivalent sexism inventory. They argued that, in addition to old-fashioned sexism, and distinct from the modern forms of sexism discussed in the previous section, there is also **benevolent sexism**, a form of prejudice which seems to be very positive on the surface but which deep down reflects a view of women as essentially inferior to men. Benevolent sexism, in this view, has three aspects: *paternalism* – the idea that, since women are believed to be less powerful and to have less authority than men, they deserve men's protection; *gender differentiation* – a phenomenon familiar to us now as a consequence of categorization (see Chapter 3), in which men and women are seen as exaggeratedly different and where women may even be viewed as possessing more of certain positive attributes (warmth, emotional sensitivity), so long as these

Table 7.4   Sample items from the ambivalent sexism inventory

Hostile sexism

1   Women are too easily offended.
2   Women exaggerate problems they have at work.
3   Feminists are making entirely reasonable demands of men (reversed item).

Benevolent sexism

1   In a disaster, women ought not necessarily to be rescued before men (reversed item).
2   Women, compared to men, tend to have a superior moral sensibility.
3   Every man ought to have a woman whom he adores.

Source: From Glick and Fiske (1996), Appendix

do not threaten the main basis of men's 'superiority'; and *heterosexual intimacy* – the strongly normative tendency in most, if not all, human societies for men to seek romantic and sexual relationships with women. Since such relationships will require some minimal co-operation from women (except in cases of sexual violence, about which more presently), benevolent sexists' attitudes will often emphasize women's sexual allure and beauty.

With these thoughts in mind, Glick and Fiske (1996) devised a number of items, half of which were designed to capture old-fashioned sexism, or what they call **hostile sexism** (HS), and the remainder tapping this more positive seeming benevolent sexism (BS). Some sample items are shown in Table 7.4, where it can be seen that HS items are obviously negative in flavour and resemble those used to measure modern sexism or neo-sexism (Tougas et al., 1995; Swim et al., 1995). BS items, on the other hand, are more positive in tone and superficially seem to express rather favourable attitudes towards women.

In some extensive psychometric work, Glick and Fiske (1996) found that the eleven HS items tended to correlate well together and to form a single unitary scale. The eleven BS items, on the other hand, while correlating well with each other, did seem to be sub-divisible into paternalistic, gender differentiation and intimacy subscales. Nevertheless, the overall BS scale was internally reliable. A few other findings from this initial research are noteworthy. First, both men and women showed similar patterns of responding on the scales, in the sense that HS and BS factors could be identified for both, even if men tended to score higher than women. Secondly, HS and BS tended to be positively correlated to each other moderately well (in the .30–.50 range).[6] Thirdly, HS was correlated to modern sexism but BS was not, at least once people's level of HS was controlled for. Fourthly, HS was negatively correlated with overall evaluations of women whilst BS was *positively* correlated. These last two points are important in Glick and Fiske's argument that HS and BS are in fact measuring rather different kinds of prejudice – the one overtly negative, the other seemingly positive but subtly demeaning. These broad empirical findings have largely been borne out by others (see Conn et al., 1999; Masser and Abrams, 1999).

The publication of the ambivalent sexism inventory stimulated a minor explosion of interest into the workings and consequences of contemporary sexism, which was due in no small measure to the assiduousness and ingenuity of Glick and his colleagues. I will focus first on research that has used the scale at an individual level, then turn to some findings at societal level.

Recall that the ambivalent sexist is thought to have simultaneously positive and negative views of women, which reflect the benevolent and hostile aspects of his[7] overall attitude. If this is so, then, as in Katz and colleagues' (1986) racial ambivalence theory, one would expect ambivalent sexists to show more polarized evaluations of women, more extremely positive *and* negative. Glick and colleagues (1997) found exactly this when they asked male participants to generate up to ten 'types' of women ('career women', 'feminists', 'housewives' and so on) and then to rate these sub-types on positive and negative scales. As expected, the men's ambivalent sexism scores correlated positively with the variance in these ratings, indicating that more sexist men showed a greater range in their evaluations (in both directions).

More worryingly, HS and BS have been found to be correlated to several distinctly unflattering attitudes towards women, particularly in domains involving their sexual conduct. Nowhere is this more evident than in men's views about rape and rape victims. It is a well established fact that most rape perpetrators are known to their victims, either as a current boyfriend or as a casual acquaintance (Temkin and Krahe, 2008). This is in stark contrast to the conventional stereotype of the rapist as 'the stranger in a dark alley'. Now, although in law 'acquaintance' and 'stranger' rape should not be distinguished – the crucial legal issue only concerns consent – in many people's minds, and especially in the minds of sexists, there is a world of difference between the two types of offence. Viki and his colleagues have shown this in a series of studies in which they presented participants with one of two vignettes describing a hypothetical rape incident (Abrams et al., 2003; Viki and Abrams, 2002; Viki et al., 2004). In one, a woman meets a man at a party and at the end of the evening they end up at her flat and he rapes her. This was the acquaintance rape scenario. In the other, the woman is raped in an unlit street by a complete stranger. Generally participants blame the victim for her plight much less in the latter situation than in the former (Abrams et al., 2003). However, this victim blaming was particularly pronounced amongst benevolent sexists, especially in the 'acquaintance rape' situation (see Figure 7.3); in the 'stranger rape' case nobody attributed much blame to her. In another study, these views about the victim were mirrored in less blame being attributed to the perpetrator and in more lenient sentences being recommended, again primarily by benevolent sexists in the 'acquaintance' scenario (Viki et al., 2004). One interpretation of these results is that benevolent sexists' apparently favourable attitudes towards women only hold so long as they (the women) conduct themselves 'appropriately'. If they are seen to depart from the traditional script that benevolent sexists have written for them ('demure', 'chaste' and 'innocent'), then the benevolence quickly turns to blame.

What of hostile sexists? It is true that they also tend to blame the rape victim, but this is more generic blame and is not affected by the type of rape situation. Moreover, and in keeping with their more aggressive attitude towards women, they seem to show greater rape *proclivity*, but again only in the 'acquaintance' scenario (Abrams et al., 2003). That is, they were more likely to agree with suggestions that they too might have behaved similarly to the perpetrator. They are also

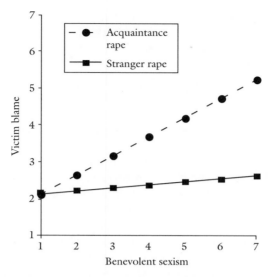

Figure 7.3 The relationship between benevolent sexism and victim blame in rape cases. From Abrams et al., 2003, Figure 1

more likely to be more tolerant of wife abuse, at least in societies with a more 'macho' attitude towards women (Glick et al., 2002). In employment settings also, hostile sexists are more likely to be openly discriminatory, since for them women in the workplace may appear as a direct threat to their superiority. So Masser and Abrams (2004) found that hostile sexists tended to rate female candidates for a managerial position as less employable, and Wiener and Hurt (2000) found that they regarded sexual harassment at work in a less severe way. In none of these instances were there any reliable correlations with BS, at least not once the effects of HS had been controlled for.

In addition to these effects at an individual level, Glick and Fiske (1996) speculated that sexism serves an ideological function by justifying and perpetuating gender inequalities in society. Moreover, because such gender inequalities seem to exist the world over, albeit in varying degrees, it should be possible not only to identify ambivalent sexism cross-culturally but also to observe a link between the prevailing levels of HS and BS in a country and the level of inequality in that country. This is exactly what Glick and his many international collaborators (in twenty-five countries in total) have found (Glick et al., 2000, 2004). In all countries except one (Peru), analysis of the ambivalent sexism inventory yielded a clear HS–BS structure. In most countries HS and BS were positively correlated, as they had been in the original Glick and Fiske (1996) study. There were some marked country differences in the average levels of HS and BS from highs (for men) of three or more in countries like Cuba, South Africa, Nigeria and Botswana, and lows of around two in Australia, England and the Netherlands.[8] Tellingly, though, these country differences in both HS and BS were correlated to country differences in objective indicators of gender inequality compiled by the United Nations. These indices included such figures as differences in percentages of men and women in managerial jobs, parliament, and different levels of education. The correlations were not always significant because of the relatively small number of countries involved, but the fact that they could be observed at all, and their respectable magnitude (all > .40), is quite remarkable.

In summary, what can we say about ambivalent prejudice? We should note, first of all, that ambivalent racism (Katz and Hass, 1988) and ambivalent sexism (Glick and Fiske, 1996) are rather differently conceived and very differently measured. The pro and anti-black scales of ambivalence measure are taken at their face value, as reflecting genuinely positive or negative sentiments to the outgroup, and are weakly and *negatively* correlated. In contrast, the HS and BS scales of Glick and Fiske's (1996) Ambivalent Sexism Inventory (ASI) measure, although apparently different in valence, are both thought to tap a desire to put women down and are usually moderately and *positively* correlated. Perhaps the most controversial element of Glick and Fiske's theory is their contention that the positive affect inherent in benevolent sexism actually belies an underlying disparagement, and therefore that the traditional definition of prejudice as antipathy is no longer adequate, if it ever was (see Chapter 1).

I find this a somewhat complicated matter to resolve. On the one hand, there can be no disputing the fact that aggregate benevolent sexism scores are associated with some negative outcomes for women (victim-blaming in rape cases, societal gender inequalities). This much clearly supports Glick and Fiske's view that BS is a disguised form of prejudice. However, the face validity of some of the BS items seems to me to be questionable. I believe it is possible for people to endorse several of the gender differentiation and heterosexual intimacy items for genuinely non-sexist reasons. For example, it is conceivable to me that a man could honestly believe in the 'superior moral sensibility' and 'more refined sense of culture and good taste' of women – to name two BS items – without at the same time believing that they should, as a consequence, be consigned to lower-status nurturing or domestic roles. Similarly, to agree that it is desirable to have and adore a romantic partner – two other BS items – does not, in itself, necessarily entail a paternalistic attitude towards women. This ambiguity of some of the BS items suggests that it might be fruitful to develop further the distinction between the three components of benevolent sexism. A hint that this may be necessary comes from Chapleau and colleagues' (2007) study of correlates of the 'rape myth acceptance' (a constellation of beliefs that justifies rape in certain circumstances: Burt, 1980). Instead of lumping together the three sub-scales of BS into a single index, Chapleau and colleagues (2007) used each of them as separate predictors, alongside HS. Hostile sexism, unsurprisingly, was positively correlated with rape myth acceptance. However, the three sub-scales of BS showed very different associations: zero for heterosexual intimacy; positive for gender differentiation; and negative for paternalism. At the very least, these findings suggest that benevolent sexism is a less unitary form of prejudice than it is often claimed to be.

Aversive prejudice

Earlier in this chapter I reviewed evidence from a variety of sources that indicated that differential reactions to white and black people – for example in offering them help – were most likely to occur when there were no very explicit social norms prescribing appropriate behaviour. In that same section I also noted research which had identified subtle differences in whites' non-verbal and relatively spontaneous behaviours when the interaction involved black rather than white participants. It was findings like these that prompted Gaertner and Dovidio (1986) to re-investigate Kovel's (1970) concept of 'aversive racism', a form of prejudice which, they thought, might underlie many white (American) people's contemporary behaviour towards members of ethnic minorities (see also Dovidio and Gaertner, 2004).

Like modern racism theorists, Gaertner and Dovidio believe that overt and blatant prejudice has been on the wane for some time. Many white people, they suggest, do genuinely endorse principles of tolerance and ethnic equality, and indeed may even support progressive public policies. On the other hand, coexisting with these liberal attitudes is some residual anxiety in their dealings with minority group members, an unease stemming from culturally socialized negative images associated with them. It is this anxiety that is thought to colour white people's interactions with blacks (and other outgroups), betraying itself in certain behavioural indicators of avoidance and coolness. However, this is only likely to happen in those situations where there are ambiguous or conflicting norms, because then the aversive reaction may more easily be rationalized as non-prejudiced. Where anti-discrimination norms are more salient, even aversive racists are expected to adhere to them.

Notice the differences and similarities between this approach and some of the theories I considered in the previous sections. Somewhat like Katz and Hass' (1988) 'ambivalent' racists, 'aversive' racists may really want to endorse some progressive intergroup attitudes on such questions as bussing and affirmative action. Such an orientation contrasts with that of 'modern' racists, for whom, according to Sears (1988) and McConahay (1986), these are linchpin issues because of their dissonance with traditional individualistic values. Gaertner and Dovidio believe that aversive racism reveals itself unconsciously, and only in situations with no obvious normative constraints. Because of this, there are inherent difficulties in measuring it with a reactive instrument like a questionnaire. Moreover, there is little emphasis in Gaertner and Dovidio's model on stable individual differences in aversive racism; rather, it is assumed that most people will display aversive reactions in particular, normatively ambiguous situations. In contrast, as we have seen, all the other approaches assume that these 'new' forms of prejudice are part of a consciously worked out ideology, which can be measured through conventional attitude scales along which individuals can be rank ordered. Finally, on the aversive racism thesis, as in Pettigrew and Meerten's (1995) subtle racism construct, the main emotions are fear, discomfort or a lack of warmth; in some of the other approaches, especially in that of modern racism, the underlying affect is still hostility or dislike.

In support of their theory, Dovidio and Gaertner (2004) have marshalled a considerable body of evidence. Some of it comes from naturalistic settings in which they have listened to white respondents' reactions to receiving a bogus 'wrong number' telephone call to a garage requesting help with a car breakdown. The ethnicity of the person requesting the help is systematically varied. Discrimination is evident if a 'black' caller receives a less helpful response than a 'white' caller. In several studies, this is exactly what has been observed (see for example Gaertner, 1973; Gaertner and Bickman, 1971). Notice that in this 'remote victim' situation there are no strong normative guidelines to indicate that help should be given.

There was one other intriguing finding from these 'wrong number' studies. By dint of calling people who were publicly registered as democrat (liberal) or republican (conservative) voters, Gaertner (1973) was able to hazard a guess as to the political

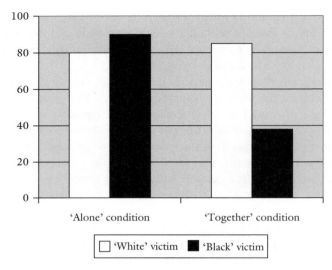

Figure 7.4 Help-giving to 'white' and 'black' victims as an index of aversive racism. Adapted from Table 1 in Gaertner and Dovidio, 1977

sympathies of the respondents to his bogus calls. Perhaps not surprisingly, the conservative respondents showed more helping to white 'callers' than to black ones, while the liberals showed no clear differentiation. However, a more careful analysis of the data revealed that, amongst those respondents who hung up prematurely (that is, before even ascertaining what the caller wanted, but not before his/her ethnicity could be recognized), it was the *liberals* who discriminated against the black callers, hanging up on them more frequently than on the white callers. On this measure, the conservatives did not discriminate. This rather serendipitous finding paved the way for the formulation of the theory of aversive racism. Here were liberals, who would surely have strenuously denied being prejudiced had they been asked outright, showing clear evidence of discrimination in a situation where no clear norms of behaviour exist. Remember, these premature hang-ups occurred before the help had been requested, and hence before any social responsibility norms could kick in.

Similar effects have been observed in laboratory studies. In one study, Gaertner and Dovidio (1977) created a mock extra-sensory perception experiment in which subjects had to try to receive telepathic messages from a 'sender' (who could be black to white). Half the subjects believed that they and the 'sender' were the only participants in the situation; the remainder believed there were two other 'receivers' as well. Then, half-way through the experiment, a stack of chairs was heard to fall, with accompanying sounds of distress from the 'sender'. Those hearing the emergency 'alone' probably perceived strong norms to intervene, and indeed a very high proportion of them (about 90 per cent) did so, irrespective of whether the victim was white or black. On the other hand, as we know from Latane and Darley's (1970) pioneering work on bystander intervention, where others are present social responsibility norms are much less keenly felt. Consistently with this, in the 'together' conditions the level of helping was lower, *and* it discriminated between the 'white' and 'black' victim: the latter was half as likely to receive help as former (see Figure 7.4). Moreover, these effects occurred irrespective of the participants' previously measured prejudice levels. Thus the situational contingencies of norm salience and the victim's ethnicity proved more significant than the participants' prior disposition to be prejudiced or not (see also Dovidio and Gaertner, 1981, 1983; Frey and Gaertner, 1986; Snyder et al., 1979).

Aversive prejudice, then, tends to rear its ugly head only in somewhat ambiguous situations. One can observe it at work in hypothetical employment or in judicial decision-making. Dovidio and Gaertner (2000) presented white participants with an application form purporting to be from an applicant for a peer counselling position. The details on the form were rigged so that the person applying was clearly a strong candidate, clearly a weak one, or ambiguously qualified. From other information on the form it was possible to infer that the applicant was white or black. Participants had to evaluate the applicant on a number of scales and finally to recommend the applicant (or not) for the position. These evaluations and recommendations were more or less consistent with the quality of the applications: very strong applicants were rated much more favourably and recommended for appointment more frequently than the ambiguous applicants, who, in turn, were graded more highly than the weak ones. At the extremes – very strong or very weak – no differentiation between black or white candidates was shown; it was so obvious what the appropriate decision should be that any ethnic bias would immediately be visible. However, for the ambiguous candidates, where the correct decision was less apparent, a clear-cut bias in favour of the white candidates emerged. Moreover, this bias was not predictable from the participant's scores on an explicit prejudice measure. Even more fascinating were the results of an exact replication of this study ten years later: they were more or less identical.

A more realistic employment discrimination test was devised by Hebl and colleagues (2002), this time using gay applicants as the target group. Carefully trained men and women visited dozens of stores enquiring after jobs vacancies. Half the time they wore hats with a 'Gay and Proud' prominently displayed on them; for the remaining visits hats read 'Texan and Proud' (the study was conducted in a Texan town in the USA). These confederates were given a hat prior to each store visit, in such a way that they could put it on without knowing which version they were wearing; this ensured that they themselves could not influence the behaviour of others. At each store there were four formal opportunities for them to be discriminated against: Would they be told that there was a vacancy? Would they be allowed to fill out an application form? Would the store call them back later, to discuss their application? And – 'oh by the way, could I use the bathroom'? The responses of the store personnel to these questions were carefully noted, as were the impressions of the 'applicants' as to how they were treated, how long the interaction lasted and so on. In addition, each encounter was witnessed by independent observers, who also rated it for warmth, helpfulness and so on. In the formal tests, where any discrimination against the gay applicant would have been obvious, the kind of hat worn made no discernible difference. But on the more subtle indicators it did. When a confederate was wearing the 'Gay and Proud' hat, interactions were more than two minutes shorter, and they were more negative in tone – as rated both by the applicants themselves and the observers. Again, then, on the indirect – less easily verifiable – indicators, a form of aversive homophobia was visible.

A similar kind of aversive prejudice has been observed in quasi-legal settings, manifesting itself not in blatant discrimination against minority defendants but in a systematic bias against them in situations of legal uncertainty. Aficionados of courtroom dramas on television will be familiar with the clever ploy adopted by some lawyers to try to have 'inadmissible evidence' introduced in the trial. 'Objection!', comes the cry from the opposing lawyer, and perhaps the judge will instruct the jury to disregard what they just have heard. As if! This dubious legal strategy was exploited in an experiment by Hodson and colleagues (2005), where the transcript of a trial involving a black and a white defendant was presented to participants who had to put forth their own judgements concerning guilt, recommended sentence length and likelihood of re-offending. In half the transcripts, some crucial evidence pointing to the defendant's guilt was stated to be 'inadmissible' and hence should be disregarded; in the remainder, the same evidence appeared to be perfectly admissible. In the latter transcripts, the guilt of the defendant was apparent and so no difference emerged in the 'verdicts' against the black and the white defendants. However, in the former transcripts, where the crucial to-be-disregarded evidence introduced a large element of ambiguity, the black defendants were more likely to be found guilty, were given longer sentences and were considered more likely to re-offend than their white counterparts who had the same evidence stacked up against them. Importantly, this anti-black bias was not predictable from the participants' scores on a modern racism measure (see also Johnson et al., 1995).

Aversive racists are thought to be prejudiced in spite of themselves. This may reveal itself in various uncontrollable autonomic responses to the presence or, even more clearly, to the actual touch of, an ethnic minority person. This was first observed in an early study by Rankin and Campbell (1955), where they found that white participants showed a larger galvanic skin response, a commonly used measure of arousal, when touched by a black experimenter as compared to a white experimenter. Although such differential galvanic skin responses to same and different ethnicity interactants has not always been found (Guglielmi, 1999), other autonomic indicators have yielded more consistent results. For example, Vrana and Rollock (1998) found that white participants' heart rate increased even when a black assistant entered the room (to take their pulse), and it went up still further whilst their pulse was actually being taken. Vrana and Rollock also observed some electromyographic changes (sub-dermal muscle activity in the face, especially in the 'smile' zones) to the same situation. In the first ten seconds after the assistant entered the room, there was greater 'smiling' activity to a white than to a black assistant. Thereafter, the black assistant elicited greater 'smiling'. Vrana and Rollock interpreted this as an initial spontaneous discrimination (aversive prejudice), followed by a more controlled social display. Finally, and in a nice echo of the Gaertner (1973) findings which had sparked off this whole line of enquiry, Nail and colleagues (2003), using the same paradigm as Vrana and Rollock (1998), found that only white 'liberal' participants, and not 'moderate' or 'conservative' ones, showed increased skin conductance and heart rate increase when touched by a black as compared to a white experimenter. Despite their self-professed progressive attitudes, they were apparently unable to control their physiological responses to the touch of a black person. As Allport (1954) memorably put it: 'defeated intellectually, prejudice lingers emotionally' (p. 311).

Integrating recent types of prejudice

In the above discussion of aversive prejudice I concentrated on the situational factors likely to allow people to discriminate covertly between ingroup and out-group members. This is the main direction taken by Dovidio and Gaertner (2004), the principal originators of the concept. Indeed, as noted earlier, they specifically eschew the use of questionnaire instruments designed to distinguish between those high and those low in aversive racism. However, their situational emphasis could perhaps be reconciled with the individual difference approach favoured by proponents of the modern prejudice models. One hint that this might be so comes from some work by Monteith and her colleagues (see Devine et al., 1991; Monteith, 1993; Monteith et al., 1993). Drawing upon an idea first floated by Allport (1954), these researchers have suggested that what distinguishes high and low (modern) prejudiced people is their reactions to discrepancies between how they think they should and how they think they actually *would* behave. One of the techniques used in these studies is to present people with mini-scenarios – for example, a black or a gay person comes and sits next to participants on a bus – and to obtain ratings as to how the latter should and would react. The next step is to elicit their emotional reactions to discrepancies between these two ratings, the most important of which are feelings of guilt, embarrassment, and self-criticism. Monteith and her colleagues showed that what differentiates high and low prejudiced people (as measured by previously administered modern racism or homophobia scales) is their response to these would/should discrepancies: low and moderately prejudiced people feel much more self-blame, or 'compunction' as Allport (1954) called it, than high prejudiced people. As one of Monteith's (1993) participants put it:

> When I was younger [...] my brother, who[m] I idolized, used 'fag' as an insulting comment. I picked it up but as I aged and slowly began to assimilate knowledge about homosexuality [...] I began to feel bad about myself. I felt that this was not how I wanted to respond toward minorities. (Monteith, 1993, p. 84)

On this conception, people's feelings associated with *particular*, situationally determined would/should discrepancies might correspond to aversive prejudice; their habitual levels of compunction across *several* such situations would be related more to modern forms of prejudice.

Further evidence that aversive and modern racism are related has been provided by Kleinpenning and Hagendoorn (1993). They developed questionnaire measures of old-fashioned (biological) racism, ethnocentrism (comprising cultural assimilation of minorities and mild own-nationality bias), symbolic racism and aversive racism, for use with Dutch school children. In addition, they administered scales enquiring into their participants' likely behavioural intentions towards minority group members (for example dating them, or avoiding people who tell racist jokes), their attitudes towards affirmative action, and their endorsement of some conventional ethnic stereotypes. Although Kleinpenning and Hagendoorn found that their various racism measures were all intercorrelated, more careful analysis revealed that they could be ordered in degree of severity. That is, biological racism encapsulated all the other forms of racism; next came symbolic racism, which also incorporated ethnocentrism and aversive racism; and aversive racism was the mildest form of the four. In agreement with this rank order, Kleinpenning and Hagendoorn found that scores on behavioural intention, affirmative action and stereotype measures varied systematically across the four types of respondents, 'aversive' racists generally giving the least discriminatory responses and 'biological' racists the most discriminatory ones. They concluded that prejudice can be regarded as a cumulative dimension, beginning with the discreet avoidance of ethnic minorities in private contexts (aversive prejudice), running through beliefs in the superiority of one's own group and convictions that ethnic groups have more social and economic benefits than they deserve (modern prejudice), and ending up with the full-blown racist ideology, which decrees the genetic inferiority of certain groups and demands for their repatriation or segregation (old-fashioned prejudice).

Implicit Measures of Prejudice

As we saw earlier in this chapter, an important stimulus for the development of theories of 'new' prejudice was the suspicion that the apparent decline in prejudice, as captured by large-scale surveys and by experimental studies alike, was masking a change either in the nature of contemporary prejudice or in the willingness of people to express bigoted views in public. This suspicion led researchers to devise new measures and techniques which, they claimed, would be more valid indicators of the true face of prejudice, because they were felt to be less direct and more subtle in their application. But these new measures themselves could be criticized for not being subtle enough, for still being vulnerable to social desirability effects. Certainly, taken at face value, many of the items that comprise them obviously concern socially sensitive issues, and it is hard to imagine that respondents are not aware of this and would not adjust their responses accordingly. Recall the findings of Fazio and colleagues (1995), which indicated that scores on the modern racism scale were affected by the ethnicity of the person administering it.

Considerations like these led to the development of **implicit** measures of **prejudice**. They are called 'implicit' because it is presumed that participants' performance on them is less – or, in some cases, definitely *not* – under conscious control. If this presumption is correct, then it should mean that any scores derived from these measures should be less susceptible to self-presentation or political correctness effects, and hence should be 'truer' indicators of prejudice. In this section I will review some of the more popular of these implicit measures of prejudice. As I do so, several issues will recur: What is the relationship of these implicit measures to their more explicit counterparts? How do different implicit measures relate to one another? How immutable are they really, especially in the face of social desirability pressures or different contextual cues? And what about construct validity, the most acid test of all? How do they relate to known indicators of prejudiced attitudes, emotions or behaviour?

One class of implicit measures relies on various physiological reactions which indicate prejudice. Some of these are already familiar to us: studies that have used changes in heart rate or galvanic skin resistance to infer negative intergroup attitudes (see Kleck et al., 1966; Nail et al., 2003; Rankin and Campbell, 1955; Vrana and Rollock, 1998). Along similar lines, there is a technique that uses electromyography. This involves recording electrical activity from different muscle groups in the face. According to Cacioppo and colleagues (1986), the activity of different facial muscles gives a subtle indication of people's likings and dislikings for various stimuli. Two areas of the face are thought to be especially significant: the corrugator muscles above the eyes, which are used when we frown, and the zygomatic muscles in the cheek, which are used in smiling; these are indicative respectively of negative and positive affect. Vanman and colleagues (1997) made recordings from these two muscle groupings whilst white participants were viewing pictures of black and white people with whom they had to imagine interacting. After each picture, participants also rated the stimulus people on various scales, including how much they liked them. These self-report ratings revealed a pro-black bias: people professed to like the blacks more than the whites. The electromyographic readings told a different story, however. Whenever a black photograph appeared, there tended to be more activity from the 'frown' muscles and less from the 'smile' muscles, compared to the levels recorded for the white photographs. Intriguingly, in the third of the experiments reported, this pro-white (or anti-black) electromyographic bias was only shown by participants scoring above the median on a modern racism measure. If this latter result can be replicated with a larger sample (there were only twenty-five participants in this study), then it suggests that the prejudice seemingly picked up by this particular physiological measure may partly correspond to people's more enduring and explicit social attitudes. Moreover, such a result is also consistent with findings I reported in Chapter 4 when discussing automatic stereotype activation. I noted there how the nature of that activation also seems to depend on people's prior prejudice levels (Brown et al., 2003; Lepore and Brown, 1997; Locke et al., 1994; Wittenbrink et al., 1997).

Physiological measures like these appear to be detecting some kind of prejudice literally 'under the skin': responses that we are unable to control and, indeed, are unaware of producing. However, there is a crucial interpretative problem with these kinds of measures, a problem that we will encounter again with other implicit indices: what is it that they are really measuring? Is it, as their proponents claim, some negative affect towards the outgroup target? Or might it be simply less positive affect, but no clear antipathy? Or, even more problematically from a validity point of view, might they be detecting instead some greater apprehension, perhaps born out of guilt or cognitive uncertainty, rather than any hostile feelings or negative evaluation? Without more robust validation, ideally triangulated with the help of more than one criterion, answers to these questions remain ambiguous.

Electromyographic measurement involves placing several electrodes on the participants' faces and recording the electrical activity associated with various stimuli, while participants keep their heads perfectly still. It is thus rather a lengthy and cumbersome procedure, not very practical for most kinds of experimentation. A second class of implicit measures suffers rather less from these disadvantages. What these measures have in common is a reliance on response times (RTs), measured in milliseconds, to pairs of stimuli, which are presented either simultaneously or with a very short interval between them. The underlying logic of these techniques is that stimuli which are closely associated in a person's cognitive system will be reacted to more quickly than stimuli that are semantically or affectively more distant. By comparing RTs to different stimulus pairings – for example, ingroup symbols and positively (or negatively) valenced stimuli, and outgroup symbols associated with those same stimuli – inferences can be drawn as to how those ingroups and outgroups are internally represented. Furthermore, because the stimuli are presented rather briefly and participants are required to respond as quickly as possible, it is assumed that participants are unable consciously to monitor or control their behaviour. Thus, it is claimed, the prejudice measures that are derived from such procedures can be regarded as implicit.

Fazio and colleagues (1995) devised one such technique, known as **associative priming**. In this technique, participants first have to make some rapid classifications of various words as positive or negative. The RTs for these judgements serve as the baseline against which subsequent RTs can be assessed. In the critical 'priming' phase of the procedure, before the words are presented, black or white faces are shown for 300 ms or so. Participants are supposed to ignore these faces and to concentrate only on categorizing each word as positive or negative. Fazio and colleagues (1995) found that white participants were noticeably slower to classify words as positive when they were preceded by black faces than when they were preceded by white faces (as compared to the baseline RTs). From this, Fazio and colleagues concluded that the participants harboured an automatic associative preference for whites over blacks. Three other findings from this research were of interest. The first was that the magnitude of individuals' automatic biases was negatively correlated to the friendliness of their behaviour towards a black confederate in a subsequent interaction. The second was that, across all participants, the automatic prejudice (if prejudice it be) was barely correlated to an explicit measure like modern racism. However, when the participants were sub-divided according to their expressed willingness or reluctance to control their prejudiced thoughts or feelings, the group which was little motivated to control its prejudice did show a clear relationship between its implicit and its explicit levels of prejudice.

In Fazio and colleagues' procedure, both the primes and the target words were presented long enough to be visible to participants. Although the gap between the disappearance of the face and the onset of the word was quite short (135 ms), and probably short enough to prevent any consciously controlled strategies, the fact remains that the supraliminal presentation of the primes may have made the purpose of the study somewhat transparent to participants. To circumvent this problem, Wittenbrink and colleagues (1997) presented their primes so briefly (for 15 ms) that they made them subliminal. This time the primes were words ('black' or 'white'), and the subsequent task was simply to judge whether various words and nonsense strings were or were not words. Once again, the crucial issue was the speed with which positive and negative words were judged to be real when preceded by different primes. Wittenbrink and colleagues found clear response facilitation for negative words to be preceded by black primes and for positive words by white primes. Unlike Fazio and colleagues (1995), they also observed that the degree of this automatic bias was clearly correlated to modern racism. The size of this correlation, although 'moderate' (around .40), was respectably higher by comparison with what is often found in experimental research.

Probably the most popular implicit prejudice measure of all is the implicit association test (IAT), invented by Greenwald and colleagues (1998).[9] The essence of the IAT is simplicity itself. After various practice trials, a first crucial task follows in which respondents are asked to use one response key for two different categorizations – for example, an ingroup name/face or a positive word – and another key for an outgroup name/face or a negative word. These trials are designated 'compatible', on the assumption that ingroup-positive and outgroup-negative are the default cognitive associations for most people. After several such compatible trials, a change is introduced: now one of the concepts is reversed and another couple of practice trials follow. In the second reversed crucial task, one response key is allocated to ingroup or negative stimuli and another to outgroup or positive stimuli.[10] These are the so-called 'incompatible' trials. Throughout, people should respond as quickly and as accurately as possible. The central idea of the IAT is that RTs for incompatible trials will be larger than for compatible trials because of the presumed closer mental associations that the latter represent compared to the former. Thus the temporal discrepancy between incompatible and compatible trial blocks is considered to give an implicit measure of prejudice against the particular outgroup in question.

In a very large number of studies using a wide variety of target groups, such a discrepancy is reliably found (Nosek et al., 2007). In one of the original experiments, Greenwald and colleagues (1998) found that white participants responded to compatible trials (white-positive, black-negative) anywhere between 100 ms and 200 ms faster than to incompatible trials (white-negative, black-positive), and these seem to be fairly typical IAT effects. Moreover, this anti-black (or pro-white) bias did not seem to correspond to prejudice as captured by more explicit measures. The same participants showed little or no ingroup bias on a semantic differential measure, and much weaker (though significant) bias on a feeling thermometer. And the correlations between the explicit measures and the IAT score were all negligible, although the rather small sample meant that the relevant tests lacked statistical power. The results from other studies, summarized by Hofmann and colleagues (2005), indicate that the correlation between implicit prejudice measured by the IAT and explicit prejudice measured by a variety of pencil and paper measures averages out at around .20. In other words, although there is some link between the two types of measure, the correlation is sufficiently low to indicate that they seem to be tapping different constructs. And the fact that the IAT consistently detects bias when **explicit measures** do not leads Greenwald and his colleagues to believe that the former is able to circumvent the social desirability factors that bedevil many explicit measures.

In the years since its first publication, the IAT has attracted an enormous amount of research attention from devotees and critics alike. One issue that has preoccupied researchers is the psychometric adequacy of the technique, especially its reliability. Unlike for explicit prejudice scales, where internal consistency is routinely noted, many scientific articles concerned with the IAT do not report its reliability. An exception was a detailed psychometric examination of the IAT, associative priming and an explicit prejudice measure (the modern racism scale) made by Cunningham and colleagues (2001). They administered three measures to the same group of participants, four times, over the space of six weeks. In fact the IAT proved to have an adequate internal reliability, as high as that of the modern racism measure. Only the associative priming measure had questionable reliability (< .70). On the other hand, the temporal stability of the implicit measures – that is, the extent to which scores at one time point correlated with scores at another – was rather low (< .30), and considerably lower than the stability of the explicit measure (> .80). Although Cunningham and colleagues (2001) attempt to rescue the test/re-test reliability of the implicit measures through some complex statistical analysis, the fact remains that these measures seem to contain enough measurement error to make the prediction of a person's score at a later time point from their earlier score a hazardous business. For a test purporting assess people's stable intergroup attitudes, this is undesirable to say the least.

A second issue is the relationship of people's IAT scores to their discriminatory behaviour. If the IAT is a genuine measure of prejudice, then it should allow us to predict how people will act towards outgroup members. Earlier in the chapter I noted how Dovidio and colleagues (2002) had found that an associative priming measure of prejudice correlated with non-verbal indicators of prejudice and with judges' ratings of an intergroup interaction, but not with people's more controlled verbal behaviour. The same may be true of the IAT. McConnell and Liebold (2001) found that the IAT correlated with various paralinguistic features in an interethnic encounter (such as speaking time, smiling, speech errors and hesitations), in a way in which an explicit measure of prejudice simply failed to correlate. Taken together with the earlier work by Dovidio and colleagues (1997a, 2002), these results suggest that responses to implicit measures, because they are less controllable, can give us an insight into people's more spontaneous intergroup behaviours.

But, note, this does not mean that the IAT, or any other implicit measure, is a 'truer' indicator of prejudice than explicit attitude measures. After all, people will sometimes manifest their prejudice quite deliberately, especially when they believe that they can escape censure for so doing (Dovidio and Gaertner, 2004). I will return shortly to the question of what implicit measures really measure, but first let me consider the results of an intriguing experiment by Karpinski and Hilton (2001). Although far removed from the prejudice domain, it does raise questions about how well the IAT can predict people's voluntary behaviour. Karpinski and Hilton measured people's implicit attitudes towards apples or candy bars by using an IAT. They found a clear implicit preference for apples. For half the participants they also measured people's *explicit* attitudes towards apples and candy bars. These also indicated a mild preference for apples, but much less strongly than shown by the IAT. Then, on their way out of the laboratory, participants were invited to choose an apple or a candy bar; just under half chose an apple, the remainder a candy bar. But the critical issue concerned the correlations between their prior attitudes and their behavioural choices: the explicit attitudes significantly predicted the choice of apple or candy bar, whilst the IAT did not at all. Even in the condition where there were no explicit attitudes to create a behavioural intention, the correlation between IAT preference and actual choice of apple or candy was effectively zero.

A third issue concerns the stability or malleability of IAT measures. In the early years of the IAT's existence, there was a widespread assumption that the IAT was able to detect stable individual differences in people's implicit attitudes towards various groups. Indeed one of the advantages of the technique, stressed by its proponents, was precisely that the IAT would be much less influenced by immediate situational factors than were explicit measures of prejudice. In recent years there has been a growing realization that this emphasis on the relative immutability of IAT scores (and of scores from other implicit measures) has been misplaced (Blair, 2002). I have already noted that the IAT does not have high test/re-test reliability, at least in the way that is conventionally established. The IAT is also susceptible to a range of situational interventions. Dasgupta and Greenwald (2001) found that implicit prejudice towards black people could be reduced by first exposing participants to a series of pictures of famous and positively viewed black people (such as Martin Luther King, or Denzel Washington) under the guise of a general knowledge test. Similar changes were also induced by showing pictures of positive elderly role models; this time a reduction in age bias was found. Gawronski and LeBel (2008) found similar changes in IAT scores after repeated subliminal presentations of ingroup-negative and

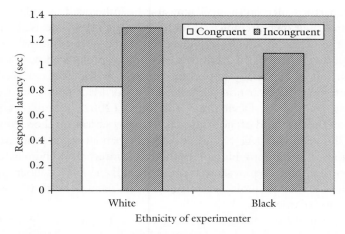

Figure 7.5 Implicit prejudice (IAT) influenced by ethnicity of experimenter. A modified pencil-and-paper version of the IAT was used in this experiment. Participants were required to categorize simultaneously category exemplars (typical white or black names) and positive or negative words. They had to do this as quickly and accurately as possible for 20 seconds. Response latencies have been derived by dividing 20 by the number of correct categorizations. Adapted from Figure 1 in Lowery et al., 2001

outgroup-positive word pairings (see also Karpinski and Hilton, 2001 and Olson and Fazio, 2006). It seems that it is also possible to reduce the implicit bias measured by the IAT simply by engaging in some prior counter-stereotypical mental imagery (Blair et al., 2001).

The fact that the IAT is sensitive to various kinds of 'reconditioning' interventions like these ones may not pose much of a challenge to the processes thought to underlie it. Such interventions are probably temporarily changing the mental associations between the target of the attitude (some social category) and positive and negative attributes. These changed associations were then picked up by the IAT. However, there are other reliable influences on the IAT, which are much more problematic for its claim to be a measure of people's core attitudes, namely one uncontaminated by social desirability factors. Perhaps the most damning of these influences have been reported by Lowery and colleagues (2001), who used a pencil and paper version of the IAT. They found that white participants' IAT scores (using blacks and whites as the focal categories) were significantly reduced by the simple expedient of changing the experimenter's ethnicity from white to black (see Figure 7.5). Interestingly, Asian participants were not affected by experimenter ethnicity, presumably because they were less implicated in the black–white intergroup relationship. In another experiment, Lowery and colleagues (2001) found that IAT scores for both Asian and whites could be reduced by instructing these participants to try not to be prejudiced. In other words, the IAT may not be as immune to self-presentational and other 'controlled' strategies as its proponents believe (see Fiedler, 2006 for a detailed and coruscating critique of the IAT; and De Houwer and colleagues, 2007 for further evidence of the IAT's susceptibility to participants' efforts to fake their scores).

Moreover, performance on the IAT may also be influenced by individuals' inclinations to control their own prejudice. Plant and Devine (1998) devised an instrument that assesses the extent to which people are motivated to respond without prejudice for internal personal reasons ('I attempt to act in non-prejudiced ways towards black people because it is personally important to me') *or* for external social influence reasons ('I attempt to appear non-prejudiced towards black people in order to avoid disapproval from others'). Devine and colleagues (2002) found that people who scored high on the first kind of motivation (internal) but low on the second (external) consistently showed lower IAT bias against blacks than all other combinations of the two motivations (low on both, high on both, or low internal and high external). Once again, the fact that the IAT appears to be influenced by people's deliberative strategies to control (or not) their prejudice is damaging for its claim to be a truly automatic and implicit indicator of prejudice.

What, then, should we make of all these different kinds of implicit measures of prejudice? In these final paragraphs I would like to make a few last comments about their construct validity (what is it that they are really measuring?) and their practical utility (when and how are they most usefully employed?).

Implicit measures are often criticized because of doubts about whether they really capture prejudice as commonly defined – that is, a person's negative orientation towards an outgroup (see Chapter 1; Arkes and Tetlock, 2004; Brendl et al., 2001; Fiedler, 2006). To begin with, we should note that any implicit measure that relies on some difference score, whether this is derived from response latencies to ingroup and outgroup pairings with differently valenced stimuli or from discrepancies in autonomic responses to various stimuli, is inherently ambiguous. It could indicate, as is usually assumed, an association between the outgroup and something negative, which is coupled with an ingroup-positive association. Such an association might reasonably be called prejudice. However, an identical difference score could also be derived from an outgroup-positive association that is simply less strong than the ingroup-positive association. This we might not want so readily to label prejudice. Similarly, as I noted earlier, differences in spontaneous behaviours to members of ingroups and outgroups (eye-gaze, speech disfluencies) may well reflect some outgroup aversion or intergroup anxiety, but they might also indicate guilt or embarrassment, which are not necessarily indicative of prejudice at all (Arkes and Tetlock, 2004).

Other doubts focus on whether implicit measures tap into people's personally held attitudes or instead merely reflect cultural associations between different groups and positive and negative attributes (Arkes and Tetlock, 2004; Karpinski and Hilton, 2001; Olson and Fazio, 2004). In other words, such measures may not be able to differentiate between people's *knowledge* of negative outgroup stereotypes and their *endorsement* of them, to use a well known distinction (Devine, 1989). There are several pieces of evidence that have provoked these concerns. Recall Karpinski and Hilton's (2001) finding that, despite a clear implicit (cultural?) preference for apples over sweets, people's explicit preferences were more ambivalent and proved to be more predictive of which of the two they actually chose. Olson and Fazio (2004) introduced a subtle but important modification to the traditional IAT procedure in order to make a similar point. In the double category phase of the procedure, where ingroup and outgroup examples have to be categorized with pleasant or unpleasant words, they replaced the 'pleasant/unpleasant' classification with things 'I like' and things 'I don't like'. In this way Olson and Fazio 'personalized' the IAT and, they claimed, made it more reflective of people's privately endorsed attitudes. In four experiments, the personalized procedure produced significantly lower IAT scores than the conventional IAT, and these scores proved also to be more in line with people's explicit attitudes.

Prejudice scores derived from implicit procedures are also seen to be susceptible to context effects, by which I mean that the same categorical stimuli presented against one background can yield very different results from those obtained when the stimuli are presented against another background (Barden et al., 2004; Wittenbrink et al., 2001). Barden and colleagues (2004) showed this most dramatically. Using a version of Fazio and colleagues' (1995) associative priming procedure, they presented black and white facial primes and the following valenced target words against a background picture of a factory, a church or a prison. Their assumption was that the black primes (especially) would be respectively positively, neutrally or negatively associated with these three contexts, and that these stereotypical associations would yield very different response time biases. So it proved. A pro-black bias was observed in the 'factory' condition, no bias was found in the 'church' condition and an anti-black bias was found in the 'prison' condition. If implicit measures are intended to give an accurate indication of someone's general attitude towards a given group, it is strange indeed that that attitude can be so radically affected by something as trivial as the background against which the stimuli are presented.

It seems clear, then, that implicit measures of prejudice cannot live up to some of the more extravagant claims made for them. They are not immune to contextual influences, whether these come in the form of social aspects of the situation or of characteristics of the stimulus presentation; they seem also to be affected by participants' deliberative strategies; and their exact meaning is often ambiguous. Still, even if they are not quite the 'holy grail' of attitude measurement, they are far from being worthless. As we have seen, they are often reliably correlated to people's spontaneous or less controlled behaviours and to the impressions gained both by fellow interactants and by disinterested observers. In that sense, they can make a useful research tool as a proxy for those behavioural indicators, especially since such observational data are notoriously labour-intensive to collect.

Of course, implicit measures themselves are not always the most convenient ones to administer. They usually involve lengthy individual testing with computers or other technologies. Thus they do not lend themselves readily to group data collection when time may be limited. Here explicit measures come into their own: these are simpler to administer and allow large numbers of people to be tested simultaneously. Nevertheless, even if they have some predictive validity in the sense of being moderately correlated to other explicit measures and deliberative behaviours, explicit measures are not without their drawbacks either. Even when attempts are made to reduce social desirability effects (for instance through anonymous responding in large group situations), because their content is so much more transparent than that of implicit measures, they can be vulnerable to the respondents' 'faking good'.

Finally, the generally weak but non-zero correlations that are observed between explicit and implicit measures suggest that it may be profitable to combine them as independent assessments of prejudice in the same study. Such, anyway, was the idea of Son Hing and colleagues (2008). They suggested that people who score high on both explicit and implicit measures may be regarded as out and out bigots; people who score low on explicit measures but above average on implicit measures may correspond to Dovidio and Gaertner's (2004) 'aversive' racists. And people who score low on both might be regarded as genuinely non-prejudiced. The final combination, high on explicit and low on implicit, may be that of the 'principled conservatives' described by Sniderman and colleagues (1991). Son Hing and colleagues (2008) used this taxonomy to show that these four groups could be reliably distinguished in their endorsement of various political values and in their responses on an employment discrimination task. In sum, then, neither implicit nor explicit measures are 'true' indicators of prejudice; they can each provide glimpses of different facets of the phenomenon (Dovidio et al., 2001; Fazio and Olson, 2003).

Summary

1   Surveys of ethnic and gender attitudes and stereotypes reveal a steady decline in prejudice over the past forty years. However, less reactive unobtrusive behavioural measures indicate that some of this decline may be attributable to changing social desirability norms rather than to internalized non-prejudiced beliefs.

2   Theories of modern prejudice have been proposed to account for the new manifestations of prejudice. Some of these theories place emphasis on the fact that prejudice takes on indirect symbolic forms, in place of the outright intergroup hostility and beliefs in outgroups' inferiority, which constitute old-fashioned prejudice. The origins of this modern prejudice are thought to be a negative affect coupled with perceived violations (by minority groups) of traditional individualistic values.

3   Another approach suggests that contemporary forms of prejudice are typically ambivalent in nature, comprising both negative and positive attitudes towards outgroups. However, such favourability may be more apparent than real. It may be a convenient 'front' whose goal is to reinforce existing intergroup status inequalities.

4   Still other conceptualizations of new prejudice place more emphasis on situational factors which permit dominant group members to avoid close contact with outgroups. This aversive prejudice is thought to stem from intergroup anxiety rather than hostility. It is possible that these different forms of prejudice are related in a hierarchy of increasing severity.

5   Implicit measures of prejudice have become very fashionable in recent years. These rely on differential autonomic responses to ingroup and outgroup targets, or on reaction time differences to various stimulus pairings. Implicit measures correlate moderately well with less controllable social behaviours, but only weakly with more traditional explicit measures of prejudice. Despite their popularity, they have not escaped criticism on theoretical and methodological grounds.

Notes

1   Although, as the authors admit, it is a moot point whether the optimal solution was really two separate factors or two sub-factors of a single superordinate prejudice construct.

2   This measure is rather akin to group relative deprivation, since it assesses men's perception that affirmative action programmes put men at a disadvantage in relation to women (see

Chapter 6). Note, however, that it is a measure of collective and not personal interests, which may explain why it correlated with attitudes to affirmative action in our study (cf. Jacobson, 1985; Kluegel and Smith, 1983).

3　Leach (2005) has made a rather different argument against new variants of prejudice. Drawing on historical evidence, he claims that so-called 'modern' prejudice could be found in earlier time periods and that 'old-fashioned' prejudice is still in evidence today. Although there is some truth in this, it is the matter of their relative prevalence that is critical. I think there is no doubt that some of the more extreme and explicit forms of outgroup denigration are clearly much less common in the latter half of the twentieth century than they were in the first half, even if they are by no means extinct. Consequently, the need for more symbolic forms of expression would have been less apparent in earlier times, even if one can identify occasional historical instances of them.

4　The idea, that ambivalence creates inner conflict and leads to amplified reactions, can also be found in psychoanalytic theory (see Freud, 1915).

5　This was the strategy used by Richard III in marrying the enemy, so well described by Shakespeare. In the Prologue to her book, Jackman (1994) presents one of Aesop's fables, 'The Wind and the Sun', as an analogy to her argument. I reproduce it here:

The Wind and the Sun

A dispute once arose between the wind and the sun over which was the stronger of the two. There seemed to be no way of settling the issue. But suddenly they saw a traveller coming down the road.

'This is our chance', said the sun, 'to prove who is right. Whichever of us can make that man take off his coat shall be the stronger. And just to show you how sure I am, I'll let you have the first chance.'

So the sun hid behind a cloud, and the wind blew an icy blast. But the harder he blew the more closely did the traveller wrap his coat around him. At last the wind had to give up in disgust. The sun came out from behind the cloud and began to shine down on the traveller with all his power. The traveller felt the sun's genial warmth, and as he grew warmer and warmer he began to loosen his coat. Finally, he was forced to take it off altogether and sit down in the shade of a tree and fan himself. So the sun was right, after all!

Application: Persuasion is better than force.

Aesop's Fables, 1947 (reproduced from Jackman, 1994, p. 1)

The title of Jackman's book itself uses an equally telling metaphor: *The Velvet Glove* (which disguises the iron fist within).

6　In this original research, there were two samples of men, both non-student, which did not show this positive correlation between HS and BS (Glick and Fiske, 1996). However, this appears to be an anomalous finding, since other research with non-student samples *has* typically found a moderate positive correlation between HS and BS (Glick et al., 2002; Moya et al., 2007; Masser and Abrams, 1999, 2004; Wiener and Hurt, 2000).

7　Actually the use of the male pronoun here is possibly misleading. One of the ironic features of Glick and Fiske's theory is that women too can be both benevolently and hostilely sexist towards their own gender, even if typically at lower levels than men (Glick et al., 2000). Still, in keeping with the focus of this book on intergroup aspects of prejudice, I will ignore for the moment this apparent 'ingroup disparaging' phenomenon of women being sexist against themselves. I will nevertheless touch on it in the next chapter.

8　The ambivalent sexism inventory uses a 0–5 scale, so that the mid-point (neutral point) is 2.5. Thus most sample means are clustered around this neutral point, indicating little evidence of extreme scoring on either the HS or BS scale (Petrocelli, 2002).

9 In the first ten years after its publication, a Psych Info search indicated that more than 250 articles have been published referring to the IAT in their titles or abstracts. Thanks to its online accessibility (at www.yale.edu/implicit), Nosek and colleagues (2007) estimate that over 2.5 million participants have undertaken an IAT. By any standards, this is an impressive corpus of research, a testament to the tireless promulgation and defence of the technique by Greenwald and his colleagues.

10 Of course, the full procedure involves counterbalancing the order of the compatible and incompatible trial blocks as well as various other controls for left and right response keys.

Further Reading

Dovidio, J. F., and Gaertner, S. L. (2004) Aversive racism. *Advances in Experimental Social Psychology* 36: 1–52.

Glick, P., and Fiske, S. T. (2001) Ambivalent sexism. *Advances in Experimental Social Psychology* 33, 115–88.

Henry, P. J., and Sears, R. R. (2005) Over thirty years later: A contemporary look at symbolic racism. *Advances in Experimental Social Psychology* 35: 95–150.

Fazio, R. H., and Olson, M. A. (2003) Implicit measures in social cognition research: Their meaning and use. *Annual Review of Psychology* 54: 297–327.

8

Prejudice from the Recipients' Point of View

Up until this point, I have concentrated mainly on the processes and factors that influence the kind and amount of prejudice people will show towards various outgroups. Such a focus on the perpetrators of prejudice is perfectly reasonable, since we want to know when prejudice is most likely to occur, how it works and how we can reduce it. Still, as they say, there are two sides to every story, and there is certainly a second side to the prejudice story. What is it like to be a member of a group that is regularly targeted as the object of prejudiced thinking, antipathy and discriminatory behaviour? It is this victim's perspective that is the focus of this chapter.

I begin with a review of the main research findings that have documented the experience of those who suffer inconvenience, discomfort or downright physical harm just because they happen to belong to groups which are socially devalued. A term often used to describe such groups is 'stigmatized', since their members may feel that they carry some physical or metaphorical sign which marks them out for mistreatment. How members of stigmatized groups cope with this situation is a second issue I will investigate. A third question will be to understand why members of stigmatized groups often manifest behaviour that appears to confirm some of the negative stereotypes about them. This recalls the phenomenon of self-fulfilling prophecies, which I discussed in Chapter 4. These prophecies have proved especially perplexing – and socially problematic – on various intellectual tasks, where the merest hint or reminder of negative societal stereotypes about the ingroup can be enough to trigger a worsened performance. Finally, I look at another seemingly paradoxical phenomenon: an apparent tendency for members of disadvantaged groups to be more avid supporters of the system that oppresses them than those who benefit from it.

The Experience of Prejudice

Before beginning our analysis of the complex set of processes implicated in being at the receiving end of prejudice and discrimination, it is probably worth reminding ourselves of the daily reality of life as the member of a group that is liable to be the object of disparagement, if not outright hostility, from others. Regrettably, there is an over-abundance of anecdotal, autobiographical and more systematic evidence from research that I could present here, so let me focus on a few telling examples. These range from the mundane prejudice that subtly – or occasionally not so subtly – insinuates itself into minority group members' everyday social encounters to more extreme, sometimes fatal, instances of being a victim of violent hate crime.

Diary studies, interviews and questionnaire surveys conducted with women, members of ethnic minorities and other marginalized groups reveal evidence of a steady stream of low-grade derogatory comments and behaviours directed towards them by members of other groups. These include being stared at, sexist or racist jokes, casual remarks made in conversation or by strangers in the street, inappropriate physical contact, deliberate exclusion from social and play activities and, thankfully more rarely, verbal or physical abuse. For example Swim and colleagues (1998) reported that African American students experience on average at least one racist event per fortnight, and women approximately twice as many sexist incidents per fortnight. Moreover, a very high percentage of women (over 90 per cent) felt that they had been the target of unwanted sexist comments or behaviours at least once. Perhaps not surprisingly, the sheer number of sexist incidents experienced seems to be associated with various socio-emotional outcomes: in one study, women who had experienced more sexist hassles became angrier and more anxious and had lower social self-esteem (Swim et al., 2001).

Such everyday prejudice is not confined to American college students. In a recent study we conducted with young ethnic minority children in Britain (aged 5–11 years), between 25 and 40 per cent of the children reported having had at least one negative experience due to their ethnicity (Brown et al., 2007a). This experience might have consisted in being left out of a playground game or in being the victim of some name-calling, as in this child's recollection: 'they might say "I'm brainier than you" or "you're from a different country, you have weird food" and stuff […] this boy has [said this] in the playground when I was small. He said, all to my friends, "you've got a different skin colour"' (Brown et al., 2007a).

Interestingly, reports of such discrimination were noticeably less frequent in schools which were ethnically more diverse – a finding perhaps attributable to the greater opportunities for intergroup contact that such schools afford (see Chapter 9).

Unemployed people, a seemingly ubiquitous and growing group in most western countries, also encounter much prejudice in their daily lives (Herman, 2007). Whether from off-hand comments made by officials in health or welfare agencies, or from explicit discrimination that they face in the labour or housing market, these people are constantly reminded that they belong to a socially devalued category. The daughter of a man who was made redundant in his early fifties describes the effects of unemployment on her father:

> He was hardly able to eat, and lost so much weight it seemed as though he was consumed by despair. He began smoking compulsively and abandoned his bracing cold water shaves, allowing a grey beard to grow. Schooled in northern self-reliance, he blamed himself for failing our family – and to my intense shame, I blamed him too. (Ruth Sutherland, *Observer*, 16 November 2008)

People who weigh more than average, being either 'overweight' or clinically 'obese', are also often subjected to unwanted negative attention or social exclusion (Miller and

Myers, 1998; Neumark-Sztainer and Haines, 2004). They may attract unflattering comments from children, they may get teased or bullied at school or at work, and sometimes they find it harder to form romantic relationships. Here is one girl's experience:

> I'm trying to think of how I'm treated differently because I'm big. Um, there's an assumption that all big people stink [...] that's the worst one I don't like, because I know I don't stink [...] that's an assumption that everybody has, they automatically think I'm going to smell like something [...]. (Quoted in Neumark-Sztainer and Haines, 2004, p. 351)

Sometimes the exposure to prejudice takes a more directly damaging, if not deadly form. In 2006–7 there were over 41,000 reports of ethnically or religiously motivated offences committed in England and Wales (Home Office, 2008). These were 'official' statistics collated by the British Home Office; the true incidence is almost certainly higher, due to considerable under-reporting of these kinds of crimes (Chakraborti and Garland, 2003; Virdee, 1997). Here are the experiences of two Pakistani families living in a rural area in the east of England, which give a flavour of some of the abuse that members of ethnic minorities have to put up with:

> We were getting dog's mess thrown at the door, stones at the window, and then you stood at the door one night, didn't you, and they threw an egg at you. And I chased after them and they called me a 'Paki loving bitch' who needed shooting.

> We had graffiti [...]'Wogs die', 'Pakis out', 'Jews smell', 'Scum', 'Burn'. On the second incident which was ten days later it was a pot of paint. On the third occasion we had 'US Killers', 'Death', 'Get out Pakis'. (Interview excerpts quoted in Chakraborti and Garland, 2003, p. 7)

These are examples of **hate crime**,[1] which is officially defined in Britain as 'any criminal offence against a person or property that is motivated by an offender's hatred of someone because of their race, colour, ethnic origin, nationality or national origins, religion, gender or gender identity, sexual orientation or disability' (Home Office, 2008). Hate crime is by no means a uniquely British disease. Several other European countries have also witnessed an increase in ethnically related crimes in recent years (Bleich, 2007). Because hate crimes are, by definition, an intergroup phenomenon, one can expect to observe temporal variations in their frequency – variations depending on changes in wider intergroup relationships. A particularly vivid example of such historical changes was the rise in islamophobia noticed after the terrorist attacks in the United States in September 2001. Kaplan (2006) extracted data from official FBI crime statistics for the years 2000–2002. Figure 8.1 shows the number of incidents recorded against four different groups over those three years. The most notable feature of that graph is the seventeen-fold increase in anti-Islamic crimes between 2000 and 2001. That sudden spike in hate crime against Muslims contrasts strongly with the stable incidence rates recorded for the other three groups.

Figure 8.1 also shows that, after anti-black crime, **homophobic** incidents are the second most frequent form of hate crime in the USA. There is evidence to suggest that being a victim of hate crime on the basis of one's sexual orientation has more

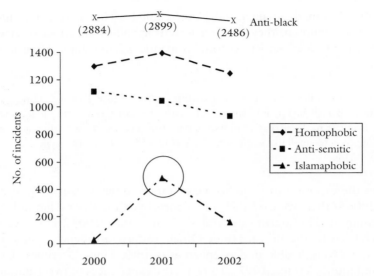

Figure 8.1 Hate crime in USA before and after 11 September 2001. Adapted from Tables 1, 3 and 6 in Kaplan, 2006

serious psychological consequences than being a victim of a comparable crime without the hate element. Herek and colleagues (1999) found that lesbians and gay men reported greater depression, stress, anxiety, anger and perceived vulnerability to future crime if they had experienced a hate crime in the past five years than if they had experienced a non-hate crime (see also McDevitt et al., 2001). And the more severe the degree of victimization due to sexual orientation, the more adverse the mental health consequences are (Hershberger and D'Augelli, 1995). Although these associations all derive from cross-sectional correlational studies, which have their usual interpretive ambiguity, they do indicate that being victimized on account of one's group membership may have additional adverse consequences over and above simply being a victim – which is already traumatic enough. Moreover, because hate crime is group-based, it is possible that its negative implications extend beyond the immediate victims themselves, to other members of the victims' group. As yet, this has been a little studied issue (Craig, 1999).

The most extreme form of hate crime is genocide, where one group attempts the systematic annihilation of another. In a few months in 1994 the world witnessed a horrific genocide in Rwanda, when over a million Tutsis were murdered by Hutus. Even now, the people of Rwanda are still trying to rebuild their society after the trauma of those months. As part of that reconstruction process they are using a traditional form of justice, known as the Gacaca Tribunals. In these tribunals members of a local community, survivors of the genocide and its alleged perpetrators meet together to discuss particular incidents and to hear testimony both from the victims of those incidents (or their families) and from those accused of carrying them out. If defendants plead guilty and ask for forgiveness from the community, they can expect to receive lighter sentences. In a truly remarkable study, Kanyangara and colleagues (2007) were able to gain access to fifty survivors and fifty alleged perpetrators before

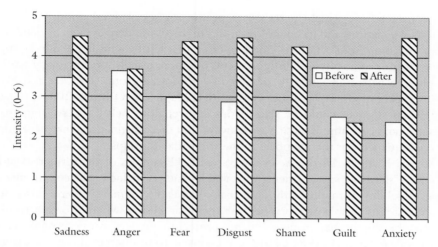

Figure 8.2   Changes in emotions experienced by survivors of genocide before and after participation in Gacaca Tribunals. Adapted from Table 1 in Kanyangara et al., 2007

and after their participation in a Gacaca Tribunal. In their questionnaire the researchers included questions concerning the participants' emotions and their stereotypes of the outgroup. Perhaps not surprisingly, those accused of genocidal crimes showed an increase in guilt after taking part in a Gacaca Tribunal. They also showed a decrease in anger. More interesting for our present purposes were the changes in emotions felt by the victim group: after the tribunal they felt markedly more sadness, fear, disgust, anxiety and, most curiously, *shame* (see Figure 8.2).

Most of these emotional changes make intuitive sense. It is perfectly understandable that survivors of a genocide should show more fear, disgust and anxiety when confronted with those thought to have slaughtered their friends and family. Less obvious, perhaps, is the increase in shame, an emotion signifying a sense of self-worthlessness and moral inferiority (Tangney, 1991). Although it seems strange that victims of barbarous acts should suffer such feelings, this is apparently not an infrequent survivor response, for example among rape victims (Janoff-Bulman, 1979; Páez et al., 2006). It seems that suffering extremes of degradation can lead victims to lose any sense of control over their lives and to experience an almost complete loss of their own humanity.

The Gacaca Tribunals appear to have resulted in generally negative emotional changes amongst survivors. Interestingly, though, these emotional changes were associated with some *improvements* in intergroup attitudes. After the trials, the survivors viewed the prisoners in a less negative and homogenous fashion, and indeed there were reliable correlations between changes in two of those negative emotions – shame and fear – and the changed intergroup perceptions (see also Rimé et al., 2008). According to Kanyangara and colleagues (2007), the social sharing of emotions permitted by the Gacaca Tribunals facilitates the development of social cohesion by encouraging a perception of common humanity between victims and perpetrators.

It is useful to consider all these diverse experiences of prejudice and discrimination as examples of what it is to posses some **social stigma**. In social psychology, a stigma is any characteristic which marks out a person for social devaluation. As both its religious associations and its etymology indicate (the word derives from ancient Greek *stigma*, meaning 'spot', 'tattoo', 'mark' – often that left by a healing wound), stigma can be a scar or some physical disfigurement, but more usually it refers to any attribute that places a person in a socially devalued or oppressed group (Crocker and Major, 1989; Crocker et al., 1998; Jones et al., 1984; Major and O'Brien, 2005). Obvious examples of stigmas would be skin colour and religious belief. These stigmatizing attributes can be distinguished in various ways, and these distinctions may have important consequences for the members of the stigmatized groups.

A stigma is either *concealable* or always visible. Examples of the former would be one's HIV status or sexual orientation; visible stigmas include skin colour, age and physical disability. It might be thought that concealable stigmas will have fewer negative sequelae for their possessors, because these can choose whether or not to reveal their membership of that group and hence protect themselves from exposure to social disapproval (Jones et al., 1984). However, choosing to be discreet about one's stigmatized group membership can also mean that one is denying oneself some potential avenues for self-protection, such as social support from friends and fellow group members (Crocker and Major, 1989). The *time since the acquisition* of the stigma is another important factor. A stigma which is inherited or acquired early in life, such as Downs syndrome, may give its bearer more time to develop coping strategies than one which arrives unexpectedly, later in life, being due, say, to accident or infection. Moreover, the late onset of a stigmatizing condition may involve the person's becoming a member of a group which he or she might previously have disparaged (ibid.). A third factor is the perceived *responsibility* for the possession of the stigma or its maintenance. People outside the stigmatized group – or even within it, in some circumstances – may regard members of that group as being responsible for their plight: overweight people or unemployed workers are often subjected to this perception. In such cases the stigmatized group will usually attract more disapproval than when possession of the stigma is regarded as being outside the person's control (for instance skin colour: ibid.). Of course, this does not mean that members of an 'uncontrollable' stigma group will escape prejudice altogether. Far from it, as the earlier examples showed. It is just that norms inhibiting the expression of prejudice may be somewhat less strict in the case of 'controllable' stigmas.

In the next section I will consider in more detail some of the consequences of belonging to a stigmatized group. Before I do so, there is one more phenomenon that deserves examination. This phenomenon is a common tendency for members of some stigmatized groups actually not to perceive the discrimination that is staring them in the face. An early illustration of this was provided by Crosby (1982). In surveying working women's perceptions of and reactions to gender inequalities, she was surprised to discover that, while most of her respondents agreed that women in general were worse off than men in terms of pay and conditions in the workplace, very few of them *personally* felt any sense of grievance. Several others have observed something similar in other intergroup contexts, and the phenomenon has come to be called the **person–group discrepancy** (Kessler et al., 2000; Moghaddam et al., 1997; Operario and Fiske, 2001; Taylor et al., 1990): in general people seem reluctant to see themselves as hard done by even when they recognize that their group is the object of systematic discrimination.

Perhaps the most vivid illustration of this phenomenon was provided by Ruggiero and Taylor (1997). They arranged for participants – in one study they were women, in another, East Asians and West Indians – to undertake a task on which they subsequently received very negative feedback from a panel of eight judges. Depending on the experimental condition, the participants were told that all, most, half, few or none of these judges were prejudiced against their group. Then they were asked to attribute the reasons for their poor performance grade either to the quality of what they had done in the task or to the judges' prejudice. Surprisingly, only those participants confronted with a unanimously prejudiced panel of judges attributed their negative feedback to discrimination on the judges' part; in all the other conditions, including those where half or three-quarters of the judges were known to be prejudiced, participants resolutely attributed their low score to their own failings on the task.[2] As we shall see, this failure to attribute negative outcomes to a plausible external source has interesting theoretical implications for how members of stigmatized groups are thought to cope with their position.

It is one thing to notice the discrimination; it is quite another to say or do something about it. As we have just seen, members of stigmatized groups seem not to be generally inclined to attribute their misfortunes to the prejudice of others. And even when they may privately do so, they may be even less ready to say something in public about the discrimination, to complain or confront. Swim and Hyers (1999) showed this in an experiment in which women participated in a group decision-making task side by side with three other people (confederates of the experimenter). During the task, one of these confederates, a man, made several rather offensive remarks. In half the groups these were clearly sexist in nature; in the remainder they were not. The sex composition of the group was also varied. Half the time the confederates were all men, so that the participant was a solo woman; in the other condition two of the confederates were women. The central interest of the experiment was to observe how the participants responded to the offensive comments, and also to record their subsequent private reactions. Overall, only a minority (less than 30 per cent) ever said anything in response to the comments and, while those in the sexist comment condition were more likely to say something, still less than half chose to do so. Perhaps surprisingly, there were signs that the women were more likely to make their displeasure known when they were on their own in the group than when they had the moral support of two other women. However, the apparent acquiescence, in public, to the confederate's sexist attitude did not mean that the participants failed to notice it. When asked later to reflect on their experience in the group, the vast majority commented negatively on the offensive male confederate, even if they had said nothing at the time.

Members of stigmatized groups, then, may feel restrained from openly confronting the prejudice they face, perhaps from fear of being seen as a 'complainer' (Kaiser and Miller, 2001; Kowalski, 1996). Such restraint may be especially keenly felt in the presence of other outgroup members. Stangor and colleagues (2002) arranged for participants to take a creativity test and to fail it, and their failure was designed to seem to be attributable to the prejudice of the experimenter, since the test feedback was accompanied by a derogatory comment (for instance: 'like many African Americans, you exhibit traditional thinking where creative thinking is more appropriate'). Participants were subsequently asked to rate the extent to which their failure on the test was attributable to their ability or effort or to discrimination on the part of the tester. Depending on experimental condition, participants underwent the whole procedure on their own or in the presence of another person, either a fellow ingroup member or someone from the outgroup. In these last two conditions, an added wrinkle was that the participants believed that they would have to read their ratings out loud, thus making their opinions very public. There were two notable findings from this study. First, overall, participants showed remarkably little inclination to attribute their failure to the experimenter's bias. Across all conditions, the highest mean value for 'attribution to discrimination' was only just above the mid-point of the scale. This was quite surprising in itself, given the experimenter's obvious prejudice; but it mirrors what Ruggiero and Taylor (1997) had found a few years before. Nevertheless, stigmatized group members did at least attribute their failure more to discrimination than to their own incapacity, *unless they were in the presence of an outgroup member*. In the latter condition, their ratings underwent a complete reversal: now they clearly attributed their poor performance to themselves rather than to the experimenter.

These laboratory findings may give us some insight into why it is that people are often reluctant to report instances of harassment and bullying in the workplace (Magley et al., 1999) and experiences of hate crime (Herek et al., 2002). Publicly confronting prejudice can be socially costly, because it has the potential to disrupt ongoing social relationships with colleagues; because it may be feared to lead to devaluation in the eyes of others; or because it may instigate further discrimination and victimization from those who are complained about.

Consequences of Stigmatization

Well-being

A stigmatized person's lot is not a happy one. One might think, therefore, that members of stigmatized groups, faced with daily reminders of their inferior social status, would have lower levels of self-esteem and well-being by comparison with members of non-stigmatized groups. This is certainly a point of view with a long and distinguished representation. Many psychologists, from Mead (1934) onwards, have assumed that people's self-concepts derive mainly from the way they are seen by others (see for instance Jones et al., 1984). Allport (1954) was in no doubt about this:

> Ask yourself what would happen to your own personality of you heard it said over and over again that you were lazy, a simple child of nature, expected to steal, and had inferior blood. Suppose this opinion were forced on you by the majority of your fellow citizens. And suppose nothing that you could do would change this opinion – because you happen to have black skin […] One's reputation, whether false or true, cannot be hammered, hammered, hammered, into one's head without doing something to one's character. (p. 142)

Despite the common sense of this view, it turns out to be largely incorrect. When careful comparisons are made between stigmatized and non-stigmatized groups, they reveal that, in general, the former do not consistently differ from the latter on such indicators as self-esteem and well-being (Crocker and Major, 1989; Diener and Diener, 1996). Probably the most intensively studied groups are ethnic groups in the

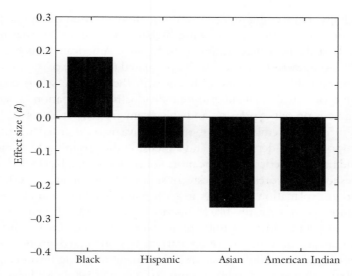

Figure 8.3 Ethnic group differences in self esteem. This figure shows the size of the difference between whites and each of four other ethnic groups. A positive effect size indicates that the ethnic group in question had higher self-esteem than the whites. Results were obtained from a meta-analysis of over 700 samples. From Twenge and Crocker, 2002, Figure 1

USA and elsewhere in the West (see for example Gray-Little and Hafdahl, 2000; Twenge and Crocker, 2002; Verkuyten, 1994). Twenge and Crocker (2002) conducted a comprehensive **meta-analysis** involving several hundred studies in which the self-esteem levels of black, white, Asian, Hispanic and native American people of various ages were compared. Most, but not all, of the respondents lived in the USA. If the traditional view – that minority groups would internalize their societally stigmatized status – were correct, one would expect that all four minority groups should show lower self-esteem than the white majority and that Asians, a somewhat less stigmatized group than blacks or Hispanics, should show a rather smaller decrement than that of the other minority groups. In fact the overall picture was completely at variance with this prediction (see Figure 8.3). As can be seen, blacks actually had *higher* self-esteem than whites in general; and, out of the remaining three minority groups, Asians showed the largest decrement compared to the whites.

Some other findings from Twenge and Crocker's (2002) meta-analysis are interesting. First, age made a difference. For example the relatively higher levels of self-esteem amongst blacks did not emerge until after 10 years of age and, intriguingly, were actually reversed amongst older blacks (over 60 years). This latter group would have been born before the Second World War, when anti-black racism in the USA was more pervasive and institutionalized than it was after the impact of the Civil Rights movement of the 1960s. Conceivably, this was the generation of black children studied by Horowitz (1936) and Clark and Clark (1947), whose work I discussed in Chapter 5. In agreement with this historical change perspective, Twenge and Crocker (2002) also found that studies conducted before 1970 showed almost no black–white difference, whereas later studies did, and increasingly so with each succeeding decade.

These findings are puzzling indeed from the 'internalization of stigma' perspective. Not only is one ethnic minority showing higher self-esteem than the majority, but arguably the least discriminated against group (Asian Americans) has the lowest self-esteem of all. Twenge and Crocker (2002) speculated that some of this between-group variation is attributable to cultural differences in the way the self is conceived and expressed. In groups which favour a more individualistic orientation, where there is a constant emphasis on self-expression and enhancement, self-esteem is likely to be elevated. In cultures which emphasize a more collectivistic or interdependent outlook, it is more usual to find self-deprecation and a focus on the group's achievement. Asians, Hispanics and native Americans may be more collectivistic than blacks and whites, with consequences for their scores on self-esteem scales (Oyserman et al., 2002).

Still, such an explanation, based as it is on cultural values, cannot be the whole story. It cannot account for the black superiority in self-esteem or for the historical changes that this superiority has undergone. Nor can it account for the self-esteem decrements that are observed in other particular stigmatized groups. Overweight women, especially during adolescence or if they manifest eating disorders, often have chronically low self-esteem (Friedman and Brownell, 1995; Miller and Downey, 1999). It may be no coincidence that being overweight, as a stigma, is often thought to be under the stigmatized person's control, and hence attracts more victim blaming and teasing than some other conditions. Recall the evidence from Chapter 5 which suggested that overweight children may be victims of prejudice from a very early age (Powlishta et al., 1994).

However, as I noted at the beginning of this section, such self-esteem deficits amongst stigmatized groups are the exception rather than the rule. This suggests that members of these groups typically develop coping strategies to protect themselves from a hostile social environment, which it is their misfortune to have to face every day. Crocker and Major (1989) envisaged three such strategies. The first one is for such people to attribute their negative outcomes (poor grades, lower pay, unpopularity) to the prejudice of others rather than to their own inadequacies. By externalizing the blame for their plight in this way, stigmatized people can continue to believe in their own self-worth. A second strategy is to restrict their self-comparisons to comparing themselves to other members of the stigmatized group. By so constraining their points of reference, the disparities between their own outcomes and those of others may be lessened. Finally, they may devalue, or disengage from, certain evaluative dimensions (like academic achievement), so that their poor performance on them is less detrimental to self-esteem.

Of these strategies, it is the first one that has excited the most controversy and, since this is also the coping mechanism that involves the prejudice of outgroups, it is probably the one most germane to the focus of this chapter. One of the earliest experimental investigations into the phenomenology of being a target of prejudice was conducted by Dion and Earn (1975). They arranged for some Jewish participants to play a game, supposedly with three other people. The game involved exchanging 'reward' and 'punishment' tokens with one's partner, with the goal of accumulating as many 'rewards' as possible. Actually the game was rigged by the experimenter so that participants always came out of the game badly, presumably – so they believed – because of the actions of the other players. The important manipulation that Dion and Earn introduced was to vary the religious affiliation of the other players: in half the conditions these were made out to be Christians, in the other half no mention was made of their religion (remember, all the participants were Jewish). This simple introduction of a religious outgroup identity had a dramatic effect on the participants' interpretation of, and reactions to, their poor game result: in the 'Christian' condition, over 70 per cent of the participants mentioned that their being Jewish was a likely reason for their failure; in the 'no information' condition, not a single participant mentioned this reason. Moreover, in the 'Christian' condition, participants reported being more aggressive, sad and anxious, confirming, as I already noted earlier in the chapter, that it is no fun to feel you are a victim of discrimination. However, and crucially for the Crocker–Major hypothesis, those same participants showed no negative effects in their overall self-esteem. In fact, on one single item – how good/ bad are you? – those in the 'Christian' condition actually scored noticeably higher than those in the 'no information' control condition. Conceivably, then, their external attributions of failure to the prejudice of the other players protected their self-esteem, just as Crocker and Major (1989) would have predicted.

When stigmatized people fail to make such an external attribution, their self-esteem can suffer. Crocker and colleagues (1993) recruited some 'overweight' women to take part in a 'dating relationships' study in which they had to exchange some personal and biographical information – including on their weight and height – with a man in the room next door. After this exchange of information, participants learned that the man either was or was not interested in going out with them on a romantic date. Their reactions to this positive or negative feedback were interesting. In the positive condition, the overweight women did not differ from normal weight women in their attributions or their emotional responses. However, in the negative condition the overweight women were more likely than normal weight women to attribute their rejection to weight (an internal factor), and they showed little additional tendency to attribute it to the man himself (an external factor). Consequently, those rejected overweight women showed enhanced negative affect, depression and anxiety.

If these two studies supported the Crocker–Major hypothesis, other findings have been more ambiguous, and still others directly contradicted it (Major et al., 2002a; Schmitt and Branscombe, 2002). Crocker and colleagues (1991) could find only weak evidence linking one's external attributions of failure to the prejudice of an outgroup to the protection of one's self-esteem. The stigmatized groups in these two studies were African Americans and women. Also working with women participants, Dion (1975) found that those who experienced severe defeat in a game conducted with a male opponent showed lower self-esteem than those whose defeat was milder. Only through an internal analysis, in which those male opponents were classified as 'highly prejudiced' or 'less prejudiced', were these (non-significant) indications of self-esteem after defeat 'buffered' by blaming the defeat on the prejudice of the male opponent.

Other studies have provided evidence which seems inconsistent with the Crocker–Major point of view. Earlier on I described a study by Ruggiero and Taylor (1997) in which members of stigmatized groups seemed reluctant to attribute their poor performance to the prejudice of those evaluating them. In that same study, the measures of self-esteem did not unequivocally support the Crocker–Major idea. It is true that the self-esteem connected to performance on the task was consistently and positively correlated with tendencies to attribute poor performance to the prejudice of others, as Crocker and Major would have expected. But a measure of 'social' self-esteem (as expressed for instance in 'I am not worried about what other people think of me') correlated *negatively* with attributions to prejudice. Ruggiero and Taylor (1997) speculated that their participants' unwillingness to blame their failure on others may have been related to a desire to retain some sense of control. Indeed a measure of perceived control showed elevated scores in all the conditions where participants had resolutely refused to make external attributions, and was noticeably lower in the one condition where they made such an attribution (when there could have been no doubt that their failure reflected the judge's bias). There is evidence from other domains that retaining a feeling of control over one's life is positively associated with various indicators of well-being (Langer, 1975; Thompson and Spacapan, 1991).

Although it would be foolish to generalize too readily from this kind of experimental setting, Ruggiero and Taylor's findings that members of disadvantaged groups may occasionally blame themselves for their plight, even in the face of contrary evidence, finds echoes in other research with stigmatized groups. Recall the so-called 'person–group discrepancy' phenomenon I noted earlier (Crosby, 1982). Here members of lower-status groups, while acknowledging that their group suffered discrimination in general, resolutely deny that they themselves are victims of any discrimination. Then there were those seemingly paradoxical findings that victims of rape and genocide sometimes experience feelings of shame – an inwardly directed self-denigrating emotion (Janoff-Bulman, 1979; Kanyangara et al., 2007; Páez et al., 2006). None of these observations sits easily with the idea that people need to protect themselves from the consequences of negative life events by assigning the blame for them elsewhere.

A further challenge to the Crocker–Major theory has come from Branscombe and her colleagues (Branscombe et al., 1999; Schmitt and Branscombe, 2002a and 2002b). According to Branscombe, believing that one is the target of discrimination, far from being self-protective, is actually deleterious for self-esteem. It is so, she believes, because it implies that others devalue one's ingroup and hence, by extension, that they devalue their person too. That this belief is not always irrevocably damaging for stigmatized group members is explained by a second process, that of enhanced identification (Branscombe et al., 1999). Groups which experience threats and discrimination from outside typically show increases in cohesion and identification, as we saw in Chapter 6. This bolstered identification can then restore self-esteem to its former level. For this reason, this account is called the **'rejection–identification model'** (Schmitt and Branscombe, 2002b). There are several, mostly correlational, studies to support this model (ibid.). Perhaps most well known is Branscombe and colleagues' (1999) survey of a small sample of African American students. They were asked how often they had experienced prejudice on account of their ethnicity. As expected from the rejection–identification model, this index was negatively correlated with their well-being. However, it was also *positively* correlated with how strongly they identified themselves as African Americans. And, once this heightened identification was factored into the analysis, the negative link to self-esteem disappeared. In technical terms, identification acted as a mediator variable, suppressing the previous negative relationship between attributions to discrimination and self-esteem.

What sense can we make of this controversy? Fortunately, Major and colleagues (2002a), in a careful re-analysis of the literature, have offered several useful insights that suggest that some of this confusion is apparent rather than real. A recurring theme in their analysis is the importance of different situational conditions and individual variables that are likely to affect the impact that experiences and perceptions of discrimination will have on well-being. In the initial research on stigmatization and self-esteem, such moderating factors had rarely been examined.

The first among these factors – somewhat ironically, in view of its role in Branscombe and colleagues' (1999) model – is group identification itself. It is reasonable to suppose that those for whom the stigmatized group identity is more central or more important to their self-definition would be more alert to the many forms that discrimination against them might take, and might also feel the pain of that social rejection more keenly. There is evidence that this is the case. More strongly identified group members seem to perceive more prejudice against them, especially in situations where there is some interpretive ambiguity about its presence (McCoy and Major, 2003; Operario and Fiske, 2001). Moreover, exposure to such prejudice is associated with a worsened mood for those more strongly identified people (McCoy and Major, 2003).

Different ideological beliefs also affect people's responses to group-based discrimination. Those who hold fast to a belief system in which the possibility and desirability of individual advancement based on merit is central are less likely to perceive discrimination, but are more vulnerable to it if its existence is undeniable (Major et al., 2002a, 2007). And there may be personality variables that cause some individuals to be more sensitive to stigmatizing behaviour than others (Mendoza-Denton et al., 2002; Pinel, 1999).

How do these moderator variables help to reconcile the seemingly contradictory theories – and evidence – on the likelihood of attributing negative outcomes to discrimination, and on the psychological consequences of doing so? Let me take the oft-cited paper by Branscombe and colleagues (1999), which showed a negative correlation between perceived discrimination and self-esteem in African Americans. Following Major and colleagues' (2002a) analysis of potential moderator variables, we would infer that the participants in this study either were especially high in ethnic identification or strongly endorsed meritocratic beliefs; or both. Similarly, the reluctance of participants in Ruggiero and Taylor's (1997) study to see the discrimination under their noses might well be attributable to a rather low level of initial group identification. Given the laboratory nature of an experiment in which group identities cannot have been very salient, such an assumption is plausible enough.

In summary, then, Allport's (1954) and others' fears about the inevitably deleterious consequences of belonging to a stigmatized group seem to have been misplaced. The number and complexity of identity protecting (and sensitizing) mechanisms mean that such a simple equation of stigma with depressed well-being is seldom valid.

Task performance

In many countries it is not unusual to find that different ethnic groups perform very differently at school. In Britain, for example, when one tallies the number of school students obtaining at least five GCSE examination passes at grades A–C, stark differences emerge between the best and worst performing groups (see Figure 8.4). Roma gypsies and Irish travellers do worst: only about one fifth of these children obtain five GCSEs. At the other end of the league table, Indian and Chinese students easily

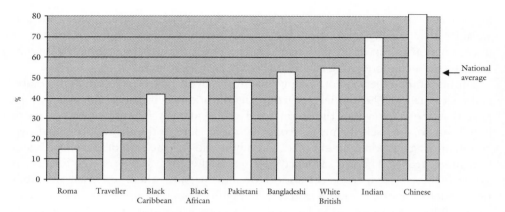

Figure 8.4 Ethnic group differences in examination performance among British school students. The figures show the percentage of each group achieving five GCSE exam passes (grades A–C). Adapted from Table 8 in Department for Education and Skills, 2006

outperform their peers, with 70 per cent and 81 per cent respectively achieving the same standard. These group averages conceal other disparities. Girls outperform boys in every group; and those from the poorest backgrounds (who are in receipt of free school meals) do worst of all – white British boys in this category perform worse than Irish travellers overall.

There are obviously many reasons for these discrepancies in academic achievement. Presumably socio-economic deprivation is taking its toll, although this cannot be the whole story, since groups with rather similar economic positions (Indians and Pakistanis) perform very differently. The different value that cultural groups place on education may well be another causal factor, which might explain why Indians and Chinese do so well. However, Steele and Aronson (1995) suggested that another cause may also contribute to ethnic group differences in academic success. They speculated that the awareness in certain ethnic groups that there are pervasively held cultural stereotypes about their lack of intellectual ability might be enough to cause them to under-perform. To test this controversial hypothesis, Steele and Aronson (1995) invited black and white students – they happened to be from Stanford University, one of the most prestigious institutions in the USA – to undertake a difficult verbal reasoning test. For half the participants, the experiment was described as being part of research into 'psychological factors involved in solving verbal problems'. This condition Steele and Aronson labelled 'non-diagnostic', since the test appeared to the participants to be part of a standard piece of scientific research. The remaining participants received a subtly different description of the experiment. Now the test was described as a 'genuine test of your verbal abilities and limitations'. Steele and Aronson dubbed this condition 'diagnostic', since performance on the test now seemed to be genuinely reflective of the ability to reason. This simple instructional variation had a dramatic effect on the black participants' test performance, as can be seen in Figure 8.5. Those in the 'diagnostic' condition solved, on average, around four items fewer than their counterparts in the 'non-diagnostic' condition. They also did worse then the whites in the 'diagnostic' condition. Two other features of this result are noteworthy: first, the participants' scores were adjusted for their actual academic ability as measured by

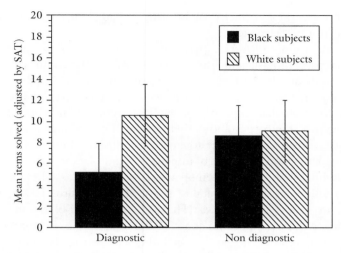

Figure 8.5 Effects of stereotype threat on the test performance of black and white students. From Steele and Aronson, 1995, Figure 2

a standardized scholastic aptitude test. Moreover, since participants were randomly assigned to the experimental conditions, there should have been no individual differences in ability between the 'diagnostic' and the 'non-diagnostic' conditions. Secondly, as I noted above, the participants were all Stanford students and Stanford is notoriously difficult to gain entry to. In other words these were highly talented and highly achieving students. And yet the blacks of this elite group – and only the blacks – reacted adversely to that simple instructional variation.

Steele and Aronson (1995) ascribed this performance decrement to **stereotype threat** – that is, to the (threatening) knowledge that in American society there are commonly held and believed stereotypes about the intellectual inferiority of black people. Black participants in the 'diagnostic' condition were reminded of these negative cultural stereotypes and, for some reason or another, performed in such a way as to be consistent with them. That such stereotypes were implicated in the lowered performance was indicated by some findings from other studies conducted by Steele and Aronson (1995). In one experiment the standard stereotype threat procedure was followed ('diagnostic' versus 'non-diagnostic' test-taking instructions), except that participants never actually took the test. Instead, they undertook an implicit stereotype activation assessment directly after receiving the diagnostic/non-diagnostic instructions. This consisted of them completing a number of word fragments that could form different works (for example – - C E (RACE or FACE); – - A C K (BLACK or SLACK)). Black participants in the diagnostic condition were more likely to complete the fragments in a stereotypically or categorially relevant manner than those in the non-diagnostic condition, thus indicating that their ethnicity and its associated stereotypes were more salient for them. In another study, Steele and Aronson (1995) replaced the diagnostic/non-diagnostic procedure with an ethnic category priming manipulation. Before taking the verbal reasoning test, participants were asked to provide some demographic information (say, age, subject major, parents' education). In the ethnic prime condition only, one of the demographic items asked for was their ethnicity. Again, this one additional question was enough to lower their test performance.

Steele and Aronson's (1995) experiments provoked a minor storm of interest amongst social psychologists and educationalists. At the last count, in 2009, I found over 300 scientific articles with the words 'stereotype threat' in their title or in the abstract. Stereotype threat effects – that is, worsened task performance due to some instructional variation that implicitly or explicitly reminds members of stigmatized groups of negative stereotypes about them – have been found in a wide variety of group settings: women on tests of mathematical ability (Cadinu et al., 2005; Spencer et al., 1999), elderly people on tests of intelligence and memory (Abrams et al., 2006; Levy, 1996; Rahhal et al., 2001), men on a social sensitivity task (Leyens et al., 2000), working-class students on verbal ability (Croizet and Claire, 1998), unemployed workers on a text comprehension task (Herman, 2007), and blacks and whites on an athletic task like golf putting (Stone et al., 1999). Women's performance in a real life educational test has also been found to be influenced by the seemingly trivial matter of eliciting from them socio-demographic information (including their gender) before or after the test (Danaher and Crandall, 2008). These and many other studies have been well reviewed by Maass and Cadinu (2003), Steele and colleagues (2002) and Shapiro and Neuberg (2007).

Stereotype threat phenomena remind us immediately of self-fulfilling prophecy effects, which I discussed in Chapter 4. There, it will be recalled, one of the more insidious consequences of stereotypes turned out to be their power to bring about, in the stereotyped people, behavioural changes that are consistent with the stereotypes themselves. Thus the stereotypes are reinforced and the social world is reshaped in their image. But there is an important difference between the self-fulfilling prophecy effects and those due to stereotype threat. When stereotypes that we hold bring about expectancy-confirming changes in others, this is probably due to *our* behaviour. We treat those people differently, whether due to intergroup anxiety, ignorance or downright hostility, and they react accordingly. However, the origins of stereotype effects seem to lie more within the targets of the stereotype themselves. When something in the situation makes stigmatized group members more aware of the prevailing negative stereotype about their group, their behaviour comes more into line with that stereotype. Quite how, why and when this happens is something that I shall consider shortly.

Before I do so, though, there is one other related phenomenon that needs to be mentioned. This is **stereotype lift**, called so because it seems that, in many of the very same situations where performance decrements in the negatively stereotyped group have been found, it is possible to observe performance *increments* in the other group. Recall Figure 8.5, which showed the results of one of the original Steele and Aronson (1995) studies. The performance of the white participants was slightly (and non-significantly) higher in the 'diagnostic' condition. This turns out to be the case in many stereotype threat experiments. According to Walton and Cohen (2003), who conducted a meta-analysis of stereotype threat studies, over 80 per cent of the studies they examined showed a similar non-significant 'lift' effect in the non-stereotyped group. However, such was the consistency of those effects that Walton and Cohen concluded that it was unlikely for them to have happened by chance. To be sure, stereotype 'lift' is noticeably weaker than stereotype 'threat' – less than half its magnitude – but it appears to be real enough.

Early attempts to explain stereotype threat phenomena proved frustrating (Steele et al., 2002). There was no evidence that stigmatized group members tried less hard in the more 'threatening' conditions; if anything, the opposite was the case. Another explanation could be that people feel more anxious when their social identity is on the line, as it is in the 'diagnostic' condition. Actually in the early Steele and Aronson (1995) studies there was little evidence of this, from self-report measures of stress and anxiety; and other studies have also failed to find that anxiety is what drives stereotype threat task deficits (Steele et al., 2002). Still, it may be that people's self-reports of how anxious they are feeling are not a wholly accurate guide as to their actual state of bodily arousal. Studies using physiological measures have found alterations in heart rate and blood pressure in the stereotype threat paradigm, which suggests that people do react adversely when they are aware that their group's stereotype is 'in the air', as Steele (1997) put it (Blascovich et al., 2001; Croizet et al., 2004; Murphy et al., 2007).

In any case, the idea that all stereotype threat effects can be explained by something like heightened anxiety, or indeed by any one single factor, is probably too simplistic. The sheer diversity of contexts that seem to elicit performance decrements and the wide range of different tasks on which they have been found (for example intellectual, social, sensorimotor) all point to a rather complex set of causal processes that underlie them. Schmader and colleagues (2008) have proposed an interesting model, which goes a long way towards capturing that complexity. They suggest that being exposed to a stereotype threatening situation sets in train both emotional and cognitive processes that combine to affect task performance in different ways. Taking cognitive ability tasks first, since these have been used in the majority of stereotype threat studies, Schmader and colleagues believe that the primary cause of under-performance on such tasks is disruption to the efficiency of people's working memory. This disruption could emanate from a number of sources. It might come from the elevated physiological arousal or stress responses to threatening situations. These, by themselves, might constitute something of a mental load and leave less cognitive capacity for dealing with the task at hand.

In addition, becoming, or being made, more aware of one's group membership in an evaluative setting might trigger more cognitively oriented processes. One of these could be an increased tendency to monitor one's performance, especially in order to avoid making errors. On many of the tasks used in stereotype threat experiments, being especially careful not to make mistakes may result in lowered performance. Seibt and Förster (2004) found some evidence that people in stereotype threat situations become focused on not making mistakes – what they call having a *prevention focus* – rather than on maximizing their attainments (*promotion focus*).

But disruption to working memory does not seem a very plausible explanation for performance decrements on physical tasks. On the face of it, being able to put a golf ball accurately, to cite one of the tasks that has displayed stereotype threat effects (Stone et al., 1999), would not seem to depend very much on working memory capacity! In fact one could make the argument, as Schmader and colleagues (2008) do, that for such well learned sensorimotor tasks it is the *absence* of cognitive activity that is normally what is required for success. As soon as we start thinking too much about hitting a golf ball or kicking a football, our performance is likely to suffer. Thus Schmader and colleagues suggest that, in sensorimotor tasks, stereotype threat decrements are most probably due to an excess of thinking brought about by the situational cues that activate the stereotype. In support of this explanation, Beilock and colleagues (2006) found that expert golfers actually performed *better* in a stereotype threatening situation if they had simultaneously to perform a second, word monitoring task while they were putting. Depleting their cognitive resources in this way led them to perform their well learned skills more automatically and hence better, as they were unencumbered by too much self-awareness.[3]

If Schmader and colleagues' (2008) model can help us to understand why members of stigmatized groups often under-perform in task situations, it is less easy to see how it explains those slight but apparently consistent 'lift' effects in the 'other' group. Schmader and colleagues suggest that such 'lift' effects may be due to the activation of a *positive* stereotype for the non-targeted group. This positive stereotype might counteract performance inhibiting processes such as arousal, over-monitoring and suppression. But, as Walton and Cohen (2003) point out, this assumption – that stereotype threat situations typically involve a positive stereotype for the non-targeted group as well as a negative stereotype for the stigmatized group – may not be warranted. Very often there is *no* particular stereotype associated with the 'other' group (Aronson et al., 1999). Instead, argue Walton and Cohen (2003), those small stereotype 'lift' effects may be due to some kind of downward comparison process – an awareness in the white (or male, or middle-class) participants that the stigmatized group (black, female, or working-class) is reputed for being poor at the task at hand. There are suggestions from other domains that downward comparisons can make people feel better about themselves and perhaps perform better as a result (Tesser et al., 1988; Wills, 1981).

Let us return to the main focus of our discussion: performance decrements due to stereotype threat. Not surprisingly, because of the potentially serious social and educational implications of this effect for the life chances of particular groups, much attention has been devoted to discovering methods of diminishing it. One good idea may be to reduce one's identification with the stigmatized category. Just as the effect of stigma on well-being seems to be especially acute for those who identify more strongly with their group, so, too, stereotype threat effects may be stronger for more strongly identified group members (Schmader, 2002). However, it may be neither practical nor desirable to encourage minority group members to disidentify with their group, and so other techniques hold more promise.

One such technique is called **self-affirmation** (Sherman and Cohen, 2006; Steele, 1988). Here people are invited to reaffirm their self-integrity by thinking about, and then writing about, their most important value(s). This simple exercise has been found to have measurable beneficial effects in a wide variety of domains, including health behaviours, stress, attitude change and reduced tendencies to engage in self and group serving attributions (Sherman and Cohen, 2006). Cohen and colleagues (2006) implemented a self-affirmation intervention for white and black students in an American middle school. The intervention employed a **randomized double-blind design** in an actual classroom setting, the teachers being unaware of which students had been assigned to which condition. This one short intervention – apparently the self-affirmation exercise took only fifteen minutes to complete – was enough to alter the subsequent grade point average of the black students (by between 0.25 and 0.35 of a grade point). The white students' performance was unaffected. Remarkably enough, the difference between the black students in the intervention condition and those in the control condition was still visible several weeks after the self-affirmation exercise.

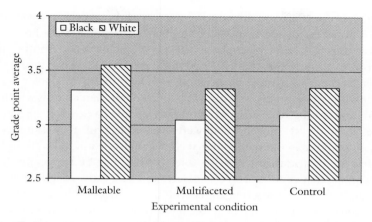

Figure 8.6 Changing views about the nature of intelligence and improved academic performance. Adapted from Table 1 in Aronson et al., 2002

Another possibility is to change the lay theories of members of stigmatized group about the nature of the task-relevant ability. In the case of intellectual tasks – which is where most stereotype threat effects have been observed – this might involve persuading people that intelligence is less fixed, more malleable, than they originally believed. In general, people who hold such beliefs about intelligence seem to be less anxious, try harder and do better at various cognitive tasks (Dweck, 1999). Aronson and colleagues (2002) set about trying to change some Stanford University students' views about intelligence by having them write encouraging letters to deprived middle-school students as part of an educational scheme called 'Scholastic Pen Pals'. In one condition (malleable), the Stanford students were asked to write letters that stressed the malleable, constantly changing nature of intelligence because, it was said, this would be particularly helpful to their younger correspondents. In another condition, the participants were asked to write instead that intelligence consisted of several different components (multi-faceted). These different 'theories' of intelligence were backed up with realistic and scientifically plausible videos. And, of course, there was a control condition, where participants wrote no letters at all. The inspiration for this letter-writing procedure might have come from some classic attitude change techniques derived from **cognitive dissonance theory** (Festinger, 1957). According to Festinger, more often than not we change our attitudes and beliefs to bring them into line with our behaviour rather than the other way around. By asking their participants to write convincing letters to those disadvantaged youngsters, Aronson and colleagues (2002) hoped (and succeeded) to change the Stanford students' views about the nature of intelligence. And, crucially, those same students' grades improved over the next few months! (See Figure 8.6.) This improvement was most obvious – and statistically significant – for the black students, those most vulnerable to stereotype threat. But even the white students improved a little in the 'malleable theory' condition.

So far I have focused on interventions which seek to bring about change within the stigmatized group members, in their views of themselves or about the nature of intelligence. But it is possible that changes in their *relationship* with the non-stigmatized group might also be efficacious in reducing stereotype threat performance decrements. Earlier on I noted in passing that Abrams and colleagues (2006) had observed stereotype threat effects in elderly people on various cognitive tasks. Another interesting finding from that study was that those performance deficits were greatly reduced – even virtually absent – for those participants who habitually had a great deal of pleasant contact with younger people. This was confirmed in a later study, which looked at the amount and quality of contact which elderly people had with their grandchildren (Abrams et al., in press). Indeed, there were even indications that asking elderly people simply to *imagine* an intergenerational contact episode might be enough to buffer them against stereotype threat deficits (ibid.). What may be happening here is that increased contact may reduce people's anxiety; and lessened anxiety, as we saw earlier, may be beneficial in counteracting stereotype threat effects. There is now much evidence that one consequence of favourable intergroup contact is indeed lessened intergroup anxiety (Brown and Hewstone, 2005). I will return to this issue in more detail in the next chapter.

Justifying, accepting or challenging the status quo

A recurring theme of this chapter has been the impact on members of stigmatized groups of knowing that their groups are devalued by society at large. In this final section I want to consider a claim, made by some, that people who belong to such socially devalued groups not only accept their inferior status, but actively conspire to support the very system that gives rise to it. This idea forms the heart of **system justification theory**, first proposed by Jost and Banaji (1994) and energetically promulgated by Jost and his colleagues since (see Jost et al., 2004; Jost and Hunyady, 2002).

The starting assumption of system justification theory is that ideologies, belief systems, group stereotypes – call them what you will – often serve the function of justifying some social arrangement or the mistreatment of others. We have already encountered literally dozens of examples of this phenomenon elsewhere in the book: seeing an ethnic minority as 'stupid', or the unemployed as 'lazy', or immigrants as 'threatening our way of life', are all convenient perceptions for legitimating various forms of discrimination against the groups in question (see Chapters 4, 6 and 7). Such an assumption is hardly controversial when applied to those who do the discriminating – members of larger or more powerful groups who, by and large, are the main agents of prejudice and discrimination. From Marx and Engels (1965 [1846]) onward, there has been a widespread acceptance of the idea that people's views about society and about the groups that comprise it will tend to reflect their interests, and hence to justify any social relationships which perpetuate those interests (LeVine and Campbell, 1972; Tajfel, 1981b). What is less obvious is Jost and colleagues' (2004) claim that members of *stigmatized* groups will often endorse those same negative stereotypes about themselves and will have a propensity to be even more enthusiastic supporters of the status quo than people in more privileged groups.

What arguments could support such an apparently paradoxical hypothesis? There are several (Jost and Banaji, 1994; Jost et al., 2003b; Jost and Hunyady, 2002). One is inspired by the conventional Marxist notion of **false consciousness** (Jost and Banaji, 1994). If ruling elites are sufficiently powerful to own and control all the institutions of the state and of the private sector, including the mass media, they can do much to ensure that consensual views about how the world is also become views about how the world should be. As Jost and Banaji (1994) put it, 'the ideas of the dominant tend to become the ideas of the dominated' (p. 10). Or, to put it more crudely, stigmatized groups get brainwashed into believing all the bad press about them.

Other arguments for system justification theory are more psychological in nature. Jost and colleagues (2003b) suggest that a mix of cognitive and motivational processes will conspire to make members of disadvantaged groups more likely to want to justify the system than those higher up in the system. These processes include needs for the reduction of uncertainty and for structure and control, together with a strong desire to reduce dissonance. According to Jost and colleagues, living in a stable and orderly system, even one which is apparently doing you no favours, is more comfortable and hence preferable to the prospect of a society in flux, where the future position of the ingroup may be unpredictable and hence unsettling. Cognitive dissonance may also be at work. Just as new group members who have endured a painful initiation into the group will often say that they like the group more than those whose entry was less uncomfortable (Aronson and Mills, 1959; Gerard and Mathewson, 1966), members of stigmatized groups will justify and defend the system that oppresses them more than those who actually benefit from the system. Jost and colleagues (2003b) concede that any such system dissonance reduction must operate differently from the individual dissonance reduction involved in attitude change and in decision-making (Festinger, 1957). The reason is that, in the classic demonstrations of dissonance-induced effects, a key element of the dissonance equation is always the person's (perceived) choice over one of the dissonant cognitions: 'I chose to join this group; I have just been through an extremely painful/embarassing experience to enter it; therefore, the group must be *really* attractive to me' (Cooper and Fazio, 1984). But this element of volition or choice would seem to be absent for most disadvantaged groups in society. Nevertheless, Jost and colleagues (2003b) still believe that 'those who suffer the most must also have the most to explain, justify and rationalize' (p. 16). As they put it, system justification is 'the ideological equivalent of eating grasshopper and then justifying one's appetite' (Jost et al., 2003b, p. 16; compare Zimbardo et al., 1965).

So much for the arguments; what about the evidence? The starting point for system justification theory was the well attested phenomenon that members of subordinate groups often show **out**group bias in their intergroup judgements (Hinkle and Brown, 1990; Mullen et al., 1992; Tajfel and Turner, 1986; see Chapter 6). Such outgroup preferences can also be observed on quasi-implicit indicators like the IAT (Jost et al., 2004; Jost et al., 2002; Rudman et al., 2002; see Chapter 7). System justification theorists take these findings at face value, to mean that members of disadvantaged groups actually believe in their inferiority and, by implication, endorse the system that has given rise to it (Jost et al., 2004).

A second line of evidence adduced in support of the theory comes from a series of American surveys, which seem to show that poorer people hold attitudes which are less critical and more supportive of the government than higher earners (Jost et al., 2004). For example, in one early study, respondents who earned less than $6,000 a year were twice as likely to want to limit the rights of individuals or of the press to criticize the government as those earning more than $16,000 a year were. A later study, this time involving Hispanic respondents – already a deprived group – found that those earning less than $9,000 seemed to believe more strongly than those earning $40,000 (or over) that the government was run for the benefit of all. In some – but not all – of these surveys, the apparently more deferential attitudes of lower-income groups disappeared once the education level was controlled for.

In summary, then, system justification theory is a species of functionalist explanation in which the continued existence of the current social order is posited as a factor motivating subordinate group members to view their group in a less favourable light than they view privileged groups, and to endorse political positions which would seem to run counter to their group's interests. To paraphrase all those anonymous graffiti writers: 'the system rules, OK!'

How plausible is this theory? To begin with, we can note that, like all functionalist theories, system justification theory has some difficulty in accounting for social change, especially for reforms or revolutions that seem to be instigated from below. Examples would include the wholesale introduction of the successful battles for independence of former British colonies like India and Kenya in the 1940s and 1950s; the welfare state in Britain after the Second World War; the demand for greater civil rights and equal opportunities made by African Americans in the 1960s; the collapse of one communist state after another in the late 1980s; and the abolition of apartheid in South Africa in the 1990s. If people are always so enamoured of the status quo, how could these changes ever have occurred?

Some of the evidence adduced in support of system justification theory is also open to other interpretations. This is particularly true of the outgroup favouritism data. As Spears and colleagues (2001) and Rubin and Hewstone (2004) point out, just because members of subordinate groups will often rate their group less favourably than a demonstrably higher-status group does not mean that they have internalized their inferiority.[4] Instead, they may just be reluctantly acknowledging a current, and maybe only temporary, social reality.[5] Rubin and Hewstone (2004) adduce the useful example of sporting contests. As I gloomily survey the premier league table in 2009, I am forced to concede that Manchester United has amassed more points this year than my beloved Liverpool. But this grudging recognition of the reality of the teams' respective league positions is a far cry from my believing that Manchester is inherently superior to us! Moreover, the vast majority of studies finding outgroup favouritism in subordinate groups have used rating dimensions such as perceived competence, which are closely related to the way the groups' respective status positions are defined. Yet, as Leach and colleagues (2007) have argued, such rating dimensions have overlooked what may be the most important attribute of all: the ingroup's perceived morality. Leach and colleagues suggest that a more widespread use of moral evaluations by intergroup researchers might well reveal much less of the allegedly system justifying outgroup favouritism, which is so critical for the validity of the theory.

A further difficulty for system justification theory is the existence of ***schadenfreude***, the malicious pleasure that subordinate groups sometimes get from witnessing the discomfiture or defeat of privileged groups at the hands of others (Leach et al., 2007). If everyone is content with their lot and desirous that the existing social order should continue, why should they be so happy about misfortunes befalling the 'top dogs' in the system?

What of the survey data in which poorer groups seem to be stronger supporters of the government than the better off groups (Jost et al., 2004)? At first sight these findings are indeed puzzling. Still, they do not provide unambiguous support for system justification theory either. The fact that the relationship between income level and deferential attitudes is considerably diminished when the education level is controlled for is not so easy to explain in terms of system justification theory. Moreover, there are few, if any, studies that actually include some measure of cognitive dissonance – one of the processes thought to underlie these system favouring beliefs. Finally, we should note that the central tenet of system justification theory – the idea that stigmatized groups believe in their relative inferiority, and also in the system that produces it – is rather at odds with one of the theories of coping with stigma which I discussed earlier in this chapter (Crocker and Major, 1989; Major et al., 2002a). As we saw there, one potent strategy open to members of groups which are at the wrong end of society's pecking order is to seek external reasons for their plight (for instance in the discrimination of others) – precisely the opposite of what system justification theory would have us believe to be the case.

Summary

1   Much research exists that documents the daily and unpleasant reality of being on the receiving end of prejudice. From verbal harassment in the street to hate crime and genocide, there is no doubt that being a victim of prejudice has aversive consequences.

2   It is useful to consider these experiences under the overarching concept of stigma. Stigma is an attribute that places a person in a socially devalued group. Stigma may be visible, as in skin colour, or concealed, as in HIV status. It may also be perceived as something that the person had (or had not) responsibility for acquiring. These different aspects of stigma may carry different consequences for its bearer.

3   Belonging to a stigmatized group was once thought to have mainly negative consequences for well-being. However, the self-esteem of stigmatized group members is often as high as that of members of other groups. This is because members of stigmatized groups can adopt a variety of coping strategies to protect themselves.

4   Members of stigmatized groups often under-perform in various academic domains. One cause of this may be 'stereotype threat', a heightened awareness of the prevailing negative stereotype about the capacity of the ingroup to undertake the task in question. Stereotype threat effects are forms of self-fulfilling prophecy. Their explanation probably lies in a mixture of emotional and cognitive processes that disrupt optimal performance on the task.

5   Members of lower-status groups may sometimes appear to endorse beliefs which seem to reinforce and justify the system that has disadvantaged them. Whether this is a genuine phenomenon is a matter of dispute.

Notes

1   In the USA, hate crime is also known as 'bias crime' (Herek et al., 2002).
2   It should be noted that it has not always proved easy to replicate these findings (Inman, 2001; Kaiser and Miller, 2001). Moreover, some have cast doubt on Ruggiero's research in general,

because of her public retractions of other papers as containing fraudulent data (Major et al., 2002a). The retractions, which do not include Ruggiero and Taylor (1997) or the earlier Ruggiero and Taylor (1995), may be found in Ruggiero and Major (2002), Ruggiero and Marx (2001), Ruggiero and colleagues (2002), Ruggiero and colleagues (2001).

3 It strikes me that England footballers might well want to try this technique the next time they are involved in a penalty shoot out. Following their disastrous penalty-taking at a succession of international tournaments (such as World Cup 1990, 1998; European Championship, 1996, 2004), they have gained a well deserved reputation for being quite hopeless at this aspect of the game. Perhaps, as each English player now steps up to take a penalty, he is only too well aware of this negative stereotype, suffers from an excess of intrusive self-doubting thoughts, and then blasts the ball over the bar as a result. I can even report that British social psychologists are not immune from this particular stereotype. At the now traditional international football match at the General Meeting of the European Association of Experimental Social Psychology in Wurzburg, 2005, a British team lost to the Dutch on penalties. Modesty prevents me from saying whether I was one of the penalty-missing culprits.

4 I am reminded here of some lines from Leonard Cohen's heavily ironic song *Everybody Knows*:

> Everybody knows that the dice are loaded
> Everybody rolls with their fingers crossed
> Everybody knows the war is over
> Everybody knows the good guys lost
> Everybody knows that the fight was fixed
> Everybody knows the poor stay poor and the rich get rich
> Everybody knows.
>
> (Leonard Cohen and Sharon Robinson,
> 1988; From *I'm Your Man*)

5 And the many studies using the IAT which also show outgroup favouritism cannot really be taken as evidence for internalized inferiority either. As we saw in Chapter 7, there is a far from resolved controversy about whether the differential reaction times that comprise the IAT index of prejudice actually imply an endorsement of particular attitudes towards an outgroup.

Further Reading

Jost, J. T., and Hunyady, O. (2002) The psychology of system justification and the palliative function of ideology. *European Review of Social Psychology* 13: 111–53.

Major, B., Quinton, W. J., and McCoy, S. (2002a) Antecedents and consequences of attributions to discrimination: Theoretical and empirical advances. *Advances in Experimental Social Psychology* 34: 251–330.

Steele, C. M., Spencer, S. J., and Aronson, J. (2002) Contending with group image: The psychology of stereotype and social identity threat. *Advances in Experimental Social Psychology* 34: 379–440.

9

Reducing Prejudice

I began this book with a tribute to Allport's *The Nature of Prejudice* (1954). As I embark on this final chapter (in 2009), it is over fifty years since that milestone publication. It is also over fifty years since a momentous Supreme Court decision in the USA, which declared ethnically segregated schools to be unconstitutional (*Brown* v *Board of Education*, Topeka, Kansas [1954]). Allport himself was one of the contributors to the expert testimony to that legal decision – a carefully argued statement by a group of social scientists on the deleterious social and educational consequences of segregated education (Clark et al., 2004). It is therefore fitting that this chapter should be devoted almost exclusively to Allport's most enduring contribution to social psychology: the **contact hypothesis**. A recurring theme of Allport's writing, and a theme certainly echoed throughout this book, is that of the mundanity and pervasiveness of prejudice. Because of our limited cognitive capacities and because of important social motivations inherent in our membership of different groups, the propensity for prejudiced thinking and behaviour is never far away. However, does a recognition of the human potential for prejudice mean that we have to accept its inevitability? Allport himself, and the generations of social psychologists he inspired, believed passionately that it does not. He argued that there are powerful social interventions which will both reduce the intensity of prejudice and counter its worst effects.

I begin the chapter with a detailed examination of the social conditions which research has demonstrated to be so important for ensuring that intergroup contact has the positive effect we intend it to have. In a second section I focus specifically on contact in educational settings, exploring why some desegregation attempts have not lived up to their promise and what techniques have proved more successful. A third section is devoted to a re-evaluation of the contact hypothesis in light of the fifty years of theory and research it has provoked. In that reassessment I shall consider such questions as: What factors promote – and what factors inhibit – the generalization of attitudes instigated by the experience of contact with members of the outgroup we have not yet met? How and why does contact have the effects it does? Why does it work better for some groups than for others? Is it in fact necessary to have direct contact with an outgroup at all? Would it be enough that some of our friends have it?

The Contact Hypothesis

One of the most long-lived and successful ideas in the history of social psychology has been the contact hypothesis. As might be discerned from its name, its central premise is that the best way to reduce tension and hostility between groups is to bring them into contact with each other. However, the phrase 'contact hypothesis' is actually somewhat of a misnomer, because it implies that mere contact is a sufficient panacea in itself. As Allport (1954) was quick to realize, this is far from being the case. In his discussion of the effects of intergroup contact, Allport cited some unpublished data on the relationship between residential proximity amongst blacks and whites in Chicago and anti-black attitudes amongst white respondents. These data showed a clear correlation between proximity and anti-black sentiment: the nearer the respondents lived to the black community the more prejudiced they were. I dare say the same pattern could be replicated in many other cities around the world today.

To these anecdotal examples we can add the many studies already described elsewhere in this book, which testify both to the ease with which intergroup bias can spring up when two groups meet and to the subsequent difficulty of reducing that bias (see Chapters 3, 5 and 6). Especially notable are the summer camp studies of Sherif (1966) and his colleagues (see Chapter 6). Prior to the successful implementation of superordinate goals designed to reduce the conflict created through intergroup competition, these researchers had attempted to attenuate the friction between the groups by arranging for the boys to get together in what should have been enjoyable circumstances. A big feast was organized on one day; a firework display on another. However, these 'mere contacts' did little to ease the hostilities. Indeed, as Sherif (1966) noted: 'far from reducing conflict, these situations served as occasions for the rival groups to berate and attack each other' (p. 88).

So contact alone is not enough. Allport (1954) identified a number of conditions which, he believed, needed to be satisfied before we could expect contact to have its desired effects of reducing prejudice. These have been added to and refined by subsequent commentators (Amir, 1969; Cook, 1962, 1978; Pettigrew, 1998). Let us examine the four most important of these conditions.

Social and institutional support: Getting those in authority to back integration

The first condition is that there should be a framework of social and institutional support for the measures which are designed to promote greater contact. By this is meant that those in authority – the school headteachers and their staff, the politicians implementing new legislation and the judges monitoring its administration – should all be unambiguous in their endorsement of the goals of the integration policies. There are at least three reasons why this is important.

The first is that those in authority are usually in a position to administer sanctions (and rewards) for actions which hinder (or promote) the achievement of the desired objectives. Given that businesses, school boards and the like are often receptive to matters which affect their material interests, they can be expected at least to be seen to be following the agreed policies. This, in itself, can often be a useful first step in breaking the vicious cycles of social deprivation and prejudice which many minority groups experience: academic underachievement and unemployment reinforcing the dominant group's negative stereotypes of them as 'stupid' and 'lazy'; stereotypes which are likely to justify yet further educational and occupational discrimination.

The second advantage of institutional support, particularly of new anti-discrimination legislation, is that, by forcing people to behave in a less prejudiced manner, such measures may eventually lead them to internalize those behaviours as their own attitudes. Festinger (1957) suggested that most people have a need to bring their beliefs into line with their behaviour in order to avoid experiencing dissonance. So it may be with prejudice. Being obliged to work alongside a minority group co-worker or to go to school with someone of a different religion may eventually bring about a change of heart in the prejudiced person: 'we work/study together successfully, therefore they cannot be as bad as I thought'.

The third and most important reason for providing institutional support for contact measures is that this helps to create a new social climate, in which more tolerant norms can emerge. Thus the significance of that momentous US Supreme Court decision in 1954, or of the British Race and Sex Discrimination Acts of 1965 and 1975, or of the anti-hate crime legislation introduced in Britain in the late 1990s may not have been that they were in themselves effective in outlawing discrimination. Indeed, many legislatures and employers did their damnedest to avoid having to implement them for years (Pettigrew, 2004). But they did have a profound impact on public attitudes, so that it became increasingly less acceptable to discriminate openly against minority groups or women, and even less acceptable to denigrate them in public (see Chapter 7).

Research demonstrating the impact of institutional support for integration at the level of prejudice has not been very plentiful, in the main because of the insuperable methodological difficulties involved. When a new piece of legislation is introduced in a country, where does one find a comparable control group against which to measure its effects? At a more microscopic level some studies do exist, which at least point to the importance of institutional support in creating new norms, even if they do not show this conclusively. For example, two early studies of ethnically integrated housing schemes documented how, in the experimental projects where the integration was taking place, people commented on the fact that the social expectations favoured tolerance and intermixing. In contrast, in the segregated areas, whites made such comments as 'it just isn't done' or 'people would think you're crazy' in response to questions about mixing with blacks (Deutsch and Collins, 1951; Wilner et al., 1952). In agreement with these different norms, the whites' intergroup attitudes were markedly more tolerant in the integrated housing projects. As we shall see later in the chapter, changing social norms proves to be an important vehicle for reducing people's prejudice.

Acquaintance potential: The power of cross-group friendships

The second condition for successful contact is that it be of sufficient frequency, duration and closeness to permit the development of meaningful relationships between members of the groups concerned. In Cook's words, it should have 'high **acquaintance potential**' (Cook, 1978, p. 97). This optimal condition can be contrasted with the infrequent, short and casual quality of some intergroup contact situations. These, it is supposed, will do little to foster more favourable attitudes and may even make things worse. Once again, there is a three-fold rationale for this condition, although there is less agreement amongst contact researchers as to the relative importance of its three components.

One component is that the development of close interpersonal relationships is thought to be positively rewarding in itself. Thus, the argument runs, the positive affect generated by these relationships will 'spill over' to encompass the outgroup as a whole (Cook, 1962). Running alongside this affective response is the acquisition of new and more accurate information about the outgroup. According to some theorists, this will lead to the discovery of many hitherto unknown similarities between the ingroup and the outgroup. Hence, according to the similarity–attraction hypothesis (Byrne, 1971), greater liking for the outgroup should result (Pettigrew, 1971; Stephan and Stephan, 1984). As we shall see, this second claim is somewhat controversial. The third reason why contacts with high-acquaintance potential are important is that they can lay the ground for the disconfirmation of some negative stereotypes about the outgroup. Again, contacts may do this by providing new information; but it is not assumed that this information will necessarily lead to perceptions of greater intergroup similarity – only to the revision of stereotypical beliefs (Brown and Hewstone, 2005; see Chapter 4).

The evidence testifying to the importance of high acquaintance potential is readily available. Early research on integrated housing projects pointed the way (Deutsch and Collins, 1951; Wilner et al., 1952). These studies found that the relative proximity between black and white families was an important correlate of positive attitude change. Also, and of relevance here, greater proximity was usually associated with more frequent and more intimate contact between the ethnic groups involved. Stephan and Rosenfield (1978) confirmed this relationship between closeness of contact and changes in prejudice in a longitudinal study (over two years) of white American elementary school children's attitudes towards Mexican Americans. The biggest single predictor of positive attitude change was increase in the frequency of interethnic contact – for example how often the children played at each other's houses. Stephan and Rosenfield were also able to demonstrate that it was the contact that caused the attitude change rather than vice versa: contact at time 1 was positively correlated with attitudes at time 2; however, attitudes at time 1 were *not* related to contact at time 2. This asymmetrical pattern is suggestive of a causal relationship in which contact determines the attitude.

Nevertheless, despite these findings, we should be a little cautious about placing too much weight on the role of direct acquaintance in the contact/prejudice-reduction process (Hewstone and Brown, 1986). Some of the reasons for caution will become apparent later; just now, the findings of Hamilton and Bishop's (1976) longitudinal study of residential integration should give us pause for thought. Hamilton and Bishop interviewed around 200 white residents, some of whom had recently acquired new black neighbours. After one year, this group had significantly lower modern racism scores than the remaining residents, even though both groups had started out with similar scores. This might seem to support a simple acquaintance/prejudice-reduction model, were it not for some additional information that Hamilton and Bishop had the foresight to collect. The information verified a number of 'acquaintanceship' measures such as whether the residents knew the names of their neighbours. The interaction measure turned out to be related to modern racism, but in a surprising way. It only had an effect within the first three months of the new residents moving in, and the effect was as strong, if not stronger, for those with new white neighbours as it was for those with new black neighbours: those who interacted had lower racism scores than those who did not. At the end of a year this variable had ceased to have an effect and, as Hamilton and Bishop point out, in any case it could hardly explain the final black–white neighbour difference in racism. The reason for this state of affairs is that there was rather *less* knowledge of the black neighbours than of the white. Hamilton and Bishop suggest that what caused reductions in racism may have been the disconfirmation of stereotypical expectations provided by the black neighbours rather than changes mediated by actually getting to know them.

Equal status

The third condition necessary for contact to be successful is that it should take place, as far as possible, between equal-status participants. The reason for this requirement is simple. Many prejudiced stereotypes of outgroups comprise beliefs about their inferior ability to perform various tasks. If, then, the contact situation involves an unequal-status relationship between the ingroup and outgroup members, the outgroup person being in the subordinate role, the existing stereotypes are likely to be reinforced rather than weakened. This is one of the reasons why prejudice against blacks in the southern states of the US proved so resistant to change. Many whites had a great deal of contact with blacks, but always with the latter in subservient positions – as nanny, cook, doorman, and so on. On the other hand, if it can be arranged that the groups meet on an equal footing – as peers in the classroom or co-workers in the factory – then the prejudiced beliefs become hard to sustain in the face of the daily experience of the outgroup people's obvious competence at their task.

There is a wealth of evidence showing the advantages of equal-status contact for reducing prejudice (Amir, 1976). For example, when blacks and whites work together relationships between them are often harmonious, as was demonstrated by Harding and Hogrefe (1952) and by Minard (1952). Both of these studies are interesting because, although they were conducted in very different settings (a city department store and a coal mine in West Virginia), they both revealed how context-specific changes induced by contact can be. The positive attitudes engendered at work did not seem to generalize beyond the factory gate. One of the miners interviewed by Minard gave a nice illustration of this:

> Do you see that bus there? [pointing to the miners' bus which took them to and from the pit]. The men ride in that bus all mixed up together and pay no attention. A white man sits with a Negro or anyway just however it comes handy. Nobody cares or pays any attention. But the white man will get right off that bus and on the interstate bus and he will not sit near a Negro. (Minard, 1952, p. 31)

This issue of generalization is absolutely central to any discussion of the effects of intergroup contact, and I shall return to it at some length in a later section.

Experimental evidence has also confirmed the value of equal-status contact. In Chapter 6 I described a study of mine which showed that school children anticipating

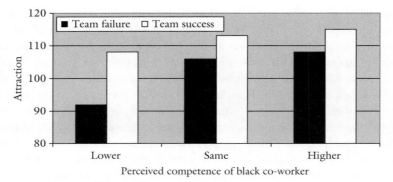

Figure 9.1   The effects of relative status and team success on liking for a black co-worker. Adapted from Table 1 in Blanchard et al., 1975

a co-operative encounter with another equal-status school showed less bias and slightly more liking than those expecting to meet a better or a worse school (Brown, 1984a). In a series of summer camps reminiscent of those of Sherif (1966), Clore and colleagues (1978) found that 8–12-year-old children, split into small, ethnically balanced groups for the duration of the camp, showed improved intergroup attitudes on several indices. For instance their choice of partners in various games displayed significant ingroup preferences (that is, preference for one's own ethnicity) at the start of four out of the five camps; but by the end of the camps these preferences were much more evenly balanced between ethnic groups, showing a significant bias in only one camp.

Perhaps the definitive study demonstrating the effect of equal-status contact is that of Blanchard and colleagues (1975). They arranged for some white American airmen to play a management training game with two confederates, one white and one black. The perceived competence of these confederates was varied, so that they appeared to be similar to, worse than, or better than the participants. At the conclusion of each game it was announced that the team of three had either done well or badly. The white participants' attraction for the black confederate was affected both by his perceived competence and by his team's alleged success (see Figure 9.1). When he was seen to be the same or better than the participant, he was liked more than when he was thought to be relatively incompetent; and members of successful teams liked their black team-mates more than members of unsuccessful teams did.

Co-operation: Working *with* rather than *against*

These studies on equal-status contact all included another element: co-operation. This is the fourth condition that Allport had identified as being necessary for successful prejudice reduction. The reason for this claim follows directly from realistic group conflict theory (see Chapter 6). In so far as members of different groups are dependent on each other for the achievement of some jointly desired objective, they have instrumental reasons to develop friendlier relationships with each other. This common goal is usually something concrete and small-scale, achievable through a joint task performance. We shall consider several examples of such cooperative tasks presently. But superordinate goals can also arise out of larger-scale threats, which are experienced by the groups concerned. This was the case in central India in October 1993, when the region was devastated by a huge earthquake in which 30,000 people were estimated to have died. In the face of a disaster of such proportions, the sectarian hatred between Hindus and Muslims was submerged in the common rescue effort. As one youth said: 'It doesn't matter to me whether this house belongs to a Hindu or a Muslim. Whoever it is, they need our help' (*Independent*, 3 October 1993).

Research has unambiguously supported this co-operation condition. From Sherif (1966) onwards, field and laboratory studies alike have demonstrated that intergroup co-operation leads to more friendliness and less ingroup bias than competition (Brown, 2000a). The only qualification we need to note at this stage is that the outcome of the co-operative endeavour needs to be successful in order to maximize positive attitude change. As we saw earlier in the study of Blanchard and colleagues (1975), the black colleague was always liked better if the team did well rather than badly, whatever his individual competence was. Indeed, Worchel and colleagues (1977) showed that ingroup members' liking for outgroup members with whom they had been co-operating was somewhat diminished after failure if that failure had been preceded by a history of competition between the groups. What may happen in these cases is that we find it convenient to blame the outgroup member(s) for our collective shortcomings.

By way of summarizing these four additional components of the optimal contact situation, let me conclude this section with two studies – one carried out in the laboratory, the other in the field – both of which tried to incorporate these components into their design. The first was by Cook (1978) and involved a prolonged series of co-operative activities between some fairly prejudiced white participants and black confederates. The activities themselves lasted for twenty days, and there were unobtrusive follow-up tests several months later. Consistent with the contact hypothesis, it was arranged that the task roles assigned to the black and to the white participants were of equal status. There were repeated opportunities for them to get to know each other, not only during the co-operative task but also in the lunch breaks, during which the black confederates made specific efforts to interact with the real participants. Social norms favouring egalitarianism and ethnic tolerance were promoted through the use of ethnically mixed supervisory staff and of a white confederate expressing pro-integration views. The whites' attitudes and behaviour towards the black confederates became uniformly more positive over the duration of the experiment. Some of this positive change was reflected in the post-test measures of their ethnic attitudes. Compared to control participants, who had not participated in the contact intervention, they showed significant decreases in their prejudice scores, although these were not consistent on all measures. In subsequent studies, Cook (1978) was to confirm the imperfect relationship between attitude change towards the particular people with whom one has had contact and attitudes towards the groups as a whole. I shall return to this issue again shortly.

The second study was conducted in a refugee camp in Ghana. Most of the inhabitants of this camp were Liberians, people who had fled from the brutal civil wars of the 1990s. There were members of several different Liberian tribes living in the camp, and some of these groups had been on opposing sides in the conflict. Under the auspices of a local non-governmental organisation comprising refugees from Liberia, a peace education programme was introduced. This programme involved members of different groups working together on a series of equal-status cooperative activities, all designed to increase intergroup trust and understanding. An evaluation of this programme revealed that it had many positive outcomes (Feuchte et al., 2008). Compared to a control group – people who had wanted to join the programme but for various reasons couldn't – participants showed clear reductions in the importance they attached to ethnic and tribal differences and increases in their desire for intergroup contact, their readiness for reconciliation, trust, and positive evaluation of outgroups. These changes are remarkable, given the trauma that so many of the participants had experienced at the hands of another group only a few years earlier.

Contact in Schools

For a few short weeks at the end of 2008 and beginning of 2009, the citizens of Gaza City and other parts of the Gaza Strip were subjected to aerial bombardment and ground invasion by Israeli armed forces. Several hundreds of Palestinians were killed, and many more were injured or lost their homes. Sadly, this tragic episode is all too typical of the long and bloody history of Israeli–Palestinian relations over the past sixty years. Much less typical of that troubled part of the world was the opening in Jerusalem, a few years earlier, of an integrated school where both the students and the teachers were drawn from the Israeli and Palestinian communities. Lessons were taught both in Hebrew and in Arabic, and the school observed the main festivals of the Christian, Jewish and Muslim faiths. The effects of being educated in such an environment are explained by Aviv Pek, a Jewish girl, and Yazid Ershed, an Arab boy:

AVIV: I have lots of Arab friends. One of my best friends is an Arab girl and, of course, she comes to my house.

YAZID: I have Jewish friends too. We go to each other's houses. We play football, we play with computers or we just talk.

(*The Independent*, 18 October 2007)

Unfortunately, integrated schools are a rarity in Israel and Palestine – just as they are in Northern Ireland, where over 90 per cent of children still go to religiously segregated schools (Smith, 1994), and as they were in the southern United States prior to that momentous Supreme Court decision in 1954. It could be foolish to pretend that desegregating education in the world's troublespots would do much to resolve immediately the intractable conflicts that underlie them. At the same time, it would be equally foolish – and socially irresponsible – to conclude that nothing is worth undertaking with a view to promoting greater school integration. As we have seen, the central proposition of the contact hypothesis is that, unless members of different groups find themselves in situations which challenge their mutually derogatory stereotypes or promote more positive affective bonds between them, prejudice is likely to continue unabated. Continuing to educate children of different faiths or ethnicities in separate schools is a policy exactly contrary to that proposition. What is the evidence for the view that **desegregated schooling** results in more favourable intergroup attitudes?

The outcomes of school desegregation

Unfortunately, there is precious little evidence from Israel and Palestine themselves, mainly because of the extreme scarcity of desegregated schools: the existing ones are not enough to provide a basis for proper evaluation. One qualitative study of two bilingual schools in Israel like the one described above did suggest that the schools were having some success in sustaining the cultural identities of the Arab and Jewish children under the common umbrella of a strong identification with the school (Bekerman and Horenczyk, 2004). Interestingly, however, despite sustained efforts from the teachers to develop mixed learning groups in the classroom, the researchers noted: 'a recurring pattern observed during the recess periods showed Jewish and Arab children playing separately: the Jewish children playing tag while the Arab ones mostly played soccer' (ibid., p. 399). Cross-group home visits were also apparently rather rare. As we shall see, such voluntary resegregation, even in integrated schools, is not an uncommon phenomenon.

If school desegregation in such divided societies as Israel and Northern Ireland is conspicuous by its absence, there are other milieux where it is much more common and where social scientists have been able to study its impact systematically. One such society is the United States, where the past fifty years have seen an enormous research effort directed at assessing the effects of integrated schooling on levels of prejudice and on cross-ethnic friendship choices.

Reviews of this work have reached rather equivocal conclusions as to whether desegregation has led to a reduction in prejudice. Stephan (1978), for example, was able to locate eighteen studies of the effect of desegregation on prejudice and concluded that about half of them showed that desegregation actually *increased* the whites' prejudice towards blacks; only a minority of the studies (13 per cent) showed the expected decrease in prejudice. Looking at the effects of desegregation on the blacks' prejudice towards whites produced a slightly more encouraging, but equally ambiguous picture: about half of them showed a decrease in prejudice, and slightly less than half showed an increase. Some years later, Schofield and Eurich-Fulcer (2001) reached a similar conclusion: the effects of desegregation on inter-group attitudes were often not demonstrable, and were certainly not always beneficial.

In a moment I shall consider why this might be so and why, on the other hand, such a conclusion should not cause us to feel unduly pessimistic about fifty years of desegregation policies. Before I do so, let me present the findings from three studies which illustrate the conclusions I have just summarized. The first is by Gerard and Miller (1975). This was a massive longitudinal study (spanning five years) of the effects of desegregating elementary schools in Riverside, California. Much of the research focused on school achievement outcomes, and hence is not of immediate concern here. However, the researchers were able to obtain socio-metric data from over 6,000 children, both before the desegregation programme took effect and then again after. On two socio-metric measures, the effects of desegregation seemed to be not overly positive. For example the percentage of 'unpopular' Mexican American children actually increased after desegregation. Similarly, the number of cross-ethnic friendship nominations for black and Mexican American children declined somewhat after desegregation, whilst the white (Anglo) children's popularity was unchanged. Three years of post-desegregation saw little change in these findings. Thus, despite the increased contact brought about by integrating these Riverside schools, there was little measurable benefit on cross-group friendships.

A second study was conducted in a single school, in a city to the north-east of the United States (Schofield, 1979, 1982; Schofield and Sagar, 1977). This school was unusual in that it was created with an explicitly integrationist ideology in mind (for example, numerical balance of black and white students; teachers of different ethnicities; explicit endorsement of desegregation by authority figures; minimization of competition). Nevertheless, despite these favourable conditions, Schofield's careful observation of the children's behaviour revealed considerable evidence of ethnic resegregation in their informal interactions. For instance black and white children generally preferred to sit next to (or opposite) a peer of the same ethnicity rather than someone of different ethnicity (Schofield and Sagar, 1977). However, despite this ethnic cleavage, there were some positive indications in these seating aggregation data. One came from a comparison between grade 7 (12-year-old) children, who were taught in heterogeneous mixed ability classes, and grade 8 (13-year-old) children who, despite the school's otherwise egalitarian philosophy, were 'streamed' by ability – this resulted in disproportionate numbers of whites in the 'accelerated' track and in higher numbers of blacks in the 'regular' track. Over the four-month observation period, Schofield and Sagar observed a significant increase in cross-ethnic seating patterns in grade 7, but no increase at all and, if anything, a *decrease* in cross-ethnic interaction in grade 8. This shows the importance of maintaining equal-status contact for improving intergroup relations. The second encouraging finding concerned the persistence of changes brought about by the school's integrationist policies. Schofield (1979) compared the seating aggregation indices of two cohorts of grade 8 children separated by one year. The significance of this comparison was that the later cohort (1976–7) had had two years' experience of the integrated school, compared with only one year for the 1975–6 cohort. Recall also that in grade 8 children tended to become ethnically more segregated, perhaps because of the academic streaming that began there. However, despite these adverse conditions, the 1976–7 cohort showed significantly less ethnic aggregation than the 1975–6 cohort, which gave some hope that prolonged exposure to favourable intergroup contact conditions can generate lasting changes in behaviour.

By way of a contrast, consider the results of a study we conducted in some British primary schools (Brown et al., 2007a). The ethnic composition of these schools varied from virtually all-white to over 50 per cent minority children (mainly of South Asian descent). Comparisons of the social life in the more diverse schools (over 20 per cent minority children) with the less diverse ones (20 per cent or less) were revealing. Majority *and* minority children in the more diverse schools had higher self-esteem, reported fewer instances of discrimination and were reported by their teachers to have fewer peer problems and to be more pro-social. One of the children in our study charmingly explained how such mixed schools gave her the opportunity to have several cross-ethnic friendships:

> Because we sit with our friends. Sometimes I've got these two friends in school dinners, Ellie and Tyler […]; and I've got this other friend Ramandeep and I sit with her as well. So, 'cos we're all friends and we're all mixed up so we sit like that with English and Indian.

This recent and encouraging set of results aside, some of the findings of those earlier American studies make rather pessimistic reading for those of us who have always supported the idea of integrated schools. Nevertheless there is a number of reasons why those findings should not cause us to abandon the principle of desegregated education.

First and foremost, we need to recognize that what happens in schools, even if it is arranged for optimal effect, is only a part of the children's experience of intergroup relationships. Thus, however well designed the curriculum and its accompanying paedagogic activity may be, if children from different groups return daily to a world outside the school gates which is still largely segregated and dominated by prejudiced values, it would be surprising indeed to find much general change in their intergroup attitudes (Dixon et al., 2005). Recall those studies I discussed earlier, which showed how changed attitudes at the workplace did not always survive the transition to other social contexts (Harding and Hogrefe, 1952; Minard, 1952).

Secondly, there is a variety of methodological reasons why studies attempting to evaluate the effects of desegregation may often record little or no change in children's attitudes. Some of these reasons are of a rather technical nature and have to do with the difficulties of measuring attitude change in this domain (see Schofield and Eurich-Fulcer, 2001).

A third difficulty with some evaluation studies is that they are aiming to detect changes over quite a short time period, perhaps too short for the intended consequences of desegregation to take effect. It would be unrealistic to expect a few months', or even a whole year's experience of integrated schooling to rectify many years of segregation and (perhaps) mutual suspicion. There is also the possibility that some integration programmes actually militate against producing generalized changes in intergroup attitudes by concentrating too hard on trying to ignore category differences in their activities and teaching materials. As I shall argue in a later section, there is a risk that such 'colour blind' programmes will generate positive changes in social relations which are confined only to those outgroup members with whom one has had immediate contact.

A fourth reason for not becoming too depressed about the apparent outcome of school desegregation policies in the USA is the realization that few are actually being implemented in anything approaching the 'ideal' conditions we identified in the first section. Many school districts in the USA only abandoned segregation unwillingly and under the threat of legal sanction. Moreover, some courts explicitly or tacitly gave succour to those who wished to resist desegregation (Pettigrew, 2004). Thus there was little of the 'institutional support' which Allport (1954) had proposed as being so important. Furthermore, the furore created by all the legal controversies surrounding school bussing, often an inherent component of desegregation programmes, is hardly the ideal atmosphere in which to introduce a new social policy.

Other features of the ways in which schools have gone about the business of integration have also, all too often, fallen far short of the optimal contact conditions. Typical classroom activities in many schools involve little co-operation between students. Indeed the reverse may often be the case, as students compete with each other for prizes – or, more routinely, for the teachers' attention or approval (Aronson et al., 1978). Furthermore, children from different groups may not interact on an equal-status footing. Some ethnic groups experience social and economic deprivation, which will put their members at a potential disadvantage in the classroom in relation to members of dominant or privileged groups unless curricula are carefully designed to avoid this. To compound these problems, teachers themselves may favour academic streaming even within integrated schools, especially if they themselves are not very supportive of integration in the first place (Epstein, 1985). Such streaming will inevitably be correlated with ethnicity, further reinforcing the existing inequalities of status between the groups.

In short, much school desegregation has been introduced in less than ideal circumstances and has seldom incorporated the features necessary for successful intergroup contact. In fact, when these features are included, there is now good evidence that prejudice intervention programmes can have some success in reducing prejudice. A recent meta-analysis of over sixty such studies concluded that the programmes in question can indeed have highly reliable effects (Beelmann and Heinemann, 2008). Let us now examine one set of interventions which have set out to maximize the chances of success of desegregation by deliberately structuring student activities around co-operation through the use of learning groups mixed by sex, ethnicity or other relevant categories.

Co-operative learning groups

There is a number of different ways in which **co-operative learning groups** can be used in schools (Aronson et al., 1978; Johnson and Johnson, 1975; Slavin, 1983). However, from the point of view of the contact hypothesis, all these techniques share four essential characteristics. Most crucially of all, they organize the learning experience of students so that these become co-operatively interdependent in a small group. This can be achieved by devising learning tasks which are structured so as to involve a division of labour among students whereby each one needs the others for the successful achievement of the group task. Thus, in a project, say, on some particular historical event, each student might be given a different facet to research: one would have to locate some demographic information, another, some economic data, yet another, the political situation at the time, and so on. The aim is to make them pool the results of each others' work so as to create a group report. Alternatively, the interdependence can be created simply by allocating rewards to the group as a whole, according to its overall performance. Either way, the key feature is that the students are dependent on each other for the achievement of their goals. A second aspect of co-operative learning activities is that they frequently necessitate a high degree of student–student interaction, in contrast to the student–teacher interaction pattern typical of most whole-class teaching methods. This greater amount of social interaction amongst students of different backgrounds is, of course, likely to generate the 'acquaintance potential' thought to be so important for successful contact. Thirdly, some co-operative learning techniques attempt to establish equal status amongst the group members. This is achieved either through role differentiation or by emphasizing the importance of each member's contribution to the overall group product (or score on an achievement test). Finally, because co-operative learning is introduced and managed by the teacher, it implicitly receives institutional support in the eyes of the students. Thus all the key conditions of the contact hypothesis are satisfied.

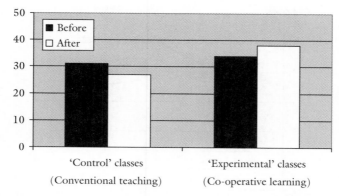

Figure 9.2 The effects of co-operative learning groups on cross-ethnic friendships. Adapted from Table 1 in Slavin, 1979

There is by now a sizeable body of evidence which demonstrates unambiguously the effectiveness of co-operative learning groups for increasing the attraction among members of different social categories. Slavin (1983) located fourteen studies, all of them conducted in ethnically mixed classroom settings in the United States, which had compared the effects of a co-operative learning programme with 'normal' classroom teaching methods on cross-ethnic friendship. Eleven of these studies demonstrated a statistically significant advantage to the co-operative group interventions; the remaining three showed no difference (see also Johnson et al., 1984). A few years later, Miller and Davidson-Podgorny (1987) were able to find a further eleven studies, and conducted a meta-analysis on the accumulated data set. The overall effect was hugely significant and showed that co-operative learning groups produced reliably higher levels of interethnic attraction than the comparable 'control' groups did. Using the statistical precision afforded by meta-analysis, Miller and Davidson-Podgorny found out that it was the kind of interdependence related to the task rather than to the reward that had the strongest effect on liking, and also that assigning specific task roles and ensuring a roughly equal distribution of different ethnicities within the groups had beneficial effects. To give some flavour of the kind of research included in these reviews, let me now present the results of two individual studies evaluating the effects of co-operative learning. One study was conducted in the area of ethnic relations, the other was concerned with attitudes towards students with disabilities.

Slavin (1979) evaluated the effects of introducing a ten-week co-operative learning programme into the English curriculum of two desegregated junior high schools in an American city. Half the class worked together in small, ethnically mixed groups, on such topics as grammar and punctuation. They were tested regularly and the scores of the team members were pooled to form a team score; the team scores were then announced to the class. The remaining 'control' classes were taught in conventional ways, and their test results were returned to them individually. It is important to note that the intervention only took place in the English classes; the remainder of the school curriculum continued as normal. The key outcome measure was simply the proportion of cross-ethnic friends whom each student nominated in answer to the question, 'Who are your friends in this class?' Figure 9.2 presents Slavin's (1979)

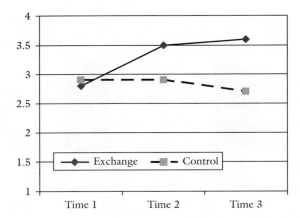

Figure 9.3 Effects of a structured contact programme on children's attitudes towards peers with disabilities. Adapted from Table 6 in Maras and Brown, 1996

results. Notice that, at the start of the intervention, the proportions of cross-ethnic friendship choices were about equal in the control and in the experimental groups. By the end of the intervention, the figure had risen slightly in the experimental classes, but it had actually *fallen* in the control classes. Slavin (1979) was able to conduct a follow-up study some nine months later. Although unfortunately there was substantial attrition of data – an endemic problem in longitudinal studies – the long-term results were quite remarkable. In the experimental students, the level of cross-ethnic friendship remained stable, at just under 40 per cent. In the control students, however, it fell still further, to under 10 per cent.

Subsequently we were able to confirm these findings in a study involving a school for children with very severe learning disabilities (Maras and Brown, 1996). These were children who, by reason of genetic, congenital or other accident, had a wide range of physical and cognitive impairments. Some had little or no physical mobility; others had only very limited language skills; most demonstrated some behavioural disturbance. In a pioneering experiment, this school was linked to a nearby mainstream primary school, in an exchange programme. Each year a number of mainstream children were randomly selected to spend some part of each week working in pairs with the disabled children, on some carefully planned co-operative activities. We administered a series of attitude measures over the first three months of this exchange programme, both to those who participated in the exchanges and to those who did not. On a number of rating dimensions, the 'exchange' children showed a progressive decline in how differently they assessed the abilities of disabled and non-disabled children; the 'control' children's perceptions of these groups changed very little over the same period. When we presented some standardized photographs of children with different disabilities – these were children not known to the participants – the exchange students rated them as increasingly more attractive play partners; the 'control' children's ratings remained unchanged (see Figure 9.3). These play preferences were for *unknown* children, and hence they showed that the programme was having some general effects on the mainstream children's attitudes: it was not restricted merely to those disabled children with whom they were interacting (see also Armstrong et al., 1981).

In sum, therefore, there is ample evidence showing that, when school integration takes place in a manner consistent with the tenets of the contact hypothesis, and particularly if it involves a change in teaching methods to incorporate co-operative learning groups, then improvements in intergroup relationships are very likely to occur. An added bonus of employing more co-operation in the classroom is that the academic achievement of both advantaged and disadvantaged students will also increase (Johnson et al., 1981; Slavin, 1983). To this optimistic conclusion I would add just one cautionary note. The vast majority of evaluation studies reporting positive effects of co-operative learning experiences have measured these effects by observing the students' socio-metric preference for *known* peers. Those few studies which have attempted to assess a more general attitude change have generally reported null results (see DeVries et al., 1979; Weigel et al., 1975).

There are several factors which could explain this. Interventions involving co-operative learning programmes often last for only a few weeks, and this may simply be too short a time for any change in entrenched attitudes to happen. Also, the interventions usually form a part, and frequently only a minor part, of the students' school experience. Typically, they are introduced in just a single academic subject or for just a few hours each week. Thus the majority of the same students' time is spent in conventional classroom settings which, as I noted earlier, may be antithetical to the goals of desegregation. In addition to these two constraints, a third limiting factor is the extent to which the experience of contact permits or inhibits the cognitive generalization of the positive attitudes generated towards members of one particular co-operative learning group. This issue has preoccupied researchers of intergroup contact over the years, and it is considered in some detail in the next section.

The Contact Hypothesis Reconsidered

It is more than half a century since the ideas which form the contact hypothesis first gained currency in the social sciences and in the minds of legislators and policy-makers. Pettigrew and Tropp (2006) conservatively estimate that during this timespan more than 500 studies have been published which have investigated different facts about the contact hypothesis, and its popularity as a research topic shows no sign of abating (Brown and Hewstone, 2005). It is probably time, therefore, to take stock of the contact hypothesis: to consider how it has been modified in the light of that huge body of work and to speculate how it might need to be developed still further, as its limitations as a policy instrument become exposed.

Pettigrew and Tropp (2006) carried out an impressive meta-analysis on those 500 studies. Their first conclusion was that there is indeed a reliable relationship between contact and prejudice. True, it is not a very strong one – on average the correlation is around −0.22 – but, given the large number of studies and even the larger number of participants (>250, 000), it is statistically indisputable. Further analyses by Pettigrew and Tropp (2006) revealed that, just as Allport predicted, that correlation rose to nearly −0.29 if Allport's optimal conditions for contact were also present. Furthermore, the relationship was stronger if the contact involved cross-group friendships than if it did not. Finally, Pettigrew and Tropp also observed that the overwhelming preponderance of contact studies had focused on attitude (and behaviour) change in members of majority or higher-status groups. When they extracted the much smaller number of studies that took the minority group's perspective, they found that the effects of contact on reducing prejudice towards majority groups were slightly weaker; the average correlation here was –0.18 (Tropp and Pettigrew, 2005).

These meta-analyses have performed a valuable service in synthesizing a large and heterogeneous research literature. They have also raised several new issues. The first among these concerns the direction of causality underlying those correlations: does contact *lead to* reduced prejudice, as Allport (1954) supposed, or is it perhaps that the more prejudiced people avoid having too much contact with members of the outgroup? Secondly, when and where does contact have its strongest effects, particularly for instigating generalized attitude change? In other words, what are the key *moderators* of contact effects? Thirdly, how and why does contact have effects on prejudice? This entails a search for the psychological processes which underlie or *mediate* the contact–prejudice relationship. A fourth issue concerns the asymmetry observed between majority and minority groups. Why does contact apparently not work for the latter as well as it does for the former? Fifthly, I consider whether direct contact is actually necessary for the reduction of prejudice. As I shall show, it is sometimes enough for us to know someone else, who has that contact, for prejudice to diminish.

The direction of causality: Contact effects or prejudice effects?

The contact hypothesis and most of the researchers who have been inspired by it hold that the number and quality of our relationships with outgroup members play a causal role in reducing our prejudice towards those outgroups. Certainly Pettigrew and Tropp (2006), whilst acknowledging that the reverse direction is also plausible (less prejudiced people seek out more intergroup contact), veer on the side of the traditional viewpoint. They do so partly on the basis of some experimental studies of contact, where contact is manipulated with predictable effects on prejudice (see Brown et al., 1999; Wolsko et al., 2003), and partly from examining studies where different statistical models have been tested against patterns of intercorrelations between contact and prejudice. Often models specifying paths *from* contact *to* prejudice fit the data better than alternative models (Pettigrew, 1997; Powers and Ellison, 1995). Nevertheless, the fact remains that the vast majority of research on intergroup contact has employed cross-sectional correlational designs, where strong causal inferences are impossible to draw. Fortunately a few longitudinal studies exist which can help us to ascertain whether the causal arrow runs from contact to prejudice reduction ('contact effects'), or from prejudice to contact avoidance ('prejudice effects') – or maybe whether it points in both directions ('reciprocal causality'). It may be recalled that earlier in the chapter I presented two longitudinal studies which clearly evinced contact effects (Maras and Brown, 1996; Stephan and Rosenfield, 1978; see also Brown et al., 2007b). However, subsequent studies with larger samples paint a different picture. Levin and colleagues (2003) tracked college students' cross-group friendships and intergroup attitudes over five years and found both contact and prejudice effects: those with less favourable attitudes in their first year had fewer outgroup friends in their second and third years; however, those with more outgroup friends in years two and three were less prejudiced in year five. Similarly, in a large cross-national study of school students in Belgium, Britain and Germany, we found that majority–minority contact predicted lessened prejudice six months later, *and* vice versa (Binder et al., 2009). If anything, the prejudice effects were a little stronger than the contact effects (see also Eller and Abrams, 2003, 2004). It seems safe to conclude, then, that in many contexts, and especially in those where a degree of choice can be exercised about whom to interact with, reciprocal causality will be the rule.

The 'when' and the 'where' of contact: The problem of generalization

From the very beginning, proponents of the contact hypothesis were aware of a particularly thorny problem: getting members of different groups to like and respect each other more in the classroom or workplace was one thing; finding ways of translating those positive interpersonal changes into lessened prejudice towards the outgroup as a whole was quite another (Allport, 1954, pp. 262–3; Chein et al., 1948, p. 49). This is the problem of **generalization**, and it has preoccupied contact researchers for decades. What are the conditions that will best promote broader attitude and stereotype change on the basis of the particularities of people's everyday intergroup encounters? Or, as I have titled this section, *when* and *where* does contact produce most change? Put more formally, this question is really concerned with variables that *moderate* the effects of contact on generalized prejudice reduction.

One answer to this question was offered by Brewer and Miller (1984). They took as their starting point the observation that enhanced intergroup discrimination and negative stereotyping are frequently seen to be triggered when social categories become psychologically salient (see Chapters 3, 4 and 6). It follows from this, they argued, that during contact the boundaries between the groups should be made less rigid, ultimately to be dissolved altogether. In this way the situation should become **decategorized**, and all interactions should take place at an interpersonal level. In this 'personalized' form of contact the participants should be more likely to attend to idiosyncratic information about each individual and should be correspondingly less attentive to group-based – that is, stereotypical – information. Repeated interpersonal contact of this kind, they thought, would result in the disconfirmation of pre-existing (negative) stereotypes of the outgroup – a process which ultimately is

> more likely to generalize to new situations because extended and frequent utilization of alternative informational features in interactions undermines the availability and usefulness of category identity as a basis for future interactions with the same or different individuals. Thus permanent changes occur in both the cognitive and motivational aspects of social interaction with outgroup members. (Brewer and Miller, 1984, pp. 288–9)

In support of this model Brewer and Miller have carried out a number of studies using a similar paradigm (Bettencourt et al., 1992, 1997; Miller et al., 1985). Typically, two artificial categories are created (for example 'overestimators' and 'underestimators'). Then members of these two categories are brought together into co-operative work groups, so both overestimators and underestimators are represented in each group. The participants are given different instructional sets for the group tasks: some are encouraged to focus on each other in order to find out what the 'fellow team members must really be like' (Bettencourt et al., 1992, pp. 305–6); others are told to concentrate particularly on the task at hand. In this way it is hoped that the contact situation will be respectively 'personalized' and 'depersonalized'. After the task, participants allocate rewards to the members of their own team, and also to members of another team unknown to them, portrayed on a short video clip. The key dependent measure in these experiments is the degree of bias in the allocations between overestimators and underestimators, both for the known team members and for the 'strangers' shown on video. A consistent finding has been that those who undertake the task with the 'personalization' instructions show less bias than those who are concentrating much more on the task, although there are indications that this effect may be restricted to majority group members (Bettencourt et al., 1997). As we shall see later, such an asymmetry between majorities and minorities in the efficacy of contact is a recurring theme in the literature.

Despite the empirical support for this decategorization model (Miller, 2002), it seemed to us that there was an inherent problem in trying to eliminate all vestiges of categorial differences in contact situations (Hewstone and Brown, 1986; Brown and Hewstone, 2005). Suppose I interact with an outgroup person under truly decategorized conditions. To the extent that these conditions have been successful in preventing me from perceiving that person as a member of an outgroup (or indeed of any group at all), no change in attitudes which I experience towards that person can be easily extrapolated to other members of his or her group, whom I have not yet met. Thus my more general intergroup attitudes may remain intact, being unaffected by the contact situation. It was this consideration that led Hewstone and myself to propose a rather different model of intergroup contact (Brown and Hewstone, 2005; Hewstone and Brown, 1986). We suggest that, rather than attempting to eliminate the existing ingroup–outgroup division, there may be some virtue in keeping it salient, at least minimally, whilst simultaneously optimizing the various conditions for successful contact established by Allport (1954). In this way the contact will take place at an intergroup rather than at an interpersonal level, between people acting somewhat as group representatives rather than as unaffiliated individuals (see Chapter 1). If this can be successfully arranged, then any positive change engendered during contact is likely to transfer readily to other members of the outgroup, because one's contact partners will be seen as somehow typical of that group (see Rothbart and John, 1985, for a similar argument).

In some ways this seems a somewhat paradoxical strategy. In order to reduce prejudice towards an outgroup, we are suggesting that it can be advantageous to maintain the psychological salience of the intergroup distinction – a proposal that appears to run directly contrary to Brewer and Miller's (1984) decategorization hypothesis. As we shall see, however, it is possible for the two approaches to be reconciled. Indeed, it may be that some combination of the two strategies is desirable if one is to avoid a potential danger inherent in promoting too much **group salience** in contact situations – namely the risk that this factor may exacerbate rather than reduce intergroup tension. Before I discuss such a resolution, let me review the evidence for the counterintuitive idea that creating conditions which maintain group salience and which foster perceptions that the people one is interacting with are typical of their group is actually conducive to greater prejudice reduction.

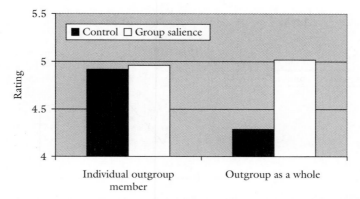

Figure 9.4 Effects of group salience during intergroup contact on outgroup ratings. Adapted from Table 1 in Van Oudenhoven et al., 1996

Wilder (1984b) set the scene with an early experiment, in which he varied how typical a member of a rival college was seen to be during a co-operative encounter. In addition, this outgroup member behaved pleasantly or unpleasantly. Only the pleasant encounter with a 'typical' outgrouper produced significant improvements in the evaluation of the outgroup as a whole. Unpleasant interaction, or contact with an atypical person, produced little change in attitude. Since then, more than a dozen experiments and field studies have confirmed the same basic finding in such diverse contexts as attitudes towards immigrants, foreigners, gays, elderly people and people with mental illness (a review of this work can be found in Brown and Hewstone, 2005). Let me pick out three of those studies by way of illustration.

Van Oudenhoven and colleagues (1996) arranged for Dutch school students to interact in a co-operative learning group with a Turkish peer (who was a confederate of the researchers). In conditions of group salience, the participants and the confederate introduced themselves to each other by making explicit reference to their respective ethnicities. In the control condition no reference was made to ethnicity. After two hours of working co-operatively with the confederate, the Dutch participants evaluated both him and Turks in general. The ratings of the individual confederate did not vary across conditions – he was always evaluated rather positively – but the general attitudes towards Turks were reliably more favourable in the group salience conditions[1] than they were in control (see Figure 9.4).

In our longitudinal study of majority–minority relations in Europe, we asked our respondents not only to assess the quality of their relationship with their outgroup friend(s), but also to rate how typical they thought these friends were of the group as a whole (Binder et al., 2009). As we had expected, those who saw their friends as more typical of the outgroup showed stronger contact effects than those who thought of them as less typical. In fact, the contact effect in the latter group was barely noticeable (Figure 9.5). Importantly, this moderation of the contact–prejudice relationship by **typicality** held both for majority and for minority groups.

In the above studies the evidence for generalization was indirect. We infer that generalization must have occurred, because attitudes towards the outgroup as a whole were more favourable under conditions of salience or typicality. More direct

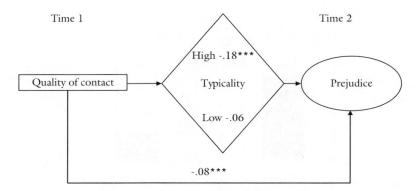

Figure 9.5 Typicality moderates the effects of contact on prejudice. Figures show standardized regression coefficients. Prejudice levels at time 1 were controlled for; *** $p < .001$. From Binder et al., 2009

evidence of the individual–group generalization process was obtained in two large surveys we conducted in Europe and Chile (González et al., 2009). In both of them we asked respondents to rate, on a number of scales, the individuals whom they knew from the outgroup (this was defined as another country in the European study, another political party in the Chilean study). We also asked them to say how typical those people were of their groups. Finally, we got them to rate the groups as a whole on the very same scales. To assess generalization, we simply correlated the individual and the group ratings. The more closely they corresponded, the greater the generalization that must have occurred. Perfectly in line with the Hewstone–Brown hypothesis, those who saw the outgroup people as more typical showed consistently stronger individual–group correlations than those who saw them as less typical. This effect was highly consistent and it held across several different outgroups.

Although the Hewstone–Brown model seems to offer a promising way of tackling the generalization problem, it is an approach not without its own difficulties. One of these follows directly from the very same argument that provided the rationale for the model in the first place. If **intergroup** (as opposed to **interpersonal) contact** permits greater generalization of the attitudes promoted by the encounter, then, in principle, both positive *and* negative attitudes can be generalized. Indeed, if the co-operative interaction goes wrong – perhaps by failing to achieve the common goal, or because it turns competitive – then structuring the interaction so as to place it more at the intergroup level could well make matters worse. Not only might one's fellow interactant(s) be disparaged, but there is a risk of the negative stereotypes of the outgroup being reinforced precisely because those people are seen as typical of it (see for instance Maras and Brown, 2000). This danger is heightened by a second problem: intergroup encounters may be more anxiety-provoking than interpersonal ones and, as I will show in the next section, such anxiety is not conducive to harmonious social relations. In studying Muslim–Hindu contact in Bangladesh, Islam and Hewstone (1993a) found that features indicative of 'intergroup' relationships tended to be correlated with increased anxiety, which in turn was correlated with less favourable attitudes towards the outgroups (see also Greenland and Brown, 1999). Finally, how can a strategy that seeks to promote perceived typicality and category salience be compatible with the evidence for the Brewer–Miller model that I reviewed earlier, in which just the opposite approach was taken with seemingly beneficial outcomes?

There are several answers to this last question. To begin with, it is important to realize that in the studies supporting the Brewer–Miller model there were elements of the experimental procedure which probably maintained some group salience, even in the decategorized conditions. For example, in the experiment undertaken by Bettencourt and colleagues (1992), team members wore large badges around their necks for duration of the study, thus proclaiming their original group affiliations. Similarly, the 'strangers' viewed on the video recording also wore badges.

A second answer is that there is now a growing realization that the most effective form of contact for the purposes of reducing prejudice is that which begins with inter-personal friendships between ingroup and outgroup members (Brown and Hewstone, 2005; Hewstone, 1996; Miller, 2002; Pettigrew, 1998). In fact Pettigrew (1998) has proposed a formal stage model of contact in which the Brewer–Miller decategorization approach precedes the Hewstone–Brown category salience approach. One argument in favour of such a sequence is that levels of intergroup anxiety may be lessened in more personalized (decategorized) settings, a process thus paving the way for conditions which would favour generalization. In this framework, the Brewer–Miller and Hewstone–Brown models are seen as complementing rather than competing with each other.

Further recognition of this complementarity was provided by Ensari and Miller (2002). In two experiments – one based in Turkey, in the context of secular and religious Muslims, the other set in the USA and looking at members of different political parties – they simultaneously manipulated variables that might vary the 'interpersonal' nature of the situation (by encouraging or discouraging self-disclosure between participants) *and* the 'intergroup' aspects (for instance typicality of outgroup member, group salience). Interestingly, they found that self-disclosing behaviour combined with salience and typicality to produce the most favourable generalized outgroup attitudes. In other words, it seems that some combination of interpersonal and inter-group features of a contact situation is optimal for generating the most positive attitude change (Miller, 2002).

The 'how' and the 'why' of contact: Mediating processes

The previous section focused on factors which moderate the effects of contact in order to make it more or less effective as a prejudice reduction agent. Now I want to turn my attention to the processes that underlie the contact–prejudice relationship: how and why does contact have the effects that it does? For ease of exposition I have grouped the mediators into those which operate mainly in the *cognitive* domain and those which are *affective* in nature.

One of the earliest ideas about how contact might bring about a reduction in prejudice, pre-dating even Allport's formal statement of the contact hypothesis, was that it dispelled people's ignorance about the outgroup (Williams, 1947). The argument was that, when people came into contact with members of other groups, they would inevitably learn more about them and their culture, and that this increased knowledge would then contribute to the weakening of pre-existing stereotypes and to the generation of friendlier attitudes (Stephan and Stephan, 1984). As I noted earlier, some believe that the acquisition of new information about outgroups also leads to the discovery of intergroup similarities, and from there to greater attraction (Pettigrew, 1971; Stephan and Stephan, 1984). Stephan and Stephan were not able to locate many studies that provided unambiguous support for the role of knowledge as a mediating mechanism. However, they did report the results of a small cross-sectional study of their own, carried out amongst white American secondary school children, where increased contact with Hispanic students was associated with improved knowledge of Hispanic culture and also with a more favourable attitude towards Hispanics in general. Subsequently Pettigrew and Tropp (2008) were able to track down seventeen attempts to test the effect of knowledge as a mediator, and they concluded that there was indeed statistically reliable evidence for such an effect, even it if was rather modest in size and certainly much weaker than two other, more emotionally laden mediators – as we shall see shortly.

Notwithstanding this meta-analytic conclusion, there are two reasons for being cautious about attributing too much importance to knowledge as a mediator. The first is that contact between groups will sometimes lead to the discovery of as many cultural *differences* as similarities. This is particularly likely to be the case in multicultural societies, where a wide range of ethnic and religious groups are co-existing. Any positive effects of increased knowledge in such contexts must therefore stem from a greater appreciation of diversity than from any simple similarity–attraction process. Secondly, sometimes enhanced knowledge may prove discomforting for its owner. This can happen if it makes us realize that the other group's view of us is something less than complimentary (Vorauer et al., 2009); I will come back to this aspect later. Another ironic effect of increased knowledge about the outgroup is that it can make us aware, if we happen to belong to a privileged group, how we may have inadvertently contributed to the outgroup's disadvantaged position. Such an awareness might instigate feelings of guilt, and hence possibly anxiety, about how we should now behave towards members if that outgroup. We discovered this when we surveyed non-indigenous Chilean students' attitudes towards the indigenous minority in that country, the Mapuche (Zagefka et al., 2008). The more contact they had had with the minority group, the more they claimed to know about them. So far, so good. But this extra knowledge was also correlated to increases in collective guilt about how the Mapuche had been mistreated over the years, and that guilt seemed to lead to higher anxiety and ultimately to slightly *more* (rather than less) prejudice towards the Mapuche.

A second cognitive mediator offers more promise as an effective prejudice mechanism. This is recategorization. The idea was first proposed by Gaertner and colleagues (1989) and has been extensively developed by Gaertner and Dovidio (2000) since then. In contrast to the Brewer and Miller (1984) model, which suggests that category boundaries should be dissolved in favour of a more personalized form of interaction, and to the Hewstone and Brown (1986) model, which argues for the retention of some category salience, Gaertner and Dovidio propose that category lines be redrawn so that previous ingroup–outgroup divisions become subsumed under a new superordinate category. In this way, they believe, members of the former inrgroup ('us') and outgroup ('them') come now to be seen as ingroup members (a new 'we'), with corresponding reductions in intergroup bias. Because of this emphasis on creating

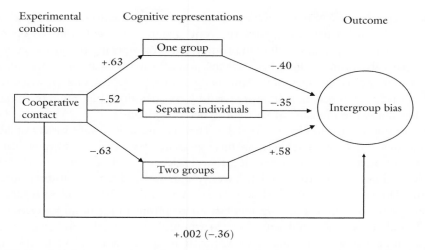

Figure 9.6 Cognitive mediators of the effect of cooperative contact on bias. Adapted from Figure 1 in Gaertner et al., 1990

larger and more inclusive categories, Gaertner and Dovidio call their model the **common ingroup identity model**.

To validate their model, Gaertner and Dovidio have conducted an impressively large number of experiments and field studies where they have explored the ramifications of those conditions which foster the perception of a common ingroup identity (see Gaertner and Dovidio, 2000 for a lucid summary of this work). In Chapter 3 I briefly described one of their typical experiments (Gaertner et al., 1989); here let me present another one, which shows clearly how co-operative contact seems to reduce intergroup bias by changing people's cognitive representations of the situation they find themselves in (Gaertner et al., 1990). As is usual in their paradigm, Gaertner and his colleagues first created two artificial groups and gave them a few minutes to interact by themselves, so as to develop some ingroup cohesion. They then brought these groups into contact, *either* in a situation which involved little or no co-operation (just listening in to two other groups who discussed the task at hand), *or* in a situation in which they actively had to co-operate with each other as equal-status partners, thus fulfilling two of Allport's (1954) conditions for ideal contact. Subsequently the participants rated everyone present in terms of likeability, honesty and so on, as well as giving their impressions of how much it felt like there were two distinct groups, one group, or merely several separate individuals working on the task. Not surprisingly, the levels of intergroup bias were noticeably lower in the co-operation condition. More interesting was a follow-up analysis in which Gaertner and colleagues (1990) were able to demonstrate how that reduction in bias came about. Looking at the effects of the co-operation–no co-operation manipulation on how participants viewed the situation, Gaertner and colleagues showed that being in the co-operation condition made people perceive the intergroup situation *more* as one involving a single group, and *less* as one involving two groups or discrete individuals. In turn, these perceptions were systematically related to ingroup bias (see Figure 9.6). In technical terms, we can say that the cognitive representations of the situation mediated the effects of co-operative contact on bias. In terms of bias reduction, as can be seen, the most effective mediator was clearly the 'one group' representation: co-operation increased that perception, which then promoted less bias. Seeing the situation in individual terms also promoted less bias, but this perception was itself somewhat inhibited by the experience of co-operation. And the 'two groups' representation worked only in a negative way: it was mostly suppressed by co-operation, but any remaining vestiges of it tended to increase rather than to decrease the bias.

The common ingroup identity model has proved useful in a wide variety of laboratory settings, mostly with artificial groups especially created for the purpose. In such contexts, recategorizing the situation into a single superordinate group reduces bias reliably, and also seems to stimulate positive behaviours such as self-disclosure and helping (Dovidio et al., 1997b; Gaertner and Dovidio, 2000). Also, in several field settings where real life groups are involved, perceptions of a common ingroup have been found to be associated with more harmonious social relations in multiethnic schools and colleges, stepfamilies and corporate mergers (ibid.). Nevertheless, for all its undoubted potency as a mediator of contact, recategorization is not without its problems as a strategy for reducing prejudice.

To begin with, we can note that much of the research supporting it has used artificial groups of relatively little significance to their members. It may be easier to get people to abandon such group identities in favour of a superordinate identity than it would be to persuade members of a particular ethnic minority (say) to give up that identity for another. As we shall see in the next section, in its purest form the common ingroup identity approach to prejudice reduction is an assimilationist strategy and, as such, it may prove more attractive to majorities than to minorities.

Secondly, it is not clear how – or if – this approach solves the generalization problem. To the extent that some intervention is completely successful in dissolving the previous sub-group boundaries in a contact situation, it will then be difficult to make the connection between those particular members of a sub-group with other not yet encountered (Brown and Hewstone, 2005).

Thirdly, there is a risk with recategorization that one simply displaces the conflict to a higher level. Suppose there is a country which is informally or institutionally sub-divided into two regions. Germany would be a case in point. Even though the iron curtain dividing that country into East and West Germany was torn down in those momentous days of November 1989, the East–West division still exists in the minds of many Germans, perhaps not unconnected to the real socio-economic differences between the two halves of the country, which still persist (see news. BBC.co.uk/3 October 2005). Will these psychological wounds be healed through the cultivation of a single unifying German identity? Perhaps they may; but this could be at the expense of an increase in xenophobia towards all non-Germans. Kessler and Mummendey (2001) found evidence for this in a longitudinal study of East German attitudes undertaken in the late 1990s. The more these respondents thought of themselves as German, the more xenophobic they became a year or two earlier.

A final possible difficulty with trying to stimulate a recategorization of the world into larger superordinate categories stems from a phenomenon known as **ingroup projection** (Wenzel et al., 2007). This phrase refers to people's tendency to assume that the attributes which best define the superordinate category are those which also happen to define their sub-group category best. So, if someone is a West German, he/she will tend to think that Germany as a whole is made up from all the best aspects of their West German identity, and will probably conveniently overlook any more typically East German attributes (Waldzus, et al., 2004). From there it is but a short step to disparaging all those East Germans who fail to match up adequately to the person's ethnocentric conception of what makes a 'good' German. Across several different intergroup contexts there does seem to be a consistent tendency to do this: the more people see their ingroup to be prototypical of the superordinate group, the less favourable their evaluations of the other sub-group will be (Wenzel et al., 2007).

Still, I doubt that these difficulties are insuperable. One way of avoiding some of them may be to follow Pettigrew's (1998) advice of structuring contact situations in a temporal fashion. Just as there may be advantages to combining the Brewer–Miller formula with the Hewstone–Brown idea, Pettigrew suggests that the Gaertner–Dovidio common ingroup strategy may be most effective when first preceded by the other two interventions. In that way, he argues, one can reap the benefits of cross-group friendship, achieve some generalization and culminate by building the bridges afforded by a shared collective identity. In effect, such an approach implies that neither maintaining sub-group salience (Hewstone–Brown) nor creating a single superordinate identity (Gaertner–Dovidio) will be sufficient by themselves. Rather, it may be more beneficial to find ways of fostering **dual** or **bicultural identities**, in which *both* the sub-groups and the superordinate group retain some psychological significance (Gaertner and Dovidio, 2000; González and Brown, 2006). I will return to this idea in the next section.

Let me now turn to mediators of the contact–prejudice nexus which operate more in the emotional domain. Pettigrew and Tropp (2008) conclude from their meta-analysis that affective mediation is noticeably more powerful than that due to increased knowledge about the outgroup. The most intensively studied of these affective mediators has been intergroup anxiety. First coined by Stephan and Stephan (1985), this phrase refers to the complex mix of apprehension over behaving inappropriately towards, fear of being rejected or exploited by, and some residual, learned, negative affect associated with, members of an outgroup. Apprehension can arise because we may feel ignorant about the cultural sensitivities of the outgroup in question, and hence we may worry that we will do or say something offensive. Fear of rejection or exploitation can come about if we are aware of a historically conflictual or oppressive relationship between one group and the other. This may prompt us to anticipate, sometimes with good reason, that the people we are interacting with may not like us very much, or may seek to take advantage of us. And in relation to some groups, as we saw in Chapters 4 and 7, we may harbour some mild (or not so mild) antipathy simply as a result of having been socialized in a particular racist society.

Perhaps I can interject a personal anecdote at this point. A year or two ago, a student with cerebral palsy attended one of my classes and was assigned to do his project with me. Such was the nature of his disability – he was confined to a wheelchair, he was unable to speak, and his lack of physical coordination meant that he sometimes made surprisingly loud vocalizations or dribbled uncontrollably – that the usual norms of social interaction did not apply. I will admit that I found teaching and supervising this student quite a challenge. Everything was mediated through his extremely able assistants, who interpreted for him via a Perspex board, on which he laboriously spelt out words and sentences. Due to my woeful unfamiliarity with this particular condition,

I found myself constantly worrying about whether I was behaving appropriately towards him: was I making sufficient allowance for his disabilities, or was I being unbearably patronizing? How could I tell if he was appreciating my advice or seeing me, with disappointment, as yet another ignorant – if well intentioned – able-bodied person? This became a very vivid personal illustration of how intergroup anxiety can disrupt normal social relations.

Stephan and Stephan (1985) hypothesized that intergroup anxiety would have negative consequences on our attitudes and behaviour towards outgroups. It might lead us to avoid them because of the discomfort we experienced when meeting them. If avoidance is not possible, our behaviour towards outgroups members might become stilted and overly reserved, with predictable consequences for their behaviour towards us. If we habitually feel uncomfortable around members of the outgroup, we may come to attribute the cause of that discomfort to the outgroup itself, which would lead us to a negative intergroup attitude. And, finally, all this emotional preoccupation consumes our cognitive resources. As we saw in Chapter 4, depletion of cognitive resources usually inclines us to fall back on familiar – and probably negative – stereo-typical judgements about those we are interacting with. In short, intergroup anxiety leads to prejudice.

The good news, though, is that intergroup anxiety is not inevitable. Stephan and Stephan (1985) argued that a powerful antidote to it is good quality intergroup con-tact. Contact can reduce anxiety, partly because it may dispel some ignorance about outgroup customs and behavioural norms. It will also reduce anxiety because, if it is structured according to Allport's conditions, it will generate its own positive affect, which can then counteract the anxiety. For these reasons, intergroup anxiety looks like a prime candidate for being the mediator of the effects of contact on prejudice: more contact leads to less anxiety, and lessened anxiety means lowered prejudice.

Stephan and Stephan (1985) provided some preliminary evidence of this mecha-nism with the help of a small sample of Hispanic students. As they had expected, contact was negatively correlated to intergroup anxiety, which in turn was positively correlated to stereotyping (but, surprisingly enough, not to ethnocentrism). Since that early study, intergroup anxiety has been repeatedly found to be a mediator of the contact/prejudice reduction relationship (Brown and Hewstone, 2005; Pettigrew and Tropp, 2008). In contexts as diverse as the relations between Hindus and Muslims in Bangladesh (Islam and Hewstone, 1993a), British and Japanese students (Greenland and Brown, 1999), attitudes towards immigrants in Italy (Voci and Hewstone, 2003), Protestants and Catholics in Northern Ireland (Paolini et al., 2004), straight people's attitudes towards gays (Vonofakou et al., 2007), majority group members' attitudes towards ethnic minorities in Europe (Binder et al., 2009), or Peruvian–Chilean atti-tudes in Chile (González et al., in press), increased contact is associated with dimin-ished anxiety, and diminished anxiety is associated with less prejudice.

Let me single out one of those studies for special scrutiny, because it uncovered one other interesting finding – which harks back to the previous section on moderator vari-ables. Voci and Hewstone (2003) surveyed some Italian hospital workers about their attitudes towards those of their co-workers who came from outside the EU (*extracom-munitari*), as well as towards such immigrants in general. Consistently with the gen-eral trends I have just described, the more contact these workers had with their immigrant colleagues, the less anxious they felt about interacting with them and the

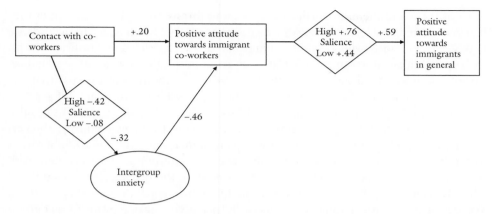

Figure 9.7 Intergroup anxiety mediates the effect of contact on prejudice, and category salience moderates it. Adapted from Figure 2 in Voci and Hewstone, 2003

more favourable their attitudes towards them and towards immigrants in general were
(see Figure 9.7). Importantly, those relationships were noticeably stronger for respondents who reported higher than average awareness of group memberships in their dealings with their foreign colleagues. Thus, group salience, which, as I showed in section
3.2, moderates the effects of contact so as to make it promote greater generalization,
also seems to amplify the beneficial effects of contact in reducing intergroup anxiety
(for similar results, see also Harwood et al., 2005 and Vonofakou et al., 2007).

A second emotionally laden mediator of contact effects is **empathy**. Batson and
colleagues (1997) argue that, the more we are able – or want – to put ourselves in the
shoes of outgroup members, the more we will see the world from their point of view,
and perhaps experience something of what they might be feeling. When that outgroup is a stigmatized group, such an empathic orientation should evoke sympathy,
and hence a more favourable, less prejudiced, attitude towards them. Because empathy involves a shift from one's own to another's perspective, it is often equated with
perspective-taking, although the latter implies a slightly more cognitively driven
process (Galinsky and Moskowitz, 2000).

A classic demonstration of empathy's power to change intergroup attitudes was
made by Batson and colleagues (1997). They invited participants to listen to a radio
interview featuring a woman with AIDS. They had to do this under one of two conditions: *either* by imagining how the AIDS victim felt *or* by taking a more objective
point of view. As they had expected, the researchers found that people subsequently
expressed more favourable attitudes towards patients with AIDS in general in the
former, perspective-taking condition. Similar results were found using homeless people and convicted murderers as the stigmatized groups. In several field studies the
links between contact, empathy and prejudice reduction have been clearly demonstrated (Pettigrew and Tropp, 2008). Empathy also seems to facilitate the effects of
contact in promoting intergroup forgiveness in post-conflict societies. We found this
in Bosnia, when we examined Bosniak (Bosnian Muslim) attitudes towards Bosnian
Serbs in the aftermath of the war in Bosnia in the 1990s (Cehajic et al., 2008). The
more contact the Bosniaks had had with the Serbs, the more empathic they felt

towards them and the more inclined they were to forgive them for the atrocities they
had committed. Such forgiveness, in turn, led to lessened prejudice. In accordance
with Gaertner and Dovidio's common ingroup identity model, an identification with
the superordinate Bosnian category also led to more forgiveness and less prejudice.
Another important mediator of contact proved to be the degree of trust that the
Bosniaks felt able to muster towards the Serbs (see also Hewstone et al., 2004).

I should just enter one qualification before concluding this discussion on the positive
effects of perspective-taking. There may be some circumstances where taking the perspective of the other can disrupt an intergroup encounter, especially if one of the parties
to the interaction has good reason to think that the outgroup might view them with
some suspicion. Vorauer and her colleagues alerted us to this problem in their studies of
white Canadians' interactions with Canadian aboriginal people (Vorauer et al., 2009).
Vorauer and colleagues speculated that successful perspective-taking by the former group
would lead its members to appreciate that aboriginal attitudes towards them might be
somewhat negative. Counter-intuitively, Vorauer and her colleagues suggested that this
realization would be stronger amongst more highly prejudiced people, because they
might regard those negative attitudes as a reaction to their own somewhat prejudiced
attitudes towards aboriginal people; less prejudiced people, in contrast, because their
own attitudes are more favourable, might have more difficulty in imagining that the
outgroup would dislike them. This line of reasoning led Vorauer and colleagues to the
ironic conclusion that highly prejudiced people might work harder to be nicer to outgroup people if forced to take their perspective, whilst low prejudiced people would
complacently assume that the relationship would be harmonious anyway, and thus they
would make fewer efforts to develop much acquaintanceship. Across four studies, using
a variety of cognitive and affective measures, Vorauer and colleagues (2009) found consistent evidence for this paradoxical phenomenon. One of the most telling findings came
from a study involving actual interaction with an aboriginal Canadian in which the white
participants were given *either* a perspective-taking *or* an objectivity instruction, closely
modeled on Batson and colleagues' (1997) procedure described above. The aboriginal
partners in the interaction reported that they felt *less* happy when interacting with a low
prejudiced white Canadian operating under the perspective-taking instructions than
with one operating under the more neutral objectivity instructions. With the higher
prejudiced white Canadians, the trend was in the opposite direction: with them, perspective-taking marginally increased the aboriginal partner's satisfaction.

I would be hesitant to generalize this result to all intergroup situations, since I suspect that very often more highly prejudiced people may not care very much about
what the outgroup thinks of them. Still, the result does underline an important feature of a great many intergroup encounters: they do not always comprise participants
from groups of equal standing in society. It is to the nature and consequences of such
contact – between majorities and minorities – that I now turn.

Majority–minority contact: Different concerns, different outcomes

In the cross-national study I described earlier (Binder et al., 2009), we were able to
survey both majority group members (indigenous Belgians, Britons and Germans)
and minority groups members (North Africans, several British ethnic minorities and
Turks). We found clear, if modest, contact effects amongst the former but, to our

surprise, virtually none at all amongst the minority groups. This is an extreme – but by no means unique – illustration of the general trend reported by Tropp and Pettigrew (2005) in their meta-analysis of the sub-set of contact studies which have focused on minorities (see also Lopez, 2004; Molina and Wittig, 2006). As I noted earlier, Tropp and Pettigrew (2005) concluded that minority groups do show contact effects, but these are somewhat weaker than the contact effects shown by majority groups. So what accounts for these minority–majority differences in the effectiveness of contact as a prejudice reduction intervention?

To answer this question, we must first appreciate that **majority** and **minority group** members do not come to intergroup encounters as equals, nor do they bring with them the same experiences and expectations. Whatever attempts may be made to equalize their status and to optimize the quality of their interaction within the contact situation, the fact remains that, in the bad old world *outside* the classroom or work-place, the two groups do not enjoy the same power or status. As a rule, members of majority (or dominant) groups have greater prestige and are more likely to be in posi-tions of power and influence – as bosses, policy-makers, teachers and the like. These extra-situational inequalities mean that, in their everyday lives, members of majority groups may have had a greater number of experiences involving persuading or coerc-ing members of minority groups into adhering to certain normative standards. In contrast, the minority group members are likely to be more familiar with attending to, and perhaps trying to negotiate with, those in authority.

According to Vorauer (2006), these differences in power will cause members of major-ity and minority groups to pay attention to different aspects of an intergroup interaction. Pragmatically, it may often be more important for minority groups to monitor the way they are being viewed and evaluated by their interaction partner(s) than it will be for majority members. On the other hand, majority groups may be more concerned about 'managing' the interaction in as smooth and conflict-free fashion as possible.

It is not just disparities in status that distinguish majority from minority groups. By virtue of their simple numerical difference, minority group members are likely to have had more prior contact with majority groups than the other way around. Some of that contact, we may hope, will have been relatively benign; much of it, given the some-what racist nature of many societies, will have been decidedly less positive. As we saw in the previous chapter, members of minority groups are more likely to experience prejudice and discrimination than members of majority groups. Either way, as Vorauer (2006) points out, the two groups arrive at an intergroup encounter with very differ-ent life experiences – and hence expectations – as to how the interaction will proceed. From the majority perspective, there may be some apprehension, born of unfamiliar-ity and concern to avoid appearing prejudiced. As I noted in Chapter 7 in the discus-sion of aversive racism (on which see Dovidio and Gaertner, 2004), many well meaning majority group members may manifest just this kind of orientation. From the minor-ity's point of view, lack of familiarity is seldom the issue; indeed, perhaps too much familiarity may be more of the problem! Their concerns may be initially to check how prejudiced the outgroup person seems to be, and subsequently to be watchful for any signs of bias, be it subtle or blatant.

Another set of concerns, and this time peculiar to the minority group, relates to phenomena associated with belonging to a stigmatized group. As we saw in Chapter 8, the repeated experience of discrimination can lead to self-protective coping strategies. In addition, the awareness of certain negative stereotypes about one's group is often associated with performance inhibiting stereotype threat effects, as people seek to avoid confirming those stereotypes (Steele et al., 2002). Some or all of these processes may be operative as members of minority groups meet majority group members for the first time.

We are now in a position to appreciate why intergroup contact is differentially effective in reducing prejudice for majority and minority groups. Earlier on I noted how intergroup anxiety appears to be an important mediator of the contact/prejudice reduction relationship. Generally speaking, the more contact we have with outgroups, the less anxious we feel about interacting with them and the lower our prejudice towards them becomes. Perhaps this process only works well for members of majority groups. Due to their greater unfamiliarity with minority groups, we might expect their levels of intergroup anxiety to be higher and the links of the contact–anxiety–prejudice chain to be stronger than would be the case in minority groups.

The evidence here is somewhat equivocal. In our European contact study we did find greater intergroup anxiety amongst majority group adolescents than in the minority groups (Binder et al., 2009). Although the difference was highly significant due to the large size of the sample, its magnitude was not great. Still, the mediation of the contact–prejudice link was only apparent for the majority groups. But other studies have not observed the same majority–minority difference in anxiety (Hyers and Swim, 1998; Shelton, 2003), and at least two have found greater intergroup anxiety in a minority group (Hindus in Bangladesh: Islam and Hewstone, 1993a; Japanese students in the UK: Greenland and Brown, 2005; compare Greenland and Brown, 1999). One reason for these inconsistencies may be that the typical ways of measuring intergroup anxiety in these studies, which often use variations of Stephan and Stephan's (1985) useful scale, may not be able to capture the different quality of the anxiety liable to be experienced by the two groups.[2] Stephan and Stephan's measure invites participants to record their feelings of 'anxiety', 'nervousness', 'awkwardness' and so on as they anticipate or recall interactions with an outgroup. If, as I suggested above, the anxiety of majority group members derives mainly from their worry about appearing prejudiced (in other words, about their self-image), whilst minority group people are more concerned about how the other person will view or treat them (in other words, about what difficulties the other person may create for them), such global affect items may not be sufficiently precise.

Findings from other research support the differential contact experience account. Hyers and Swim (1998) invited African Americans and European Americans to work together on an involving problem-solving task. Post-task measures indicated that the biggest difference between the two groups was in how much attention people paid to the situation and to their partner; African American participants scored higher. Shelton and colleagues (2005) focused just on American minority group members in a diary study of room-mate relationships. For those who had a white roommate, the more they expected to be a target of prejudice, the more negative affect they experienced. Interestingly, amongst that same sub-set of respondents, the more they expected to be a target of prejudice, the more self-disclosure they engaged in with their room-mate, perhaps as a strategy to ward off the prejudice they were anticipating. Turning to majority groups members, Vorauer and colleagues (2000) found that merely warning white Canadian participants that they would shortly interact with an aboriginal Canadian person was enough to trigger various negative **meta-stereotypes** about the white Canadian

Table 9.1 Four acculturation orientations

	Desire for intergroup contact	
Desire to maintain culture	*High*	*Low*
High	Integration	Separation
Low	Assimilation	Marginalization

Source: Adapted from Figure 1 in Berry, 1997

ingroup (for example as 'prejudiced', 'arrogant'). A meta-stereotype is the view that one believes the other group to have of one's ingroup. In other words, the anticipation of an intergroup interaction led these majority group members to activate concerns that they would be regarded as being prejudiced (see also Vorauer and Kumhyr, 2001).

In an earlier section I discussed how the fostering of a common ingroup identity can help to reduce prejudice. When we consider this common ingroup strategy from the different vantage points of majority and minority group members, a difficulty arises. Recall from Chapter 6 that a powerful motive at work in intergroup relations is the desire to create, maintain or enhance the distinctiveness of the ingroup (Tajfel and Turner, 1986). Any attempt to impose a single superordinate identity is directly antithetical to such needs for distinctiveness in the sub-groups involved, since these sub-groups risk being swallowed up in the larger entity. This risk is particularly acute for minority sub-groups; majority sub-groups might have less to fear, since they may be in a position to fashion the superordinate category in their own image (Wenzel et al., 2007). A consequence of these distinctiveness threats could be an *increase* in intergroup bias, as groups try to retain their unique identities. The results of several laboratory studies and at least one field study seem to support this reasoning: minority sub-groups seem to show the least bias in conditions which favour the simultaneous maintenance of the superordinate identity and of the sub-group identity (Dovidio et al., 2007; González and Brown, 2006; Hornsey and Hogg, 2000, 2002; although compare Guerra et al., in press).

The efficacy of this dual identity strategy is underlined in research which has studied how minority (and immigrant) and majority groups with different cultural traditions mutually accommodate each other. In this research it is common to distinguish between two kinds of question that these groups may face: How much contact do the members of the groups wish to have with each other? And how much do they wish to maintain (or relinquish) their own cultural heritage? Berry (1997) has suggested that any particular group's answers to these two questions represents its preferred **acculturation orientation** and that such acculturation orientations have important consequences for its members' well-being and, as we shall see, for their intergroup attitudes too. Berry (1997) proposed a simple four-fold taxonomy of acculturation strategies, based on people's affirmative or negative answers to the two questions (see Table 9.1). If people are eager for intergroup contact *and* simultaneously desire to maintain their own culture, this is known as the **integration** strategy, also sometimes known as **multiculturalism**. Perhaps they are less interested in maintaining their own culture but still wish to have a lot to do with the other group. This option is known as **assimilation**, especially when applied to a minority group. On the other hand, the outgroup may hold little interest (or people may feel excluded from it), and they may have a strong desire not to lose their cultural heritage. This is called '**separation**'. Finally, if people show little interest in either contact or cultural maintenance, they are said to be '**marginalized**'. A similar scheme has been proposed by Hutnik (1991), although there more emphasis is placed on the locus of people's identifications: sub-group identification (high or low) and superordinate group identification (high or low). In such a model, the high–high combination corresponds to the integration or dual identity orientation.

A large amount of research now firmly points to the psycho-social benefits for minority group members of adopting an integrationist orientation (Berry, 1997; Liebkind, 2001). Such an orientation seems also to be associated with more harmonious intergroup attitudes on the part of both minority and majority group members, especially when compared to the other three orientations (Pfafferott and Brown, 2006; Zagefka and Brown, 2002; Zagefka et al., 2009).

Still, whatever the psychological and social costs and benefits of different acculturation orientations, it is important to establish which orientations seem to be generally preferred by majority and minority groups (Arends-Toth and van de Vijver, 2003; Pfafferott and Brown, 2006; Verkuyten, 2006; Zagefka and Brown, 2002). When one reviews the findings from these several studies, a consistent pattern emerges which points to a potential problem for majority–minority contact: in general, we find that the integration (or dual identity) orientation is noticeably more popular among minority groups than it is in majority ones. Typically one finds anything between 67 per cent and 90 per cent of minority group members opting for integration, whilst usually only 50 per cent of majority group members favour this choice. For assimilation, the picture is inverted: assimilation is adopted by only a small proportion of minority groups, and certainly much less frequently than it is by majority groups. To complicate matters still further, it seems that preferred minority group acculturation orientations may greatly depend on context. In the private sphere of home and family, they may veer more towards separation (speaking one's heritage language, engaging in particular cultural practices), whilst in the more public domains of work and community these orientations will be more firmly integrationist. Majority groups seem to display less difference between these public and private contexts (Arends-Toth and van de Vijver, 2003).

In the light of these findings, let us now imagine typical encounters between minority and majority group members. The former may come to the contact situation wanting and expecting an integrationist outlook to prevail; with the latter, there is a good chance that they will bring with them a more assimilationist set of expectations. As Dovidio and colleagues (2007) point out, these divergent acculturation perspectives may well have deleterious consequences for the ease with which social consensus will be reached on items such as how the intergroup interaction will be managed, what the appropriate topics for discussion and negotiation are, and so on (see also Johnson et al., 2009).

Observing or imagining cross-group friendships: The effects of indirect contact

As we have seen, intergroup contact works best when it permits the development of meaningful relationships with outgroup members, especially if those relationships still retain some intergroup salience. But such cross-group friendships can also have other, *indirect*, effects by signalling to other ingroup members that it is possible and appropriate to be friends with members of the outgroup. By changing social norms in this way, these friendships may reduce prejudice.

Wright and his colleagues (1997) called this process ***extended contact***, to distinguish it from the direct contact described by Allport (1954). In extended contact, my attitudes change not because I have any outgroup friends myself, but because I know some ingroup members who do. According to Wright and colleagues (1997), extended contact reduces prejudice in four ways. Like direct contact, it may help to dispel people's anxiety about the prospect of getting to know, and then of interacting with, members of an outgroup. Knowing or observing other ingroup members apparently enjoying easily harmonious relations with outgroup members may allow me to contemplate having a similar relationship too. Secondly, extended contact can change people's self-concept. As we known from social identity theory (Tajfel and Turner, 1986; see Chapter 6), people readily include members of the ingroup into their identity, their sense of themselves (Smith and Henry, 1996). The awareness that some of those ingroup members have a close relationship with people in another group may widen the scope of the self-concept, so that the latter are also included within it. Wright and colleagues (1997) call this process '**inclusion of other in the self**' (IOS). Thirdly, the observation that it is possible to have friends from another group can make it seem *permissible* also. In other words, extended contact has the potential to change the way we perceive ingroup norms about the desirability of having a more diverse network of friendships. Lastly, it may change people's perceptions about the norms that prevail in the *outgroup* concerning the appropriateness of having cross-group friendships. Studies of perceived acculturation preferences – that is, of the acculturation orientations which one group believes to be held by another – have found that members of majority groups exaggerate the extent to which they think minority groups wish not to have contact with them and 'separate' themselves from the rest of society (Pfafferott and Brown, 2006; Zagefka and Brown, 2002). When one witnesses cross-group friendships in others, such misperceptions may change and one may come to believe that the norms prevailing in the outgroup are not so exclusive after all.

Wright and colleagues (1997) themselves provided some of the first pieces of evidence in favour of the extended contact hypothesis. They found that American college students who knew at least one member of their own group to have a friendship with someone from another ethnic group showed lower levels of prejudice towards that ethnic group than students who knew no one with such a cross-group friendship. This held true even when controlling for the students' own, direct cross-group contacts. Moreover, the extended contact effect worked even with artificial laboratory groups. Merely observing a fellow ingroup member (from a blue/green group) interacting warmly with an outgroup member (from a green/blue group) was enough to change the participants' evaluation of that outgroup.

Since then, studies conducted in several other countries have confirmed these findings. Whether in Germany, Northern Ireland, England or Norway, and whether involving adults in large representative surveys or university, secondary and primary school students, having ingroup friends with outgroup friends seems to be reliably associated with lessened prejudice, at least in cross-sectional correlations (Feddes et al., 2009; De Tezanos Pinto et al., 2009; Paolini et al., 2004; Pettigrew et al., 2007;

Turner et al., 2007b, 2008). The studies conducted by Turner and colleagues (2008) are particularly noteworthy, since they incorporated all four of the mediators originally proposed by Wright and colleagues (1997): intergroup anxiety, IOS, ingroup and outgroup norms. Each one of these proved to be a reliable and independent mediator of the link between extended contact and more favourable intergroup attitudes.

There is another form of indirect contact, which is even more tenuous than extended contact: it may be possible merely to fantasize about a positive intergroup interaction to effect some attitude change. Crisp and Turner (2009) call this **'imagined contact'**, and have conducted several studies to demonstrate its effects. In a typical experimental paradigm, participants are asked to 'take a minute to imagine yourself meeting an elderly stranger for the first time. Imagine their appearance, the conversation that follows and, from what you learn, all the different ways you could classify them into different groups of people' (Turner et al., 2007a, p. 481). In control conditions, participants have to imagine a scene in nature, with no intergroup interaction. Using this simple mental imagery instruction, or slight variants of it, Turner and her colleagues have found that people's attitudes or behavioural intentions towards the outgroup become a little more positive. So far they have applied the technique to prejudice towards the elderly, gay people, Muslims, Mexican Mestizos and international students in the UK (Stathi and Crisp, 2008; Turner et al., 2007a; Turner and Crisp, in press). There is even evidence that an imagined contact procedure can affect people's responses on an implicit measure of prejudice like the IAT (Turner and Crisp, in press).

How does imagined contact work? Turner and colleagues (2007a) suggest that the mental imagery exercise might prepare people for the prospect of an actual cross-group interaction and thereby lessen their intergroup anxiety, in the same way in which direct contact also seems to work (see the section on the 'how' and the 'why' of contact above).

This is an intriguing technique. Indeed, it almost seems too good to be true! Simply by getting people to create positive intergroup scenarios in their heads, their prejudice is apparently imagined away. It is still too early to say whether this idea will make a genuine contribution to prejudice reduction endeavours, and certainly Crisp and Turner (2009) are too sensible to make exaggerated claims for it. I have the suspicion that some of the laboratory results may be partly attributable to demand characteristics, although the findings of Turner and Crisp (in press) with an implicit measure speak against a simple methodological explanation of the effects of imagined contact. I also wonder how feasible imagined contact would be in some particularly intense conflictual contexts, where people may have difficulty in engaging in the requisite mental activity. Crisp and Turner (2009) suggest that imagined contact may be best used in conjunction with other forms of contact rather than as an intervention in its own right. And, in situations where there are few opportunities for actual contact, it may be better than nothing.

How effective is indirect contact compared to its direct cousin? If one compares the simple correlations between direct and indirect contact and prejudice, there appears little to choose between them (De Tezanos Pinto et al., 2009; Pettigrew et al., 2007; Turner et al., 2007b, 2008). However, as Turner and colleagues (2007b) point out, direct contact generally seems to have stronger links with prejudice reduction, once other variables are controlled for. Take for example the study by Feddes and colleagues (2009). This is one of the very few longitudinal studies of extended contact, and it studied young German and Turkish children in three ethnically mixed primary schools in Germany. Its longitudinal design means that we can infer here some causality from the data in a way that is impossible in cross-sectional studies. It turned out that initial *direct* contact was correlated with positive intergroup attitudes seven months later, at least for the German majority children (for the Turkish children there was no equivalent effect, just as we had observed in another longitudinal study; see Binder et al., 2009). However, no such longitudinal effect could be observed for extended contact, either for the German or for the Turkish children.

Nevertheless, this is not to say that indirect contact will always be less efficacious than direct contact. In some contexts the normal prevalence of contact between members of different groups may be rather low. This may happen because of institutional segregation, which virtually eliminates the opportunities for cross-group friendship formation. The almost completely segregated school system in Northern Ireland would be a case in point. Informal or voluntary resegregation, even after formal desegregation has occurred, can also limit the possibilities for actual contact. Dixon and Durrheim (2003) observed such resegregation on a beach in a South African holiday resort. Black, white and Indian families spontaneously grouped themselves into ethnically separate clusters on this beach, despite the fact that apartheid had been abolished several years before. Moreover, the absolute numbers of the same outgroups in any given culture may be rather small, a situation which makes it statistically unlikely that the majority will have the chance to meet them. In contexts such as these, the chances of direct intergroup contact happening in the normal course of everyday life are limited. It may also be difficult to engineer opportunities for contact through social policy interventions. This is where extended and imagined contact come into their own. It is possible to draw on the principles of indirect contact to design effective – and economical – interventions, which can initiate the process of prejudice reduction.

One such intervention was devised by Liebkind and McAlister (1999) for use in six secondary schools in Finland – a country which, at the time of the research, was quite intolerant of foreigners. In half the schools the researchers arranged for stories to be distributed in which a Finnish boy or girl had close friendships with foreigners (for instance Iranians or Somalis). Classroom discussions of these stories were led by slightly older Finnish students, who took every opportunity to make and encourage positive comments about these cross-group friendships. In this way, the stories and the discussants acted as peer models for extended contact. In the remaining (control) schools no such intervention occurred. The effects of the intervention were clear: over a seven-month period the intergroup attitudes of the students in the experimental schools remained stable or improved; in the control schools they deteriorated for the most part.

We followed up this idea by designing a story-book intervention in some British primary schools (Cameron et al., 2006). We wanted to see whether the effectiveness of indirect contact would be enhanced through the incorporation of the dual identity strategy that I discussed in the section on majority–minority contact above. In our stories, the outgroup protagonist was a refugee child who had made friends with a white British child. In the dual identity versions of the stories, constant references were made to the children's respective cultural identities, whilst at the same time their common identity as students at the same school was emphasized. Other stories focused just on the common school identity (the common condition), or it highlighted the children's individual characteristics (the decategorized condition). And, of course,

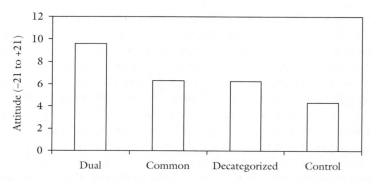

Figure 9.8   Changing children's attitudes with an extended contact intervention. The figure shows positive attitudes towards refugees. Adapted from Table 1 in Cameron et al., 2006

there was a control condition, in which the children heard no stories at all. The stories and the subsequent discussion of them occurred once a week, for a period of six weeks. A week or two later we assessed the children's attitudes towards refugees. As can be seen in Figure 9.8, all three of the experimental groups had more favourable intergroup attitudes than the no-story control group. But, strikingly, those in the dual condition had the most favourable attitudes of all (and they were significantly more positive than the other two experimental groups). A similar technique has been successfully used to change children's attitudes towards people with disabilities (Cameron and Rutland, 2006).

An even more dramatic example of how media interventions using extended contact ideas can be used to change even the most entrenched attitudes was provided by Paluck (2009). She carried out an evaluation of the impact of a radio programme in Rwanda, a country that is even now trying to rebuild itself after the genocide of 1994, in which hundreds of thousands of Tutsis were slaughtered in a few brutal months. The radio programme, called 'Musekeweya' ('New Dawn'), featured a soap opera involving people from the Hutu and Tutsi communities and, of course (it being a soap opera) there was a romantic storyline with a boy and a girl from the different ethnic groups. Paluck arranged for four twenty-minute episodes of this radio programme to be played on transistor radios in a number of village communities. Other communities listened to another soap opera, whose focus was on changing attitudes about HIV and AIDS. At the end of a year, members of these communities were interviewed in order for Paluck to assess their beliefs about the origins and panaceas of group violence and their endorsement of social norms about trust and intermarriage.[3] Paluck found that, although people's beliefs appeared to be little affected by having been exposed to the 'Musekeweya' programme, their norms about the permissibility of intermarriage, about the possibility of trust and about having empathy for other Rwandans had all changed for the better by comparison with the corresponding norms of those who had listened to the health soap opera. Paluck notes a pleasing symmetry in these findings: it proved possible to use a radio programme as a tool for intergroup reconciliation when, by common consent, radio broadcasts depicting the Tutsi as cockroaches and other vermin played a not insignificant role in the 1994 genocide.

Last Words

I chose that study by Paluck for the end of this chapter – and of my book – because I find it a particularly inspiring example of what social psychology can contribute, both by way of theoretical ideas which can inform the design of an effective intervention and by way of methodological tools with which to evaluate it. Let me quickly temper that rather optimistic conclusion with a note of caution about the limits of what social psychology can achieve in the comprehension and eventual eradication of the social problem of prejudice. As I pointed out in Chapter 1, it would be foolish to pretend that any one academic discipline has a monopoly on wisdom when it comes to unravelling a phenomenon as complex and as deeply enmeshed in historical, economic and political forces as is prejudice. Indeed, it is my view that it is quite likely that the world's long-standing conflicts and their associated prejudices will first require some radical socio-political transformation before any intergroup contact, be it direct or extended, is even remotely conceivable. Still, as the saying goes, all roads eventually lead to Rome. And if the path of the social psychological road is narrow and its direction as yet uncertain, it is a journey we must surely make if we are serious about doing something to reduce prejudice in today's conflict-ridden world. My rather immodest hope is that this book may serve as something of a guide for others who think of embarking on this project.

Summary

1   A substantial body of research has shown that contact between groups can reduce prejudice, provided that it takes place under certain conditions. These are: there should be social and institutional support for the measures designed to promote the contact; the contact should be of sufficient frequency, duration and closeness to permit the development of meaningful relationships between members of the groups concerned; as far as possible, the participants in the contact situation should be of equal status; the contact should involve co-operative activity.

2   A major focus of contact research have been integrated schools. Some of this research, particularly on the effects of school desegregation in the United States, suggests that integration has not always had the hoped-for effects on interethnic relations. The reason for this is that desegregation has seldom met all the four optimal conditions for successful contact. However, specific intervention programmes, especially those involving co-operative learning groups, have been very successful in increasing the attraction between members of different social categories.

3   The contact hypothesis has undergone substantial modification and extension in recent years. It is now clear that the causal effects are bidirectional: contact reduces prejudice, but prejudice reduces contact just as well.

4   To promote the maximum generalization of contact effects, it is important to retain some category salience in intergroup encounters. The ways in which contact achieves its effects seem to be: reducing intergroup anxiety; promoting a common ingroup identity; and allowing the development of empathy. However, these mediating

processes may not work in the same way, or as effectively, in minority groups as they do in majority groups.

5   Finally, it is possible to reduce prejudice without any direct outgroup contact at all; simply knowing other people who have friends in the outgroup, or imagining oneself to have such friends, may be sufficient to improve intergroup attitudes.

Notes

1   There were actually two conditions of group salience, depending on the point in the inter-action at which those references to ethnicity were made salient. In the event the two conditions did not differ from each other, so I treat them here as one.
2   I am grateful to Jack Dovidio and the other members of my work-group at the 2009 Summer School of the International Graduate College for these insights.
3   Because of the extreme sensitivity of intergroup relations in Rwanda, it was felt that interethnic attitudes could not be assessed directly.

Further Reading

Brown, R., and Hewstone, M. (2005) An integrative theory of intergroup contact. *Advances in Experimental Social Psychology* 37: 255–343.
Gaertner, S., and Dovidio. J. (2000) *Reducing Intergroup Bias: The Common Ingroup Identity Model*. Hove: Psychology Press.
Oskamp, S. (2000) *Reducing Prejudice and Discrimination*, esp. Part III. Mahwah, NJ: Erlbaum.
Turner, R. N., Hewstone, M., Voci, A., Paolini, S., and Christ, O. (2007c) Reducing prejudice via direct and extended cross-group friendship. *European Review of Social Psychology* 18: 212–55.

Glossary of Key Terms

Accessibility The ease with which a given cognitive construct comes to someone's mind defines its accessibility.

Acculturation orientation A strategy which group members may adopt in relation to other groups in a context of immigration. Traditionally, acculturation orientations are seen as deriving from people's preference for maintaining (or relinquishing) their own culture and for interacting with the other group and adopting facets of its culture (or not).

Acquaintance potential A social setting that can facilitate the development of cross-group friendships.

Acquiescence response set A tendency to answer items on a questionnaire in the 'agreeing' direction, irrespective of the content of the items.

Aetiological Pertaining to the origins or causes of a phenomenon.

Ageism A particular form of prejudice, in which the target is defined by age, usually elderly people.

Ambivalent prejudice (racism/sexism) A form of prejudice which contains a mixture of both positive and negative attitudes towards the outgroup.

Anti-Semitism A particular form of prejudice, in which the target is Jewish people.

Assimilation An acculturation orientation or social policy that favours the absorption of minority cultures into the majority culture.

Associative priming A technique for measuring prejudice implicitly. Group labels or stimuli serve as primes in a task where people have to judge various words as positive or negative. Response times in the primed task can be compared to baseline response times without the primes, and from these differences an implicit measure of prejudice can be derived.

Attribution theory A theory which is concerned with lay people's beliefs about the causes of human behaviour.

Authoritarian personality (authoritarianism) Derives from a theory which holds that prejudice is mostly explained by a personality trait (authoritarianism), and that this trait derives from a particular kind of family environment, in which the child is subject to a very strict and morally censorious upbringing.

Automatic process/behaviour   Something which occurs without effort or will, often without awareness.

Aversive racism   A form of prejudice in which people, while genuinely endorsing principles of tolerance, still display evidence of avoidance or apprehension in intergroup encounters, especially if there are no clear norms for how one should behave in those situations.

Belief (in)congruence   The extent to which the beliefs of two (or more) people are seen as (dis)similar. In one theory (the belief congruence theory) this is thought to determine people's prejudice.

Benevolent sexism   A form of sexism which appears to consist of favourable attitudes towards women, but which disguises an underlying wish to maintain gender inequality.

Bogus pipeline   An experimental paradigm in which participants believe that their true feelings can be detected by a machine. Differences between responses in this paradigm and responses from people under normal conditions are thought to reveal tendencies towards social desirability in people's responding.

Categorization   The cognitive process of segmenting the (social) world into discrete units.

Category awareness   Knowledge of the existence of categorial differences amongst people.

Category identification   A person's self-defining in terms of some category membership.

Category preference   A person's favouring of one category over another.

Civic nationalism   A form of national identification in which the nation is defined in terms of citizenship, through a commitment to respect and participate in institutional and legal frameworks.

Cognitive busyness   A state of mind where one's present cognitive resources are taken up by ('busy with') some ongoing mental activity.

Cognitive closure (need for)   A strong desire to arrive at a definite answer to a problem rather than being able to tolerate some ambiguity in the solution.

Cognitive dissonance theory   A theory which proposes that a major motivation for human behaviour is the need to avoid holding two or more contradictory beliefs. The state of holding such beliefs is an aversive state known as cognitive dissonance.

Common fate   The perception that different people undergo similar experiences, especially in how they are treated by others.

Common ingroup identity model   A theory according to which contact will be most successful if it succeeds in redrawing category boundaries in such a way that members of an ingroup and members of an outgroup come to be seen as belonging to the same superordinate category.

Concrete operational period   A stage in the child's cognitive development in which, according to Piaget, the child's perceptions and cognitions of people and objects are dominated by the physical appearance of these people and objects.

Conflict of interests   A situation where what one group seeks or desires conflicts with, and would come at the expense of, another group's goals.

Conservation   The child's ability to understand that, despite a change in a person's or an object's physical appearance, the underlying properties of the person or object in question remain unchanged. A classical conservation task is to transfer liquid from a tall thin jar into a shorter wider jar and to ask the child whether the amount of liquid has changed as a result.

Contact hypothesis   The idea that prejudice can be reduced by bringing members of different groups together, under conditions that favour equal-status co-operation and friendship formation and where there is institutional support for the goals of integration.

Co-operative learning groups   Small groups of students working together; such groups are organized as part of a method of teaching in which students are positively interdependent on each other for their learning outcomes.

Creative ingroup bias   A method of seeking positive distinctiveness for an ingroup by drawing attention to hitherto overlooked positive attributes it may possess.

Cross-cutting categorization   A manner of classifying where two or more systems of categorization overlap, so that people can be seen as belonging to more than one group simultaneously (e.g. to gender and ethnicity).

Decategorization   Process of de-emphasizing the social categories, which thus become less salient.

Desegregated schooling   School systems that foster ethnic or religious diversity within schools.

Discriminant validity   The validity of a test or measure, when that test or measure is correlated to variable(s) on relevant criteria but not to variables on less relevant criteria.

Displacement   A process, articulated in psycho-dynamic theory, in which the aggression or prejudice towards a powerful target is re-directed towards substitute and less powerful targets.

Dogmatism   A personality trait similar to authoritarianism, but thought to be equally applicable to people with strong left or right-wing political views.

Dual (or **bicultural**) **identities**   A form of identity which results when people identify with two or more categories simultaneously.

Empathy   The ability to experience the emotions of another person by being able to take their perspective.

Entitativity   The extent to which a set of stimuli are seen as forming a single unit or group.

Ethnic constancy   The ability to understand that some of the physical characteristics which define people's ethnicity (e.g. skin colour) are unlikely to change with age.

Ethnic nationalism   A form of national identification in which the nation is defined in terms of some supposed shared ancestral, linguistic or cultural distinctiveness.

Ethnocentrism   Technically, an outlook in which everything is seen from the perspective of the person's ingroup. It is often used to denote a prejudiced attitude towards outgroups in general.

Explicit prejudice   A direct form of prejudice, which is usually under the person's control.

Expressive ingroup bias   A method of seeking positive distinctiveness for an ingroup by emphasizing the positive attributes it is already widely seen as possessing.

Extended contact   An indirect form of intergroup contact, which derives from a person's knowledge that other members of the ingroup have outgroup friends.

Factor analysis   A form of statistical analysis that seeks to find an underlying structure in a set of intercorrelated variables.

False consciousness   A Marxist concept describing a situation where subordinate group members hold beliefs about the existing social order that are at variance with reality and run against their material interests.

Fit   The extent to which a category relates functionally to real differences amongst stimuli in any given situation.

Frustration–aggression theory   A theory which holds that prejudice is caused by people being unable to satisfy their basic needs or to achieve desired goals.

Generalization   Transferral of an attitude change towards one individual onto other members of that person's group, or to the group as a whole.

Group (or **fraternalistic**) **deprivation**   The feeling which arises when people perceive a discrepancy between their *group* 's current social standing and the one to which they feel it is entitled.

Group essence/essentialism   An attribute which is presumed to be possessed by all or most of the members of a group on account of the fact that the group is partially defined by that attribute. In some cases, an 'essence' may be perceived to be biologically associated with the group.

Group identification (**strength of**)   The extent to which people see themselves as belonging to a group; their evaluation of that group; and their emotional commitment to it.

Group salience   A state in which one or more groups become readily available or accessible in people's minds.

Habituation paradigm   An experimental technique, used in the study of very young children, in which a given stimulus is shown repeatedly until the child appears to lose interest in it. In the test phase, the same stimulus is shown in conjunction with a new test stimulus, and the times of looking both at the new and at the original one are recorded. Differential looking time between the two stimuli indicates that the child sees something different in the test stimulus.

Hate crime   Any criminal offence which is motivated by an antipathy towards the victim's group membership (e.g. ethnicity, religion, sexual orientation).

Homophobia   A particular form of prejudice, in which the target is a group defined by its members' sexual orientation (e.g. gay, lesbian, transgender).

Homophobic   Prejudiced against gay people.

Hostile sexism   A form of sexism in which negative attitudes towards women are explicitly stated.

Illegitimate status differences   A situation where a group's position in a hierarchy is seen to be based on arbitrary criteria or unfair practices.

Illusory correlation   An erroneous belief that members of a minority group are more likely than members of a majority group to possess certain infrequently occurring attributes.

Image theory   A theoretical perspective in political science in which the prevailing stereotypic images of an outgroup derive from the ingroup's functional relationship to that outgroup as an 'ally', an 'enemy', a 'dependant' or a 'barbarian'.

Imagined contact   A technique in which people are asked to imagine having a pleasant interaction with a member of an outgroup.

Impermeable group boundaries   Groups which are defined in such a way that exit from or entry into them is difficult to achieve by individual choice are said to have impermeable boundaries.

Implicit association test   An indirect measure of prejudice, based on people's speed to categorize various categorial and positive/negative attributes presented in different combinations.

Implicit prejudice   An indirect form of prejudice, which typically is not (much) under the person's control.

Inclusion of other in the self (IOS) A process whereby other people, especially from outgroups, become incorporated into a person's self concept.

Individual (or **egoistic**) **deprivation**   The feeling which arises when people perceive a discrepancy between *their own personal* current social standing and the one to which they feel entitled.

Ingroup bias   A tendency to favour the ingroup over an outgroup in perceptions, judgements or behaviour.

Ingroup over-exclusion effect   A tendency to categorize someone as belonging to an outgroup rather than to the ingroup.

Ingroup homogeneity   The extent to which members of the ingroup are seen as similar to each other.

Ingroup projection   A cognitive process in which attributes of the ingroup are perceived also as belonging to another, usually superordinate, category.

Integrated threat theory   A theory which proposes that prejudice arises primarily from different kinds of threat to the ingroup – e.g. symbolic or realistic.

Integration   A social policy that favours positive intergroup relations and ethnic diversity. When applied to a person's acculturation orientation, it indicates a wish both to maintain one's own culture and to engage actively with the culture of the other group.

Integrative complexity   A cognitive style which recognizes the existence of multiple perspectives and hypothesizes how they might be interrelated.

Intercategory differentiation   The tendency to see members of different categories to be more dissimilar than they really are.

Intergroup anxiety   The feeling of apprehension which may be experienced while anticipating an interaction with members of an outgroup.

Intergroup contact   Contact that takes place under conditions of group salience and where the interactants are seen as typical of their groups.

Intergroup discrimination   Any behaviour which treats members of two (or more) groups differently, usually by way of favouring one group over the other(s).

Intergroup emotions   Emotions that may be experienced because of something that has happened or may happen to the ingroup, but not necessarily directly to any single ingroup member.

Internal reliability   The extent to which the sub-components of a measure correlate well to each other. A commonly used index of internal reliability is Cronbach's alpha.

Interpersonal contact   Contact which takes place under conditions of low group salience and where the interactants are seen as individuals and not especially typical of their group.

Intolerance of ambiguity   A cognitive style associated with authoritarianism, in which the person has a preference for viewing the world in very clearly defined ways and finds ambiguity aversive.

Intracategory assimilation   The tendency to see members of the same category to be more similar than they really are.

J-curve hypothesis The contention that relative deprivation will be highest when a period of increasing prosperity for a group is followed by a sharp downturn in the group's fortunes.

Linguistic intergroup bias A tendency to describe positive ingroup and negative outgroup actions in abstract generalized terms, and negative ingroup and positive outgroup actions in a more concrete manner (*see* ultimate attribution error).

Majority group Literally the larger of two (or more) groups in a social context; but more usually a group with higher status and more power.

Marginalization An acculturation orientation or social policy that favours neither engagement with minority groups nor the maintenance of their cultural traditions.

Maximizing difference An evaluative or behavioural strategy which seeks to establish a positive difference between the ingroup and the outgroup.

Mediator A variable which can help to explain the effect of an independent variable on the dependent variable.

Meta-analysis A statistical method for combining the results of several independent research studies.

Meta-contrast ratio The degree to which a certain categorization maximizes the perceived differences between members of different groups whilst simultaneously minimizing the differences between members of the same groups.

Meta-stereotype The perception of another group's stereotypes about the ingroup.

Minimal group paradigm An experimental setting involving the creation of two (or more) artificial groups, where participants have no knowledge of or interaction with members of their group or of the other(s), and then are asked to allocate resources (usually money) to anonymous members of the different groups.

Minority group Literally the smaller of two (or more) groups in a social context; but more usually a group with lower status and less power.

Moderator A variable which can alter (moderate) the effects of an independent variable on the dependent variable.

Multiculturalism An ideology or social policy that favours integration as an acculturation orientation, particularly by promoting respect for cultural diversity.

Nationalism A form of national identification which stresses one's positive attachment to one's own country and also involves one's disparagement of other countries.

Negative interdependence A situation where the achievement of one group's goals prevents another group from achieving its goals.

Old-fashioned/blatant prejudice (racism/sexism) A form of prejudice in which the negative attitudes towards the outgroup are explicitly stated, often in very derogatory terms.

Outgroup bias A situation where an outgroup is judged or treated more favourably than the ingroup.

Outgroup homogeneity effect A perception that members of the outgroup are more similar to each other than members of the ingroup are.

Patriotism A form of national identification which stresses one's positive attachment to one's own country but involves no concomitant disparagement of other countries.

Perceived intragroup homogeneity   The degree to which members of one group are seen as similar to each other.

Person–group discrepancy   The tendency to feel that other members of one's group are discriminated against more than one personally is.

Perspective-taking   Seeing things from another person's point of view.

Positive distinctiveness   The ingroup's being seen or treated in such a way that it can be regarded as different from, and better than, some outgroup.

Positive interdependence   A situation where the achievement of one group's goals depends on the active contribution of another group.

Positive–negative asymmetry effect   The phenomenon in which behavioural or attitudinal discrimination is different and usually stronger along positively valued dimensions than along negatively valued dimensions.

Prejudice   Any attitude, emotion or behaviour towards members of a group, which directly or indirectly implies some negativity or antipathy towards that group.

Prevention focus   A cognitive orientation that focuses on not making errors in some task.

Priming   A procedure by which the presentation of one stimulus is made to affect the processing of a subsequent stimulus.

Promotion focus   A cognitive orientation that focuses on trying to optimize performance on some task.

Racism   A particular form of prejudice, in which the target is an ethnic group.

Randomized double-blind design   A research design in which neither the participants nor the researchers collecting the data are aware of the experimental condition the participants are in. Assignment of participants to treatment conditions is done randomly.

Reactive distinctiveness   A form of biased judgement or behaviour which seeks to establish positive distinctiveness for an otherwise ambiguously defined ingroup.

Realistic group conflict theory   A theory which holds that prejudice stems from various groups' competition for scarce material resources. Accordingly, on this perspective, prejudice may best be reduced by aligning the groups' real interests.

Realistic threats   Any threats to the material well-being or physical security of the ingroup.

Rebound effects   A situation where the intention to avoid stereotyping someone results in even greater stereotype activation or usage than before.

Refencing   Redefining a category and its associated attributes so that (apparent) disclaimers as to its validity or applicability can be accommodated or explained away.

Reflective distinctiveness   A form of biased judgement or behaviour which seeks to re-assert the positive distinctiveness of an already well defined ingroup.

Rejection–identification model   A theory which predicts that members of stigmatized groups will normally suffer negative consequences for their well-being, unless that phenomenon can be buffered by a heightened group identification, caused by discrimination targeted at their group.

Relative deprivation   The feeling which arises when people perceive a discrepancy between their current standard of living and the one to which they feel entitled.

Relative gratification   The opposite of relative deprivation – i.e. a situation where people perceive that their current standard of living is better than the one to which they feel entitled.

Response amplification   A heightened or exaggerated response, which is due to some variable.

Right-wing authoritarianism   A modern variant of the traditional authoritarianism personality trait; it comprises submission to authorities, aggression towards deviants or 'outsiders' and adherence to orthodox moral codes.

Schadenfreude   The pleasure that members of lower-status groups may feel when they learn of some misfortune befalling a higher-status group.

Self-affirmation   An experimental induction that invites people to think about their most important values.

Self-categorization theory   A theoretical perspective which holds that a primary determinant of people's group and intergroup behaviour is the manner in which and the level at which they categorize themselves as members of a group.

Self-fulfilling prophecy   A situation where stereotypic expectancies from a target bring about in it changes which are in line with, and hence reinforce, those expectancies.

Separation   An acculturation orientation or social policy that favours the segregation of minority cultures from the majority culture.

Sexism   A particular form of prejudice, in which the target is gender; usually directed at women.

Social dominance theory   A theory according to which prejudice and discrimination are thought to be manifestations of a universal human tendency to form unequal group-based structures, in which members of some groups have the power to subjugate members of others.

Social dominance orientation (SDO) A measure of the extent to which an individual endorses an ideological viewpoint which favours unequal social relationships, especially between groups.

Social identity   Those aspects of people's self-concepts that derive from their membership of various social categories.

Social identity theory   A perspective which claims that a major determinant of prejudice and intergroup behaviour stems from the way people's identities are constructed and defined and from the way they may be affected by particular social contexts.

Social stigma   Any characteristic that marks out a person for social devaluation.

Stereotype activation   The triggering and setting into operation of some stereotypic attribute or expectancy about a group.

Stereotype lift   A perception by members of a higher-status group that another group may be judged in terms of some negative stereotype – perception which then leads to better task performance in the higher-status group.

Stereotype suppression   The active attempt not to use a particular group stereotype in making a social judgement.

Stereotype threat   A perception by members of a stigmatized group that they may be judged in terms of some negative stereotype(s) of their group – perception which then leads to poorer task performance.

(Stereotypical) expectancies   Beliefs about what members of a group are like or about how they can be expected to behave typically.

Stereotyping/stereotypes   The attribution of various features to people on the basis of their membership of a particular group.

Subliminal   Below the threshold of awareness.

Subtle prejudice (racism/sexism)   A form of prejudice which is characterized by the defence of traditional individualistic values, an exaggeration of cultural intergroup differences and a denial of positive emotions towards the outgroup.

Sub-typing   The creation of sub-groups within a category so as to accommodate category members who do not easily fit within the broader category definition.

Superordinate goals   Goals which cannot be achieved by one group on its own or in competition with another group, but depend on the other group for their successful attainment.

Symbolic/modern prejudice, neo-prejudice (racism/sexism)   A form of prejudice which is characterized by opposition to social policies seen to favour disadvantaged groups or perceived to be inconsistent with the traditional values of individual freedom of choice or of meritocracy.

Symbolic threats   Challenges to the way the ingroup chooses to define itself and to the cultural practices which symbolize that identity.

System justification theory   A theory which holds that one source of intergroup attitudes is people's need to believe in the legitimacy and stability of existing social structures.

Temporal relative deprivation   A form of relational deprivation, which stems from unfavourable comparisons of the present situation with the past or the likely future.

Test/re-test reliability   The extent to which a measure yields similar results on two separate occasions; it is often measured by the correlation between scores at different time points.

Typicality   The extent to which a person is perceived to be representative of his/her group.

Ultimate attribution error   A tendency to ascribe the positive behaviours of ingroup members to internal causes and negative behaviours to external causes. Correspondingly, positive outgroup behaviours are attributed externally, while negative behaviours are seen to have internal origins.

Unstable status differences   A situation where changes to groups' respective positions in a hierarchy are perceived to be possible, or even imminent.

V-curve hypothesis   The contention that prejudice can arise from both relative deprivation and relative gratification.

Validity   A measure is said to be valid if it provides a good indication or approximation of the construct it is aiming to measure.

Xenophobia   A particular form of prejudice, in which foreigners are the target group.

References

Aboud, F. E. (1977) Interest in ethnic information: A cross-cultural developmental study. *Canadian Journal of Behavioral Science* 9: 134–46.

Aboud, F. E. (1980) A test of ethnocentrism with young children. *Canadian Journal of Behavioral Science* 12: 195–209.

Aboud, F. E. (1988) *Children and Prejudice*. Oxford: Basil Blackwell.

Aboud, F. E. (2003) The formation of in-group favoritism and out-group prejudice in young children: Are they distinct attitudes? *Developmental Psychology* 39(1): 48–60.

Aboud, F. E., and Doyle, A.-B. (1996) Parental and peer influences on children's racial attitudes. *International Journal of Intercultural Relations* 20: 371–83.

Aboud, F., and Amato, M. (2001) Developmental and socialization influences on intergroup bias. In R. Brown and S. Gaertner (eds), *Blackwell Handbook of Social Psychology: Intergroup Processes*, pp. 65–85. Oxford: Blackwell.

Aboud, F. E., and Sankar, J. (2007) Friendship and identity in a language-integrated school. *International Journal of Behavioral Development* 31: 445–53.

Aboud, F. E., Mendelson, M. J., and Purdy, K. T. (2003) Cross-race relations and friendship quality. *International Journal of Behavioral Development* 27: 165–73.

Abrams, D., Eller, A., and Bryant, J. (2006) An age apart: The effects of intergenerational contact and stereotype threat on performance and intergroup bias. *Psychology and Aging* 21: 691–702.

Abrams, D., Viki, G. T., Masser, B., and Bohner, G. (2003) Perceptions of stranger and acquaintance rape: The role of benevolent and hostile sexism in victim blame and rape proclivity. *Journal of Personality and Social Psychology* 84: 111–125.

Abrams, D., Rutland, A., Cameron, L., and Ferrell, J. (2007) Older but wilier: Ingroup accountability and the development of subjective group dynamics. *Developmental Psychology* 43: 134–148.

Abrams, D., Crisp, R. J., Marques, S., Fagg, E., Bedford, L., and Provias, D. (2008) Threat inoculation: Experienced and imagined intergenerational contact prevent stereotype threat effects on older people's math performance. *Psychology and Aging* 23: 934–9.

Ackerman, N. W., and Jahoda, M. (1950) *Anti-Semitism and Emotional Disorder*. New York: Harper.

Adorno, T. W., Frenkel-Brunswik, E., Levinson, D. J., and Sanford, R. M. (1950) *The Authoritarian Personality*. New York: Harper.

Alexander, M. G., Brewer, M. B., and Hermann, R. K. (1999) Images and affect: A functional analysis of out-group stereotypes. *Journal of Personality and Social Psychology* 77: 78–93.

Allen, V. L., and Wilder, D. A. (1975) Group categorization, belief similarity and group discrimination. *Journal of Personality and Social Psychology* 32: 971–7.

Allen, V. L., and Wilder, D. A. (1979) Group categorization and attribution of belief similarity. *Small Group Behavior* 10: 73–80.

Allport, G. W. (1954) *The Nature of Prejudice*. Reading, MA: Addison-Wesley.

Allport, G. W., and Kramer, B. B. (1946) Some roots of prejudice. *Journal of Psychology* 22: 9–39.

Altemeyer, B. (1988) *Enemies of Freedom: Understanding Right-Wing Authoritarianism*. San Francisco: Jossey-Bass.

Altemeyer, B. (1996) *The Authoritarian Specter*. Cambridge, MA: Harvard University Press.

Altemeyer, B. (1998) The other 'authoritarian personality'. *Advances in Experimental Social Psychology* 30: 47–92.

Amir, Y. (1969) Contact hypothesis in ethnic relations. *Psychological Bulletin* 71: 319–342.

Amir, Y. (1976) The role of intergroup contact in change of prejudice and ethnic relations. In P. A. Katz (ed.), *Towards the Elimination of Racism*, pp. 245–308. New York: Pergamon.

Angelou, M. (1969) *I Know Why a Caged Bird Sings*. London: Hutchinson.

Appelgryn, A. E., and Nieuwoudt, J. M. (1988) Relative deprivation and the ethnic attitudes of blacks and Afrikaans-speaking whites in South Africa. *Journal of Social Psychology* 128: 311–23.

Arends-Toth, J., and van de Vijver, F. J. R. (2003) Multiculturalism and acculturation: Views of Dutch and Turkish–Dutch. *European Journal of Social Psychology* 33: 249–66.

Arkes, H. R., and Tetlock, P. E. (2004) Attributions of implicit prejudice, or 'Would Jesse Jackson "fail" the implicit association test?' *Psychological Inquiry* 15: 257–78.

Armstrong, B., Johnson, D. W., and Balour, B. (1981) Effects of co-operative versus individualistic learning experiences on interpersonal attraction between learning disabled and normal progress elementary school students. *Contemporary Educational Psychology* 15: 604–16.

Aronson, E., and Mills, J. (1959) The effect of severity of initiation on liking for a group. *Journal of Abnormal and Social Psychology* 59: 177–81.

Aronson, J., Fried, C. B., and Good, C. (2002) Reducing the effects of stereotype threat on African American college students by shaping theories of intelligence. *Journal of Experimental Social Psychology* 38: 113–25.

Aronson, E., Blaney, N., Stephan, C., Sikes, J., and Snapp, M. (1978) *The Jig-Saw Classroom*. London: Sage.

Aronson, J., Lustina, M. J., Good, C., Keogh, K., Steele, C. M., and Brown, J. (1999) Whe white men can't do math: Necessary and sufficient factors in stereotype threat. *Journal of Experimental Social Psychology* 35: 29–46.

Asch, S. E. (1952) *Social Psychology*. New Jersey: Prentice Hall.

Asher, S. R., and Allen, V. L. (1969) Racial preference and social comparison processes. *Journal of Social Issues* 25: 157–66.

Augoustinos, M., Ahrens, C., and Innes, M. (1994) Stereotypes and prejudice: The Australian experience. *British Journal of Social Psychology* 33: 125–41.

Bandura, A. (1977) *Social Learning Theory*. Englewood Cliffs, NJ: Prentice-Hall.

Banks, W. C. (1976) White preference in blacks: A paradigm in search of a phenomenon. *Psychological Bulletin* 83: 1179–86.

Banton, M. (1983) *Racial and Ethnic Competition*. Cambridge: Cambridge University Press.

Bar-Haim, Y., Ziv, T., Lamy, D., and Hodes, R. M. (2006) Nature and nurture in own-race face processing. *Psychological Science* 17: 159–63.

Barden, J., Maddux, W. W., Petty, C. R., and Brewer, M. B. (2004) Contextual moderation of racial bias: The impact of social roles on controlled and automatically activated attitudes. *Journal of Personality and Social Psychology* 87: 5–22.

Bargh, J., Chen, M., and Burrows, L. (1996) Automaticity of social behavior: Direct effects of trait construct and stereotype activation on action. *Journal of Personality and Social Psychology* 71: 230–44.

Baron, A. S., and Banaji, M. R. (2006) The development of implicit attitudes. *Psychological Science* 17: 53–8.

Barrett, M. (2007) *Children's Knowledge, Beliefs and Feelings about Nations and National Groups.* Hove: Psychology Press.

Bartsch, R. A., and Judd, C. M. (1993) Majority–minority status and perceived ingroup variability revisited. *European Journal of Social Psychology* 23: 471–83.

Bass, B. M. (1955) Authoritarianism or acquiescence? *Journal of Abnormal and Social Psychology* 51: 616–23.

Batson, C. D., Polycarpou, M. P., Harmond-Jones, E., Imhoff, H. J., Mitchener, E. C., Bednar, L. L., Klein, T. R., and Highberger, L. (1997) Empathy and attitudes: Can feeling for a member of a group improve feelings towards the group? *Journal of Personality and Social Psychology* 72(1): 105–18.

BBC Radio 4 (2004) 'Shocking' racism in jobs market. Monday 12 July, 13:46 GMT. Available at: http://news.bbc.co.uk/1/hi/business/3885213.stm.

Beauvois, C., and Spence, J. T. (1987) Gender, prejudice and categorization. *Sex Roles* 16: 89–100.

Beelmann, A., and Heinemann, K. S. (2008) Effects of educational and psychological prevention programs in childhood and adolescence: A meta-analysis. Paper presented at the International Workshop on Developmental Psychology.

Beilock, S. L., Jellison, W. A., Rydell, R. J., McConnell, A. R. and Carr, T. H. (2006) On the causal mechanisms of stereotype threat: Can skills that don't rely heavily on working memory still be threatened? *Personality and Social Psychology Bulletin* 32: 1059–71.

Bekerman, Z., and Horenczyk, G. (2004) Arab–Jewish bilingual co-education in Israel: A long-term approach to intergroup conflict resolution. *Journal of Social Issues* 60: 389–404.

Bem, D. (1972) Self-perception theory. In L. Berkowitz (ed.), *Advances in Experimental Social Psychology*, Vol. 6, pp. 1–62. New York: Academic Press.

Bennett, M., and Sani, F. (2003) The role of target gender and race in children's encoding of category-neutral person information. *British Journal of Developmental Psychology* 21: 99–112.

Bennett, M., and Sani, F. (2004) *The Development of the Social Self.* Hove: Psychology Press.

Bennett, M., Sani, F., Hopkins, N., Agostini, L., and L, M. (2000) Children's gender categorization: An investigation of automatic processing. *British Journal of Developmental Psychology* 18: 97–102.

Benokraitis, N. V., and Feagin, J. R. (1986) *Modern Sexism: Blatant, Subtle and Covert Discrimination.* Englewood Cliffs, NJ: Prentice-Hall.

Berkowitz, L. (1962) *Aggression: A Social Psychological Analysis.* New York: McGraw Hill.

Berry, J. W. (1984) Cultural relations in plural societies: Alternatives to segregation and their sociopsychological implications. In N. Miller and M. B. Brewer (eds), *Groups in Contact: The Psychology of Desegregation*, pp. 11–12. New York: Academic Press.

Berry, J. W. (1997) Immigration, acculturation, and adaptation. *Applied Psychology: An International Review* 46(1): 5–68.

Berry, J. W., Kalin, R., and Taylor, D. M. (1977) *Multiculturalism and Ethnic Attitudes in Canada.* Ottawa: Minister of Supply and Services Canada.

Bertrand, M., and Mullainathan, S. (2004) Are Emily and Greg more employable than Lakisha and Jamal? A field experiment on labor market discrimination. *The American Economic Review* 94: 991–1013.

Bettencourt, B. A., Brewer, M. B., Croak, M. R., and Miller, N. (1992) Cooperation and the reduction of intergroup bias: The role of reward structure and social orientation. *Journal of Experimental Social Psychology* 28: 301–9.

Bettencourt, B. A., Charlton, K., and Kernaham, C. (1997) Numerical representation of groups in co-operative settings: Social orientation effects on ingroup bias. *Journal of Experimental Social Psychology* 33: 630–59.

Bettencourt, B. A., Charlton, K., Dorr, N., and Hume, D. L. (2001) Status differences and in-group bias: A meta-analytic examination of the effects of status stability, status legitimacy, and group permeability. *Psychological Bulletin* 127: 520–42.

Biernat, M., and Vescio, T. K. (1993) Categorization and stereotyping: Effects of group context on memory and social judgement. *Journal of Experimental Social Psychology* 29: 166–202.

Biernat, M., and Vescio, T. K. (1994) Still another look at the effects of fit and novelty on the salience of social catagories. *Experimental Social Psychology* 30: 399–406.

Biernat, M., Manis, M., and Nelson, T. E. (1991) Stereotypes and standards of judgement. *Journal of Personality and Social Psychology* 60: 485–99.

Bigler, R., Jones, L. C., and Lobliner, D. B. (1997) Social categorization and the formation of intergroup attitudes in children. *Child Development* 68: 530–43.

Billig, M. G. (1976) *Social Psychology and Intergroup Relations*. London: Academic Press.

Billig, M. G. (1978) *Fascists: A Social Psychological View of the National Front*. London: Harcourt Brace Jovanovich.

Billig, M. G., and Tajfel, H. (1973) Social categorization and similarity in intergroup behaviour. *European Journal of Social Psychology* 3: 27–52.

Billig, M. G., and Cochrane, R. (1979) Values of political extremists and potential extremists: A discriminant analysis. *European Journal of Social Psychology* 9: 205–22.

Binder, J., Zagefka, H., Brown, R., Funke, F., Kessler, T., Mummendey, A., Maquil, A., Demoulin, S., and Leyens, J.-P. (2009) Does contact reduce prejudice or does prejudice reduce contact? A longitudinal test of the contact hypothesis amongst majority and minority groups in three European countries. *Journal of Personality and Social Psychology* 96: 843–56.

Bird, C., Monachesi, E. D., and Burdick, H. (1952) Infiltration and the attitudes of white and negro parents and children. *Journal of Abnormal and Social Psychology* 47: 688–99.

Black-Gutman, D., and Hickson, F. (1996) The relationship between racial attitudes and social–cognitive development in children: An Australian study. *Developmental Psychology* 32: 448–56.

Blair, I. (2002) The malleability of automatic stereotypes and prejudice. *Personality and Social Psychology Review* 6: 242–61.

Blair, I., Ma, J., and Lenton, A. (2001) Imagining stereotypes away: The moderation of automatic stereotypes through mental imagery. *Journal of Personality and Social Psychology* 81: 828–41.

Blanchard, F. A., Weigel, R. H., and Cook, S. W. (1975) The effect of relative competence of group members upon interpersonal attraction in cooperating interracial groups. *Journal of Personality and Social Psychology* 32: 519–30.

Blank, T., and Schmidt, P. (2003) National identity in a united Germany: Patriotism or nationalism? An empirical test with representative data. *Political Psychology* 24: 289–312.

Blascovich, J., Wyer, N., Swart, L. A., and Kibler, J. L. (1997) Racism and racial categorization. *Journal of Personality and Social Psychology* 72: 1364–72.

Blascovich, J., Spencer, S. J., Quinn, D., and Steele, C. M. (2001) African Americans and high blood pressure: The role of stereotype threat. *Psychological Science* 12: 225–9.

Bleich, E. (2007) Hate crime policy in western Europe: Responding to racist violence in Britain, Germany and France. *American Behavioral Scientist* 51: 149–65.

Boulding, K. (1959) National images and international systems. *Journal of Conflict Resolution* 3: 120–31.

Bourhis, R. Y., and Giles, H. (1977) The language of intergroup distinctiveness. In Giles, H. (ed.), *Language, Ethnicity and Intergroup Relations*, pp. 119–36. London: Academic Press.

Bourhis, R. Y, Sachdev, I., and Gagnon, A. (1994) Intergroup research with the Tajfel matrices: Methodological notes. In M. Zanna and J. M. Olson (eds), *The Psychology of Prejudice: The Ontario Symposium*, Vol. 7, pp. 209–32. Hillsdale, NJ: Erlbaum.

Bourhis, R. Y., Giles, H., Leyens, J. P., and Tajfel, H. (1978) Psycholinguistic distinctiveness: Language divergence in Belgium. In H. Giles and R. St Clair (eds), *Language and Social Psychology*, pp. 158–85. Oxford: Blackwell.

Braha, V., and Rutter, D. R. (1980) Friendship choice in a mixed-race primary school. *Educational Studies* 6: 217–23.

Branch, C. W., and Newcombe, N. (1980) Racial attitudes of black pre-schoolers as related to parental civil rights activism. *Merrill–Palmer Quarterly* 26: 425–8.

Brand, E. S., Ruiz, R. A., and Padilla, A. (1974) Ethnic identification and preference. *Psychological Bulletin* 81: 860–90.

Branscombe, N. R., and Wann, D. L. (1994) Collective self-esteem consequences of outgroup derogation when a valued social identity is on trial. *European Journal of Social Psychology* 24: 641–57.

Branscombe, N. R., and Doosje, B. (2004) *Collective Guilt: International Perspectives*. New York: Cambridge University Press.

Branscombe, N. R., Schmitt, M. T, and Harvey, R. D. (1999) Perceiving pervasive discrimination among African Americans: Implications for group identification and well-being. *Journal of Personality and Social Psychology* 77: 135–49.

Branscombe, N. R., Schmitt, M. T., and Schiffhauer, K. (2007) Racial attitudes in response to thoughts of white privilege. *European Journal of Social Psychology* 37: 203–15.

Branthwaite, A., Doyle, S., and Lightbown, N. (1979) The balance between fairness and discrimination. *European Journal of Social Psychology* 9: 149–63.

Breakwell, G. (1978) Some effects of marginal social identity. In H. Tajfel (ed.), *Differentiation between Social Groups*, pp. 301–36. London: Academic Press.

Breakwell, G. (1988) Strategies adopted when identity is threatened. *Revue internationale de psychologie sociale* 1: 189–203.

Brendl, C. M., Markman, A. B., and Messner, C. (2001) How do indirect measures of evaluation work? Evaluating the inference of prejudice in the implicit association test. *Journal of Personality and Social Psychology* 81: 760–73.

Brewer, M. B. (1979) Ingroup bias in the minimal intergroup situation: A cognitive–motivational analysis. *Psychological Bulletin* 86: 307–24.

Brewer, M. B. (1986) The role of ethnocentrism in intergroup conflict. In S. Worchel and W. G. Austin (eds), *Psychology of Intergroup Relations*, 2nd edn, pp. 88–102. Chicago: Nelson Hall.

Brewer, M. B. (1991) The social self: On being the same and different at the same time. *Personality and Social Psychology Bulletin* 17: 475–82.

Brewer, M. B. (1999) The psychology of prejudice: Ingroup love or outgroup hate? *Journal of Social Issues* 55: 429–44.

Brewer, M. B., and Campbell, D. T. (1976) *Ethnocentrism and Intergroup Attitudes: East African Evidence*. New York: Sage.

Brewer, M. B., and Miller, N. (1984) Beyond the contact hypothesis: Theoretical perspectives on desegregation. In N. Miller and M. B. Brewer (eds), *Groups in Contact: The Psychology of Desegregation*, pp. 281–302. Orlando, FL: Academic Press.

Brewer, M. B., Dull, V., and Lui, L. (1981) Perceptions of the elderly: Stereotypes as prototypes. *Journal of Personality and Social Psychology* 41: 656–70.

Brewer, M. Sibieta, L., and Wren-Lewis, L. (2008) *Racing Away? Income Inequality and the Evolution of High Incomes.* London: Institute for Fiscal Studies, Briefing Note No. 76.

Brewer, M. B., Ho, H.-K., Lee, J.-Y., and Miller, N. (1987) Social identity and social distance among Hong Kong schoolchildren. *Personality and Social Psychology Bulletin* 13: 156–65.

Brief, A. P., Dietz, J., Cohen, R. R., Pugh, S. D., and Vaslow, J. B. (2000) Just doing business: Modern racism and obedience to authority as explanations for employment discrimination. *Organizational Behavior and Human Decision Processes* 81: 72–97.

Brown, C. S., and Bigler, R. (2002) Effects of minority status in the classroom on children's intergroup attitudes. *Journal of Experimental Child Psychology* 83: 77–110.

Brown, Roger (1953) A determinant of the relationship between rigidity and authoritarianism. *Journal of Abnormal and Social Psychology* 48: 469–76.

Brown, Roger (1965) *Social Psychology.* New York: Macmillan.

Brown, R. J. (1978) Divided we fall: An analysis of relations between sections of a factory workforce. In H. Tajfel (ed.), *Differentiation between Social Groups: Studies in the Social Psychology of Intergroup Relations.* London: Academic Press.

Brown, R. J. (1984a) The effects of intergroup similarity and cooperative vs. competitive orientation on intergroup discrimination. *British Journal of Social Psychology* 23: 21–33.

Brown, R. J. (1984b) The role of similarity in intergroup relations. In H. Tajfel (ed.), *The Social Dimension: European Developments in Social Psychology*, pp. 395–429. Cambridge: Cambridge University Press.

Brown, R. J. (1995) *Prejudice: Its Social Psychology.* Oxford: Blackwell.

Brown, R. J. (2000a) *Group Processes: Dynamics within and between Groups*, 2nd edn. Oxford: Blackwell.

Brown, R. J. (2000b) Social identity theory: Past achievements, current problems and future challenges. *European Journal of Social Psychology* 30(6): 745–78.

Brown, R. J., and Turner, J. C. (1979) The criss-cross categorization effect in intergroup discrimination. *British Journal of Social and Clinical Psychology* 18: 371–83.

Brown, R. J., and Deschamps, J. C. (1981) Discrimination entre individus et entre groupes. *Bulletin de psychologie* 34: 185–95.

Brown, R. J., and Turner, J. C. (1981) Interpersonal and intergroup behaviour. In J. C. Turner and H. Giles (eds), *Intergroup Behaviour*, pp. 33–65. Oxford: Blackwell.

Brown, R. J., and Ross, G. F. (1982) The battle for acceptance: An investigation into the dynamics of intergroup behaviour. In H. Tajfel (ed.), *Social Identity and Intergroup Relations*, pp. 155–78. Cambridge: Cambridge University Press.

Brown, R. J., and Abrams, D. (1986) The effects of intergroup similarity and goal interdependence on intergroup attitudes and task performance. *Experimental Social Psychology* 22: 78–92.

Brown, R. J., and Smith, A. (1989) Perceptions of and by minority groups: The case of women in academia. *European Journal of Social Psychology* 19: 61–75.

Brown, R. J., and Wootton-Millward, L. (1993) Perceptions of group homogeneity during group formation and change. *Social Cognition* 11: 126–49.

Brown, R. J., and Haeger, G. (1999) 'Compared to what?' Comparison choice in an internation context. *European Journal of Social Psychology* 29: 31–42.

Brown, R. J., and Hewstone, M. (2005) An integrative theory of intergroup contact. *Advances in Experimental Social Psychology* 37: 255–343.

Brown, R. J., and Zagefka, H. (2006) Choice of comparisons in intergroup settings: The role of temporal information and comparison motives. *European Journal of Social Psychology* 36: 649–71.

Brown, R. J., and Cehajic, S. (2008) Dealing with the past and facing the future: Mediators of the effects of collective guilt and shame in Bosnia and Herzegovina. *European Journal of Social Psychology* 38: 669–84.

Brown, R. J., Vivian, J., and Hewstone, M. (1999) Changing attitudes through intergroup contact: The effects of group membership salience. *European Journal of Social Psychology* 29: 741–64.

Brown, R. J., Rutland, A., and Watters, C. (2007a) *Identities in Transition: A Longitudinal Study of Immigrant Children. Final Report.* Swindon: Economic and Social Research Council.

Brown, R. J., Capozza, D., Paladino, M.-P., and Volpato, C. (1996) Identificazione e favoritismo per il proprio gruppo: Verifica del modello di Hinkle e Brown. In P. Boscolo, F. Cristante, A. Dellantinio, and S. Soresi (eds), *Aspetti qualitativi e quantitativi nella ricerca psicologica*, pp. 307–18. Padova: Il Poligrafo.

Brown, R. J., Eller, A., Leeds, S., and Stace, K. (2007b) Intergroup contact, perceived typicality and intergroup attitudes: A longitudinal study. *European Journal of Social Psychology* 37: 692–703.

Brown, R. J., Condor, S., Matthews, A., Wade, G., Williams, J. A. (1986) Explaining intergroup differentiation in an industrial organisation. *Journal of Occupational Psychology* 59: 273–86.

Brown, R. J., Maras, P., Masser, B., Vivian, J., and Hewstone, M. (2001) Life on the ocean wave: Testing some intergroup hypotheses in a naturalistic setting. *Group Processes and Intergroup Relations* 4(2): 81–97.

Brown, R. J., Croizet, J.-C., Bohner, G., Fournet, M., and Payne, A. (2003) Automatic category activation and social behavior: The moderating role of prejudiced beliefs. *Social Cognition* 21: 167–93.

Brown, R. J., González, R., Zagefka, H., Manzi, J., and Cehajic, S. (2008) *Nuestra culpa*: Collective guilt and shame as predictors of reparation for historical wrong-doing. *Jounal of Personality and Social Psychology* 94: 75–90.

Brown, R. J., Hinkle, S., Ely, P., Fox-Cardamone, L., Maras, P., and Taylor, L. A. (1992) Recognising group diversity: Individualist–collectivist and autonomous–relational social orientations and their implications for intergroup processes. *British Journal of Social Psychology* 31: 327–42.

Bruner, J. S. (1957) On perceptual readiness. *Psychological Review* 64: 123–51.

Buhl, T. (1999) Positive–negative asymmetry in social discrimination: Meta-analytic evidence. *Group Processes and Intergroup Relations* 2: 51–8.

Bureau of Labor and Statistics (2005) *Women in the Labor Force: A Data Book.* Washington: Department of Labor.

Burnstein, E., and McRae, A. V. (1962) Some effects of shared threat and prejudice in racially mixed groups. *Journal of Abnormal and Social Psychology* 64: 257–63.

Burt, M. R. (1980) Cultural myths and supports for rape. *Journal of Personality and Social Psychology* 38: 217–30.

Byrne, D. (1971) *The Attraction Paradigm.* New York: Academic Press.

Byrne, D., and Wong, T. J. (1962) Racial prejudice, interpersonal attraction and assumed dissimilarity of attitudes. *Journal of Abnormal and Social Psychology* 65: 246–53.

Cacioppo, J. T., Petty, R. E., Losch, M. E., and Kim, H. S. (1986) Electromyographic activity over facial muscle regions can differentiate the valence and intensity of affective reactions. *Journal of Personality and Social Psychology* 50: 260–8.

Caddick, B. (1982) Perceived illegitimacy and intergroup relations. In H. Tajfel (ed.), *Social Identity and Intergroup Relations*, pp. 137–54. Cambridge: Cambridge University Press.

Cadinu, M., Maass, A., Rosabianca, A., and Kiesner, J. (2005) Why do women underperform under stereotype threat? Evidence for the role of negative thinking. *Psychological Science* 16: 572–8.

Calitri, R. (2005) *Nationalism and Patriotism: The Effects of National Identification on Implicit and Explicit Ingroup Bias.* Unpublished PhD, University of Kent.

Cameron, J. A., Alvarez, J. M., Ruble, D. N., and Fuligni, A. J. (2001) Children's lay theories about ingroups and outgroups: Reconceptualizing research on prejudice. *Personality and Social Psychology Review* 5: 118–28.

Cameron, L., and Rutland, A. (2006) Extended contact through story reading in school: Reducing children's prejudice towards the disabled. *Journal of Social Issues* 62: 469–88.

Cameron, L., Rutland, A., Brown, R., and Douch, R. (2006) Changing children's attitudes towards refugees: Testing different models of extended contact. *Child Development* 77: 1208–19.

Campbell, B., Schellenberg, E. G., and Senn, C. Y. (1997) Evaluating measures of contemporary sexism. *Psychology of Women Quarterly* 21: 89–102.

Campbell, D. T. (1956) Enhancement of contrast as a composite habit. *Journal of Abnormal and Social Psychology* 53: 350–5.

Campbell, D. T. (1958) Common fate, similarity and other indices of the status of aggregates as social entities. *Behavioral Science* 3: 14–25.

Campbell, D. T. (1965) Ethnocentric and other altruistic motives. *Nebraska Symposium on Motivation* 13, 283–311. Lincoln: Universtiy of Nebraska.

Campbell, D. T., and McCandless, B. R. (1951) Ethnocentrism, xenophobia, and personality. *Human Relations* 4: 185–92.

Caplan, N. (1970) The new ghetto man: A review of recent empirical studies. *Journal of Social Issues* 26: 59–73.

Capozza, D., Voci, A., and Licciardello, O. (2000) Individualism, collectivism and social identity theory. In D. Capozza and R. Brown (eds), *Social Identity Processes*, pp. 62–80. London: Sage.

Castano, E., Yzerbyt, V. Y., Bourguignon, D., and Seron, E. (2002) Who may enter? The impact of in-group identification on in-group/out-group categorization. *Journal of Experimental Social Psychology* 38: 315–22.

Castelli, L., De Dea, C., and Nesdale, D. (2008) Learning social attitudes: Children's sensitivity to the nonverbal behaviors of adult models during interracial interactions. *Personality and Social Psychology Bulletin* 34: 1504–13.

Castelli, L., Zogmaister, C., and Tomelleri, S. (2009) The transmission of racial attitudes within the family. *Developmental Psychology* 45: 586–91.

Cehajic, S., Brown, R., and Castano, E. (2008) Forgive and forget? Antecedents, mediators and consequences of intergroup forgiveness in Bosnia and Herzegovina. *Political Psychology* 29: 351–68.

Chakraborti, N., and Garland, J. (2003) An 'invisible' problem: Uncovering the nature of racist victimisation in rural Suffolk. *International Review of Victimology* 10: 1–17.

Chambers 20th Century Dictionary (1979) Edinburgh: W. and R. Chambers Ltd.

Chapleau, K. M., Oswald, D. L., and Russell, B. L. (2007) How ambivalent sexism toward women and men supports rape myth acceptance. *Sex Roles* 57: 131–6.

Chapman, L. J. (1967) Illusory correlation in observational report. *Journal of Verbal Learning and Verbal Behavior* 6: 151–5.

Chein, I., Cook, S. W., and Harding, J. (1948) The field of action research. *American Psychologist* 3: 43–50.

Chen, M., and Bargh, J. (1997) Nonconscious behavioral confirmation processes: The self-fulfilling consequences of automatic stereotype activation. *Journal of Experimental Social Psychology* 33: 541–560.

Chiesi, F., and Primi, C. (2006) Italian children's ethnic stereotyping: Age differences among 4–10 year-olds. *Review of Psychology* 13: 3–7.

Christie, R. (1954) Authoritarianism re-examined. In R. Christie and M. Jahoda (eds), *Studies in the Scope and Method of 'The Authoritarian Personality'*, pp. 123–96. Glencoe, IL: Free Press.

Christie, R., and Cook, P. (1958) A guide to published literature relating to the authoritarian personality through 1956. *Journal of Psychology* 45: 191–9.

Christie, R., and Jahoda, M. (eds) (1954) *Studies in the Scope and Method of 'The Authoritarian Personality'*. Glencoe, IL: The Free Press.

Cialdini, R. B., Borden, R. J., Thorne, A., Walker, M. R., Freeman, S., and Sloan, L. R. (1976) Basking in reflected glory: Three (football) field studies. *Journal of Personality and Social Psychology* 34: 366–74.

Clark, K. B., and Clark, M. P. (1947) Racial identification and preference in negro children. In H. Proshansky and B. Seidenberg (eds), *Basic Studies in Social Psychology*, pp. 308–17. New York: Holt Rinehart and Winston.

Clark, A., Hocevar, D., and Dembo, M. H. (1980) The role of cognitive development in children's explanations and preferences for skin color. *Developmental Psychology* 16: 332–9.

Clark, K. B., Chein, I., and Cook, S. W. (2004) The effects of segregation and the consequences of desegregation: A (September 1952) social science statement in the *Brown* v. *Board of Education of Topeka Supreme Court* case. *American Psychologist* 59: 495–501.

Clore, G. L., Bray, R. M., Itkin, S. M., and Murphy, J. (1978) Interracial attitudes and behaviour at a summer camp. *Journal of Personality and Social Psychology* 36: 107–16.

Coenders, M., Scheepers, P., Sniderman, P. M., and Verberk, G. (2001) Blatant and subtle prejudice: Dimensions, determinants and consequences; Some comments on Pettigrew and Meertens. *European Journal of Social Psychology* 31: 281–97.

Cohen, G. L., Garcia, J., Apfel, N., and Master, A. (2006) Reducing the racial achievement gap: A social–psychological intervention. *Science* 313: 1307–10.

Cohen, J., and Streuning, E. L. (1962) Opinions about mental illness. *Journal of Abnormal and Social Psychology* 64: 349–60.

Cole, C. F., Arafat, C., Tidhar, C., Tafesh, W. Z., Fox, N. A., Killen, M., Ardila-Rey, A., Leavitt, L. A., Lesser, G., Richman, B. A., and Yung, F. (2003) The educational impact of Rechov Sumsum/Shara'a Simsim: A Sesame Street television series to promote respect and understanding among children living in Israel, the West Bank, and Gaza. *International Journal of Behavioral Development* 27: 409–22.

Colman, A., and Lambley, P. (1970) Authoritarianism and race attitudes in South Africa. *Journal of Social Psychology* 82: 161–4.

Conn, A. B., Hanges, P. J., William, P. S., and Salvaggio, A. M. (1999) The search for ambivalent sexism: A comparison of two measures. *Educational and Psychological Measurement* 59: 898–909.

Cook, S. W. (1962) The systematic analysis of socially significant events: A stragegy for social research. *Journal of Social Issues* 18: 66–84.

Cook, S. W. (1978) Interpersonal and attitudinal outcomes in cooperating interracial groups. *Journal of Research and Development in Education* 12: 97–113.

Cooper, J., and Fazio, R. H. (1984) A new look at dissonance theory. *Advances in Experimental Social Psychology* 17: 229–65.

Corenblum, B., and Annis, R. C. (1993) Development of racial identity in minority and majority children: An affect discrepancy model. *Canadian Journal of Behavioral Science* 25: 499–521.

Correll, J., Park, B., Wittenbrink, B., and Judd, C. M. (2002) The police officer's dilemma: Using ethnicity to disambiguate potentially threatening individuals. *Journal of Personality and Social Psychology* 83: 1314–29.

Cottrell, C. A., and Neuberg, S. L. (2005) Different emotional reactions to different groups: A sociofunctional threat-based approach to 'prejudice'. *Journal of Personality and Social Psychology* 88: 770–89.

Cowan, G., Heiple, B., Marquez, C., Khatchadourian, D., and McNevin, M. (2005) Heterosexuals' attitudes toward hate crimes and hate speech against gays and lesbians: Old-fashioned and modern heterosexism. *Journal of Homosexuality* 49: 67–82.

Cowen, E. L., Landes, J., and Sachet, D. E. (1958) The effects of mild frustration on the expression of prejudiced attitudes. *Journal of Abnormal and Social Psychology* 58: 33–8.

Craig, K. M. (1999) Retaliation, fear, or rage: An investigation of African American and white reactions to racist hate crimes. *Journal of Interpersonal Violence* 14: 138–51.

Cramer, P., and Steinwert, T. (1998) Thin is good, fat is bad: How early does it begin? *Journal of Applied Developmental Psychology* 19: 429–51.

Crandall, C. S. (1994) Prejudice against fat people: Ideology and self-interest. *Journal of Personality and Social Psychology* 66: 882–94.

Crano, W. D., and Mellon, P. M. (1978) Causal influence of teachers' expectations on children's academic performance: A cross-lagged panel analysis. *Journal of Educational Psychology* 70(1): 39–49.

Crawford, M. T., Sherman, S. J., and Hamilton, D. L. (2002) Perceived entitativity, stereotype formation, and the interechangeability of group members. *Journal of Personality and Social Psychology* 83: 1076–94.

Crawford, T. J., and Naditch, M. (1970) Relative deprivation, powerlessness, and militancy: The psychology of social protest. *Psychiatry: Journal for the Study of Interpersonal Processes* 33: 208–23.

CRE (1990) *'Sorry It's Gone': Testing for Racial Discrimination in the Private Rented Housing Sector*. London: Commission for Racial Equality.

Crisp, R. J., and Hewstone, M. (2000) Crossed categorization and intergroup bias: The moderating roles of intergroup and affective context. *Journal of Experimental Social Psychology* 36: 357–83.

Crisp, R. J., and Hewstone, M. (2001) Multiple categorization and implicit intergroup bias: Differential category dominance and the positive–negative asymmetry effect. *European Journal of Social Psychology* 31: 45–62.

Crisp, R. J., and Turner, R. N. (2009) Can imagined interactions produce positive perceptions? Reducing prejudice through simulated social contact. *American Psychologist* 64: 231–40.

Crisp, R. J., Hewstone, M., and Rubin, M. (2001) Does multiple categorization reduce intergroup bias? *Personality and Social Psychology Bulletin* 27: 76–89.

Crisp, R. J., Ensari, N., Hewstone, M., and Miller, N. (2002) A dual-route model of crossed categorization effects. *European Review of Social Psychology* 13: 35–74.

Crocker, J., and Major, B. (1989) Social stigma and self-esteem: The self-protective properties of stigma. *Psychological Review* 96(4), 608–30.

Crocker, J., Cornwell, B., and Major, B. (1993) The stigma of overweight: Affective consequences of attributional ambiguity. *Journal of Personality and Social Psychology* 64: 60–70.

Crocker, J., Major, B., and Steele, C. (1998) Social stigma. In D. T. Gilbert, S. T. Fiske and G. Lindzey (eds), *The Handbook of Social Psychology*, 4th edn, Vol. 2, pp. 504–53. Boston: McGraw Hill.

Crocker, J., Voelkl, K., Testa, M., and Major, B. (1991) Social stigma: Affective consequences for attributional ambiguity. *Journal of Personality and Social Psychology*, 60: 218–28.

Croizet, J.-C., and Claire, T. (1998) Extending the concept of stereotype threat to social class: The intellectual underperformance of students from low socioeconomic background. *Personality and Social Psychology Bulletin* 24: 588–94.

Croizet, J.-C., Despres, G., Gauzins, M., Huguet, P., and Leyens, J. P. (2004) Stereotype threat undermines performance by triggering a disruptive mental load. *Personality and Social Psychology Bulletin* 30: 721–31.

Crosby, F. (1976) A model of egoistical relative deprivation. *Psychological Review* 83: 85–113.

Crosby, F. (1979) Relative deprivation revisited: A response to Miller, Bolce and Halligan. *American Political Science Review* 73: 103–12.

Crosby, F. (1982) *Relative Deprivation and Working Women*. New York: Oxford University Press.

Crosby, F., Bromley, S., and Saxe, L. (1980) Recent unobtrusive studies of black and white discrimination and prejudice. *Psychological Bulletin* 87: 546–63.

Cuddy, A. J. C., Fiske, S. T., and Glick, P. (2007) The BIAS map: Behaviors from intergroup affect and stereotypes. *Journal of Personality and Social Psychology* 92: 631–48.

Cunningham, W. A., Preacher, K. J., and Banaji, M. R. (2001) Implicit attitude measures: Consistency, stability, and convergent validity. *Psychological Science* 12: 163–70.

Curseu, P. L., Stoop, R., and Schalk, R. (2007) Prejudice towards immigrant workers among Dutch employees: Integrated threat theory revisited. *European Journal of Social Psychology* 37: 125–40.

Dambrun, M., Taylor, D. M., McDonald, D. A., Crush, J., and Meot, A. (2006) The relative deprivation–gratification continuum and the attitudes of South Africans towards immigrants: A test of the V-curve hypothesis. *Journal of Personality and Social Psychology* 91: 1032–44.

Danaher, K., and Crandall, C. S. (2008) Sterotype threat in applied settings re-examined. *Journal of Applied Social Psychology* 38: 1639–55.

Daniels, W. W. (1968) *Racial Discrimination in England*. Harmondsworth: Penguin.

Darley, J. M., and Fazio, R. H. (1980) Expectancy confirmation processes arising in the social interaction sequence. *American Psychologist* 35: 867–81.

Darley, J. M., and Gross, P. H. (1983) A hypothesis-confirming bias in labeling effects. *Journal of Personality and Social Psychology* 44: 20–33.

Dasgupta, N., and Greenwald, A. G. (2001) On the malleability of automatic attitudes: Combating automatic prejudice with images of admired and disliked individuals. *Journal of Personality and Social Psychology* 81: 800–14.

Davey, A. (1983) *Learning to Be Prejudiced*. London: Edward Arnold.

Davies, J. C. (1969) The J-curve of rising and declining satisfactions as a cause of some great revolutions and a contained rebellion. In H. D. Graham and T. R. Gurr (eds), *The History of Violence in America: Historical and Comparative Perspectives*, pp. 670–730. New York: Praeger.

Davies, J. C. (1978) Communication. *American Political Science Review* 72: 1357–8.

Davies, J. C. (1979) Comment. *American Political Science Review* 73: 825–6.

Davis, J. A. (1959) A formal interpretation of the theory of relative deprivation. *Sociometry* 20: 280–96.

De Houwer, J., Beckers, T., and Moors, A. (2007) Novel attitudes can be faked on the implicit association test. *Journal of Experimental Social Psychology* 43: 972–8.

De Tezanos Pinto, P., Bratt, C., and Brown, R. (2009) What will the others think? Ingroup norms as a mediator of the effects of intergroup contact. *British Journal of Social Psychology*.

Deaux, K. (2006) *To Be an Immigrant*. New York: Russell Sage Foundation.

DES [Department for Education and Skills] (2003) *The Future of Higher Education*. Norwich: Her Majesty's Stationery Office.

Deschamps, J. C., and Doise, W. (1978) Crossed category memberships in intergroup relations. In H. Tajfel (ed.), *Differentiation between Social Groups*. London: Academic Press.

Deutsch, M., and Collins, M. E. (1951) *Interracial Housing*. Minneapolis: University of Minneapolis Press.

Deutscher, I. (1959) *The Prophet Unarmed: Trotsky 1921–1929*. London: Oxford University Press.

Devine, P. G. (1989) Stereotypes and prejudice: Their automatic and controlled components. *Journal of Personality and Social Psychology* 56: 5–18.

Devine, P. G., and Sherman, S. J. (1992) Intuitive versus rational judgement and the role of stereotyping in the human condition: Kirk or Spock? *Psychological Inquiry* 3: 153–9.

Devine, P. G., Monteith, M. J., Zuwerink, J. R., and Elliot, A. J. (1991) Prejudice with and without compunction. *Journal of Personality and Social Psychology* 60: 817–30.

Devine, P. G., Plant, E. A., Amodio, D. M., Harmon-Jones, E., and Vance, S. L. (2002) The regulation of explicit and implicit race bias: The role of motivations to respond without prejudice. *Journal of Personality and Social Psychology* 82: 835–48.

DeVries, D. L., Edwards, K. J., and Slavin, R. E. (1979) Biracial learning teams and race relations in the classroom: Four field experiments on Teams–Games-Tournament. *Journal of Educational Psychology* 70: 356–62.

Diehl, M. (1988) Social identity and minimal groups: The effects of interpersonal and intergroup attitudinal similarity on intergroup discrimination. *British Journal of Social Psychology* 27: 289–300.

Diehl, M. (1990) The minimal group paradigm: Theoretical explanations and empirical findings. *European Review of Social Psychology* 1: 263–92.

Diener, E., and Diener, C. (1996) Most people are happy. *Psychological Science* 7: 181–5.

Dijker, A. J. M. (1987) Emotional reactions to ethnic minorities. *European Journal of Social Psychology* 17: 305–25.

Dijksterhuis, A., and van Knippenberg, A. (1998) The relation between perception and behavior or how to win a game of trivial pursuit. *Journal of Personality and Social Psychology* 74: 865–77.

Dijksterhuis, A., and van Knippenberg, A. (2000) Behavioral indecision: Effects of self-focus on automatic behavior. *Social Cognition* 18: 55–74.

Dijksterhuis, A., Spears, R., and Lepinasse, V. (2001) Reflecting and deflecting stereotypes: Assimilation and contrast in automatic behavior. *Journal of Experimental Social Psychology* 37: 286–99.

Dion, K. L. (1973) Dogmatism and intergroup bias. *Representative Research in Social Psychology* 4: 1–10.

Dion, K. L. (1975) Women's reactions to discrimination from members of the same or opposite sex. *Journal of Research in Personality* 9: 294–306.

Dion, K. L., and Earn, B. M. (1975) The phenomenology of being a target of prejudice. *Journal of Personality and Social Psychology* 32: 944–50.

Dittmar, H. (2007) *Consumer Culture, Identity and Well-Being*. Hove: Psychology Press.

Dixon, J., and Durrheim, K. (2003) Contact and the ecology of racial division: Some varieties of informal segregation. *British Journal of Social Psychology* 42: 1–23.

Dixon, J., Durrheim, K., and Tredoux, C. (2005) Beyond the optimal contact strategy: A reality check for the contact hypothesis. *American Psychologist* 60: 697–711.

Doise, W. (1976) *L'Articulation psychosociologique et les relations entre groupes/ Groups and Individuals: Explanations in Social Psychology*. Brussels/Cambridge: De Boeck/Cambridge University Press.

Doise, W., Deschamps, J. C., and Meyer, G. (1978) The accentuation of intracategory similarities. In H. Tajfel (ed.), *Differentiation between Social Groups: Studies in the Social Psychology of Integroup Relations*, pp. 159–68. London: Academic Press.

Dollard, J., Doob, L., Miller, N. E., Mowrer, O. H., and Sears, R. R. (1939) *Frustration and Aggression*. New Haven: Yale University Press.

Doosje, B., Branscombe, N. R., Spears, R., and Manstead, A. S. R. (1998) Guilty by association: When one's group has a negative history. *Journal of Personality and Social Psychology* 75: 872–86.

Doosje, B., Branscombe, N. R., Spears, R., and Manstead, A. S. R. (2006) Antecedents and consequences of group-based guilt: The effects of ingroup identification. *Group Processes and Intergroup Relations* 9: 325–38.

Doty, R. M., Peterson, B. E. A., and Winter, D. G. (1991) Threat and authoritarianism in the United States, 1978–1987. *Journal of Personality and Social Psychology* 61: 629–40.

Dovidio, J. F., and Fazio, R. H. (1992) New technologies for the direct and indirect assessment of attitudes. In J. M. Tanur (ed.), *Questions about Questions: Inquiries into the Cognitive Bases of Surveys*, pp. 204–37. New York: Russell Sage Foundation.

Dovidio, J. F., and Gaertner, S. L. (1981) The effects of race, status, and ability on helping behavior. *Social Psychology Quarterly* 44: 192–203.

Dovidio, J. F., and Gaertner, S. L. (1983) The effects of sex, status, and ability on helping behavior. *Journal of Applied Social Psychology* 13: 191–205.

Dovidio, J. F., and Gaertner, S. L. (2000) Aversive racism and selection decisions: 1989 and 1999. *Psychological Science* 11: 315–19.

Dovidio, J. F., and Gaertner, S. L. (2004) Aversive racism. *Advances in Experimental Social Psychology* 36: 1–52.

Dovidio, J. F., Kawakami, K., and Beach, K. R. (2001) Implicit and explicit attitudes: Examination of the relationship between measures of intergroup bias. In R. Brown and S. L. Gaertner (eds), *Blackwell Handbook of Social Psychology: Intergroup Processes*, pp. 175–97. Oxford: Blackwell.

Dovidio, J. F., Kawakami, K., and Gaertner, S. L. (2002) Implicit and explicit prejudice and interracial interaction. *Journal of Personality and Social Psychology* 82: 62–68.

Dovidio, J. F., Gaertner, S. L., and Saguy, T. (2007) Another view of 'we': Majority and minority group perspectives on a common ingroup identity. *European Review of Social Psychology* 18: 296–330.

Dovidio, J. F., Brigham, J. C., Johnson, B. T., and Gaertner, S. L. (1996) Stereotyping, prejudice and discrimination: Another look. In C. N. Macrae, C. Stangor and M. Hewstone (eds), *Stereotypes and Stereotyping*, pp. 276–319. New York: Guilford Press.

Dovidio, J. F., Kawakami, K., Johnson, C., Johnson, B., and Howard, A. (1997a) On the nature of prejudice: Automatic and controlled processes. *Journal of Experimental Social Psychology* 33: 510–40.

Dovidio, J. F., Gaertner, S. L., Validzic, A., Matoka, K., Johnson, B., and Frazier, S. (1997b) Extending the benefits of re-categorization: Evaluations, self-disclosure and helping. *Journal of Experimental Social Psychology* 33: 401–20.

Doyle, A.-B., and Aboud, F. E. (1995) A longitudinal study of white children's racial prejudice as a social–cognitive development. *Merrill–Palmer Quarterly* 41: 209–28.

Doyle, A.-B., Beaudet, J., and Aboud, F. (1988) Developmental patterns in the flexibility of children's ethnic attitudes. *Journal of Cross-Cultural Psychology* 19: 3–18.

Driedger, L. (1976) Ethnic self-identity. *Sociometry* 39: 131–41.

Duckitt, J. (1988) Normative conformity and racial prejudice in South Africa. *Genetic, Social and General Psychology Monographs* 114: 413–37.

Duckitt, J. (1989) Authoritarianism and group identification: A new look at an old construct. *Political Psychology* 10: 63–84.

Duckitt, J. (2001) A dual-process cognitive–motivational theory of idelogy and prejudice. *Advances in Experimental Social Psychology* 33: 41–113.

Duckitt, J., and Mphuthing, T. (1998) Group identification and intergroup attitudes: A longitudinal analysis in South Africa. *Journal of Personality and Social Psychology* 74: 80–85.

Duckitt, J., and Mphuthing, T. (2002) Relative deprivation and intergroup attitudes: South Africa before and after the Transition. In I. Walker and H. Smith (eds), *Relative Deprivation: Specification, Development and Integration*, pp. 69–90. Cambridge: Cambridge University Press.

Duckitt, J., and Fisher, K. (2003) The impact of social threat on worldview and ideological attitudes. *Political Psychology* 24: 199–222.

Dumont, M., Yzerbyt, V., Wigboldus, D., and Gordijn, E. (2003) Social categorization and fear reactions to the September 11th terrorist attacks. *Personality and Social Psychology Bulletin* 29: 1509–20.

Duncan, B. L. (1976) Differential social perception and attribution of intergroup violence: Testing the lower limits of stereotyping of blacks. *Journal of Personality and Social Psychology* 34: 590–8.

Duriez, B., Van Hiel, A., and Kossowska, M. (2005) Authoritarianism and social dominance in western and eastern Europe: The importance of the socio-political context and of political interest and involvement. *Political Psychology* 26: 299–320.

Durkin, K. (1985) *Television, Sex roles, and Children*. Milton Keynes: Open University Press.

Duveen, G., and Lloyd, B. (1986) The significance of social identities. *British Journal of Social Psychology* 46: 219–30.

Dweck, C. S. (1999) *Self-Theories: Their Role in Motivation, Personality and Development*. Philadelphia: Taylor and Francis.

DWP [Department for Work and Pensions] (2009) *A Test for Racial Discrimination in Recruitment Practice in British Cities* Norwich: Her Majesty's Stationery Office.

Eagly, A. (1987) *Sex Differences in Social Behavior: A Social Role Interpretation*. Hillsdale, NJ: Erlbaum.

Eagly, A., and Wood, W. (1982) Inferred sex differences in status as a determinant of gender stereotypes about social influence. *Journal of Personality and Social Psychology* 43: 915–28.

Eagly, A., and Steffen, V. J. (1984) Gender stereotypes stem from the distribution of women and men into social roles. *Journal of Personality and Social Psychology* 46: 735–54.

Eagly, A., and Mladinic, A. (1994) Are people prejudiced against women? Some answers from research on attitudes, gender stereotypes, and judgements of competence. *European Review of Social Psychology* 5: 1–35.

Easterbrook, J. A. (1959) The effect of emotion on cue utilization and the organization of behavior. *Psychological Review* 66: 183–201.

Eccles-Parsons, J., Adler, T., and Kaczala, C. (1982) Socialization of achievement attitudes and beliefs: Parental influences. *Child Development* 53: 310–21.

Eccles, J. S., Jacobs, J. E., and Harold, R. D. (1990) Gender role stereotypes, expectancy effects, and parents' socialization of gender differences. *Journal of Social Issues* 46: 183–201.

Echebarria-Echabe, A., and Guede, E. F. (2007) A new measure of anti-Arab prejudice: Reliability and validity evidence. *Journal of Applied Social Psychology* 37: 1077–91.

Eiser, J. R. (1971) Enhancement of contrast in the absolute judgement of attitude statements. *Journal of Personality and Social Psychology* 17: 1–10.

Eiser, J. R., and Stroebe, W. (1972) *Categorisation and Social Judgement*. London: Academic Press.

Elashoff, J., and Snow, R. (1971) *Pygmalion Reconsidered*. Worthington, OH: C. A. Jones.

Ellemers, N., and Bos, A. E. R. (1998) Social identity, relative deprivation, and coping with the threat of position loss: A field study among native shopkeepers in Amsterdam. *Journal of Applied Social Psychology* 28(21): 1987–2006.

Ellemers, N., Kortekaas, P., and Ouwerkerk, J. K. (1999a) Self-categorisation, commitment to the group and group self-esteem as related but distinct aspects of social identity. *European Journal of Social Psychology* 29: 371–89.

Ellemers, N., Spears, R., and Doosje, B. (eds) (1999b) *Social Identity: Context Commitment, Content.* Oxford: Blackwell.

Eller, A., and Abrams, D. (2003) 'Gringos' in Mexico: Cross-sectional and longitudinal effects of language school-promoted contact on intergroup bias. *Group Processes and Intergroup Relations* 6: 55–75.

Eller, A., and Abrams, D. (2004) Come together: Longitudinal comparisons of Pettigrew's reformulated intergroup contact model and the common ingroup identity model in Anglo-French and Mexican–American Contexts. *European Journal of Social Psychology* 34: 1–28.

Enesco, I., Navarro, A., Paradela, I., and Guerrero, S. (2005) Stereotypes and beliefs about different ethnic groups in Spain. A study with Spanish and Latin American children living in Madrid. *Applied Developmental Psychology* 26: 638–59.

Ensari, N., and Miller, N. (2001) Decategorization and the reduction of bias in the crossed categorization paradigm. *European Journal of Social Psychology* 31: 193–216.

Ensari, N., and Miller, N. (2002) The out-group must not be so bad after all: The effects of disclosure, typicality, and salience on intergroup bias. *Journal of Personality and Social Psychology* 83: 313–29.

Equal Opportunities Commission (2006) *Facts about Women and Men, 2006.* London: Equal Opportunities Commission.

Epstein, I. M., Krupat, E., and Obudho, C. (1976) Clean is beautiful: Identification and preference as a function of race and cleanliness. *Journal of Social Issues* 32: 109–18.

Epstein, J. L. (1985) After the bus arrives: Resegregation in desegregated schools. *Journal of Social Issues* 41: 23–43.

Esmail, A., and Everington, S. (1993) Racial discrimination against doctors from ethnic minorities. *British Medical Journal* 306: 691–2.

Espenshade, T. J., and Hempstead, K. (1996) Contemporary American attitudes towards US immigration. *International Migration Review* 30 535–70.

Esses, V. M., Jackson, L. M., and Armstrong, T. L. (1998) Intergroup competition and attitudes toward immigrants and immigration: An instrumental model of group conflict. *Journal of Social Issues* 54(4): 699–724.

Esses, V. M., Dovidio, J., Jackson, L. M., and Armstrong, T. L. (2001) The immigration dilemma: The role of perceived group competition, ethnic prejudice, and national identity. *Journal of Social Issues* 57: 389–412.

Eysenck, H. J. (1954) *The Psychology of Politics.* London: Routledge Kegan Paul.

Fazio, R. H., and Olson, J. M. (2003) Implicit measures in social cognition. *Annual Review of Psychology* 54: 297–327.

Fazio, R. H., Jackson, J. R., Dunton, B. C., and Williams, C. J. (1995) Variability in automatic activation as an unobtrusive measure of racial attitudes: A *bona fide* pipeline? *Journal of Personality and Social Psychology* 69: 1013–27.

Feddes, A. R., Noack, P., and Rutland, A. (2009) Direct and indirect friendship effects on minority and majority children's interethnic attitudes: A longitudinal study. *Child Development* 80: 377–90.

Ferraresi, L. (1988) *Identità sociale, categorizzazione e pregiudizio.* Unpublished thesis. Bologna: University of Bologna.

Ferraresi, L., and Brown, R. (2008) Spontaneous categorisation in 4–9 year old Italian children. Unpublished MS, Sussex University.

Festinger, L. (1954) A theory of social comparison processes. *Human Relations* 7: 117–40.

Festinger, L. (1957) *A Theory of Cognitive Dissonance.* Evanston, IL: Row, Peterson and Co.

Feuchte, F., Beelmann, A., and Brown, R. (2008) Evaluation of a peace education programme in a Liberian refugee camp in Ghana. Paper presented at the Understanding Conflicts: Cross-Cultural Perspectives. Aarhus University, Denmark, 19–22 August 2008.

Fiedler, K. (2006) Unresolved problems with the 'I', the 'A' and the 'T'. *European Review of Social Psychology* 17: 74–147.

Fiedler, K., and Walther, G. (2004) *Stereotyping as Inductive Hypothesis Testing*, Hove: Psychology Press.

Fiedler, K., Freytag, P., and Unkelbach, C. (2007) Pseudocontingencies in a simulated classroom. *Journal of Personality and Social Psychology* 92: 655–77.

Finkel, S. E. (1995) *Causal Analysis with Panel Data*. Thousand Oaks: Sage.

Fiske, S. T. (1998) Stereotyping, prejudice and discrimination. In D. T. Gilbert, S. T. Fiske, and G. Lindzey (eds), *The Handbook of Social Psychology*, 4th ed., Vol. 2, pp. 357–411. New York: McGraw-Hill.

Fiske, S. T., and Taylor, S. E. (1991) *Social Cognition*, 2nd edn. New York: McGraw Hill.

Fiske, S. T., Cuddy, A. J. C., Glick, P., and Xu, J. (2002) A model of (often mixed) stereotype content: Competence and warmth respectively follow from perceived status and competition. *Journal of Personality and Social Psychology* 82: 878–902.

Förster, J., and Liberman, N. (2001) The role of attribution of motivation in producing post-suppressional rebound. *Journal of Personality and Social Psychology* 81: 377–90.

Förster, J., and Liberman, N. (2004) A motivational model of post-suppressional rebound. *European Review of Social Psychology* 15: 1–32.

Forbes, H. D. (1985) *Nationalism, Ethnocentrism, and Personality*. Chicago: University of Chicago Press.

Frable, D. E. S., and Bem, S. L. (1985) If you are gender schematic, all members of the opposite sex look alike. *Journal of Personality and Social Psychology* 49: 459–68.

Frenkel-Brunswik, E. (1949) Intolerance of ambiguity as an emotional and perceptual personality variable. *Journal of Personality* 18: 108–43.

Frenkel-Brunswik, E. (1953) Prejudice in the interviews of children: Attitudes towards minority groups. *Journal of Genetic Psychology* 82: 91–136.

Freud, S. (1915) Thoughts for the times on war and death. In S. Freud (ed.), *The Complete Psychological Works of Sigmund Freud: Standard Edition*, Vol. 4, pp. 273–300. London: Hogarth Press.

Freud, S. (1921) *Group Psychology and the Analysis of the Ego*. London: Hogarth Press.

Frey, D., and Gaertner, S. L. (1986) Helping and the avoidance of inappropriate interracial behavior: A strategy that can perpetuate a non-prejudiced self-image. *Journal of Personality and Social Psychology* 50: 1083–90.

Friedman, M. A., and Brownell, K. D. (1995) Psychological correlates of obesity: Moving to the next research generation. *Psychological Bulletin* 117: 3–20.

Funke, F. (2005) The dimensionality of right-wing authoritarianism: Lessons from the dilemma between theory and measurement. *Political Psychology* 26: 195–218.

Furnham, A. (1982) Explanations for unemployment in Britain. *European Journal of Social Psychology* 12: 335–52.

Gaertner, S. L. (1973) Helping behavior and discrimination among liberals and conservatives. *Journal of Personality and Social Psychology* 25: 335–52.

Gaertner, S. L., and Bickman, L. (1971) Effects of race on the elicitation of helping behavior: The wrong number technique. *Journal of Personality and Social Psychology* 20: 218–22.

Gaertner, S. L., and Dovidio, J. F. (1977) The subtlety of white racism, arousal and helping behavior. *Journal of Personality and Social Psychology* 35: 691–707.

Gaertner, S. L., and McGlaughlin, J. P. (1983) Racial stereotypes: Associations and ascriptions of positive and negative characteristics. *Social Psychology Quarterly* 46: 23–30.

Gaertner, S. L., and Dovidio, J. F. (1986) The aversive form of racism. In J. F. Dovidio and S. L. Gaertner (eds), *Prejudice, Discrimination, and Racism*, pp. 61–86. Orlando: Academic Press.

Gaertner, S. L., and Dovidio, J. (2000) *Reducing Intergroup Bias: The Common Ingroup Identity Model*. Hove: Psychology Press.

Gaertner, S. L., Mann, J., Murrell, A., and Dovidio, J. (1989) Reducing intergroup bias: The benefits of recategorization. *Journal of Personality and Social Psychology* 57: 239–49.

Gaertner, S. L., Mann, J. A., Dovidio, J., Murrell, A. J., and Pomare, M. (1990) How does cooperation reduce intergroup bias? *Journal of Personality and Social Psychology* 59: 692–704.

Galinsky, A. D., and Moskowitz, G. B. (2000) Perspective-taking: Decreasing stereotype expression, stereotype accessibility, and in-group favoritism. *Journal of Personality and Social Psychology* 78: 708–24.

Gardham, K., and Brown, R. (2001) Two forms of intergroup discrimination with positive and negative outcomes: Explaining the positive–negative asymmetry effect. *British Journal of Social Psychology* 40: 23–34.

Gawronski, B., and LeBel, E. P. (2008) Understanding patterns of attitude change: When implicit measures show change, but explicit measures do not. *Journal of Experimental Social Psychology* 44: 1355–61.

Gerard, H. B., and Mathewson, G. C. (1966) The effects of severity of initiation on liking for a group: A replication. *Journal of Experimental Social Psychology* 2|: 278–87.

Gerard, H. B., and Miller, N. (1975) *School Desegregation*. New York: Plenum.

Gergen, K. J., and Jones, E. E. (1963) Mental illness, predictability, and affective consequences as stimulus factors in person perception. *Journal of Abnormal and Social Psychology* 67: 95–104.

Ghosh, E. S. K., Kumar, R., and Tripathi, R. C. (1992) The communal cauldron: Relations between Hindus and Muslims in India and their reactions to norm violations. In R. DeRidder and R. C. Tripathi (eds), *Norm Violation and Intergroup Relations*, pp. 70–89. New York: Clarendon Press.

Gibbons, F. X., Stephan, W. G., Stephenson, B., and Petty, C. R. (1980) Reactions to stigmatized others: Response amplification vs sympathy. *Journal of Experimental Social Psychology* 16, 591–605.

Gilbert, D. T., and Hixon, J. G. (1991) The trouble of thinking: Activation and application of stereotypic beliefs. *Journal of Personality and Social Psychology* 60: 509–17.

Gilbert, G. M. (1951) Stereotype persistence and change among college students. *Journal of Abnormal and Social Psychology* 46, 245–54.

Glick, P., and Fiske, S. T. (1996) The ambivalent sexism inventory: Differentiating hostile and benevolent sexism. *Journal of Personality and Social Psychology* 70: 491–512.

Glick, P., and Fiske, S. T. (2001) An ambivalent alliance: Hostile and benevolent sexism as complementary justifications for gender inequality. *American Psychologist* 56: 109–18.

Glick, P., Zion, C., and Nelson, C. (1988) What mediates sex discrimination in hiring decisions? *Journal of Personality and Social Psychology* 55: 178–86.

Glick, P., Diebold, J., Bailey-Werner, B., and Zhu, L. (1997) The two faces of Adam: Ambivalent sexism and polarized attitudes toward women. *Personality and Social Psychology Bulletin* 23: 1323–34.

Glick, P., Sakalli-Ugurlu, N., Ferreira, M. C., and de Souza, M. A. (2002) Ambivalent sexism and attitudes toward wife abuse in Turkey and Brazil. *Psychology of Women Quarterly* 26: 292–7.

Glick, P., Fiske, S. T., et al. (2000) Beyond prejudice as simple antipathy: Hostile and benevolent sexism across cultures. *Journal of Personality and Social Psychology* 79: 763–75.

Glick, P., Lameiras, M., Fiske, S. T., Eckes, T., Masser, B., Volpato, C., et al. (2004) Bad but bold: Ambivalent attitudes toward men predict gender inequality in 16 nations. *Journal of Personality and Social Psychology* 86: 713–28.

Gluckman, M. (1956) *Custom and Conflict in Africa*. Oxford: Blackwell.

González, R., and Brown, R. (2006) Dual identities in intergroup contact: Group status and size moderate the generalization of positive attitude change. *Journal of Experimental Social Psychology* 42: 753–67.

González, R., Brown, R., and Christ, O. (2009) *Intergroup Contact and Individual–Group Generalization: The Role of Group Membership Salience*. Santiago, Chile: Pontificia Universidad Católica de Chile.

González, R., Sirlopú, D., and Kessler, T. (in press) Prejudice among Peruvians and Chileans as a function of identity, intergroup contact, acculturation preferences and intergroup emotions. *Journal of Social Issues*.

Goodman, M. E. (1952) *Race Awareness in Young Children*. New York: Collier Macmillan.

Grant, P. R. (1992) Ethnocentrism between groups of unequal power in response to perceived threat to social identity and valued resources. *Canadian Journal of Behavioural Science* 24: 348–70.

Grant, P. R. (1993) Reactions to intergroup similarity: Examination of the similarity–differentiation and the similarity–attraction hypotheses. *Canadian Journal of Behavioural Science* 25: 28–44.

Grant, P. R., and Brown, R. (1995) From ethnocentrism to collective protest: Responses to relative deprivation and threats to social identity. *Social Psychology Quarterly* 58(3): 195–211.

Grant, P. R., and Holmes, J. G. (1981) The integration of implicit personality theory schemes and stereotypic images. *Social Psychology Quarterly* 44: 107–15.

Graves, S. B. (1999) Television and prejudice reduction: When does television as a vicarious experience make a difference? *Journal of Social Issues* 55: 707–25.

Gray-Little, B., and Hafdahl, A. R. (2000) Factors influencing racial comparisons of self-esteem: A quantitative review. *Psychological Bulletin* 126: 26–54.

Green, D. P., Glaser, J., and Rich, A. (1998) From lynching to gay bashing: The elusive connection between economic conditions and hate crime. *Journal of Personality and Social Psychology* 75: 82–92.

Greenland, K., and Brown, R. (1999) Categorization and intergroup anxiety in contact between British and Japanese nationals. *European Journal of Social Psychology* 29: 503–22.

Greenland, K., and Brown, R. (2005) Acculturation and contact in Japanese students studying in the United Kingdom. *Journal of Social Psychology* 145: 373–89.

Greenwald, A. G., McGhee, D. E., and Schwartz, J. L. K. (1998) Measuring individual differences in implicit cognition:The implicit association test. *Journal of Personality and Social Psychology* 74: 1464–80.

Griffiths, J. A., and Nesdale, D. (2006) In-group and out-group attitudes of ethnic majority and minority children. *International Journal of Intercultural Relations* 30: 735–49.

Grofman, B. N., and Muller, E. N. (1973) The strange case of relative gratification and potential for political violence: The V-curve hypothesis. *American Political Science Review* 67: 514–39.

Guerra, R., Rebelo, Monteiro, M. B., Riek, B. M., Mania, E. W., Gaertner, S. L., and Dovidio, J. F. (in press) How should intergroup contact be structured to reduce bias among majority and minority children? *Group Processes and Intergroup Relations*.

Guglielmi, R. S. (1999) Psychophysiological assessment of prejudice: Past research, current status, and future directions. *Personality and Social Psychology Review* 3: 123–57.

Guimond, S., and Dube-Simard, L. (1983) Relative deprivation theory and the Quebec nationalist movement: The cognition–emotion distinction and the personal–group deprivation issue. *Journal of Personality and Social Psychology* 44: 527–35.

Guimond, S. and Dambrun, M. (2002) When prosperity breeds intergroup hostility: The effects of relative deprivation and relative gratification on prejudice. *Personality and Social Psychology Bulletin* 28: 900–12.

Guimond, S., Dif, S., and Aupy, A. (2002) Social identity, relative group status and integroup attitudes: When favourable outcomes change intergroup relations ... for the worse. *European Journal of Social Psychology* 32: 739–60.

Guimond, S., Dambrun, M., Michinov, N., and Duarte, S. (2003) Does social dominance generate prejudice? Integrating individual and contextual determinants of intergroup cognitions. *Journal of Personality and Social Psychology* 84: 697–721.

Guinote, A., Judd, C. M., and Brauer, M. (2002) Effects of power on perceived and objective group variability: Evidence that more powerful groups are more variable. *Journal of Personality and Social Psychology* 82: 708–21.

Gurr, T. (1970) *Why Men Rebel.* Princeton, NJ: Princeton University Press.

Gurwitz, S. B., and Dodge, K. A. (1977) Effects of confirmations and disconfirmations on stereotype-based attributions. *Journal of Personality and Social Psychology* 35: 495–500.

Hagendoorn, L., and Henke, R. (1991) The effect of multiple category membership on intergroup evaluations in a north-Indian context: Class, caste and religion. *British Journal of Social Psychology* 30: 247–60.

Hall, N. R., and Crisp, R. J. (2005) Considering multiple criteria for social categorization can reduce intergroup bias. *Personality and Social Psychology Bulletin* 31: 1435–44.

Hamilton, D. L. (ed.) (1981) *Cognitive Processes in Stereotyping and Intergroup Behavior.* Hillsdale, NJ: Erlbaum.

Hamilton, D. L., and Bishop, G. D. (1976) Attitudinal and behavioral effects of inital integration of white suburban neighbourhoods. *Journal of Social Issues* 32: 47–67.

Hamilton, D. L., and Gifford, R. K. (1976) Illusory correlation in interpersonal perception. *Journal of Experimental Social Psychology* 12: 392–407.

Hamilton, D. L., and Rose, T. L. (1980) Illusory correlation and the maintenance of stereotypic beliefs. *Journal of Personality and Social Psychology* 39: 832–45.

Hamilton, D. L., and Sherman, S. J. (1989) Illusory correlations: Implications for stereotype theory and research. In D. Bar-Tal, C. F. Graumann, A. W. Kruglanski, and W. Stroebe (eds), *Stereotypes and Prejudice: Changing Conceptions.* New York: Springer.

Hanson, D. J., and Blohm, E. R. (1974) Authoritarianism and attitudes towards mental patients. *International Behavioural Scientist* 6: 57–60.

Harding, J., and Hogrefe, R. (1952) Attitudes of white departmental store employees toward negro co-workers. *Journal of Social Issues* 8: 18–28.

Harkness, S., and Super, C. M. (1985) The cultural context of gender segregation in children's peer groups. *Child Development* 56: 219–24.

Harris, J. R. (1995) *Where is the Child's Environment: A Study of Small Groups and Policy Failure.* Amsterdam: Swets and Zeitlinger.

Harris, M. J., Milich, R., Corbitt, E. M., Hoover, D. W., and Brady, M. (1992) Self-fulfilling prophecy effects of stigmatizing information on children's social interactions. *Journal of Personality and Social Psychology* 63: 41–50.

Harth, N. S., Kessler, T., and Leach, C. W. (2008) Advantaged group's emotional reactions to intergroup inequality: The dynamics of pride, guilt, and sympathy. *Personality and Social Psychology Bulletin* 34: 115–29.

Hartstone, M., and Augoustinos, M. (1995) The minimal group paradigm: Categorization into two versus three groups. *European Journal of Social Psychology* 25: 179–93.

Harwood, J., Hewstone, M., Paolini, S., and Voci, A. (2005) Grandparent–grandchild contact and attitudes towards older adults: Moderator and mediator effects. *Personality and Social Psychology Bulletin* 31: 393–406.

Haslam, N., Rothschild, L., and Ernst, D. (2000) Essentialist beliefs about social categories. *British Journal of Social Psychology* 39: 113–27.

Haslam, N., Rothschild, L., and Ernst, D. (2002) Are essentialist beliefs associated with prejudice? *British Journal of Social Psychology* 41: 87–100.

Hass, R. G., Katz, I., Rizzo, N., Bailey, J., and Eisenstadt, D. (1991) Cross-racial appraisal as related to attitude ambivalence and cognitive complexity. *Personality and Social Psychology Bulletin* 17: 83–92.

Hass, R. G., Katz, I., Rizzo, N., Bailey, J., and Moore, L. (1992) When racial ambivalence evokes negative affect, using a disguised measure of mood. *Personality and Social Psychology Bulletin* 18: 787–97.

Hayden-Thomson, L., Rubin, K. H., and Hymel, S. (1987) Sex preferences in sociometric choices. *Developmental Psychology* 23: 558–62.

Heaven, P. C. L. (1983) Individual versus intergroup explanations of prejudice amongst Afrikaners. *Journal of Social Psychology* 121: 201–10.

Hebl, M. R., Foster, J. B., Mannix, L. M., and Dovidio, J. F. (2002) Formal and interpersonal discrimination: A field study of bias toward homosexual applicants. *Personality and Social Psychology Bulletin* 28: 815–25.

Heinmann, W., Pellander, F., Vogelbusch, A., and Wojtek, B. (1981) Meeting a deviant person: Subjective norms and affective reactions. *European Journal of Social Psychology* 11: 1–25.

Henderson-King, E., Henderson-King, D., Zhermer, N., Posokhova, S., and Chiker, V. (1997) In-group favoritism and perceived similarity: A look at Russians' perceptions in post-Soviet era. *Personality and Social Psychology Bulletin* 23: 1013–21.

Hendrick, C., Bixenstine, V. E., and Hawkins, G. (1971) Race vs belief similarity as determinants of attraction: A search for a fair test. *Journal of Personality and Social Psychology* 17: 250–8.

Hendricks, M., and Bootzin, R. (1976) Race and sex as stimuli for negative affect and physical avoidance. *Journal of Social Psychology* 98: 111–20.

Henry, P. J., and Sears, R. R. (2002) The symbolic racism 2000 scale. *Political Psychology* 23: 253–83.

Henry, P. J., and Sears, R. R. (2005) Over thirty years later: A contemporary look at symbolic racism. *Advances in Experimental Social Psychology* 35: 95–150.

Hepworth, J. T., and West, S. G. (1988) Lynchings and the economy: A time-series reanalysis of Hoyland and Sears (1940). *Journal of Personality and Social Psychology* 55: 239–46.

Herek, G. M., Cogan, J. C., and Gillis, J. R. (2002) Victim experiences of hate crimes based on sexual orientation. *Journal of Social Issues* 58, 319–39.

Herek, G. M., Gillis, J. R., and Cogan, J. C. (1999) Psychological sequelae of hate-crime victimization among lesbian, gay and bisexual adults. *Journal of Consulting and Clinical Psychology* 67, 945–51.

Herman, G. (2007) *Travail, chomage et stigmatisation*. Brussels: De Boeck and Larcier.

Hermann, R. K., Voss, J., Schooler, T., and Ciarrochi, J. (1997) Images in international relations: An experimental test of cognitive schemata. *International Studies Quarterly* 41, 403–33.

Hershberger, S. L., and D'Augelli, A. R. (1995) The impact of victimization on the mental health and suicidality of lesbain, gay and bisexual youth. *Developmental Psychology* 31: 65–74.

Hewstone, M. (1989) *Causal Attribution*. Oxford: Blackwell.

Hewstone, M. (1994) Revision and change of stereotypic beliefs: In search of the elusive subtyping model. *European Review of Social Psychology* 5: 69–109.

Hewstone, M. (1996) Contact and categorization: Social psychological interventions to change intergroup relations. In N. Macrae, C. Stangor and M. Hewstone (eds), *Stereotypes and Stereotyping*, pp. 323–68. New York: Guildford.

Hewstone, M., and Ward, C. (1985) Ethnocentrism and causal attribution in southeast Asia. *Journal of Personality and Social Psychology* 48: 614–23.

Hewstone, M., and Brown, R. (1986) Contact is not enough: An intergroup perspective on the 'contact hypothesis'. In M. Hewstone and R. Brown (eds), *Contact and Conflict in Intergroup Encounters*, pp. 1–44. Oxford: Blackwell.

Hewstone, M., Johnston, L., and Aird, P. (1992) Cognitive models of stereotype change 2: Perceptions of homogeneous and heterogeneous groups. *European Journal of Social Psychology* 22: 235–50.

Hewstone, M., Islam, M. R., and Judd, C. M. (1993) Models of crossed categorization and intergroup relations. *Journal of Personality and Social Psychology* 64: 779–93.

Hewstone, M., Rubin, M., and Willis, H. (2002) Intergroup bias. *Annual Review of Psychology* 53: 575–604.

Hewstone, M., Cairns, E., Voci, A., McLernon, F., Niens, U., and Noor, M. (2004) Intergroup forgiveness and guilt in Northern Ireland: Social psychological dimensions of 'the Troubles'. In N. Branscombe and B. Doosje (eds), *Collective Guilt: International Perspectives*, pp. 193–215. Cambridge: Cambridge University Press.

Hewstone, M., Crisp, R. J., Contarello, A., Voci, A., Conway, L., Marletta, G., and Willis, H. (2006) Tokens in the tower: Perceptual processes and interaction dynamics in academic settings with 'skewed', 'tilted' and 'balanced' sex ratios. *Group Processes and Intergroup Relations* 9: 509–32.

Higgins, E. T. (1989) Knowledge accessibility and activation: Subjectivity and suffering from unconscious sources. In J. S. Uleman and J. A. Bargh (eds), *Unintended Thought*, pp. 75–123 New York: Guildford.

Himmelweit, H. T., Oppenheim, A. N., and Vince, P. (1958) *Television and the Child: An Empirical Study of the Effect of Television on the Young*. Oxford: Oxford University Press.

Hinkle, S., and Brown, R. (1990) Intergroup comparisons and social identity: Some links and lacunae. In D. Abrams and M. A. Hogg (eds), *Social Identity Theory. Constructive and Critical Advances*, pp. 48–70. London: Harvester-Wheatsheaf.

Hodson, G., Hooper, H., Dovidio, J. F., and Gaertner, S. L. (2005) Aversive racism in Britain: The use of inadmissable evidence in legal decisions. *European Journal of Social Psychology* 35: 437–48.

Hoffman, C., and Hurst, N. (1990) Gender stereotypes: Perception or rationalization? *Journal of Personality and Social Psychology* 58: 197–208.

Hofmann, W., Gawronski, B., Gschwendner, T., Le, H., and Schmitt, M. (2005) A meta-analysis on the correlation between the implicit association test and explicit self-report measures. *Personality and Social Psychology Bulletin* 31: 1369–85.

Hoge, D. R., and Carroll, J. W. (1973) Religiosity and prejudice in Northern and Southern churches. *Journal of Scientific Study of Religion* 12: 181–97.

Home Office (2008) Hate crime. from www.homeoffice.gov.uk/crime-victims/reducing-crime/hate-crime.

Hornsey, M. J., and Hogg, M. A. (2000) Subgroup relations: A comparison of mutual inter-group differentiation and common ingroup identity models of prejudice reduction. *Personality and Social Psychology Bulletin* 26: 242–56.

Hornsey, M. J., and Hogg, M. A. (2002) The effects of group status on subgroup relations. *British Journal of Social Psychology* 41: 203–18.

Horowitz, E. L. (1936) The development of attitude towards the negro. *Archives of Psychology* 194: 5–47.

Horowitz, E. L., and Horowitz, R. E. (1938) Development of social attitudes in children. *Sociometry* 1: 301–38.

Horwitz, M., and Rabbie, J. M. (1982) Individuality and membership in the intergroup system. In H. Tajfel (ed.), *Social Identity and Intergroup Relations*, pp. 241–74. Cambridge: Cambridge University Press.

Hovland, C., and Sears, R. R. (1940) Minor studies in aggression: VI. Correlation oflynchings with economic indices. *Journal of Psychology* 9: 301–10.

Howard, J. W., and Rothbart, M. (1980) Social categorization and memory for ingroup and outgroup behaviour. *Journal of Personality and Social Psychology* 38: 301–10.

Hraba, J., and Grant, G. (1970) Black is beautiful: A re-examination of racial preference and identification. *Journal of Personality and Social Psychology* 16: 398–402.

Hunter, J. A., Stringer, M., and Watson, R. P. (1991) Intergroup violence and intergroup attributions. *British Journal of Social Psychology* 30: 261–6.

Hutnik, N. (1991) *Ethnic Minority Identity. A Social Psychological Perspective.* Oxford: Clarendon Press.

Hyers, L. L., and Swim, J. K. (1998) A comparison of the experiences of dominant and minority group members during an intergroup encounter. *Group Processes and Intergroup Relations* 1: 143–63.

Hyman, H., and Sheatsley, P. B. (1954) 'The authoritarian personality': A methodological critique. In R. Christie and M. Jahoda (eds), *Studies in the Scope and Method of 'The Authoritarian Personality'*, pp. 50–112. Glencoe, IL: Free Press.

Inman, M. L. (2001) Do you see what I see? Similarities and differences in victims' and observers' perceptions of discrimination. *Social Cognition* 19, 521–46.

Insko, C. A., Nacoste, R. W., and Moe, J. L. (1983) Belief congruence and racial discrimination: Review of the evidence and critical evaluation. *European Journal of Social Psychology* 13: 153–74.

The Irish News (2004) Racist attacks result in vetting of tenants. 24 October, p. 1.

Islam, M. R., and Hewstone, M. (1993a) Dimensions of contact as predictors of intergroup anxiety, perceived outgroup variability, and outgroup attitude: An integrative model. *Personality and Social Psychology Bulletin* 19(6): 700–710.

Islam, M. R., and Hewstone, M. (1993b) Intergroup atributions and affective consequences in majority and minority groups. *Journal of Personality and Social Psychology* 64: 936–50.

Iyer, A., and Leach, C. W. (2008) Emotion in inter-group relations. *European Review of Social Psychology* 19: 86–125.

Jacklin, C. N., and Maccoby, E. (1978) Social behavior at thirty-three months in same-sex and mixed-sex dyads. *Child Development* 49: 557–69.

Jackman, M. (1994) *The Velvet Glove: Paternalism and Conflict in Gender, Class and Race Relations.* Berkeley, CA: University of California Press.

Jackson, J. W. (2002) Intergroup attitudes as a function of different dimensions of group identification and perceived intergroup conflict. *Self and Identity* 1: 11–33.

Jackson, J. W., and Smith, E. R. (1999) Conceptualizing social identity: A new framework and evidence for the impact of different dimensions. *Personality and Social Psychology Bulletin* 25, 120–35.

Jackson, L. A., Sullivan, L. A., Harmish, R. and Hodge, C. N. (1996) Achieving positive social identity: Social mobility, social creativity, and permeability of group boundaries. *Journal of Personality and Social Psychology* 70: 241–54.

Jacobson, C. K. (1985) Resistance to affirmative action: Self-interest or racism? *Journal of Conflict Resolution* 29: 306–29.

Jahoda, G. (1963) The development of children's ideas about country and nationality. *British Journal of Educational Psychology* 33: 47–60.

Jahoda, G., Thomson, S. S., and Bhatt, S. (1972) Ethnic identity and preferences among Asian immigrant children in Glasgow: A replicated study. *European Journal of Social Psychology* 2: 19–32.

Janoff-Bulman, R. (1979) Characterological versus behavioral self-blame: Inquiries into depression and rape. *Journal of Personality and Social Psychology* 37: 1798–809.

Jetten, J., and Spears, R. (2003) The divisive potential of differences and similarities: The role of intergroup distinctiveness in intergroup differentiation. *European Review of Social Psychology* 14: 203–41.

Jetten, J., Spears, R., and Manstead, A. S. R. (1997) Strength of identification and intergroup differentiation: The influence of group norms. *European Journal of Social Psychology* 27: 603–9.

Jetten, J., Spears, R., and Manstead, A. S. R. (1998) Defining dimensions of distinctiveness: Group variability makes a difference to differentiation. *Journal of Personality and Social Psychology* 74: 1481–92.

Jetten, J., Spears, R., and Manstead, A. S. R. (2001) Similarity as a source of differentiation: The role of group identification. *European Journal of Social Psychology* 31: 621–40.

Jetten, J., Spears, R., and Postmes, T. (2004) Intergroup distinctiveness and differentiation: A meta-analytic integration. *Journal of Personality and Social Psychology* 86: 862–79.

Johnson, C. S., Olson, M. A., and Fazio, R. H. (2009) Getting acquainted in interracial interactions: Avoiding intimacy but approaching race. *Personality and Social Psychology Bulletin* 35: 557–71.

Johnson, D. W., and Johnson, R. T. (1975) *Learning Together or Alone*. Englewood Cliffs, NJ: Prentice Hall.

Johnson, D. W., Johnson, R. T., and Maruyana, G. (1984) Group interdependence and interpersonal attraction in heterogeneous classrooms: A meta-analysis. In N. Miller and M. Brewer (eds), *Groups in Contact: The Psychology of Desegregation*. Orlando: Academic Press.

Johnson, D. W., Maruyama, G., Johnson, R. T., Nelson, D., and Skon, L. (1981) Effects of cooperative, competitive, and individualistic goal structures on achievement: A meta-analysis. *Psychological Bulletin* 89: 47–62.

Johnston, J., D., and Ettema, J. S. (1982) *Positive Images: Breaking Stereotypes with Children's Television*. Beverly Hills, CA: Sage.

Johnson, J. D., Whitestone, E., Jackson, L. A., and Gatto, L. (1995) Justice is still not colorblind: Differential racial effects of exposure to inadmissable evidence. *Personality and Social Psychology Bulletin* 21: 893–8.

Johnston, L. and Hewstone, M. (1992) Cognitive models of stereotype change: III. Subtyping and the perceived typicality of disconfirming group members. *Journal of Experimental Social Psychology* 28: 360–86.

Joly, S., Tougas, F., and Brown, R. (1993) L'Effet de la catégorisation croisée sur la discrimination intergroupe en milieu universitaire. Unpublished manuscript, Unpublished MS, University of Ottawa.

Jones, E. E., Wood, G. C., and Quattrone, G. A. (1981) Perceived variability of personal characteristics in ingroups and outgroups: The role of knowledge and evaluation. *Personality and Social Psychology Bulletin* 7: 523–8.

Jones, E. E., Farina, A., Hastorf, A. H., Markus, H., Miller, D. T., and Scott, R. A. (1984) *Social Stigma: The Psychology of Marked Relationships*. New York: Freeman.

Jones, F., Annan, D., and Shah, S. (2008) The distribution of household income 1977 to 2006/07. *Economic and Labour Market Review* 2: 18–31.

Jones, J. M. (1972) *Prejudice and Racism*. Reading, MA: Addison-Wesley.

Jones, J. M. (1997) *Prejudice and Racism*, 2nd edn. New York: McGraw Hill.

Jost, J. T., and Banaji, M. R. (1994) The role of stereotyping in system justification and the production of false consciousness. *British Journal of Social Psychology* 33: 1–27.

Jost, J. T., and Hunyady, O. (2002) The psychology of system justification and the palliative function of ideology. *European Review of Social Psychology* 13: 111–53.

Jost, J. T., Pelham, B. W., and Carvallo, M. (2002) Non-conscious forms of system justification: Cognitive, affective and behavioral preferences for higher status groups. *Journal of Experimental Social Psychology* 38: 586–602.

Jost, J. T., Banaji, M. R., and Nosek, B. A. (2004) A decade of system justification theory: Accumulated evidence of conscious and unconscious bolstering of the status quo. *Political Psychology* 25: 881–919.

Jost, J. T., Glaser, J., Kruglanski, A. W., and Sulloway, F. J. (2003a) Political conservatism as motivated social cognition. *Psychological Bulletin* 129: 339–75.

Jost, J. T., Pelham, B. W., Sheldon, O., and Sullivan, B. N. (2003b) Social inequality and the reduction of ideological dissonance on behalf of the system: Evidence of enhanced system justification among the disadvantaged. *European Journal of Social Psychology* 33: 13–36.

Judd, C. M., and Park, B. (1993) Definition and assessment of accuracy in social stereotypes. *Psychological Review* 100, 109–28.

Jussim, L. (1989) Teacher expectations: Self-fulfilling prophecies, perceptual biases and accuracy. *Journal of Personality and Social Psychology* 57: 469–80.

Jussim, L. (2005) Accuracy in social perception: Criticisms, controversies, criteria, components, and cognitive processes. *Advances in Experimental Social Psychology* 37: 1–93.

Jussim, L., and Harber, K. D. (2005) Teacher expectations and self-fulfilling prophecies: Knowns and unknowns, resolved and unresolved controversies. *Personality and Social Psychology Review* 9: 131–55.

Kahn, W., and Crosby, F. (1985) Change and stasis: Discriminating between attitudes and discriminating behaviour. In L. Larwood, B. A. Gutek and A. H. Stromberg (eds), *Women and Work: An Annual Review*, Vol. 1, pp. 215–38. Beverly Hills, CA: Sage.

Kaiser, C. R., and Miller, C. T. (2001) Reacting to impending discrimination: Compensation for prejudice and attributions to discrimination. *Personality and Social Psychology Bulletin* 27: 1357–67.

Kanter, R. M. (1977) Some effects of proportions on group life: Skewed sex ratios and responses to token women. *American Journal of Sociology* 82: 965–90.

Kanyangara, P., Rimé, B., Philippot, P., and Yzerbyt, V. Y. (2007) Collective rituals, emotional climate and intergroup perception: Participation in 'Gacaca' Tribunals and assimilation of the Rwandan genocide. *Journal of Social Issues* 63: 387–403.

Kaplan, J. (2006) Islamophobia in America? September 11 and islamophobic hate crime. *Terrorism and Political Violence* 18: 1–33.

Karlins, M., Coffman, T. L., and Walters, G. (1969) On the fading of social stereotypes: Studies in three generations of college students. *Journal of Personality and Social Psychology* 13: 1–16.

Karpinski, A., and Hilton, J. L. (2001) Attitudes and the implicit association test. *Journal of Personality and Social Psychology* 81: 774–88.

Katz, D., and Braly, K. (1933) Racial stereotypes of one hundred college students. *Journal of Abnormal and Social Psychology* 28: 280–90.

Katz, I., and Hass, R. G. (1988) Racial ambivalence and American value conflict: Correlational and priming studies of dual cognitive structures. *Journal of Personality and Social Psychology* 55: 893–905.

Katz, I., Hass, R. G., and Wackenhut, J. (1986) Racial ambivalence, value duality, and behavior. In J. F. Dovidio and S. L. Gaertner (eds), *Prejudice, Discrimination and Racism*, pp. 35–59. New York: Academic Press.

Katz, I., Glass, D. C., Lucido, D., and Farber, J. (1979) Harm-doing and victim's racial or orthopedic stigma as determinants of helping. *Journal of Personality* 47: 340–64.

Katz, P. A. (1983) Developmental foundations of gender and racial attitudes. In R. Leahy (ed.), *The Child's Construction of Social Inequality*, pp. 41–77. New York: Academic Press.

Katz, P. A. (2003) Racists or tolerant multiculturalists? How do they begin? *American Psychologist* 58: 897–909.

Katz, P. A., and Zalk, S. R. (1974) Doll preferences: An index of racial attitudes? *Journal of Educational Psychology* 66: 663–8.

Kawakami, K., Dion, K. L., and Dovidio, J. F. (1998) Racial prejudice and stereotype activation. *Personality and Social Psychology Bulletin* 24: 407–16.

Kawakami, K., Dovidio, J. F., and van Kamp, S. (2005) Kicking the habit: Effects of nonstereotypic association training and correction processes on hiring decisions. *Journal of Experimental Social Psychology* 41: 68–75.

Kawakami, K., Dovidio, J. F., Moll, J., Hermson, S., and Russin, A. (2000) Just say no (to stereotyping): Effects of training in the negation of stereotypic associations on stereotype activation. *Journal of Personality and Social Psychology* 78: 871–88.

Kedem, P., Bihu, A., and Cohen, Z. (1987) Dogmatism, ideology and right-wing radical activity. *Political Psychology* 8: 35–47.

Keller, J. (2005) In genes we trust: The biological component of psychological essentialism and its relationship to mechanisms of motivated social cognition. *Journal of Personality and Social Psychology* 88: 686–702.

Kelly, C. (1988) Intergroup differentiation in a political context. *British Journal of Social Psychology* 27: 319–32.

Kelly, C. (1989) Political identity and perceived intragroup homogeneity. *British Journal of Social Psychology* 28: 239–50.

Kelly, D. J., Quinn, P. C., Slater, A. M., Lee, K., Gibson, A., Smith, M., Ge, L., and Pascalis, O. (2005) Three-month olds, but not newborns, prefer own-race faces. *Developmental Science* 8: 31–6.

Kelly, D. J., Liu, S., Ge, L., Quinn, P. C., Slater, A. M., Lee, K., Liu, Q., and Pascalis, O. (2007) Cross-race preferences for same-race faces extends beyond the African versus Caucasian contrast in 3-month-old infants. *Infancy* 11: 87–95.

Kessler, T., and Mummendey, A. (2001) Is there any scapegoat around? Determinants of intergroup conflict at different categorization levels. *Journal of Personality and Social Psychology* 81: 1090–102.

Kessler, T., Mummendey, A., and Leisse, U.-K. (2000) The personal/group discrepancy: Is there a common information basis for personal and group judgment? *Journal of Personality and Social Psychology* 79(1): 95–109.

Kinder, D. R., and Sears, R. R. (1981) Prejudice and politics: Symbolic racism versus racial threats to the good life. *Journal of Personality and Social Psychology* 40: 414–31.

Kleck, R., Ono, H., and Hastorf, A. H. (1966) The effects of physical deviance upon face to face interaction. *Human Relations* 19: 425–36.

Kleinpenning, G., and Hagendoorn, L. (1993) Forms of racism and the cumulative dimension of ethnic attitudes. *Social Psychology Quarterly* 56: 21–36.

Kluegel, J. R., and Smith, E. R. (1983) Affirmative action attitudes: Effects of self-interest, racial affect and stratification on whites' views. *Social Forces* 61: 797–824.

Kohlberg, L. (1966) A cognitive developmental analysis of children's sex-role concepts and attitudes. In E. Maccoby (ed.), *The Development of Sex Differences*, pp. 82–173. Stanford, CA: Stanford University Press.

Koomen, W., and Fränkel, E. G. (1992) Effects of experienced discrimination and different forms of relative deprivation among Surinamese, a Dutch ethnic minority group. *Journal of Community and Applied Social Psychology* 2: 63–71.

Kosterman, R., and Feshbach, S. (1989) Towards a measure of patriotic and nationalistic attitudes. *Political Psychology* 10: 257–74.

Kovel, J. (1970) *White Racism: A Psychohistory*. London: Allen Lane.

Kowalski, R. M. (1996) Complaints and complaining: Functions, antecedents and consequences. *Psychological Bulletin* 119: 179–96.

Krueger, J., and Clement, R. W. (1994) Memory-based judgements about multiple categories: A revision and extension of Tajfel's accentuation theory. *Journal of Personality and Social Psychology* 67: 35–47.

Krueger, J., and Rothbart, M. (1988) Use of categorical and individuating information in making inferences about personality. *Journal of Personality and Social Psychology* 55: 187–95.

Kunda, Z., Sinclair, L., and Griffin, D. (1997) Equal ratings but separate meanings: Stereotypes and the construal of traits. *Journal of Personality and Social Psychology* 72: 720–34.

La Freniere, P., Strayer, F. F., and Gauthier, R. (1984) The emergence of same-sex affiliative preferences among pre-school peers: A developmental/ethological perspective. *Child Development* 55, 1958–65.

Lalonde, R. N., and Gardner, R. C. (1989) An intergroup perspective on stereotype organization and processing. *British Journal of Social Psychology* 28: 289–303.

Lambert, A. J., Cronen, S., Chasteen, A. L., and Lickel, B. (1996) Private vs public expressions of racial prejudice. *Journal of Experimental Social Psychology* 32: 437–59.

Lambert, W. E., and Klineberg, O. (1967) *Children's Views of Foreign Peoples*. New York: Appleton Century Crofts.

Langer, E. J. (1975) The illusion of control. *Journal of Personality and Social Psychology* 32: 311–28.

Langer, E. J., Fiske, S., Taylor, S. E., and Chanowitz, B. (1976) Stigma, staring, and discomfort: A novel-stimulus hypothesis. *Journal of Experimental Social Psychology* 12: 451–63.

Latane, B., and Darley, J. M. (1970) *The Unresponsive Bystander: Why Doesn't He Help?* New York: Appleton-Crofts.

Leach, C. W. (2005) Against the notion of a 'new racism'. *Journal of Community and Applied Social Psychology* 15: 432–45.

Leach, C. W., Ellemers, N., and Barreto, M. (2007) Group virtue: The importance of morality (vs. competence and sociability) in the positive evaluation of in-groups. *Journal of Personality and Social Psychology* 93, 234–49.

Leach, C. W., Snider, N., and Iyer, A. (2002) 'Poisoning the consciences of the fortunate': The experience of relative advantage and support for social equality. In I. Walker and H. Smith (eds), *Relative Deprivation: Specification, Development and Integration*, pp. 136–63. Cambridge: Cambridge University Press.

Leach, C. W., van Zomeren, M., Zebel, S., Vliek, M. L. W., Pennekamp, S. F., Doosje, B., Oewerkerk, J. W., and Spears, R. (2008) Group-level self-definition and self-investment: A hierarchical (multi-component) model of in-group identification. *Journal of Personality and Social Psychology* 95: 144–65.

Lee, R. E., and Warr, P. (1969) The development and standardization of a balanced F-scale. *Journal of General Psychology* 18: 109–29.

Lee, Y.-T., Jussim, L. J., and McCauley, C. R. (eds) (1995) *Stereotype Accuracy: Toward Appreciating Group Differences*. Washington, DC: American Psychological Association.

Lemaine, G. (1966) Inégalité, comparaison et incomparabilité: Esquisse d'une théorie de l'originalité sociale. *Bulletin de Psychologie* 20: 1–9.

Lepore, L., and Brown, R. (1997) Category activation and stereotype accessibility: Is prejudice inevitable? *Journal of Personality and Social Psychology* 72: 275–87.

Lepore, L., and Brown, R. (2000) Exploring automatic stereotype activation: A challenge to the inevitability of prejudice. In D. Abrams and M. A. Hogg (eds), *Social Identity and Social Cognition*, pp. 140–163. Oxford: Blackwell.

Levin, S., van Laar, C., and Sidanius, J. (2003) The effects of ingroup and outgroup friendships on ethnic attitudes in college: A longitudinal study. *Group Processes and Intergroup Relations* 6: 76–92.

LeVine, R. A., and Campbell, D. T. (1972) *Ethnocentrism: Theories of Conflict, Ethnic Atttitudes and Group Behaviour*. New York: Wiley.

Levy, B. R. (1996) Improving memory in old age by implicit self-stereotyping. *Journal of Personality and Social Psychology* 71: 1092–107.

Levy, B. R., and Langer, E. (1994) Aging free from negative stereotypes: Successful memory in China and among the American deaf. *Journal of Personality and Social Psychology* 66: 989–97.

Leyens, J. P., and Yzerbyt, V. Y. (1992) The ingroup overexclusion effect: Impact of varaince and confirmation on stereotypical information search. *European Journal of Social Psychology* 22: 549–69.

Leyens, J.-P., Yzerbyt, V. Y., and Schadron, G. (1992) The social judgeability approach to stereotypes. *European Review of Social Psychology* 3: 91–120.

Leyens, J.-P., Yzerbyt, V. Y., and Schadron, G. (1994) *Stereotypes and Social Cognition*. London: Sage.

Leyens, J. P., Desert, M., Croizet, J.-C., and Darcis, C. (2000) Stereotype threat: Are lower status and history of stigmatization preconditions of stereotype threat? *Personality and Social Psychology Bulletin* 26: 1189–99.

Liberman, N., and Förster, J. (2000) Expression after suppression: A motivational explanation of post-suppressional rebound. *Journal of Personality and Social Psychology* 79: 190–203.

Lickel, B., Hamilton, D., Wieczorkowska, G., Lewis, A., Sherman, S. J., and Uhles, A. N. (2000) Varieties of groups and the perception of group entitativity. *Journal of Personality and Social Psychology* 78: 223–46.

Liebkind, K. (2001) Acculturation. In R. Brown and S. Gaertner (eds), *Blackwell Handbook of Social Psychology*, Vol. 4, pp. 387–405. Oxford: Blackwell.

Liebkind, K., and McAlister, A. (1999) Extended contact through peer modelling to promote tolerance in Finland. *European Journal of Social Psychology* 29: 765–80.

Linville, P. W., Fischer, F. W., and Salovey, P. (1989) Perceived distributions of characteristics of ingroup and outgroup members: Empirical evidence and a computer simulation. *Journal of Personality and Social Psychology* 42: 193–211.

Lippman, W. (1922) *Public Opinion*. New York: Harcourt Brace.

Livingstone, A., and Haslam, S. A. (2008) The importance of identity content in a setting of chronic social conflict: Understanding intergroup relations in Northern Ireland. *British Journal of Social Psychology* 47, 1–21.

Locke, V., Macleod, C. and Walker, I. (1994) Automatic and controlled activation of stereotypes: Individual differences associated with prejudice. *British Journal of Social Psychology* 33: 29–46.

Locksley, A., Hepburn, C. and Ortiz, V. (1982) On the effects of social stereotypes on judgments of individuals: A comment on Grant and Holmes' 'The integration of implicit personality theory schemes and stereotypic images'. *Social Psychology Quarterly* 45: 270–3.

Locksley, A., Borgida, E., Brekke, N., and Hepburn, C. (1980) Sex stereotypes and social judgement. *Journal of Personality and Social Psychology* 39: 821–31.

Lopez, G. E. (2004) Interethnic contact, curriculum, and attitudes in the first year of college. *Journal of Social Issues* 60: 75–94.

Lowery, B. S., Hardin, C. D., and Sinclair, S. (2001) Social influence efects on automatic racial prejudice. *Journal of Personality and Social Psychology* 81: 842–55.

Maass, A. (1999) Linguistic intergroup bias: Stereotype-perpetuation through language. In M. Zanna (ed.), *Advances in Experimental Social Psychology*, Vol. 31, 79–121. New York: Academic Press.

Maass, A., and Cadinu, M. (2003) Stereotype threat: When minority members underperform. *European Review of Social Psychology* 14: 243–75.

Maass, A., Salvi, D., Arcuri, L. and Swim, G.R. (1989) Language use in intergroup contexts: The linguistic intergroup bias. *Journal of Personality and Social Psychology* 57, 981–93.

Maass, A., Cadinu, M., Guarnieri, G., and Grasselli, A. (2003) Sexual harassment under social identity threat: The computer harassment paradigm. *Journal of Personality and Social Psychology* 85: 853–70.

Maccoby, E. (1980) *Social Development.* New York: Harcourt Brace Jovanovich.

Maccoby, E. (1988) Gender as a social category. *Developmental Psychology* 24: 755–65.

Maccoby, E. (1998) *The Two Sexes: Growing Up Apart, Coming Together.* Cambridge, MA: Harvard University Press.

Maccoby, E., and Jacklin, C. N. (1974) *The Psychology of Sex Differences.* Stanford: Stanford University Press.

Maccoby, E., and Jacklin, C. N. (1987) Gender segregation in childhood. *Advances in Child Development and Behaviour* 20: 239–87.

Macdonald, A. M. (1988) (ed.) *Chambers Twentieth Century Dictionary.* Edinburgh: W. and R. Chambers.

Mackie, D. M., and Smith, E. R. (2002) *From Prejudice to Intergroup Emotions: Differentiated Reactions to Social Groups.* Hove: Psychology Press.

Mackie, D. M., Devos, T., and Smith, E. (2000) Intergroup emotions: Explaining offensive action tendencies in an intergroup context. *Journal of Personality and Social Psychology* 79(4): 602–16.

Mackie, D. M., Hamilton, D. L., Schroth, H. H., Carlisle, L. J., Gersho, B. F., Meneses, L. M., Nedler, B. F., and Reichel, L. D. (1989) The effects of induced mood on expectancy-based illusory correlations. *Journal of Experimental Social Psychology* 25: 524–44.

Mackie, D. M., and Hamilton, D. L. (eds) (1993) *Affect, Cognition and Stereotyping: Interactive Processes in Group Perception.* San Diego: Academic Press.

Macrae, C. N., and Shepherd, J. W. (1989) Stereotypes and social judgements. *British Journal of Social Psychology* 28: 319–25.

Macrae, C. N., Hewstone, M., and Griffiths, R. J. (1993) Processing load and memory for stereotype-based information. *European Journal of Social Psychology* 23: 77–87.

Macrae, C. N., Milne, A., and Bodenhausen, G. V. (1994a) Stereotypes as energy-saving devices: A peek inside the cognitive toolbox. *Journal of Personality and Social Psychology* 66: 37–47.

Macrae, C. N., Stangor, C., and Milne, A. (1994b) Activating stereotypes: A functional analysis. *Journal of Experimental Social Psychology* 30: 370–89.

Macrae, C. N., Bodenhausen, G. V., and Milne, A. (1995) The dissection of selection in person perception: Inhibitory processes in social stereotyping. *Journal of Personality and Social Psychology* 69: 397–407.

Macrae, C. N., Bodenhausen, G. V., and Milne, A. (1998) Saying no to unwanted thoughts: Self-focus and the regulation of mental life. *Journal of Personality and Social Psychology* 74: 578–89.

Macrae, C. N., Bodenhausen, G. V., Milne, A., and Jetten, J. (1994c) Out of mind but back in sight: Stereoytpes on the rebound. *Journal of Personality and Social Psychology* 67: 808–17.

Macrae, C. N., Stangor, C., and Hewstone, M. (eds) (1996) *Stereotypes and Stereotyping.* New York: Guilford.

Madon, S., Guyll, M., Aboufadel, K., Motiel, E., Smith, A., Palumbo, P., and Jussim, L. (2001a) Ethnic and national stereotypes: The Princeton trilogy revisited. *Personality and Social Psychology Bulletin* 27: 996–1010.

Madon, S., Smith, A., Jussim, L., Russell, D. W., Eccles, J., Palumbo, P., and Walkiewicz, M. (2001b) Am I as you see me or do you see me as I am? Self-fulfilling prophecies and self-verification. *Personality and Social Psychology Bulletin* 27: 1214–24.

Magee, J. C., and Tiedens, L. Z. (2006) Emotional ties that bind: The roles of valence and consistency of group emotion in inferences of cohesiveness and common fate. *Personality and Social Psychology Bulletin* 32: 1703–15.

Magley, V. J. Hulin, C. L., Fitzgerald, L. F., DeNardo, M. (1999) Outcomes of self-labeling sexual harassment. *Journal of Applied Psychology* 84: 390–402.

Major, B., and O'Brien, L. T. (2005) The social psychology of social stigma. *Annual Review of Psychology* 56: 393–421.

Major, B., Quinton, W. J., and McCoy, S. (2002a) Antecedents and consequences of attributions to discrimination: Theoretical and empirical advances. *Advances in Experimental Social Psychology* 34: 251–330.

Major, B., Kaiser, C. R., O'Brien, L. T., and McCoy, S. K. (2007) Perceived discrimination as world-view threat or world-view confirmation: Implications for self-esteem. *Journal of Personality and Social Psychology* 92: 1068–86.

Major, B., Gramzow, R. H., McCoy, S., Levin, S., Schmader, T., and Sidanius, J. (2002b) Perceiving personal discrimination: The role of group status and legitimising ideology. *Journal of Personality and Social Psychology* 82(3): 269–82.

Maras, P. (1993) *The Integration of Children with Disabilities into the Mainstream.* Unpublished PhD, University of Kent, Canterbury.

Maras, P., and Brown, R. (1996) Effects of contact on children's attitudes toward disability: A longitudinal study. *Journal of Applied Social Psychology* 26: 2113–34.

Maras, P., and Brown, R. (2000) Effects of different forms of school contact on childrens attitudes towards disabled and non-disabled peers. *British Journal of Educational Psychology* 70: 337–51.

Marx, K., and Engels, F. (1965) *The German Ideology* [1846] London: Lawrence Wishart.

Masser, B., and Abrams, D. (1999) Contemporary sexism: The relationship among hostility, benevolence, and neosexism. *Psychology of Women Quarterly* 23: 503–17.

Masser, B., and Abrams, D. (2004) Reinforcing the glass ceiling: The consequences of hostile sexism for female managerial candidates. *Sex Roles* 51: 609–15.

Maykovich, M. K. (1975) Correlates of racial prejudice. *Journal of Personality and Social Psychology* 32: 1014–20.

McConahay, J. B. (1982) Self-interest versus racial attitudes as correlates of anti-busing attitudes in Louisville: Is it the buses or the blacks? *Journal of Politics* 44: 692–720.

McConahay, J. B. (1986) Modern racism, ambivalence and the modern racism scale. In J. F. Dovidio and S. L. Gaertner (eds), *Prejudice, Discrimination and Racism*, pp. 91–126. Orlando: Academic Press.

McConahay, J. B., Hardee, B. B., and Batts, V. (1981) Has racism declined in America? It depends on who is asking and what is asked. *Journal of Conflict Resolution* 25: 563–79.

McConnell, A. R., and Liebold, J. M. (2001) Relations among the implicit association test, discriminatory behavior, and explicit measures of racial attitudes. *Journal of Experimental Social Psychology* 37: 435–42.

McCoy, S., and Major, B. (2003) Group identification moderates emotional responses to perceived prejudice. *Personality and Social Psychology Bulletin* 29: 1005–17.

McDevitt, J., Balboni, J., Garcia, L., and Gu, J. (2001) Consequences for victims: A comparison of bias and non-bias motivated assaults. *American Behavioral Scientist* 45: 697–713.

McFarland, S. G., Agehev, V. S., and Abalakina-Paap, M. A. (1992) Authoritarianism in the former Soviet Union. *Journal of Personality and Social Psychology* 63: 1004–10.

McGarty, C., Haslam, S. A., Turner, J. C., and Oakes, P. J. (1993) Illusory correlation as accentuation of actual intercategory difference: Evidence for the effect with minimal stimulus information. *European Journal of Social Psychology* 23: 391–410.

McGarty, C., Pederson, A., Leach, C. W., Mansell, T., Waller, J., and Bliuc, A.-M. (2005) Group-based guilt as a predictor of commitment to apology. *British Journal of Social Psychology* 44: 659–80.

McGarty, C., and Penny, R. E. C. (1988) Categorization, accentuation and social judgement. *British Journal of Social Psychology* 27: 147–57.

McGlothlin, H., and Killen, M. (2006) Intergroup attitudes of European American children attending ethnically homogeneous schools. *Child Development* 77: 1375–86.

McGlothlin, H., Killen, M., and Edmonds, C. (2005) European–American children's intergroup attitudes about peer relationships. *British Journal of Developmental Psychology* 23: 227–49.

McGuire, W. J., McGuire, C. V., Child, P., and Fujioka, T. (1978) Salience of ethnicity in the spontaneous self concept as a function of one's ethnic distinctiveness in the social environment. *Journal of Personality and Social Psychology* 36: 511–20.

McLaren, L. (2003) Anti-immigrant prejudice in Europe: Contact, threat perception, and preferences for the exclusion of migrants. *Social Forces* 81: 909–36.

McLaren, L., and Johnson, M. (2007) Resources, group conflict and symbols: Explaining anti-immigration hostility in Britain. *Political Studies* 55: 709–32.

Mead, G. H. (1934) *On Social Psychology.* Chicago: University of Chicago Press.

Meertens, R. W., and Pettigrew, T. F. (1997) Is subtle prejudice really prejudice? *Public Opinion Quarterly* 61: 54–71.

Meeus, J., Duriez, B., Vanbeselaere, N., Phalet, K., and Kuppens, P. (2008) Where do negative outgroup attitudes come from? Combining an individual differences and an intergroup relations perspective. Paper presented at the General Meeting of the European Association of Social Psychology, Optajia, Croatia, July.

Meleon, J. D., Hagendoorn, L., Raaijmakers, Q., and Visser, L. (1988) Authoritarianism and the revival of political racism: Reassessments in the Netherlands of the reliability and validity of the concept of authoritarianism by Adorno et al. *Political Psychology* 9(3): 413–29.

Mendoza-Denton, R., Downey, G., Purdie, V. J., Davis, A., and Pietrzak, J. (2002) Sensitivity to status-based rejection: Implications for African American students' college experience. *Journal of Personality and Social Psychology* 83: 896–918.

Migdal, M., Hewstone, M., and Mullen, B. (1998) The effects of crossed categorization on intergroup evaluations: A meta-analysis. *British Journal of Social Psychology* 37: 303–24.

Miles, R. (1989) *Racism.* London: Routledge.

Miller, A., and Bolce, L. (1979) Reply to Cosby. *American Political Science Review* 73: 818–22.

Miller, A., Bolce, L. and Halligan, M. (1977) The J-curve theory and the black urban riots: An empirical test of progressive relative deprivation theory. *American Political Science Review* 71: 964–82.

Miller, C. T., and Myers, A. M. (1998) Compensating for prejudice: How heavyweight people (and others) control outcomes despite prejudice. In J. K. Swim and C. Stangor (eds), *Prejudice: The Target's Perspective*, pp. 191–218. San Diego: Academic Press.

Miller, C. T., and Downey, K. T. (1999) A meta-analysis of heavyweight and self-esteem. *Personality and Social Psychology Review* 3: 68–84.

Miller, N. (2002) Personalization and the promise of contact theory. *Journal of Social Issues* 58: 387–410.

Miller, N., and Davidson-Podgorny, F. (1987) Theoretical models of intergroup relations and the use of co-operative teams as an intervention for desegregated settings. In C. Hendrick (ed.), *Group Processes and Intergroup Relations: Review of Personality and Psychology*, Vol. 9, pp. 41–67. Beverley Hills: Sage.

Miller, N., Brewer, M. B., and Edwards, K. (1985) Cooperative interaction in desegregated settings: A laboratory analogue. *Journal of Social Issues* 41: 63–79.

Miller, N. E., and Bugelski, R. (1948) Minor studies in aggression: The influence of frustrations imposed by the ingroup on attitudes toward out-groups. *Journal of Psychology* 25: 437–42.

Milner, D. (1983) *Children and Race: Ten Years On*. London: Ward Lock.

Minard, R. D. (1952) Race relationships in the Pocahontas coal field. *Journal of Social Issues* 8: 29–44.

Ministry of Industry (2005) *Women in Canada: A Gender Based Statistical Report*, 5th edn. Ottawa: Statistics Canada.

Mischel, W. (1966) A social learning view of sex differences in behavior. In E. Maccoby (ed.), *The Development of Sex Differences*. Stanford, CA: Stanford University Press.

Mischel, W. (1970) Sex typing and socialization. In P. H. Mussen (ed.), *Carmichael's Manual of Child Psychology*, Vol. 2. New York: Wiley.

Moghaddam, F. M., Fathali, M., Stolkin, A. J., and Hutcheson, L. S. (1997) A generalized personal/group discrepancy: Testing the domain specificity of a perceived higher effect of events on one's group than on oneself. *Personality and Social Psychology Bulletin* 23: 743–50.

Molina, L. E., and Wittig, M. A. (2006) Relative importance of contact conditions in explaining prejudice reduction in a classroom context. *Journal of Social Issues* 62: 489–509.

Monteith, M. J. (1993) Self-regulation of prejudiced responses: Implications for progress in prejudice-reduction efforts. *Journal of Personality and Social Psychology* 65: 469–85.

Monteith, M. J. (1996) Contemporary forms of prejudice-related conflict: In search of a nutshell. *Personality and Social Psychology Bulletin* 22: 461–73.

Monteith, M. J., Devine, P. G., and Zuwerink, J. R. (1993) Self-directed versus other-directed affect as a consequence of prejudice-related discrepancies. *Journal of Personality and Social Psychology* 64: 198–210.

Monteith, M. J., Sherman, J. W., and Devine, P. G. (1998a) Suppression as a stereotype control strategy. *Personality and Social Psychology Review* 2: 63–82.

Monteith, M. J., Spicer, C. V., and Tooman, G. D. (1998b) Consequences of stereotype suppression: Stereotypes on AND not on the rebound. *Journal of Experimental Social Psychology* 34: 355–77.

Morgan, M. (1982) Television and adolescents' sex-role stereotypes: A longitudinal study. *Journal of Personality and Social Psychology* 43: 947–55.

Morgan, N. (1988) *The Equality Game: Women in the Federal Public Service (1908–1987)*. Ottawa: Canadian Advisory Council on the Status of Women.

Morrison, K. R., and Ybarra, O. (2008) The effects of realistic threat and group identification on social dominance orientation. *Journal of Experimental Social Psychology* 44: 156–63.

Mosher, D. L., and Scodel, A. (1960) Relationships between ethnocentrism in children and authoritarian rearing practices of their mothers. *Child Development* 31: 369–76.

Moya, M., Glick, P., Exposito, F., de Lemus, S., and Hart, J. (2007) It's for your own good: Benevolent sexism and women's reactions to protectively justified restrictions. *Personality and Social Psychology Bulletin* 33: 1421–34.

Mullen, B., and Hu, L. (1989) Perceptions of ingroup and outgroup variability: A meta-analytic integration. *Basic and Applied Social Psychology* 10: 233–52.

Mullen, B., Brown, R. and Smith, C. (1992) Ingroup bias as a function of salience, relevance, and status: An integration. *European Journal of Social Psychology* 22: 103–22.

Mummendey, A., and Otten, S. (1998) Positive–negative asymmetry in social discrimination. In W. Stroebe and M. Hewstone (eds), *European Review of Social Psychology*, Vol. 8, pp. 107–43. Chichester: Wiley.

Mummendey, A., Klink, A., and Brown, R. (2001a) Nationalism and patriotism: National identification and outgroup rejection. *British Journal of Social Psychology* 40: 159–72.

Mummendey, A., Klink, A., and Brown, R. (2001b) A rejoinder to our critics and some of their misapprehensions. *British Journal of Social Psychology* 40: 187–91.

Mummendey, A., Simon, B., Dietze, C., Grünert, M., Haeger, G., Kessler, T., Lettgen, S., and Schäferhoff, S. (1992) Categorization is not enough: Intergroup discrimination in negative outcome allocations. *Journal of Experimental Social Psychology* 28: 125–44.

Murphy, M., Steele, C. M., and Gross, J. (2007) Signaling threat: How situational cues affect women in math, science and engineering. *Psychological Science* 18: 879–85.

Myrdal, G. (1944) *An American Dilemma*. New York: Harper Row.

Nail, P. R., Harton, H. C., and Decker, B. P. (2003) Political orientation and modern versus aversive racism: Tests of Dovidio and Gaertner's (1998) integrated model. *Journal of Personality and Social Psychology* 84: 754–70.

Nakanishi, D. T. (1988) Seeking convergence in race relations research: Japanese–Americans and the resurrection of the internment. In P. A. Katz and D. Taylor (eds), *Eliminating Racism: Profiles in Controversy*, pp. 159–80. New York: Plenum.

Nelson, T. E., Biernat, M., and Manis, M. (1990) Everyday base rates (sex stereotypes): Potent and resilient. *Journal of Personality and Social Psychology* 59: 664–75.

Nesdale, D. (2004) Social identity processes and children's ethnic prejudice. In M. Bennett and F. Sani (eds), *The Development of the Social Self*, pp. 219–45. Hove: Psychology Press.

Nesdale, D., and Flesser, D. (2001) Social identity and the development of children's group attitudes. *Child Development* 72: 506–17.

Nesdale, D., Durkin, K., Maass, A., and Griffiths, J. (2005a) Threat, group identification, and children's ethnic prejudice. *Social Development* 14: 189–205.

Nesdale, D., Maass, A., Durkin, K., and Griffiths, J. (2005b) Group norms, threat, and children's racial prejudice. *Child Development* 76: 652–63.

Neuberg, S. L., and Fiske, S. T. (1987) Motivational influences on impression formation: Outcome dependency, accuracy-driven attention, and individuating processes. *Journal of Personality and Social Psychology* 53: 431–44.

Neumark-Sztainer, D., and Haines, J. (2004) Psychosocial and behavioral consequences of obesity. In J. K. Thompson (ed.), *Handbook of Eating Disorders and Obesity*, pp. 349–71. Hoboken, NJ: Wiley.

Nier, J. A., Mottola, G. R., and Gaertner, S. L. (2000) The O. J. Simpson criminal verdict as a racially symbolic event: A longitudinal analysis of racial attitude change. *Personality and Social Psychology Bulletin* 26: 507–16.

Nosek, B. A., Smyth, F. L., Hansen, J. J., Devos, T., Lindner, N. M., Ranganath, K. A., Tucker Smith, C., Olson, K. R., Chugh, D., Greenwald, A. G., and Banaji, M. R. (2007) Pervasiveness and correlates of implicit attitudes and stereotypes. *European Review of Social Psychology* 18: 36–88.

Nunez, J., and Gutierrez, R. (2004) Class discrimination and meritocracy in the labor market: Evidence from Chile. *Estudios de Economia* 31: 113–32.

Oakes, P. J. (1994) The effects of fit versus novelty on the salience of social categories: A response to Biernat and Vescio (1993). *Journal of Experimental Social Psychology* 30: 390–8.

Oakes, P. J., and Turner, J. (1986) Distinctiveness and the salience of social category membership: Is there an automatic bias towards novelty? *European Journal of Social Psychology* 16: 325–44.

Oakes, P. J., and Reynolds, K. J. (1997) Asking the accuracy question: Is measurement the answer? In R. Spears, P. J. Oakes, N. Ellemers, and S. A. Haslam (eds), *The Social Psychology of Stereotyping and Group Life*, pp. 51–71. Oxford: Blackwell.

Oakes, P. J., Haslam, A., and Turner, J. C. (1994) *Stereotyping and Social Reality*. Oxford: Blackwell.

Olson, J. M., and Fazio, R. H. (2004) Reducing the influence of extrapersonal associations on the implicit association test: Personalizing the IAT. *Journal of Personality and Social Psychology* 86: 653–67.

Olson, M. A., and Fazio, R. H. (2006) Reducing automatically activated racial prejudice through implicit evaluative conditioning. *Personality and Social Psychology Bulletin* 32: 421–33.

Operario, D., and Fiske, S. T. (2001) Ethnic identity moderates perceptions of prejudice: Judgments of personal versus group discrimination and subtle versus blatant bias. *Personality and Social Psychology Bulletin* 27(5): 550–61.

Ostrom, T. M., and Sedikides, C. (1992) Outgroup homogeneity effects in natural and minimal groups. *Psychological Bulletin* 112: 536–52.

Otten, S., and Moskowitz, G. B. (2000) Evidence for implicit evaluative in-group bias: Affect-biased spontaneous trait inference in a minimal group paradigm. *Journal of Experimental Social Psychology* 36: 77–89.

Oyserman, D., Coon, H. M., and Kemmelmeier, M. (2002) Rethinking individualism and collectivism: Evaluation of theoretical assumptions and meta-analyses. *Psychological Bulletin* 128, 3–72.

Padgett, V. R., and Jorgenson, D. O. (1982) Superstition and economic threat: Germany 1918–1940. *Personality and Social Psychology Bulletin* 8, 736–41.

Páez, D., Marques, J. M., Valencia, J., and Vincze, O. (2006) Dealing with collective shame and guilt. *Psicologia Politica* 32: 59–78.

Paluck, E. L. (2009) Reducing intergroup prejudice and conflict using the media: A field experiment in Rwanda. *Journal of Personality and Social Psychology* 96: 574–87.

Paolini, S., Hewstone, M., Cairns, E., and Voci, A. (2004) Effects of direct and indirect cross-group friendships on judgments of Catholics and Protestants in Northern Ireland: The mediating role of an anxiety-reduction mechanism. *Personality and Social Psychology Bulletin* 30: 770–86.

Park, B., Judd, C. M., and Ryan, C. S. (1991) Social categorization and the representation of variability information. *European Review of Social Psychology* 2: 211–45.

Park, R. E. (1924) The concept of social distance as applied to the study of racial attitudes and racial relations. *Journal of Applied Sociology* 8: 339–44.

Patterson, M. M., and Bigler, R. (2006) Preschool children's attention to environmental messages about groups: Social categorization and the origins of intergroup bias. *Child Development* 77: 847–60.

Payne, B. K. (2001) Prejudice and perception: The role of automatic and controlled processes in misperceiving a weapon. *Journal of Personality and Social Psychology* 81: 181–92.

Payne, B. K., Shimizu, Y., and Jacoby, L. L. (2005) Mental control and visual illusions: Toward explaining race-biased weapon misidentifications. *Journal of Experimental Social Psychology* 41: 36–47.

Pederson, A., Beven, J., Walker, I., and Griffiths, B. (2004) Attitudes toward indigenous Australians: The role of empathy and guilt. *Journal of Community and Applied Social Psychology* 14: 233–49.

Pehrson, S., Brown, R., and Zagefka, H. (2009a) When does national identification lead to the rejection of immigrants? Cross-sectional and longitudinal evidence for the role of essentialist ingroup definitions. *British Journal of Social Psychology* 58: 61–76.

Pehrson, S., Vignoles, V., and Brown, R. (2009b) National identification and anti-immigrant prejudice: Individual and contextual effects of national definitions. *Social Psychology Quarterly* 72, 24–38.

Pendry, L. F., and Macrae, C. N. (1994) Stereotypes and mental life: The case of the motivated but thwarted tactician. *Journal of Experimental Social Psychology* 30: 303–25.

Pendry, L. F., and Macrae, C. N. (1996) What the disinterested perceiver overlooks: Goal-directed social categorization. *Personality and Social Psychology Bulletin* 22: 249–56.

Penny, H., and Haddock, G. (2007) Anti-fat prejudice among children: The 'mere proximity' effect in 5–10 year-olds. *Journal of Experimental Social Psychology* 43: 678–83.

Perdue, C. W., Dovidio, J., Gurtman, M. B., and Tyler, R. B. (1990) 'Us' and 'them': Social categorization and the process of intergroup bias. *Journal of Personality and Social Psychology* 59: 475–86.

Perrin, A. J. (2005) National threat and political culture: Authoritarianism, anti-authoritarianism, and the September 11 attacks. *Political Psychology* 26: 167–94.

Petrocelli, J. V. (2002) Ambivalent sexism inventory: Where's the ambivalence? *American Psychologist* 57: 443–4.

Pettigrew, T. F. (1958) Personality and sociocultural factors in intergroup attitudes: A cross-national comparison. *Journal of Conflict Resolution* 2: 29–42.

Pettigrew, T. F. (1971) *Racially Separate or Together?* New York: McGraw Hill.

Pettigrew, T. F. (1979) The ultimate attribution error: Extending Allport's cognitive analysis of prejudice. *Personality and Social Psychology Bulletin* 5: 461–76.

Pettigrew, T. F. (1985) New patterns of racism: The different worlds of 1984 and 1964. *Rutgers Law Review* 1: 673–706.

Pettigrew, T. F. (1997) Generalised intergroup contact effects on prejudice. *Personality and Social Psychology Bulletin* 23(2): 173–85.

Pettigrew, T. F. (1998) Intergroup contact theory. *Annual Review of Psychology* 49: 65–85.

Pettigrew, T. F. (2004) Justice deferred: A half century after *Brown* v. *Board of Education*. *American Psychologist* 59: 521–9.

Pettigrew, T. F., and Meertens, R. W. (1995) Subtle and blatant prejudice in western Europe. *European Journal of Social Psychology* 25: 57–75.

Pettigrew, T. F., and Meertens, R. W. (2001) In defense of the subtle prejudice concept: A retort. *European Journal of Social Psychology* 31: 299–309.

Pettigrew, T. F., and Tropp, L. (2006) A meta-analytic test of intergroup contact theory. *Journal of Personality and Social Psychology* 90: 751–83.

Pettigrew, T. F., and Tropp, L. (2008) How does intergroup contact reduce prejudice? Meta-analytic tests of three mediators. *European Journal of Social Psychology* 38: 922–34.

Pettigrew, T. F., Christ, O., Wagner, U., and Stellmacher, J. (2007) Direct and indirect intergroup contact effects on prejudice: A normative interpretation. *International Journal of Intercultural Relations* 31: 411–25.

Pettigrew, T. F., Christ, O., Wagner, U., Meertens, R. W., van Dick, R., and Zick, A. (2008) Relative deprivation and intergroup prejudice. *Journal of Social Issues* 64: 385–401.

Pettigrew, T. F., Jackson, J. S., Brika, J. B., Lemaine, G., Meertens, R. W., Wagner, U., Lemain, G., Meertens, R.W., Wagner, U., and Zick, A. (1998) Outgroup prejudice in western Europe. In W. Stroebe and M. Hewstone (eds), *European Review of Social Psychology*, Vol. 8, pp. 241–73. Chichester: John Wiley.

Pfafferott, I., and Brown, R. (2006) Acculturation preferences of majority and minority adolescents in Germany in the context of society and family. *International Journal of Intercultural Relations* 30: 703–17.

Piaget, J. (1954) *The Construction of Reality in the Child*. New York: Basic Books.

Pilger, J. (1989) *A Secret Country*. London: Vantage.

Pinel, E. C. (1999) Stigma consciousness: The psychological legacy of social stereotypes. *Journal of Personality and Soial Psychology* 76(1): 114–28.

Plant, E. A., and Devine, P. G. (1998) Internal and external motivation to respond without prejudice. *Journal of Personality and Social Psychology* 75: 811–32.

Plomin, R. (1990) *Nature and Nurture: An Introduction to Human Behavioral Genetics.* Pacific Grove, CA: Brooks/Cole.

Popper, K. (1963) *Conjectures and Refutations: The Growth of Scientific Knowledge.* London: Routledge and Kegan Paul.

Populus (2008) *Poll for BBC Newsnight: Executive Summary.*

Porter, J. D. R. (1971) *Black Child, White Child: The Development of Racial Attitudes.* Cambridge, MA: Harvard University Press.

Powers, D. A., and Ellison, C. G. (1995) Interracial contact and black racial attitudes: The contact hypothesis and selectivity bias. *Social Forces* 74: 205–26.

Powlishta, K. K., Serbin, L. A., Doyle, A.-B., and White, D. R. (1994) Gender, ethnic and body type biases: The generality of prejudice in childhood. *Developmental Psychology* 30: 526–36.

Pratto, F., Sidanius, J., Stallworth, L. M., and Malle, B. F. (1994) Social dominance orientation: A personality variable predicting social and political attitudes. *Journal of Personality and Social Psychology* 67: 741–63.

Pratto, F., Stallworth, L. M., Sidanius, J., and Siers, B. (1997) The gender gap in occupational role attainment: A social dominance approach. *Journal of Personality and Social Psychology* 72: 37–53.

Quanty, M. B., Keats, J. A., and Harkins, S. G. (1975) Prejudice and criteria for identification of ethnic photographs. *Journal of Personality and Social Psychology* 32: 449–54.

Quattrone, G. A. (1986) On the perception of a group's variability. In S. Worchel and W. G. Austin (eds), *Social Psychology of Intergroup Relations*, pp. 25–48. Chicago: Nelson.

Quillian, L. (1995) Prejudice as a response to perceived group threat: Population composition and anti-immigrant and racial prejudice in Europe. *American Sociological Review* 60: 586–611.

Quinn, P. C., Yahr, J., Kuhn, A., Slater, A. M., and Pascalis, O. (2002) Representation of the gender of human faces by infants: A preference for female. *Perception* 31: 1109–21.

Raabe, T., and Beelmann, A. (2009) Age differences and development of prejudice among children and adolescents: A meta-analysis. Paper presented at the Society for Research in Child Development (SRCD), Denver, USA (April).

Rabbie, J. M., and Horwitz, M. (1969) Arousal of ingroup bias by a chance win or loss. *Journal of Personality and Social Psychology* 13: 269–77.

Rahhal, T. A., Hasher, L., and Colcombe, S. J. (2001) Instructional manipulations and age differences in memory: Now you see them, now you don't. *Psychology and Aging* 16: 697–706.

Rankin, R. E., and Campbell, D. T. (1955) Galvanic skin response to negro and white experimenters. *Journal of Abnormal and Social Psychology* 51: 30–3.

Ratazzi, A. M. M., and Volpato, C. (2003) Social desirability of subtle and blatant prejudice scales. *Psychological Reports* 92: 241–50.

Reicher, S. (1986) Contact, action and racialization: Some British evidence. In M. Hewstone and R. Brown (eds), *Contact and Conflict in Intergroup Encounters*, pp. 152–68. Oxford: Blackwell.

Reicher, S. (2004) The context of social psychology: Domination, resistance, and change. *Political Psychology* 25: 921–45.

Reicher, S., and Hopkins, N. (2001) *Self and Nation.* London: Sage Publications.

Repetti, R. L. (1984) Determinants of children's sex-stereotyping: Parental sex-role traits and television viewing. *Personality and Social Psychology Bulletin* 10: 457–68.

Reynolds, K. J., Turner, J. C., Haslam, S. A., and Ryan, M. K. (2001) The role of personality and group factors in explaining prejudice. *Journal of Experimental Social Psychology* 37: 427–34.

Richardson, S. A., and Green, A. (1971) When is black beautiful? Coloured and white children's reactions to skin colour. *British Journal of Educational Psychology* 41(1): 62–9.

Rimé, B., Kanyangara, P., Yzerbyt, V. Y., Philippot, P., and Páez, D. (2008) Social rituals and collective expression of emotion after a collective trauma. Paper presented at the European Association of Experimental Social Psychology, Opatija, Croatia, July.

Robinson, J. P., Shaver, P. R., and Wrightsman, L. S. (1991) *Measures of Personality and Social Psychological Attitudes*. San Diego: Academic Press.

Roccas, S., Klar, Y., and Liviatan, I. (2006) The paradox of group-based guilt: Modes of national identification, conflict vehemence, and reactions to the in-group's moral violations. *Journal of Personality and Social Psychology* 32: 1674–89.

Roccas, S., and Schwartz, S. H. (1993) Effects of intergroup similarity on intergroup relations. *European Journal of Social Psychology* 23, 581–95.

Roese, N. J., and Jamieson, D. W. (1993) Twenty years of bogus pipeline research: A critical review and meta-analysis. *Psychological Bulletin* 114: 363–75.

Rojahn, K., and Pettigrew, T. F. (1992) Memory for schema-relevant information: A meta-analytic resolution. *British Journal of Social Psychology* 31: 81–109.

Rokeach, M. (1948) Generalized mental rigidity as a factor in ethnocentrism. *Journal of Abnormal and Social Psychology* 43: 259–78.

Rokeach, M. (1956) Political and religious dogmatism: An alternate to the authoritarian personality. *Psychological Monographs* 70(18) (whole issue).

Rokeach, M. (1960) *The Open and Closed Mind*. New York: Basic Books.

Rokeach, M. (1973) *The Nature of Human Values*. New York: Free Press.

Rokeach, M., and Mezei, L. (1966) Race and shared belief as factors in social choice. *Science* 151: 167–72.

Rokeach, M., Smith, P. W., and Evans, R. I. (1960) Two kinds of prejudice or one? In M. Rokeach (ed.), *The Open and Closed Mind*. New York: Basic Books.

Rombough, S., and Ventimiglia, J. C. (1981) Sexism: A tri-dimensional phenomenon. *Sex Roles* 7: 747–55.

Rosch, E. (1978) Principles of categorization. In E. Rosch and B. Lloyd (eds), *Cognition and Categorization*, pp. 27–48. Hillsdale, NJ: Lawrence Erlbaum.

Rosenberg, M., and Simmons, R. G. (1972) *Black and White Self-Esteem: The Urban School Child*. Washington, DC: American Sociological Association.

Rosenthal, R. (1966) *Experimenter Effects in Behavioral Research*. New York: Appleton.

Rosenthal, R., and Jacobson, L. (1968) *Pygmalion in the Classroom: Teacher Expectations and Student Intellectual Development*. New York: Holt, Rinehart and Winston.

Ross, L. D. (1977) The intuitive psychologist and his shortcomings: Distortions in the attribution process. In L. Berkowitz (ed.), *Advances in Experimental Social Psychology*, Vol. 10, pp. 173–220. New York: Academic Press.

Rothbart, M. (1981) Memory processes and social beliefs. In D. L. Hamilton (ed.), *Cognitive Processes in Stereotyping and Intergroup Behavior*, pp. 145–81. Hillsdale, NJ: Erlbaum.

Rothbart, M., and John, O. P. (1985) Social categorization and behavioural episodes: A cognitive analysis of the effects of intergroup contact. *Journal of Social Issues* 41: 81–104.

Rothbart, M., and Park, B. (1986) On the confirmability and disconfirmability of trait concepts. *Journal of Personality and Social Psychology* 50: 131–42.

Rubin, M., and Hewstone, M. (2004) Social identity, system justification, and social dominance: Commentary on Reicher, Jost et al., and Sidanius et al. *Political Psychology* 25: 823–44.

Ruble, D. N., Boggiano, A., Feldman, N., and Loebl, J. (1980) A developmental analysis of the role of social comparisons in self-evaluation. *Developmental Psychology* 12: 192–7.

Rudman, L. A., Feinberg, J., and Fairchild, K. (2002) Minority members' implicit attitudes: Automatic ingroup bias as a function of group status. *Social Cognition* 20: 294–320.

Ruggiero, K., and Taylor, D. M. (1995) Coping with discrimination: How disadvantaged group members perceive the discrimination that confronts them. *Journal of Personality and Social Psychology* 68: 826–38.

Ruggiero, K., and Taylor, D. M. (1997) Why minority group members perceive or do not perceive the discrimination that confronts them: The role of self-esteem and perceived control. *Journal of Personality and Social Psychology* 72: 373–89.

Ruggiero, K. M., and Marx, D. M. (2001) Retraction: 'Less pain and more to gain': Why high status group members blame their failure on discrimination. *Journal of Personality and Social Psychology* 81: 178.

Ruggiero, K. M., and Major, B. (2002) Retraction. Group status and attributions to discrimination: Are low or high status group members more likely to blame their failures on discrimination? *Personality and Social Psychology Bulletin* 28: 284.

Ruggiero, K. M., Steele, J., Hwang, A., and Marx, D. M. (2001) 'Why did I get a "D"?' The effects of social comparisons on women's attributions to discrimination: Retraction. *Personality and Social Psychology Bulletin* 27: 1237.

Ruggiero, K. M., Mitchell, J. P., Krieger, N., Marx, D. M., and Lorenzo, M. L. (2002) 'Now you see it now you don't: Explicit versus implicit measures of the personal/group discrimination discrepency': Retraction. *Psychological Science* 13: 511–14.

Runciman, W. G. (1966) *Relative Deprivation and Social Justice. A Study of Attitudes to Social Inequality in Twentieth Century England.* London: Routledge and Kegan Paul.

Rutland, A., Cameron, L., Bennett, L., and Ferrell, J. (2005a) Interracial contact and racial constancy: A multi-site study of racial intergroup bias in 3–5 year old Anglo-British children. *Applied Developmental Psychology* 26: 699–713.

Rutland, A., Cameron, L., Milne, A., and McGeorge, P. (2005b) Social norms and self-presentation: Children's implicit and explicit attitudes. *Child Development* 76: 451–66.

Rutland, A., Brown, R., Ahmavaara, A., Arnold, K., Samson, J., and Cameron, L. (2007) Development of the positive–negative asymmetry effect: Ingroup exclusion norm as a mediator of children's evaluations on negative attributes. *European Journal of Social Psychology* 37: 171–90.

Ryan, C. S. (2002) Stereotpye accuracy. *European Review of Social Psychology* 13: 75–109.

Ryan, M. K., and Haslam, A. (2007) The glass cliff: Exploring the dynamics surrounding women's appointment to precarious leadership positions. *Academy of Management Review* 32: 549–72.

Ryen, A. H., and Kahn, A. (1975) Effects of intergroup orientation on group attitudes and proxemic behavior. *Journal of Personality and Social Psychology* 31: 302–10.

Sachdev, I., and Bourhis, R. (1987) Status differentials and intergroup behaviour. *European Journal of Social Psychology* 17: 277–93.

Sachdev, I., and Bourhis, R. (1991) Power and status differentials in minority and majority group relations. *European Journal of Social Psychology* 21: 1–24.

Sagar, H. A., and Schofield, J. W. (1980) Racial and behavioral cues in black and white children's perceptions of ambiguously aggressive acts. *Journal of Personality and Social Psychology* 39: 590–8.

Sales, S. M. (1973) Threat as a factor in authoritarianism: An analysis of archival data. *Journal of Personality and Social Psychology* 28: 44–57.

Samson, E. E. (1999) *Dealing with Differences: An Introduction to the Social Psychology of Prejudice.* New York: Harcourt Brace.

Sangrigoli, S., and de Schonen, S. (2004) Recognition of own-race and other-race faces by three-month-old infants. *Journal of Child Psychology and Psychiatry* 45: 1219–27.

Sassenberg, K., Moskowitz, G. B., Jacoby, J., and Hansen, N. (2007) The carry-over effect of competition: The impact of competition on prejudice towards uninvolved outgroups. *Journal of Experimental Social Psychology* 43: 529–38.

Saucier, G. (1994) Separating description and evaluation in the structure of personality attributes. *Journal of Personality and Social Psychology* 66: 141–54.

Schaller, M. (1991) Social categorization and the formation of group stereotypes: Further evidence for biased information processing in the perception of group-behaviour correlations. *European Journal of Social Psychology* 21: 25–35.

Schaller, M., and Maass, A. (1989) Illusory correlation and social categorization: Toward an integration of motivational and cognitive factors in stereotype formation. *Journal of Personality and Social Psychology* 56: 709–21.

Schatz, R. T., Staub, E., and Lavine, H. (1999) On the varieties of national attachment: Blind versus constructive patriotism. *Political Psychology* 20: 151–74.

Scheepers, D., Spears, R., Doosje, B., and Manstead, A. S. R. (2006) The social functions of ingroup bias: Creating, confirming, or changing social reality. *European Review of Social Psychology* 17: 359–96.

Schmader, T. (2002) Gender identification moderates stereotype threat effects on women's math performance. *Journal of Experimental Social Psychology* 38: 194–201.

Schmader, T., Johns, M., and Forbes, C. (2008) An integrated process model of stereotype threat effects on performance. *Psychological Review* 115: 336–56.

Schmitt, M., and Branscombe, N. (2002a) The internal and external causal loci of attributions to prejudice. *Personality and Social Psychology Bulletin* 28: 620–8.

Schmitt, M. T., and Branscombe, N. R. (2002b) The meaning and consequences of perceived discrimination in disadvantaged and privileged social groups. In W. Stroebe and M. Hewstone (eds), *European Review of Social Psychology*, Vol. 12, pp. 167–199. Chichester: John Wiley and Sons.

Schmitt, M. T., Branscombe, N., and Kappen, D. M. (2003) Attitudes toward group-based inequality: Social dominance or soical identity. *British Journal of Social Psychology* 42: 161–86.

Schofield, J. W. (1979) The impact of positively structured contact on intergroup behavior: Does it last under adverse conditions? *Social Psychology Quarterly* 42: 280–4.

Schofield, J. W. (1982) *Black and White in school: Trust, Tension, or Tolerance.* New York: Praeger.

Schofield, J. W., and Sagar, H. A. (1977. Peer interaction patterns in an intergrated middle school. *Sociometry* 40: 130–8.

Schofield, J. W., and Eurich-Fulcer, R. (2001) When and how school desegregation improves intergroup relations. In R. Brown and S. Gaertner (eds), *Blackwell Handbook of Social Psychology: Intergroup Processes*, pp. 475–94. Oxford: Blackwell.

Schuman, H., Steeh, C., Bobo, L., and Krysan, M. (1997) *Racial Attitudes in America: Trends and Interpretations.* Cambridge, MA: Harvard University Press.

Schütz, H., and Six, B. (1996) How strong is the relationship between prejudice and discrimination? A meta-analytic answer. *International Journal of Intercultural Relation,* 20: 441–62.

Seago, D. W. (1947) Stereotypes: Before Pearl Harbor and after. *Journal of Social Psychology* 23: 55–63.

Sears, R. R. (1988) Symbolic racism. In P. Katz and D. Taylor (eds), *Eliminating Racism: Profiles in Controversy*, pp. 53–84. New York: Plenum.

Sears, R. R., and Kinder, D. R. (1971) Racial tensions and voting in Los Angeles. In W. Z. Hirsch (ed.), *Los Angeles: Viability and Prospects for Metropolitan Leadership*, pp. 51–88. New York: Praeger.

Sears, R. R., and Henry, P. J. (2005) Over thirty years later: A contemporary look at symbolic racism. *Advances in Experimental Social Psychology* 37: 95–150.

Sears, R. R., Maccoby, E. E., and Levin, H. (1957) *Patterns of Child Rearing.* Oxford, England: Row, Peterson and Co.

Seibt, B., and Förster, J. (2004) Stereotype threat and performance: How self-stereotypes influence processing by inducing regulatory foci. *Journal of Personality and Social Psychology* 87: 38–56.

Semyonov, M., Raijman, R., and Gorodzeisky, A. (2006) The rise of anti-immigrant sentiment in European societies, 1988–2000. *American Sociological Review 71*: 426–49.

Serbin, L. A., Tonick, I. J., and Sternglaz, S. H. (1978) Shaping cooperative cross-sex play. *Child Development* 48: 924–9.

Shapiro, J. R., and Neuberg, S. L. (2007) From stereotype threat to stereotype threats: Implications of a multi-threat framework for causes, moderators, mediators, consequences and interventions. *Personality and Social Psychology Review* 11: 107–30.

Shelton, J. N. (2003) Interpersonal concerns in social encounters between majority and minority group members. *Group Processes and Intergroup Relations* 6: 171–85.

Shelton, J. N., Richeson, J. A., and Salvatore, J. (2005) Expecting to be the target of prejudice: Implications for interethnic interactions. *Personality and Social Psychology Bulletin* 31: 1189–202.

Sherif, M. (1966) *Group Conflict and Cooperation: Their Social Psychology*. London: Routledge and Kegan Paul.

Sherif, M., and Sherif, C. W. (1953) *Groups in Harmony and Tension*. New York: Harper.

Sherif, M., White, B. J., and Harvey, O. J. (1955) Status in experimentally produced groups. *American Journal of Sociology* 60: 370–9.

Sherif, M., Harvey, O. J., White, B. J., Hood, W. R., and Sherif, C. W. (1961) *Intergroup Conflict and Cooperation: The Robbers Cave Experiment*. Norman, Oklahoma: University of Oklahoma Book exchange.

Sherman, D. K., and Cohen, G. L. (2006) The psychology of self-defense: Self-affirmation theory. *Advances in Experimental Social Psychology 38*: 183–242.

Shils, E. A. (1954) Authoritarianism: 'Left' and 'right'. In R. Christie and M. Jahoda (eds), *Studies in the Scope and Method of 'The Authoritarian Personality'*, pp. 24–49. Glencoe, IL: Free Press.

Sidanius, J., and Pratto, F. (1999) *Social Dominance: An Intergroup Theory of Social Hierarchy and Oppression*. Cambridge: Cambridge University Press.

Sidanius, J., Liu, J., Pratto, F., and Shaw, J. (1994) Social dominance orientation, hierarchy-attenuators and hierarchy-enhancers: Social dominance theory and the criminal justice system. *Journal of Applied Social Psychology* 24: 338–366.

Sidanius, J., Levin, S., Liu, J., and Pratto, F. (2000) Social dominance orientation, anti-egalitarianism and the political psychology of gender: An extension and cross-cultural replication. *European Journal of Social Psychology* 30: 41–67.

Sidanius, J., Pratto, F., van Laar, C., and Levin, S. (2004) Social dominance theory: Its agenda and method. *Political Psychology* 25: 845–80.

Siegel, A. E., and Siegel, S. (1957) Reference groups, membership groups and attitude change. *Journal of Abnormal and Social Psychology* 55: 360–4.

Sigall, H., and Page, R. (1971) Current stereotypes: A little fading, a little faking. *Journal of Personality and Social Psychology* 18: 247–55.

Simon, B. (1992a) Intragroup differentiation in terms of ingroup and outgroup attributes. *European Journal of Social Psychology* 22: 407–13.

Simon, B. (1992b) The perception of ingroup and outgroup homogeneity: Reintroducing the intergroup context. *European Review of Social Psychology* 3: 1–30.

Simon, B., and Brown, R. (1987) Perceived intragroup homogeneity in minority–majority contexts. *Journal of Personality and Social Psychology* 53: 703–11.

Simon, B., Glassner-Boyerl, B., and Stratenworth, I. (1991) Stereotyping self-stereotyping in a natural intergroup context: The case of heterosexual and homosexual men. *Social Psychology Quarterly* 54: 252–66.

Simpson, G. E., and Yinger, J. M. (1972) *Racial and Cultural Minorities: An Analysis of Prejudice and Discrimination* New York: Harper Row.

Sinclair, L., and Kunda, Z. (1999) Reactions to a black Professional: Motivated inhibition and activation of conflicting stereotypes. *Journal of Personality and Social Psychology* 77: 885–904.

Sinclair, S., Dunn, E., and Lowery, B. S. (2005) The relationship between parental racial attitudes and children's implicit prejudice. *Journal of Experimental Social Psychology* 41: 283–9.

Sinha, R. R., and Hassan, M. K. (1975) Some personality correlates of social prejudice. *Journal of Social and Economic Studies* 3: 225–31.

Skowronski, J. J., Carlston, D. E., and Isham, J. T. (1993) Implicit versus explicit impression formation: The differing effects of overt labelling and covert priming on memory and impressions. *Journal of Experimental Social Psychology* 29: 17–41.

Slaby, R. G., and Frey, K. S. (1975) Development of gender constancy and selective attention to same-sex models. *Child Development* 46: 849–56.

Slavin, R. E. (1979) Effects of biracial learning teams on cross-racial friendships. *Journal of Educational Psychology* 71: 381–7.

Slavin, R. E. (1983) *Cooperative Learning*. New York: Longman.

Smith, A. (1994) Education and conflict in Northern Ireland. In S. Dunn (ed.), *Facets of the Conflict in Northern Ireland*, pp. 168–86. London: Macmillan.

Smith, A. D. (2001) *Nationalism: Theory, Ideology, History*. Cambridge: Polity Press.

Smith, A. E., Jussim, L., and Eccles, J. (1999) Do self-fulfilling prophecies accumulate, dissipate or remain stable over time? *Journal of Personality and Social Psychology* 77: 548–65.

Smith, E. R. (1993) Social identity and social emotions: Toward new conceptualizations of prejudice. In D. M. Mackie and D. L. Hamilton (eds), *Affect, Cognition and Stereotyping*, pp. 297–315. San Diego: Academic Press.

Smith, E. R., and Henry, S. (1996) An ingroup becomes part of the self: Response time evaluation. *Personality and Social Psychology Bulletin* 22: 635–42.

Smith, E. R., Murphy, J., and Coats, S. (1999) Attachment to groups: Theory and management. *Journal of Personality and Social Psychology* 25: 873–82.

Smith, H., and Ortiz, D. J. (2002) Is it just me? The different consequences of personal and group relative deprivation. In I. Walker and H. Smith (eds), *Relative Deprivation: Specification, Development and Integration*, pp. 91–115. Cambridge: Cambridge University Press.

Smith, H. J., and Leach, C. W. (2004) Group membership and everyday social comparison experiences. *European Journal of Social Psychology* 34: 297–308.

Sniderman, P. M., and Tetlock, P. E. (1986) Symbolic racism: Problems of motive attribution in political debate. *Journal of Social Issues* 42: 129–50.

Sniderman, P. M., Piazza, T., Tetlock, P. E., and Kendrick, A. (1991) The new racism. *American Journal of Political Science* 35: 423–47.

Snyder, C. R., Lassegard, M., and Ford, C. E. (1986) Distancing after group success and failure: Basking in reflected glory and cutting off reflected failure. *Journal of Personality and Social Psychology* 51: 382–8.

Snyder, M. L. (1981) On the self-perpetuating nature of social stereotypes. In D. L. Hamilton (ed.), *Cognitive Processes in Stereotyping and Intergroup Behavior*, pp. 183–212. New York: Lawrence Erlbaum.

Snyder, M. L., and Swann, W. B. (1978) Hypothesis-testing processes in social interaction. *Journal of Personality and Social Psychology* 36: 1202–12.

Snyder, M. L., Tanke, E. D., and Berscheid, E. (1977) Social perception and interpersonal behavior: On the self-fulfilling nature of social stereotypes. *Journal of Personality and Social Psychology* 35: 656–66.

Snyder, M. L., Kleck, R. E., Strenta, A., and Mentzer, S. J. (1979) Avoidance of the handi-
    capped: An attributional ambiguity analysis. *Journal of Personality and Social Psychology*
    37: 2297–306.
Son Hing, L. S., Chung-Yan, G. A., Hamilton, L. K., and Zanna, M. (2008) A two-
    dimensional model that employs explicit and implicit attitudes to characterize prej-
    udice. *Journal of Personality and Social Psychology* 94: 971–87.
Spears, R., Jetten, J., and Doosje, B. (2001) The (il)legitimacy of ingroup bias: From social
    reality to social resistance. In J. T. Jost and B. Major (eds), *The Psychology of Legitimacy:
    Emerging Perspectives on Ideology, Justice and Intergroup Relations*, pp. 332–62. Cambridge:
    Cambridge University Press.
Spears, R., Oakes, P. J., Ellemers, N., and Haslam, S. A. (eds) (1997) *The Social Psychology of
    Stereotyping and Group Life*. Oxford: Blackwell.
Spencer-Rodgers, J., Hamilton, D. L., and Sherman, S. J. (2007) The central role of entitativity
    in stereotypes of social categories and task groups. *Journal of Personality and Social
    Psychology* 92: 369–88.
Spencer, M. B. (1983) Children's cultural values and parental rearing strategies. *Developmental
    Review* 3: 351–70.
Spencer, S. J., Steele, C. M., and Quinn, D. M. (1999) Stereotype threat and women's math
    performance. *Journal of Experimental Social Psychology* 35: 4–28.
Spielman, D. A. (2000) Young children, minimal groups, and dichotomous categorization.
    Personality and Social Psychology Bulletin 26: 1433–41.
Stagner, R., and Congdon, C. S. (1955) Another failure to demonstrate displacement of aggres-
    sion. *Journal of Abnormal and Social Psychology* 51: 695–6.
Stangor, C. (1988) Stereotype accessibility and information processing. *Personality and Social
    Psychology Bulletin* 14: 694–708.
Stangor, C. (1995) Content and application inaccuracy in social stereotyping. In Y. T. Lee, L.
    Jussim and C. R. McCauley (eds), *Stereotype Accuracy*, pp. 275–92. Washington, DC:
    American Psychological Association.
Stangor, C., and Ford, T. E. (1992) Accuracy and expectancy-confirming processing orienta-
    tions and the development of stereotypes and prejudice. *European Review of Social
    Psychology* 3: 57–89.
Stangor, C., and McMillan, D. (1992) Memory for expectancy-congruent and expectancy-
    incongruent information: A review of the social and social–developmental literature.
    Psychological Bulletin 111: 42–61.
Stangor, C., Sullivan, L. A., and Ford, T. E. (1991) Affective and cognitive determinants of
    prejudice. *Social Cognition* 9: 359–80.
Stangor, C., Lynch, L., Dunn, C., and Glass, B. (1992) Categorization of individuals on the
    basis of multiple social features. *Journal of Personality and Social Psychology* 62: 207–18.
Stangor, C., Swim, J., Van Allen, K., and Sechrist, G. (2002) Reporting discrimination in
    public and private contexts. *Journal of Personality and Social Psychology* 82(1): 69–74.
Stathi, S. and Crisp, R. J. (2008) Imagining intergroup contact promotes projection to out-
    groups. *Journal of Experimental Social Psychology* 44: 943–57.
Steele, C. M. (1988) The psychology of self-affirmation: Sustaining the integrity of the self.
    Advances in Experimental Social Psychology 21: 261–302.
Steele, C. M. (1997) A threat in the air: How stereotypes shape intellectual identity and
    performance. *American Psychologist* 52: 613–29.
Steele, C. M., and Aronson, J. (1995) Stereotype threat and the intellectual test performance
    of African Americans. *Journal of Personality and Social Psychology* 69: 797–811.
Steele, C. M., Spencer, S. J., and Aronson, J. (2002) Contending with group image: The
    psychology of stereotype and social identity threat. *Advances in Experimental Social
    Psychology* 34: 379–440.

Stein, D. D., Hardyck, J. A., and Smith, M. B. (1965) Race and belief: An open and shut case. *Journal of Personality and Social Psychology* 1: 281–9.

Steiner, I. D. (1986) Paradigms and groups. *Advances in Experimental Social Psychology* 19: 251–89.

Stellmacher, J., and Petzel, T. (2005) Authoritarianism as a group phenomenon. *Political Psychology* 26: 245–74.

Stephan, W. G. (1977) Cognitive differentiation in intergroup perception. *Sociometry* 40: 50–8.

Stephan, W. G. (1978) School desegregation: An evaluation of predictions made in *Brown* vs. *Board of Education*. *Psychological Bulletin* 85: 217–38.

Stephan, W. G., and Rosenfield, D. (1978) Effects of desegregation on racial attitudes. *Journal of Personality and Social Psychology* 36: 795–804.

Stephan, W. G., and Stephan, C. W. (1984) The role of ignorance in intergroup relations. In N. Miller and M. Brewer (eds), *Groups in Contact: The Psychology of Desegregation*, pp. 229–55. New York: Academic Press.

Stephan, W. G., and Stephan, C. W. (1985) Intergroup anxiety. *Journal of Social Issues* 41: 157–75.

Stephan, W. G., and Stephan, C. W. (2000) An integrated threat theory of prejudice. In S. Oskamp (ed.), *Reducing Prejudice and Discrimination*, pp. 23–46). Mahwah, NJ: Erlbaum.

Stephan, W. G., and Renfro, C. L. (2002) The role of threat in intergroup relations. In D. M. Mackie and E. R. Smith (eds), *From Prejudice to Intergroup Emotions: Differentiated Reactions to Social Groups*, pp. 191–207. New York: Psychology Press.

Stephan, W. G., Ybarra, O., and Bachman, G. (1999) Prejudice towards immigrants: An integrated threat analysis. *Journal of Applied Social Psychology* 29: 2221–37.

Stephan, W. G., Demitrakis, K. M., Yamada, A. M., and Clason, D. L. (2000) Women's attitudes towards men: An integrated threat theory analysis. *Psychology of Women Quarterly* 24: 63–73.

Stephan, W. G., Ybarra, O., Martinez, C., Schwarzwald, J., and Tur-Kaspa, M. (1998) Prejudice towards immigrants to Spain and Israel: An integrated threat theory analysis. *Journal of Cross-Cultural Psychology* 29: 559–76.

Stephan, W. G., Renfro, C. L., Esses, V. M., Stephan, C. W., and Martin, T. (2005) The effects of feeling threatened on attitudes towards immigrants. *International Journal of Intercultural Relations* 29: 559–76.

Stephan, W. G., Boniecki, K. A., Ybarra, O., Bettencourt, A., Ervin, K. S., Jackson, L. A., McNatt, P. S., and Renfro, C. L. (2002) The role of threats in the racial attitudes of blacks and whites. *Personality and Social Psychology Bulletin* 29: 1242–54.

Stone, J., Lynch, C. I., Sjomeling, M., and Darley, J. M. (1999) Stereotype threat effects on black and white athletic performance. *Journal of Personality and Social Psychology* 77: 1213–27.

Stouffer, S. A., Suchman, E. A., DeVinney, L. C., Star, S. A., and Williams, R. M. (1949) *The American Soldier: Adjustment during Army Life*, Vol. 1. Princeton, NJ: University Press.

Stroessner, S. J., Hamilton, D. L., and Mackie, D. M. (1992) Affect and stereotyping: The effect of induced mood on distinctiveness-based illusory correlations. *Journal of Personality and Social Psychology* 62: 564–76.

Stroop, J. (1935) Studies of interference in serial verbal reactions. *Journal of Experimental Psychology* 18: 643–62.

Struch, N., and Schwartz, S. H. (1989) Intergroup aggression: Its predictors and distinctness from ingroup bias. *Journal of Personality and Social Psychology* 56: 364–73.

Suls, J., and Mullen, B. (1982) From the cradle to the grave: Comparison and self-evaluation across the life-span. In J. Suls (ed.), *Psychological Perspectives on the Self*, Vol. 1, pp. 97–125. London: Erlbaum.

Sumner, W. G. (1906) *Folkways*. New York: Ginn.

Sutton, C. D., and Moore, K. K. (1985) Probing opinions: Executive women 20 years later. *Harvard Business Review* 63: 43–66.

Swim, J. K., and Hyers, L. L. (1999) Excuse me – what did you say? Women's public and private responses to sexist remarks. *Journal of Experimental Social Psychology* 35: 68–88.

Swim, J. K., and Miller, D. L. (1999) White guilt: Its antecedents and consequences for attitudes toward affirmative action. *Personality and Social Psychology Bulletin* 25: 500–14.

Swim, J. K., Cohen, L. L., and Hyers, L. L. (1998) Experiencing everyday prejudice and discrimination. In J. K. Swim and C. Stangor (eds), *Prejudice: The Target's Perspective*, pp. 37–60. San Diego: Academic Press.

Swim, J. K., Aikin, K. J., Hall, W. S., and Hunter, B. A. (1995) Sexism and racism: Old fashioned and modern prejudices. *Journal of Personality and Social Psychology* 68: 199–214.

Swim, J. K., Hyers, L. L., Cohen, L. L., and Ferguson, M. J. (2001) Everyday sexism: Evidence for its incidence, nature, and psychological impact from three daily diary studies. *Journal of Social Issues* 57(1): 31–53.

Tajfel, H. (1959) The anchoring effects of value in a scale of judgements. *British Journal of Psychology* 50: 294–304.

Tajfel, H. (1969a) Cognitive aspects of prejudice. *Journal of Social Issues* 25: 79–97.

Tajfel, H. (1969b) Social and cultural factors in perception. In G. Lindzey and E. Aronson (eds), *Handbook of Social Psychology*, Vol. 3, pp. 315–94. Reading, MA: Addison-Wesley.

Tajfel, H. (1978a) Interindividual and Intergroup Behaviour. In H. Tajfel (ed.), *Differentiation between Social Groups: Studies in the Social Psychology of Integroup Relations*, pp. 27–60. London: Academic Press.

Tajfel, H. (1978b) Social categorisation, social identity and social comparison. In H. Tajfel (ed.), *Differentiation between Social Groups: Studies in the Social Psychology of Intergroup Relations*, pp. 61–76. London: Academic Press.

Tajfel, H. (1981a) *Human Groups and Social Categories*. Cambridge: Cambridge University Press.

Tajfel, H. (1981b) Social stereotypes and social groups. In J. C. Turner and H. Giles (eds), *Intergroup Behaviour*, pp. 144–67. Oxford: Blackwell.

Tajfel, H. (1982) Social psychology of intergroup relations. *Annual Review of Psychology* 33: 1–30.

Tajfel, H., and Wilkes, A. L. (1963) Classification and quantitative judgement. *British Journal of Psychology* 54: 101–14.

Tajfel, H., and Turner, J. C. (1986) The social identity theory of intergroup behavior. In S. Worchel and W. G. Austin (eds), *Psychology of Intergroup Relations*, pp. 7–24. Chicago: Nelson Hall.

Tajfel, H., Flament, C., Billig, M. G., and Bundy, R. P. (1971) Social categorization and intergroup behaviour. *European Journal of Social Psychology* 1: 149–78.

Tajfel, H., Jahoda, G., Nemeth, C., Rim, Y., and Johnson, N. B. (1972) The devaluation by children of their own national and ethic group: Two case studies. *British Journal of Social and Clinical Psychology* 2: 235–43.

Tangney, J. P. (1991) Moral affect: The good, the bad, and the ugly. *Journal of Personality and Social Psychology* 61: 598–607.

Tarman, C., and Sears, R. R. (2005) The conceptualization and measurement of symbolic racism. *Journal of Politics* 67: 731–61.

Taylor, D. M., and Jaggi, V. (1974) Ethnocentrism and causal attribution in a South India context. *Journal of Cross-Cultural Psychology* 5: 162–71.

Taylor, D. M., Wright, S. C., Moghaddam, F. M., and Lalonde, R. N. (1990) The personal/ group discrimination discrepancy: Perceiving my group, but not myself, to be a target for discrimination. *Personality and Social Psychology Bulletin* 16(2): 254–62.

Taylor, M. C. (2002) Fraternal deprivation, collective threat and racial resentment. In I. Walker and H. Smith (eds), *Relative Deprivation: Specification, Development and Integration*, pp. 13–43. Cambridge: Cambridge University Press.

Taylor, S. E. (1981) A categorization approach to stereotyping. In D. L. Hamilton (ed.), *Cognitive Processes in Stereotyping and Intergroup Behavior*, pp. 83–114. Hillsdale, NJ: Erlbaum.

Taylor, S. E., and Falcone, H. T. (1982) Cognitive bases of stereotyping: The relationship between categorization and prejudice. *Personality and Social Psychology Bulletin* 8: 426–36.

Taylor, S. E., Fiske, S. T., Etcoff, N. L., and Ruderman, A. J. (1978) Categorical and contextual bases of person memory and stereotyping. *Journal of Personality and Social Psychology* 36: 778–93.

Temkin, J., and Krahe, B. (2008) *Sexual Assault and the Justice Gap: A Question of Attitude*. Oxford: Hart Publishing.

Tesser, A., Millar, M., and Moore, J. (1988) Some affective consequences of social comparison and reflection processes: The pain and pleasure of being close. *Journal of Personality and Social Psychology* 54: 49–61.

Tetlock, P. E. (1983) Cognitive style and political ideology. *Journal of Personality and Social Psychology* 45: 118–26.

Tetlock, P. E. (1984) Cognitive style and political belief systems in the British House of Commons. *Journal of Personality and Social Psychology* 46: 365–75.

Thompson, S. C., and Spacapan, S. (1991) Perceptions of control in vulnerable populations. *Journal of Social Issues* 47: 1–21.

Thompson, S. K. (1975) Gender labels and early sex-role development. *Child Development* 46: 339–47.

Thorndike, R. L. (1968) Review of Rosenthal and Jacobson's 'Pygmalion in the classroom'. *American Educational Research Journal* 5: 708–11.

Tougas, F., and Beaton, A. (2002) Personal and group relative deprivation: Connecting the 'I' to the 'we'. In I. Walker and H. Smith (eds), *Relative Deprivation: Specification, Development and Integration*, pp. 119–35. Cambridge: Cambridge University Press.

Tougas, F., Brown, R., Beaton, A., and Joly, S. (1995) Neo-sexism: *Plus ça change, plus c'est pareil*. *Personality and Social Psychology Bulletin* 21: 842–9.

Triandis, H. C., and Davis, E. F. (1965) Race and shared belief as shared determinants of behavior intentions. *Journal of Personality and Social Psychology* 2: 715–25.

Tripathi, R. C., and Srivastava, R. (1981) Relative deprivation and intergroup attitudes. *European Journal of Social Psychology* 11: 313–18.

Tropp, L., and Pettigrew, T. F. (2005) Relationships between integroup contact and prejudice among minority and majority groups. *Psychological Science* 16: 951–7.

Turner, J. C. (1978) Social comparison, similarity and ingroup favouritism. In H. Tajfel (ed.), *Differentiation between Social Groups*, pp. 235–50. London: Academic Press.

Turner, J. C. (1980) Fairness or discrimination in intergroup behaviour? A reply to Branthwaite, Doyle and Lightbown. *European Journal of Social Psychology* 10: 131–47.

Turner, J. C. (1981) The experimental social psychology of intergroup behaviour. In J. Turner and H. Giles (eds), *Intergroup Behaviour*, pp. 66–101. Oxford: Blackwell.

Turner, J. C. (1999) Some current issues in research on social identity and self categorization theories. In N. Ellemers, R. Spears and B. Doosje (eds), *Social Identity*, pp. 6–34. Oxford: Blackwell.

Turner, J. C., and Brown, R. (1978) Social status, cognitive alternatives, and intergroup relations. In H. Tajfel (ed.), *Differentiation between Social Groups: Studies in the Social Psychology of Intergroup Relations*, pp. 201–34. London: Academic Press.

Turner, J. C., and Reynolds, K. J. (2003) Why social dominance theory has been falsified. *British Journal of Social Psychology* 42: 199–206.

Turner, J. C., Hogg, M. A., Oakes, P. J., Reicher, S. D., and Wetherell, M. S. (1987) *Rediscovering the Social Group: A Self-Categorization Theory*. Oxford: Blackwell.

Turner, R. N. and Crisp, R. J. (in press) Imagining intergroup contact reduces implicit prejudice. *British Journal of Social Psychology*.

Turner, R. N., Crisp, R. J. and Lambert, E. (2007a) Imagining intergroup contact can improve intergroup attitudes. *Group Processes and Intergroup Relations* 10: 427–41.

Turner, R. N., Hewstone, M., and Voci, A. (2007b) Reducing explicit and implicit outgroup prejudice via direct and extended contact: The mediating role of self-disclosure and intergroup anxiety. *Journal of Personality and Social Psychology* 93: 369–88.

Turner, R. N., Hewstone, M., Voci, A., and Vonofakou, C. (2008) A test of the extended intergroup contact hypothesis: The mediating role of intergroup anxiety, perceived ingroup and outgroup norms, and inclusion of the outgroup in the self. *Journal of Personality and Social Psychology* 95: 843–60.

Turner, R. N., Hewstone, M., Voci, A., Paolini, S., and Christ, O. (2007c) Reducing prejudice via direct and extended cross-group friendship. *European Review of Social Psychology* 18: 212–55.

Twenge, J. M. (1997) Attitudes towards women, 1970–1995. *Psychology of Women Quarterly* 21, 35–51.

Twenge, J. M., and Crocker, J. (2002) Race and self-esteem: Meta-analyses comparing whites, blacks, Hispanics, Asians, and American Indians and comment on Gray-Little and Hafdahl (2000). *Psychological Bulletin* 128: 371–408.

Urban, L. M., and Miller, N. M. (1998) A theoretical analysis of crossed categorization effects: A meta-analysis. *Journal of Personality and Social Psychology* 74: 894–908.

US Department of Labor (1992) Trends in wage and salary inequality: 1967–1988. *Monthly Labor Review* 115: 23–39.

van Avermaet, E., and McLintock, L. G. (1988) Intergroup fairness and bias in children. *European Journal of Social Psychology* 18: 407–27.

van den Berghe, P. L. (1967) *Race and Racism*. New York: Wiley.

van Oudenhoven, J. P., Groenewoud, J. T., and Hewstone, M. (1996) Cooperation, ethnic salience and generalisation of interethnic attitudes. *European Journal of Social Psychology* 26: 649–61.

Vanman, E. J., Paul, B. Y., Ito, T. A., and Miller, N. (1997) The modern face of prejudice and sturctural features that moderate the effect of cooperation on affect. *Journal of Personality and Social Psychology* 73 (941–59).

Vanneman, R., and Pettigrew, T. F. (1972) Race and relative deprivation in the urban United States. *Race* 13: 461–86.

Vaughan, G. M. (1964a) The development of ethnic attitudes in New Zealand school children. *Genetic Psychology Monographs* 70: 135–75.

Vaughan, G. M. (1964b) Ethnic awareness in relation to minority group membership. *Journal of Genetic Psychology* 105: 119–30.

Vaughan, G. M. (1978) Social change and intergroup preferences in New Zealand. *European Journal of Social Psychology* 8: 297–314.

Vaughan, G. M. (1987) A social psychological model of ethnic identity development. In J. S. Phinney and M. J. Rotheram (eds), *Children's Ethnic Socialization: Pluralism and Development*, pp. 73–91. Beverly Hills, CA: Sage.

Vaughan, G. M., Tajfel, H., and Williams, J. (1981) Bias in reward allocation in an intergroup and interpersonal context. *Social Psychology Quarterly* 44: 37–42.

Verkuyten, M. (1994) Self-esteem among ethnic minority youth in western countries. *Social Indicators Research* 32: 21–47.

Verkuyten, M. (2006) Multicultural recognition and ethnic minority rights: A social identity perspective. *European Review of Social Psychology* 17: 148–84.

Verkuyten, M., and Hagendoorn, L. (1998) Prejudice and self-categorization: The variable role of authoritarianism and in-group stereotypes. *Personality and Social Psychology Bulletin* 24: 99–110.

Verkuyten, M., Masson, K., and Elffers, H. (1995) Racial categorization and preference among older children in the Netherlands. *European Journal of Social Psychology* 25: 637–56.

Viki, G. T., and Abrams, D. (2002) But she was unfaithful: Benevolent sexism and reactions to rape victims who violate traditional gender role expectations. *Sex Roles* 47 289–293.

Viki, G. T., Abrams, D., and Masser, B. (2004) Evaluating stranger and acquaintance rape: The role of benevolent sexism in perpetrator blame and recommended sentence length. *Law and Human Behavior* 28: 295–303.

Virdee, S. (1997) Racial harassment. In T. Madood, R. Berthoud, J. Lakey, J. Nazroo, P. Smith, S. Virdee, and S. Beishon (eds), *Ethnic Minorities in Britain: Diversity and Disadvantage*, pp. 259–89. London: Policy Studies Institute.

Voci, A. (2000) Perceived group variability and the salience of personal and social identity. *European Review of Social Psychology* 11: 177–221.

Voci, A. (2006) The link between identification and ingroup favouritism: Effects of threat to social identity and trust-related emotions. *British Journal of Social Psychology* 45: 265–84.

Voci, A., and Hewstone, M. (2003) Intergroup contact and prejudice towards immigrants in Italy: The mediational role of anxiety and the moderational role of group salience. *Group Processes and Intergroup Relations* 6: 37–54.

Vollebergh, W. (1991) *The Limits of Tolerance*. Utrecht: Rijksuniversiteit te Utrecht.

Vonofakou, C., Hewstone, M., and Voci, A. (2007) Contact with outgroup friends as a predictor of meta-attitudinal strength and accessibility of attitudes towards gay men. *Journal of Personality and Social Psychology* 92: 804–20.

Vorauer, J. (2006) An information search model of evaluative concerns in intergroup interaction. *Psychological Review* 113: 862–86.

Vorauer, J., and Kumhyr, S. M. (2001) Is this about you or me? Self versus other-directed judgements and feelings in response to intergroup interaction. *Personality and Social Psychology Bulletin* 27: 706–19.

Vorauer, J., Martens, V., and Sasaki, S. J. (2009) When trying to understand detracts from trying to behave: Effects of perspective taking in intergroup interaction. *Journal of Personality and Social Psychology* 96: 811–27.

Vorauer, J., Hunter, A. J., Main, K. J., and Roy, S. A. (2000) Metastereotype activation: Evidence from indirect measures for specific evaluative concerns experienced by members of dominant groups in intergroup interaction. *Journal of Personality and Social Psychology* 78: 690–707.

Vrana, S. R., and Rollock, D. (1998) Physiological response to a minimal social encounter: Effects of gender, ethnicity, and social context. *Psychophysiology* 35: 462–9.

Waldzus, S., Mummendey, A., Wenzel, M., and Boettcher, F. (2004) Of bikers, teachers and Germans: Groups' diverging views about their prototypicality. *British Journal of Social Psychology* 43: 385–400.

Walker, I., and Pettigrew, T. F. (1984) Relative deprivation theory: An overview and conceptual critique. *British Journal of Social Psychology* 23: 301–10.

Walker, I., and Mann, L. (1987) Unemployment, relative deprivation and social protest. *Personality and Social Psychology Bulletin* 13: 275–83.

Walker, I., and Smith, H. J. (eds) (2002) *Relative Deprivation: Specification, Development, and Integration*. Cambridge: Cambridge University Press.

Walton, G. M., and Cohen, G. L. (2003) Stereotype lift. *Journal of Experimental Social Psychology* 39: 456–67.

Wason, P. C., and Johnson-Laird, P. N. (1972) *Psychology of Reasoning*. London: Batsford.

Weber, R., and Crocker, J. (1983) Cognitive processes in the revision of stereotypic beliefs. *Journal of Personality and Social Psychology* 45: 961–77.

Wegner, D. M., Schneider, D. J., Carter, S., and White, L. (1987) Paradoxical effects of thought suppression. *Journal of Personality and Social Psychology* 53: 5–13.

Weigel, R. H., Wiser, P. L., and Cook, S. W. (1975) The impact of cooperative learning experiences on cross-ethnic relations and attitudes. *Journal of Social Issues* 31: 219–44.

Weitz, S. (1972) Attitude, voice and behavior: A repressed affect model of interracial interaction. *Journal of Personality and Social Psychology* 24: 14–21.

Wenzel, M., Mummendey, A., and Waldzus, S. (2007) Superordinate identities and intergroup conflict: The ingroup projection model. *European Review of Social Psychology* 18: 331–72.

Wetherell, M. (1982) Cross-cultural studies of minimal groups: Implications for the social identity theory of intergroup relations. In H. Tajfel (ed.), *Social Identity and Intergroup Relations*, pp. 207–40. Cambridge: Cambridge University Press.

White, L. A. (1949) *The Science of Culture: A Study of Man and Civilization*. New York: Farrar Strauss.

Whitley, B. E. (1999) Right-wing authoritarianism, social dominance orientation and prejudice. *Journal of Personality and Social Psychology* 77: 126–34.

WHO [World Health Organization] (2000) *Obesity: Preventing and Managing the Global EpidemicReport of a WHO Consultation* (WHO Technical Report Series 894). Geneva: WHO.

Wiener, R. L., and Hurt, L. E. (2000) How do people evaluate social sexual conduct at work? A psycholegal model. *Journal of Applied Psychology* 85: 75–85.

Wilder, D. A. (1984a) Intergroup contact: The typical member and the exception to the rule. *Journal of Experimental Social Psychology* 20: 177–94.

Wilder, D. A. (1984b) Predictions of belief homogeneity and similarity following social categorization. *British Journal of Social Psychology* 23: 323–33.

Wilder, D. A. (1986) Social categorization: Implications for creation and reduction of intergroup bias. *Advances in Experimental Social Psychology* 19: 291–355. New York: Academic Press.

Wilder, D. A., and Shapiro, P. N. (1989a) Effects of anxiety on impression formation in a group context: An anxiety assimilation hypothesis. *Journal of Experimental Social Psychology* 25: 481–99.

Wilder, D. A., and Shapiro, P. N. (1989b) Role of competition-induced anxiety in limiting the beneficial impact of positive behavior by an outgroup member. *Journal of Personality and Social Psychology* 56: 60–9.

Williams, J. E., and Morland, J. K. (1976) *Race, Color and the Young Child*. Chapel Hill: University of North Carolina Press.

Williams, R. M. (1947) *The Reduction of Intergroup Tensions*. New York: Social Science Research Council.

Williams, T. M. (1986) *The Impact of Television: A Natural Experiment in Three Communities*. New York: Academic Press.

Wills, T. A. (1981) Downward comparison principles in social psychology. *Psychological Bulletin* 90: 245–71.

Wilner, D. M., Walkley, R. P., and Cook, S. W. (1952) Residential proximity and intergroup relations in public housing projects. *Journal of Social Issues* 8: 45–69.

Wilson, M. S., and Liu, J. H. (2003) Social dominance orientation and gender: The moderating role of gender identity. *British Journal of Social Psychology* 42: 187–98.

Witt, L. A. (1989) Authoritarianism, knowledge of AIDS, and affect towards people with AIDS: Implications for health education. *Journal of Applied Social Psychology* 19: 599–607.

Wittenbrink, B., Judd, C. M., and Park, B. (1997) Evidence for racial prejudice at the implicit level and its relationship with questionnaire measures. *Journal of Personality and Social Psychology* 72: 262–74.

Wittenbrink, B., Judd, C. M., and Park, B. (2001) Spontaneous prejudice in context: Variability in automatically activated attitudes. *Journal of Personality and Social Psychology* 81: 815–27.

Wolsko, C., Park, B., Judd, C. M., and Bachelor, J. (2003) Intergroup contact: Effects on group evaluations and perceived variability. *Group Processes and Intergroup Relations* 6: 93–110.

Worchel, S., Andreoli, V. A., and Folger, R. (1977) Intergroup cooperation and intergroup attraction: The effect of previous interaction and outcome of combined effort. *Journal of Experimental Social Psychology* 13: 131–40.

Word, C. O., Zanna, M. P., and Cooper, J. (1974) The non-verbal mediation of self-fulfilling prophecies in interracial interaction. *Journal of Experimental Social Psychology* 10: 109–20.

Wright, S. C., Aron, A., Mclaughlin-Volpe, T., and Ropp, S. A. (1997) The extended contact effect: Knowledge of cross-group friendships and prejudice. *Journal of Personality and Social Psychology* 73: 73–90.

Wyer, N., Sherman, J. W., and Stroessner, S. J. (2000) The roles of motivation and ability in controlling the consequences of stereotype suppression. *Personality and Social Psychology Bulletin* 26: 13–25.

Wyer, R. S., and Gordon, S. E. (1982) The recall of information about persons and groups. *Journal of Experimental Social Psychology* 18: 128–64.

Yee, M., and Brown, R. (1988) *Children and Social Comparisons*. Swindon: Economic and Social Research Council.

Yee, M., and Brown, R. (1992) Self-evaluations and intergroup attitudes in children aged three to nine. *Child Development* 63: 619–29.

Yee, M., and Brown, R. (1994) The development of gender differentiation in young children. *British Journal of Social Psychology* 33: 183–96.

Yzerbyt, V. Y., Leyens, J. P., and Bellour, F. (1995) The ingroup overexclusion effect: Identity concerns in decisions about group membership. *European Journal of Social Psychology* 25: 1–16.

Yzerbyt, V. Y., Corneille, O., and Estrada, C. (2001) The interplay of subjective essentialism and entitativity in the formation of stereotypes. *Personality and Social Psychology Review* 5: 141–55.

Zagefka, H., and Brown, R. (2002) The relationship between acculturation strategies, relative fit and intergroup relations: Immigrant–majority relations in Germany. *European Journal of Social Psychology* 32: 171–88.

Zagefka, H., González, R., and Brown, R. (2009) Antecedents and consequences of acculturation preferences of non-indigenous Chileans in relation to an indigenous minority: Longitudinal survey evidence. *European Journal of Social Psychology* 39: 558–75.

Zagefka, H., González, R., Brown, R., and Manzi, J. (2008) *To Know You Is to Love You? Differential Longitudinal Effects of Intergroup Contact and Knowledge on Intergroup Anxiety and Prejudice among Indigenous and Non-Indigenous Chileans*. London: Royal Holloway, University of London.

Zander, A., Stotland, E., and Wolfe, D. (1960) Unity of group, identification with group, and self-esteem of members. *Journal of Personality* 28: 463–78.

Zimbardo, P. G., Weisenberg, M., Firestone, I., and Levy, B. (1965) Communicator effectiveness in producing public conformity and private attitude change. *Journal of Personality* 33: 233–55.

Zuckerman, D. M., Singer, D. G., and Singer, J. L. (1980) Children's television viewing, racial and sex-role attitudes. *Journal of Applied Social Psychology* 10: 281–94.

Subject Index

Numbers in **bold** indicate where the concept is defined or discussed extensively.

Author Index